GREAT EVENTS
FROM
HISTORY II

GREAT EVENTS FROM HISTORY II

Arts and Culture
Series

Volume 5
1969-1992

Edited by

FRANK N. MAGILL

SALEM PRESS

Pasadena, California   Englewood Cliffs, New Jersey

Library of Congress Cataloging-in-Publication Data
Great events from history II. Arts and culture series / edited by Frank N. Magill.
    p.   cm.
Includes bibliographical references and index.
    1. Arts, Modern—20th century. 2. Arts and so-
ciety—History—20th century. I. Magill, Frank Northen,
1907-   . II. Title: Great events from history. 2. Arts
and culture series.

NX456.G72   1993
700′.9′04—dc20
ISBN 0-89356-807-4 (set)   93-28381
ISBN 0-89356-812-0 (volume 5)   CIP

LIST OF EVENTS IN VOLUME V

1969	*Sesame Street* Revolutionizes Children's Programming	2185
1970's	New York's SoHo Develops into a Center for Contemporary Art	2191
1970's	Relevance Programs Change Entertainment Standards	2197
1970's	Spanish Art Explodes After Years of Suppression	2203
1970	*Design for the Real World* Reorients Industrial Design	2208
1970	Sondheim's *Company* Is Broadway's First "Concept" Musical	2213
1970-1977	*Mary Tyler Moore Show* Examines Women's Roles, *The*	2218
1970	Trudeau's *Doonesbury* Popularizes Topical Comic Strips	2223
1971	Led Zeppelin Merges Hard Rock and Folk Music	2228
1971-1976	*All in the Family* Introduces a New Style of Television Comedy	2234
1971	Guare's *The House of Blue Leaves* Combines Comedy with Horror	2239
1971-1977	*Sonny and Cher Comedy Hour* Brings Glitz to Television, *The*	2244
1971	Mortimer's *A Voyage Round My Father* Is Embraced by Audiences	2249
1971	*Jesus Christ Superstar* Establishes the Rock Opera	2254
1972	Syndication Turns *Star Trek* into a Cult Classic	2260
1972, 1974, 1990	Coppola Revives Gangster Films with *The Godfather* Trilogy	2265
1972	*M*A*S*H* Reflects 1970's Sentiments	2271
1973-1975	*Gulag Archipelago* Exposes Soviet Atrocities, *The*	2277
1973	Pynchon's *Gravity's Rainbow* Is Published	2283
1973	Tharp Stages *Deuce Coupe* for the Joffrey Ballet	2288
1973	Wonder Releases *Innervisions*	2294
1974-1976	Punk's Antifashion Style First Appears	2299
1974-1984	*Happy Days* Exemplifies Escapist Television	2305
1974	Dalí Museum Opens in Figueras, Spain, A	2310
1974	*Dog Soldiers* Portrays Vietnam in Fiction	2315
1975	Forman Adapts *One Flew Over the Cuckoo's Nest* for Film	2320
1975	Springsteen's *Born to Run* Reinvigorates Mainstream Rock	2325

1975-1979   Violent Action-Adventure Television Series Flourish 2330
1975   *Wiz* Brings African-American Talent to Broadway, *The* 2334
1975-1985   *Jeffersons* Signals Success of Black Situation
      Comedies, *The* 2339
1975   Marley's *Natty Dread* Establishes Reggae's Popularity 2344
1975   Joplin's *Treemonisha* Is Staged by the Houston Opera 2350
1975   *Saturday Night Live* Is First Broadcast 2355
1975-1978   Sex Pistols Spark Punk Rock's Musical Insurrection, The ... 2360
1976   *Wanted: The Outlaws* Revitalizes Country Music 2365
1976   Shange's *for colored girls* . . . Is a Landmark 2370
1976   *Einstein on the Beach* Is a Triumph of Minimalism 2375
1977   Allen's *Annie Hall* Captures Complexities of 1970's Life ... 2381
1977   *Saturday Night Fever* Epitomizes the Disco Craze 2386
1977-1983   *Star Wars* Trilogy Redefines Special Effects, The 2391
1977   *Roots* Dramatizes the African-American Experience 2397
1977   Pompidou Center Opens in Paris, The 2402
1978   AT&T Building Exemplifies Postmodernism, The 2407
1978-1979   Shepard's *Buried Child* Promotes Off-Broadway
      Theater 2413
1978-1991   *Dallas* Popularizes the Prime-Time Soap Opera 2418
1978   Singer Wins the Nobel Prize in Literature 2423
1979   *Apocalypse Now* Is Hailed as the Ultimate Vietnam
      War Film 2428
1979   Sondheim Uses Operatic Techniques in *Sweeney Todd* 2433

Early 1980's   Schnabel Emerges as a Celebrity Artist 2438
1980's   Female Directors Attain Prominence 2443
1980's   Madonna Revolutionizes Popular Fashion 2449
1980's   Wynton Marsalis Revives Acoustic Jazz 2454
1980   Baryshnikov Becomes Artistic Director of American Ballet
      Theatre 2459
1980   Four Modern Masters Affirm Germany's Place in the Art
      World 2464
1981-1987   *Hill Street Blues* Defines Hard-Reality Television 2470
1981   MTV Changes the Look of American Popular Culture 2475
1981   New Dance U.S.A. Festival Celebrates Contemporary
      Dance, The 2480
1982   Scott's *Blade Runner* Is a Visual Masterpiece 2486
1982   *E.T.: The Extraterrestrial* Breaks Box-Office Records 2491
1982   *"MASTER HAROLD"* . . . *and the boys* Examines
      Apartheid 2496
1982   Fierstein's *Torch Song Trilogy* Meets with Unexpected
      Success 2502

1982	*USA Today* Is Launched	2507
1982	*Thriller* Marks Michael Jackson's Musical Coming-of-Age	2512
1983	Laurie Anderson's *United States* Popularizes Performance Art	2517
1983-1984	Festivals Mark a Peak in the Dance Created by Black Artists	2521
1984	*Sixteen Candles* Starts a Wave of Teen Films	2527
1984-1992	*Cosby Show* Makes Television History, *The*	2532
1984	Simon's *Biloxi Blues* Emphasizes Serious Themes	2537
1985	Live Aid Generates Millions for Famine Relief	2543
1985	Christo Wraps the Pont Neuf	2548
Late 1980's	Decline of the Big Three Networks Becomes a Fall, The	2554
Late 1980's	Multiculturalism Dominates the Dance World	2559
Late 1980's-early 1990's	Innovative Black Filmmakers Achieve Success	2565
1986	Akalaitis' *Green Card* Confronts Audiences with Harsh Realities	2571
1986	*Platoon* Explores the Vietnam Experience	2576
1986	Rap Goes Platinum with Run-D.M.C.'s *Raising Hell*	2582
1986	Musée d'Orsay Opens, The	2588
1986	Soyinka Wins the Nobel Prize in Literature	2594
1987	Adams' *Nixon in China* Premieres	2599
1987	Van Gogh's *Irises* Sells for $53.9 Million	2603
1987	National Museum of Women in the Arts Opens Amid Controversy, The	2608
1988	Deconstructivists Exhibit at the Museum of Modern Art	2614
1988	Pei Creates a New Entrance to the Louvre	2619
1988	Mahfouz Wins the Nobel Prize in Literature	2625
1989	Khomeini Calls for Rushdie's Death	2630
1989	Mapplethorpe's Photographs Provoke Controversy	2636
1989	*Do the Right Thing* Establishes Lee as a World-Class Director	2641
Early 1990's	Disney Emerges as an Architectural Patron	2646
1990	*Simpsons* Debuts, Anchoring the Fledgling Fox Network, *The*	2652
1990	*Civil War* Rivets the Attention of the United States, *The*	2657
1990	Baryshnikov's White Oak Dance Project Debuts	2663
1991	Gordimer Wins the Nobel Prize in Literature	2668
1992	Columbus Day Debates Reflect Cultural Diversity	2673

GREAT EVENTS FROM HISTORY II

CHRONOLOGICAL LIST OF EVENTS LXIX
ALPHABETICAL LIST OF EVENTS LXXXIV
SUBJECT / KEY WORD INDEX XCIV
CATEGORY INDEX CV
GEOGRAPHICAL INDEX CXV
PRINCIPAL PERSONAGES CXXVI

SESAME STREET REVOLUTIONIZES CHILDREN'S PROGRAMMING

Category of event: Television and radio
Time: November 10, 1969
Locale: New York, New York

Blending skills of educators and television producers, Sesame Street *emerged as television's most successful combination of education and entertainment for preschoolers*

Principal personages:
JOAN GANZ COONEY (1929-   ), a television producer, the president of Children's Television Workshop and one of the show's creators
LLOYD MORRISETT (1929-   ), a psychologist and executive who was one of the show's creators
GERALD S. LESSER (1926-   ), an educational psychologist, Children's Television Workshop adviser, and force for the show's creation

Summary of Event

The *Sesame Street* children's television show was in gestation years before it premiered over National Educational Television (NET) on November 10, 1969, and subsequently triumphed before many educators, social scientists, television critics, and its foundation sponsors as well as before general audiences of children and adults. The desire for experimentation with children's television and the commitments required of talented and experienced educators, psychologists, television executives, producers, and performers were, in substantial measure, elicited or encouraged by the social turbulence and attendant reformism of the 1960's. President John F. Kennedy's "New Frontier" and President Lyndon B. Johnson's "Great Society"—despite their increasing erosion by the Vietnam War and the domestic controversies it engendered—were widely perceived as responses to the nation's need to address costly and embarrassing social problems: racial injustice, discrimination against minorities and women, urban blight and decay, endemic poverty, epidemic crime and violence, and, underlying them all, perceived failures in American education marked by a "reading crisis."

Nowhere was educational failure understood to be more apparent than it was among the deprived, most especially among the preschool, children of America's inner cities. This deficiency appeared the more acute because of children's increasing addiction to television. Widespread concerns were voiced about the low quality of the television children were watching and about its purportedly pernicious effects upon their educations, character, and social interactions. These alarms were sounded despite a general acceptance of such programs as *Ding Dong School, Captain Kangaroo, Exploring,* and *Misterogers' Neighborhood,* presentations of high quality for nursery or preschool children.

Under the auspices of the nonprofit Children's Television Workshop (CTW), and with handsome initial funding from the U.S. Office of Education as well as from the private Carnegie and Ford foundations and from the Corporation for Public Broadcasting (CPB), Joan Ganz Cooney and Lloyd Morrisett in 1966 began preparations for a new preschoolers' program combining education and entertainment. Cooney, the planned show's producer, was an educator and a journalist and had experience in noncommercial television. Cooney would soon be president of CTW. Morrisett was a University of California at Berkeley psychologist who would become CTW's board chairman. They were joined by Gerald Lesser, a Harvard University professor of education and developmental psychology, who filled a vital advisory role and later analyzed the production's evolution.

Conceived as a weekday, hour-long show, *Sesame Street* was directed primarily at preschool inner-city children. Its purpose was to raise preschoolers' reading and numbers skills and to do so by entertaining. Cooney, Morrisett, and Lesser, conscious of children's infatuation with fast-paced television commercials and with the kaleidoscopic comedy flashes characterizing such shows as *Rowan and Martin's Laugh-In*, thought such approaches might be interesting to children, particularly when joined with the tested storytelling and fable traditions of writers such as Sophocles, Aesop, Daniel Defoe, Charles Dickens, and Mark Twain.

The permanent set chosen by the program's executive producers replicated an inner-city, racially and ethnically mixed neighborhood. The real set, a brownstone structure with an adjacent fenced lot, was on Manhattan's West Side. Neighborhood "residents" acted as program hosts. A young black couple, Susan and Gordon (a high school science teacher), along with Bob, a white neighbor, were usually found sitting on the front steps talking about local people—and creatures. A nearby candy store was operated by Mr. Hooper (the original show's only professional actor), who often joined them. Jim Henson, famed as the voice of Kermit the Frog, further populated the show with his brilliant collection of Muppets: principally Big Bird, a friendly but incompetent seven-foot yellow canary, Oscar the Grouch, a denizen of local garbage cans, and the Cookie Monster. Other characters, including a deaf girl, were added later and were accompanied by an eventual score or more of other Henson creations. The accomplished Joe Raposo supplied the theme and other music.

The show was designed as a fast-paced attention grabber consisting of between thirty and fifty segments of less than three minutes each; some segments lasted only seconds. Much of the hour of show time was composed of rapid sequences of songs, skits, stories, games, puns, and wordplay involving the street's residents and its fantastic creatures. "Commercials," dedicated each day to a letter or to numbers, were regularly inserted to teach preschoolers the alphabet and to instruct them on numbers from one to ten. Since one of the producers' objectives was to appeal particularly to minority children, the show's characters were richly representative of a racially and ethnically plural society.

Within two years, *Sesame Street* had earned plaudits from a remarkably wide spectrum of the television viewing community. At the close of its first season, the program won a Peabody Award, which was followed by seventeen Emmy Awards and, by 1985, more than a hundred further honors. Equally impressive were estimates of the size of the audiences drawn to the 250 public television stations that carried the show. At the end of *Sesame Street*'s first decade, nine out of ten preschoolers, representing equal percentages of minority and white children and boys and girls, reportedly watched the program.

Impact of Event

No other children's television show had ever enjoyed either the sensational, instantaneous success or the subsequent praise and emulation that came to *Sesame Street*. If the challenge confronting its producers was to gain a huge audience while openly using the show to educate young children, that challenge was splendidly met. Indeed, the show represented the largest educational experiment ever undertaken. There is also no doubt that it entertained hugely, within the United States and, by 1988, in seventy-three other countries.

Proponents of the show believed that it yielded the first hard evidence that preschool children were capable of learning from visual media at previously unbelievable rates. Unexpectedly, very young chidren with early exposure to television were found to have brought a startling degree of media literacy to viewing the show. This appeared to be especially true not only of three- to five-year-olds but also of even younger children. Accordingly, data from the show's producers raised questions about prevailing professional educational and psychological concepts as to what constituted normal childhood development. Since the effects of television—except for a few monographs on the impact of television advertising and violence upon younger children—had scarcely been studied, the show provided fresh sources of research material that caused an explosion of data-heavy publications across the United States and in Europe. Not least, many show participants, in company with other observers, felt that the quality and success of their production lent new measures of respectability to studies of television's impact on children and raised the prestige of people in the television trade who chose to work on children's shows. Certainly, the show's conceptions and production methods set new standards for other educational series.

The continuous innovation and the self-criticisms of its professionals doubtless contributed to *Sesame Street*'s growing audience strength. Several new characters and creatures were added, as were celebrity guests; skits were dropped or revised, and many other adjustments—the show's pace was slowed somewhat, for example—were made in light of self-analyses or external complaints. Moreover, when the models of what constituted successful educational television experiments in several European and Asian countries were evaluated by *Sesame Street*'s producers, they found their own criteria comparable.

Field research, furthermore, indicated that *Sesame Street*'s preschool viewers did enjoy easier transitions into school and had better preparation for reading and learning numbers than did nonviewers. The extent to which viewers were affected, if at all, by the implicit social pluralism of the show remains unclear, but more than other children's programs, *Sesame Street* persistently addressed issues of social relationships, race and ethnicity, women's roles, traditional perspectives on gender difference, and the environment.

While for years *Sesame Street* garnered extraordinary numbers of honors and maintained its huge audience, it also provoked acerbic debate and criticism from a variety of qualified observers, from some parents and children, and even from the British Broadcasting Corporation. Some critics found the show to be too fast-paced, with the result that children could barely absorb the contents of one segment before another confronted them. In this regard, the program was deemed overstimulating and likely to produce a generation of "speed freaks." Others condemned the show because it failed in its declared mission of narrowing the gap between disadvantaged inner-city minority children and those who were advantaged. Specially devised tests did seem to indicate educational gains by minority children, but the gains were minor. There were further complaints that the show's contents were redundant, merely teaching materials children already were learning or shortly would learn from life experiences. The show's high expenses also drew fire for having yielded too little of quantifiable social or educational value in contrast to the sums expended. Each twenty-six-week season rang up an average bill of $8 million, and by the mid-1980's the show's total costs exceeded $100 million—although when reduced to production costs per viewer or when compared with other producers' production costs per animated cartoon, for example, *Sesame Street*'s budgets seemed cost-effective.

Friends of the show, including media historians, have tried speaking and writing objectively about what they believed were its real failures. First, whether the show's producers should have assumed so or not—indeed, whether they could have or not—they did not significantly influence most educational theorists, teachers, principals, or educational systems. For their own reasons, professional educators prefer teaching, which certainly includes television, to proceed in the schools. Neither did *Sesame Street*'s creators either encourage or drive the commercial networks to devoting more time and money to children's educational programming; the networks' considerations of profitability prevailed.

The consensus seems to be that *Sesame Street* remains the most massive educational experiment of its kind and that it is a worthy enterprise with worthy, if often unmeasurable, results. Nevertheless, given the dimensions of the problems the program sought to alleviate, it represents a very small effort. Bright children still learn more from television, as they do from all experiences, than do the less bright, and the problem the show seeks to remedy may not be the immense gaps between the needs of the advantaged and the disadvantaged. It may be, as the show's coproducers came to believe, that so many minority children fall below any educational floor that, in a formal sense, they become uneducable for joining effectually in twentieth century life. *Sesame Street*'s mission of contributing to the improvement of literacy at the earliest stages of childhood though, was pragmatically sound. For, as Cooney explained, "There's a literacy line. Once you're above that line you can participate in American life; below it, you can't."

Bibliography

Chester, Giraud, Garnet R. Garrison, and Edgar E. Willis. *Television and Radio.* 4th ed. New York: Appleton-Century-Crofts, 1971. A useful general look at television and radio through the late 1960's, including a discussion of women's and children's programming and of *Sesame Street.* Includes a reproduction of one of the show's scripts. A scholarly survey, though opinions are muted, and it is hardly profound. Good if somewhat dated bibliography, many illustrations, useful index.

Grossman, Gary H. *Saturday Morning TV.* New York: Dell, 1981. Provides a survey of children's programs during the "prime day" allocated to them by commercial networks. Provides a basis for understanding one aspect of what Newton Minnow castigated as the "wasteland" of television as it continued into the opening of the 1980's. Illustrations, adequate bibliography, index.

Lesser, Gerald S. *Children and Television: Lessons from "Sesame Street."* New York: Vintage Books, 1974. By far the best, most authoritative, and most interesting work on the subject and the show, by one of *Sesame Street*'s principal advisers. Prefatory observations by Cooney and Morrisett. Clear, uncluttered, and reflective work. Illustrations, cartoons, photographs, and graphs, along with a splendid bibliography and extensive index. A thoughtful study that is essential—and enjoyable—reading.

MacDonald, J. Fred. *One Nation Under Television: The Rise and Decline of Network TV.* New York: Pantheon Books, 1990. A study of television as America's principal window upon itself and the world, a story shaped by a few evolving networks. In this context, *Sesame Street* and analogous children's programs are covered, ominously, under the title "The Politics of Television." Some of the influences and failures of the show are noted. A useful read in its entirety. Good chapter notes, excellent bibliography, and extensive subject and program indexes.

Mayer, Martin. *About Television.* New York: Harper & Row, 1972. A reportorial analysis of television's evolution as a vital component of American culture. Much fascinating material, including a chapter on *Sesame Street* that is laudatory but critical of network reactions to children's educational television. Raises important questions about the show and its effects. Brief chapter notes; no illustrations or bibliography. Useful index.

Palmer, Edward L. *Television and America's Children: A Crisis of Neglect.* New York: Oxford University Press, 1988. Author helped Cooney and others launch *Sesame Street*, then served with CTW for sixteen years. Excellent, authoritative, well-written, and shocking book concerning the state of children's television. Must reading. Annotated chapter notes and a fine bibliography, rich in monographs on the show. Useful double-columned index. A balanced, reflective insider's views.

Clifton K. Yearley

Cross-References

Capra Releases *It's a Wonderful Life* (1946), p. 1335; *Kukla, Fran, and Ollie* Pioneers Children's Television Programming (1948), p. 1400; *Captain Kangaroo* Debuts (1955), p. 1678; *The Flintstones* Popularizes Prime-Time Cartoons (1960), p. 1840; *The Simpsons* Debut, Anchoring the Fledgling Fox Network (1990), p. 2652.

NEW YORK'S SOHO DEVELOPS INTO
A CENTER FOR CONTEMPORARY ART

Category of event: Art
Time: The 1970's
Locale: New York, New York

During the 1970's, SoHo became the principal location for New York's trade in contemporary art, a trade that provided the economic basis of the SoHo community and gave it cultural orientation

Principal personages:
RICHARD L. FEIGEN (1930-   ), a Park Avenue art dealer who established the first dealer presence in SoHo in 1968
PAULA COOPER (1938-   ), a staffer in uptown galleries of New York City who established SoHo's first gallery in the fall of 1968
LEO CASTELLI (1907-   ), one of the most influential art dealers in New York City, who moved all of his business in contemporary art to SoHo in 1976

Summary of Event

The SoHo area, a forty-three-block district in lower Manhattan, originated with urban planners who as late as 1962 referred to this area as the South Houston Industrial District. The acronym designates the structurally intact but socially transformed district where most of New York's and much of the United States' visual art is created and marketed. A residential population of approximately seven thousand people (according to the 1990 census), predominantly artists and their families, works and lives in renovated factory lofts. Residents have created a community with an economic foundation resting on the demand for contemporary fine art and with a cultural identity rooted in the dynamics and contradictions of the American middle class.

The artists of SoHo first drifted into the district in the late 1950's. A few of the new breed of artists, such as Jackson Pollock, Mark Rothko, and Franz Klein, lived and worked in factory buildings in the Coenties Slip area of lower Manhattan, near the Battery. The postwar years brought an influx of artists into lower Manhattan and into SoHo specifically.

The artists settled into the midst of industrial decay, into what was then a zone of doll makers and dress manufacturers, rag balers and wastepaper processors. Painters, sculptors, and dancers found that the deserted factory lofts were uniquely adaptable to their needs for unrestricted space. Landlords found artists to be useful scavengers of otherwise unmarketable upper floors in poorly maintained buildings. They were occupants who renovated the lofts they inhabited and who legally were in no position to ask for anything but to be left alone, beneath the notice of the law. A symbiotic relationship was struck. Landlords received modest rents and could count on leaky roofs being fixed by the tenants; artists in search of cheap but ample studio space found it on a scale commensurate with their needs.

In the decade of the 1960's, SoHo's population of artists grew. The industrial base of the area declined and, simultaneously, more and more middle-class youth set out on an artistic trek that led them inevitably to New York City, the nation's center for art education, museums, and art sales. Having perfected the techniques of coping with life in lofts, and finding that more of the district's spaces were losing their attraction for manufacturing tenants, painters and sculptors formed cooperative associations in order to purchase and remodel entire factory buildings for studio and residential purposes. The "art world," the urban subculture to which artists belong by virtue of their shared commitments, was expanded by a new basis of interaction: finding, renovating, and collectively financing loft studios in SoHo.

The extent of the growing renovation brought artists new problems. At first, they had only to supplant the established rat population and provide heat and hot water in buildings with coal furnaces long rusted into uselessness. As greater numbers of artists moved in, open confrontation with the city became the artists' most pressing difficulty. In the early period, fire and building inspectors had been third parties to the illegal housing accommodation between artist and landlord. The inspectors took their portion of petty graft or simply attended to higher priorities elsewhere in the city, thus informally licensing the residency. The increasing numbers of artists and the growing publicity surrounding their residency, however, inevitably made the artists' occupancy a political issue. Parties with an interest in the course of urban change—planners protecting their professional prerogatives, developers, urban reformers of varied types, and elected officials—generated opposition that made the place of artists in the city an important issue.

The SoHo artists, trading on the patron relationship between art and its sponsors, won legal sanction of their residency by 1971 in a contest that reveals much about the position of the artist in urban society and national culture. The artists had won a political struggle to defeat demolition schemes and to secure a residential monopoly in what was otherwise a manufacturing zone.

SoHo subsequently became an attractive location for art dealers. The gallery display technique and the storage of art require extensive but moderately priced space. This is particularly true when, as with contemporary art, much of a dealer's inventory is speculative in value and executed on the large scale that had been established by abstract expressionism. SoHo offered dealers more space for their money than was available in the established gallery district along Manhattan's Fifty-seventh Street. More important, the surrounding artistic community facilitated interaction between artists, dealers, and clients, generating an ambience that drew clients away from the more fashionable uptown art neighborhood with the prospect of investing in new trends at their very source, a concept that had been promoted by the garment industry in its use of the Manhattan "factory showroom." During the 1970's, new galleries opened in SoHo, and the contemporary art operations of many established uptown dealers, such as Leo Castelli, were relocated among the artists' lofts, making the area the focus of the city's trade in the work of living artists.

The galleries, in their turn, attracted art lovers as well as the professional and managerial populations of Manhattan, which were growing with the completion of each new office tower. Having established themselves as a part of the urban design, however, the artists discovered that complete control of the area was beyond their economic and political resources. The middle class exacted a tribute in return for its sponsorship. Although the law only permits certified artists to live in SoHo, severe budget cutbacks at the Department of Cultural Affairs, plus a Loft Board mired in owner-tenant disputes, meant a gray area in enforcement. As a result, the area became by the 1990's a mix of early pioneers, arts-related residents from the 1980's, and those among the internationally rich who saw SoHo as a "finishing school."

Impact of Event

As a result of the increasing migration of artists and dealers into the area, SoHo became the national center for the contemporary fine arts. It is the focus for many status communities within the arts, each distinguished by its own medium. As the location of New York's largest concentration of painters and sculptors, and of the galleries that display their work, SoHo most notably became a center for the visual arts, central to the dynamics of the contemporary art world.

The impact of SoHo upon the environment in which contemporary art was viewed was enormous. Dealers wanted to distinguish themselves from the conservative, formal atmosphere of uptown galleries. Galleries in SoHo became simpler and larger, with 5,000-square-foot floors and 10-foot ceilings. As a result, dealers were able to exhibit works without concern for their size. In addition, the atmosphere was more relaxed. The galleries welcomed students, professionals, and tourists as well as art connoisseurs. Doors were kept open, and visitors were free to come and go without being observed or questioned. SoHo dealers were highly visible. Most remained on hand to answer questions and to discuss the works on display. This accessibility to the public became one of the major differences between SoHo galleries and uptown galleries.

The artists, in turn, benefited because exhibitions of experimental works by unknown artists became financially less risky for the dealers. Because the galleries were evolving as showcases for an increasing diversity of styles, artists had the opportunity to exhibit larger, more innovative art not considered to be mainstream.

SoHo has the reputation of exhibiting art that is original, art that demands exposure and feedback from the audience. The work that is shown often sets new trends or is the start of a new movement. To view these pieces, preconceived notions of art must be set aside, since the SoHo art community is dedicated to the exchange of ideas. Rarely in the history of art has such a tightly knit support system developed, and nowhere else in the world is there such a high concentration of artistically talented people.

Neighborhood artists frequent the galleries and, in speaking about the works, influence both dealers and fellow artists. This interaction of ideas and opinions is crucial for young artists. SoHo has become a mecca for art students and recent graduates who come to study new art movements; it is a place where conceptions about art are continually being challenged and invented.

Unlike uptown galleries, the neighborhood of SoHo prides itself on exhibiting the works of unestablished artists alongside the renowned names. The term "unestablished" signifies that the artist is young in terms of career; that is, the artist has not yet exhibited widely or received critical attention. There is no connotation of lack of merit, only of merit that has not yet been discovered.

Another byproduct of the development of SoHo is the proliferation of artist-managed "alternative space," or cooperative galleries. These developed as a result of the tight caste system of private galleries. Because of the limited number of private galleries and restricted exhibition spaces, a large number of artists went without representation. Cooperative galleries allowed groups of artists to represent themselves. SoHo grew to have the largest concentration of cooperative galleries in the world, as the artists were attracted by the same economic factors that brought private galleries to the area.

The development of the SoHo community and its galleries has coincided with specific changes in the art world—the growth and openness of the market since the advent of abstract expressionism, the introduction of a new contemporary art buyer who seeks artistic coordinates from the market itself, and the absence of any single critical definition of what is important or correct avant-garde art or theory. The result of these changes has been elevation of the dealer to the central position as arbiter of taste in contemporary art.

The elevation of the dealer role is possible because of critical fluctuations in the art world. What is common to all the contemporary styles and movements of the late twentieth century, including earthworks, minimalist art, conceptual art, the random scattering of found objects, and the appropriation of nonartistic "reality" into art in the form of commercial iconography, is an emancipation of the work of art from control by the professional critic. Either the work can be immediately comprehended in nonaesthetic terms, or the artist or the dealer has taken on the function of generating the conceptual notion that makes such items as stacked railroad ties "art." In either case, the critic as a powerful and autonomous participant in the dialogue about art has lost his or her power. The new art found in SoHo frequently employs either material speaking for itself or concepts defined at some length by the artist and illustrated by intrinsically uninteresting material. The gallery installations present the art objects as "reality" or as supported by explanations which themselves are "meta-art."

Art has become an unabashedly and increasingly entrepreneurial field as a consequence of the SoHo art world. Some artists have become entrepreneurs and even celebrities, either through showmanship or by articulating their own theories about art and their own context of interpretation. The celebrity artist may use a dealer, but only as a representative, and will conduct his or her own salesmanship and conceptual defense.

Bibliography

Bilgore, Ellen. "The Boom Town of Bohemia: SoHo." *Town and Country Magazine* (September, 1977): 118-123. Bilgore gives an interesting historical perspective on the growth and development of SoHo in the twentieth century. She discusses social, economic, and cultural changes in the area as well as its reputation as a mecca for bohemians.

Edens, S. T. "Alternative Spaces—SoHo Style." *Art in America* 61 (November, 1973): 36-40. Compares and contrasts uptown galleries to those of SoHo, noting the advantages of SoHo alternative spaces. The advantages of exhibiting works without concern for their size are discussed. The diversity of styles exhibited in SoHo galleries and the relaxed atmosphere of the galleries is viewed as an advantage, as is accessibility to the public.

Hoffman, Katherine. *Explorations: The Visual Arts Since 1945.* New York: Harper-Collins, 1991. An excellent history of the period. Details the development of the various postwar movements and the artists who shaped them.

Hughes, Robert. *The Shock of the New.* New York: Alfred A. Knopf, 1980. The companion to a widely acclaimed television series narrated by Hughes. Provides an excellent background on the development of modern art.

Price, Brenda. "An Artist's Gallery." *The Feminist Art Journal* 5 (Spring, 1976): 21-26. The author surveys thirty galleries; twenty had taken in no new "unreferred" artists in 1975. She focuses primarily on female artists and their gallery representation in New York City.

Rapkin, Chester. *South Houston Industrial Area.* New York: City of New York, 1963. This is an excellent historical study of the growth of industry in SoHo from the 1880's to the 1950's. It focuses on the development of the quiet residential area into one filled with a million-dollar textile industry and its commercial and industrial buildings.

Siegfried, Alanna, and Helene Zucker Seeman. *SoHo: A Guide.* New York: Neal-Schuman, 1978. In addition to being a guidebook to museums and galleries in the area, this book also provides useful information on the history, architecture, and residential neighborhood of SoHo. Contains numerous photographs and maps as well as an extensive bibliography.

Simpson, Charles R. *SoHo: The Artist in the City.* Chicago: University of Chicago Press, 1981. This is a scholarly longitudinal study that extends from the initial phases of artist residency in SoHo in the early 1960's to the culturally heterogeneous community of the 1980's. The work discusses the cultural renovation of SoHo, the structure of the SoHo art market, the historical movement from industry to art, and family life in the area. Contains several appendices.

Genevieve Slomski

Cross-References

Stein Holds Her First Paris Salons (1905), p. 129; Duchamp's "Readymades" Challenge Concepts of Art (1913), p. 349; Avant-Garde Art in the Armory Show Shocks American Viewers (1913), p. 361; Minimalism Emphasizes Objects as Art (1963), p. 1949; Warhol's *The Chelsea Girls* Becomes a Commercial Success (1966), p. 2053.

RELEVANCE PROGRAMS CHANGE
ENTERTAINMENT STANDARDS

Category of event: Television and radio
Time: The 1970's
Locale: The United States

Television programs dealing with contemporary social problems and concerns became very popular in the 1970's, reflecting the social and political tensions of those times

Principal personages:
> NORMAN LEAR (1922-   ), the creator of many relevance programs such as *All in the Family, Maude, The Jeffersons,* and *Good Times*
> ROBERT D. WOOD (1925-1986), the president of the Columbia Broadcasting System, who insisted that his network shift to broadcasting more relevant programs in order to reach a wider audience
> BUD YORKIN (1926-   ), a television producer/director who believed that the national climate was right for television programs that confronted current issues
> MARY TYLER MOORE (1937-   ), a television actress turned producer who took a more moderate approach to relevance programming than did Norman Lear

Summary of Event

Television executives are part of the same general culture as everyone else in the United States. Their ideas about society come from the same sources as do those of everyone else. When these sources show, or are perceived as showing, a change in the public mood, television executives want their industry to change to meet the mood. This desire to change rests on the fact that the major networks tailor their schedules of shows toward what they think people want to see. For this reason, hit shows soon spawn numerous imitators. Although the public mood keeps changing, there is a limited number of types, or genres, of television programs. When a new public mood is perceived to be developing, therefore, television producers try to develop programs that can use the old genres and still suit the new mood.

In the early 1970's, the Columbia Broadcasting System (CBS), led by its president, Robert D. Wood, correctly sensed the shifting public mood and began to change its programming. At the beginning of the decade, CBS broadcast a large number of shows with rural orientations because its audience was basically small-town and rural people over the age of fifty. Popular programs of the time included *Mayberry RFD* and *The Beverly Hillbillies.* Advertisers on CBS were becoming concerned for two reasons. The network's aging audience was spending less and less money on advertisers' products, and the CBS shows did not appeal to younger audiences in urban areas who had more money to spend.

Wood perceived that the social mood of America was ready for television that combined anxiety with hope. Producer/director Bud Yorkin agreed. He thought that young people especially were ready for a new approach to television entertainment. Many young people were challenging established assumptions, or knew peers who were, and they wanted entertainment that dealt with the issues of the day and that could prompt debate.

In Norman Lear, CBS found a producer who knew how to develop these kinds of programs. Lear described himself as a social and political liberal whose politics informed his sense of comedy. His *All in the Family*, an adaptation of the British comedy show *Till Death Do Us Part*, was the first of the relevance programs. Its main characters, Archie and Edith Bunker and their daughter and son-in-law, Gloria and Mike Stivic, became one medium through which the United States could confront controversial topics ranging from abortion to impotence to racism. Viewers often were offended by ideas espoused by conservative Archie Bunker or liberal Mike Stivic, and that was the point—to get viewers to examine ideas.

Nor was Lear confined to producing a single show. Edith Bunker had a fictional cousin whose guest appearances on *All in the Family* led to a spin-off show, *Maude*. On her own show, Maude had a maid, Flora, who became so popular that she was given her own show, *Good Times*. The Bunkers' next-door neighbors, an African-American family, made a success of their neighborhood business and moved from Queens to the Upper East Side of Manhattan, where their own show, *The Jeffersons*, was set.

Other networks followed the CBS success formula. The National Broadcasting Company (NBC) produced *The Mary Tyler Moore Show*, which in fact began airing in 1970, several months before *All in the Family*. NBC's show, however, took longer to develop an issue orientation and throughout its run featured relevance with a softer edge. It focused on the feminist movement, showing a single career woman. The lead character was, however, also a traditional female in being the "heart" of her work group. She was young enough to attract young female viewers but pliant enough not to be a threat to traditional males and housewives. On *The Mary Tyler Moore Show*, Mary was not a virgin, was not vapid, and was not always intimidated by her boss, all characteristics notably different from previous single female characters. There were concessions made to the conservatives of the 1970's, but Mary Tyler Moore remained a relevant figure in moderate guise.

An entirely different kind of relevance show was *M*A*S*H*, which quickly developed a cultlike following. The show was born on a wave of antiwar and antiauthoritarian feeling, but it was so popular that it was rarely attacked by the political and religious right wing despite its clearly pacificist and liberal orientation.

The Jeffersons reflected the realism given to life-styles by the relevance approach to television. In 1968, *Julia* featured Diahann Carroll as a nurse with a middle-class life-style living in a modern, integrated apartment building. That show introduced black leading characters with middle-class jobs. In *All in the Family*, George Jefferson ran a dry-cleaning shop in a blue-collar neighborhood until business success struck; *The Jeffersons* portrayed him as owner of a chain of shops. *Good Times* dealt with the world of "temporary lay-offs, easy credit rip-offs," as its theme song put it.

These shows and their imitators changed the course of television programming in the United States. By 1975, relevance programs had swept much of the silliness of the 1960's from the screen. Although the American Broadcasting Company took a different approach with its nostalgic *Happy Days* and its spin-offs, even there relevance gained an occasional footing. Relevance programs destroyed the old taboos and set television free to deal with current problems.

Impact of Event

In order to judge the impact that relevance programs had on television, one should consider the change in shows popular with the public. In the 1950's and 1960's, the most popular programs included *I Love Lucy*, *Dragnet*, and *Gunsmoke*; the most popular actors included Lucille Ball, Jack Benny, Dean Martin, and Red Skelton. These had been industry leaders for years with little or no change in content or in characters. With the first broadcast of *All in the Family* on January 12, 1971, CBS completely changed the rules. The old verities in the industry changed.

The programs of the 1960's involved a good deal of silliness, as in *I Love Lucy*, or dealt in unambiguous confrontations between good guys and bad guys, as on *Dragnet* or the nostalgic *Gunsmoke*. The new relevance programs all had conflict at the heart of their appeal. The conflict, however, involved controversy rather than clear-cut issues. The positions presented by the relevance programs were open to varied interpretations. Archie Bunker was either a boorish bigot or a hardworking, lower-middle-class male, depending on the viewer's perspective. Surveys of audiences who watched relevance shows indicated that viewers generally received reinforcement for whatever views they brought to the show. This was a major change from the single clear message sent by shows in the preceding decade.

In part, the impact of relevance programming was a measure of changes in society. Programming of the 1960's reflected the stable society of the 1950's. As the Civil Rights movement, Vietnam, and urban violence destroyed that stability, society began to look for programs that would reflect the world viewers lived in every day. Of the top ten shows of the 1968-1969 season, none remained on the top ten list for 1973-1974.

Because reality was often grim as well as confusing, television viewers still wanted some degree of escape. The greatest success of relevance programming came when serious contemporary problems were dealt with in a humorous context. The use of humor made problems bearable.

Perhaps the best example of humor in the midst of gritty reality was *M*A*S*H*, a program set in Korea during the 1950's conflict while the real world was watching the bloody scenes from Vietnam on the nightly news. The *M*A*S*H* characters expressed the rising doubts, growing opposition, and increasing horror of the society associated with war but tempered these sentiments with quiet humor and regular doses of slapstick. As shifting middle-class values made it harder to envisage the nuclear family as a weekly center of excitement, the contemporary single working woman, portrayed by Mary Tyler Moore, came on the TV screen. This shift in emphasis in programming from pure entertainment to entertainment with a message is one major impact of relevance programming.

Even as the use of humor forced the television-viewing public to think seriously about some current situations, another impact was taking place in program content. Television of the 1960's was largely populated by whites. When other racial or ethnic groups appeared, it was usually on shows featuring only that group or with minority group members playing minor roles as menial workers. With relevance programming came more diverse racial and ethnic portrayals. This was not just on entertainment shows but on educational programs as well. The Bunkers, on *All in the Family*, had black neighbors. *The Jeffersons* had white neighbors, and the show featured an interracial marriage. Perhaps the ultimate example of racial and ethnic integration was found on the children's show *Sesame Street*. This program featured, at various times, Native Americans, Asian Americans, African Americans, Caucasian Americans, and Hispanic Americans in its urban setting. Its treatment of issues, even though at a child's level, qualifies it as relevance programming.

Relevance programming sounded different, too, with the use of everyday language that was frequently ungrammatical and crudely vigorous. In the 1950's and 1960's, standard grammatical English was the regular fare on television unless the character was given deliberately "picturesque" speech, as with the Clampetts on *The Beverly Hillbillies*. On relevance programs, dialogue sounded very much like what would be heard on a typical street. As is often the case in relevance programming, Norman Lear was the pioneer in introducing new language. Racial epithets flew freely on *All in the Family* as Archie Bunker spoke in the words used by many people. The groups referred to in these terms did not take offense at their use because Archie was clearly a bigot and such language was to be expected of his character. In addition, his views were rebutted by son-in-law Mike Stivic and others, providing balance. Lear's opinion was that by using these words openly he was depriving them of their power to shock and to offend.

Relevance programming also had an impact on nonverbal communication. Good guys no longer wore white hats. The man wearing old clothes and sporting long hair and a beard might be a policeman or an attorney or schoolteacher. Television styles of grooming and dress suddenly changed to reflect the styles seen across America.

Relevance programming faced limits, however. It lent itself to humor better than to realism. Relevance drama (still mixed with comedy) endured better, with shows such as *Hill Street Blues* and *L.A. Law* creating a genre of their own. Even in humor-oriented shows, relevance programming faced problems. Relevance easily became trivial or idiotic, as sometimes happened on *Good Times* or *Maude*.

Relevance programming was ideal for the 1970's, but when the mood of the United States became more conservative, as indicated by the election of President Ronald Reagan in 1980, the public lost its taste for many of these shows. Networks began to take fewer chances, and relied more on noncontroversial programming. Scriptwriters, however, retained their new freedom to express controversial opinions at least occasionally.

Bibliography

Barnouw, Erik. *Tube of Plenty: The Evolution of American Television.* Oxford, England: Oxford University Press, 1982. The author was head of the section of the Library of Congress that dealt with broadcasting. His book is a thorough coverage and analysis of television from *I Love Lucy* to the Jimmy Carter-Ronald Reagan debates.

Fiske, John. *Television Culture.* London: Routledge, 1989. This is a heavily sociological work that analyzes television through technical sociological research and studies.

Gitlin, Todd. *Inside Prime Time.* New York: Pantheon Books, 1983. An analysis of how television is produced, describing the power held by small groups of top executives, writers, producers, and agents. Gitlin looks at what makes good shows good and why some catch on while others fail.

Goldstein, Fred, and Stan Goldstein. *Prime-Time Television.* New York: Crown, 1983. Combines text and pictures to present a vivid history of television from 1948 to 1983. Almost every program or series that was on the air for at least one season is included in this comprehensive work.

Hefzallah, Ibrahim M. *Critical Viewing of Television: A Book for Parents and Teachers.* Landham, Md.: University Press of America, 1987. The author, a teacher of critical viewing of television, writes about how to understand television, how it affects viewers, and how to become a critical viewer.

Lowe, Carl, ed. *Television and American Culture.* New York: H. H. Wilson, 1981. A reprint of articles, addresses, and excerpts from books on television as a social force in American society. Covers such diverse topics as politics, religion, news, and education.

Miranda, Fred, and Bill Ginch. *TV Trivia.* New York: Ballantine Books, 1984. The title of the book accurately describes its contents, but there are many interesting nuggets of information scattered throughout its pages. An index will help the reader find shows of interest.

Mitz, Rick. *The Great TV Sitcom Book.* New York: Richard Marek, 1980. This book covers virtually every situation comedy shown on television from 1949 to 1980. In addition to describing the shows, the author discusses social reference points and proposes reasons why the shows succeeded or failed.

O'Connor, John, ed. *American History, American Television.* New York: Frederick Ungar, 1985. Television is presented both as a force in recent social history and as a matter to be studied. This collection of essays came out of Columbia University's Seminar on Cinema, but all relate to television. This book deals with a wide range of topics, from the *Amos 'n' Andy* show to coverage of Watergate.

Rose, Brian G., ed. *TV Genres: A Handbook and Reference Guide.* Westport, Conn.:

Greenwood Press, 1985. Attempts to explain how and why television shows fall into a limited number of formats. The cross-fertilizing of formats, or genres, is discussed. Genres from police shows to church services are discussed.

Michael R. Bradley

Cross-References

The Mary Tyler Moore Show Examines Women's Roles (1970), p. 2218; *All in the Family* Introduces a New Style of Television Comedy (1971), p. 2234; *M*A*S*H* Reflects 1970's Sentiments (1972), p. 2271; *The Jeffersons* Signals Success of Black Situation Comedies (1975), p. 2339; *Hill Street Blues* Defines Hard-Reality Television (1981), p. 2470.

SPANISH ART EXPLODES AFTER YEARS OF SUPPRESSION

Category of event: Art
Time: The 1970's
Locale: Spain

Following the death of Francisco Franco in 1975, Spanish art underwent an explosive transformation and growth that brought with it international recognition and acceptance

Principal personages:
FRANCISCO FRANCO (1892-1975), the Spanish dictator whose regime stifled artistic expression
LUIS GORDILLO (1934-   ), a Spanish painter who inspired a generation of artists in the 1970's
GUILLERMO PÉREZ VILLALTA (1948-   ), a Spanish artist who broadened the range of figurativist art
RAFAEL PÉREZ-MINGUEZ (1951-   ), a Spanish artist who was strongly influenced by Gordillo

Summary of Event

From the end of the Spanish Civil War in 1938, it was evident that Spain's new Nationalist state would find it difficult to attain intellectual respectability. The majority of the European and Spanish intelligentsia had sympathized with the defeated Spanish republic. Moreover, the assassination of the poet and dramatist Federico García Lorca engendered a permanent indictment of the Francisco Franco regime by European liberals; the assassination became a symbol of the fate of culture at the hands of Franco and his supporters.

Nearly all the poets and painters of García Lorca's generation, considered by many to have been the potential architects of a new Spanish golden age, fled into exile. Intellectuals and artists with a European reputation joined the "other Spain," the Spain of the exiles who saw themselves as the true bearers of Spanish civilization while their homeland lay in the grip of despotism.

The Franco regime became more concerned with control of possible alternative cultures through censorship than with the creation of an original culture. The "official" art that the new state wished to impose on Spain expressed the aesthetic, intellectual, and artistic principles of the groups that supported Franco. A common style emerged, marked by exalted nationalism, the glorification of the military spirit, a fervent Catholicism, and a preference for classical and traditional styles.

In the 1950's, while the "official" culture still dominated the rhetoric of the regime, its failure to capture the public mind—much less the imagination of creative artists—was increasingly evident. Repression did not entirely succeed in eradicating the liberal tradition; Franco's regime was forced to combat the emergence of an alternative culture as well as the spread of "foreign" ideas. A censorship policy set up under wartime directives continued functioning for nearly thirty years of peace. Its purpose—the control of all information—produced a culture of almost inconceivable mediocrity.

During the 1940's, the artistic canons of official art were simply neglected, since no artist of integrity could work within them. It was artists who first established a direct connection with the lost world of the 1930's. Joan Miró returned to Spain from exile in 1940; his 1937 Civil War poster *Aidez l'Espagne* had been a frontal attack on Francoism. The work of Miró, the most famous living Spanish painter after Pablo Picasso, was totally neglected by the regime. As for Picasso, he was dismissed as an enemy of not only the regime but also of all things divine and human.

While the Spanish writers of the postwar period turned to an introspective realism and discussed—as far as governmental censorship would allow—the effects of the war and its aftermath on the people of Spain, Spanish painters tended to concentrate on representing the physical landscape of the Spanish countryside. The olive trees of Andalusia, the plains of Castile, and the rocky vistas of the Costa Brava dominated the paintings of the day, as artists searched the landscape for uniquely Spanish qualities. Painting styles were still influenced by the weak imitations of cubism and post-impressionism that had marked prewar Spain but were distinguished by an exaggeration of the paint surface, which was often used for the direct imitation of the textures of the soil. Many younger artists were to develop this technique as a major characteristic of the abstract painting of the 1950's.

The International Exhibit of Abstract Art in 1953 heralded a national breakthrough in the new spirit of the avant-garde in Spain, and during the following four years, the movement began to accelerate. At this point, the new Spanish art was finally accorded recognition abroad. From 1959 to 1962, the Spanish boom continued, prompting a series of popular exhibitions in Paris, London, Tokyo, New York, and nearly every major city in Europe and Latin America.

Joining the international abstract expressionist movement as late as they did, Spanish artists found themselves in a strange position. Their work was classified as a late and exotic regional movement. Spain's abstract art (known as "Informalism") was an extension of a tradition, a revolt against technique. Yet a lack of success caused by a falling off of international interest in the early 1960's proved a deadly blow to the movement. The majority of artists involved decided to reject those aspects of the movement with which they had never really identified, and soon new styles were evolving from the old.

In the early 1970's, Spain was still ruled by a political regime that prohibited all kinds of democracy and freedom. Although Franco died in 1975 and the policies he had set up during nearly forty years of rule were gradually dismantled and discredited, social, political, and cultural repression in Spain did not cease immediately. Spain still suffered from a lack of cultural information. Books did not reach major bookshops in Madrid and Barcelona; films were censored or banned, especially those focusing on sex, religion, or morals. The atmosphere was stifling and drab. Almost every week, a journalist, critic, or editor was taken to court and charged with a string of offenses. Despite these obstacles, many Spanish writers, filmmakers, theater directors, and artists traveled abroad in order to continue their craft uncensored. If exile was impossible, they managed to find ways of getting the information they were denied at home.

Thus, the new developments of Spanish art in the 1970's took the art world almost completely by surprise. No one writing a retrospective of Spanish art at the end of the 1960's would have seriously expected that a new art that replaced objects with actions could attract more than a few isolated practitioners, yet both conceptual art (art that emphasizes the exploration of ideas, notions, and rational motives) and Arte Povera ("Poor Art," a movement begun in Italy that used materials that were considered aesthetically impoverished or irredeemable) found a great many followers in a very short time. Much of the inspiration came from outside the country, a consequence of the new generation's unusual mobility and open-mindedness, yet the new art was not without some basis in both traditional and contemporary Spanish attitudes.

Conceptual art attracted attention between 1971 and 1975 largely because it was associated with acts of political opposition to the Franco dictatorship such as the signing of petitions and participation in demonstrations. This was especially true of the Catalan Grup de Treball composed of Antoni Muntadas, Francesc Abad, and Francesc Torres, among others. Many artists, however, found themselves in a dilemma. Should they make conventional work to please the narrow-minded taste of Spanish art dealers, or should they follow such aesthetic tendencies as neoconstructivism (so-called cybernetic art) or the critical figurative trend termed "Chronicle of Reality"? This latter movement was represented by two Valencian groups, Equipo Cronica and Equipo Realidad, as well as by some well-known individual artists. These two main currents, despite their differences, had a common point of reference in Spain's ever-growing industrial and consumer society.

During the ensuing period of transition to democracy, there was a considerable slackening of the political tension that had provided a certain justification for creativity in the arts; a tension, moreover, that was so intense that some of the more nostalgic combatants later maintained that they were "better off" (more creative) under Franco. The vast majority of young creative artists in the country were either neofigurativists, and thus poles apart from critical realism and political pop art, or abstract artists of some type or another. All of them, in any case, were returning to the idea of painting as an end in itself, a notion accepted even by those who still believed in painting as a revolutionary political practice.

It was at this juncture, in Madrid, that the liberating influence of Luis Gordillo, a little-known painter of the previous generation, stimulated several younger men— Rafael Pérez-Minguez, Carlos Alcolea, Carlos Franco, Herminio Molero, Manolo Quejido, and Guillermo Pérez Villalta—to lay the foundations of a new figurative art and, in general, to open up a new horizon of concerns, tastes, and cultural references.

Gordillo, a painter born in 1934, helped to catalyze and liberate the attitudes of the younger artists. By 1971, when Gordillo held an exhibition of drawings in Madrid, his work had already developed considerably in breadth and complexity. Gordillo's work in the 1960's was the paradigmatic embodiment of the general crisis of art in the decade. He was one of the artists of his generation who had most intensely and originally confronted the avant-garde assumptions current in the 1960's. As a result of his artistic theories and practice, painting was able to recover its independence as the surface on which body and consciousness are reflected.

Impact of Event

More than any other individual painter, Luis Gordillo influenced a generation of young Spanish artists in the 1970's. Spanish figurative painting during that time possessed a surprising strength and originality. The automatic drawings of Gordillo exhibited in 1971 showed that he had broken his ties with simple expressionism; they both affirmed and denied spontaneity, showing the dual nature—the folding and unfolding—of creative art. As a result, he propitiated the development of a versatility that was to be the watchword of the generation of the 1970's. It was a generation of mannerists, in concept or in feeling, and even, in some cases, in both.

A major impact of the artistic boom of the 1970's was the decentralization of Spanish art. Although other cities had been major art centers in other areas, the postwar period was both aesthetically and economically dominated by Madrid—even though the community of artists consisted almost entirely of people who had been born and reared in the provinces. This influence continued, with the number of galleries more than doubling, but the provincial movements and markets also gained strength. Barcelona reaffirmed and expanded its rebellious role, emphasizing its own unique culture while at the same time opening up to new ideas from outside the country. After going nearly two decades without producing another generation of young artists, Barcelona was suddenly deluged by a wave of conceptualists and became, along with a number of neighboring towns, home to the newest Spanish art. Valencia and Seville likewise built up numbers of young artists and established both representational and geometric tendencies that were capable of bearing comparison with those in Madrid and Barcelona. Even the Basques, spurred by the teachings and example of Jorge de Oteiza, came to unify themselves into something resembling a regional movement.

All things considered, Spain's contemporary art of the 1970's was both exciting and astonishing. It managed to achieve and maintain a high level of quality in spite of the circumstances in which it developed and the immense indifference that it encountered. Until the early 1970's, the Spanish public showed no interest in contemporary art—except to ridicule or attack it. Moreover, support from the government was largely limited to exhibitions that made use of the art to give the country a more progressive image abroad. Censorship, which remained negligible as long as art remained abstract, was revived with figuration and resulted in the occasional closing of exhibitions and even in prosecution of artists. Right-wing groups succeeded in vandalizing galleries and bookstores without notable opposition from the police.

As a result of the explosion of new ideas in the post-Franco era, artists working in traditional media of painting and sculpture achieved a high and fashionable profile. Yet there were also lesser known, more subversive forces at work that questioned and opened up the parameters of fine art for decades to come.

Bibliography

Aliaga, Juan Vincente. "Conceptual Art in Spain: Traditionalism Subtly Undermined." *Art International* 6 (Spring, 1989): 28-31. Author traces the roots of the conceptual movement in the early 1970's and follows it through the 1980's. Discusses the two major trends in contemporary Spanish art: artists working in the traditional media of painting and sculpture as well as artists who question the parameters of fine art.

Lippard, Lucy R., ed. *Six Years: The Dematerialization of the Art Object from 1966 to 1972.* New York: Praeger, 1973. Interesting study by a reputable art historian. Provides useful information on the growth and development of the conceptual art movement in the twentieth century. Cross-references, numerous illustrations, and a bibliography.

Meyers, Ursula. *Conceptual Art.* New York: E. P. Dutton, 1972. An excellent survey of conceptual art, primarily focusing on the movement in the United States. Provides insight into the works of individual artists as well as the general period. Contains numerous illustrations and a bibliography.

Serraller, Calvo. "Spanish Painting Today: The New Figurativists." *Flash Art* 107 (May, 1982): 43-46. Comments on the Spanish artistic crisis of the 1970's that was partly caused by the fact that artists no longer had to fight Franco. The author sees Luis Gordillo as the stimulus for the foundation of a new figurative art in Madrid. He explains why he concentrates on the Madrid group and speculates on why there has not been a broad exhibition of Spanish figurative art outside Spain.

Tager, Alisa. "Spain's Lost Generation: The Artists of *La Nueva Figuracion.*" *Journal of Art* 4 (February, 1991): 27-30. The author calls attention to a group who inspired many Spanish artists of the productive era after Franco's death. Tager argues that Spain's cultural isolation during Franco's rule led to the underestimation of the public stature of this group of artists and calls for a reconsideration of their work.

Genevieve Slomski

Cross-References

The New Objectivity Movement Is Introduced (1925), p. 631; Buñuel and Dalí Champion Surrealism in *Un Chien andalou* (1928), p. 750; Picasso Paints *Guernica* (1937), p. 1062; García Lorca's *Poet in New York* Is Published (1940), p. 1179; A Dalí Museum Opens in Figueras, Spain (1974), p. 2310.

DESIGN FOR THE REAL WORLD REORIENTS INDUSTRIAL DESIGN

Category of event: Architecture
Time: 1970
Locale: New York, New York; Helsinki, Finland; and Stockholm, Sweden

Victor J. Papanek's Design for the Real World *decried the wastage and ecological disaster flowing from what he perceived as the socially delinquent values of industrial designers*

Principal personages:
> VICTOR J. PAPANEK (1925-   ), an influential industrial designer, educator, and author
> R. BUCKMINSTER FULLER (1895-1983), an innovative architect/structural designer; a friend of Papanek
> FRANK LLOYD WRIGHT (1867-1959), a major modern architect who taught and influenced Papanek
> RAYMOND FERNAND LOEWY (1893-1986), a distinguished industrial designer

Summary of Event

Victor J. Papanek began his career as a well-trained product designer but left industry for academia in 1954. During his early years, he had been exposed to the finest design instruction available in America, at New York's Cooper Union as well as at the Massachusetts Institute of Technology. In addition, he had studied with genuine masters, including Frank Lloyd Wright, one of the modern world's seminal architects and designers, and French-born Raymond Loewy, for years a regnant figure in American product design. Moreover, as Papanek's career ripened, he gained considerable experience in countries and cultures in which design societies had originated, among them Sweden, his native Austria, Germany, Denmark, the United Kingdom, Norway, and Finland. He therefore was sensitive to his profession's historical foundations, its principles, and its evolved responsibilities.

Papanek's major popular work, *Design for the Real World: Human Ecology and Social Change* (1971), initially appeared in a Swedish edition (*Miljön och Miljonerna,* 1970) while its author was chairman and professor of the environmental and industrial design department of Purdue University. Publication of the book's first American edition in 1971 coincided with his becoming dean of the California Institute of the Arts' school of design. Papanek's indictment of the arrogant trivialities, sycophancy, and social irresponsibility of industrial designers, of their educators, of their Western corporate employers, and of their middle-class customers therefore was lent credence by his familiarity with the sources and objects of his revelations.

Provocative and occasionally strident, Papanek's *Design for the Real World*, while drawing its examples from the follies and lethal failings of industrial designers, more broadly and impressionistically critiques cultures with distorted capitalist values. It was these values, Papanek believed, that promised the certain extinction of his own profession. Far more tragically, these values had murderous consequences within the Western world and threatened to produce further worldwide genocidal horrors and attendant miseries, which by the 1960's were already visibly affecting billions of people.

Papanek organized these generic observations more substantively around three major propositions. First, most product or industrial design, in his view, chiefly reflected nothing more than the fantasies and social blindness of bourgeois cultures. Design therefore almost exclusively pandered to the tastes—rather than genuine needs—of relatively affluent, middle-class, middle-aged people whose lives were spent in Western postindustrial societies. Papanek saw that as explaining the seduction and bamboozlement of large numbers of poorer people into purchasing shoddy or soon-to-be-obsolete products at exorbitant prices. The cultivation and propitiation of bourgeois consumers, worse yet, led to the neglect of vast areas of human needs even within developed economies. With their energies channeled toward a middle-class clientele, designers (and those who employed them) thus notoriously ignored development of products that might have alleviated the plights of the physically disabled, retarded children and babies, left-handed persons, the obese, the elderly, or the poor. On a larger scale, the vast and swelling populations of developing countries were almost entirely excluded from consideration, the mitigation of their circumstances and needs almost entirely ignored.

Papanek's second theme stressed the necessity of bringing multidisciplinary talents and insights to bear upon industrial design. Isolated from all but the near-sighted ambitions and objectives of their corporate masters, designers tended to function in the barren cloisters of their own overspecialization. Accordingly, they were ignorant of the requirements of production and how design choices would affect manufacturing of the products they designed. They were similarly ignorant of the prevailing cultural conditions and the capacities and needs of their designs' final users. Papanek thought it essential that designers be trained as generalists, that they work as teams in interdisciplinary environments, and that their designs emanate from products' prospective users.

Papanek's third theme enlarged upon implications in the first two. Basically, it decried the fantasy worlds that enveloped postindustrial nations' product design to the exclusion of the stark necessities of the grossly underresourced, fearful, and miserable "real" world—that is, the underdeveloped countries known collectively as the Third World. Papanek's examples of follies, inefficiencies, and waste attributable to Western nations' addiction to fantasies—and the profits flowing from them—were abundant. He cited hundreds of millions of lives and trillions of dollars worth of scarce resources squandered in the designs dedicated to the twentieth century's murderous wars and the attrition of raw materials through the planned obsolescence of mass-produced goods. The "Kleenex culture," as Papanek dubbed it, was characterized by the prodigalities and ecological disasters hatched by badly designed technology of the ludicrous Ford Edsel or supersonic transport variety. Less obvious were the design of high-priced pens that failed to write and had no refills; of life-sized, inflatable plastic "play girls" for men; of lethal toys for children; of diapers for pet parakeets; of luxury hotels on the ocean floor; of more than twenty thousand types of chairs, few of which were designed for human comfort; of safety helmets that were untested and provided little safety; of indoor "jogging" equipment; and of excessive packaging that grossly inflated product prices and led to pollution. Like his friend, architect and designer R. Buckminster Fuller, Papanek was outraged by the trivialization of life on a planet that he believed confronted imminent ecological destruction. In that regard, he spoke for many others.

Impact of Event

Eliciting widespread, if mixed, media reviews, *Design for the Real World* served to swell the substantial chorus of discontent in postindustrial nations that marked much of the 1960's and 1970's. Papanek, both by his tenor and by his specifics, furnished additional evidence of failures of the establishment to reformers, whether their focus was upon alternative life-styles, saving the earth, outreach to the poor and other neglected populations, disassembling corporate capitalism, mitigating racial conflict, erasing vestiges of colonialism, bringing equal status to women, or ending the Vietnam War.

Although some of his examples had not been previously exploited, Papanek's general perspectives, by 1970, had already entered into the public domain. Ralph Nader's revelations about the automotive industry, contained in *Unsafe at Any Speed: The Designed-in Dangers of the American Automobile* (1965), were more calmly reasoned and accurate than Papanek's material. His book doubtless helped to inform Papanek's efforts. Similarly, R. Buckminster Fuller, who wrote a rambling introduction to *Design for the Real World*, had long sounded the tocsin against ecological damage ensuing from the wastes and inefficiencies identified with American economic life. His campaign culminated with the compilation of the *Inventory of World Resources, Human Trends, and Needs: The Design Initiative* (1966), the first in a multivolume set. The title only lightly masked the book's varied ecological warnings for what Fuller described elsewhere as "Spaceship Earth." Many other critical authors likewise had preceded Papanek in voicing their skepticism, concerns, or outrage concerning the deleterious effects of design on consumers, humanity, and the environment. Among them were Lewis Mumford (beginning in 1934); Vance Packard, who exposed the nation's "hidden persuaders," "status seekers," and "wastemakers" in the 1950's; Paul Ehrlich, who made dire predictions in *Eco-Catastrophe* (1969); and Russell Lynes, who denounced America's "tastemakers" in 1954 and whose views were subsequently matched by those of James Alexander Campbell Brown's *Techniques of Persuasion: From Propaganda to Brainwashing* (1963). Paul Goodman wrote on "growing up absurd" and "compulsory miseducation," and Robert Lindner assaulted conformity and gave his prescription for rebellion during the early 1950's.

If such works constituted some of the immediate context for the reception of Papanek's book, Papanek nevertheless reached beyond them to embrace the themes of one of the most learned and trenchant of America's critics, Thorstein Veblen. A masterful satirizer of nineteenth century capitalism's institutional barbarities—and later the inspiring force behind development of an American (engineering) technocracy—Veblen had published his scathing indictment of capitalist mores and manners in *The Theory of the Leisure Class* in 1899. In the process, he had coined phrases that had become part of American speech, such as "conspicuous consumption," "conspicuous leisure," "conspicuous waste," "acquisitive instinct," and "pecuniary emulation." By the 1960's, Veblen's classic work—as well as a spate of studies on Veblen himself—enjoyed unprecedented popularity, providing an intellectual framework and pertinent caricatures for reindictment of American values. This, in turn, prepared the ground for readier acceptance of Papanek's views as well as those of kindred reformers.

Papanek's book certainly gained currency within his profession and was in vogue on campuses during the early 1970's. Like Nader's spectacularly successful exposé of the American automotive industry, which was aimed at a general public audience, Papanek's book also avoided narrow address solely to his profession and related industries. For several reasons, however, its potential impact may have been softened. In tone it was more strident and less carefully reasoned than Nader's book. From the outset, it was suffused with dubious, sweeping generalizations, for example, that "population sinks" in city ghettos shared "absolutely none" of the middle class's "motivations and aspirations." In response, reviewers suggested that the urban poor may indeed aspire to higher incomes, decent housing, economic mobility, extensive health care, consumer goods, and equal education. Further, Papanek marred the book with his own gratuitousness. If, as he frequently proclaimed, he preferred the art of North Vietnam, Cuba, and China to that of Western postimpressionists and cubists—Piet Mondrian in particular was ridiculed—or the architecture of Paolo Soleri to that of the Bauhaus, those constituted legitimate personal tastes. His insistence upon the superiority of his own choices, however, led him to the same narrow advocacy of taste for which he condemned his own profession and its corporate associates. In addition to being unreflective and sweeping in approach, Papanek also littered his work with the hallmarks of haste and carelessness, slips that even sympathetic professionals as well as media reviewers dutifully noted. Zeppelins, for example, were not phased out in the 1930's because they used highly flammable helium; aspects of mass production require qualification but mass production itself was scarcely "a myth," as Papanek claimed. Papanek could not cite some important sources and miscited others: John Mitchell, for example, was credited with seven books that were written, in fact, by Lewis Mumford, and there were similar misattributions of John Kouwenhoven's writings. These shortcomings obscured rather than negated the validity of the issues raised by Papanek. Those who shared some of his anxieties were heartened when, with different emphases and examples, he re-addressed and embellished them in 1983 with publication of his *Design for Human Scale.*

Bibliography

Fuller, R. Buckminster, ed. *Inventory of World Resources, Human Trends, and Needs: The Design Initiative.* Carbondale: Southern Illinois University Press, 1966. Fuller, a friend of Papanek, raises in this first of a multivolume series many of the issues that concerned Papanek, but both more broadly and more substantively. Interesting reading from an accomplished intellect.

Nader, Ralph. *Unsafe at Any Speed: The Designed-in Dangers of the American Automobile.* New York: Grossman, 1965. This classic exposé of the automotive industry and its relationships with government, carefully researched and reasoned, places Papanek's work in proper perspective as a reformist piece. Nader not only produced better reformist research but also became the most persistent, articulate, visible, and successful consumer advocate in the United States. Illustrations, notes, and index.

Papanek, Victor J. *Design for Human Scale.* New York: Van Nostrand Reinhold, 1983. Meeting with better professional reception than his earlier work, this book deals less with what design had become and why than with how to design efficiently and humanely. Stress remains upon user participation, ecological realities, cultural differences, and the scarcity of resources. Many illustrations and photos. Good index but a poor bibliography.

_____. *Design for the Real World: Human Ecology and Social Change.* New York: Pantheon Books, 1971. Worth reading if only as a "tract for its times." Many photos and illustrations, several of interesting designs by Papanek and his students. No index. Confused, often inaccurate bibliography. Generally available in major libraries.

Veblen, Thorstein. *The Theory of the Leisure Class.* New York: Macmillan, 1899. Still widely available, this classic continues to provide a major frame of reference for critics (such as Papanek) of the consequences of the inefficiencies and distorted values at work in American society. Reading requires close attention, as Veblen was one of the more broadly learned men of his day. There are many recent paperback editions, many with impressive introductions. No notes, illustrations, or bibliography. Veblen put his learning directly into his text.

Clifton K. Yearley

Cross-References

Loewy Pioneers American Industrial Design (1929), p. 777; Wright Founds the Taliesin Fellowship (1932), p. 902; Dreyfuss Designs the Bell "300" Telephone (1937), p. 1057; The Guggenheim Museum Opens in a Building Designed by Wright (1959), p. 1806; Expo 67 Presents Innovative Architectural Concepts (1967), p. 2081.

SONDHEIM'S *COMPANY* IS BROADWAY'S FIRST "CONCEPT" MUSICAL

Category of event: Music
Time: April 26, 1970
Locale: Alvin Theater, New York, New York

In Company, *Stephen Sondheim emphasized plot-driven songs that were integrated into an overriding thematic focus, or "concept"*

Principal personages:
STEPHEN SONDHEIM (1930-   ), a lyricist and composer who moved the Broadway musical into the modern era
GEORGE FURTH (1932-   ), a dramatic writer turned librettist who wrote the first concept "book" for *Company*
HAL PRINCE (1928-   ), the producer and director of *Company*

Summary of Event

The Broadway musical had coasted for several decades on the Richard Rodgers and Oscar Hammerstein II approach to theater: cardboard characters in elaborate plots moved forward by the "book" and not by the songs, which were included solely in hopes of providing hits for Tin Pan Alley. Although such musicals as *Oklahoma!* (1943) and *Carousel* (1945) had once been noteworthy and innovative, imitators had watered down the form, and the theatrical world had moved past the pastel niceness of the upbeat, happy-ending product. Even experimental Broadway fare such as *Hair* (1968) followed essentially the same formula: "moments" in the play that could be culled or inserted almost at random, moments that froze the play's action as they were sung and danced.

Some signals of a desire for change in the theater-going public were apparent in the successes of *Man of La Mancha* (1965), *Fiddler on the Roof* (1964), and *Cabaret* (1966). In these musicals, plot was subordinated to mood and to a more introverted psychological message, with characters more complex and fully defined.

In the old mode, however, was *West Side Story* (1957), a modernization of the Romeo and Juliet story set on the rough West Side of New York City. Its young lyricist was Stephen Sondheim, and the complexity and sophistication of the lyrics he provided signaled a new talent on Broadway. The success of the musical afforded Sondheim the opportunity to expand his contribution and his distinct style in a string of subsequent successes.

The next musical with Sondheim lyrics was *Gypsy* (1959), with music by Jule Styne, another success in the Rodgers and Hammerstein form but moving toward more serious, more substantial songwriting. By this time, Sondheim had gained a reputation that allowed him to try both music and lyrics. *A Funny Thing Happened on the Way to the Forum* (1962), the first musical for which Sondheim contributed both lyrics and music, was successfully produced by Hal Prince and directed by George Abbott. Though the production was still episodic and superficial in characterization, the clever lyrics and the unexpectedly convoluted musical forms became the signature of Sondheim's unique personality.

The play that truly changed the face of American musicals, however, was *Company*, which opened on Broadway on April 26, 1970, after a Boston tryout. Sondheim wrote both the music and lyrics for the work while George Furth wrote the book, in this case a loosely woven, virtually plotless series of scenes focusing on the marriage prospects and the development of the central character, Robert. Unlike in other musicals, however, the lion's share of song and dialogue was given not to the central figure but to the characters surrounding him. In addition, the songs were distinctly integral to the movement of the play and could not be comfortably removed from the musical and performed as individual pieces. Even the show-stopping "The Ladies Who Lunch" demanded the urban, cynical setting that Elaine Stritch gave it in performance.

The play was produced and directed by Hal Prince, who had enjoyed several successes in collaboration with these artists in the past. Michael Bennett was chosen as choreographer, although there were no chorus numbers in the strict sense. The set was designed by Boris Aronson and the costumes by D. D. Ryan.

A Boston tryout revealed several problems with the script; one song ("Happily Ever After") was dropped as being too negative and was replaced by "Being Alive." Every segment of the play's parts, from the musical harmonies to the structure of the moments through the play, were worked on in minute detail by the whole creative team involved. No single voice overrode the piece; it was truly a collaboration of creative spirits. Never before had a musical been talked about in terms of its integrity, its overall message, its texture. Heretofore, the box office had been the only consideration. Now, with Prince and Sondheim both approaching the project in terms of its artistic unity, the work became a model for more complex, richer artistic experiences on the part of the artists as well as the audience. The ratio of spoken to sung dialogue was closer to that of opera than to that of standard musical fare.

The Alvin Theater was chosen as the site, and the cast was assembled. Notable among the cast were Elaine Stritch (Joanne), Beth Howland (Amy), and George Coe (David), but the entire cast consisted of professionals, not celebrities, who knew their way around the Broadway musical stage.

The play opened to mixed reviews. Reserved but intrigued, Clive Barnes of *The New York Times* wrote, "It is a very New York show" that, despite his reservations, deserved to be a hit. Barnes noted that Sondheim's lyrics stood out and that "they have a lyric suppleness, sparse, elegant wit, and range from the virtuosity of a patter song to a kind of sweetly laconic cynicism in a modern love song." Barnes also commented that Sondheim "must be one of the most sophisticated composers ever to write Broadway musicals, yet the result is slick, clever and eclectic rather than exciting."

The original Robert was Dean Jones, but he was replaced a few weeks after the opening by Larry Kert. Mel Gussow, then a second-string reviewer for *The New York Times*, reviewed the play after Jones's departure and wrote:

> This is, by design, not a musical about a man, but about a theme: marriage and non-marriage in an urban society. Intentionally, the hero is underwritten, which makes him especially difficult to play. . . . The scenes whose impulse comes from the music, and not from the book, seem distinctly superior."

Gussow's remarks became the basis for the term "concept musical," a production in which a theme or idea is examined in musical and dramatic terms. What the audience saw was not what they expected. There were no leading man and lady singing their way through a plot with songs popping up at arbitrary occasions. Instead, five couples, all married or committed in some way, take turns arguing in favor of the institution of marriage to their bachelor friend Robert. The musical numbers identify the specific relationships between members of each pair and articulate the couples' various and complicated relationships with Robert. At the same time, Robert is shown involved in superficial ways with three girlfriends, each a candidate for marriage but none fulfilling Robert's expectations completely. The theme, or "concept," of the musical, then, is the examination of the variety of marriage contracts, the ways in which people commit or do not commit to each other. Nor is there the typical happy ending—Robert does not "get the girl" in the end. Instead, Robert simply disappears, never showing up at his surprise party. The audience is left to wonder if suicide, a change of identity, or simply an elopement has brought this stage in Robert's life to its conclusion.

Also absent from the new musical form was the big dance number, with dancing that showed off the choreographer's virtuosity rather than providing movement integral to the show itself. Michael Bennett, the show's choreographer, painstakingly structured the actors' movements into an ensemble, highlighting the structure and rhythm of the individual scenes. The show's structure was not interrupted by the typical full-cast spectacular number, with extras in ethnic or historical costume showing off everything but the sense of the drama.

Company's story and music are extremely sophisticated, by which is meant that the complexities of the art form are explored—there are no easy solutions, no cartoon characters, no hummable tunes. For example, one of the most successful songs in the musical, "Getting Married Today," is sung at a double-staccato pace; it is a tour de force for the actress who sings it but is hardly a Top-Forty candidate. Another hit, "The Ladies Who Lunch," is so cynical in tone and so arhythmic and atonal in musical structure that it takes a hard-edged singer such as Elaine Stritch, and a jaundiced audience, to recognize the truth in the complex social image it captures.

Impact of Event

Theatergoers and critics acknowledged the quality and innovation of *Company* by giving it several awards at season's end. The musical won Tony Awards for best musical, best music, best lyrics, best director of a musical, and best scenic design. The play also won the New York Drama Critics Circle Award for best musical that year.

Company was a moderate box-office success. The 690 performances set no records, but a relatively modest budget and daily cost of production made the musical turn a profit for its investors. As the Sondheim hits continued, it became clear that there was a new kind of musical in the making, one far removed from the niceness of the old. Sondheim followed *Company* with another ensemble show, *Follies* (1971), which focused on the reminiscences of mature people whose love lives were now being remembered and experienced through the past rather than the present. *Follies* was followed by *A Little Night Music* (1973), *Pacific Overtures* (1976), *Sweeney Todd* (1979), *Merrily We Roll Along* (1981), *Sunday in the Park with George* (1984), *Into the Woods* (1987), and *Assassins* (1990).

The string of musicals was by no means universally successful—*Merrily We Roll Along*, for example, closed after only sixteen performances, and *Assassins* never got to Broadway—but they marked a singular voice in American musical theater. A bare handful of songs from these musicals ever made their way to the mass-media public ("Send in the Clowns," from *A Little Night Music*, was recorded by Judy Collins, and "Not a Day Goes By," from *Merrily We Roll Along*, was recorded by Carly Simon), but Broadway musical fans bought the full show recordings in substantial numbers. Two televised celebrations of Sondheim's work are available in videotape: a 1985 concert recital of *Follies* and a 1992 Carnegie Hall retrospective and celebration.

What all these musicals had in common was the central theme or idea that was not easily paraphrased. Each was also structured to accommodate a multiple perspective, driven by complex musical and lyrical creativity, and aimed at artistic expression rather than box-office success.

The old style of musical, though, was not gone completely. When the "unhummable" songs of Sondheim seemed to have overtaken the theater, the Tony Awards of 1985 showed otherwise. *Sunday in the Park with George*, despite many nominations for best musical in several categories, was overshadowed by the more traditional *La Cage Aux Folles* (1983). Nevertheless, small-cast musicals did become more musically sophisticated in ensuing years. They held the Broadway musical market in place until the invasion of British products such as *Cats* (1981), *Les Misérables* (1980), *Phantom of the Opera* (1986), and *Chess* (1986), plays in which the technical skills, sets, costumes, special effects, and spectacle of the stage overtook the plot and songs.

Sondheim himself has summed up his contribution by remarking that "The biggest challenge for me is the opportunity to constantly try new things. I believe it's the writer's job to educate the audience . . . to bring them things they would never have expected to see."

Bibliography

Green, Stanley. *The World of Musical Comedy.* 4th rev. ed. San Diego, Calif.: A. S.

Barnes, 1980. Best for the history of the form as it moves through pairs of collaborators chapter by chapter. Sondheim's contributions are placed in perspective with those of Richard Rodgers and Lorenz Hart, Rodgers and Hammerstein, and others. Discography and index.

Kislan, Richard. *The Musical: A Look at the American Musical Theater.* Englewood Cliffs, N.J.: Prentice-Hall, 1980. Sondheim is discussed at great length as a mature artist who has contributed to the complexities of the elements of musical theater. More than simple stage history; especially valuable as a guide to the collaborative process.

Spurrier, James Joseph. *The Integration of Music and Lyrics with the Book in the American Musical.* Ann Arbor, Mich.: University Microfilms, 1982. An important book for the study of "the techniques by which and the degree to which the musical elements" of Sondheim and others advance the plots of their musicals. Best for explaining Sondheim's unique contributions. Appendices and bibliography.

Swain, Joseph P. *The Broadway Musical: A Critical and Musical Survey.* New York: Oxford University Press, 1990. A sophisticated examination of the relation of music to theme in the American musical. Mostly post-*Oklahoma!* selections are discussed; requires an ability to read music for full appreciation of the thesis and its thorough treatment.

Zadan, Craig. *Sondheim and Co.* 2d ed. New York: Harper & Row, 1986. A thorough, informative, conversational overview of Sondheim's career, told primarily in interview form by those who worked with Sondheim. Rehearsal problems, backstage controversies, and reviewers' comments are surveyed. Illustrated throughout with production stills and candid photographs. Full appendices of production information and cast albums; index.

Thomas J. Taylor

Cross-References

Show Boat Introduces American Musical Theater (1927), p. 745; *Oklahoma!* Opens on Broadway (1943), p. 1256; Porter Creates an Integrated Score for *Kiss Me, Kate* (1948), p. 1404; Bernstein Joins Symphonic and Jazz Elements in *West Side Story* (1957), p. 1731; The Radical Musical *Hair* Opens on Broadway (1968), p. 2121; *Jesus Christ Superstar* Establishes the Rock Opera (1971), p. 2254; Sondheim Uses Operatic Techniques in *Sweeney Todd* (1979), p. 2433.

THE MARY TYLER MOORE SHOW
EXAMINES WOMEN'S ROLES

Category of event: Television and radio
Time: September 19, 1970-September 3, 1977
Locale: The United States

The Mary Tyler Moore Show *further established television situation comedies featuring independent women*

Principal personages:
MARY TYLER MOORE (1937-   ), an actress who portrayed Mary Richards on *The Mary Tyler Moore Show*
GRANT TINKER (1926-   ), Moore's then-husband and corporate vice president of CBS, also cofounder of MTM Enterprises
JAMES L. BROOKS (1940-   ), a writer who, with Allan Burns, created *The Mary Tyler Moore Show*
ALLAN BURNS (1929-   ), a writer who, with James L. Brooks, created *The Mary Tyler Moore Show*
ED ASNER (1929-   ), an actor who played Lou Grant on *The Mary Tyler Moore Show* and *Lou Grant*
VALERIE HARPER (1940-   ), an actress who played Rhoda Morgenstern on *The Mary Tyler Moore Show* and *Rhoda*

Summary of Event

The Mary Tyler Moore Show began airing on September 19, 1970, and went off the air on September 3, 1977. It was one of the most literate and lasting situation comedies of the 1970's. More important, it was one of the pioneers of the "independent woman" television genre. Mary Richards (Mary Tyler Moore) is the idealized single career woman. She moves to Minneapolis, Minnesota, after her fiancé leaves her, then gets a job as assistant producer of the local news show on television station WJM-TV. She moves into an old apartment building and finds friendship with Rhoda Morgenstern (Valerie Harper), an interior decorator for a local department store. Rhoda also is single, but unlike Mary, she desperately seeks a husband. Phyllis Lindstrom (Cloris Leachman) is Mary's busybody landlady.

At the office, Mary finds another family to rely on. Her boss, Lou Grant (Ed Asner), is a cantankerous and mildly sexist man, soft underneath his gruff exterior. Murray Slaughter (Gavin McLeod) is the head newswriter at the station. He is happily married and has a positive attitude about work and life, along with a snide sense of humor, especially when it is aimed at his colleague Ted Baxter (Ted Knight). Ted is the "pretty boy" anchorman who is less than average in intelligence but makes up for this lack with an inflated ego. Ted has a long courtship with Georgette Franklin

(Georgia Engels), a vacuous blonde whom he eventually marries.

The program had a cast of other recurring characters, including Bess Lindstrom (Lisa Gerritsen), who played Phyllis' daughter on the show from 1970 to 1975. John Amos played Gordy Howard, WJM-TV's weatherman, from 1970 to 1973. Sue Ann Nivens, played by Betty White, arrived at the station in 1973 with her "Happy Home-maker Show." Sue Ann is a foil for Mary's role as the independent woman. She is in her late forties and very man-hungry, spending the bulk of her time outlandishly pursuing men. Joyce Bulifont portrayed Murray's wife, Marie, from 1971 to 1977, and Priscilla Morrill played Lou's wife, Edie, in 1973 and 1974. Robbie Rist played David Baxter in 1976 and 1977. Along with the cast of regulars, *The Mary Tyler Moore Show* often employed guest stars for specific episodes, among them Nancy Walker as Rhoda's mother, Slim Pickens, Michael Constantine, Jack Cassidy, Jerry Van Dyke, Louise Lasser, Penny Marshall, and John Ritter, along with Johnny Carson and Wal-ter Cronkite playing themselves.

Although Moore was the star, *The Mary Tyler Moore Show* had no single perspec-tive. Moore's role often was to react to others, to play within the framework of a solid ensemble to sharpen and define herself and the other characters. James L. Brooks, a cocreator of the show, believed that its success stemmed from its plausible characters. Where Norman Lear would have made a big point of Mary's sex life, Brooks and Allan Burns decided to deal with issues more subtly. Rather than facing large issues, *The Mary Tyler Moore Show* was more interested in dealing with small problems of daily life. Brooks also stressed that the show was more attuned to verbal comedy than were Lear's programs, which dealt more with situations than with subtlety. Even though *The Mary Tyler Moore Show* theoretically did not take on problems of magnitude, it did tackle issues within an individual framework. One episode dealt with Rhoda coming to terms with one of Mary's friends who is preju-diced, and another focused on Phyllis trying to get her brother interested in Mary, not knowing that he is gay. Others dealt with Lou's divorce and Murray's thoughts of infidelity. These big issues were treated on a small scale, but they are big issues nevertheless.

Mary Tyler Moore as an actress was not new to television success. She played Laura Petrie, wife of television writer Robert Petrie, on the highly successful *The Dick Van Dyke Show* (1961-1966). She won an Emmy Award for her work on the series in 1964 and 1965. Having the popularity of *The Dick Van Dyke Show* under her belt, she wanted to branch out into something different. In 1963, she married Grant Tinker, who became corporate vice president of the Columbia Broadcasting System (CBS) and then founder of MTM (Mary Tyler Moore) Enterprises, the pro-duction company responsible for *The Mary Tyler Moore Show*. Ironically, Moore intended Mary Richards to be a divorcée, but CBS complained that the public would never accept a divorcée as a funny heroine. This resulted in a compromise making Richards a jilted lover, ambitious and ready to make a new life for herself.

Grant Tinker was married to Mary Tyler Moore from 1963 until they divorced in 1981. MTM Enterprises was founded by Moore, Tinker, and Arthur Price. Tinker's philosophy for MTM was to maintain a high standard of quality and creativity. This idea remained evident as he took the helm as president of the National Broadcasting Company (NBC) from 1981 to 1986. Tinker tried to stay within his standards for quality programming during his tenure as president of NBC but found he had to make compromises for the sake of profits.

Tinker was very influential in making *The Mary Tyler Moore Show*, but the writers who created the series also deserve credit for being the driving forces behind the new type of television series pioneered by the program. Writers Allan Burns and James L. Brooks had been successful with the popular television series *Room 222* in the late 1960's and early 1970's, so they were seasoned and ready to take on the responsibilities of creating a new program for CBS. Brooks was executive producer and cocreator of *The Mary Tyler Moore Show*. Later he cocreated *Rhoda*, sharing the title of executive producer for that show as well as for *Lou Grant*. Brooks would also become known for writing and directing *Broadcast News* (1987).

A shift in viewing habits in the early 1970's caused television executives to seek innovative types of programming. Demographics were coming into use, breaking down audiences by age, sex, income, and other sociological variables. These data described networks' target audiences. The Brooks and Burns concept for *The Mary Tyler Moore Show* fit into this new mold, appealing to upscale audiences with more refinement and sophistication than previously seen on network television. Programs like *The Mary Tyler Moore Show* set the tone for prime-time entertainment for decades to come.

The Mary Tyler Moore Show did not magically appear on the airwaves without having had some formidable influences. *That Girl*, starring Marlo Thomas, was the prototype for the influx of the "independent woman" series. It ran from September 8, 1966, until September 10, 1971, and was a huge success. Marlo Thomas played Ann Marie, an eager actress who left the comfort and stability of her parents' home for the bright lights of New York City. Don Hollinger (Ted Bessell), a junior executive for *Newsview Magazine*, was her steady boyfriend. Don and Ann Marie finally got engaged during the final season of the program, but they never married. The series ended with Don's stag party.

Like *The Mary Tyler Moore Show*, *That Girl* dealt with different aspects of a woman's life by looking at her family, work associates, friends, and neighbors. For the first time, television audiences got a glimpse of a working woman's life. Even if it was often a rather shallow representation, just the idea that a woman could have a happy and productive life outside of being a wife and mother was a startling image for television to represent. *The Doris Day Show* (1968-1973) also helped establish the marketability of the "independent woman" genre.

Another popular series that debuted soon after *The Mary Tyler Moore Show* began its run was *All in the Family* (1971-1983). Norman Lear's series was the foundation for television's format for the domestic comedy, while Tinker's MTM Enterprises pioneered the format for the workplace series. Programs produced by MTM concentrated more on showing an alternative to the nuclear family, while Lear simply worked within that framework. Together, Lear's Tandem Productions and MTM Enterprises dominated programming in these areas, for years offering many programs in the top ten spots in ratings.

Impact of Event

As a direct result of *The Mary Tyler Moore Show*'s popularity, a cascade of spin-offs, television's answer to the sequel, populated the screen. Valerie Harper won three Emmy Awards as supporting actress (1971, 1972, and 1973) for her role as Rhoda Morgenstern on *The Mary Tyler Moore Show*. Harper left the show in 1974 for her own spin-off series, *Rhoda*, which aired until 1978. Many scripts for her program were partly or wholly written by women, making it a more consciously feminist-focused program than *The Mary Tyler Moore Show*. *Phyllis*, based on Cloris Leachman's character as Mary's landlady, spun off from *The Mary Tyler Moore Show* in 1975. *The Nancy Walker Show*, a short-lived spin-off airing in 1976, revolved around Rhoda's meddling mother, played by Nancy Walker. The last in line was *Lou Grant*, starring Ed Asner reprising his role as the tough yet vulnerable boss.

Lou Grant ran for five seasons, from 1977 to 1982. It was, along with *Rhoda*, the most popular of the spin-offs. Asner played Lou Grant, formerly Mary Richards' boss at WJM-TV, and now editor of the city desk at the *Los Angeles Tribune*, a family-owned daily newspaper. The series strived for realism, paying close attention to the details of journalistic life. The program dealt with relevant social and political issues such as rape, environmental pollution, exploitation of migrant workers and illegal aliens, and corruption of big business and corporations. Like *The Mary Tyler Moore Show*, *Lou Grant* relied on its ensemble cast as a vital element of its success. Through the responses of individual characters, political issues were made relevant, bringing the problems and possible solutions to a personal level.

The impact *The Mary Tyler Moore Show* has had on viewers and on television itself is enormous. The series probably is one of the most influential in television history. The success of the show itself and of the MTM production company established a nurturing environment for the writers, producers, and actors dedicated to this particular style of presentation, mixing comedy and drama. That influence remained evident into the 1990's in series ranging from *Cheers* to *Alf* to *The Cosby Show* to *The Tracey Ullman Show* to *Family Ties*. All these programs had MTM offspring as members of their production teams.

Not only did members of MTM Enterprises continue personally to influence production values of television series, but the subject matter introduced by *The Mary Tyler Moore Show* also remained of vital importance to later programming. Shows about women such as *Murphy Brown, The Days and Nights of Molly Dodd, Designing Women*, and *The Golden Girls*; ensemble shows such as *Hill Street Blues* and *L.A. Law*; and even *Charlie's Angels* owed their opportunity to have women in central roles and show alternative life-styles for women in part to the success and influence of *The Mary Tyler Moore Show*.

The Mary Tyler Moore Show remained popular in syndicated reruns. Although

Mary Tyler Moore had less success with her later television series *Mary* (1985-1986) and two variety shows, she already had made her mark in television history.

Bibliography

Harris, Jay S., ed. *TV Guide: The First Twenty-five Years.* New York: Simon & Schuster, 1978. Interesting collection of articles about and photographs of television programs and personalities from 1953 through 1977. Includes color reprints of *TV Guide* covers and essays by performers and personalities about their work in television. Wonderfully dated material gives the reader a taste of the journalistic style of the time. Contains critical arguments about the impact of television upon society as well as information about a wide variety of personalities and programs.

McCrohan, Donna. *Prime Time, Our Time: America's Life and Times Through the Prism of Television.* Rocklin, Calif.: Prima, 1990. Good collection of essays on different phases of television history. Deals with individual programs within a larger framework. Cites interesting trivia and top-rated programs for past years. No photographs.

Newcomb, Horace, ed. *Television: The Critical View.* 3d ed. New York: Oxford University Press, 1982. This collection of essays on various themes in television delves into specific programs as well as more abstract criticism of television's effects on its audience. Included in this edition are essays on soap operas, *Happy Days*, and *Laverne and Shirley*; the politics of *Lou Grant*; and television's aesthetics, ideology, and role in popular culture.

Settel, Irving, and William Laas. *A Pictorial History of Television.* New York: Grosset & Dunlap, 1969. Good pictures combined with commentary on the history of television. Combines facts about television in general mixed with stories about the stars.

Taylor, Ella. *Prime-Time Families: Television Culture in Postwar America.* Berkeley: University of California Press, 1989. A feminist-oriented discussion about the portrayal of family life on television. Fascinating cultural and social analysis, featuring chapters on episodic series (1946-1969), entertainment programming in the 1970's, television's changing families (1970-1980), and television families in workplace settings, along with a section comparing and contrasting television families of different eras. Cohesive and intelligent analysis of its topic. Each chapter is placed in historical context for a broader understanding of the driving forces behind particular modes of programming.

Felicia Bender

Cross-References

Situation Comedies Dominate Television Programming (1960's), p. 1835; *The Dick Van Dyke Show* Popularizes Situation Comedy (1961), p. 1908; *All in the Family* Introduces a New Style of Television Comedy (1971), p. 2234; *M*A*S*H* Reflects 1970's Sentiments (1972), p. 2271; *The Jeffersons* Signals Success of Black Situation Comedies (1975), p. 2339; *The Cosby Show* Makes Television History (1984), p. 2532.

TRUDEAU'S *DOONESBURY* POPULARIZES
TOPICAL COMIC STRIPS

Categories of event: Literature and journalism
Time: October, 1970
Locale: The United States

With the creation of the Doonesbury *comic strip, satirist Garry Trudeau brought political satire to a peak and transformed comic-strip art in the United States*

Principal personage:
GARRY TRUDEAU (1948-   ), the cartoonist, writer, and satirist who created the *Doonesbury* characters

Summary of Event

In October, 1970, Garry Trudeau, a master of fine arts candidate at the Yale University School of Art, signed a contract with the Universal Press Syndicate to produce a comic strip entitled *Bull Tales*, which had originally been a comic strip Trudeau had done for the Yale student paper. Because the syndicate feared the name *Bull Tales* would offend some readers, the strip took a new name from one of its major characters, Mike Doonesbury. The name derived from a Yale slang term, "doone," which meant a good-natured fool.

As a syndicated comic strip, *Doonesbury* considered subjects covering a wide range of topics, from the Watergate scandal to the war in Vietnam. Almost immediately, the strip was involved in controversy. The *Indianapolis Star* and other conservative newspapers dropped the strip almost immediately. Other papers did not object to the strip until it dealt with some especially touchy subject. For many papers, this point came in May, 1972, when character Zonker Harris speculated that the responsibility for the deaths of four students at Kent State University in Ohio during a 1970 antiwar demonstration was to be laid at the feet of Attorney General John Mitchell. By this time, however, the strip had a large and vocal following, and some editors found themselves so besieged by protest that they reversed their decisions to drop *Doonesbury*.

In response to criticism about his presentation of the Kent State issue and to criticism concerning his' depictions of a trial of Black Panther members, Trudeau replied that the truth was often to be found in hyperbole. This seems to have been the guiding philosophy of Trudeau in producing *Doonesbury*. Because electronic media bring the harshest realities into every home, Trudeau assumed that there was no need to avoid a satirical, humorous approach to these same topics in the comics.

Such a philosophy, though, offended many people who perceived comics as for entertainment only. Trudeau replied to such critics that cartoons concern themselves with truth, but that truth delivered straight would destroy the cartoonist's role as humorist. Moreover, Trudeau noted, as humorists, cartoonists do not have an obligation to discuss all sides of an issue.

As the Watergate scandal grew more intense in 1973, *Doonesbury* became increasingly controversial for its depiction of President Richard Nixon and his associates. At the time, many newspapers moved the strip to their editorial pages. Yet the insights provided by the cartoon proved to be so powerful that, in 1975, Trudeau won a Pulitzer Prize for *Doonesbury*, the first time since the awards began to be given that the prize for cartooning went to a comic-strip artist.

The style of *Doonesbury* was obviously inspired by the more sophisticated comics of the 1950's and 1960's, such as *Feiffer* from *The New Yorker* magazine. Trudeau's drafting style was to reduce the drawings to simple forms; this style was well suited to the content of *Doonesbury*, since the strip was more literary than visual.

As a Pulitzer Prize winner only four years into his career, Trudeau described himself as "a thoughtful, concerned, and highly creative young man who is out to make a fast buck." A less self-deprecating analysis came from *The Washington Post*, which called Trudeau "the youngest and most successful of the new wave of comic strip artists appearing in today's newspapers."

Although frequently complained about by conservatives, Trudeau is not ideological in the usual sense. The *Doonesbury* characters have made iconoclastic assaults on liberal ideas and figures as well as on right-wing concepts. From 1976 to 1980, the comic strip frequently pointed out that the Democratic administration of President Jimmy Carter was long on symbolism and short on accomplishments.

Doonesbury is often described as "liberal," an epithet that is in some ways misleading. Trudeau does have a personal commitment to an open and frank discussion of ideas and an accompanying willingness to laugh at the ridiculous inconsistencies and posturings of public figures; this is, historically, a liberal attitude, but not an ideological one. Moreover, since *Doonesbury* entered public view in 1970, most U.S. presidential administrations have been conservative. Such administrations have been the natural targets of Trudeau's satire, not because they are conservative but because they provide national leadership.

The end of Watergate was not the end of satire in *Doonesbury*. In 1983, Trudeau took a sabbatical to rethink his characters and their futures. At the end of that time, he returned to have them graduate from college and enter business life. The new setting gave Trudeau a platform from which to address the national events of the Ronald Reagan years. Trudeau satirized Frank Sinatra's alleged ties to mobsters when the singer received a presidential medal; led viewers on a mountain-climbing-style cartoon expedition through the brain of Ronald Reagan (which was found to be vacant); dealt humorously and sensitively with the plight of acquired immune deficiency syndrome (AIDS) victims; poked fun at critics of the National Endowment for the Arts; and depicted Vice President Dan Quayle as a feather floating in the air. When Trudeau pointed out that President George Bush avoided payment of state income tax by claiming as his legal residence a hotel suite in Texas, which has no state income tax, more than thirty thousand fans wrote to the Texas state comptroller asking for Texas citizenship.

Trudeau's satire has not been without its price. In 1990, he was dropped from a

United Service Organization (USO) trip to visit troops in Saudi Arabia during the Gulf War, even though *Doonesbury* was carried by the U.S. military newspaper *Stars and Stripes*. At that time, *Doonesbury*'s character B. D. was an army reservist deployed to the Persian Gulf, and his girlfriend, Boopsie, was learning to cope with the problems of managing on her own.

Impact of Event

Trudeau's *Doonesbury* is both a continuation of and a departure from tradition. It has spawned a host of imitators and transformed the landscape of the comics. Comics writers have always dealt with the ambiguities of life and with the need for human beings to triumph over, or at least to endure, the conditions of contemporary life. Comics, however, have the privilege of creating a fantasy world within which these ambiguities are examined. *Doonesbury* has used this privilege to undertake a provocative analysis of American life.

The presentation of Trudeau's views in comic form has enormously extended the audience for those views. It has been estimated that eighty percent of all Americans who live in towns of more than twenty-five hundred people read the comics on a regular basis. Furthermore, people with more education show more interest in comics. More than half of all Americans say they have a favorite comic-strip character, and about three times as many Americans read the comics as read the news. It has been estimated that more than seventy million people read *Doonesbury* every day, far more than normally watch a nationally televised address by the president of the United States.

Many comics have given birth to film cartoons, radio serials, television specials, and popular songs based on their characters. Trudeau has seen *Doonesbury* produce a Broadway play based on his strip that ran for four months, and an anti-Reagan play inspired by his work toured the country for four years. Comic-strip spin-offs such as lunch boxes, Thermos bottles, and paperback collections of strips are big business, but for many years, Trudeau resisted the production of commercial spin-offs from *Doonesbury*. In the early 1990's, however, he began to permit these developments, with the understanding that the profits would go to the numerous charities he supports.

Comics often have characters that become real to readers or that suggest solutions to real-life problems. During the Great Depression, a comic-strip character named Gordo enjoyed a nutritious dish made with beans and cheese; more than eighty-five thousand readers wrote in to request the recipe. In the 1940's and 1950's, the character Jiggs in *Maggie and Jiggs* enjoyed corned beef and cabbage at a corner saloon named Dinty Moore's; soon a line of canned goods was successfully marketed under that brand name. *Doonesbury* has exerted a similarly strong influence, as demonstrated by the thousands who requested Texas citizenship at Trudeau's suggestion.

By dealing with real issues in the comic-strip format, Trudeau performed an important task. Most Americans get their news from brief television presentations; Trudeau brings selected events to a wide audience and highlights these events vividly. As a satirist, Trudeau sees no reason for *Doonesbury* to be balanced so as to avoid offending those who disagree with his views. He has stated that "to fault a satirist for being unfair is like faulting a nose-guard in football for being physical."

Of course, Trudeau did not create this ability to deal with contemporary issues in *Doonesbury*; comics have long used familiar themes from the news as well as from everyday life. *Doonesbury*, though, set new standards in the complexity and controversial nature of many of its real-life-inspired topics. Thus, Mike Doonesbury, working in an advertising agency, is troubled by the health hazards of smoking, but he nevertheless draws up an advertising campaign making cigarettes appear glamorous so he can keep his job. The presentation of such a dilemma speaks to the human condition much more forcefully than do the stock situations so common in older comics such as *Blondie*.

In many modern comics, reader response goes beyond enjoyment. Comics mirror life as the readers understand it and as it is presented by the writer. This is obvious in *Doonesbury*. The strip originated in and was set in an academic culture. Although the characters have long since graduated and left college, educated, young, socially and economically mobile people still find the strip appealing because it reflects their world. When Trudeau, therefore, has his characters comment on politics, he is saying what many of his readers actually feel. This is what makes *Doonesbury*'s satire biting—so biting, in fact, that Bush has said Trudeau is the one critic he can never forgive.

The perceived failure of public leadership in the post-Vietnam War era has made the American public ready to learn about and laugh about the foibles of public people. Private life too, with its many fads, philosophies and generational conflicts, invites introspection of both serious and comic sorts. With *Doonesbury*, Trudeau makes people laugh.

Bibliography

Alter, Jonathan. "Real Life with Garry Trudeau." *Newsweek* 116 (October 15, 1990): 60-66. Trudeau has been a rather shy person most of his career, making this relatively lengthy interview unusual. Trudeau reveals a little about his personal beliefs and his family life with his wife, television personality Jane Pauley.

Botkin, Benjamin. *Standard Dictionary of Folklore, Mythology, and Legend*. New York: Funk & Wagnalls, 1949. A good discussion of many aspects of popular culture in America, including the comics.

Luedtke, Luther S., ed. *The Study of Contemporary Culture Conflicts*. Deland, Fla.: Everett/Edwards, 1977. A conference at the American Studies Institute at the University of Southern California produced these essays. Twelve writers explore various aspects of conflict as presented in popular culture, including the comics.

Waugh, Coulton. *The Comics*. New York: Macmillan, 1947. A substantial study of the comics that deals with their history in a scholarly, analytical fashion; nevertheless, good reading.

White, David Manning, and Robert H. Abel. *The Funnies: An American Idiom*. New

York: Free Press, 1963. Examines newspaper comics to see what they say about American culture. Notes that American comics have a worldwide following and are a window for much of the world on American humor, drama, adventure, and fantasy.

Michael R. Bradley

Cross-References

The First Pulitzer Prizes Are Awarded (1915), p. 407; *Catch-22* Illustrates Antiwar Sentiment (1961), p. 1866; Vonnegut's *Cat's Cradle* Expresses 1960's Alienation (1963), p. 1939; McLuhan Probes the Impact of Mass Media on Society (1964), p. 1973; *M*A*S*H* Reflects 1970's Sentiments (1972), p. 2271; *The Simpsons* Debuts, Anchoring the Fledgling Fox Network (1990), p. 2652.

LED ZEPPELIN MERGES HARD ROCK AND FOLK MUSIC

Category of event: Music
Time: 1971
Locale: England and the United States

Led Zeppelin established itself as more than merely a hard-rock band by including songs on its fourth album—especially "Stairway to Heaven"—that are rooted in folk music

Principal personages:
JIMMY PAGE (1944-), the innovative guitarist and producer who formed the group
ROBERT PLANT (1948-), the band's vocalist and lyricist
JOHN BONHAM (1948-1980), the band's drummer
JOHN PAUL JONES (JOHN BALDWIN, 1946-), the band's bass and keyboard player

Summary of Event

By May, 1970, Led Zeppelin had reached the pinnacle of rock status. At a mountain cottage called Bron-Y-Aur, Wales, Jimmy Page and Robert Plant worked on material for the group's third album. With the breakup of the Beatles and the tax problems of the Rolling Stones, Led Zeppelin had become the number-one rock band in the world. For the band's third album, Page wanted more emphasis on acoustic material. Even though Page had used an acoustic guitar to some degree on the band's first two albums, both critics and fans alike were surprised by the results they heard on *Led Zeppelin III* (1970). Released on October 23, 1970, the third album went to the top of the *Billboard* and British charts. Led Zeppelin took a short holiday break before the initial recording sessions for the band's fourth release were held at London's Island Studios in December, 1970.

In January, 1971, the group had the Rolling Stones' mobile studio moved to Headley Grange, a country house located in Hampshire, England. Page pushed himself to make the new album a perfect blend of power rock—for which the band was famous—and folk music. Since both Page and Plant were fans of folk singer and songwriter Joni Mitchell, they wanted to incorporate folk elements into the total mix. With the fourth album, Led Zeppelin was determined to prove to its critics that the band could succeed at more than exciting the teenage libido. The band immersed itself in mysticism and Celtic lore.

Page had entertained the notion of making a double album, but eventually this idea was scratched in favor of a single album. The members of Led Zeppelin moved to the rural setting of Headley Grange in order to remove all of London's distractions. The recording sessions lasted through January, 1971. In February, the overdub sessions were moved back to Island Studios. As Led Zeppelin's producer, Page was not yet totally satisfied with what was already on tape, so he traveled with the tapes to Los Angeles to do more mixing at Sunset Sound Studios. The band played "Stairway to Heaven" for the first time live on March 5, 1971, at Belfast's Ulster Hall. In July, more mixing was done on the album. The fourth album was finally released on November 12, 1971. The band had decided that the album was not to have an official title, a decision that angered Led Zeppelin's record company, Atlantic. Instead of a real title, Page suggested that each member of the band select a symbol from a book of runes that he had in his possession. The symbols would then be placed on the inside of the record jacket.

Over the years, the album has been variously referred to as *Untitled*, *Led Zeppelin Four*, *The Runes*, *Four Symbols*, and *Zoso* (after Page's mysterious symbol). Eight songs made the final album: "Black Dog," "Rock and Roll," "The Battle of Evermore," "Stairway to Heaven," "Misty Mountain Hop," "Four Sticks," "Going to California," and "When the Levee Breaks." Written by Page, Plant, and John Paul Jones, "Black Dog" proved to critics that Led Zeppelin could still produce songs that were a pure adrenaline rush; the power of "Black Dog" made it an instantly recognizable Led Zeppelin song. The title of the song came from a hound that had adopted Headley Grange as its home.

All four members of the group contributed to the song "Rock and Roll," which was more of an improvisation than anything else. It grew out of a jam session with the Rolling Stones' piano player, Ian Stewart. With the tape still running, John Bonham played the introduction of Little Richard's "Good Golly Miss Molly," and Page was inspired to add a guitar riff that seemed to fit. With Stewart banging out a great boogie piano, Plant came up with the appropriate lyrics on the spot. The initial improvisation produced the structure for the song, which Page massaged into shape without losing what had been captured on the original taping. "The Battle of Evermore" was written by Page and Plant. Page came up with the tune while he tried his hand at playing Jones's mandolin, and Plant's lyrics were inspired by a book he had been reading at the time concerning Scottish wars. Sandy Denny of the group Fairport Convention (an English folk group) was asked to share the vocals with Plant, adding a wonderful touch to the overall arrangement.

"Stairway to Heaven" has come to be thought of as the quintessential Led Zeppelin song. Written by Page and Plant, it melds the diverse strengths of the group. Page had almost completed the chord progression when the group started recording at Island Studios in December, 1970. The various parts of the song came together after Led Zeppelin moved to Headley Grange. Plant was inspired to write lyrics that told a mythic tale of a lady's search for perfection. Parallels can be drawn with famous female creations from Western literature, such as Edmund Spenser's Faerie Queen, the Lady of the Lake, Rhiannon, and many others. That is not to say that the lyrics stand up as great poetry, but as they were intended to be wedded to music, the ethereal quality of the lyrics works supremely well. The song builds from an acoustic beginning which gradually—but inevitably—builds to a muscular rock crescendo. There are different sections in "Stairway to Heaven." Page employs a six-string guitar in one section, a twelve-string guitar in another, and an electric guitar, solo, in the other distinct section. Page has said that the song "crystallized the essence of the band."

The next song on the album was an uptempo piece written by Page, Plant, and Jones entitled "Misty Mountain Hop." On the song, Jones played electric piano. The song has a funk quality to it that is catchy and joyous. On "Four Sticks," Bonham made use of four drum sticks to create a driving rhythm track. Taking their inspiration on "Going to California" from Joni Mitchell, Page contributed tender acoustic guitar work while Plant came up with poignant lyrics concerning California and the search for the perfect lady. The last song on the album, "When the Levee Breaks," was constructed by the group around an old blues song of the same name written by Memphis Minnie. On the song, Bonham pushed his pounding drum sound to the limit. Page added bottleneck guitar, while Plant contributed a dynamic mouth harp.

The fourth album was produced by Page, who meticulously worked the tracks over while keeping the improvisational feel, and engineered by Andy Johns. The album entered the English music charts at number one and remained on the charts for sixty-two weeks. In the United States, the album went as high as number two and stayed on the *Billboard* charts longer than any other album by the group.

Impact of Event

By the time Led Zeppelin entered London's Island Studios in December, 1970, to commence the recording sessions that would result in its fourth album, the band already had established itself as one of the world's most popular hard-rock bands. Led Zeppelin had been the brainchild of guitarist Jimmy Page in 1968. In the early 1960's, Page had made a reputation for himself as a remarkable session player. He joined the Yardbirds in 1966 as its bass player. At the time Page joined the group, Jeff Beck was its lead guitar player, but eventually he and Page played dual lead guitars for the group. Later in that same year, Beck left the Yardbirds, leaving Page to shoulder the lead guitar work. In 1967, Page already was thinking about forming a new group. Some of his discussions had been with the Who's drummer, Keith Moon, who suggested that the new group be called Lead Zeppelin (as in "go over like a lead balloon"). By the middle of 1968, the Yardbirds were ready to disband. On June 22, 1968, both Keith Relf and Jim McCarty announced that they were leaving the Yardbirds. With the old Yardbirds in disarray, Page went about the business of pulling together a group that would be known as the New Yardbirds for the time being.

After talking to various musicians, Page finally settled on John Paul Jones on bass, Robert Plant on vocals, and John Bonham on drums. Page had known Jones from session work they had done together. Plant was offered the job as vocalist after Page and some associates heard him perform at a Birmingham teacher-training college. It was Plant who recommended Bonham, and thus the lineup was complete for the New Yardbirds. They began rehearsing together in September, 1968, and soon agreed that they would have to find a new name for the group. Page and manager

Peter Grant decided to use Keith Moon's suggestion but dropped the "a" in "Lead." Thus "Led Zeppelin" was born.

The group entered Olympic studios in October, 1968, to record its first album. Led Zeppelin's approach to music grew out of the blues-rock explosion that had hit England in the late 1960's. Similar in some degree to other English bands such as Cream, the Jeff Beck Group, and even the Yardbirds, the group went beyond all the others in creating a calculated and lumbering musical style—which incorporated amplified distortion—that has come to be known as "heavy metal." *Led Zeppelin* was released in the United States on January 17, 1969; by February, the album was climbing up the *Billboard* charts. By May, it would reach the top ten. Led Zeppelin's popularity was driven by the group's live performances. In the spring of 1969, Led Zeppelin went back into the studio to begin recording its second album. Because of the band's heavy touring schedule, the second album was not completed until September. It has been estimated that *Led Zeppelin II* had an advance order of 400,000. The second album was released on October 31, 1969, and before long it went to number one on both the American and British charts. The song "Whole Lotta Love" became Led Zeppelin's anthem and would remain so until it was eclipsed by "Stairway to Heaven."

Led Zeppelin continued to exist until 1980, when Bonham died and the remaining members decided that Led Zeppelin could not continue without him. The announcement came on December 4, 1980, and the music world was stunned. The group had not toured the United States since 1977. During the mid-1970's and culminating with Bonham's death, the band had more than its share of mishaps. The misadventures seemed to be never-ending, and there was even speculation that since members of the group had dabbled in the occult, something evil was at work. These rumors contributed to Led Zeppelin's allure and mystique. The group's reputation for excess was legendary, whether on stage or behind the scenes. The group thrilled millions of rock fans with every new and outrageous direction it took. If Led Zeppelin had simply played "heavy metal" and left it at that, then it probably would be remembered as merely another example of hedonistic rock. The tough, take-no-prisoners approach to music had its fans, but the members of Led Zeppelin felt compelled to blend musical styles. The untitled fourth album was the group's shining creation. Through the vision and drive of Jimmy Page, Led Zeppelin made a quantum leap beyond run-of-the-mill loud rock music. The fourth album brought the group respectability.

The eight-minute "Stairway to Heaven" became the most-requested song of all time on FM rock stations. The song also sells more sheet music than any other in the history of rock music. On radio stations that compile lists of the top rock songs of all time and then play them, "Stairway to Heaven" has consistently placed at the top. The acoustic strumming, the lyrics that defy clear interpretation, the inserted rock explosions that eventually build into a fury that sweeps the listener away—all these elements and more make "Stairway to Heaven" one of the most innovative songs in rock history. The song has continued to mean different things to different listeners. The song was supposedly written by Plant in a fit of automatic writing. The idea that some power greater than the individual lyricist helped to produce the song helped to fuel the flames of its mystique.

During the 1970's and 1980's, hundreds of bands cropped up attempting to emulate Led Zeppelin. Unfortunately, most of these bands were poor imitations of the original. The creativity of rock music was tossed aside by senseless purveyors of noise. With "Stairway to Heaven," Led Zeppelin entered the pantheon of rock groups that produced something that mattered. The texture and power of its fourth album surpassed what any other heavy metal band had ever done. In what Led Zeppelin created, there was actual tenderness that counterbalanced the blustery bombast. In a real sense, Led Zeppelin never was a true heavy-metal band, and the fourth album proved that point. The band was not afraid to venture into musical areas uncharted by other hard-rock outfits. A listener can find dashes of folk, slices of country, a hearty helping of blues, and musical influences from exotic countries. Endlessly curious, the band was not willing to settle for the middle path. Each member contributed a wealth of musical knowledge to the whole, giving it a unique shape. Led Zeppelin was raw and distorted but also—especially on the fourth album—delicate. In 1990, a boxed set of the band's music was released, selling nearly a million copies in the next several years. Page and George Marino digitally remastered the songs for the set. The fourth album has continued to be popular and, as of 1993, had sold more than ten million copies. Led Zeppelin has continued to exert its hold over millions of fans who like their music to incorporate both heavy guitar riffs and gentle, more mystical, acoustic fare.

Bibliography

Cole, Richard, with Richard Trubo. *Stairway to Heaven: Led Zeppelin Uncensored.* New York: HarperCollins, 1992. Led Zeppelin's tour manager recounts his twelve-year association with the band. Cole's story concentrates primarily on the outrageous excesses of Led Zeppelin's tour life-style.

Considine, J. D. "Led Zeppelin." *Rolling Stone* 587 (September 20, 1990): 56-60, 109. The three surviving members of Led Zeppelin reflect on their days in the band and also do their best to correct a few misconceptions about the group.

Davis, Stephen. *Hammer of the Gods: The Led Zeppelin Saga.* New York: Ballantine, 1986. Thoroughly researched, this is the definitive biography of the band. It makes the point that Led Zeppelin has become just as famous for its excesses as for its music. The paperback edition includes a new chapter concerning Led Zeppelin's reunion at the Live Aid concert in 1985.

Karbo, Karen. "'Stairway to Heaven': Is This the Greatest Song of All Time?" *Esquire* 116 (November, 1991): 128-132. The article playfully and seriously discusses the popularity of Led Zeppelin's most famous song.

Lewis, Dave. *Led Zeppelin: A Celebration.* New York: Omnibus Press, 1991. A beautifully produced oversized paperback book that includes a wealth of information on the band. There are chapters on the group in the studio and about the band live, a complete chronology, various discographies, and an equipment file.

Resnicoff, Matt. "Jimmy Page: My Life in Led Zeppelin." *Musician* 145 (November, 1990): 48-64, 72. An extended interview with the reclusive guitarist who was the driving force of Led Zeppelin. Page reveals some of his musical secrets and also talks about the work that went into remastering the group's songs for Led Zeppelin's four-CD boxed set released in 1990.

Jeffry Jensen

Cross-References

Berry's "Maybellene" Popularizes Rock and Roll (1955), p. 1635; Presley Becomes a Rock-and-Roll Sensation (1956), p. 1705; The Beatles Revolutionize Popular Music (1963), p. 1944; The Rolling Stones Release *Out of Our Heads* (1965), p. 2027; Dylan Performs with Electric Instruments (1965), p. 2038; Hendrix Releases *Are You Experienced?* (1967), p. 2092; The Beatles Release *Sgt. Pepper's Lonely Hearts Club Band* (1967), p. 2098; The Monterey Pop Festival Inaugurates the "Summer of Love" (1967), p. 2104; The Sex Pistols Spark Punk Rock's Musical Insurrection (1975), p. 2360; Live Aid Generates Millions for Famine Relief (1985), p. 2543.

ALL IN THE FAMILY INTRODUCES A NEW STYLE OF TELEVISION COMEDY

Category of event: Television and radio
Time: January 12, 1971-September 16, 1976
Locale: The United States

All in the Family *revolutionized the content of television situation comedies by dealing with currently controversial topics in both humorous and touching ways*

Principal personages:
NORMAN LEAR (1922-   ), the creator of *All in the Family*
ROBERT D. WOOD (1925-1986), the president of the Columbia Broadcasting System (CBS), who insisted that his network shift to broadcasting programs that were more socially relevant
BUD YORKIN (1926-   ), the producer and director of *All in the Family*, who believed that the national climate was right for television programs that confronted current issues
CARROLL O'CONNOR (1924-   ), the actor who played Archie Bunker, the narrow-minded conservative father with a soft heart, on *All in the Family*
JEAN STAPLETON (JEANNE MURRAY, 1923-   ), the actress who played Archie's bumbling wife
SALLY STRUTHERS (1948-   ), the actress who played Gloria, Archie and Edith's daughter
ROB REINER (1947-   ), the actor who played Mike Stivic, Gloria's boyfriend and later husband

Summary of Event

On January 12, 1971, the Columbia Broadcasting System (CBS) broadcast the first episode in a situation comedy series that would soon change the course of television comedy. Critic Dwight Newton said of this show, *All in the Family*, "In one half-hour CBS destroyed old taboos and liberated comedy writing."

This program had a simple premise. A working-class family of father, mother, and daughter, in a blue-collar neighborhood of New York City, portrayed the ambitions, concerns, and fears of millions of Americans who faced the changing social values and conditions of the 1970's. The father, Archie Bunker, was especially concerned over the changes wrought by the Civil Rights movement and the youth culture prevalent on many college campuses at that time. The very forces he feared were brought into his own home as his daughter, Gloria, fell in love with and eventually married Mike Stivic, a liberal college student. When the young couple moved in with Archie and his wife, Edith, the stage was set for regular confrontations between the reactionary views of Archie and the liberal opinions of "Meathead," as Archie referred to Mike.

Television critics and social commentators noted that the broadcast of this program represented a new peak in the social revolution of the 1960's and that the medium of television entertainment would now aid in spreading the revolutionary liberal views. The basic theme of the show was that of young people with 1960's values trying to make a life for themselves while being forced by circumstances to live under an imposed arbitrary authority. Unlike the popular television series of the 1950's *Father Knows Best*, on *All in the Family* daughter, son-in-law, and even mother all had something to say about what was best.

Jean Stapleton, in the role of Edith Bunker, portrayed the changes affecting millions of American women at that time. Edith was a housewife, and she knew herself to be one of a dying breed. Many of her fictional contemporaries worked outside the home. Edith did not expect her daughter, Gloria, to have the same relationship with her husband, Mike Stivic, that she had with Archie. Though not ready to join the National Organization for Women or to demonstrate in the streets, Edith still saw new vistas of opportunity opening before her as a woman, and she occasionally shocked her husband by exploring one of those new avenues. Although bumbling in physical actions and often under assault from her husband as a "dingbat," Edith maintained her essential personal dignity and often brought to the resolution of problems a warmhearted dose of common sense.

If television critics and social commentators thought *All in the Family* to be new and wonderful, the public had different views. The pilot film had been offered to the American Broadcasting Company (ABC), which had showed it to a test audience. The results from this showing were so poor that ABC declined to purchase the show. Some sociologists have suggested that this test audience actually liked the show but was ashamed to say so because some of the opinions expressed by the actors were not considered socially proper, even though many viewers agreed with those opinions.

Robert Wood, president of CBS, was determined to replace the aging stories and actors making up the CBS lineup with fresh, contemporary material. He saw the social mood of the United States in 1971 as a mixture of anxiety and hope. To him, *All in the Family* caught and reflected these dual notes. Bud Yorkin, producer and director of *All in the Family*, agreed. He believed that young people in particular were ready for a new approach to television entertainment. Many of them were challenging established assumptions or had peers who were, and they wanted entertainment that dealt with these same real issues.

On these assumptions, CBS purchased the show. In a move unusual for television, the network allowed the show to stay on the air despite a slow start. Its audience grew as viewers became accustomed to the radical change in television conventions represented by the show. These changed conventions included episodes in which the show dealt with abortion, homosexuality, impotence, menopause, civil disobedience, and a host of other topics not previously dealt with in any depth by television shows, either drama or comedy. Archie Bunker's blatant racism was featured on virtually every episode, and other previously taboo topics were fair game. Among other "firsts" on the show was the sound of a toilet flushing and a discussion of toilet paper. Never before had there been any evidence on television that Americans went to the bathroom.

All in the Family was not an original idea. Norman Lear, creator of the series, stated that he was inspired by a British program, *Till Death Do Us Part,* which featured a blue-collar worker in an urban setting. Topics were updated, however, for relevance to contemporary American life.

Despite its ever-increasing popularity, CBS was not always comfortable with the content and direction of the show. Numerous battles were fought within the standards and practices division of CBS over the content of various episodes. *All in the Family,* however, became the nation's most-watched regular television show in its first season. It retained that position for five seasons. After that, it was consistently in the top fifteen shows in viewership until it was canceled at the beginning of the 1982-1983 season.

Impact of Event

With the broadcast of *All in the Family,* a new fact became obvious about television entertainment in the United States. The enormous popularity of the show made it clear that people were ready for a new approach that dealt with contemporary issues in a way that reflected the concerns of the society. *All in the Family* allowed reality to tint comedy to some extent, rather than restricting comedy to sanitized presentations of family life as in previous shows. This does not mean that the show offered solutions to social problems. Archie Bunker was a narrow-minded character who often expressed bigoted views. He portrayed those views honestly and unapologetically. Because he was also a lovable and ineffective character, his views were not taken seriously or viewed as threatening. Some viewers saw Archie as a hero, able to express opinions no longer socially acceptable even though they were still commonly held. Others reveled in the put-downs that Archie suffered as a racist.

In the same way, Mike Stivic represented new liberal values but also could not support his views completely. As a student who had not yet assumed the responsibility of holding a job and supporting a family, his liberal views could be seen as theoretical but not practical. This meant that the controversies of the 1970's could be presented without the show being didactic. The approach reflected the social and political interests of the show's creator, Norman Lear. Lear described himself as a social and political liberal whose politics informed his sense of comedy. Lear believed that people laugh hardest when they are the most concerned.

Going beyond his television presentations, Lear founded the political lobbying organization People for the American Way. He brought to this organization all the skills of Hollywood in raising money, recruiting celebrities, and producing advertisements capable of conveying a powerful message in a short time. The most obvious activity of this group was to lead the successful opposition to the nomination of

Robert Bork to the Supreme Court of the United States. Such political involvement, along with continuing frank discussion of sexuality and changing forms of the family, made Lear, by the 1980's, one of the chief targets of the religious and political fundamentalist right. Such controversy, however, did not prevent Lear from producing other shows in the mold of *All in the Family* or from keeping up his constant barrage of social commentary from the mouths of his characters. Lear and *All in the Family* proved that controversy can be the stuff of comedy.

All in the Family had a continuing impact by bringing social tensions into the open. Many critics have assumed that Lear meant to discredit conservative views by placing support for them in the hands of Archie Bunker, an obviously flawed character tending toward bigotry. Other critics argued that *All in the Family* took on issues only tangentially instead of confronting them head-on. These critics point to evidence that there was widespread sympathy for Archie Bunker and his views. For many, Archie became a reactionary hero.

In reality, Archie Bunker could raise sensitive social issues and get people to talk about them by being an ignorant, narrow-minded figure. Carroll O'Connor, in a superbly shrewd performance, kept Archie from becoming a buffoon. This allowed huge numbers of viewers to watch Archie with sympathy. They found someone somewhat like themselves, who lived in a neighborhood like theirs and who had ideas somewhat like theirs. They too were worried about the changes sweeping across the nation. As these changes and issues were introduced on the show, and as various aspects of them were raised by the show's characters, the fallacies of beliefs of both the left and the right were exposed. As one critic stated, "the best preachers deliver sermons without preaching." Lear and his show helped the nation look at problems and deal with them within the family.

The popularity of *All in the Family* seems to have come from its ability to transform, or even deform, the tensions of real-life conflicts. The predictable, almost ritual, confrontations between Archie Bunker and Mike Stivic were actually taking place across the country. The social and psychological cracks in the nation's cultural landscape were real. The reaction to the show, and its characters, was ambivalent because the United States was and is a mixed culture, with few ideas approaching anything near universal acceptance.

The most obvious impact of *All in the Family* was that it prompted a new wave of television situation comedies dealing with relevant subjects. Having proved that society would accept such shows, *All in the Family* produced spin-offs and imitators such as *Sanford and Son, Maude, M*A*S*H, The Jeffersons, Good Times, Married . . . with Children, Roseanne*, and *The Simpsons.* Lear himself tried to re-create the power of *All in the Family* with *Sunday Dinner*, which lasted only a few episodes. Images on television were permanently changed by *All in the Family*. Social relevance and an acceptance of controversy have been made part of television comedy and are no longer subjects limited to drama or documentaries. Lear showed an uncanny ability to reach, to touch, and to stimulate American audiences through comedy.

Bibliography

Fiske, John. *Television Culture.* New York: Methuen, 1987. An interesting analysis of the fantasy culture that television creates and the ways in which that culture is accepted as true and valid by viewers. The key to this process is that television uses some elements from real life to lend credibility to its fictitious worlds.

Gitlin, Todd. *Inside Prime Time.* New York: Pantheon Books, 1983. The author interviewed more than two hundred people who work in television. They describe their search for a hit show. Provides a good description and analysis of how television functions and deals with the impact of the "religious right" on programming.

Goldstein, Fred, and Stan Goldstein. *Prime-Time Television.* New York: Crown, 1983. Presents the history of television from 1946 to 1983 on a year-by-year basis.

O'Connor, John, ed. *American History, American Television.* New York: Frederick Ungar, 1983. Presents television both as a force in recent social history and as a matter to be studied. This collection of essays came out of Columbia University's Seminar on Cinema, but all of the essays in this volume relate to television. They deal with a wide range of topics, from the *Amos 'n' Andy* show to Watergate.

Rose, Brian G., ed. *TV Genres: A Handbook and Reference Guide.* Westport, Conn.: Greenwood Press, 1985. This useful guide discusses various genres of television programs, including police shows, docudramas, and news. Specific shows are analyzed with differences between types of programs discussed. The ways in which lines between various genres have been blurred, as in the case of socially relevant comedy programs, is also discussed.

Michael R. Bradley

Cross-References

Rowan and Martin's Laugh-In Is the Top Show on Television (1968), p. 2115; Relevance Programs Change Entertainment Standards (1970's), p. 2197; *The Mary Tyler Moore Show* Examines Women's Roles (1970), p. 2218; *M*A*S*H* Reflects 1970's Sentiments (1972), p. 2271; *The Jeffersons* Signals Success of Black Situation Comedies (1975), p. 2339.

GUARE'S *THE HOUSE OF BLUE LEAVES*
COMBINES COMEDY WITH HORROR

Category of event: Theater
Time: February 10, 1971
Locale: New York, New York

Some drama critics were baffled by John Guare's play because of its mixture of comedy and pain and its nonrepresentational style, but many still saw it as a significant dramatic statement

> *Principal personages:*
> JOHN GUARE (1938-), a playwright and film writer widely recognized as an important American voice
> MEL SHAPIRO (1937-), the director of *The House of Blue Leaves* and an interpreter of Guare's plays
> HAROLD GOULD (1923-), an actor who played the part of the main character, Artie Shaughnessy
> ANNE MEARA (1924-), an actress and comedienne who played the part of Artie's mistress, Bunny Flingus
> KATHERINE HELMOND (1933-), an actress who played the part of Artie's wife, Bananas Shaugnessy

Summary of Event

After some modest success with such plays as *Muzeeka* (1967) and *Cop-Out* (1968), John Guare attracted the attention of the American theatergoing public with the first production of *The House of Blue Leaves*, not only because of the blackness of the play's comedy but also because of the originality of its style, which left audiences confused, disturbed, and intrigued.

The play is a devastating farce set in the apartment in Sunnyside, Queens, New York, of an Irish Catholic family on October 4, 1965, the day of the Pope's visit to New York to speak before the United Nations on the subject of world peace. In order to get from the airport to Manhattan, the Pope must pass through Queens, and the streets outside the apartment are full of local residents and others who are excited over the prospect of getting a glimpse of the Pope. Artie Shaughnessy, the middle-aged head of the household, works as a zookeeper, but his real passion is for song-writing. Artie's wife, Bananas, has gone insane, and Artie wants to commit her to a mental hospital, the "house" of the title, so that he can then be free to travel to Hollywood with his mistress and downstairs neighbor, Bunny Flingus, in order to "make it big" as a songwriter in show business.

Artie's son, Ronnie, who is AWOL from Fort Dix and now dressed like an altar boy, has plans to "blow up" the Pope. Moreover, three nuns who were stationed on top of Artie's apartment building in order to see the Pope wander into Artie's apartment. In addition, Corrinna Stroller, the wife of Billy Einhorn, a Hollywood producer, has become deaf during the filming of a bomb scene in one of Billy's movies, and she stops by to visit Artie while on her way to the airport. The action of the play turns bizarre. Ronnie's bomb kills two of the nuns and Corrinna, but Ronnie escapes to Rome with plans to blow up the Vatican. Bananas is taken away to a "house," and Billy arrives from Hollywood to tell Artie that he must stay in Queens. At the end, Billy takes Bunny with him to Australia to make another movie.

The implications of much of the play depend not so much on action as on more subtle reactions and behavior. For example, Artie's wife Bananas, although insane, has moments of extraordinary perception, of lucidity of painful memories, and revelation of human feeling that wrenches the heart—all of which Artie realizes and tries to ignore. Moreover, Corrinna deals with her deafness by wearing a hearing aid that, when the batteries become defunct, places her in the position of either admitting to her disability or smiling bravely and pretending to understand what is going on. She chooses the latter alternative, which results in puzzling non sequiturs and a strange awareness on the audience's part of seeing the scene from her deaf perspective. Meanwhile, Artie persists in his dreams; at one point, however, he is made to realize by his mistress Bunny that the melody of one of his songs is that of the famous song "White Christmas"—thus bringing the audience to the realization that Artie is talentless, his dreams are fraudulent, and his sacrificing of those around him for his false dreams is ironic, cruel, and strangely pathetic.

Yet it is not just the action alone that endows the play with its historical significance. Guare employs devices that violate the apparent realistic feel of the play. There are times when characters step out of character and speak directly to the audience; at other moments, there are songs, slow-motion pantomimes, slapstick routines, and bizarre, dreamlike sequences. In addition, the statement made by the play is extremely negative, if not cynical, especially as it seems to address questions of hopes and dreams, materialism, relationships, exploitation, and, ultimately, American culture.

The reaction of drama critics to the play was significant for its stridency and inconsistency. One reviewer declared that the production was a "farce with a serious intent, but at heart it's hollow," and another wrote, "I really don't have much to say about *The House of Blue Leaves*. It affected me that way . . . which is no way at all." On the other hand, some critics saw the play's merit. Julius Novick, after analyzing its "black comedy," proclaimed that "it is not an insignificant play," while Clive Barnes perceived that Guare's "black inversions have a Joe Orton air to them, but his tone is all-American emanating from a mind riotously littered with the detritus of a civilization, its comic books, its radio serials, its movies, indeed all of its advertisements." Barnes also notes that "Mr. Guare is so funny because he goes for broke" and is almost "unendurably savage."

Impact of Event

The House of Blue Leaves takes its historical significance from Guare's original application of style, technique, tone, subject matter, and themes. The modern drama was born out of the nineteenth century's revolt against the popular and commercially successful melodrama. Since melodrama presented such a false picture of real life, the thrust of the nineteenth century theater was toward greater and greater realism. With the advent of Henrik Ibsen's naturalistic period, such an approach became the established style for plays attempting to deal in a serious way with the conflicts of people, society, and life. "Naturalism" may be defined as a style that creates a stage-picture that looks exactly like life itself: The room depicted on stage looks like a room in a real house, the only difference being that one wall has been removed in order for the audience to observe the action. Moreover, nothing in the action of the play can happen that would remind the audience that it is not, in fact, watching real life. The development of naturalistic techniques on stage gained support from such advocates as Konstantin Stanislavsky, John Galsworthy, and George Bernard Shaw, and naturalism became the conventional style of drama for the twentieth century.

Soon after the advent of naturalism, the limitations of the style became apparent, and experimenters began to search for and explore other styles. August Strindberg was one of the earliest dramatists to break with naturalism, and shortly after the turn of the century, he wrote a sequence of plays in which he attempted to create on stage the world of the dreamer. Other experimenters followed. Alfred Jarry in France (who actually preceded Strindberg), the expressionists in Germany, Luigi Pirandello in Italy, the Futurists, the Dadaists, and the Surrealists all contributed to the exploration of nonrealistic forms and sought to push the twentieth century stage to its limits.

Two of the most influential figures on modern drama were Bertolt Brecht and Samuel Beckett. In his plays, Brecht developed the idea of epic theater, in which he sought to alienate the audience so that it would not fall under any theatrical illusion and would remain in control of its intellectual and critical faculties. Writing primarily from the 1920's to the 1950's, Brecht attempted to jar his audiences to their senses by using frequent scene changes, minimalistic sets, music, songs, dance, and nonnaturalistic devices. Samuel Beckett created a type of drama in the 1950's that came to be known as absurdism. Beckett too used abstract and minimal settings, nonrealistic situations and dialogue, and plotless structures, all infused with a seeming sense of despair. By the 1960's, however, the heavily propagandistic plays of Brecht had lost much of their appeal, and absurdism, with its depressing message, had somewhat run its course.

While Guare invented neither naturalism nor nonrepresentational theater, his use of both techniques within the same play in *The House of Blue Leaves* in 1971 offered a rather refreshing and original stage style that confused some and satisfied others. On the surface, the play has something of the appearance of being realistic, although it seems at times to be a reality that is exaggerated and grotesquely distorted. There is nothing in the action of the play that could not happen in real life. At the same time, characters do nonnaturalistic deeds, such as speaking directly to the audience, which make the audience aware that it is in a theater and watching a play. It is the juxtaposition of styles that makes Guare's work seem so original.

Juxtaposition, in point of fact, is one of the key elements that lends novelty to Guare's work. The audience is often kept off balance by the play's mixture of comedy and tragedy, humor and pathos, and hope and despair.

The tone of Guare's play is characterized by contrast. On the one hand, there resides within the play an element of hope and bright optimism. For example, the characters are charged with excitement over the Pope's visit and the prospect of getting a glimpse of him and receiving his blessing. Moreover, Artie is full of hope and confidence as he makes plans to escape with his mistress to the West Coast in order to start a new life, get into show business, and become wealthy. All seems well, and the future unlimited. On the other hand, the Pope's visit turns out to be a massive disappointment. The nuns who have traveled far to see him in person cannot see him because the crowds are too thick, and they end up watching him on Artie's black-and-white television when they could have, as one nun says, stayed home, watched him in color, and drunk imported beer. One particularly powerful tableau occurs when Artie is seen hugging his television set in order to receive the Pope's blessing. What is worse, all the nuns but one are killed by Ronnie's bomb intended for the Pope. In addition, Artie's enthusiasm for escaping with his mistress is tempered by the appearance of his deranged wife and, at the end, by the betrayal of his friend Billy, who steals Artie's mistress away from him. It is the juxtaposition of desire and perversion that lends the play its unusual tone.

The historical event out of which Guare's play emerges is the Vietnam War, and while the play does not deal directly with the war itself, aside from several references to it, the play does concern itself indirectly with issues related to the era. Violence, exploitation, manipulation, materialism, false dreams, and a sense of despair and alienation speak to the heart of the period in which it was written.

Bibliography

Friend, Tad. "The Guare Facts." *Vogue* 182 (March, 1992): 326-329. Account of a visit with Guare in his own apartment. Reveals various aspects of his writing, plays, personal habits, and attributes, mixing in observations from Guare's wife, friends, and director Peter Hall. Attempts to give insight into the person behind the plays, especially the connection between the bizarre in Guare's own life and its presence in his plays.

Guare, John. "John Guare: Playwright." *Esquire* 110 (September, 1988): 122-125. A brief statement by Guare regarding his basic views on art and playwriting. The artist's soul desires to "give people a new pair of eyes with which to look at the world." Theater, Guare says, is composed of strangers sitting together in the dark, trying to figure out who they are and how they fit into things.

_____. *Three Exposures: Plays by John Guare.* Foreword by Louis Malle. New York: Harcourt Brace Jovanovich, 1982. Contains the text of *The House of Blue Leaves.* In addition to a statement by Louis Malle on Guare's work and their relationship, the volume also contains an invaluable introduction by the playwright himself.

Hewes, Henry. "The Playwright as Voyager." *Saturday Review/World* 1 (November 20, 1973): 48. Guare comments on various aspects of his writing, his work habits ("by writing, without censoring, in pocket-size notebooks"), working in the theater, and his work itself ("work for me is all voyaging, a kind of emotional serendipity").

Kroll, Jack. "Laugh When It Hurts." *Newsweek* 93 (May 14, 1979): 85-86. After reviewing *Bosoms and Neglect* (pr. 1979, pb. 1980), Kroll gives a profile of Guare's background, his work, and his opinions on contemporary theater. Guare states that New York critics are "besotted" with English plays and cannot appreciate what American playwrights are trying to do.

Rose, Lloyd. "A New American Master." *Atlantic* 253 (March, 1984): 120-124. Discusses much of Guare's work in general, including *The House of Blue Leaves.* Places Guare in relation to other major American playwrights, emphasizing Guare's love of language, his free structures, and his sense of American culture, history, and art.

Tony J. Stafford

Cross-References

The Ghost Sonata Influences Modern Theater and Drama (1908), p. 199; Pirandello's *Six Characters in Search of an Author* Premieres (1921), p. 534; *Our Town* Opens on Broadway (1938), p. 1099; *Waiting for Godot* Expresses the Existential Theme of Absurdity (1953), p. 1573; Esslin Publishes *The Theatre of the Absurd* (1961), p. 1871; *The American Dream* Establishes Albee as the Voice of Pessimism (1961), p. 1903; Baraka's *Dutchman* Dramatizes Racial Hatred (1964), p. 2000; Shange's *for colored girls . . .* Is a Landmark (1976), p. 2370; Shepard's *Buried Child* Promotes Off-Broadway Theater (1978), p. 2413.

THE SONNY AND CHER COMEDY HOUR BRINGS GLITZ TO TELEVISION

Category of event: Television and radio
Time: August 1, 1971-August 29, 1977
Locale: The United States

Sonny and Cher Bono launched a second career for themselves by bringing the spectacular staging of motion-picture musicals to television with huge sets and lush costuming

Principal personages:

CHER (CHERILYN LAPIERE, 1946-   ), the lead singer, comic wit, and costar of *The Sonny and Cher Comedy Hour*

SONNY BONO (1935-   ), the songwriter, singer, and comic straight man who was costar of *The Sonny and Cher Comedy Hour*

FRED SILVERMAN (1937-   ), the network executive who recognized Sonny and Cher's talent and brought them to prime-time television

Summary of Event

On August 1, 1971, the Columbia Broadcasting System (CBS) introduced a new comedy-variety show as part of its summer replacement lineup. The show, *The Sonny and Cher Comedy Hour*, featured Sonny and Cher Bono, a husband and wife team. The show won public approval, especially from younger audiences, and became a regular part of the fall schedule. It was to run for three seasons before being interrupted by personal problems in the lives of its stars; it would later return for a short time.

The introduction of *The Sonny and Cher Comedy Hour* to the television viewers of America was another of the intuitive strokes of genius of Fred Silverman. As head of CBS, Silverman was attempting to revamp his network to attract a younger, more urban audience. This group had more money to spend and so would allow CBS to attract more advertisers. To accomplish this goal, Silverman was changing the orientation of CBS toward the production of "relevance" shows such as *All in the Family*.

Of course, the entire lineup of the network could not be the same type of show, and Silverman was looking for something in a different genre that would also appeal to his target audience. While watching *The Merv Griffin Show*, Silverman was impressed by the style and hip appearance of the temporary hosts of the show, Sonny and Cher Bono. Silverman contacted the pair and asked them to host a prime-time comedy and variety program for the rest of the 1971 summer season. Younger viewers reacted positively, and Silverman made a bold decision. On December 27, 1971, Sonny and Cher entered the regular CBS programming schedule, replacing *The Ed Sullivan Show* in a time period that Sullivan had held for two decades. Every week, the young couple came on the air for an hour, dazzling viewers with comic routines, well-timed putdowns, and Cher's decolletage and belting delivery of songs, many written by Sonny. In less than a month, the show had reached a forty percent Nielsen rating, making it one of the top twelve shows on television. Its producers, Chris Bearde and Allan Blye, kept the pace of the show fast and uncluttered. They also made clever use of animation and videotape.

On the show, Sonny appeared to be a good-natured, bumbling buffoon who was constantly outwitted by his sharp-tongued but glamorous wife. Actually, he was a shrewd show-business manager who had rescued the couple's career. Cher, his svelte wife whose exotic appearance reflected her mixed American Indian, Armenian, and French ancestry, had a powerful singing voice, which one critic called "a cross between a mating call and a sonic boom."

The basic premise behind the show was that of the fall guy who succumbs to the mischievous woman. Despite its toned-down hippie roots, critic Henry Ehrlich wrote "the show sometimes echoes *Laugh-In* but its real ancestors are George Burns and Gracie Allen." The show also depended on elaborate costumes, lavishly staged production numbers, and comedy skits with celebrity guest performers. The elaborate nature of the costumes was reflected in the show's production costs; Cher wore about ten thousand dollars' worth of clothes during each week's show.

By and large, the critics liked the show as much as the audience did. *Life* magazine noted that "Cher is better looking and sings better than Ed Sullivan," whose place *The Sonny and Cher Comedy Hour* took. *Time* magazine wrote that "the salvation of the show is Cher's singing ability." Another critic noted, "There is about the Sonny and Cher show that inspired comic touch to production numbers only CBS seems capable of doing."

There were also, however, problems with the show. *Time* also noted that "the trouble comes in the comedy, which consists mostly of Cher putting down Sonny in skits that would be rejected by any self-respecting high-school drama coach." The general critical consensus was that the show would have been stronger if the producers had not insisted that Cher try to be funny. Too many of the comic skits revolved around the incongruity of the couple's size and personality, contrasting the tall, cool Cher with the short, zany Sonny. This basic theme was used so frequently that critics soon began to complain.

If the skits were often corny, the public usually laughed anyway. The show had going for it the same running comedy appeal that had made Burns and Allen a show-business institution. The actors and producers combined a casual tone with stunts, state-of-the-art visual effects, and glossy production, and the combination was tremendously popular.

While such success was taking place in the public eye, however, in private the two stars were beginning to diverge; Cher began to contend that Sonny was inhibiting her professional development. In February, 1974, the couple filed for divorce. CBS canceled the show in April of the same year. Cher commented, "People ask me if I left Sonny for another man. I tell them, no, I left for another woman. Me."

When the pair split, each tried to repeat the success of *The Sonny and Cher Com-*

edy Hour on a separate show. Cher stayed with CBS, while Sonny moved to the rival American Broadcasting Company (ABC). Sonny's show soon flopped, and Cher's, although initially successful, began to slip in the ratings. In 1976, the two again appeared on a joint show, but success eluded them. Their trademark song, "I Got You Babe," written by Sonny for Cher in the 1960's, had no punch when the audience knew they did not have each other.

Impact of Event

The Sonny and Cher Comedy Hour had a great impact on the career of Cher; from 1971 until mid-1974, she was the most glamorous sex symbol on television. She emerged from the status of singing partner to Sonny to become a superstar in her own right. Her latent talent had begun to emerge prior to the couple's television debut; even in the failed 1969 film *Chastity*, some observers were impressed by Cher's acting ability. One noted, "Her marvelous quality makes you forget the lines you are hearing. Her manner can be described as a combination of tough, disinterested, unhappy, self-critical, and deadpan." Cher had long been determined to develop her career. Following the 1974 divorce, even her mother remarked that to Cher "the quality of her career is much more important than the quality of any human tie." To this extent, Cher was a show-business creation, and she found success in becoming a stereotypical star.

The glamour of show business overlay an unhappy childhood. Cher's mother wed and divorced Cher's father, a heroin addict, three times. Cher left high school after the tenth grade to pursue her own life-style; she met Sonny Bono just after her eighteenth birthday, and they were married over family opposition. When the two reached stardom in a singing career, Cher was on the road she had wished to travel—but the road would go downhill before she reached the heights on *The Sonny and Cher Comedy Hour*. Cher became a megastar only after the television show gave the couple a second career in show business.

Sonny Bono's parents were poor immigrants from Sicily who could not always feed their family. Sonny dropped out of high school to work at menial jobs while trying his hand at writing songs and producing records. He had some success at this and also at singing back-up for better-known performers. Sonny was working for a record company when he met Cher on a double date. In addition to experiencing a personal attraction, he immediately recognized her star potential.

The first step on the road to success as singers came when Sonny and Cher borrowed $168 to finance the recording of "Baby Don't Go" in 1964. When the song caught on in Los Angeles and Dallas, they hurriedly recorded more, including their big hit "I Got You Babe." By the fall of 1965, Sonny and Cher had five records on the charts at one time, and they were also drawing large crowds to their concerts. By the end of 1967, the two had sold more than forty million records.

Shifting musical fashions, though, soon cost the duo much of their popularity. Sonny and Cher's success had been built on a string of lightweight pop hits, and the rise of "acid rock" and other harder styles soon made the couple's music seem outdated. Along with acid rock came the drug culture, a development that was appalling to Sonny and Cher, who neither drank nor smoked tobacco; the pair even made an antimarijuana film for use in schools. They had fallen out of step with the times; in fact, though, Sonny and Cher had never been heavyweights in the world of rock. Though they had been embraced by rock audiences, they were musicians who used a variety of styles and even occasionally sang standards, to the horror of many rock critics. The duo's style was always far removed from those of the leading rock bands of the day.

As their recording career fell apart, Sonny tried to reestablish their position in the youth culture with a 1969 film, *Chastity*, which he wrote and directed. The film, starring Cher, dealt with a teenage runaway. The critics panned the film, and the public ignored it; Sonny and Cher lost half a million dollars on the venture.

Sonny realized that something had to be done to salvage the duo's career. "The biggest mistake a performer makes is to try to stay a teenager," he noted. "Young kids have a new idol every year. Someone always takes your place next year." He thus suggested to Cher that they should switch from making records to performing as nightclub entertainers. He was confident the two could put their career back at the top in five years; in fact, it took less than four.

The idea was entirely Sonny's. "I've got to admit it, I fought him all the way," Cher later recalled. Nightclub appearances, sometimes to audiences as small as forty-five persons, led to guest appearances on television shows. Then came the invitation to host *The Merv Griffin Show*, and Fred Silverman was watching.

The Sonny and Cher Comedy Hour brought spectacular, motion-picture-style production values to television. Sonny and Cher used sets that cost as much as $250,000 for each week's show. The costumes and decor matched the sets; Cher was always the centerpiece of these productions. The full orchestration and use of spectacle set the show's tone, which not only made a success of the program but also encouraged other producers and other networks to imitate the genre. After more than a decade of the down-home comedy and bare stage performance of the Ed Sullivan variety, *The Sonny and Cher Comedy Hour* brought glamour to American television.

Bibliography

Allen, Bonnie. "Cher Struck!" *Ms.*, July, 1988, pp. 54-55. A feature article in a popular feminist magazine that extols Cher as a "real" woman who has attained success on her own terms. Focuses on Cher's later film career.

Bono, Sonny. *And the Beat Goes On.* New York: Pocket Books, 1991. Sonny's account of his years with Cher, written after he had attained renewed celebrity as the mayor of Palm Springs, California. In many ways a "get-even" book; portrays Cher as ambitious and insecure.

Brooks, Tim, and Earle Marsh. *The Complete Directory to Prime Time Network TV Shows, 1946-Present.* 4th ed. New York: Ballantine Books, 1988. Gives a brief discussion of *The Sonny and Cher Comedy Hour* and lists the show's cast members and broadcast history. Provides similar information for hundreds of other programs; helpful in understanding the broader context in which *The Sonny and Cher Comedy Hour* was produced.

"The Cher Effect." *Maclean's*, March 6, 1989, pp. 38-42. An illustrated biographical feature on Cher that serves as a counterweight to Bono's book. Contains an interview section.

Green, Michele. "Sonny on Cher." *People*, August 5, 1991, pp. 83-85. Another shot in the decades-long war between the two stars. Illustrated.

Michael R. Bradley

Cross-References

Variety Shows Dominate Television Programming (1948), p. 1383; "Mr. Television," Milton Berle, Has the Top-Rated Show (1948), p. 1394; *The Red Skelton Show* Becomes a Landmark on Network Television (1951), p. 1520; *Rowan and Martin's Laugh-In* Is the Top Show on Television (1968), p. 2115; *Saturday Night Live* Is First Broadcast (1975), p. 2355.

MORTIMER'S *A VOYAGE ROUND MY FATHER* IS EMBRACED BY AUDIENCES

Category of event: Theater
Time: August 4, 1971
Locale: Haymarket Theatre, London, England

Spanning two decades and dramatizing a symbiotic relationship between the playwright and his blind father, A Voyage Round My Father *was an unusual work for the English stage: an autobiographical memory play*

Principal personage:
JOHN MORTIMER (1923-   ), a novelist, screenwriter, and dramatist

Summary of Event

Because his plays had been regularly produced in West End theaters since 1958, John Mortimer was well known to British audiences by the time *A Voyage Round My Father* opened in London in 1971. He also had written a number of favorably received novels and screenplays and many radio and television dramas for the British Broadcasting Corporation (BBC), one of which (in 1963) was an early, briefer version of *A Voyage Round My Father.* In addition, as a leading barrister, he frequently had argued for the defense in highly publicized freedom of speech and press cases. None of his previous literary work, however, prepared audiences for this play. Whereas his novels of the 1940's and early 1950's had skirted the edge of the mystery genre, most of his plays had been one-act comedies of manners and sex farces, and even the three full-length works that preceded *A Voyage Round My Father* were Chekhovian portraits of the middle class in decline. Only a year earlier, in a study of the contemporary English theater, John Russell Taylor wrote that Mortimer's "world is consistently and instantly knowable" and wondered whether he would use it "as a launching-pad to the discovery of fresh worlds elsewhere." What is more, the autobiographical memory play, long an established form in the United States, was uncommon in Great Britain. In the event, *A Voyage Round My Father* was an immediate critical and popular success as well as an innovative advance for Mortimer, and it endures as his major stage achievement and as a landmark work in the English theater.

When the play opened at the Greenwich Theatre near London on November 25, 1970, in a production directed by Claude Whatham and starring Mark Dignam as the father, Betty Huntley Wright as the mother, and David Wood as the grown son, *The Times* of London called it Mortimer's most successful full-length play and expressed the hope that the playwright would make "future returns to his past." With minor revisions, the play came to London's Haymarket Theatre on August 4, 1971, in a production directed by Ronald Eyre and starring Alec Guinness, Leueen MacGrath, and Jeremy Brett. (A 1982 television adaptation—scripted by the playwright—starred Laurence Olivier as the father, Jane Asher as the mother, and Alan Bates as their son.) *The Times'* critic of the London production recalled the "splendid launching" of the play in Greenwich and again was laudatory. He also noted that *A Voyage Round My Father* was "far from an obvious choice for the Haymarket" and did not pander "to the plot-loving public." Nevertheless, West End theatergoers loved the play, which ran for 501 performances.

A Voyage Round My Father's episodic action spans two decades and is unified by a reflective narrator who bridges past and present. Through his chronological recollection of events, he cumulatively demonstrates a symbiotic, yet peculiarly distant and unemotional, relationship between the father and son. As the title suggests, the son—as boy and man—never can get as close to his father as he desires, not only because of the father's blindness but also because the older man treats life as a game and creates an impenetrable emotional barrier between himself and everyone else, including his wife, on whom he is totally dependent. Notwithstanding the father's coldness, self-absorption, and lack of meaningful involvement with others, Mortimer clearly wants the play to be considered an act of love.

The story begins with the old man, blinded long ago in an accident, having his adult son describe the family garden. The son then tells the audience that his father was a barrister who went daily to London's law courts and returned nightly to his flowers and a ritualistic earwig hunt. The action reverts to the past with the presentation of a number of youthful initiation episodes, the most fully developed of which deal with the son's school experiences with a simpleminded headmaster and inept teachers, veterans of World War I, who are afflicted with the aftereffects of shell shock and battle fatigue. When the time comes for the son to choose a profession, the old barrister, although he regards the law with contempt, encourages his boy to follow in his footsteps, primarily so the son will have spare time for writing. At the end of the first act, as they walk arm in arm, the son informs his father that in lieu of military service (his eyesight is bad), he may get work as assistant director with a wartime propaganda film unit.

The second act opens on a film production set, where the young man is assigned to fetch snacks for the crew and maintain silence during takes. Failing at this role, he is sent to the writer's section, where he meets Elizabeth, a scriptwriter supporting her husband and children. By the next episode, the son has been a barrister for nine months, Elizabeth has divorced her husband, and she and the son plan to marry, despite the father's attempts to dissuade both. As the old man foresaw, financial problems bear down upon the couple; busy though the son is with divorce cases, he sees little money, for a clerk collects fees and dispenses payments in a quixotically parsimonious manner. To support his new family, the son works part-time for a legal aid society and starts to write plays, though the father warns him to "hold hard on the law" and instructs him in nuances of timing in cross-examinations. He eventually wins a major domestic case, but Elizabeth reacts equivocally, since the victor did not deserve to prevail. The son responds, "*I* won," and she concludes that he is becoming more like his father every day: one who plays games, makes jokes, and takes nothing seriously. The son agrees, later telling the audience: "He had no message. I think he had no belief. He was the advocate who can take the side that comes to him first and always discover words to anger his opponent." The penultimate sequence in the play has the old man regaling his grandchildren with songs and stories, an atypical display of warmth and *joie de vivre*. The last scene describes the garden deteriorating in tandem with the dying father, and the play concludes with the son telling the audience:

> I'd been told of all the things you're meant to feel. Sudden freedom, growing up, the end of dependence, the step into the sunlight when no one is taller than you and you're in no one else's shadow. . . . I know what I felt. Lonely.

A decade later, in his autobiography, Mortimer recalled anxieties he had about the work and noted that "a man who had filled so much of my life seemed to have left me and become someone for other people to read about and perform." Mortimer has also said that publishing his autobiography meant that the first half century of his life was lost to him, that by writing about those years he "made them public property, just as I lost my father when I wrote that play about him." As an ironic coda, Kathleen Mortimer, the playwright's mother, died on the opening night of the play in Greenwich.

Impact of Event

Introspective and usually autobiographical, memory plays are more common to the American theater, which can boast such examples as Thornton Wilder's *Our Town* (1938), Tennessee Williams' *The Glass Menagerie* (1944), Arthur Miller's *After the Fall* (1964), and Robert Anderson's *I Never Sang for My Father* (1968), than to the English stage. Whereas these American dramas are basically products of their authors' imaginations, with highly stylized autobiographical elements and with Oedipal and other psychological concerns as thematic centerpieces, Mortimer's play, which has been described as a personal essay in dramatic form, is largely reportorial. While Mortimer altered some details, the play's situations and events closely parallel the past as he records it in *Clinging to the Wreckage: A Part of Life*, his 1982 autobiography. The play, therefore, was a departure for Mortimer, whose previous dramas had been much more traditional in form. That the play ran for more than a year at the Haymarket is testimony to London audiences' willingness, following earlier stage breakthroughs by John Osborne and Harold Pinter, to embrace the unfamiliar once more. Critical and popular success notwithstanding, the play did not spawn a movement on the part of Mortimer's contemporaries, so both the immediate and long-range impact was largely upon Mortimer's career.

The 1971 success of *A Voyage Round My Father* definitively demonstrated Mortimer's mastery of the full-length serious play and testified to the foresight of a 1958 *Encore* magazine story that had included him in a survey of eight promising new British playwrights. (A quarter of a century later, only two were figures of international stature, Mortimer and Pinter.) The success of *A Voyage Round My Father*, coupled with the wide popularity of the stories and teleplays starring Old Bailey barrister Horace Rumpole that he began to write soon after, encouraged Mortimer to retire from the law. He became, for the first time in his life, a full-time writer of short stories, novels, criticism, television plays, newspaper interviews, and even an opera libretto. His 1981 television adaptation of Evelyn Waugh's novel *Brideshead Revisited* was critically acclaimed and watched by millions not only in Great Britain and the United States but also throughout the world. When *Paradise Postponed*, his first novel in thirty years, came out in 1985, it was widely praised as a Dickensian saga of post-World War II Great Britain. Its sequel, *Titmuss Regained* (1991), and *Summer's Lease* (1988) established him as a leading novelist, and he also did successful television adaptations of the three books.

More than any of his contemporaries in drama, fiction, criticism, or journalism, Mortimer has become an influential public personage, taking active leadership roles in cultural activities (such as the management of the Royal Court Theatre and the chairmanship of the Royal Society of Literature) and speaking out on such major social issues as prison, educational, and legal reform. This public persona was accorded an official imprimateur when Mortimer was made a Commander of the British Empire in 1986; a portrait of him was hung in the National Portrait Gallery in 1991.

A Voyage Round My Father stands as the centerpiece of John Mortimer's concurrent multiple careers, which, though widely divergent, have enriched one another. All of his work is connected by common threads: a social conscience that is sometimes iconoclastic but that is less interested in destroying institutions than in reforming them; a sympathy for the underdog or outcast; and a humor that echoes such varied predecessors as William Shakespeare, Charles Dickens, Anthony Trollope, and P. G. Wodehouse.

Bibliography

Hayman, Ronald. *British Theatre Since 1955: A Reassessment.* Oxford, England: Oxford University Press, 1979. A useful book, not only for its judgments about plays but also for its discussion of the London stage milieu of the time. Hayman's pessimism about the future of the English theater, however, has been proven to be unfounded.

Herbert, Rosemary. "The Art of Fiction CVI: John Mortimer." *Paris Review* 109 (Winter, 1988): 97-128. Introduced by a lengthy biographical note, this is a wide-ranging interview that is up to the high standards of the *Paris Review* series. While the focus is on the Rumpole stories and later novels, many of Mortimer's responses, including some revealing biographical asides, relate directly to *A Voyage Round My Father* and to relevant aspects of his work as a dramatist.

Mortimer, John. *Clinging to the Wreckage: A Part of Life.* New Haven, Conn.: Ticknor & Fields, 1982. Witty and engaging, Mortimer's autobiography is frequently conversational in its tone and discursiveness. At the same time, its anecdotes provide insights into, and likely sources of, characters and events in *A Voyage Round My Father* and other plays and novels. As the subtitle indicates, the book does not pretend to be a full memoir, and Mortimer's recollections are not always factually accurate.

Rusinko, Susan. *British Drama, 1950 to the Present: A Critical History.* Boston: Twayne, 1989. A comprehensive study of modern drama in England that includes insightful discussions of some forty playwrights. Mortimer is classified as an "establishment traditionalist" and is considered in a chapter with such men as Alan Ayckbourn, Michael Frayn, Christopher Hampton, and Anthony and Peter Shaffer.

Taylor, John Russell. *The Angry Theatre: New British Drama.* New York: Hill & Wang, 1969. Primarily covers the period from the 1956 opening of John Osborne's *Look Back in Anger.* The lengthy section on Mortimer, part of a chapter entitled "In the Air," provides a thorough analysis of his first decade as a dramatist for the stage and also discusses the radio and television plays of the period. Though Taylor's book preceded *A Voyage Round My Father,* its discussion of Mortimer's early plays is helpful for an appreciation of Mortimer's art as it emerges in that work.

Gerald H. Strauss

Cross-References

Our Town Opens on Broadway (1938), p. 1099; "Angry Young Men" Express Working-Class Views (1950's), p. 1454; Osborne's *Look Back in Anger* Opens in London (1956), p. 1721; *Long Day's Journey into Night* Revives O'Neill's Reputation (1956), p. 1726; Behan's *The Hostage* Is Presented by the Theatre Workshop (1958), p. 1757; The Theatres Act Ends Censorship of English Drama (1968), p. 2131.

JESUS CHRIST SUPERSTAR ESTABLISHES THE ROCK OPERA

Categories of event: Theater and music
Time: October 12, 1971
Locale: Mark Hellinger Theater, New York, New York

Jesus Christ Superstar *generated intense controversy, but it legitimized rock music as a resource for theater composers, revitalized musical theater, and created a worldwide market for musicals*

Principal personages:

ANDREW LLOYD WEBBER (1948-   ), a British composer who brought classical, theater, and rock music traditions together to establish a new kind of musical theater

TIM RICE (1944-   ), a British lyricist who combined the techniques for writing rock and show lyrics to establish a new kind of book for musical theater

ROBERT STIGWOOD (1934-   ), a music and theater producer who became Lloyd Webber and Rice's manager, handling all legal and business negotiations for *Jesus Christ Superstar*

TOM O'HORGAN (1926-   ), a director who conceived and staged the controversial, flamboyant Broadway production of *Jesus Christ Superstar*

ROBIN WAGNER (1933-   ), a designer who created the stage settings for the Broadway production

RANDY BARCELO (1946-   ), a designer who created the costumes for the Broadway production

BEN VEREEN (1946-   ), an actor who originated the role of Judas Iscariot in the Broadway production, winning a Theater World Award for outstanding new talent

Summary of Event

In April, 1965, seventeen-year-old Andrew Lloyd Webber, who had a classical music background and a desire to compose for the musical theater, was introduced to twenty-year-old Tim Rice, who had an encyclopedic knowledge of pop music and a desire to write hit lyrics. After three years of unprofitable collaboration, they were asked to write a short cantata, with at least some minimal religious significance, for Colet Court, a preparatory school. The result was a twenty-five-minute work called *Joseph and the Amazing Technicolor Dreamcoat*, in the composing of which the two discovered they could relate action entirely in song without a narrative line. They experimented, changing musical styles freely throughout the piece, and discovering a kind of opera in the popular idiom. An expanded *Joseph* was recorded and unexpectedly became a hit album in England.

With the success of *Joseph*, Rice and Lloyd Webber concentrated on finding a suitable new project. Rice was struck by a question posed in a Bob Dylan song: "Did Judas Iscariot have God on his side?" Thinking it over, Rice had got the idea to relate the story of the Passion of Jesus from the viewpoint of Judas. Lloyd Webber liked the idea, and the pair wrote *Jesus Christ Superstar*. First released as a double record album in November, 1969, it became an instant hit in England and the United States, creating a religious controversy over its relative reverence.

When a production of *Jesus Christ Superstar* opened on Broadway on October 12, 1971, new controversies erupted over the quality of the music and lyrics as musical theater and especially over the staging. Some denounced Rice's lyrics as limp doggerel and Lloyd Webber's music as not only bad theater but also bad rock and roll. Others praised the achievement of using rock lyrics in a theatrical idiom and rock music as a flexible framework for the show. There was, however, almost universal disdain for Tom O'Horgan's staging. Christ made his first entrance, draped in a silver robe, emerging upright from a silver chalice; Herod was a campy drag queen on platform shoes; gigantic caterpillar-like creatures wormed their way onto the stage for no apparent reason; and Judas returned from the grave on a trapeze, surrounded by feathered chorus girls. It was agreed that the direction served primarily to obscure the text of the libretto. Despite the negative reviews, the public's enthusiasm sustained the Broadway production for almost two years. Lloyd Webber hated the irrelevant spectacle and moved to ensure that the Broadway staging was never revived. Nevertheless, he remained saddled with a widespread reputation that his musicals required overblown spectacle to succeed.

After *Jesus Christ Superstar*, Lloyd Webber decided to venture in a completely new direction, writing the music for Alan Ayckbourn's *Jeeves* (1975). He completely abandoned the rock idiom, trying to write a score in the style of Jerry Herman. When *Jeeves* flopped, Lloyd Webber decided never to write for a book musical again, and he resolved to try out everything he wrote before taking it public. It was a wiser but humbler Lloyd Webber who went back to Tim Rice, agreeing to write the music for a show about Eva Peron.

Evita (1976) solidified the artistic approach that had been so successful in *Jesus Christ Superstar*. Every aspect of Rice and Lloyd Webber's technique, however, had advanced, from the musical style and cohesiveness of the score to the dramatic structure of the libretto, which related character and narrative through lyrics. They did not want another O'Horgan to subvert the musical with an appliquéd concept, so they contacted veteran Hal Prince, who listened to the music and wrote a three-thousand-word memo with his suggestions for rewrites. Lloyd Webber and Rice did not want to be subservient to anyone, though, so they finished writing the show and recorded the album before beginning a production. This unique approach became the pair's method for ensuring artistic control whether working on projects alone or together: They would write a show and then record it, releasing singles to become hits and using the album to generate public interest, before stage production began. For better or worse, producers could thus make few changes in the work.

Lloyd Webber and Rice believed that *Jesus Christ Superstar* had alienated the New York critics, so they established another precedent, opening the show in London and allowing it to become established before moving it to Broadway. *Evita* opened in London in June, 1978, to generally positive reviews. The American production opened in Los Angeles and then San Francisco. As with *Jesus Christ Superstar*, some theater critics were confused by the operatic quality of a musical that had no dialogue and doubted the theatricality of a production that had first been a record. When *Evita* opened on Broadway on September 25, 1979, the pair's worst nightmares proved true. The critics savaged everything about Lloyd Webber and Rice's abilities, from their subject matter to their ability to write music and lyrics. Once again, though, popular response to *Evita* established it as a solid hit.

Although Lloyd Webber and Rice did not continue to collaborate after *Evita*, they remained business partners. *Jesus Christ Superstar* and *Evita* established the artistic approach that both would use on their independent projects. During the 1980's, Rice wrote the librettos for two musicals, *Blondel* (1983) and *Chess* (1986); *Chess* was an enormous hit in England but ran for less than two months on Broadway. Lloyd Webber, on the other hand, became the most financially successful composer in the history of musical theater by composing the music for *Cats* (1981), *Song and Dance* (1985), *Requiem* (1985), *Starlight Express* (1984), *Phantom of the Opera* (1987), and *Aspects of Love* (1989). Yet he continued to be criticized for pandering to the lowest common denominator of an undiscerning public, for relying on repetitive and derivative themes, and for requiring overblown technical theatrics to mask his deficiencies. His supporters have countered that he has displayed a genius for melody and a unique ability to combine classical, show, and popular music in a way that appeals to a universal audience.

Impact of Event

When *Jesus Christ Superstar* opened in September, 1971, almost three million double record albums of the music had already been sold. The show's "I Don't Know How to Love Him" was an established hit single. Unauthorized concert productions of the album's music were being closed by the copyright holders on a weekly basis, while the professional tour sold thousands of tickets at unprecedented prices. Many religious organizations condemned the blasphemy of a rock music version of the Passion of Christ, while others praised its reverence. No one could foretell the impact that *Jesus Christ Superstar* was to have on both the art and business of musical theater.

The content and status of rock music had changed rapidly from 1965 to 1970. Bob Dylan had given rock intellectual respectability, and the Beatles had stretched the boundaries of rock recording when they released the first concept album, *Sgt. Pepper's Lonely Hearts Club Band*, in 1967. The Who had released the first rock opera, *Tommy* (1969), which was performed only in concert because it was not theatrically cohesive. Broadway had its first successful rock musical, *Hair* (1968), full of hit songs that commented upon, but did not develop, the action or characters. It was the logical extension of these events for Andrew Lloyd Webber and Tim Rice to incorporate such developments in a rock opera for the stage.

When the Broadway theater season began in 1971, Broadway had witnessed a decade of declining ticket sales, the fragmentation of its audience, few openings, and even fewer hits. The traditional Broadway musical had stagnated. Stephen Sondheim had scored in 1970 with *Company*, his first "concept musical," which the elite theater community had hailed as the dawning of a new era. They were less than optimistic about the arrival of *Jesus Christ Superstar*, viewing it as nothing more than the opportunistic staging of a hit record album written by a pair of young British rock-and-rollers with no background in the musical theater. When the production opened on October 12, it was generally panned and dismissed, but it did not go away; instead, it ran for seven hundred and twenty performances. As a record, a concert, and again as a Broadway musical, it found its audience—a young, fresh audience for an otherwise ailing theater. Its impact would not be acknowledged for another decade.

Recognizing that Tom O'Horgan's Broadway staging obscured the libretto, the writers worked for continually more restrained productions. When *Jesus Christ Superstar* moved to London, Jim Sharman directed a scaled-down version that enhanced the score and libretto. Sharman's production ran for eight years, becoming the longest-running musical in British history and establishing the British reputation of Lloyd Webber and Rice in musical theater. *Jesus Christ Superstar* went international with profesional productions in twenty countries, developing audiences for musical theater everywhere it went.

When Lloyd Webber and Rice returned to Broadway in 1979 with *Evita*, the New York theater was in much better health. Broadway had discovered a new audience, but it was no longer homogeneous; the new Broadway provided a variety of shows for a fragmented audience. The critics, though, still tried to rule as the arbiters of taste, and they ruled that *Evita*, even though directed by Hal Prince, had no place on Broadway. Yet Lloyd Webber and Rice had anticipated this by carefully creating a popular demand for the show that again transcended critical response, and *Evita* enjoyed a four-year run.

As it was generally too expensive and risky to originate a show on Broadway, many other producers followed the pattern of developing a show elsewhere: in regional theaters, universities, and showcases and in Off-Broadway and London productions. In New York, Sondheim's sophisticated, complex musicals continued to garner high praise from the critics but had limited box-office appeal. Other British producers such as Cameron Mackintosh noticed what had happened with *Evita* and followed its pattern of development. Through the 1980's, Great Britain nourished its contemporary theater and sent its best to Broadway, creating a theatrical "British invasion" much as the Beatles had done in pop music two decades earlier. Almost unbelievably, the British producers shifted the center of musical theater from Broadway to London. It seemed as though every substantial Broadway musical had been preceded by a record album, successful London run, and unprecedented advance ticket sales. Among others, Broadway imported Lloyd Webber's *Cats*, *Starlight Express*, and *Phantom of the Opera*, and Alain Boubil and Claude-Michel Schönberg's *Les Misérables* (1987) and *Miss Saigon* (1991). Even L. Arthur Rose, Douglas Furber, and Noel Gay's old-fashioned *Me and My Girl* (1986) was a long-running hit, while no new American musical of the season lasted more than six weeks. Although Broadway looked for a "great American hope," pumped-up critical response and advertising could not save Jerome Alden's tepid *Teddy and Alice* (1987), with music by John Philip Sousa.

The success of the British musical became an international phenomenon. Criticized in New York as nothing more than titillating spectacles, these same musicals succeeded even in greatly scaled-down versions on the road and in such locations as Reykjavik, Iceland, creating audiences where none had existed before. As many as twenty professional productions of *Cats* were playing simultaneously, opening in at least seven countries that had never experienced musical theater.

Artistically, *Jesus Christ Superstar* began the movement toward merging opera and musical theater later exemplified by *Phantom of the Opera*, Sondheim's *Sweeney Todd* (1979), and Boubil and Schönberg's *Les Misérables*. Lloyd Webber and Rice legitimized rock as a tool for the contemporary musical theater composer and songwriter, demonstrating the medium to have great versatility for theatrical application. The success of professional revivals in honor of *Jesus Christ Superstar*'s twentieth anniversary demonstrated the work to have retained its excitement and relevance, and the show remained an active part of the worldwide musical theater repertoire.

Bibliography

Horn, Miriam, with John Lee. "Broadway's Age of Wit and Glitter." *U.S. News and World Report* (February 1, 1988): 52-54. Compares and contrasts the work and success of Andrew Lloyd Webber and Stephen Sondheim.

Kasha, Al, and Joel Hirschhorn. "Tim Rice." In *Notes on Broadway: Conversations with the Great Songwriters*. Chicago: Contemporary Books, 1985. Rice comments on the relationship between theater and rock music on the modern stage, his approach to writing the libretto and lyrics, and his collaboration with Lloyd Webber.

Kerr, Walter. "Quality Camped." In *Journey to the Center of the Theater*. New York: Alfred A. Knopf, 1979. A collection of criticism originally published in *The New York Times* from 1971 to 1978, the years in which a dying Broadway was resurrected. The review of *Jesus Christ Superstar* is representative in that it captures both the praise and criticism following the Broadway opening.

Polkow, Dennis. "Andrew Lloyd Webber: From *Superstar* to *Requiem*." *The Christian Century* 104 (March 18, 1987): 272-276. An important interview with Lloyd Webber examining the theological and theatrical differences between the earlier and later musical scores. Some exclusive information such as the fact that *Jesus Christ Superstar* had its origins in Bob Dylan's "With God on Our Side."

Rice, Tim. *Jesus Christ Superstar*. In *Great Rock Musicals*, edited by Stanley Richards. New York: Stein & Day, 1979. The complete book and lyrics for this and seven other rock musicals. Richards' brief but informative introductions include opening-night credits, background and production history, and excerpts of representative critical response.

Walsh, Michael. *Andrew Lloyd Webber: His Life and Works.* New York: Harry N. Abrams, 1989. An oversized book featuring an excellent collection of photographs from Lloyd Webber's life and productions. The text is informative, providing biographical details along with descriptive and critical commentary.

Gerald S. Argetsinger

Cross-References

Bernstein Joins Symphonic and Jazz Elements in *West Side Story* (1957), p. 1731; The Beatles Release *Sgt. Pepper's Lonely Hearts Club Band* (1967), p. 2098; The Radical Musical *Hair* Opens on Broadway (1968), p. 2121; Sondheim's *Company* Is Broadway's First "Concept" Musical (1970), p. 2213; Sondheim Uses Operatic Techniques in *Sweeney Todd* (1979), p. 2433.

SYNDICATION TURNS *STAR TREK* INTO A CULT CLASSIC

Category of event: Television and radio
Time: 1972
Locale: The United States

After Star Trek *premiered on network television, it sank nearly to the bottom of the ratings, but syndication transformed it into a force in popular culture*

Principal personages:
GENE RODDENBERRY (1921-1992), the creator and producer of *Star Trek* and *Star Trek: The Next Generation*
WILLIAM SHATNER (1931-   ), the Canadian-born actor who portrayed Captain James Kirk in *Star Trek*
LEONARD NIMOY (1931-   ), the actor who portrayed *Star Trek*'s half-human, half-Vulcan science officer, Mr. Spock
MAJEL BARRETT (1932-   ), Roddenberry's wife, who portrayed Nurse Christine Chapel in *Star Trek*

Summary of Event

First broadcast on September 8, 1966, *Star Trek* aired for three seasons and seventy-nine episodes on the National Broadcasting Company (NBC) before its cancellation by the network. Series creator and producer Gene Roddenberry peopled the program with the most international and interracial ensemble ever seen on television. The cast included a Japanese-American chief helmsman, Mr. Sulu (George Takei); an African communications officer, Lieutenant Uhura (Nichelle Nichols), who ranked fourth in command of the Starship *Enterprise* and whose name meant "freedom" in Swahili; a Scottish chief of engineering, Lieutenant Commander Montgomery "Scotty" Scott (James Montgomery Doohan); a Russian navigator, Pavel Chekov (Walter Koenig), who joined the series its second season after *Pravda*, the official newspaper of the Communist Party in the Soviet Union, lambasted the show for ignoring the Soviets; a half-human, half-alien science officer, Mr. Spock (Leonard Nimoy); and a testy Southern physician and surgeon, Dr. Leonard "Bones" McCoy (DeForest Kelley), who was also analyst to Captain James Kirk and whose operating instruments in the original series were made of salt shakers.

The *Star Trek* concept was rejected in 1964 by the Columbia Broadcasting System (CBS), and the show itself was not an immediate commercial success. Shortly after its premiere, the show sank to fifty-second place in the ratings, and it continued to hold a low position in the ratings for three seasons.

Set in the twenty-third century, the series, which cost an estimated $180,000 per episode, eventually did achieve success with a formula rare on series television. At the heart of each episode was neither crime nor doctors, neither love nor money. Instead of a crime of the week, *Star Trek* episodes were built around an idea. The idea of the week frequently was woven into a moral tale that pointed toward open-mindedness, the wonders of cultural diversity, and the blessings of peace.

The original series ran during the Vietnam War's bitterest days, and in one episode called "The Day of the Dove," an alien entity that fed on hatred and aggressive instincts provoked hostilities between the crew of the *Enterprise* and their alien enemies, the Klingons. In order to avoid mutual destruction, the *Enterprise* crew and the Klingons cooperated, ended their fighting, and actually laughed the creature out of existence. "A Taste of Armageddon" portrayed two planets that conducted their warfare with each other via computer simulation: No blood was spilled in actual battle, no buildings were devastated by missiles or bombs. After a successful military strike had been made, the victims selected by the computers would be notified to turn themselves in and make the casualty figures real. After Kirk and Spock destroyed their computers, the two contending worlds began to talk peace. "Is There in Truth No Beauty?" sensitively and subtly explored how differences between life forms could be resolved for the benefit of all concerned. "Let That Be Your Last Battlefield" featured a genocidal rivalry between a space race pigmented white on the right side and black on the left and another race in which those colors were reversed. Even the last episode of the original series, "Turnabout Intruder," which aired on June 3, 1969, investigated philosophical questions of mind transfer and of personal identity. Space, time, prejudice, parent-youth conflict, racism, sexism, pacifism, and political despotism—all these and other ideas were explored in a future that was akin to an idealized present.

The series foresaw no malicious or grotesque transformation of human society. Instead, no matter what the manifestation of evil or extraterrestrial power encountered each week, the series portrayed a future in which democracy, private enterprise, decency, and humanity clearly prevailed. People liked this message of hope and reassurance about the future. The planet-hopping, time-warping crew of the *Enterprise* gave hope to viewers in the turbulent 1960's that the human species would not only manage to survive but would also create a better tomorrow.

The visionary plots and themes of Gene Roddenberry showed a future in which people of various races and planets worked together harmoniously, and the show's multiethnic stars provided role models, specifically for black women and for minorities in general. Ironically, Nichelle Nichols planned to quit *Star Trek* after its first season because she perceived her role as underdeveloped. After a chance meeting with the civil rights leader Martin Luther King, Jr., she changed her mind. Nichols later recalled, "He told me, 'You *must* stay. You have opened a door that can never be closed again. Do it not only for black children, black adults and for all women— but for the non-ethnic people who are seeing us as we're *supposed* to be.'" Not long afterward, she and William Shatner shared the first interracial kiss on series television.

Star Trek engendered a loyal and dedicated following. When the series was to be canceled in 1968, fans of the program, who prefer to be referred to as "Trekkers" rather than as "Trekkies," wrote a million letters to NBC urging that it remain on the air, which it did for an additional season.

Impact of Event

Above all else, what enabled the series to survive and to prosper was the power of syndication. *Star Trek* originally had been marketed exclusively to NBC's affiliate stations in the United States. Under that arrangement, the program could be shown only on days and at times specified by the network. With syndication, the seventy-nine original episodes were sold to various independent local stations throughout the nation, which opened up additional markets and time slots. Independent television stations caught on quickly, aided in part by the real-life space program, which had made substantial progress since the series' cancellation. Men had walked on the moon, and ideas once appealing only to a few science-fiction fans had come to interest millions of people around the world. Subsequent to syndication, the television series could be seen on 145 independent television stations in the United States and also in thirty-nine additional countries. The show was particularly popular in Japan.

Ever since the original series went into syndication, it had generated a fanatical cult following in Trekkers. Fans formed clubs all over the United States. Club Starbase Houston alone numbered more than one thousand adult members who had their own flag, anthem, and jackets. The head of the Amherst, Massachusetts, Star Trek Welcommittee reportedly had a model of a Klingon warship hanging from the ceiling of her home and could help interested fans find out what combination Captain Kirk used to open his safe aboard the *Enterprise*. More than four hundred *Star Trek* conventions have been held throughout the world each year.

These fans wanted information, a need that was partly satisfied by the creation of several slick commercially produced *Star Trek* fan magazines as well as by countless low-budget "fanzines." Fanzines are no-frills periodicals containing long articles about various aspects of the *Star Trek* universe, reviews of new *Star Trek* films and books, and news about forthcoming *Star Trek* projects and about the doings of the show's stars. They report on activities of other fan groups and provide fans a forum in which to discuss their hobby and exchange information.

Trekkers also hungered for memorabilia. Fans could purchase a wide variety of such items at *Star Trek* conventions, at conventional retail stores, and through fan magazines: scale models of the *Enterprise*, plastic Vulcan ears, board games, greeting cards, model kits, bedspreads, shower curtains, comic books, records, commemorative coins, Vulcan harps, pinball machines, T-shirts, and wristwatches. By 1991, merchandise sales totaled half a billion dollars.

Star Trek eventually permeated the cultural fabric beyond the level of a fanatic fringe. It spawned a theme-park attraction and a short-lived Saturday-morning cartoon show; the program was the basis for a variety of video games, from arcade games to those designed specifically for home computers. The word "Trekkie" entered the Oxford English Dictionary. In the autumn of 1990, the U.S. Postal Service produced a set of ten stamps with the image of the Starship *Enterprise*. The Smithsonian Institution has hung the original scale model of the *Enterprise* from its ceiling, not far from the Wright brothers' biplane and Charles Lindbergh's *Spirit of St. Louis*. In

1976, the National Aeronautics and Space Administration (NASA) named the nation's first space shuttle *Enterprise* after having received approximately four hundred thousand letters from *Star Trek* fans. As the shuttle was rolled out for its first public viewing at Edwards Air Force Base, a band played the theme from *Star Trek*. One of the senators speaking at the ceremony remarked that none of the astronauts was qualified to fly the craft because they lacked pointy ears. In 1978, NASA hired Nichelle Nichols to recruit women and minority astronauts for the space-shuttle program. Courses on *Star Trek* that could be taken for academic credit appeared at major American universities. Tom Rush could write a song called "Beam Me Up, Scotty" and have people around the world know what he was talking about. Among those influenced by the original series was a star-struck New York girl inspired by Nichelle Nichols' character who would grow up and change her name to Whoopi Goldberg.

More than two hundred books have been written about *Star Trek*. At one point, Simon & Schuster published an official *Star Trek* novel every other month. The series also has spawned a highly successful series of motion pictures, including *Star Trek—The Motion Picture* (1979), *Star Trek II—The Wrath of Khan* (1982), *Star Trek III—The Search for Spock* (1984), *Star Trek IV—The Voyage Home* (1986), *Star Trek V—The Final Frontier* (1989), and *Star Trek VI—The Undiscovered Country* (1991). These films and their videos have grossed more than $600 million, a figure that was aided in part by the rapid growth in the number of homes with videocassette recorders (VCRs). In little more than a decade, more than seventy percent of all television households in the United States had acquired VCRs, a growth rate more rapid than that of radios, color televisions, microwave ovens, or even toasters; the *Star Trek* films proved among the most popular in the booming video-rental industry.

A second television series, *Star Trek: The Next Generation*, premiered in 1986. This series was set one hundred years after the original and had a completely different set of characters. Costing an estimated $1.5 million per episode, the second series caught on quickly to become the highest-rated first-run series in television syndication. According to Paramount Pictures, which owns all three incarnations of *Star Trek*, the highly successful second series was broadcast to ninety-eight percent of television households in the United States in 1990. What once had been popular with a few dedicated fans had been transformed by the power of syndication into a worldwide phenomenon, a monumental event in popular culture.

Bibliography

Asherman, Allan. *Star Trek Compendium.* New York: Pocket Books, 1989. An oversized paperback book with many black-and-white photos. Provides a good synopsis of each of the original seventy-nine episodes. Short chapters on syndication, conventions, the cartoon series, and the first five films.

Cohen, Daniel. *Strange and Amazing Facts About Star Trek.* New York: Pocket Books, 1986. An entertaining, readable, informative book with several black-and-white photos. History of the first series; biographical sketches of the *Enterprise* crew and of the actors who portray them. Interesting chapters on aliens and alternate universes, villains, and the fans of the original series.

Cooper, Nancy, and Charles Leerhsen. "Star Trek's Nine Lives." *Newsweek* 108 (December 22, 1986): 66-71. Readable, entertaining exploration of the appeal, extent, and staying power of the *Star Trek* concept. Color photos accompany the article.

Logan, Michael. "Star Trek XXV: The Craze Continues." *TV Guide* 39 (August 31, 1991): 4-12. A perceptive report on television's most enduring science-fiction series. Full of trivia, including the observation that no character in any episode of *Star Trek* ever said "Beam me up, Scotty!"

Van Hise, James. *The Trek Crew Book.* Las Vegas, Nev.: Pioneer Books, 1989. An oversized paperback book providing in-depth biographical profiles of the original crew of the *Enterprise* and of the actors and actresses who portrayed them. Completing the book are interviews with the cast members themselves, including William Shatner, Leonard Nimoy, DeForest Kelley, Nichelle Nichols, and George Takei.

Marjorie Donovan

Cross-References

Le Voyage dans la lune Introduces Special Effects (1902), p. 57; Huxley's *Brave New World* Reflects Fears About the Future (1932), p. 896; American Science Fiction Enjoys Its Golden Age (1938), p. 1094; Welles Broadcasts *The War of the Worlds* (1938), p. 1103; Heinlein Publishes *Stranger in a Strange Land* (1961), p. 1883; Kubrick Becomes a Film-Industry Leader (1964), p. 1989; The *Star Wars* Trilogy Redefines Special Effects (1977), p. 2391; Scott's *Blade Runner* Is a Visual Masterpiece (1982), p. 2486; *E.T.: The Extraterrestrial* Breaks Box-Office Records (1982), p. 2491.

COPPOLA REVIVES GANGSTER FILMS
WITH *THE GODFATHER* TRILOGY

Category of event: Motion pictures
Time: 1972, 1974, 1990
Locale: Hollywood, California, and New York, New York

Three popular movies explored criminal violence and corruption in politics, business, and religion

Principal personages:
  FRANCIS FORD COPPOLA (1939-   ), the Hollywood filmmaker who directed and cowrote *The Godfather* trilogy
  MARIO PUZO (1920-   ), writer on whose best-selling novel the film trilogy was based
  MARLON BRANDO (1924-   ), the actor who played Don Vito Corleone, a Sicilian immigrant who founds a crime family in America
  AL PACINO (1940-   ), the actor who played Michael Corleone, a son who takes over the family business
  ROBERT DE NIRO (1943-   ), the actor who played the young Vito in flashbacks
  TALIA SHIRE (1946-   ), the actress who played Connie Corleone, Michael's sister
  ROBERT DUVALL (1931-   ), the actor who played Tom Hagen, a foundling, who serves the Don as a counselor

Summary of Event

The Godfather trilogy is an epic tale of one family's sojourn in America. The characters take on mythic proportions as their deeds assume national and international dimensions.

In 1945, Connie, the daughter of Don Vito Corleone, the "Godfather," is being wed to Carlo Rizzi. Her brother Michael, who has not been involved in his father's criminal organization, has brought his girlfriend, Kay Adams, to the wedding. The Godfather receives well-wishers, some with requests for help. Singer Johnny Fontane wants the Godfather to coerce producer Jack Woltz to cast him in a war film. Tom Hagen is dispatched to make Woltz "an offer he can't refuse." The next morning Woltz wakes up to find the bloody head of his favorite horse in bed with him, and Fontane gets the part.

Later, the Godfather is visited by a gangster named Sollozzo, who wants the Corleones to join the other crime families in trafficking narcotics. Vito refuses on grounds that his political allies would desert him, but his eldest son and successor, Sonny, blunders by revealing that he would make the deal. Rivals order Vito to be killed. He takes five bullets, but survives.

On a visit to the hospital one evening, Michael finds that the police have set his father up for a second assassination attempt. He deftly thwarts the attempt, saving his father's life but enraging the corrupt police captain, who personally breaks Michael's jawbone. Michael decides to join the underworld.

Hot-tempered Sonny lashes out at the other families. Michael calmly plots his revenge. A meeting is arranged for Sollozzo, the police captain, and Michael, supposedly to work out a truce. Michael, though, uses a pistol planted at the site to shoot both men dead.

He escapes to his ancestral home in Sicily, where he meets and marries the beautiful Apollonia. His enemies, though, discover his whereabouts and plant a bomb in his car, which explodes, killing Apollonia. Years later, back in America, he marries Kay.

Meanwhile, Sonny is betrayed by Rizzi and brutally murdered. Vito makes peace with the other families and turns his organization over to Michael shortly before dying a natural death. Michael orchestrates the murder of his enemies, including Rizzi, to take place while he stands in church as godfather to Connie's baby. Later, Connie accuses him of killing her husband, and Kay demands to know if he did. Michael tells her he did not, but before the door is closed on her, Kay sees henchmen kneeling to kiss Michael's hand and call him "Godfather."

The Godfather, Part II goes backward and forward in time. Almost an hour is spent in flashbacks to Vito's youth, both in Sicily, where he sees his family murdered by a Mafia chieftain and to which he later returns to take revenge by disemboweling the old man, and in New York, where he rids the neighborhood of its overbearing mob boss and organizes his own Robin-Hood gang.

In 1958, Senator Geary thanks Michael for a large donation to a university by insulting his ethnicity and trying to overcharge him for a casino license. Michael refuses to be squeezed. He also refuses Frankie Pentangeli's request for permission to rub out rival gangsters in New York; the rivals are associated with Jewish gangster Hyman Roth, a potential partner. Pentangeli complains that the family has grown less Sicilian. Then, mysteriously, someone tries to gun Michael down in his bedroom.

Michael tries to discover which insider betrayed him. In Miami, Roth agrees that Pentangeli should be killed. In New York, Pentangeli insists on killing Roth. Actually, Michael's weak brother Fredo had been manipulated by Roth's men, who proceed to subvert Pentangeli's loyalty by nearly killing him and making him think they work for Michael.

Michael meets Roth in Cuba, discovers Fredo's perfidy, and escapes as rebels topple the government. Troubles mount. To avoid indictment, Michael perjures himself at Senate hearings and kidnaps Pentangeli's brother to silence testimony against him. Kay abandons him, confessing that she has had an abortion to end "this Sicilian thing."

Mama Corleone's funeral brings the family together again. Yet the second film, too, ends with Michael shutting the door on Kay and carrying out a series of killings, including those of Fredo, Roth, and Pentangeli, who opts for suicide.

The Godfather, Part III shows Michael twenty years later as a King Lear whose family is splintering. Son Anthony rejects his world for a career in opera. Kay lingers as a nagging reproach, yet he has no new love interest. Wanting to keep his daughter, Mary, innocent, he alienates her by forbidding her to see Vincent, Sonny's illegitimate son, the only young man with the steel to carry on as Godfather.

Michael wants to make the family legitimate by investing hundreds of millions of dollars in the Vatican bank and a multinational real-estate company. The higher he goes, however, the more crooked things get. Finally, he is swindled by European financiers, who poison the Pope to ruin Michael's deal.

Vincent loyally protects him from enemies: insubordinate enforcer Joey Zasa (whose ear he nearly bites off in one scene), old friend Don Altobello, and Sicilian boss of bosses Don Lucchese. Having evaded attempts on his life, including a helicopter assault on a penthouse in Atlantic City, and having settled scores with another series of killings, Michael is broken when Mary dies in his arms, wounded by a bullet meant for him. The film ends with Vincent the new Godfather and Michael slumped in peaceful death.

Impact of Event

The Godfather was a record-breaking event in publishing and motion-picture history. Mario Puzo's novel stayed on *The New York Times'* best-seller list for sixty-seven weeks; Francis Ford Coppola's film adaptation shattered box-office records and swept the major Academy Awards. The saga had an immediate and solid impact on American society. Seldom has the public imagination bonded so firmly with a film. For months after its release, one could hardly get through a day without hearing jokes about "an offer he can't refuse." The effects were felt by subsequent films, critics, the film industry itself, and society at large.

By exploring links with government, the church, and world finance, the trilogy injected a vein of seriousness into the gangster-film genre. It also fueled the modern craze for sequels. Many films showed its direct influence, including John Huston's *Prizzi's Honor* (1985), Sergio Leone's *Once Upon a Time in America* (1984), Martin Scorsese's *GoodFellas* (1990), and Brian De Palma's *Scarface* (1983), written by Coppola. *The Godfather* was spoofed in Andrew Bergman's *The Freshman* (1990), in which Marlon Brando himself delivered a withering parody of the role he made famous.

Critics have accounted for the saga's mass appeal by interpreting it as a mythic metaphor of America, a story that explains simply how a complex nation works. The opening line, "I believe in America," is spoken by Amerigo Bonasera, disgusted with American courts, who comes to the Godfather for justice. The films were released at a time when many people were growing cynical about politics. The Watergate scandal was simultaneously revealing the reach of criminality into the highest levels of government. Many found in Coppola's films an explanation of the ways money and power work in America.

Michael's perpetual frustration in trying to make the Corleone family legitimate indicts American capitalism; gangsterism becomes a metaphor for business. The Corleones' wealth cannot be disentangled from crime, any more than business profits can be decoupled from underpaying labor and overcharging consumers. As Don Lucchese tells Vincent, "Power wears out those that don't have it." Especially in the two sequels, Michael finds that gangsters' exploitation of vice is small potatoes compared with the corrupt machinations of politicians and financiers, supposedly respectable people, who prey upon church and state.

The changing character of Michael Corleone reflects the agonies of America. His innocent youth ends when police conspire with crooks to kill his father. As he assumes the mantle of power and grows ever more prosperous, his ideals are compromised, the ethnicity of his family is diluted, and his soul sinks into a mire of political corruption, moral decay, and internecine violence. In *Part III*, he sags with remorse and regret, his fundamental goodness washed away by lying and vengeance, his achievements mocked by his wife and heirs. He tries to purchase respectability and to dictate world affairs with his financial clout only to be swindled.

The Godfather trilogy may be viewed in several contexts: as a gangster story, a mystery thriller, a period piece, an ethnic study, and a social commentary. Critics have complained that the series romanticizes criminals, as gangster films tend to do. The violence, though, has hardly been hidden from view in several memorable scenes: Michael putting bullet holes into the forehead and neck of the police captain, blood gushing out of an eyesocket through a shattered eyeglass lens, Sonny's macabre dance of death to the riveting of machine-gun fire, Vito laying the muzzle of his gun into Fannuci's mouth, the helicopter attack in Atlantic City. Coppola complained that people pitied the decapitated horse more than the human victims of violence.

Unlike most gangster films, though, the trilogy celebrates the domestic life and ethnicity of its characters. There are good bad guys and bad bad guys. Vito is a loving father; he is seen celebrating his daughter's wedding, playing with his grandson in the garden, and doing the Christmas shopping. His business is depicted as the doing of favors for friends and the correction of social injustice; he even rejects the narcotics trade. Gangsters are neither stereotyped nor demonized, and so the public sympathized with their home life, loyalty, and Sicilian honor.

The Godfather was popular with ethnic groups, even though some characters were overtly racist and there were no black actors. Somehow, it appealed to all fragments of a society split asunder. *Part II* particularly explores the family's European roots with a respect for ethnicity rare in gangster movies. Vito's rich ethnic past is contrasted with Michael's loss of ethnicity, family, and soul.

The Godfather saga speaks to a society whose ideals have been weakened by ethnic warfare, assassinations, political corruption, and the disintegration of families. The Corleone family, in its successes and failures, mirrors the fate of nations and peoples in the New World.

Bibliography

Chown, Jeffrey. *Hollywood Auteur: Francis Coppola.* New York: Praeger, 1988. A thorough and scholarly examination of Coppola's career, film by film, from 1967's *You're a Big Boy Now* through 1987's *Gardens of Stone*. Coppola is portrayed as the central figure in a new Hollywood era dominated by directors who learned how to make films in college. Includes an annotated bibliography and extensive footnotes.

Hess, John. "*Godfather II*: A Deal Coppola Couldn't Refuse." In *Movies and Methods: An Anthology*, edited by Bill Nichols. Berkeley: University of California Press, 1976. An incisive review of *The Godfather, Part II* that interprets the film as a Marxist critique of American capitalism. Hess considers human relations in the film in four areas, family, friendships, church, and ethnic group. Then he shows how each is broken down by the needs of capitalism, as symbolized in the film by gangsterism.

Johnson, Robert K. *Francis Ford Coppola*. Boston: Twayne, 1977. A balanced criticism of Coppola's early films, with a brief chronology of his life, an annotated bibliography of sources, photographic stills from the films, and a filmography. Matter relating to *The Godfather* draws heavily on *The Godfather Papers*. Johnson considers *The Godfather* a fine gangster film but tasks it for its romanticized departures from the real underworld.

Puzo, Mario. *The Godfather*. New York: Putnam, 1969. The book on which the films were based. The Corleones are less romanticized in the novel, which has more graphic sex and violence than the films. Of special interest to anyone who wants to assess Coppola's departures from his source. Puzo believes corruption can benefit society; Coppola's attitude toward the powerful and corrupt is more angry.

_____. *The Godfather Papers and Other Confessions*. New York: Putnam, 1972. A collection of essays on immigrants, writers, criminals, and the making of the book and the film. Interesting for personal details: how the studio was against casting Brando and Pacino, how studio executives cut out the final, crucial scene, how Puzo wrote from research without actually knowing any Mafiosi, and how Coppola did not like the book at first.

Silver, Isidore. "All in the Mafia Family: *The Godfather*." In *Film in Society*, edited by Arthur Asa Berger. New Brunswick, N.J.: Transaction Books, 1980. An attempt to explain the films' wide appeal. Silver complains that the film has sanitized, falsified, and glorified the Mafia. He concludes that the story is popular because many Americans have given up on constructive social cooperation, abandoned the values of the welfare state, and regressed to uncivilized modes of life.

Zuker, Joel S. *Francis Ford Coppola: A Guide to References and Resources*. Boston: G. K. Hall, 1984. A scholarly account of Coppola's life and work. Biographical information, an annotated bibliography, a synopsis of each film with credits, and a critical survey of Coppola's achievement are included, with a useful index. Contains cogent summaries of many reviews from popular periodicals.

John L. McLean

Cross-References

Little Caesar, Public Enemy, and *Scarface* Launch the Gangster-Film Genre (1930), p. 839; The Sherlock Holmes Film Series Begins (1939), p. 1131; *The Maltese Falcon* Establishes a New Style for Crime Films (1941), p. 1223; Godard's Expressionistic *À bout de souffle* Revolutionizes Film (1960), p. 1845; *Apocalypse Now* Is Hailed as the Ultimate Vietnam War Film (1979), p. 2428.

M*A*S*H REFLECTS 1970'S SENTIMENTS

Category of event: Television and radio
Time: September 17, 1972
Locale: The United States

The first episode of M*A*S*H *aired on September 17, 1972; eleven years and 255 episodes later, the show was one of the most famous in the history of television*

Principal personages:

ALAN ALDA (1936-   ), the actor who played the role of Dr. Benjamin Franklin "Hawkeye" Pierce

LARRY GELBART (1928-   ), a prominent and prolific Hollywood comedy writer who did much to create the series and who wrote many of the episodes in the first four years of the program

LORETTA SWIT (1937-   ), the actress who served as Major Margaret "Hot Lips" Houlihan, the sexy head nurse

GARY BURGHOFF (1943-   ), the only actor from the film to join the television series, continuing in the role of Corporal Walter "Radar" O'Reilly

WAYNE ROGERS (1933-   ), the actor who played Dr. John Francis Xavier "Trapper John" McIntyre, Hawkeye's medical and playboy partner in the first three years of the series

MCLEAN STEVENSON (1929-   ), the actor who played Colonel Henry Blake, the commander of the MASH unit through the first three years of the series

GENE REYNOLDS (1925-   ), the producer and director of the *M*A*S*H* pilot

Summary of Event

One of the most popular television situation comedies in history premiered on the Columbia Broadcasting System (CBS) on September 17, 1972. This event occurred in the midst of the United States' withdrawal of combat troops from the controversial war in Vietnam and approximately six weeks before the 1972 presidential election between Richard Nixon and George McGovern. The series was based upon the 1970 film and 1968 book by Richard Hooker of the same name, with the asterisks between the letters added for the film and television productions.

The book was the work of Dr. J. Richard Hornberger, who served as a surgeon in a Mobile Army Surgical Hospital (MASH) unit during the Korean War. Published under the pseudonym Richard Hooker, the book's film rights were sold to Ingo Preminger, brother of Otto Preminger, the famous director. Ring Lardner, Jr., wrote the prize-winning screenplay that Robert Altman quickly produced as a low-budget film that was released in the fall of 1970 to great box-office success and a nomination as best picture of the year. A subplot of the book became the basis of the first television episode. The progression from book to film to television series was one of the fastest in the history of American entertainment.

The pilot episode of *M*A*S*H* was directed by Gene Reynolds, who recently had been dismissed by the American Broadcasting Company (ABC). It was written by Larry Gelbart, a prominent and prolific film and television comedy writer. Gelbart would go on to write thirty-nine of the ninety-seven episodes produced in the first four years of the series. Casting was done by Burt Metcalfe, a friend of Reynolds. A number of experienced actors were placed in key roles. McLean Stevenson took the role of Colonel Henry Blake, the easy-going commander of the 4077th MASH unit. Alan Alda played "Hawkeye" Pierce and soon emerged as the leading character in the series, in this role becoming the first person ever to win Emmy Awards for directing, for acting, and for writing. Wayne Rogers, a prominent actor since the early 1950's, was Hawkeye's wisecracking partner, "Trapper John" McIntyre. Loretta Swit was the sexy head nurse, Margaret "Hot Lips" Houlihan, and Gary Burghoff, who began his career as a singer and dancer, was Corporal Walter "Radar" O'Reilly, a shy and innocent Iowa farm boy who ran the entire unit. Burghoff was the only member of the *M*A*S*H* film cast who moved into the television series.

The pilot episode had Hawkeye and Trapper playing golf behind the 4077th Mobile Army Surgical Hospital, a few miles from enemy lines and immediately adjacent to a mine field. Their golf game was interrupted by the sound of incoming helicopters bearing wounded from the Korean War front. The dash to the hospital tents and to the helicopter pad formed the image by which the series was introduced for the next eleven years. Following surgery, Hawkeye learned that his Korean houseboy had been admitted to medical school back in the United States. The thrill of this accomplishment was dampened when Hawkeye learned that he would have to provide two thousand dollars to cover the tuition cost. To raise funds for this purpose, Hawkeye organized a raffle with alcohol and sex as the inducement to ticket sales. Nurse Houlihan intervened, however, and urged the commanding general in Tokyo to come in and break up the planned party. When the general arrived, he ordered the arrest and court-martial of Hawkeye and his accomplice Trapper John, an action interrupted by another group of helicopters bearing wounded. This medical emergency was so great that everyone on the staff had to join in, including the general, who was so impressed by the performance of Hawkeye and Trapper John that he dropped all charges.

The public response to the pilot was so poor that the series came close to being canceled. Although the overall ratings were low, CBS executives found that the show established a strong response in a segment of young Americans. Because of this clearly identified and reliable audience, even though small, CBS permitted the series to continue. By January of 1973, *M*A*S*H* was in the top thirty shows on network television and received renewal for one additional season.

For the fall season in 1973, the series was moved to Saturday night and placed between *All in the Family* and *The Mary Tyler Moore Show*. This was a crucial turning point. Within weeks, *M*A*S*H* was in the top ten in the ratings. By 1974,

Watergate, the failure of the South Vietnamese government, and the inability of the U.S. government to deal with a growing list of domestic problems made the American public more receptive to the biting commentary of *M*A*S*H*. Changes in the cast resulted in more focused roles for the actors, and a wide array of writers produced increasingly brilliant scripts. In 1975, the series moved to Monday night, taking a large audience with it and building new fans among those who did not want to watch *Monday Night Football*. By 1983, there had been 255 episodes produced. The two-and-a-half-hour farewell show garnered the largest audience for a regularly scheduled television show in history. In the decade following the halt of production, *M*A*S*H* became the most successful of all syndicated television productions, attracting millions of viewers to late-night reruns.

Although *M*A*S*H* was set in Korea, it was very much about the Vietnam War. The growing antiwar sentiment of the early 1970's contributed much to the popularity of the series. The isolation of the campsite, the closeness to the enemy, and the antagonism among the characters reflected a relevant and powerful frustration about war in general and the American government in particular. The unit often found itself unable to communicate with headquarters and had little choice but to carry on as best it could in a senseless war.

From the beginning, *M*A*S*H* was a different type of sitcom. It was unique in its combination of comedy and tragedy, it was recorded on film rather than on tape, it included indoor as well as outdoor scenes, its stories were often based upon events that came from the news of the day, and it was dedicated to an unusual degree of technical accuracy in both medicine and the military. As the series became more popular, it experimented with new ideas and new techniques. A decade after the series concluded, it was widely regarded as one of the best programs in all of television history.

Impact of Event

*M*A*S*H* had a tremendous influence upon the nature of adult sitcoms. The combination of war and medicine provided a format for exploring enduring human themes. The endless stream of torn and broken bodies and vulnerable individuals permitted an often penetrating examination of civilization and social conventions. The episodes placed people in incredible circumstances with only their humanity to turn to for the resolution of issues of war, violence, racism, bigotry, sexual freedom, patriotism, and materialism. The phoniness and artificiality of civilization were exposed amid the casualties of war in the hospital tent, and viewers frequently were left with issues unresolved. In a revealing discussion of the Korean enemy, Hawkeye stated that "I don't know why they are shooting at us. All we want to bring them is democracy and white bread, to transplant the American Dream: freedom, achievement, hyperacidity, affluence, flatulence, technology, tension, the inalienable right to an early coronary sitting at your desk while plotting to stab your boss in the back."

There would be many sitcoms to follow that included biting commentary on American social conventions, *Hill Street Blues*, *Designing Women*, *Murphy Brown*, and

China Beach among them. It is worth noting that Linda Bloodworth-Thomason, the creator of *Designing Women*, wrote a number of *M*A*S*H* scripts.

A second effect of the series came through its combination of comedy and drama. Perhaps the most enduring legacy of *M*A*S*H* is that it made comedy the principal instrument by which television sitcoms would present social criticism. In so doing, it replaced the family comedy and silly sitcom that offered laughter for the sake of laughter. *The Beverly Hillbillies*, *Petticoat Junction*, and *Bewitched* fall into this category. Examples of the new trend, which some critics have labeled "dramedy," include *Maude*, *Rhoda*, and *Mary Hartman, Mary Hartman*.

Virtually all the episodes of *M*A*S*H* had two themes intertwined, one human and enduring, the other humorous and brief. Every segment of *M*A*S*H* had at least one scene in the operating room, where wisecracking surgeons made desperate efforts to save lives. The irony of officers in uniform serving as vehicles for criticism of the system they were a part of was new and different for American television. The show's popularity could only have come in a period of transition and difficulty. The writers often used the device of a letter sent or received to permit the characters to narrate their interpretations of powerful themes. There were soon a number of military sitcoms seeking to achieve the same sort of fame that marked *M*A*S*H*'s record. Examples of these include *Baa Baa Black Sheep*, *Roll Out*, and *C.P.O. Sharkey*.

*M*A*S*H* effectively incorporated modern themes into its scripts. The characters explored contemporary themes in the framework of the Korean War. What *Gunsmoke* and *Bonanza* did rather lightly in the 1960's, *M*A*S*H* did with enthusiasm in the 1970's and 1980's. This proved effective because of the great strength of the characters. No previous sitcom developed so many sharply focused characters. On a weekly basis, viewers never knew quite what to expect from any specific episode of *M*A*S*H*, but for the farewell program in September of 1983, almost all of the one hundred twenty-five million Americans who watched that show expected and received a tribute to the strength of the characters developed over the years. There would be many sitcoms that offered strong characters that writers, producers, and directors sought to use as commentators on contemporary American society and enduring human themes. An effort would be made to have characters grow as a series progressed. *Maude*, *Rhoda*, *Designing Women*, and *Murphy Brown* are examples of this; none of these shows has approached the success of *M*A*S*H*.

Bibliography

Castleman, Harry, and Walter J. Podrazik. *Watching TV: Four Decades of American Television*. New York: McGraw-Hill, 1982. A history of television from its earliest days through the 1980 network season. The great strength of this work is a year-by-year summary, including network schedules of evening shows. Contains an excellent summary of the introduction and development of *M*A*S*H* in the 1970's.

Fass, Paula S. "Television as Cultural Document: Promises and Problems." In *Television as a Cultural Force*, edited by Richard Adler and Douglass Cater. New York: Praeger, 1976. An intelligent analysis of *M*A*S*H* based upon its first three years of production. A comparison is made with *The Mary Tyler Moore Show* as expressing American culture and society. The author emphasizes the development of human values while linking the characters to the specific problems of the day.

Gitlin, Todd. *Inside Prime Time.* New York: Pantheon Books, 1983. An examination of the network television business. Gitlin explains the emphasis upon ratings and advertising. With much biting commentary about the networks and network executives, the author frequently uses *M*A*S*H* and the Vietnam War to comment upon the greed and materialism of those who produce America's evening fare.

Kalter, Suzy. *The Complete Book of M*A*S*H.* New York: Harry N. Abrams, 1984. A book-length survey of the *M*A*S*H* television series. Contains two hundred illustrations, one hundred color photographs, and a short summary of each of the episodes aired between 1972 and 1983. The work contains interviews with the leading actors, writers, and directors. Based upon research in Twentieth Century-Fox archives and materials in the Smithsonian Institution. Anyone wanting information on the evolution of the characters in the series will find this invaluable.

Lichter, S. Robert, Linda S. Lichter, and Stanley Rothman. *Watching America.* New York: Prentice Hall Press, 1991. A study of the social meaning of television from the 1950's to 1990. Contains separate chapters on the way in which the television networks present work, crime, law enforcement, women, and public issues in America. *M*A*S*H* is used to illustrate the antiwar sentiments of the 1970's. Describes the complaints of *MASH* author J. Richard Hornberger about the television series.

Newcomb, Horace. *TV: The Most Popular Art.* New York: Anchor Books, 1974. A widely read survey of television sitcoms to 1974. Comments on the first year of *M*A*S*H.* Makes the point that programs such as *M*A*S*H* deal with greater complexities than were found in the programs of the 1950's and 1960's.

Reed, Robert M., and Maxine K. Reed. *The Encyclopedia of Television, Cable, and Video.* New York: Van Nostrand Reinhold, 1992. Contains a short summary of the series as well as brief biographies of the leading actors, writers, and producers. Asserts that *M*A*S*H* "is universally regarded by the critics and public as one of the best in the history of television."

Williams, Martin. *TV: The Casual Art.* New York: Oxford University Press, 1982. A study of television sitcoms by a television critic and reviewer. The author states that he found the film version of *M*A*S*H* to be "repellent" but the television series one of the "best shows on TV." The series evolved, according to the author, and "discovered its humanity the way most of us do, by facing up to its shortcomings." As do many commentators on the television series, Williams points to the evolution of the characters as the key to the success of the program.

Frank Nickell

Cross-References

Hašek's *The Good Soldier Švejk* Reflects Postwar Disillusionment (1921), p. 523;

All Quiet on the Western Front Stresses the Futility of War (1929), p. 767; *Catch-22* Illustrates Antiwar Sentiment (1961), p. 1866; Relevance Programs Change Entertainment Standards (1970's), p. 2197; *Apocalypse Now* Is Hailed as the Ultimate Vietnam War Film (1979), p. 2428.

THE GULAG ARCHIPELAGO EXPOSES SOVIET ATROCITIES

Category of event: Literature
Time: 1973-1975
Locale: Moscow, Union of Soviet Socialist Republics; Zurich, Switzerland; and Vermont

Aleksandr Solzhenitsyn's The Gulag Archipelago *trilogy unveiled the inhumane and arbitrary nature of the Soviet police state with a wealth of compelling personal testimony and historical analysis*

Principal personages:
ALEKSANDR SOLZHENITSYN (1918-   ), the Nobel Prize-winning novelist and social critic whose *The Gulag Archipelago* and other works brought the grim human costs of the Soviet labor-camp system under worldwide scrutiny
JOSEPH STALIN (JOSEPH VISSARIONOVICH DZHUGASHVILI, 1879-1953), the dictator who vastly expanded the Soviet prison-camp system
FELIKS DZERZHINSKY (1877-1926), the chief of the earliest Soviet prison camps and founder and head of the Soviet secret police
NIKOLAY KRYLENKO (1885-1938), a powerful Bolshevik executed for the same sort of "counterrevolutionary" crimes for which he had long been mercilessly prosecuting others

Summary of Event

Like many other works by Aleksandr Solzhenitsyn, *Arkhipelag gulag, 1918-1956* (1973-1975; *The Gulag Archipelago*, 1974-1978) was completed years before it got published. Solzhenitsyn worked on this massive tome of "literary investigation" from 1958 to 1968, a period during which acclaimed novels such as *Odin den Ivana Denisovicha* (1962; *One Day in the Life of Ivan Denisovich*, 1963) established his literary reputation. He had been putting off the publication of *The Gulag Archipelago* largely out of fear that Soviet authorities would take reprisals against some of the 227 informants with whom he had consulted while compiling the giant work. On the other hand, he believed that he had a duty to former prisoners who had died in the camps to get *The Gulag Archipelago* published in the near future, lest their sacrifices gradually fade away to dim memories amid the mists of time.

During the late 1960's and early 1970's, government harassment of Solzhenitsyn was intensifying to an intolerable point. Among other things, he was punitively ejected from the Union of Soviet Writers in 1969 and prevented from traveling to Stockholm in 1970 to receive the Nobel Prize in Literature. Finally, a close friend named Elizaveta Voronyanskaya, who had been hiding a manuscript copy of *The Gulag Archi-*

pelago, broke down under five days' interrogation in September, 1973, informed the Komitet Gosudarstvennoi Bezopasnosti (KGB) where she had hidden it, and committed suicide. Once the KGB had seized a copy of his masterwork, he reasoned, no rationale for protecting the identity of informants through delay of publication existed any longer. The first part of the trilogy was published in Paris within a couple of months, and the second part was soon to follow.

The Soviet state-controlled media quickly reacted to the release of *The Gulag Archipelago* with furious denunciations of Solzhenitsyn, who received a number of death threats during the winter of 1973-1974. KGB agents hauled him off to jail on February 12, 1974, and by the next day he had been stripped of his Soviet citizenship and deported to West Germany. Solzhenitsyn subsequently stayed in Zurich for a period before settling down for a protracted exile in rural Vermont. Both *The Gulag Archipelago* and its author would be strictly banned from entering the Soviet Union from 1974 until the late 1980's, when the work's officially sanctioned republication marked a new height for tolerance and *glasnost* under the regime of Mikhail Gorbachev.

Solzhenitsyn characterized *The Gulag Archipelago* as "literary investigation," for the work did not adequately fit the categories of either history or literature. The narrator comes across as a highly dramatized and often impassioned figure who would be out of place in a sober historical treatise. Solzhenitsyn's narrator directly addresses the reader and historical figures such as Joseph Stalin on a number of occasions, often with overtones of indignation or querulousness that would be out of place in historical narrative. Furthermore, the extended use of such imaginative metaphors as islands for labor camps and sewer pipes as conduits for prisoners' transit to the camps runs counter to the drier and more factual approach typically adopted by historians. On the other hand, Solzhenitsyn eschews the creation of literary characters and even refrains from adopting pseudonyms for the personages in his book: The furthest he is willing to go to protect the confidentiality of certain informants is to refer to a relatively small proportion of the total only by their initials. Moreover, the abundance of historical detail and testimonial anecdote prevents the text from straying very far in the direction of imaginative narrative.

The author draws on a range of methods to organize his voluminous materials, which bulk to nearly two thousand pages. At the book's outset, Solzhenitsyn includes separate chapters on the phases that the new prisoner undergoes between arrest and resettlement in a prison camp, including confinement in jail cells, interrogation, transit in paddy wagons and trains, and stopovers in transit prisons along the way to the camp destination. Combining personal recollections with the experiences of 227 informants, the author evokes the pace and texture of these stages in the new prisoner's life with verve and liveliness. At other times, he seeks to trace the origins of a relevant set of social practices, such as the implementation of Soviet counterrevolutionary suppression laws. In these sections, he draws heavily on historical source materials and imparts a chronological order to what is overall a topically organized narrative. Occasionally, he pauses to dwell at length on the stories of memorable individuals such as George Tenno, who led prison breaks on a number of occasions. Still other times, Solzhenitsyn takes on a more reflective bearing and explores the possibility of achieving something on the order of spiritual redemption through suffering the privations of camp life.

It is the redemptive side of camp life that imparts so much ambivalence to Solzhenitsyn's view of the camp system as a whole. His voice often rings indignant while piling up incident after incident suggestive of the camp system's brutality, and yet he repeatedly insists that he has gained something along the lines of spiritual or emotional growth from having suffered in the camps. Solzhenitsyn's ambivalence toward the camps stands in strong contrast to the older Soviet writer Varlam Shalamov's more thoroughgoing, if gentle, negation of the camp system's purported redemptive function.

Impact of Event

The publication of *The Gulag Archipelago* achieved one of Solzhenitsyn's major aims: to undercut the post-Stalinist line, adopted by Marxist-Leninists both within and outside the Soviet Union, that state socialism had been on a glorious course of humanity and justice until Stalin and his "personality cult" muscled in to distort the "correct" Leninist policies. Particularly in the second part of the trilogy, Solzhenitsyn sifted through a wide array of historical records and memoirs to make the case that the repressive police state that reached its apogee of brutality under Stalin had been built up from the dawn of the October Revolution by Vladimir Ilich Lenin and his chief lieutenants, notably Feliks Dzerzhinsky, the regime's first security chief. Solzhenitsyn also included Karl Marx himself among the parties to blame for the creation of the repressive Soviet police state, noting Marx's vehement advocacy of violence as a progressive force for social change. Furthermore, Solzhenitsyn extended the blame for injustices in the Soviet system to post-Stalin times, noting that in spite of various measures taken to decrease the brutality of the gulag by Stalin's successors, the basic machinery of the Soviet legal system and gulag had changed very little. Indeed, it was not until the late 1980's that Gorbachev would oversee the dismantling of most of the gulag, and Boris Yeltsin had to wait until 1992 before he could announce the release of the last political prisoner in the Russian Republic.

Marxist-Leninist intellectuals in the West had long dismissed hard-hitting critiques of the Soviet record on human rights and social justice as the propagandistic outpourings of biased "bourgeois" outsiders who were ignorant of Soviet realities. *The Gulag Archipelago* put all but the extremist fringe of Western Marxist-Leninist apologists for the Soviet system on the defensive, for even though one might disagree with Solzhenitsyn on this or that interpretation, his massive compilation of eyewitness reports from within the gulag could not be dismissed by any but the most intransigent of Communist ideologues.

The gradual decline of Marxist-Leninist philosophy as a viable intellectual force in the modern world gathered momentum and intensified; far-left political parties and individuals in the West desperately backpedaled in an effort to qualify their previous wholehearted support for Leninist doctrines that were now shown to have aided and abetted the creation of the gulag. Even for radical Western academics such as the ex-Communist Michel Foucault, who continued throughout his career to portray modern "bourgeois" Western society as terribly and insidiously repressive, Solzhenitsyn's critique of the major alternative to the Western order could not be ignored; in his *Surveiller et punir: Naissance de la prison* (1975; *Discipline and Punish: The Birth of the Prison*, 1977), Foucault attempted to dramatize the apparent repressiveness of the modern Western prison system by styling it "the carceral archipelago," thus rhetorically putting it on par with the Soviet gulag. It is a tribute to the impact of Solzhenitsyn's work that avant-garde intellectuals such as Foucault, who disdained the supposed primitivity of the Russian's humanistic and pragmatic philosophy, nevertheless eagerly borrowed the moral weight of *The Gulag Archipelago* when it suited their rhetorical interests.

Solzhenitsyn's influential trilogy underlined the potential impact of patient and detailed chronicling of human rights abuses. Although a secretive and repressive regime such as the Soviet government could continue to suppress the facts about many a political prisoner, the glare of international publicity inspired by *The Gulag Archipelago* and the acts of other dissidents would keep human rights concerns near the top of the agenda for foreign political leaders in their dealings with Soviet leaders throughout the late 1970's and all of the 1980's. Solzhenitsyn's literary close-ups of suffering inmates encouraged human rights activists to focus their efforts on the pursuit of justice for individual prisoners of conscience rather than on unrealistic demands for large-scale releases. The regime would at first find it easier to make individual and small-scale concessions rather than sweeping concessions, but incremental changes would gradually gather momentum, to the point that large-scale reforms like Gorbachev's seemed not only conceivable but even necessary. There is little doubt, therefore, that *The Gulag Archipelago* played a significant role in the monumental changes that swept over the Soviet Union in the late 1980's and early 1990's.

Bibliography

Dolgun, Alexander, and Patrick Watson. *Alexander Dolgun's Story: An American in the Gulag.* New York: Alfred A. Knopf, 1975. A vivid and accessible autobiographical account of an American foreign-service officer who was kidnapped by the Soviet secret police and forced to spend a decade under brutal conditions in the gulag. As one of Solzhenitsyn's 227 informants, Dolgun appears in the pages of *The Gulag Archipelago* as Alexander D.

Feuer, Kathryn, ed. *Solzhenitsyn: A Collection of Critical Essays.* Englewood Cliffs, N.J.: Prentice-Hall, 1976. Fine background reading and interpretive essays on Solzhenitsyn's works, including *The Gulag Archipelago*. In one of the book's chapters, the dissident scholar Roy Medvedev balances his praise for *The Gulag Archipelago* with criticism of Solzhenitsyn's apparent nostalgia for the repressive *ancièn régime* and Russian Orthodox Church. Medvedev also criticizes Solzhenitsyn's ambivalence in describing the Bolsheviks who got caught in the maw of the very purges they had once enthusiastically supported.

Moody, Christopher. *Solzhenitsyn*. New York: Harper & Row, 1975. A solid and readable treatise that contains separate chapters on Solzhenitsyn's biography and his compilation of *The Gulag Archipelago*.

Shalamov, Varlam. *Kolyma Tales*. Translated by John Glad. New York: W. W. Norton, 1980. In spite of the fact that Varlam Shalamov endured a much longer and harsher prison stay than Solzhenitsyn, this collection of delicate, low-key short stories provides a strong contrast with the bitingly satiric narrative tone of *The Gulag Archipelago*.

Solzhenitsyn, Aleksandr I. *The Gulag Archipelago, 1918-1956: An Experiment in Literary Investigation*. Vols. 1 and 2. Translated by Thomas P. Whitney. New York: Harper & Row, 1974. This first volume in the three-volume set draws on numerous personal accounts and historical records to sketch the various stages of Soviet incarceration, including arrest, frisking, interrogation, rail transit, transit prisons, and the prison camp itself.

_____. *The Gulag Archipelago, 1918-1956: An Experiment in Literary Investigation*. Vols. 3 and 4. Translated by Thomas P. Whitney. New York: Harper & Row, 1975. The second volume of the gulag trilogy traces the origins of the Soviet labor camp system back past Stalin's dictatorship to the beginning of Lenin's rule and even to Marx's polemics in favor of class warfare and dictatorship. Solzhenitsyn also discusses the prison-camp milieu, dividing it up into warders, guards, "free workers," and categories of prisoners such as women, children, returned war prisoners, political prisoners, common thieves, and stool pigeons.

_____. *The Gulag Archipelago, 1918-1956: An Experiment in Literary Investigation*. Vols. 5-8. Translated by Harry Willetts. New York: Harper & Row, 1978. The third and concluding volume covers a broad array of topics, including large and small prison breaks, mass ethnic deportations to the camps, waves of peasant prisoners, and the difficulties facing ex-inmates returning to society.

_____. *One Day in the Life of Ivan Denisovich*. Translated by Ralph Parker. New York: E. P. Dutton, 1963. It required the personal intervention of Nikita Khrushchev himself to allow the journal *Novy mir*'s publication of this controversial novel about one day in the life of a camp prisoner. The low-key tone of understatement in the novel stands in sharp contrast with the unrestrainedly sardonic rhetoric typical of *The Gulag Archipelago*.

Wu, Hongda Harry. *Laogai: The Chinese Gulag*. Translated by Ted Slingerland. Boulder, Colo.: Westview Press, 1992. The first in-depth examination of the only prison-camp system to rival the Soviet gulag in both size and harshness. While this treatise lacks the literariness of *The Gulag Archipelago*, it explores the economic dimensions of the labor-camp system in much greater detail.

Philip F. Williams

Cross-References

The Soviet Union Bans Abstract Art (1922), p. 544; *The Bedbug* and *The Bathhouse* Exemplify Revolutionary Theater (1929), p. 787; Socialist Realism Is Mandated in Soviet Literature (1932), p. 908; Stalin Restricts Soviet Composers (1932), p. 914; Shostakovich's *Lady Macbeth of Mtsensk* Is Condemned (1936), p. 1042; Zhdanov Denounces "Formalism" in Music (1948), p. 1388; *Nineteen Eighty-Four* Portrays Totalitarianism and Mind Control (1949), p. 1421; Pasternak's *Doctor Zhivago* Is Published (1957), p. 1747; Havel's *The Garden Party* Satirizes Life Under Communism (1963), p. 1967.

PYNCHON'S *GRAVITY'S RAINBOW* IS PUBLISHED

Category of event: Literature
Time: March, 1973
Locale: New York, New York

Publication of Thomas Pynchon's long, controversial novel was a major event in the history of postmodern literature, conveying a sense of imminent disaster and of the absurdities of modern life

Principal personages:
THOMAS PYNCHON (1937-   ), the reclusive postmodern author who wrote *Gravity's Rainbow*
RICHARD POIRIER (1925-   ), a critic who was among the enthusiasts of Pynchon's work, especially *Gravity's Rainbow*
RICHARD THORBURN, a critic hostile to Pynchon and *Gravity's Rainbow*

Summary of Event

Thomas Pynchon vaulted from relative obscurity to the front rank of post-World War II novelists with the publication of *Gravity's Rainbow* in 1973. Previously admired by a coterie of readers for a few short stories and his earlier novels, *V.* (1963) and *The Crying of Lot 49* (1966), Pynchon won instant recognition as a major novelist when the scope and achievement of *Gravity's Rainbow* became evident.

Upon its publication, *Gravity's Rainbow* became an immediate center of controversy. Many critics, including Richard Poirier, greeted the novel with high praise, but others, led by Richard Thorburn, raised objections to its supposed lack of morality, its explicit descriptions of deviant sexual activities, its lack of fully rounded characters, its melange of styles, and its negative portrayal of American society. Some objected also to its apparently apocalyptic view of the future. The judges for the Pulitzer Prize in fiction recommended giving the prize to the novel, but the Pulitzer advisory committee refused the recommendation, and no award was given for 1973. *Gravity's Rainbow* did, however, share the National Book Award for Fiction. Pynchon did not appear to accept the award. The controversy has continued, although the preponderance of critical opinion has regarded the novel as a modern classic.

Gravity's Rainbow was the first contemporary instance of what critics have labeled the "encyclopedic" novel to focus on war and the violence associated with war. Encyclopedic novels attempt to encapsulate an entire culture or a national experience in a single multileveled narrative; earlier modern versions of the type tended to focus on peacetime events, which their authors seemed to regard as more typical of their nations' cultures. Such novels have included the Irish author James Joyce's *Ulysses* (1922) and the American John Dos Passos' *U.S.A.* (1937). Even one of the earliest and greatest of such novels, the Russian Leo Tolstoy's *Voyna i mir* (1865-1869; *War and Peace*, 1886), depicts the Napoleonic invasion of Russia as a brief cataclysm in the life of his country, not a permanent state. For Pynchon, war is a determining and persistent condition of modern life. As several of *Gravity's Rainbow*'s most reliable characters point out, the cease-fire of 1945 does not mean the end of war; it means only a pause, probably brief, in active hostilities in one area.

In *Gravity's Rainbow*, Pynchon used a quest motif, as he has in all of his other long fictions. The quest is engaged in by virtually the entire cast of characters, all working on or seeking to find the German rocket that might change the outcome of World War II. Called the A-4, it is a further development of the famous German V-1 and V-2 rockets, which caused enormous destruction in Great Britain during the closing months of the European war in 1944 and 1945. It becomes clear late in the novel that the rocket is also capable of carrying human cargo.

What most clearly distinguishes *Gravity's Rainbow*, and what has continued to fascinate critics and readers, is Pynchon's range of styles, moods, devices, and knowledge. The style ranges from farcical to elegiac, the mood from hilarious to pathetic to tragic. Unlike other encyclopedic novels, most of which cover different levels of society but not a wide range of society's different activities, *Gravity's Rainbow* incorporates a wide and varied range of information about all kinds of things, from motion-picture history to popular songs, from drug use to nuclear physics, from local geography to the history of science and technology, from the history of German colonization in Africa to the claims of behavioral science. A reviewer for *Scientific American* wrote that he could not judge the novel as a work of fiction, but that its science was sound. The novel presents an overwhelming amount of information, some of it obscure, all of it evidently accurate, from the history of science to the layout of the streets in a small German town in 1945 to the traditional festive rites in a small Polish village.

The social fabric of Pynchon's world is also dense. Where Joseph Heller's *Catch-22* (1961), for example, provided a crude if amusing primer on the workings of capitalism, Pynchon examines the interconnections of cartels in such fields as petroleum and electricity. Where Joyce's *Ulysses* makes suggestions of a cyclical theory of history, *Gravity's Rainbow* involves, among other ways of looking at the world, a dramatic conflict between the behaviorism associated with B. F. Skinner (the theory's champion in the novel is named Ned Pointsman) and probability theory, represented by the novel's mathematician, Roger Mexico. The conflict is played out largely in the adventures of the novel's central character, an American officer named Tyrone Slothrop, who is programmed by Pointsman to seek out the A-4 rocket and whose peregrinations through Europe in the final days of World War II and the first months of the war's aftermath expose him to a wide variety of characters from various elements in society. In the highly ambiguous but menacing ending, Slothrop disappears, as does the rocket prototype, and the reader is left waiting for the missile to strike.

Impact of Event

In terms of Pynchon's reputation, the publication of *Gravity's Rainbow* created not only a controversy but also what became a critical industry. No other contemporary author attracted the volume and intensity of study that has been devoted to Pynchon's work, chiefly to *Gravity's Rainbow*. Dozens of book-length studies, two journals, several collections of essays, and hundreds of articles and essays have examined the novel and Pynchon's other works in great detail and from numerous perspectives. Because Pynchon has been successful in his choice of a reclusive lifestyle, no one has been able to interview him in order to discover precisely what his intentions might have been, so critics have been free to advance their own interpretations.

The major source of continuing controversy over *Gravity's Rainbow* has been the question of whether the novel is as hopeless as its ending, with an atomic missile about to drop on the reader's head, seems to indicate. Some critics have argued that there are no suggestions of redemption or possible mitigations of the pessimism of the novel, with its bitter critique of a violent culture, especially in view of that ending. The power of those who control events in the world, power so great that World War II is seen as a working out of their plans for renewing their technological empire, is seen by these critics as so overwhelming that nothing can stand in its way.

Other critics have found reason to believe that the novel is less than entirely bleak. They point out that while Slothrop may not be saved, he does escape the conditioning with which Pointsman has manipulated him; other characters find ways of resisting the power of the rulers, even if resistance is often brief and may be subverted. There are numerous suggestions that there are still mercies available to at least some characters, such as the young girl who survives a concentration camp and lives freely in the postwar world; moreover, the fate of castration intended for Slothrop is instead enforced on the novel's most repugnant character, Major Marvy. Most important is the idea that the book itself, like all art that conveys and encourages humane values, is itself evidence that such values can endure.

On the broader literary scene, *Gravity's Rainbow* provided the single major work that in a sense validated the postmodern novel. Literary works that combined elements of fantasy and reality, made use of a mixture of styles and genres, and called attention to their own fictional nature had been appearing since the early 1960's. Pynchon's short stories and his earlier novels had been among these fictions, as had works by Joseph Heller, John Barth, William Gass, William Gaddis, Bruce Jay Friedman, and others. At first, such works had been labeled "black humor," because many of them emphasized the grimly humorous aspects of subject matter commonly treated with great seriousness. *Gravity's Rainbow*, however, helped to establish the new style as a rejection of realism in favor of a type of work that not only acknowledged that its purpose was not to portray or imitate real life but that also emphasized that fiction had no reason to do so. Critics, searching for a label, called this type of work "fabulation" (to reflect its connection to fables) or "metafiction," indicating that it is a step beyond conventional fiction.

Postmodern fiction has remained popular. On the international scene, it has similarities to the "Magical Realism" of such Latin American writers as Gabriel García

Márquez and Carlos Fuentes; American and Latin writers alike owe a major debt to the Argentine Jorge Luis Borges. There has, however, been a reaction against metafiction in the work of so-called minimalist writers typified by Jim Harrison and Raymond Carver. Pynchon himself moved closer to something like realism with *Vineland* (1990), suggesting that the style of *Gravity's Rainbow* did not suit the urgent political message of the later work.

Bibliography

Clerc, Charles, ed. *Approaches to "Gravity's Rainbow."* Columbus: Ohio State University Press, 1983. A collection of fully developed original essays on different ways of approaching the novel, including the relations between film, comedy, science, and the themes of the novel. Also discusses Pynchon's use of war as a background in *Gravity's Rainbow.* Contributors include such well-known Pynchon critics as Khachig Tololyan, Joseph W. Slade, and Raymond M. Olderman.

Hite, Molly. *Ideas of Order in the Novels of Thomas Pynchon.* Columbus: Ohio State University Press, 1983. An excellent study of Pynchon's first three novels, especially *Gravity's Rainbow*, emphasizing the presence of various kinds of order in the apparently disorderly world of Pynchon's fiction. Hite's book is a clear statement of the position that Pynchon's worldview, while clearly not optimistic, is not without mitigation and contains suggestions that there is some hope for humanity.

Hume, Kathryn. *Pynchon's Mythography: An Approach to "Gravity's Rainbow."* Carbondale: Southern Illinois University Press, 1981. An attempt to define a pattern of myth in the novel that would provide an organizing principle and a guide to the novel's meaning. Hume believes that the Bible, in its straight-line narratives and its symbol of the rainbow as a redemptive sign, provides major organizing principles for *Gravity's Rainbow.*

Mead, Clifford. *Thomas Pynchon: A Bibliography of Primary and Secondary Materials.* Elmwood Park, Ill.: Dalkey Archive Press, 1989. A thorough and careful bibliography of Pynchon's work and the critical commentary on it, this book also includes the author's juvenilia and most of the few pictures of him known to exist, taken from Pynchon's high school yearbook. Includes listings of dust-jacket puffs Pynchon has written for others' books as well as reproductions of the jackets of all editions of Pynchon's books through *Slow Learner* (1984).

Moore, Thomas. *The Style of Connectedness: "Gravity's Rainbow" and Thomas Pynchon.* Columbia: University of Missouri Press, 1987. Using insights based on the myth psychology of Carl Jung, Moore shows that Pynchon's criticism of technology and the modern economic system is based on romantic ideas of culture. Moore argues that Pynchon makes use of the occult in the novel to provide a hope for a more positive integration of human societies.

Plater, William M. *The Grim Phoenix: Reconstructing Thomas Pynchon.* Bloomington: University of Indiana Press, 1978. One of the earliest book-length studies of Pynchon, this work is among the most persuasive of the interpretations that see *Gravity's Rainbow* as a deeply pessimistic book. Plater emphasizes the novel's argument that major wars have placed control of the planet in the hands of huge industrial enterprises that exploit natural and human resources without regard for humane values.

Schaub, Thomas. *Pynchon: The Voice of Ambiguity.* Urbana: University of Illinois Press, 1981. Schaub sees Pynchon's fiction as maintaining an uneasy balance between chaos and various kinds of order, none of which is stable or permanent. In his view, the style of the novel reflects this by holding the reader in a similar state of tension.

Weisenberger, Steven. *A "Gravity's Rainbow" Companion: Sources and Contexts for Pynchon's Novel.* Athens: University of Georgia Press, 1988. Of the various guides and companions to the novel, this is the most complete and most useful. Contains explanations of the novel's many allusions to psychology, mysticism, physics, history, and various aspects of popular culture.

John M. Muste

Cross-References

Rilke's *Duino Elegies* Depicts Art as a Transcendent Experience (1911), p. 281; Joyce's *Ulysses* Epitomizes Modernism in Fiction (1922), p. 555; Borges' *Ficciones* Transcends Traditional Realism (1944), p. 1268; The "Boom" Captures Worldwide Attention (Late 1950's), p. 1689; *Catch-22* Illustrates Antiwar Sentiment (1961), p. 1866.

THARP STAGES *DEUCE COUPE*
FOR THE JOFFREY BALLET

Category of event: Dance
Time: March 1, 1973
Locale: City Center for Music and Drama, New York, New York

Avant-garde choreographer Twyla Tharp and artistic director Robert Joffrey surprised ballet audiences with Deuce Coupe, *a fresh new ballet that changed perceptions of ballet structure*

Principal personages:
TWYLA THARP (1941-   ), an avant-garde choreographer who brought radical modern dance to the ballet stage
ROBERT JOFFREY (ABDULLAH JAFFA ANVER BEY KHAN, 1930-1988), the director of the Joffrey Ballet, a company that cultivated young American choreographers using music by American composers
MIKHAIL BARYSHNIKOV (1948-   ), a Soviet dancer and defector for whose extraordinary talents Tharp created another popular ballet

Summary of Event

On March 1, 1973, the curtain of the City Center for Music and Drama in New York rose on a landmark new ballet. The work, specially commissioned for the City Center Joffrey Ballet, was called *Deuce Coupe.* Everything about the ballet was a surprise. *Deuce Coupe* brought a little-known avant-garde choreographer before the eyes of a wide ballet public, instantly making her a star. It looked at dance, both classical and contemporary, from a skewed angle by mixing ballet vocabulary with social dance styles and ballerinas with modern dancers. Its music and decor came from popular culture, not high art.

By 1973, Robert Joffrey had succeeded in realizing his dream of creating a ballet company that would reflect the state of dance in America. From the first, Joffrey had wanted to encourage young American choreographers working with American music and American themes. As early as 1967, Joffrey himself had chosen to use acid-rock music and psychedelic decor in his unprecedented *pas de deux Astarte.* Gerald Arpino, the Joffrey Ballet's associate director, had presented an apocalyptic world vision dressed in the latest high technology stage effects with *Clowns* (1968) and had glorified the hippie years of war protest in his wildly popular ballet *Trinity* (1970). With these and other topical works, the Joffrey Ballet had become firmly established as a company performing relevant ballets for a young, "with-it" crowd. Neither Joffrey's selection of the experimental choreographer Twyla Tharp to create a new ballet for his company nor the ballet, *Deuce Coupe,* should have surprised the public, yet they did.

Twyla Tharp—born in Indiana, reared in California, educated in New York—was the iconoclastic choreographer of *Deuce Coupe*. She took the ballet's name from "Little Deuce Coupe," a popular song of the early 1960's by the Beach Boys. A tape collage of "Little Deuce Coupe" and thirteen other Beach Boys tunes formed the accompaniment. Tharp juxtaposed tradition and rebellion by having one female dancer dressed in a white tutu proceed methodically across the stage, performing all the steps of the classical ballet vocabulary in an alphabetical execution from *ailes de pigeon* to *voyagé*. Meanwhile, costumed in orange sun dresses or red beachcomber pants and Hawaiian print shirts, a maelstrom of dancers from both the Joffrey Ballet and Tharp's own small company churned around her. Sometimes their movements echoed the ballerina's, but with an odd twist. Often their movements were exaggerations—speeded up, enlarged, clarifying—of the social dances of the 1960's. Simultaneously with this apparent chaos, the scenery was created anew each night by a group of young New Yorkers who called themselves the United Graffiti Artists. As three large white panels slowly rolled upward, they applied graffiti with spray paint in a style remarkably like that of the "art" adorning apartment house stoops, the walls surrounding vacant lots, and most of the subway trains in New York.

Tharp introduced the ballerina in the opening section, "Matrix I," contrasting the formality and serene grace of that figure to two other dancers, a couple who gyrated in a semblance of contemporary rock steps. In ensuing sections of the dance, Tharp introduced the rest of the cast while maintaining the ballerina as the calm eye of a storm. Without relinquishing the ballet vocabulary, the ballerina occasionally echoed the eccentricities of the dancers surrounding her, her movements adopting briefly the syncopated rhythms and relaxed torsos of the other dancers. Occasionally, the ballerina abandoned the stage to the spastic movements of the rest, only to reappear and pick up where she had left off in her execution of the ballet lexicon.

At times, Tharp illustrated the content of the Beach Boys songs literally. For example, the piece performed to "Papa-Oom-Mow-Mow" began with a slow-motion pantomime of marijuana smoking, and "Don't Go Near the Water" contained swimming motions. Yet Tharp always broke up such images by accelerating, fragmenting, and multiplying the movement, then sending it into another part of the stage space before resolving the section. At other times, Tharp was not quite literal but was, rather, tongue-in-cheek. Her ability for self-parody emerged principally in "Long Tall Texan," during which one small female dancer (Tharp) imitated the smooth moves of a tall female dancer (Rose Marie Wright, a member of Tharp's company). Often, every dancer had his or her own path to wend and time in which to accomplish the task. If two dancers were on stage, then two movement phrases were evident; if ten dancers, then ten movement phrases—or sometimes one movement phrase performed in ten different ways.

Tharp concluded the ballet with a gradual accumulation of the entire cast performing fragments of thematic movements that had occurred throughout the ballet. Gradually, Tharp massed the dancers on one side of the stage, with the ballerina isolated from them in the center. At that moment, all the dancers froze, etched by two pools of light. Then music and dancers faded.

Impact of Event

As he had with previous commissions of choreographers for the Joffrey Ballet, Joffrey demonstrated astuteness in his choice of Tharp. The immediate reception of *Deuce Coupe*, by critics and public alike, was ecstatic. *Deuce Coupe* was a phenomenon—a ballet that pleased both the uncritical, non-dance-educated crowds and the severest of professional critics. The ballet worked for so many people for several reasons. Its surface held immense appeal. That is, it looked and sounded just right, exploiting the audience's natural tendency toward nostalgia with those eminently hummable Beach Boys tunes and capitalizing on the trend to revere urban folk art as expressed through the spray-paint cans of the United Graffiti Artists. This look and sound made the avant-garde palatable to a young audience that was as apt to attend a rock concert as the ballet. The first level, the entertainment level, of *Deuce Coupe* worked instantly. This ballet went directly to viewers' hearts, bypassing the head. The audience could sit back, relax, and enjoy *Deuce Coupe* without having to engage in great amounts of mental effort. It took people's breath away, rendering at least one usually articulate dance critic figuratively speechless and skeptical of her ability to write coherently about such a rich and complex ballet.

Part of the ballet's initial appeal was its juxtaposition of classical and contemporary dance art forms. Tharp offered a wealth of visual ideas: the image of the ballerina relentlessly pursuing her goals toward the ideal in spite of the "voices" of the latest fashions in social dancing; frenetic, unclassifiable blends of everyday gesture with pyrotechnical turns and leaps that suddenly encounter moments of stillness or fussy footwork reminiscent of tap dancing; the mingling of Joffrey Ballet dancers with Tharp's company. The movement was brash, slinky, hot, cool, elastic, tight, intricate, dreamy, direct, clever, intelligent, elegant—a veritable kaleidoscope of steps. Threaded through this brilliant array of quicksilver movement was the constancy of classicism, the ballerina, who represented the foundations of Western art forms.

Tharp's images were presented unorthodoxly. Instead of clear, geometric arrangements of even numbers of dancers in time and space, as typically happened in ballet, Tharp cluttered her work with odd numbers. She dispatched her corps to peculiar places on the stage, clumping them or spreading them out, but always in unexpected ways. Instead of gearing up for a rousing grand finale with the entire cast onstage, she slowly dispersed the dancers—an ebb rather than a flood tide. *Deuce Coupe* was visually unpredictable. More than that, it demanded a new way of looking at ballet by disregarding nineteenth century rules for structure.

Below the exciting surface, *Deuce Coupe* held further appeal. It reminded audiences of carefree teenage years before the arrival of adult responsibility, that period of growing up when life was one long moment of waiting to catch just the right wave that would carry one into a rosy future. It was about revving up car motors and looking for girls—or guys, as the case may be. It was about getting high and about innocent sexuality. In short, it was about youth. *Deuce Coupe* was a ballet not to the Beach Boys' music so much as it was about the music and a lifestyle and generation that the music extolled. These subjects waited below the surface of *Deuce Coupe* for those members of the audience willing to delve into layers of possible meaning.

In *Deuce Coupe*, Tharp investigated several preoccupations that proved fruitful in succeeding years. She sought a blend of the highly contrasting movement styles—the latest teen social dances, jazz, tap, modern dance, and ballet—that live side by side in the rich tradition of American dance. She investigated the discipline of classical ballet that comprises the technical foundation for much of America's concert dance. She commented wittily, but without moralizing, on a substratum of American culture. She employed popular music as a vehicle for her social observations. She approached the matching of movement with music in her usual idiosyncratic way; that is, she created an ebb and flow of loose-limbed, seemingly spontaneous and improvisational movement that was syncopated with the music rather than wedded to its rhythms and tempos. She also developed a structure that became her basic aesthetic stance: a presentation of order that dissolves into chaos and returns to order.

Deuce Coupe captured the hearts of public and critics alike. Its choreography was lauded, the dancers praised. One critic, with a reputation for stringently measuring each new work that she saw against her high standards, confessed to losing her head and seeing the ballet eight times during its first season in the Joffrey repertoire.

Despite its critical and popular acclaim, *Deuce Coupe* shortly became unworkable in its initial format. Touring was problematic, for Tharp and her company moved on to other projects; furthermore, taking the United Graffiti Artists on the road was unfeasible. Tharp then customized the ballet, stripping it down to a version (called, not surprisingly, *Deuce Coupe II*) that suited the Joffrey company alone and with a newly designed set by James Rosenquist. This streamlined edition became equally popular with the public—if not with the press, which tended to regard the original *Deuce Coupe* as irreplaceable.

Deuce Coupe had long-run ramifications for Tharp, for the Joffrey Ballet, for the ballet world, and even for a generalized filmgoing public. *Deuce Coupe* displayed this quirky, irreverent, go-her-own-way choreographer to groups larger than her previously small but devoted coterie of fans. The ballet helped to establish Tharp's reputation as an experimental choreographer, as a modern dancer running her own company, and as a popular phenomenon. For the Joffrey Ballet, *Deuce Coupe* solidified its reputation as the "hippest" company around. The ballet's success quickly led to Tharp's creating another work for the Joffrey company. In October of the same year, 1973, *As Time Goes By*, performed to the music of Josef Haydn, was an equal hit without resorting to the faddishness of popular music and graffiti decor.

In 1976, the American Ballet Theatre sought out Tharp to create a vehicle for the company's new superstar, Mikhail Baryshnikov. The resulting *Push Comes to Shove* indeed provided the multitalented Baryshnikov an opportunity to explore a part of the vast new dance horizon for which he had defected to the West. *Push Comes to Shove* was also a droll commentary on Baryshnikov, on backstage politics at the American Ballet Theatre, on ballet conventions and rehearsal habits. The popularity of the piece was astounding.

Subsequently, Tharp created a string of other ballets for the American Ballet Theatre. In May, 1984, the American Ballet Theatre staged an entire evening of Tharp ballets. For a brief period in the late 1980's, she shared the duties of artistic director for the American Ballet Theatre with Baryshnikov while simultaneously maintaining the existence of her own organization, the Twyla Tharp Dance Foundation.

In addition, her fame as a choreographer spread beyond the limits of a ballet audience. In 1978, she produced the choreography for Milos Forman's film of the 1960's counterculture musical *Hair* (1979). Later, she tackled another stage-to-film project as choreographer for *Amadeus* (1984) and made another essay into cinematic dance with *White Nights* (1986), which starred Baryshnikov and Gregory Hines.

Bibliography

Au, Susan. *Ballet and Modern Dance.* London: Thames and Hudson, 1988. A discussion of American avant-garde choreographers and the place of Tharp in the experimental dance scene.

Coe, Robert. *Dance in America.* New York: E. P. Dutton, 1985. Picture of American dance as presented in the series prepared by the Public Broadcasting System; describes contributions of the City Center Joffrey Ballet and analyzes the work of Tharp, who is labeled a "contemporary master."

Croce, Arlene. *Afterimages.* New York: Alfred A. Knopf, 1977. Collection of Croce's early dance criticism; reviews *Deuce Coupe* and other works by Tharp and ballets in the Joffrey Ballet repertoire. Croce is a bold critic of dance, unafraid to voice her opinion.

Gruen, John. *The World's Great Ballets.* New York: Harry N. Abrams, 1981. Descriptions of topical ballets in the Joffrey Ballet repertoire: *Astarte* and *Trinity* in addition to *Deuce Coupe.*

Harris, Dale. "Twyla Tharp." In *Contemporary Dance: An Anthology of Lectures, Interviews, and Essays with Many of the Most Important Contemporary American Choreographers, Scholars, and Critics,* edited by Anne Livet. New York: Abbeville Press, 1978. A presentation of information about fifteen experimental American choreographers who emerged in the 1960's and 1970's. The Tharp section details her career as a member of the avant-garde as well as popular ballet choreographer.

Jowitt, Deborah. *Dance Beat: Selected Views and Reviews, 1967-1976.* New York: Marcel Dekker, 1977. A compilation of reviews by the dance critic for *The Village Voice.* Alludes to Joffrey Ballet works of a topical nature and has a review of *Deuce Coupe* in which the author refers to herself as "stunned."

Siegel, Marcia B. *The Shapes of Change: Images of American Dance.* Boston: Houghton Mifflin, 1979. Attempts to preserve the heritage of twentieth century dance in America by describing, analyzing, and responding to a spectrum of dance works. This book offers the most extensive description of the events in *Deuce Coupe.*

Pegeen H. Albig

Cross-References

Balanchine and Kirstein Make New York a World Center for Ballet (1946), p. 1301; Joffrey Founds His Ballet Company (1956), p. 1694; Baryshnikov Becomes Artistic Director of American Ballet Theatre (1980), p. 2464; The New Dance U.S.A. Festival Celebrates Contemporary Dance (1981), p. 2480; Multiculturalism Dominates the Dance World (Late 1980's), p. 2559; Baryshnikov's White Oak Dance Project Debuts (1990), p. 2663.

WONDER RELEASES *INNERVISIONS*

Category of event: Music
Time: August, 1973
Locale: The United States

Innervisions *demonstrated Stevie Wonder's musical maturity and propelled him to a series of Grammy Awards and even more original music-making*

Principal personages:
STEVIE WONDER (STEVELAND JUDKINS or STEVELAND MORRIS, 1950-   ), a singer and songwriter who, after a career as a child prodigy and teenage performing sensation, went on to develop into a major force in popular music
BERRY GORDY, JR. (1929-   ), a Detroit native who started Motown Records, the leader in black popular music in the 1960's
MARTIN LUTHER KING, JR. (1929-1968), the charismatic preacher and civil rights leader who inspired Wonder

Summary of Event

The release of *Innervisions* in August, 1973, marked Stevie Wonder's musical maturity. At the age of twenty-three, he had found freedom from the formulas of the Motown Records assembly-line method of producing hits so popular and successful in the 1960's. Then he was "Little Stevie Wonder, the twelve-year-old genius." Now he was revealed as a consummate African-American musician: singer, songwriter, instrumentalist, arranger, and producer.

Innervisions remained on the pop charts for fifty-eight weeks, reaching as high as number four. Both it and *Talking Book* of 1972 sold better than any of Wonder's albums since his first back in 1963. Two top-ten singles were drawn from *Innervisions*: "Higher Ground" and "Living for the City," both of which signaled Wonder's increasing proclivity for adult songs about social conditions. The National Association of Recording Arts and Sciences (NARAS) presented Wonder with five Grammy Awards at its 1974 show: best album and best engineered recording of the year for *Innervisions*, best male pop vocal for "You Are the Sunshine of My Life" (from *Talking Book*) and best rhythm-and-blues vocal and song for "Superstition."

Wonder picked up his first Grammys. The conservative NARAS had finally recognized a Motown artist; in its prime in the 1960's, Motown had won nothing. Between 1974 and 1977, though, Wonder was to win fifteen Grammys—five a year for three years. Three albums in a row won album of the year awards.

In 1971, when he was twenty-one and out from under much of the restrictions the Motown organization had placed on him as a minor and as their "discovery," Wonder had refused to renew his Motown contract, and he moved from Detroit to New York City so that he could control all aspects of his music. Setting up his own studio and publishing company and soon working with a new electronic instrument, the synthesizer, he was able to oversee in great detail and with startling musical acuity the creation of whole albums conceived as units from start to finish. If not exactly "concept" albums in the popular sense (series of songs entirely united by theme or focus, really song cycles), they were designed less to produce singles than to allow Wonder a chance to improvise and jam, to play all the instruments on an album himself and to mix the results, to expand songs beyond the time limits of cuts aimed solely at the singles market, and to explore new themes and song types.

He did eventually sign again with Motown, but with guarantees that he would have freedom to produce his own material, which the company would then distribute. For both parties, it turned out to be an ideal arrangement. Motown had moved to Los Angeles; Berry Gordy, Jr., its charismatic founder and creative leader, had moved his headquarters there in 1971. The glory days of the 1960's were over: Even the label's star attraction the Supremes had broken up, as leader Diana Ross wanted to explore a solo career. Only the new Jackson Five created a sensation echoing that of the early and middle 1960's. The times were changing. Having started out as teenagers with Motown, the label's major stars now wanted more freedom to choose songs and the sounds they wanted behind them in the studio.

As a teenage sensation, Stevie Wonder had had his first number-one pop hit with "Fingertips (Part Two)" in 1963, and he had followed up with some lively dance tunes and love songs that featured his high-pitched young voice. Sometimes he would still play his harmonica on recordings, but more and more a kind of standard treatment was applied to his recordings, a sort of blandness creeping even into his forays into jazz and standards. He was increasingly frustrated. The new approach, however, heralded the changes and freedom that *Innervisions* best represents.

As a singer, songwriter, and instrumentalist, Wonder needed new contexts, a broader repertoire, and openness to other musical styles. By the late 1960's, the "Motown Sound" and the pop-song crossover formulas for soul music restricted Wonder too much. As a live performer, he loved to improvise and jam, demonstrating his skills on instruments that included harmonica, piano, organ, and drums. He wanted to arrange and produce his own records—an idea unheard of at Motown, with its tight control from the top down.

Wonder had pushed the parameters a bit when he recorded Bob Dylan's "Blowin' in the Wind" in 1966, but it was a hit single. After 1971, he extended his reach to a broader white audience that had grown up with the Beatles and Dylan and that expected its artists to show independence and creativity as songwriters beyond the confines of one style. With albums such as *Music of My Mind* and *Talking Book* (both released in 1972), Wonder took complete charge of his work.

Innervisions continued to chart new paths in this line with extended songs and a sharper look at life. Wonder's voice had become deeper and richer; he could still croon, but now he convincingly shouted and used a wide range to handle all kinds of material, from the soft and romantic to the raw power of tough rhythm and blues. He could put across densely worded pieces and build a sound made up of complex rhythms and cross-rhythms—largely because he could now work slowly and carefully in his own studio, at his own direction, to get just the soundscape he wanted for any particular song. Variety became the norm in Wonder's work.

"Too High" faulted a drug-taking woman; "Visions" was one of the first of Wonder's philosophical songs about dreams of a better world. At seven-and-a-half minutes, "Living for the City" was one of the highlights of the album: A rap-like mini-drama or dramatic scene, it pictured the harshness of urban life, particularly that of New York City, and incorporated actual city sounds into the musical track. "Higher Ground," with a harder rhythm-and-blues shout vocal, was a warning of potential world collapse (an apocalyptic strain in Wonder's work that would surface again). In the same manner, "Jesus Children of God" and "He's Misstra Know-It-All" represented Wonder's social and religious concerns, the first a plea for a more truly open and giving religious sensibility and the latter a sharp critique of self-centered and false authority figures. *Innervisions* was the boldest and most original album of Wonder's career to that point.

Impact of Event

Now recognized by a more mainstream and adult pop audience as a winner of five prestigious Grammy Awards, Stevie Wonder felt confident in his work. Ten more Grammys came his way by 1977.

Among others, he won a 1974 Grammy for album of the year for his follow-up to *Innervisions*, the almost equally original *Fulfillingness' First Finale*. A number-one pop album, two of its cuts were pop singles hits: "Boogie on Reggae Woman" and "You Haven't Done Nothin'." The first was a shouting dance song with extended instrumental passages in Wonder's best improvisatory manner. The second song was a piece of sharp social criticism about the lack of significant action to lessen the hardships of the disadvantaged. Another innovative cut was "Heaven Is Ten Zillion Light Years Away," an evocatively scored song about the inability to embrace humanitarianism, peace, universal brotherhood, and harmony. Lyrically, the song enunciated themes Wonder would treat many times in later albums through the 1970's and 1980's. Musically, it was a sort of chanted spiritual, with a repeated throbbing bass and chorus setting up its hypnotic effect and rich chordal harmonies.

Wonder's albums continued to integrate reggae, rap, jazz, blues, gospel, rock, and even classical elements. Echoes of Johann Sebastian Bach in some chorale-like pieces were mixed with complex African rhythms and the use of actual African instruments in his orchestrations. With his complete control of arranging and production, Wonder was in essence scoring and orchestrating his songs as complex soundscapes and as extended compositions rather than as simple songs. His double album of 1976, *Songs in the Key of Life*, went on to garner Grammys in 1977. Here, Wonder continued to explore social themes in pieces such as "Black Man," an eight-minute tribute to black leaders and heroes done in a rap-like style. "Sir Duke" (a hit single) was a tribute to jazz great Duke Ellington. "Village Ghetto Land" continued in the vein of "Living for the City," while "Love's in Need of Love Today" reiterated a favorite Wonder theme. The latter piece was a fascinating example of Wonder's studio and production art. With its pattern of lead voice overlapped by a responding or echoing chorus, the work achieved an odd and compelling effect. A seven-minute composition, it consisted of an opening plea for love and then burst into a polyphonic main segment, and throughout was marked by a flowing, gently propulsive bass rhythm. "Contusion" exemplified Wonder's instrumental jamming skills and improvisatory manner. One song used only a harp and harmonica to back the vocal; another included a long jam with a prominent flute part.

In 1978 and 1979, Wonder became actively involved in lobbying for a national holiday on the date of slain civil rights leader Martin Luther King, Jr.'s birthday. His 1980 album *Hotter than July* included his own song "Happy Birthday," a tribute to King, and also included a picture sleeve with a photo of King, a montage of scenes from the turbulent civil rights struggles of the 1960's, and Wonder's own prose comments on King's significance. At a rally held January 15, 1981, in Washington, D.C., to celebrate King's birthday and to lobby Congress for official recognition of the day as a holiday, Wonder sang his "Happy Birthday" and "We Shall Overcome." Motown then released the Wonder song as a single backed with excerpts from four speeches by King. Congress finally made the holiday official in 1986.

Wonder's albums of the 1970's and his campaign for broader recognition of King's significance are really congruent aspects of Wonder's art as singer and composer. His philosophy of love and understanding among all races and countries and his criticisms of hate and narrow religious sectarianism pervade his music. Even the less successful—and distinctly experimental—double album of 1979, *Journey Through the Secret Life of Plants*, explored his common themes of the inner life, peace, and communication with any kind of sensate world. Planned as a sound track for a documentary film about plants, the 1979 album featured Wonder on harmonica, organ, and African instruments, which were used to suggest the sensate life of plants themselves. Though not aimed at easy commercial success (though it did reach a number-four position on the charts), the album represented the achievement of Wonder as a composer and not simply as a pop songwriter.

His work through the 1980's continued in the directions set in the 1970's, without perhaps surpassing it in any deep sense. Wonder, however, had established himself as one of the few popular music figures who could break through the stereotypes and narrow musical categorizations of the music industry. Like his hero, Duke Ellington, Wonder had become a composer; Wonder's compositions were the albums he created as musical units. He absorbed many musical influences without becoming a dilettante, and he managed to create a kind of musical universalism. As a major step in Wonder's transition from child prodigy to master musician, *Innervisions* indicated that the designation "twelve-year-old genius" was not unwarranted.

Bibliography

Davis, Sharon. *Motown: The History.* Enfield, England: Guiness Publishing, 1988. The most thorough and enlightening history of the label. Covers everything in nearly three hundred double-columned pages: the label's artists, recordings, business aspects, struggles, and conflicts. Fully illustrated, with complete listing of releases; indexed.

George, Nelson. *Where Did Our Love Go?: The Rise and Fall of the Motown Sound.* New York: St. Martin's Press, 1985. George, an expert on black music, offers considerable insight into the origins of Motown's artists and sound in black music traditions. Critical yet appreciative. Illustrated, with a discography by artist; indexed.

Haskins, Jim, with Kathleen Benson. *The Stevie Wonder Scrapbook.* New York: Grosset & Dunlap, 1978. A very good text covering the 1970's period in some detail, with musical commentary as well as biographical detail. Profusely illustrated; no index.

McEwen, Joe, and Jim Miller. "Motown." In *The Rolling Stone Illustrated History of Rock and Roll*, edited by Anthony DeCurtis and James Henke. 3d ed. New York: Random House, 1992. A fine essay on the label, Gordy, and Motown's major artists down through the years. Capsule career summaries, singles and albums discography.

Rockwell, John. "Stevie Wonder." In *The Rolling Stone Illustrated History of Rock and Roll*, edited by Anthony DeCurtis and James Henke. 3d ed. New York: Random House, 1992. Like its companion piece on Motown, this essay is a fine appreciation of Wonder's work—critical where useful, but balanced and perceptive. Perhaps too brief and dismissive of Wonder's experiments, but still fully aware of the value of his 1970's work. Brief discography.

Schipper, Henry. *Broken Record: The Inside Story of the Grammy Awards.* New York: Carol, 1992. A useful history of the Grammys and the conservative nature of NARAS in general. Covers Wonder's successes with the Grammys in the 1970's. Complete listing of all Grammy Awards, and hence useful, when tied into Schipper's narrative of the inside politics of NARAS, in assessing the broader dynamics of commercial music-making and the place of African-American music in the mainstream. Illustrated; no index.

Frederick E. Danker

Cross-References

The First Successful Synthesizer Is Completed (1959), p. 1785; Gordy Founds Motown Records (1959), p. 1790; The Beatles Revolutionize Popular Music (1963), p. 1944; The Rolling Stones Release *Out of Our Heads* (1965), p. 2027; Dylan Performs with Electric Instruments (1965), p. 2038; Brown Wins a Grammy for "Papa's Got a Brand New Bag" (1966), p. 2059; Davis' *Bitches Brew* Vitalizes Jazz-Rock Fusion (1969), p. 2153; Marley's *Natty Dread* Establishes Reggae's Popularity (1975), p. 2344; *Thriller* Marks Michael Jackson's Musical Coming-of-Age (1982), p. 2512.

PUNK'S ANTIFASHION STYLE FIRST APPEARS

Category of event: Fashion and design
Time: 1974-1976
Locale: London, England

As innovative and controversial proprietors of a clothing store, Malcolm McLaren and Vivienne Westwood ignited the general public's awareness of the punk explosion in fashion and music

Principal personages:

MALCOLM MCLAREN (1946-   ), a boutique owner and manager of a rock-and-roll band, who created the punk style in fashion

VIVIENNE WESTWOOD (1941-   ), the wife of McLaren, a jewelry and clothing designer and manager of McLaren's boutique

JOHNNY ROTTEN (JOHN LYDON, 1956-   ), the lead vocalist for the Sex Pistols

STEVE JONES (1955-   ), the lead guitarist for the Sex Pistols, the first punk band named, managed, and attired by McLaren

PAUL COOK (1956-   ), the drummer for the Sex Pistols

GLEN MATLOCK (1956-   ), the original bass guitarist for the Sex Pistols

SID VICIOUS (JOHN SIMON RITCHIE, 1957-1979), a bass guitarist who replaced Matlock in 1977 and who died from an accidental drug overdose

Summary of Event

Surprisingly, the birthplace of punk's antifashion style was a boutique owned and operated by Malcolm McLaren and his wife, Vivienne Westwood. In November of 1971, McLaren purchased a shop located at 430 King's Row in the fashionable Chelsea section of London. McLaren and Westwood opened a clothing boutique they called Let It Rock. The store specialized in 1950's "teddy boys" clothing; the teddy boys style included "drapes" (long jackets trimmed with velvet), scarlet shirts, string ties, gold brocade vests, peg-legged pants, neon-green-striped socks, and "brothel creepers," thick, crepe-soled shoes. From the beginning, McLaren and Westwood wanted their shop to be more than merely a retrogressive clothing store. They designed Let It Rock to be a place where young people could congregate, shop, talk with one another, or just listen to music—the store included a jukebox that played vintage rock and roll. In addition to clothing, Let It Rock also sold 1950's rock-and-roll memorabilia such as posters, old records, books, and magazines.

In March of 1973, McLaren changed the name of his boutique to Too Fast to Live, Too Young to Die. At the same time, the clothing sold at 430 King's Row began to deviate from the teddy boys style. The teddy boys style was replaced with a strong "outlaw biker" component: black leather jackets, jeans decorated with metal studs, and T-shirts spelling out motorcycle brand-names—in letters made out of boiled chicken bones attached to the cloth by tiny chains.

During the spring of 1974, McLaren and Westwood closed and once again refurbished their store. When it reopened in the late summer of 1974, it had a new name—Sex, displayed in big pink sponge letters. It was this reincarnation of the shop at 430 King's Row that spawned the punk style.

Sex still sold "drapes" and "outlaw biker" apparel, but there was also a new clothing element added to the store's inventory by Westwood. Westwood's new designs included sadomasochistic bondage garments as well as clothing that was handmade in a deliberately crude, haphazard, or perverse manner. The "bondage suit" was made of fabric called Black Italian—a polished blend of black satin and cotton. The suit had zippers on the back of the pants up to the knee and on the thighs, buckles on the calves, a cloth strap connecting each leg of the pants, and a piece of terry-cloth material hanging down over the backside. Other punk attire and accessories included black shirts with adjustable straps crossing the chest, shirts with the sleeves dyed different colors and displaying either bleached or painted stripes on one or both sleeves, multicolor mohair sweaters with one sleeve considerably longer than the other, spandex and vinyl pants in lurid colors, rubber or leather masks with large silver zippers covering the mouth area, bicycle or dog chains, outsize safety-pins, handcuffs, and, perhaps most distinctive, a new line of T-shirts.

Producing the T-shirts was simplicity itself: Two pieces of cloth were roughly sewed together, leaving holes for the head and arms. The T-shirts were often artificially torn and the ripped material turned back and sewed or held together with safety pins. Some of the T-shirts were printed with pornographic writing; others displayed images of nude boys, half-naked cowboys, or giant swastikas. Still others contained various slogans written out in ransom-note style (the letters of the words appeared to have been cut out of and pasted together from newspapers). The slogans appearing on the T-shirts included "Only Anarchists Are Pretty," "Dangerously Close to Love," "Be Reasonable, Demand the Impossible," "Destroy," "Anarchy," and "Chaos." Frequently attached to the T-shirts were adornments such as upside-down crucifixes and hypodermic syringes.

Combining a spiky hair style with McLaren and Westwood's antifashions was the height of sartorial effrontery. For McLaren and Westwood, the effrontery was intentional, as they explained during the "Fashion Forum—New Designers" session at the Institute of Contemporary Arts on February 4, 1976. At the same time, McLaren was also quite excited about a new advertising medium for his boutique—a rock-and-roll band.

Steve Jones and Paul Cook were regular customers at Sex as well as novice musicians. They frequently told McLaren of their interest in forming a band. Glen Matlock, a part-time employee at Sex, was also interested in forming a group. Responding to McLaren's encouragement, the three began practicing with Cook on drums, Jones on lead guitar, and Matlock on the bass guitar (he was replaced in 1977 by John "Sid Vicious" Ritchie). In August of 1975, John "Johnny Rotten" Lydon auditioned for the remaining position of lead vocalist, and the group was complete. McLaren agreed to serve as the group's adviser and manager and he provided the "Sex Pistols" name. By outfitting the Sex Pistols, McLaren initially, expected the group merely to serve as a marketing vehicle for his shop. McLaren never anticipated becoming the infamous manager of England's first widely recognized punk band.

By the end of 1976, McLaren and Westwood had changed the name of their boutique from Sex to Seditionaries. Even with a change of name, the almost exclusive control of punk fashion began to slip away from McLaren and Westwood, as many other designers unveiled new collections featuring torn clothes, chains, and safety pins.

Impact of Event

The spirit and impact of punk's antifashion style can be encapsuiated in the sentiments of Jean Cocteau: "Ce que le public te reproche, cultive-le, c'est toi" (What the public rebukes you for, cultivate: it is you). When McLaren and Westwood marketed their antifashions, they not only introduced a new style of clothing but also created an entirely alien perspective on the purpose of fashion. Traditionally, fashion had been used either to accentuate or to create attractiveness. Antifashion very deliberately subverted this process; that is, antifashion was intended to accentuate or cultivate ugliness. Every aspect of punk fashion was meant to provoke and scandalize the general public.

If contrived ugliness was one defining characteristic of antifashion, the other was a do-it-yourself polemic against high fashion. High fashion originates from the salon of a couturier, and the couturier's most successful and expensive designs are often copied and manufactured in less-expensive versions for the general public. McLaren and Westwood demonstrated that anyone could be a couturier. One of the slogans stenciled on T-shirts sold at Sex was "Anarchy Is the Melody, Do-It-Yourself Is the Key." When John Lydon appeared at Sex to audition for McLaren's band, he was wearing an official T-shirt of the rock-and-roll band Pink Floyd. Lydon, however, had added his own antifashion alterations: He had torn holes in the T-shirt and, with a ballpoint pen, scrawled "I Hate" above the band's logo. Lydon had subverted an official Pink Floyd T-shirt (fashion) and created an unofficial "I Hate Pink Floyd" T-shirt (antifashion).

What were McLaren and Westwood hoping to accomplish by this nihilistic stance toward fashion? If it was merely the advocacy of a do-it-yourself ugliness, what was the overall point? Essentially, McLaren and Westwood were trying to establish a continuity with the 1960's, when youth culture was viewed as threatening to the established order of society. The young people of the 1960's, McLaren and Westwood's generation, represented a generation in protest against the conventions of society. To McLaren and Westwood, 1970's youth culture appeared too complacent, too enervated, and such fads as leisure suits and disco music seemed to symbolize the state of affairs. The calculated attack on such symbols was an effort to shake

Great Britain's youth culture out of its seeming lethargy.

Ironically, the innocuous sounds of disco music belied the economic and political turmoil that was England in the 1970's. The country was in recession, and unemployment figures were the worst since World War II. England was no longer a world power; moreover, it was on the verge of becoming the first industrialized nation to have its economy revert to that of a developing nation. The government seemed incapable of reversing the downward spiral.

Within this context, McLaren and Westwood wanted to revivify the latent resistance and dissent that they thought characterized the youth of every generation. They believed that subversive energy could be set in motion by clothes. McLaren and Westwood's clothes reflected their ideological beliefs; not only could the clothes be made by anybody, but they could be used to announce publicly one's disdain for contemporary popular culture.

McLaren's belief that antifashion was a potential form of revolutionary action reflects his exposure to the Situationist International during the 1960's. The Situationist International was an avant-garde art movement that existed in Western Europe from 1957 to 1972. This artistic and political movement indicted contemporary society for turning citizens into passive consumers rather than active participants in public life. The goal of the Situationists was to radically disrupt conventional life and to subvert and question its normal, taken-for-granted aspects. Their primary means of accomplishing this goal was through the use of *détournement* (diversion). Basically, *détournement* referred to such bizarre antics as kidnapping a priest and stealing his clothes. During the 1960's, the Situationist International focused on political organizing. The general strike of French workers and students in May of 1968 reflected Situationist ideas; those ideas were humorously displayed in the Situationist posters, slogans, and cartoons that extolled the aspirations of radical students during the strike.

McLaren, an art student at the time, was galvanized by the unruly political events that took place in France during May of 1968. The Situationist International strongly affected McLaren insofar as it demonstrated that art could effectively alter political realities, not merely document political changes after the fact. Many of the slogans that appeared on McLaren and Westwood's T-shirts ("Be Reasonable, Demand the Impossible") were originally created by members of the Situationist International. While McLaren loosely embraced the overall ideological position of the Situationist International, he decidedly implemented many of their ideas in designing clothes, organizing his store, and publicizing his band.

McLaren and Westwood's influence on popular culture has been pervasive yet indirect. While many rock-and-roll bands acknowledged a musical debt to the Sex Pistols, perhaps the band's most enduring legacy has been as the artful embodiment of McLaren's do-it-yourself philosophy—the idea that anybody can form a band and perform in public. This philosophy inspired many young people without highly polished musical skills or extensive business contacts to form bands and perform their music. The renewed political implications of rock and roll became conspicuous in the lyrics of rap performers such as Public Enemy, Ice-T, and Sister Souljah. Finally, the perceived ugliness of punk fashion diminished, as sleeveless T-shirts emblazoned with slogans and jeans ripped at the knees became commonplace apparel for young people.

Bibliography

Bromberg, Craig. *The Wicked Ways of Malcolm McLaren.* New York: Harper & Row, 1989. As the title suggests, this is a rather critical biography of McLaren. Bromberg tends to present McLaren as a shallow and manipulative individual who uses people and then discards them when they are no longer useful to him or his career. Approximately half of the book examines McLaren's life prior to and during his management of the Sex Pistols. The other half discusses McLaren's post-Sex Pistols career. Subject and name index included.

Lurie, Alison. *The Language of Clothes.* New York: Vintage, 1983. Enjoyable and easy-to-read general discussion of what the clothes people wear say about them. Lurie details the ways in which clothing can reveal information about age, personality, and opinions. Particularly germane to the topic of punk fashions is chapter 6, "Fashion and Opinion." No subject and name index, but illustrations and photographs included.

Marcus, Greil. *Lipstick Traces: A Secret History of the Twentieth Century.* Cambridge, Mass.: Harvard University Press, 1989. Detailed treatment of the history and cultural implications of the Situationist International. Carefully examines the Situationist International's link to punk rock, especially to the Sex Pistols. Contains a brief discussion of McLaren and his boutique. Useful but somewhat disjointed; jumps from one topic to another without easy transitions. Name and subject index, illustrations, and photographs.

Matlock, Glen, with Pete Silverton. *I Was a Teenage Sex Pistol.* Winchester, Mass.: Faber & Faber, 1990. Matlock's autobiography is particularly useful in describing what it was like to work for McLaren and Westwood at SEX. In addition, Matlock describes several of Westwood's designs, other aspects of punk fashion, and the various trials and tribulations of his days with the Sex Pistols. No name and subject index; photographs included.

Savage, Jon. *England's Dreaming: Anarchy, Sex Pistols, Punk Rock, and Beyond.* New York: St. Martin's Press, 1992. A massive (602-page) and perhaps definitive description of popular culture in England during the 1970's and 1980's. Savage carefully and exhaustively chronicles the precursors of punk rock, as well as most of the punk groups from England and the United States. Practically every chapter has something to say about punk fashion. Especially noteworthy are biographies of McLaren and Westwood and a fairly complete history of their shop at 430 King's Row. Name and subject index is woefully inadequate, however; illustrations, photographs, and excellent discography included.

Ernest G. Rigney, Jr.

Cross-References

Schiaparelli's Boutique Mingles Art and Fashion (1935), p. 979; The Bikini Swimsuit Is Introduced (1946), p. 1324; Laura Ashley and Her Husband Found a Fashion Company (1953), p. 1562; Quant Introduces the Miniskirt (Early 1960's), p. 1824; The Sex Pistols Spark Punk Rock's Musical Insurrection (1975), p. 2360; Madonna Revolutionizes Popular Fashion (1980's), p. 2449; MTV Changes the Look of American Popular Culture (1981), p. 2475.

HAPPY DAYS EXEMPLIFIES ESCAPIST TELEVISION

Category of event: Television and radio
Time: January 15, 1974-July 12, 1984
Locale: The United States

At a time when television programming was dominated by relevance and reality shows, Happy Days took a lighthearted, nostalgic look backward to the 1950's and early 1960's

Principal personages:
GARRY MARSHALL (1934-   ), the producer of and a writer for *Happy Days* and spin-offs from that show
HENRY WINKLER (1945-   ), the actor who played Arthur Fonzarelli, "the Fonz"
RON HOWARD (1954-   ), the actor who played Richie Cunningham
TOM BOSLEY (1927-   ), the actor who played Howard Cunningham, Richie's father
MARION ROSS (1928-   ), the actress who played Marion Cunningham, Richie's mother

Summary of Event

On January 15, 1974, and every Tuesday night for a decade thereafter, the American Broadcasting Company (ABC) sent out to a receptive audience *Happy Days*, a television show that was inoffensive, comfortable, lightweight, enjoyable, and destined to become an American institution. The show did not develop overnight. In 1973, the film *American Graffiti*, a nostalgic look at young people in the early 1960's, was well received by theater audiences. A skit on an episode of the television program *Love American Style* in February, 1972, was entitled "Love and the Happy Day" and starred Ron Howard. From that basis, the hit television show was born.

Originally, the show revolved around two stereotypical high-school students, Richie Cunningham and Potsie Weber (played by Anson Williams) of Milwaukee, Wisconsin. These two hung out after school at Arnold's, a drive-in restaurant, and discussed girls, grades, and other topics of similar concern.

The show did reasonably well in the ratings but seemed to the network to lack some vital spark. This problem was solved by adding to the cast Henry Winkler, a graduate of the Yale Drama School, to play the role of Arthur Fonzarelli, known as "Fonzie" or "the Fonz." Although conceived as a minor character, the Fonz stole the show and became its real star. Fonz was a leather-jacketed, greasy-haired 1950's-style juvenile delinquent. From the moment he gave his soon-to-be-famous thumbs-up gesture and uttered his single most famous line—"aaayyh"—he became a national hero for thousands of American kids.

In many ways, Fonzie was the antithesis of the values the show had originally set out to portray. Instead of being a clean-cut, all-American type, Fonzie was something of a teenage renegade, a dangerously attractive rogue who could score with any girl he wanted, any time he wanted to do so. Fonzie was tough, confident, independent, undominated, always free—the ultimate in 1950's cool. He cared about three things: girls, cars, and the Cunninghams. Lacking a family of his own, he adopted the Cunninghams as his surrogate family, first offering advice to Richie and eventually moving into an apartment over the Cunninghams' garage.

The presence of the Fonz as a character changed the focus of the show. Winkler quickly moved from fifth billing to third. The plots of many episodes came to center on the relationship between the straitlaced Richie and the unlaced Fonz. In many ways, this was typecasting. Ron Howard, who played Opie on *The Andy Griffith Show*, was in his personal life very much like the characters he portrayed. Fonzie, however, was well symbolized by his black leather jacket (now exhibited in the Smithsonian Institution), which became his inseparable trademark. In one episode, he was actually seen waterskiing in it. Winkler played the only character on the show who was more than one-dimensional. With great skill, Winkler infused the Fonz with both life and vulnerability. The public responded well to this portrayal. During its second season, *Happy Days* received fifteen thousand fan letters, ten thousand of them addressed to Winkler.

The rewards for Winkler were proportionate to his popularity. As the Fonz caught on, Winkler's pay rose from $750 an episode to $80,000. The network was pleased to pay this sum, however. With Fonz-induced popularity, *Happy Days* could command higher prices for commercial time. The price of a thirty-second spot on *Happy Days* rose from $50,000 to $90,000 in one year. To accommodate this growing popularity, the show's writers moved Fonz into an apartment over the Cunninghams' garage so there could be greater interaction within the group.

Happy Days was described as a recombinant program. The producers took from other shows and from literature elements that had proven audience appeal and recombined them. Garry Marshall said he conceived of *Happy Days* as a "look back, a humorous *Waltons*." He saw himself in the tradition of Norman Rockwell, Tom Sawyer, and Huckleberry Finn. Marshall was a master of formula writing and the situation comedy format.

Appealing characters, rather than plot, spelled success for *Happy Days*. Most of the episodes had highly predictable, routine plots; almost none was memorable. No one who watched the show, however, can forget the Fonz. The appealing nature of the characters also is seen in the number of spin-offs from the show. *Laverne and Shirley* and *Joanie Loves Chachi* were both developed from *Happy Days* characters.

The show was filmed before a live audience and was dependent on lots of quick, easy laughs. The pilot episode contained eight jokes and sight gags in the main titles alone, all carefully placed to get the audience laughing instantly and continuously. On some occasions, Garry Marshall actually went into the studio and threw candy to audience members to keep them in a good mood.

The program was no more about the 1950's than it was about Milwaukee. It was about nostalgia in general and the desire to solve life's everyday problems. This was what a large audience wanted, and *Happy Days* provided it.

Impact of Event

Happy Days represents one impact of a marketing change that came to television in the 1970's. At that time, demographics became important, as sponsors began to target audiences for their products. Writers saw demographic considerations as yet another restriction on their creative abilities. The challenge was to stimulate creativity while directing shows toward specifically targeted audiences that would be watching at a known hour.

Garry Marshall was able to write creatively for a specific audience, adolescents and almost-adolescents, while retaining appeal for some older viewers who would watch his shows with their children. This demographic targeting suited ABC quite well. ABC typically courted audiences that were young and urban. *Happy Days* might well have failed on the rival Columbia Broadcasting System (CBS) or National Broadcasting Company (NBC) networks.

Some critics of the content of *Happy Days* drew unkind conclusions from this demographic targeting. Regardless of criticism, *Happy Days* and its success helped to make demographic targeting a fact of television writing and scheduling. The program also spawned a plethora of shows meant specifically for adolescents and children.

Another impact of *Happy Days* was the creation of a second stream of situation comedies for the 1970's. At a time when the Norman Lear-inspired relevance shows filled the schedules of CBS and NBC, Garry Marshall created reactionary programs that ignored current problems to hark back to a supposedly simpler and purer time or invoke ideals of happy, carefree lives. These programs began with *Happy Days* and would include *Laverne and Shirley, Mork and Mindy,* and *Diff'rent Strokes.*

An interesting contrast can be made between *Happy Days* and *M*A*S*H.* Both shows were set in the 1950's and aired during many of the same years but with completely different views of life. The troubles that came up in *Happy Days* were the normal problems of growing up in "Anytown, U.S.A." and could all be handled with love, compassion, and understanding, commodities readily available in the stable nuclear family represented by the Cunninghams. *M*A*S*H* saw people caught up in circumstances of war beyond their personal control; love, compassion, and understanding could only alleviate situations. In short, *Happy Days* was a mid-1970's swing away from contemplating problems to "just for the fun of it" television.

Happy Days was apolitical in content yet aired in an era of political concern following the Watergate scandal and the war in Vietnam. *Happy Days* even avoided the political crises of the 1950's. There was never any mention of McCarthyism or the Korean War. One episode concerned fear of atomic war and the building of home bomb shelters, but few of the other societal concerns and tensions of the era received notice.

Garry Marshall was proud of the content of his show. This feeling was reinforced when the two hundredth episode of *Happy Days* was read into the *Congressional Register* as an example of a wholesome television show. Marshall also argued that the show was not devoid of serious messages. The impact of the show on its target audience cannot be denied. After Fonzie took out a library card as part of one episode, thousands of teenagers nationwide did the same thing during the next few days.

A further impact of *Happy Days* was to make Garry Marshall and ABC powerful figures in American television. At one time, Marshall had three hit shows on the air: *Happy Days, Laverne and Shirley,* and *Mork and Mindy.* All were on ABC and were largely responsible for moving ABC from third to first place in network popularity. In the 1976-1977 season, ABC had seven of the top ten shows, led by *Happy Days.*

At the height of its popularity, *Happy Days* had fifty million viewers a week. When ABC decided to take the risk of broadcasting the episodes of the miniseries *Roots* on eight consecutive nights in 1977, a major contributing factor to the decision was the knowledge that even if *Roots* flopped, *Happy Days* would hold the network's audience.

Happy Days had its negative side. Its plots were little more than sanitized nostalgia. Many of its jokes and pranks were done only for their own sake and contributed nothing to the development of the story. With minor exceptions, the show depicted an all-white America at a time when the nation was increasingly aware of cultural and racial diversity. Over the course of a decade marked by tension, however, *Happy Days* offered escape.

Bibliography

Barnouw, Erik. *Tube of Plenty: The Evolution of American Television.* Oxford, England: Oxford University Press, 1982. The author was head of the section of the Library of Congress that dealt with broadcasting. His book is a thorough coverage and analysis of television from *I Love Lucy* to the Jimmy Carter-Ronald Reagan debates.

Fiske, John. *Television Culture.* London: Routledge, 1989. A heavily sociological work analyzing television through technical sociological research and studies.

Gitlin, Todd. *Inside Prime Time.* New York: Pantheon Books, 1983. An analysis of how the television industry functions, with power plays made by small groups of top executives, writers, producers, and agents. Gitlin examines what makes good shows good and why some catch on while others fail.

Goldstein, Fred, and Stan Goldstein. *Prime-Time Television.* New York: Crown, 1983. Combines text and pictures to present a vivid history of television from 1948 to 1983. Almost every program or series on the air for a significant time is included in this comprehensive work.

Hefzallah, Ibrahim M. *Critical Viewing of Television: A Book for Parents and Teachers.* Landham, Md.: University Press of America, 1987. The author, a teacher of classes on critical viewing of television, has written about how to understand television, how it affects viewers, and how to become a critical viewer.

Lowe, Carl. *Television and American Culture.* New York: H. H. Wilson, 1981. Reprints of articles, addresses, and excerpts from books on television as a social force in American society. Covers such diverse topics as politics, religion, news, and education.

Miranda, Fred, and Bill Ginch. *TV Trivia.* New York: Ballantine Books, 1984. The title of the book accurately describes its contents, but there are many interesting nuggets of information scattered throughout its pages. An index will help the reader find shows of interest.

Mitz, Rick. *The Great TV Sitcom Book.* New York: Richard Marek, 1980. Covers virtually every situation comedy shown on American television from 1949 to 1980. In addition to describing the shows, the author discusses social reference points and proposes reasons for the shows' successes or failures.

O'Connor, John, ed. *American History, American Television.* New York: Frederick Ungar, 1985. Television is presented both as a force in recent social history and as a matter to be studied. This collection of essays came out of Columbia University's Seminar on Cinema, but the essays all relate to television. This book deals with a wide range of topics, from *Amos 'n' Andy* to Watergate.

Rose, Brian G. *TV Genres: A Handbook and Reference Guide.* Westport, Conn.: Greenwood Press, 1985. Attempts to explain to viewers how and why television shows fall into a limited number of formats. The cross-fertilizing of formats, or genres, is discussed, as are genres from police shows to religious programming.

Michael R. Bradley

Cross-References

Situation Comedies Dominate Television Programming (1960's), p. 1835; *The Dick Van Dyke Show* Popularizes Situation Comedy (1961), p. 1908; *The Mary Tyler Moore Show* Examines Women's Roles (1970), p. 2218; *M*A*S*H* Reflects 1970's Sentiments (1972), p. 2271; *The Jeffersons* Signals Success of Black Situation Comedies (1975), p. 2339; *The Cosby Show* Makes Television History (1984), p. 2532.

A DALÍ MUSEUM OPENS IN FIGUERAS, SPAIN

Category of event: Art
Time: September 28, 1974
Locale: Figueras, Spain

Dalí's native city honored him with its Teatro-Museo Dalí, a true Dalínian museum that would become the greatest repository of works produced and collected by the artist and his wife

Principal personages:

SALVADOR DALÍ (1904-1989), an internationally renowned Surrealist painter

GALA DALÍ (1893-1982), the wife of Salvador Dalí, and former wife of Surrealist poet Paul Éluard

CAMILLE GOEMANS (1900-1960), the main art dealer and a great supporter of Dalí

LUIS BUÑUEL (1900-1983), a close friend of Dalí from the Fine Arts Academy in Madrid who became a famous filmmaker

EMILIO PÉREZ PIÑERO (1936-1972), the young Spanish architect who designed the huge geodesic dome for the Teatro-Museo Dalí

Summary of Event

The year 1974 marked the inauguration of the Teatro-Museo Dalí in Figueras, a city in the northeastern Spanish province of Catalonia. The museum evolved from a former civic theater that was destroyed by fire during the Spanish Civil War. Many critics make the distinction that this is not a "Dalí museum," an institution housing artifacts by Salvador Dalí, but rather a Dalínian one that is saturated with the living ideologies and creative spirit of a true twentieth century genius. Dalí exists and breathes when one enters the structure, since there are numerous kinetic sculptures, theatrical props, and constructed environments that provoke viewer participation.

Ironically, Figueras, his native town, appears throughout Dalí's life story in mixed terms. He spent most of his childhood and early youth enjoying the splendor of the great plain of Ampurdan, in which Figueras lies, and of the olive trees and sharp rock formations of the Catalonian coast. He attended the state school in Figueras and then went to a private school. Although in 1921 he went to Madrid for studies at the Fine Arts Academy, it was at his Figueras studio in the early 1920's that he developed a Futurist fantastic style, like that of Marc Chagall. In 1923, Dalí was sent home to Figueras after charges of insubordination at the Fine Arts Academy. He was arrested and imprisoned for a month in Figueras after his involvement in a burning of the Spanish flag, after a riot at the art school in Figueras protesting the rise to power of dictator Miguel Primo de Rivera in 1923.

Figueras, however, was a source of stability for Dalí and a place to which he could return. There he painted one of his most renowned works, *The Great Masturbator*

(1929), which, according to Dalí, demonstrated his "heterosexual anxiety." Gala, the wife of poet Paul Éluard and the source of Dalí's maddening passion, had just returned to Paris, and Dalí's fears of impotence were stirred. *The Enigma of Desire: My Mother, My Mother, My Mother* (1929), painted during the same period in Figueras, was his first work sold at the Goemans Gallery during his first one-man show there.

It is therefore in a sense poetic justice that, after all of Dalí's trials and tribulations involving Figueras, his birthplace finally paid tribute to its most celebrated citizen through construction of the Teatro-Museo Dalí. Visitors are overwhelmed first by the lavish façade of the reconstructed theater. A crown of gilded Art Deco mannequins made of synthetic material encircles the roof of the entranceway; one figure at the extreme right holds a hydrogen atom. Beneath the crown in the center of the pediment are the figures of Dalí and Gala on a medallion. Nearby stands the famous Gorgot Tower, which was added in 1981 and renamed the Galatea Tower. Dalí convinced the museum administration to purchase the huge structure, formerly a middle-class housing complex. It houses Dalí books, videos, and other collectibles, also providing storage and exhibition rooms.

Part of the excitement surrounding the opening of the Teatro-Museo Dalí involved the theatrical nature of the museum, conceived as a piece of environmental sculpture. In fact, from the late 1930's onward, Dalí was excited about creating whole environments and artifacts on a monumental scale. Some of his earlier endeavors included a pavilion entitled *Dream of Venus* for the New York World's Fair in 1939. This work was to consist of a huge water tank filled with sirens, a man composed of table tennis rackets, a backdrop of surrealistic soft watches in a landscape, and magnified reproductions of Sandro Botticelli's *Birth of Venus* and Leonardo da Vinci's *Mona Lisa*.

In his Teatro-Museo Dalí, the artist had an entire room turned into a depiction of Mae West's face. The idea for such a fantastic environmental sculpture was based on a gouache by Dalí in the Art Institute of Chicago, entitled *Face of Mae West Which Can Be Used as an Apartment* (1943). Interesting to note is that Dalí, in the 1930's, did a series of paintings in which paranoiac faces protrude from landscapes sometimes formed by parts of the body. The entire Mae West environment is ingenious. Huge bulbous curtains, representing her hair, frame the room, turning the environmental piece of art into a stage set. The audience stands on a small platform to gaze at it from a designated height and angle. Catalan architect and decorator Oscar Tusquest collaborated with Dalí on this memorable project.

Another startling environmental work in the museum, which captures the eccentric, theatrical spirit of Dalí and which stimulates audience participation, is the interior court area. It houses *(Queen) Esther*, a bronze sculpture by Ernst Fuchs. A 1940 Cadillac, on which Esther serves as a huge radiator cap, is transformed into *Rainy Taxi*; a huge stage design for the ballet *Labyrinth* (1941) completes the project. Many of the rooms in the museum are filled with kinetic objects that reflect Dalí's interest in optical illusions.

Perhaps the most rewarding surprises awaiting visitors to the Dalí museum in Figueras—after the initial splendor of Emilio Pérez Piñero's reticular cupola of a dazzling Byzantine-like geodesic dome that crowns the old theater-turned-museum—are spellbinding ceiling canvases. *Foyer of the Old Theater* (1971-1972), an oil on canvas, depicts the interaction between the painter, Dalí, and his native plain. The love between artist and countrymen is immortalized. The former's fame has precipitated showers of gold coins, which dramatically fall from the sky onto the citizens of Figueras. Another spectacular sight is one of the five ceiling panels of the famed reception room, entitled *The daughter of the West Wind/ To the East Wind was wed/ When he went to see her/ Returned crying to his bed.* In this beautifully dynamic and colorful canvas, Dalí and Gala are seated together, romantically contemplating the landscape of the plain of Ampurdan. The title of the work is taken from a Catalonian poem.

Impact of Event

The effects of the 1974 opening of the Teatro-Museo Dalí, besides placing Figueras on the map as a great cultural center and immortalizing its star citizen, were varied. First, the museum gave validity to Salvador Dalí as a great exponent of Surrealism. From about 1929, after his banishment from his family (a result in part of his relationship with a foreign married woman) and his arrival in Paris, he rejoined Gala, who had just left Paul Éluard. Dalí began to participate enthusiastically in the Surrealists' activities. Even though the subject matter in his paintings clashed with the works of other exponents of Surrealism, André Breton, the organizer of this group, still acknowledged that Dalí provided a vital force to the movement, which owed much to his ingenious, fantastic imagery. Highly publicized rifts, such as the one involving Dalí's expulsion from the group in 1934 because of his erotic, obsessive, Hitler-imaged paintings, only heightened his role in Surrealism. Dalí proclaimed that he was too much of a Surrealist for the group; the members, however, needed such a publicity-getting, highly controversial figure as Dalí.

The artifacts in Dalí's museum affected or inspired other art forms and new techniques. He was an innovator who combined the pictorial medium with new ways of achieving heightened three-dimensional depth: stereoscopy, holography, and stereovideo were his favorite means. For example, his well-known *Dalí from the Back Painting Gala from the Back Eternized by Virtual Corneas Provisionally Reflected by Six Real Mirrors* (1972-1973) at the Teatro-Museo Dalí, illustrates an unusual sculptural perspective that results in binocular vision because of the optical superimposition of his two paintings. One of Dalí's holographs of the early 1970's, exhibited at his museum, is entitled *Holos! Holos! Velázquez! Gabor!* It is one of the first holographic photo montages. Dalí even worked with a holograph expert, Selwyn Lissack, on this huge project.

The museum is an expression not only of the modernistic, progressive art forms and techniques to come but also of decadence. Interspersed with the radically different conceptual, environmental approach to art and the pulsating, gyrating, kinetic machines is the presence of heavy red velvet deco and pretentious Art Nouveau objects. The Teatro-Museo Dalí also exhibits heavy, gaudy jewelry pieces. Some of these move, while others are punctuated heavily with religious themes of Dalí's own unique symbolism. Quite a few are social parodies of the decadence at the end of the previous epoch.

The entire testimony to Dalí as one of the greatest twentieth century painters depends on the ultimate disposition of the artist's (and his wife's) own personal collection. Rumors circulated that Dalí had donated his collection to his country, although the artist clarified that it was not a gift but a loan. According to Dalí's own *Salvador Dalí: A Guide to His Works in Public Museums* (1973), only the future will reveal a catalog of the important works of the Dalís in their possession and their ultimate destinations, and how society and history will finally evaluate Dalí. Some of Dalí's major works found in the Teatro-Museo Dalí in the early 1990's included *Self-Portrait* (1921), *Self-Portrait with Neck of Raphael* (1922-1923), *The Great Masturbator* (1929), *Portrait of Paul Éluard* (1929), *Imperial Monument to the Child-Woman* (1929), *The Invisible Man* (1929-1933), *Specter of Sex Appeal* (1934), *The Poetry of America* (1943), *The Endless Enigma* (1938), *Basket of Bread #2* (1945), and *Galarina* (1944-1945). Critics believe that the Dalí museum and especially the foyer ceiling panels will be an eternal testimony to the artist's rare genius.

Bibliography

Ades, Dawn. *Dalí and Surrealism.* New York: Harper & Row, 1982. An excellent text for an introduction to Dalí. Approximately two hundred pages are divided into various ideological stages of Dalí and his works. Contains 170 illustrations, 28 in color. Useful chronology, valuable select bibliography, list of illustrations, and index. Somewhat dated, as the text ends in the early 1950's.

Dalí, Salvador. *Salvador Dalí: A Guide to His Works in Public Museums.* Cleveland, Ohio: Dalí Museum, 1973. A helpful tool for locating specific Dalí paintings and the details of these works in public museum collections. Photos of major masterpieces. Written in a personal tone, with relevant interjections of Dalí gossip and intimate facts.

Descharnes, Robert. *Dalí.* Translated by Eleanor R. Morse. New York: Harry N. Abrams, 1976. A thorough introduction to the artist, including personal life, stylistic changes, and critical commentary on major works. Included are 199 reproductions, with 52 beautiful color plates. Practical select bibliography and index.

_____. *Salvador Dalí: The Work, the Man.* Translated by Eleanor R. Morse. New York: Harry N. Abrams, 1984. A monumental text with more than 1,100 illustrations, with 672 plates in full color. Direct quotations and philosophical deliveries from the artist. Includes original sketches for major works and critical comments from magazines and newspapers at the time of production of various Dalí masterpieces and of major Dalí exhibitions.

Livingston, Lida. *Dalí: A Study of His Art-in-Jewels.* Greenwich, Conn.: New York Graphic Society, 1970. Filled with thirty-three gorgeous color plates of jewelry designed by Dalí and executed by Alemany and Co. of New York in collaboration with the artist. Poetic comments by Dalí on each work and a thorough descriptive index of the jewelry.

Constance A. Pedoto

Cross-References

Freud Inaugurates a Fascination with the Unconscious (1899), p. 19; Jung Publishes *Psychology of the Unconscious* (1912), p. 309; Surrealism Is Born (1924), p. 604; Buñuel and Dalí Champion Surrealism in *Un Chien andalou* (1928), p. 750; Picasso Paints *Guernica* (1937), p. 1062; Garcia Lorca's *Poet in New York* Is Published (1940), p. 1179; Spanish Art Explodes After Years of Suppression (1970's), p. 2203.

DOG SOLDIERS PORTRAYS VIETNAM IN FICTION

Category of event: Literature
Time: November, 1974
Locale: Boston, Massachusetts

The principal characters of Stone's award-winning novel epitomized many Americans' abandonment or confusion of traditional moral values during the Vietnam era

Principal personage:
ROBERT STONE (1937-   ), the author of *Dog Soldiers*

Summary of Event

Winner of the prestigious National Book Award for 1974, Robert Stone's novel *Dog Soldiers* appeared as a terse, crisply written depiction of characters morally adrift. It is a work reflective of the questioning and confusion of values specifically identified with national ambiguities that arose over the American imbroglio in Vietnam. At other levels of artistic analysis, it also recapitulates the author's personal vision and chronicle of disturbing strains eroding what had been perceived as traditionally dominant cultural values. Phrased differently, Stone delineates more than just a decade of countercultural protest, but at the same time less. Protest activities often produced positive, generally beneficial results: greater tolerance of different races and genders, greater understanding or acceptance of disparities in personal conduct and language, a broadening of the range of artistic communication, and revisions in the mission of higher educational institutions to address new clienteles with new needs and agendas. Stone, however, concerns himself with almost totally negative characters—by definition, "dog soldiers" are renegades—representing stark caricatures, if not complete perversions, of conventional values.

Published the year prior to American military withdrawal from Vietnam, but presaging full recognition of the futility of U.S. involvement, *Dog Soldiers* in a superficial sense was successful because it was timely. More important, the novel added its own artistic perspectives on what many observers would have agreed was a palpable deterioration of the nation's will and a notable decay of its moral fiber during the Vietnam era. On both grounds, Stone's work was instantly acclaimed, however repugnant or banal its characters variously appeared to readers and critics. Several literary authorities pronounced it as the most significant novel of 1974, and nearly all major reviewers praised the distinctiveness and integrity of Stone's prose.

Born in Brooklyn and reared in Manhattan, Stone worked variously as a newspaper copyboy, an ad writer, a Navy journalist, and a free-lance writer. While holding menial jobs, he became a self-described participant in the countercultures of New Orleans and San Francisco, from which he gleaned much of the ambience, language, and characterizations embodied in his work. He likewise had firsthand experience in Vietnam during 1971, contributing materials on the war to both *The Atlantic* and *The Guardian*.

Stone's promise as a writer had won him serious literary recognition by 1970. By then, he already had been awarded a Houghton Mifflin Fellowship and a John Simon Guggenheim Fellowship for a variety of publications, most prominently for *A Hall of Mirrors* (1968), which the distinguished novelist Wallace Stegner, among others, proclaimed to be one of the two finest first novels he had ever read. In both *A Hall of Mirrors* and *Dog Soldiers*, Stone's central characters are marginal personalities morally adrift. To paraphrase *The New Republic*'s J. J. Hall, they are members of a counterculture gone sour. Almost passively, they allow themselves to be victimized by circumstance. Whatever vestigial decency they retain as they drift in and out of drugs and navigate the fringes of sober reality only further condemns them. Although the major characters are from middle-class backgrounds, they lack a commitment to or a mastery of anything. Even their drug smuggling proves less an exercise in plausible paranoia than in ineptitude. They are bunglers and losers, while both their acquaintances and their enemies are hustlers, sleazy dilettantes, and assorted riff-raff. In Stone's idiom, his players have discerned Satan but are bound indifferently for Hell or whatever dimly conceived limbo awaits them.

Stone's *Dog Soldiers* was one of the earliest serious literary efforts to depict the degenerate side of the counterculture of the Vietnam era. Although its opening chapters are set in Saigon and there are flashes of war and violence through the eyes of its chief protagonist, the novel is less a conventional war story than it is a morality play about the perversion of individual values, about the denigration of responsibilities, and about the demoralization of individuals. To Stone, America's adventure in Vietnam stands as both a cause and an effect of protagonist John Converse's confusion, derationalization, and demoralization. Although his depiction of his feckless characters is unsentimental and grippingly real, Stone nevertheless has been defined by most critics as a stringent political novelist, a point further substantiated by his two subsequent novels, *A Flag for Sunrise* (1981) and *Children of Light* (1986). In each of his books, his vision of American life and values is etched accurately in the degeneracies, the passivity, and the soullessness of his protagonists and their decadent associates.

As a missionary to the strung out, Stone has carved an important literary niche for himself. Since writing *Dog Soldiers*, he has been nominated for additional National Book Awards as well as for an American Book Award, has held the Wallace Stegner Fellowship (among others), has taught as a member of Amherst's English department, and has been a writer-in-residence at Harvard, Princeton, and Stanford universities.

It is normal for novelists to function as critical commentators on the failures or idiocies of their times and societies. What distinguishes Stone's work as it matured in *Dog Soldiers* is not only his compelling prose (critics have compared him in this regard to Ernest Hemingway, Graham Greene, Joseph Conrad, and William Faulkner, among others), but also his exploration of the underbelly of American countercultures in juxtaposition to his vision of a general erosion of traditional morality.

Impact of Event

Stone's novels continued winning literary as well as popular acclaim into the early 1990's. Because his focus has been on illuminating America's collapsing moral infrastructure, notably by concentrating on aspects of the drug cultures and, within them, on the moral drift of his characters in a soulless environment, there appears scant likelihood that his novels will rapidly become dated or that their subject matter will be dismissed. The national malaise that marked the Vietnam era persisted in preoccupying public attention in the decades following 1975.

When *Dog Soldiers* appeared, the United States already had confronted a decade of protests. Protests arose from racial discrimination and its accompanying injustice, particularly in regard to African Americans, although collective grievances were also more insistently being voiced by Hispanic Americans and other minorities. Reactions to these movements were punctuated by murders and assassinations, bombings, and maimings directed against those involved. Renascent feminism and related issues of free choice in regard to abortion, to job access, to equal pay, and to respectful treatment in the workplace represented another class of protest, as did attacks upon the credibility of official war reporting, upon the exposed deceptions of wartime administrations, and against what were construed as problems of congenital poverty. Still other class protests were mounted by college and university students as well as faculty against outmoded, nonrelevant, or discriminatory curricula and campus regulations. In addition, a multitude of urban problems, unsatisfactorily addressed, led to devastating riots in many of the country's major cities. All these uprisings in some measure were linked to and stimulated by increasingly widespread antiwar sentiments that cut across all social strata. Overarching all else were the ominous twists of the Cold War, seemingly deranged national priorities, and the public's immanent fears of nuclear holocaust.

Individual moral and behavioral protests reflected a widespread suspicion of or antipathy toward nearly every type of legal authority, from parental and marital to the broadly political and philosophical. It was fashionable to be antiestablishment. Although many people simply were confused or confounded by these tendencies, a significant number of others abandoned the regimes of traditional institutions—parents, spouses, churches, the corporate world, and governments—in favor of self-determined life-styles, whether communal, hippie, yippie, or as runaways and street people. Manifestations of this were marked by individuals flaunting traditional mores by what were perceived as their perverse mannerisms, language, and dress. An almost invariable component of such individual protests, or at least a generally negative feature of them, was the epidemic use of drugs as an integral part of everyday life, not only for relaxation and recreation—that is, for escape—but also purportedly as unique vehicles of self-exploration.

Conservative critics tend to view Stone's characters as doomed-again losers, as people who enjoyed advantages in life but who abnegated responsibilities, who are indifferent to the disciplines of conventional morality, who succumb to personal greed and vice and throw off their lines to normal society. Such deviants are not the peculiarities of the Vietnam era; such people always have existed. The whole society thus cannot be indicted legitimately for its choice of drift and disaster. They may attract attention and even sympathy, conservatives agree, but fundamentally they get what they deserve.

More liberal critics—and certainly Stone—imply that these deviant characters, symbolically, are in fact the flotsam one might expect from the dominant cynicism, venality, violence, and disorder endemic to the deficient structure of American culture. What the culture as a whole lacks—namely, a sense of purpose and direction, a mastery over drift—cannot be remedied by its individual parts. Accordingly, individuals fall prey to forces that they cannot comprehend and events that lie substantially beyond their manipulation.

Whether his setting is Saigon or Los Angeles during the Vietnam years, Hollywood's film industry, or a fictitious Central American country wracked by guerrilla warfare, Stone, sometimes with some humor, traces the self-immolation of his victimized characters, characters made more repugnant by varying addictions to hard drugs, about which Stone has nothing good to say. Neither the political themes introduced by his novels nor the attitudes of his well-drawn characters are likely to lose relevance. Widespread sentiments—and not even mainly among amoral people—that American political and legal institutions are unresponsive, soulless, and out of control have existed for decades. Stone's novels speak to those long-lived sentiments. Simultaneously, drug use and addiction, tragically, have become integrated into wide swaths of American life, as a reaction to the culture's deficiencies and to disenchantment with the validity of its old dreams.

Bibliography

Fiedler, Leslie A. "Adolescence and Maturity in the American Novel." In *Visions and Revisions in Modern American Literary Criticism*, edited by Bernard S. Old- sey and Arthur O. Lewis, Jr. New York: E. P. Dutton, 1962. Without mentioning Stone, literary critic Fiedler places Stone's work in the context of post-1940 disenchantment among writers and critics coping with the question of how writers, unsustained by tradition in atomized society, can reflect the consciousness of their age. No notes, bibliography, or index.

Hall, Joan J. "Review." *The New Republic* 172 (January 4, 1975): 29. A balanced, critical assessment of *Dog Soldiers* in terms of the intrinsic merits of the novel as well as the literary context into which it fits. This review is representative of Stone's popular reception.

Matusow, Allen J. *The Unraveling of America: A History of Liberalism in the 1960s.* New York: Harper & Row, 1984. A fine scholarly interpretation of the historical environment in which Stone and other dissident novelists were maturing as their liberal traditions seemed to decay. Fascinating reading, complete with extensive endnotes and a detailed index.

Pritchard, William. "Stone's *Dog Soldiers.*" *Hudson Review* 28 (Spring, 1975): 55-67. A serious analysis, easily read, that places Stone's work in a setting with other

1960's and 1970's political, dissident, and antiwar writings. Astute and interesting. Sale, Roger. "Bringing the News." *New York Review of Books* 22 (April 3, 1975): 9-10. An extensive and insightful review of *Dog Soldiers* that maintains good critical balance both of the novel's literary merits and of the political message conveyed by its characters. Sale depicts Stone as a nineteenth century moralist.

Clifton K. Yearley

Cross-References

Hašek's *The Good Soldier Švejk* Reflects Postwar Disillusionment (1921), p. 523; *All Quiet on the Western Front* Stresses the Futility of War (1929), p. 767; Mailer Publishes *The Naked and the Dead* (1948), p. 1373; *Catch-22* Illustrates Antiwar Sentiment (1961), p. 1866; *Apocalypse Now* Is Hailed as the Ultimate Vietnam War Film (1979), p. 2428; *Platoon* Explores the Vietnam Experience (1986), p. 2576.

FORMAN ADAPTS *ONE FLEW OVER THE CUCKOO'S NEST* FOR FILM

Category of event: Motion pictures
Time: 1975
Locale: The United States

After a moderately successful career as a director in Czechoslovakia, Miloš Forman achieved international recognition as a filmmaker with his adaptation of Ken Kesey's landmark novel

Principal personages:
MILOŠ FORMAN (1932-   ), a Czechoslovakian filmmaker
KEN KESEY (1935-   ), the author of the novel *One Flew over the Cuckoo's Nest*
MICHAEL DOUGLAS (1944-   ), an actor who acquired the production rights to the Kesey novel from his father, Kirk Douglas
KIRK DOUGLAS (ISSUR DANIELOVITCH, 1916-   ), a successful American actor who mounted a production of Kesey's novel Off-Broadway
JACK NICHOLSON (1937-   ), an actor who won an Academy Award for his memorable performance as the protagonist in Forman's film

Summary of Event

Almost from the moment of its publication in 1962, *One Flew over the Cuckoo's Nest* became, along with Jack Kerouac's *On the Road* (1957) and Allen Ginsberg's *Howl and Other Poems* (1956), one of the central documents of an American counterculture; at the same time, it received respectful reviews from serious critics in the cultural mainstream. Ken Kesey's depiction of a mental hospital as a symbolic equivalent to American society, one in which many patients voluntarily have accepted the domination of an authoritarian administration until they are inspired to reclaim their freedom by a wildly energetic, anarchic antihero, Randle Patrick McMurphy, captured the imagination of a large number of readers who felt trapped by the social and political structure of America in the early 1960's. In spite of its somewhat sexist conception of a suffocating maternal presence—the Big Nurse of the institution—as the cause of conformity and impotence, Kesey's bold vision of a man who refused to be crushed by a stagnant, fear-ridden culture had a widespread appeal. This appeal was recognized by the intelligent actor Kirk Douglas, who thrived on roles that permitted him to play principled action heroes. In anticipation of an eventual film production, he cast himself as McMurphy in an Off-Broadway stage version in 1963. Although Douglas' efforts were acknowledged by some critics, the play was neither a commercial nor a critical success. Douglas' attempts to interest a film studio were even less successful, and he eventually agreed to let his son Michael, a television star, attempt to put together a deal.

   With little experience in the industry, Michael Douglas was not limited by conventional arrangements or expectations. Instead of seeking financing from the large studios, he approached Saul Zaentz of Fantasy Records, who agreed to act as the film's coproducer after Jack Nicholson accepted the role of McMurphy for a salary of one million dollars, approximately one-third of the entire production budget. Then, citing his appreciation of Miloš Forman's sense of black humor and naturalism in previous films that were made in Europe, such as *Loves of a Blonde* (1965) and *The Firemen's Ball* (1968), as well as acting on his father's suggestion, Douglas contacted Forman, who had left Czechoslovakia after the repressive reaction to the Prague Spring in 1968. Forman had been able to make one film in the United States, *Taking Off* (1971), but since then, he had written three screenplays without finding a backer for any of them. He was not familiar with Kesey's novel, but upon reading it he liked it immensely and immediately agreed to make the film. His experiences in Czechoslovakia led him toward considerations of how institutional tyranny affects the citizens of a country, and he knew that many artists and political activists had been imprisoned by totalitarian regimes on the grounds that their resistance was a form of insanity. Commenting on the book's subject, he observed, "Why shouldn't insane people seem more appealing? Aren't we more interesting and more appealing than our government officials?"

   Douglas convinced Dean R. Brooks, the superintendent of the Oregon State Mental Hospital in Salem, to permit the crew to make the film on the hospital grounds. Brooks claimed that the therapeutic benefits for the patients outweighed the risks involved, and he insisted that the film must not denigrate the patients. Eventually, eighty-nine patients worked in the production. Brooks himself played Doctor Spivey, the chief psychiatrist. Forman, who frequently had worked with amateurs in his European productions, liked the "unforeseeable moments which first of all confused me, but later enraptured me." He accepted Douglas' offer to direct the film after Nicholson already was committed to the project, but he was involved in the remainder of the casting. He chose Louise Fletcher to play Nurse Ratched after seeing her in a small part in Robert Altman's *Thieves Like Us* (1974). The entire production company spent ten to twelve hours a day on the hospital grounds, and Nicholson spent two weeks prior to filming in the mental ward, observing that "usually I don't have much trouble slipping out of a film role, but here I don't go home from a movie studio, I go home from a mental institution." He was especially enthusiastic about the role of McMurphy, saying that he was admirable in his desire "to fight for his fellow man." Nicholson believed that the role had a "very human appeal."

   This view coincided with Forman's idea that "We have to live with the insane, so we had better accept them as human beings." He was unaware of the book's reputation, and this enabled him to create his own cinematic vision rather than to act merely as the story's illustrator. His most significant decision was to change the focus of narration from the schizophrenic mute Chief "Broom" Bromden of Kesey's novel to a more anonymous observer, possibly another patient on the ward. In describing to screenwriters Bo Goldman and Lawrence Hauben what he wanted, he said, "I hate that voice-over . . . going with the camera through somebody's head." Hauben wanted to use a less realistic approach that might be closer to the mood of Kesey's novel, but Forman believed that such an approach might confuse viewers. Forman also clashed with cinematographer Haskell Wexler, who objected to the use of a comic mode while considering issues of mental illness. Forman eventually replaced Wexler with Bill Butler, who shared his belief that the camera should not intrude upon actors and story. Although Kesey's book is at the heart of the film, the ultimate shape and form is clearly Forman's, reflecting his ideas of sanity and the relationship of an individual to a tightly structured society. He was determined to make a film in accordance with his belief that his first priority is to entertain, but he believed that he had kept the novel's essence.

The various disputes that took place during the actual filming through the autumn and winter of 1974 and 1975 were only a prelude to the controversy that occurred when the film was released in November, 1975, in a limited series of engagements designed to build a critical reputation for the film before its general distribution. The producers knew that the sensitive subject and its somewhat antic treatment, in addition to the expectations of the novel's wide readership, would generate sufficient interest to override any really strenuous objections to the film's content.

Impact of Event

Initial critical responses to the film confirmed the producer's anticipation of a volatile, mixed reaction. At first, most reviewers found some elements to admire and some aspects of the film to criticize, their tentative judgments a function of their realization that the film's power was undeniable and their concern that it might have been misused. Vincent Canby of *The New York Times*, like virtually everyone else, was very impressed with the acting but thought the ending awkward and the analogy between American society and the mental hospital unsatisfactory. Robert Hatch, writing in *The Nation*, thought the film was entertaining but had no depth. Pauline Kael of *The New Yorker* thought it lacked the visual energy Martin Scorcese might have provided. Stanley Kauffmann, writing in *The New Republic*, found the film warped, sentimental, and dangerous, but he noted that Nicholson was "tremendous" and praised Forman's sensitive handling and expert casting. In *Newsweek*, Jack Kroll argued that Forman gave the novel shape and clarity but lost the terror, black humor, and complexity that made it a "riveting allegory." Other critics were more concerned that the novel and the film were somehow not more closely aligned, responding more to the political program of Kesey's thought than the focus of the film. *Time*'s Richard Schickel thought that the film did not express Kesey's subtle understanding of revolution, and John Simon, in a typically contrarian complaint, was bothered that there was some ambiguity to McMurphy's character, even though he detested Kesey's position. As additional essays appeared in journals during the year after the film's release, the critical focus widened, with some commentators comparing McMurphy's struggle with the story of Christ, others praising Kesey and Forman's critique of society, and some regarding the film as irresponsible and anti-intellectual or dangerous in its appeal to adolescent fantasies. Others found it valuable in its depiction of an oppressed human spirit fighting against dominating institutions. The one point of agreement was that Forman's collaboration with the actors was very successful.

The validity of this position was confirmed by the Academy Award ceremony. For the first time since *It Happened One Night* in 1934, one film won the five major Oscars: Forman as director, Nicholson and Fletcher as best actor and actress, Hauben and Goldman for the screenplay, and the film as best picture. At the presentation, Forman was reunited with his two sons, whom he had not seen in five years. They had been permitted to travel because "the international publicity of the Academy Awards is important to the Communist leaders," Forman said. He added that there was a feeling that many members of the Academy did not like to give a major award to a foreigner, and he was pleased to see this notion dispelled.

The strategy of a carefully timed and placed distribution was altered to a broad, general release and an extensive publicity campaign, with some theater owners displeased by the percentage split but compelled to accept it. *Variety* noted in April, 1976, that there was a box-office improvement in major markets after the Academy Awards. Forman's career prospects were improved considerably by the award, enabling him to make another controversial adaptation, *Hair*, from the Broadway musical in 1979, and to adapt E. L. Doctorow's 1975 postmodern novel *Ragtime* in 1981. The culmination of the rise in his reputation and influence was his production of *Amadeus* (1984) in Prague, a triumphal return to the country he had left in 1968; *Amadeus* gave Forman the opportunity to employ many of his old colleagues in the Czech film industry.

The award to Nicholson on his fifth nomination ratified his reputation as a superstar, as well as a superb actor, whose earning power compared to that of Robert Redford and Al Pacino. Fletcher, on the other hand, was disappointed by questions suggesting that her role was really a supporting one. She remarked that she had not received any good offers since the film had opened. Michael Douglas made the point that the success of this offbeat project ten years in the making might send some studio heads back to reread some of the scripts they had turned down. As for himself, Douglas predicted "It's all downhill from here," but his career actually took a different turn as he became a leading actor in films including *Romancing the Stone* (1984) and *Wall Street* (1987). Although they were not mentioned much at the time, the cast included, as patients, Christopher Lloyd and Danny DeVito, before their roles in the *Taxi* television series and their success in films.

The only person involved with the project who was thoroughly displeased was Ken Kesey. Kesey wrote a script that was not used, and Zaentz gave him a small percentage of the production in return for his suggestions. Kesey claimed that Douglas did not honor a verbal agreement with him about his share of the gross and about his ability to control the adaptation. He considered a lawsuit, especially after each of the Oscar winners failed to mention him in their speeches. Kesey did benefit from increased sales of the novel that provided the story.

The passage of time since the film's release has provided a broader perspective for the issues that it raised. Kesey's novel retains its power, and the character of McMurphy can be seen as another version of the alienated post-World War II hero, akin to Yossarian in Joseph Heller's *Catch-22* (1961), Holden Caulfield in J. D. Salinger's *The Catcher in the Rye* (1951), or T. S. Garp in John Irving's *The World According to Garp* (1978). The film conveys this quality as well, and the issues of sexism, racism, and antiauthoritarian rebellion that it explores remain subjects of intense debate, so that its presentation of these issues seems less a matter of specific advocacy and more an investigation of unsettled and vital social concerns. As Forman has said in discussing the basic philosophical position of his work, "You want to be part of this cleansing process of the human soul. We will never beat the stupidity of bureaucracy, and so on, but we must never stop fighting it." The relevance of this credo is an essential element in the continuing importance of his best films.

Bibliography

Cahill, Tim. "Knocking Around the Nest." *Rolling Stone* (December 4, 1975): 48-54, 87-88. Informative first-person accounts by Forman and Douglas about selecting the cast and crew, and by Nicholson on his experiences with mental patients.

Haskel, Molly. "Kesey Cured: Forman's Sweet Insanity." In *The Modern American Novel and the Movies*, edited by Gerald Peary and Roger Shatzkin. New York: Frederick Ungar, 1978. One of the best reviews of the film, with an interview that offers some of Forman's ideas about the film's themes.

Liehm, Antonin J. *The Miloš Forman Stories.* White Plains, N.Y.: International Arts and Sciences Press, 1974. A study of the director's life and career by a knowledgeable and sympathetic authority on Eastern European cinema.

Skvorecky, Josef. *All the Bright Young Men and Women: A Personal History of the Czech Cinema.* Toronto: Peter Martin Associates, 1971. Places Forman in the context of his country's film industry. Written with sensitivity and insight by one of Forman's oldest friends and coworkers.

Slater, Thomas J. *Miloš Forman: A Bio-Bibliography.* New York: Greenwood Press, 1987. An absolutely indispensable volume for the student of Forman's work. Contains an overview of Forman's life and career, a critical filmography, and a well-annotated bibliography.

Sturhahn, Larry. "*One Flew over the Cuckoo's Nest*: An Interview with Miloš Forman." *Filmmaker's Newsletter* (December, 1975): 26-31. Forman discusses how he works with his writers, cast, and crew.

Leon Lewis

Cross-References

Psycho Becomes Hitchcock's Most Famous Film (1960), p 1855; Foucault's *Madness and Civilization* Is Published (1961), p. 1877; Havel's *The Garden Party* Satirizes Life Under Communism (1963), p. 1967; *Easy Rider* Captures the Spirit of 1960's Youth (1969), p. 2158; *Platoon* Explores the Vietnam Experience (1986), p. 2576.

SPRINGSTEEN'S *BORN TO RUN* REINVIGORATES MAINSTREAM ROCK

Category of event: Music
Time: 1975
Locale: The United States

Bruce Springsteen's Born to Run *catapulted the young rock star to national attention and introduced millions of rock fans to a figure who would decisively shape popular music for the next generation*

Principal personages:
BRUCE SPRINGSTEEN (1949-   ), a singer, guitarist, and songwriter who rose to fame with *Born to Run*
MIKE APPEL (1942-   ), the manager who landed Springsteen a record contract but who also impeded his career
CLARENCE CLEMONS (1942-   ), a saxophonist who became Springsteen's longtime friend and foil onstage
JOHN HAMMOND (1910-1987), the Columbia Records talent scout who recognized Springsteen's potential and signed him to the label
JON LANDAU (1952-   ), the rock music critic who befriended Springsteen, advised him on *Born to Run*, and later became his manager

Summary of Event

By the middle of 1974, Bruce Springsteen's fledgling music career had stalled. He had released two critically acclaimed albums for Columbia Records, but they had sold poorly. One more flop, and Springsteen might be discharged from the label altogether. Meanwhile, his notorious perfectionism was preventing him from finishing the record that could put his career back on track.

Springsteen had come a long way, though, and he had no intention of turning back. Born and reared in the decaying industrial town of Freehold, New Jersey, he had led a working-class childhood marked by a frustrating relationship with his father, a bus driver, and by a joy of music he inherited from his mother, a secretary. He developed a passion for the guitar he received as a gift in 1963—drums were too expensive—and began emulating his idol, Elvis Presley.

His life soon became music, and he played in a variety of bands during his adolescence. Remaining in New Jersey after his parents left for California, he lived an improvised, vagrant existence, dropping out of a local community college and evading the draft by intentionally filling out forms incorrectly. After a few years, he decided to try to make it on his own as a performer. In 1972, he met Mike Appel, a producer and songwriter who had enjoyed some success working with the Partridge Family, a television singing group. Appel wanted to move into managing artists, and he regarded Springsteen as a major discovery. Excited by the prospect of professional representation, Springsteen signed a contract—on the hood of a car in a parking lot. It was a move he would live to regret.

Its immediate results, however, proved fruitful. Appel arranged for Springsteen to audition for John Hammond, the legendary talent scout who had played a role in the success of Bessie Smith, Billie Holiday, Count Basie, Bob Dylan, and Aretha Franklin. Hammond was deeply impressed by Springsteen and signed him to Columbia Records.

Springsteen's first album, *Greetings from Asbury Park, N.J.*, was released in 1973 to much fanfare. Because of his prolix lyrics, Columbia publicized Springsteen as the "New Dylan" in an effort to market him in the then-popular singer-songwriter mold of such performers as James Taylor, Jackson Browne, and Joni Mitchell. The Dylan claim alienated critics, however, even including some who saw promise in Springsteen. Later the same year, he released *The Wild, the Innocent, and the E Street Shuffle*, a more musically complex record that showcased the rhythm-and-blues influences in his work. Again, many critics were impressed, but Springsteen's music still received little radio airplay or commercial attention.

Nevertheless, Springsteen's following was growing in the major cities of the Northeast, thanks largely to his live shows, which would soon become legendary. His word-of-mouth reputation attracted the attention of Jon Landau, a highly influential editor for *Rolling Stone* magazine. Landau attended a Springsteen show in Cambridge, Massachusetts, in May of 1974 and experienced an epiphany. "I saw my rock 'n' roll past flash before my eyes," Landau wrote for Boston's *Real Paper* in what became perhaps the most famous review in pop music history. "And I saw something else: I saw rock and roll future and its name is Bruce Springsteen."

Columbia seized on Landau's remark and began marketing Springsteen's work with new interest. More important, Landau befriended Springsteen and began offering eagerly solicited advice on the stalled album. Under Landau's guidance (to the chagrin of Appel), Springsteen moved forward, albeit slowly, on the project. *Born to Run* was released in the fall of 1975.

Born to Run created an immediate sensation. Critics hailed it as one of the most vibrant rock records to be released in years. Others grew increasingly skeptical of the hype surrounding the star. It was in this context that both *Time* and *Newsweek* put Springsteen on the covers of their October 27, 1975, issues. The former depicted him as an emerging artist; the latter focused on the machinery that had brought him fame. Either way, Springsteen had been transformed from an obscure rock singer into a national phenomenon.

The events that followed, however, threatened to plunge Springsteen back into obscurity. He found it difficult to focus on his work amid all the notoriety, and expectations for him were higher than ever. Meanwhile, tensions with Appel had reached the point of crisis. The contract Springsteen had signed on the hood of a car came back to haunt him; under the terms of the agreement, he did not even have the right to quote his own lyrics. It would be three years before Springsteen would untangle himself legally from Appel and release his next album, 1978's *Darkness on the Edge of Town.* By that point, the tone of his work had decisively changed from effusive excitement to grim uncertainty.

Springsteen, though, would eventually fulfill many of the hopes that were pinned on him. His appearances at a series of 1978 concerts against nuclear power (captured in the 1980 film *No Nukes*) consolidated his position as the premier performer of his generation. *The River*, released in 1980, resulted in his first top-ten single, "Hungry Heart." He detoured from mass appeal with the extraordinarily powerful *Nebraska* in 1982 before achieving towering success with 1984's *Born in the U.S.A.*, which spawned seven hit singles and established Springsteen as an American icon of integrity amid the glitter of the Ronald Reagan era. At long last, rock's future had arrived.

Impact of Event

Born to Run was one of the great rock-and-roll records of the 1970's. It reaffirmed some of rock's early traditions, but it did so in a way that was relevant to American society in the post-Watergate era. As such, the album maintained a vital center at a time when it seemed that center was dwindling.

As many historians of popular music have noted, the 1970's were not good years in the history of rock. The diverse wave of music that crested in the late 1960's broke with the collapse of the Beatles, the deaths of Jimi Hendrix and Janis Joplin, the corporate consolidation of the music industry, and the fragmentation of rock by race and genre. Moreover, even some of the most widely hailed music of the 1960's would soon seem badly dated, attenuated from its blues roots and marred by fuzzy sentiment. The most interesting music of the decade would come from society's margins; the seductive appeal of disco emanated from black and gay nightclubs, and the visceral power of punk rock was produced by Great Britain's angry, disenfranchised youth.

Growing up on the New Jersey shore, Bruce Springsteen was relatively isolated from these influences. His musical style derived largely from the classic rock of the 1950's: the seemingly effortless grace of Elvis Presley, the buoyant rhythm and blues of Gary U.S. Bonds, and the momentary pleasures of countless one-hit wonders that Springsteen would later include in his expansive live repertoire. Eschewing the watery psychedelia of the late 1960's San Francisco music scene, Springsteen's songs were imbued with a powerful proletarian sensibility that depicted the joys of working-class life as well as its frustrations. All of these elements are present on *Greetings from Asbury Park, N.J.* and *The Wild, the Innocent, and the E Street Shuffle*.

Born to Run, however, represented a quantum leap forward. Springsteen displayed increased confidence in the studio, and Jon Landau's contributions helped to polish the record. Moreover, the album showcased Springsteen's encyclopedic ability to evoke rock traditions, whether in a lyrical reference to Roy Orbison in "Thunder Road" or in the use of the Bo Diddley beat that underlay "She's the One." Springsteen was also able to take rock fundamentals (raspy vocals, prominent guitars, and the big, booming saxophone of sidekick Clarence Clemons) and augment them with novel elements such as a glockenspiel, layered keyboards, and even a violin for the elegiac "Jungleland."

The greatest source of *Born to Run*'s appeal, however, was the album's sense of urgency. Whereas Springsteen's first two albums had largely focused on the careless joys of life on the boardwalk, *Born to Run* showed an awareness of the threats to that life-style, of the likelihood that the characters who embraced it would land in dead-end jobs and see their dreams go unrealized. Nevertheless, there remained the confidence that Springsteen asserted in the title song: "Someday girl, I don't know when/ We're gonna get to that place where we really wanna go/ And we'll walk in the sun." This confidence, asserted amid vividly depicted frustrations—emblematic of those of economically weakened, politically exhausted young people in the United States— gave *Born to Run* its ongoing vitality.

In the years that followed, Springsteen would pay ever greater attention to these frustrated dreamers. *Born to Run* depicted their anxiety; *Darkness on the Edge of Town* captured their anger. *The River* suggested the joys that could coexist with failure; *Nebraska* chronicled the tragedy of resignation. By the time of *Born in the U.S.A.*, Springsteen was effectively integrating all of these elements into individual songs such as "Dancing in the Dark," "Glory Days," and the title track, a chilling portrait of a Vietnam veteran betrayed by his country but determined to carry on.

Springsteen's unwavering commitment to representing such characters, and the continuing intensity (and generosity) of his live shows, won him the admiration of Americans across the political spectrum. Both Ronald Reagan and Walter Mondale invoked Springsteen's name during the 1984 presidential campaign, and he gave considerable credibility to the U.S.A. for Africa antihunger effort by singing a duet with Stevie Wonder on the international hit "We Are the World." Springsteen also made charitable contributions in every city of his *Born in the U.S.A.* tour, and he headlined a series of benefit concerts for Amnesty International. By the end of the 1980's, he had become rock's premier figure and was widely viewed as its conscience.

To be sure, he continued to have his skeptics, and to some extent his very success enhanced that skepticism (similar doubts dogged Springsteen's biggest mid-1980's commercial rival, Michael Jackson). Moreover, Springsteen's subsequent albums such as *Tunnel of Love* (1987), *Human Touch* (1992), and *Lucky Town* (1992) indicated a clear retreat from the class-based concerns that had long been a cornerstone of his art. Still, for the millions of fans who had been provoked, moved, and inspired by Springsteen's body of work, these and subsequent records seemed likely to become valued landmarks in an ongoing journey that began with *Born to Run*.

Bibliography

Cross, Charles, ed. *Backstreets: Springsteen, the Man and his Music.* New York: Harmony Books, 1989. This book, a collection of articles, photos, and Springsteen trivia from the Springsteen fanzine *Backstreets*, is an excellent source for diehard fans. Cross approaches his project with unusual intelligence.

Cullen, Jim. "Bruce Springsteen's Ambiguous Musical Politics in the 1980's." *Popu-*

lar Music and Society 16 (Summer, 1992): 1-22. An iconoclastic reading of Springsteen's career that emphasizes the degree to which he left himself vulnerable to appropriation by the political right. Analyzes how the free agents of his early music seem to become powerless victims in his more recent work.

Frith, Simon. "The Real Thing: Bruce Springsteen." In *Music for Pleasure.* New York: Routledge, 1988. Using the multirecord set *Bruce Springsteen Live 1975-85* (1987) as a point of departure, Frith looks at the performer skeptically, arguing that Springsteen's appeal stems from a series of misleading perceptions. A bracing alternative to the idolatry of much Springsteen commentary.

Harron, Mary. "McRock: Pop as Commodity." In *Facing the Music*, edited by Simon Frith. New York: Pantheon Books, 1988. An interesting use of Springsteen (vis-à-vis Madonna) to argue for the frank commercial appeal of rock music. Harron argues that publicity and hype are central to artistic value.

Hilburn, Robert. *Springsteen.* New York: Scribner's, 1985. A handsomely illustrated critical biography. Perhaps the best brief treatment of Springsteen's life and work.

Marsh, Dave. *Born to Run: The Bruce Springsteen Story.* New York: Dell Books, 1981. Mannered, fawning, and lacking in documentation, Marsh's biography covers Springsteen's career until the time of *The River.* Nevertheless useful as the definitive record of Springsteen's life and for the author's access to his normally reticent subject.

_____. *Glory Days: Bruce Springsteen in the 1980s.* New York: Pantheon Books, 1987. The sequel to *Born to Run*, the book has many of its predecessor's weaknesses—and its strengths. The bibliography is a useful source for further investigation.

Smith, Martha Nell. "Sexual Mobilities in Bruce Springsteen: Performance as Commentary." *South Atlantic Quarterly* 90 (Fall, 1991): 833-854. A provocative analysis of the hetero- as well as homosexual currents running through Springsteen's performances and recordings. Persuasive use of contemporary cultural theory.

Winner, Langdon. "Bruce Springsteen." In *The Rolling Stone Illustrated History of Rock 'n' Roll*, edited by Jim Miller. New York: Random House, 1980. Though dated, Winner's article is nevertheless revealing for suggesting the hope—and skepticism—surrounding Springsteen in the 1970's.

Jim Cullen

Cross-References

Guthrie's Populist Songs Reflect the Depression-Era United States (1930's), p. 810; Berry's "Maybellene" Popularizes Rock and Roll (1955), p. 1635; Presley Becomes a Rock-and-Roll Sensation (1956), p. 1705; The Beatles Revolutionize Popular Music (1963), p. 1944; The Rolling Stones Release *Out of Our Heads* (1965), p. 2027; Dylan Performs with Electric Instruments (1965), p. 2038; Brown Wins a Grammy for "Papa's Got a Brand New Bag" (1966), p. 2059; The Sex Pistols Spark Punk Rock's Musical Insurrection (1975), p. 2360.

VIOLENT ACTION-ADVENTURE
TELEVISION SERIES FLOURISH

Category of event: Television and radio
Time: 1975-1979
Locale: The United States

The amount of violence shown on prime-time action-adventure television increased to unprecedented levels, raising questions about possible effects on viewers

Principal personages:
FRED SILVERMAN (1937-   ), a television executive in charge of entertainment programming at all three major U.S. networks at various times during the 1970's
AARON SPELLING (1925-   ), a television producer responsible for *Starsky and Hutch*, *The Rookies*, and many other violent shows
STEPHEN JOSEPH CANNELL (1943-   ), a producer and director who created *The Rockford Files*, *Baretta*, and other violent programs

Summary of Event

In the early 1970's, America's three major networks, the American Broadcasting Company (ABC), the National Broadcasting Company (NBC), and the Columbia Broadcasting System (CBS), established what was called the "family hour." Between 8:00 P.M. and 9:00 P.M., television programs were to be suited for family viewing. Before long, however, the networks tried to outdo one another by broadcasting more and more sensational shows, which became increasingly violent. In the 1975-1976 program season, the networks agreed to observe the family-hour restrictions more carefully, but that merely meant that violent shows were delayed until the hour's end. After 9:00 P.M., violent shows dominated prime time, the period between 7:00 P.M. and 11:00 P.M. when audiences are typically greatest.

By 1977, the television programs shown during prime time had been studied by numerous scholars and researchers. Violent television shows such as *Kojak*, *Starsky and Hutch*, and *The Rockford Files* were bringing the major networks high ratings, and concern regarding the effects of viewing these programs became a major issue among parents, researchers, and television producers. As a result of such concerns, by the end of the decade, many violent shows had been replaced by more subtle programs.

Most of the violent 1970's programs were crime dramas, and most, including such shows as *Mannix*, *Baretta*, and *Hawaii Five-O*, shared many characteristics. For example, most involved at least one eccentric, daring white male involved with private investigating or law enforcement. Such programs also often portrayed women as victims and violence as the means by which men protected women. Researchers noted numerous other features common to 1970's crime dramas.

As the popularity of violent shows increased by the late 1970's, so did the problems related to broadcasting them. Advertisers, for example, started to evaluate more closely the programs on which they chose to advertise. Violent shows came to be seen as inappropriate advertising venues for certain companies and agencies. Companies such as Best Foods and Samsonite avoided excessively violent programs when they chose their prime-time advertising slots. Evidence to support these decisions came when research began to show that violence on such programs as *The Rookies* and *Starsky and Hutch* was actually turning off consumers. One such study done by J. Walter Thompson, one of America's largest advertising firms, revealed that eight percent of the consumers surveyed had boycotted products advertised during violent shows and that ten percent more had considered the idea.

Throughout the 1970's, television sponsors, including such advertising heavyweights as Johnson & Johnson, continued monitoring prime-time programs, and some would pull their advertisements from shows that were perceived as excessively violent. Johnson & Johnson pulled advertisements from a total of twenty-four shows such as *Kojak* and *Police Story* during the height of prime-time violence. Surprisingly, though, all prime-time advertising spaces were sold during this controversial period.

The Federal Communications Commission (FCC) attempted to regulate violence by using a rating system, but the FCC's efforts were not very effective. With the advertisers on one side and television producers on the other, the issue of how much violence would be tolerated seemed likely to become a question of censorship.

Televised violence was not restricted to prime-time action shows. At almost any time of day, the networks were showing some type of violence. Morning and afternoon programs such as cartoons, Western movies, and science-fiction series were also found to contain heavy doses of violence.

By the end of the decade, the round-the-clock violence had palled on many viewers, and prime time became less concentrated with violent programs. Numerous researchers had come to the conclusion that there was an excessive and dangerous amount of violence being shown on prime-time television, and the U.S. surgeon general stated that there was a clear causal relationship between the viewing of violence on television and aggressive behavior on the part of viewers.

Impact of Event

The impact of television violence in the late 1970's was widespread. Violence on prime-time shows affected other programs, television advertisers, and viewers. The impact on the producers of the programs and the advertisers was large enough to set them at odds; many producers believed that television did not make violence real enough, whereas many advertising agencies thought that televised violence was too real. Therefore, neither party was sure if they could dictate the other's actions. The FCC became involved and created a violence rating system to keep producers and advertisers at ease, and the amount of televised violence decreased by 1980.

The television audience was also significantly affected by the violence shown on prime-time programs. Children were especially affected by the violence they observed. According to George Gerbner, a University of Pennsylvania researcher, the average American child had viewed fifteen thousand hours of television by the age of eighteen and had witnessed eighteen thousand television murders and other violent acts. The number of weapons shown, the setting of the violence, and the male-to-female ratios on the shows were all factors directly relating to audience impact. In a sample of seventy-three hours of 1977 prime-time shows, an average of almost nine weapons appeared each hour; handguns were the most common type of weapon shown. *Hawaii Five-O* was observed to have the greatest number of weapon appearances. In a study sponsored by the U.S. Conference of Mayors, crime-drama programs were compared to Western movies, cartoons, and science-fiction series and were found to be more violent, more frightening, more disturbing, and more realistic than the other types of shows. In studies comparing American crime drama with British crime drama, the American shows were rated as more violent. The series *Starsky and Hutch*, which concerned a duo of private investigators fighting crime in a city setting, was rated as the most violent of all the action/adventure programs.

Another significant finding of the studies of violent programs was the ratio of males to females involved in violent acts. Studies showed that white males were more often shown involved in violent acts than were women or members of other ethnic groups. Depictions of male violence against females were rated more realistic and more frightening than portrayals of female violence against males. Typically, unmarried women, adolescents, and elderly women were portrayed as victims. Character portrayal was also a significant factor in the effect of television violence; in general, violence instigated by a good character was rated as less serious than violence caused by a bad character.

Moreover, violent television significantly affected the perception of law enforcement in the real world. Viewers tended to perceive the level of police involvement in day-to-day life to be higher than the actual level and also tended to overestimate the extent of violence and danger in the real world. Frequent television watchers believed that the incidence of violent crimes was higher than it in fact was and also perceived themselves as likely victims. Another study sponsored by the mayor's conference showed that violence by American police was perceived as more violent and more frightening than violence by British police. In another study, viewers' perceptions of television violence that depicted harmful consequences were different from perceptions of violent acts that showed no harm to the victims. The distinction between fantasy and reality was studied by Gerbner and other researchers, who found that viewers' perceptions of reality were distorted and tended to resemble the depictions on television rather than real life. Another interesting finding was the fact that females may have become less aggressive by exposure to television violence. Evidence to support this theory was given by researchers who claimed that television acted as an outlet for aggression otherwise not socially acceptable for females.

Although research findings were often inconsistent and contradictory, the majority of studies agreed on one basic point: Television violence had a significant impact on its viewers. Although violence would continue to be a major feature of many television shows, the amount of televised violence declined as the 1970's ended, and most experts agreed that this was a good thing.

Bibliography

Feshbach, Seymour, and Robert A. Singer. *Television and Aggression.* San Francisco: Jossey-Bass, 1971. A good basis for understanding the prevalence of violence and aggression on television. Various studies show what genres of programs contained violence prior to 1971. All angles of arguments and theories are covered. Complete index.

Gunter, Barrie. *Dimensions of Television Violence.* Aldershot, England: Gower Press, 1985. The best source of information on violence in television for this time period. Wide variety of visual aids to research; bar graphs, tables, and charts are used throughout the text. A majority of studies compare British shows with American shows. Good index and complete reference list.

Higgins, Patricia B., and Marla W. Ray. *Television's Action Arsenal: Weapon Use in Prime Time.* Washington, D.C.: United States Conference of Mayors, 1978. Individual studies of violent 1970's programs. Does not discuss the effects of televised violence on viewers. Tables and figures are shown with each study. No index.

Huesmann, L. R. "Television Violence and Aggressive Behavior." In *Television and Behavior: Ten Years of Scientific Progress and Implications for the Eighties,* edited by David Pearl, Lorrain Bouthilet, and Joyce Lazar. 2 vols. Washington, D.C.: Government Printing Office, 1982. A valuable resource for theories and the basic types of research methods used to study aggression on television.

Rowland, Willard D., Jr. *The Politics of TV Violence.* Beverly Hills, Calif.: Sage Publications, 1983. A technical, politically minded work that covers television history up to the 1980's. No index or visual aids.

David Francis

Cross-References

Little Caesar, Public Enemy, and *Scarface* Launch the Gangster-Film Genre (1930), p. 839; *The Maltese Falcon* Establishes a New Style for Crime Films (1941), p. 1223; *Dragnet* Is the First Widely Popular Police Show (1951), p. 1531; Godard's Expressionistic *À bout de souffle* Revolutionizes Film (1960), p. 1845; *I Spy* Debuts to Controversy (1965), p. 2044.

THE WIZ BRINGS AFRICAN-AMERICAN TALENT TO BROADWAY

Category of event: Theater
Time: January 5, 1975
Locale: Majestic Theater, New York, New York

Opening to lukewarm reviews, The Wiz, *an African-American version of* The Wizard of Oz, *survived through audience word-of-mouth, ran for several years, and won seven Tony Awards*

> *Principal personages:*
> GEOFFREY HOLDER (1930-), the director and costume designer called in to "save" *The Wiz*
> CHARLIE SMALLS (1944-1987), a composer and lyricist
> KEN HARPER (1939-1988), the producer who conceived and developed *The Wiz*

Summary of Event

Producer Ken Harper approached Geoffrey Holder two years before *The Wiz* opened, querying him about directing an all-African-American version of *The Wizard of Oz.* Harper had trouble finding financial backing for the production but finally found a backer in Twentieth Century-Fox, which provided one million dollars, enough to fund the entire show. Early in its development, direction and choreography were in other hands, but when *The Wiz* ran into trouble, Geoffrey Holder came back and performed a show-business miracle in a few weeks, transforming the show as both director and costumer into a hit musical that ran for 1,672 performances and won seven Tony Awards, including the award for best musical. Holder himself won two Tony Awards for his work.

Initial reviews of the theatrical production were only lukewarm, but strong word-of-mouth response and a publicity campaign funded by Twentieth Century-Fox kept the show open. Eventually, these two forces resulted in enormous ticket sales, and the musical made show-business history. A letter to *The New York Times* protesting that newspaper's lack of appreciation of the musical pointed out that *The Wiz* was more faithful to the original book *The Wonderful Wizard of Oz* (1900), by L. Frank Baum, than was the "classic" Judy Garland film *The Wizard of Oz* (1939). At the same time, *The Wiz* was relevant to a 1970's black American audience. It contained "inside" jokes, and its music was African American. The Wicked Witch of the West was brought on stage by slaves yelled at by an overseer with a bullhorn. When Dorothy "freed the slaves," they headed for the North—to the Emerald City, a fantasy Harlem—reflecting the Great Migration after World War I. There they met the Wiz, dressed like a fantasy hipster or pimp in glittering white and wearing green "shades." "Follow the Yellow Brick Road" was replaced by the refrain "Ease on down, ease on down the road."

The Wiz had not one but two Good Witches. Dee Dee (Denise) Bridgewater played Glinda, the Good Witch of the South. Clarisse Taylor played the other, the "trickster" witch. Fifteen-year-old Stephanie Mills played Dorothy. Mabel King as Evillene, the Wicked Witch of the West, had a show-stopping song, "Don't Nobody Bring Me No Bad News." Hinton Battle played the Scarecrow; Tiger Haynes played the Tin Man, attired in a garbage can and a skillet hat. Ted Ross was the "signifying" Cowardly Lion, and Andre de Shields played the Wiz.

The creative artists involved met the challenge of developing a new and updated version of a story that every schoolchild knew, already a film classic shown repeatedly on television. Kansas became the cultural equivalent of Lenox Avenue in Harlem, and the Emerald City was, as the *Newsweek* drama critic said, "a kind of utopian cocktail lounge." Most reviewers praised the visual aspects of the show, the direction, the choreography, and the performances of the actors. Many, though, thought that the book by William F. Brown was weak. Some had reservations about the score, finding the songs, with several notable exceptions, too similar musically. It may be that these critics, many of them white, simply were not attuned to the black American music these songs represented.

In July, 1975, a writer for *The New York Times* described *The Wiz* as a "blaxploitation" musical, adding that "sociology surely had something to do with the tolerant reviews heaped upon . . . the insistently all-black version" of *The Wizard of Oz*. Not sharing that critic's disdain, the Antoinette Perry voters in April, 1975, awarded *The Wiz* seven "bests," more Tony Awards than any other nominated show. In addition to Geoffrey Holder's two awards for best director and best costumer, Ted Ross, the Cowardly Lion, won for best supporting actor in a musical; Dee Dee Bridgewater, Glinda the Good Witch, won for best supporting actress in a musical; Charlie Smalls won for best score; and George Faison won for best choreography. The show itself won as best musical.

Smalls's music was variously described as rock, rhythm and blues, gospel, and soul. Although William F. Brown's book was regarded by reviewers as rather weak, they liked the use of black American urban experience, language, and slang in a book that otherwise faithfully followed the original. The Tony Award for best book, however, went to James Lee Barrett for his work on *Shenandoah*.

Interviewed after winning the two Tony Awards, Geoffrey Holder explained the genesis of the show and his final contributions to it. Holder said that two years before the show opened, producer Ken Harper had asked him to recommend a director for *The Wiz*. He suggested Louis Johnson, director of the 1970 hit musical *Purlie*, based on Ossie Davis' 1961 *Purlie Victorious*, or Donald McKayle, director of *Raisin* (1973), based on Lorraine Hansberry's 1959 play *A Raisin in the Sun*. Harper asked Holder to do some costume drawings for the show. After listening to the score, Holder did a series of forty drawings. Harper then wanted Holder to direct, choreograph, design costumes, and play the role of the Wiz.

Later, Harper chose Gilbert Moses to codirect. Holder withdrew from the production except as costumer. Moses then hired choreographer George Faison. When the show ran into trouble in tryout performances in Baltimore, Holder took over for Moses. In tryouts in Detroit and Philadelphia, he reshaped the show, plucking Hinton Battle from the chorus to play the Scarecrow and restoring the tornado ballet, which had been eliminated. It became a show-stopping number on Broadway.

Holder was already well known as an actor, having appeared in the James Bond film *Live and Let Die* (1973). Born in Trinidad, he came to the United States as a member of a Trinidadian dance ensemble.

It was somewhat ironic that Dee Dee Bridgewater, winner of the best supporting actress award as Glinda, was at the time sharing an apartment with Gilbert Moses, who was removed as director and replaced by Holder. Moses said it was "just one of those things," pointing out that he had been nominated for a Tony Award in 1973 for *Ain't Supposed to Die a Natural Death* and was at the time directing *The Taking of Miss Janie* at the Lincoln Center.

Impact of Event

In 1984, *The Wiz* was revived on Broadway, but the revival was far from successful. Stephanie Mills was the only original cast member in the revival. The reviewer for *The New York Times* found the new production depressing: "*The Wiz* was hardly a great musical in 1975, but it had something to say, and it said it with verve and integrity."

In 1987, there was a minor flurry when a suburban Chicago dinner theater cast white actors in seven of the seventeen roles of *The Wiz*, including the role of Dorothy. Some of the black American actors who had toured in *The Wiz* had been available for the dinner-theater production. In its defense, the management cited its past attempts at nontraditional casting of black actors in traditionally white roles. Ernest Perry, the ethnic minorities committee chairman of the Midwest regional office of Equity, an actors' union, pointed out that the chief complaint was that the show itself had been created specifically by black American artists for black American performers.

In 1978, Universal Studios released what was described as the most expensive film musical ever made up to that time, with a budget of about $30 million. Reviewers regarded the film version of *The Wiz* as the last major black American film of the 1970's. The director was Sidney Lumet, actress Lena Horne's former-son-in-law. Lumet and the author of the film script, Joel Schumacher, were white. Some reviewers thought that the generally recognized flatness of the film version was the result of the change from African-American director and writer to white artists.

Except for Ted Ross and Mabel King, who were in the original Broadway production, major actors replaced the less-well-known Broadway actors in the film. Nipsey Russell, known for his appearances on *The Tonight Show*, played the Tin Man to excellent reviews. Michael Jackson, then nineteen years old, played the Scarecrow, and Richard Pryor played the Wiz. Diana Ross, thirty-four years old when the film was made, played twenty-four-year-old Dorothy.

The director and scriptwriter received negative criticism for changing the locales and weakening the themes. Instead of traveling from Kansas to an urbanized Emerald City, Dorothy starts uptown in Harlem, travels downtown into white New York, and finds the Wiz in the World Trade Center. Lumet also was criticized for distancing the audience from the actors and scenes with too many long shots and not enough close-ups. Joel Schumacher, who adapted William F. Brown's book, was criticized for failing to understand the nuances of black American idiom and "street humor" in the original.

Reviewers thought that Richard Pryor's talent was wasted in a virtually unwritten role, that Diana Ross was too old to play Dorothy, and that Michael Jackson, though sweet and charming, was also wasted. Nipsey Russell received the best reviews. Reviewer Pauline Kael of *The New Yorker* called his two numbers, "Slide Some Oil to Me" and "What Would I Do If I Could Feel?," the best in the film.

Lena Horne, as Glinda the Good Witch, was posed against a night sky at the end of the film to sing "Believe in Yourself." The scene recalled Metro-Goldwyn-Mayer musicals of the 1940's, in which a voice-over would announce "Ladies and Gentlemen, Miss Lena Horne" and she would appear to visually and musically dazzle the film audience, disappearing as abruptly as she came. *Newsweek* reviewer Jack Kroll commented that Horne sang the song in *The Wiz* with "fiercely exultant dignity."

Horne repeated this number in her brilliant one-woman show at the Niederlander Theater in New York City a few years later, winning a Tony Award for her performance. Her show was autobiographical and included a healthily satirical section on her days at Metro-Goldwyn-Mayer. Her singing of "Believe in Yourself" moved theater audiences to tears and to shouts of approval.

Perhaps the success of the Broadway production helped pave the way for such all-black American musicals as *Eubie!* (1978), *Bubbling Brown Sugar* (1975), and *Ain't Misbehavin'* (1978). Perhaps the success in the early 1990's of *Jelly's Last Jam*, a musical fable about the life of musician Jelly Roll Morton, might remind audiences that *The Wiz*, like the Baum book on which it was based, was a fable, too, about finding courage and self-reliance without forgetting roots. Whatever its connections, *The Wiz* stands in theater history as a shining illustration of ethnically oriented entertainment that succeeded in the mainstream.

Bibliography

Bogle, Donald. "The Wiz." In *Blacks in American Films and Television: An Encyclopedia*. New York: Garland, 1988. A fairly detailed account of the 1978 film version of the Broadway musical, including capsule reviews. Agrees with reviewers that the white director and scriptwriter altered the "blackness" of the original musical. Praises Nipsey Russell and Lena Horne.

Buckley, Tom. "About New York." *The New York Times*, April 21, 1975, p. 42. An interview with Dee Dee Bridgewater that ran the morning after she won a Tony as best supporting actress.

Douglas, Carlyle C. "'The Whiz' Behind *The Wiz.*" *Ebony* 30 (October, 1975): 114-122. A biographical profile and interview with Geoffrey Holder after he received two Tony Awards, as director and costumer of *The Wiz*. Discusses his other artistic talents as actor, dancer, and painter as well as his boyhood in Trinidad.

Gill, Brendan. "Broadway." *The New Yorker* 51 (January 13, 1975): 64-65. Gill wrote in his column, "Wolcott Gibbs once wrote in this department that a certain production of *Hamlet* was well worth taking the children to on a rainy afternoon. So is *The Wiz*, in any weather." Gill's review is mostly favorable, though it expresses many of the reservations expressed by other reviewers.

Lester, Eleanor. "Geoffrey Holder—The Whiz Who Rescued *The Wiz*." *The New York Times*, May 25, 1975, Sect. II, p. 1. This interview with Holder focuses on events leading up to his directing *The Wiz*.

Katherine Lederer

Cross-References

Hallelujah Is the First Important Black Musical (1929), p. 772; Gershwin's *Porgy and Bess* Opens in New York (1935), p. 1016; The Classic *The Wizard of Oz* Opens (1939), p. 1109; *Stormy Weather* Offers New Film Roles to African Americans (1940's), p. 1159; Hansberry's *A Raisin in the Sun* Debuts on Broadway (1959), p. 1795; *Thriller* Marks Michael Jackson's Musical Coming-of-Age (1982), p. 2512.

THE JEFFERSONS SIGNALS SUCCESS OF BLACK SITUATION COMEDIES

Category of event: Television and radio
Time: January 18, 1975-July 23, 1985
Locale: The United States

The Jeffersons, *a spin-off from* All in the Family, *became an immensely success-ful situation comedy, one of the first to put a black cast into nonstereotyped scripts*

Principal personages:

NORMAN LEAR (1922-   ), a television producer and director who cre-ated *The Jeffersons* and numerous other shows of the 1970's and 1980's

SHERMAN HEMSLEY (1938-   ), the actor who played George Jefferson, the leading character in the show

ISABEL SANFORD (1933-   ), the actress who played Louise Jefferson, the long-suffering wife of George

MIKE EVANS (1949-   ), the actor who played Lionel Jefferson when the show went on the air

MARLA GIBBS (1931-   ), the actress who played Florence, the Jeffer-sons' maid

ROXIE ROKER (1929-   ), the actress who played Helen Willis, one of the Jeffersons' neighbors

FRANKLIN COVER (1928-   ), a white actor who played Tom Willis, Helen's husband

PAUL BENEDICT (1938-   ), an actor who played Harry Bentley, the klutzy, well-meaning British neighbor of the Jeffersons

Summary of Event

"Getting taken to the cleaners" took on a whole new meaning when, in January, 1975, *The Jeffersons* came on the air. Originally, the characters George and Louise Jefferson, with their son, Lionel, had been next-door neighbors to Archie and Edith Bunker on *All in the Family.* In that capacity, they fulfilled the role of allowing a humorous discussion about urban race relations. The Jeffersons proved to be eco-nomically upwardly mobile, finding business success as their single dry-cleaning shop in Queens turned into a chain of seven shops covering several areas of New York City. In celebration of their success, they moved out of their working-class neighbor-hood to an apartment on the Upper East Side of Manhattan. This was where their own show was set.

The launching of *The Jeffersons* was testimony to the fact that, in the mid-1970's, television was producing spin-off series at a furious rate. No show produced more spin-offs than the grandfather of the socially relevant situation comedy, Norman Lear's *All in the Family.* George and Louise Jefferson bid farewell to Edith Bunker and good riddance to Archie because the characters had established a television identity of their own that could support a separate series.

The strength of situation comedies, or "sitcoms," tends to be more in characters than it is in plots. The plots of sitcoms are, generally, routine and predictable. The strength of a program can be seen when a character is able to leave the original setting and establish a free-standing spin-off. It is astonishing that Norman Lear created so many strong characters. *All in the Family* spun off *The Jeffersons* and *Maude* (Edith Bunker's cousin); *Maude* later spawned *Good Times*, which featured the character who had been Maude's maid. Gloria Bunker even had her own show, *Gloria*, in 1982 and 1983.

The basic situation pursued in *The Jeffersons* was the misplacement of a family in a social class. The Jeffersons had money, but they did not have the education or the social skills of their new associates. This was far from a new premise. Television had used the same concept a decade earlier with *The Beverly Hillbillies. The Jeffersons* was basically *The Beverly Hillbillies* in blackface. One twist was that while Jed Clampett tried to hold on to the old ways, George Jefferson was attempting to learn new ones. *The Jeffersons* also had elements reminiscent of *Father Knows Best.* George Jefferson tried to be the all-knowing father for his brood and usually made a mess of things in the attempt.

At the beginning of the series, George Jefferson was probably the most unsympathetic character on American television. He had few redeeming qualities, was devoid of warmth, was verbally abusive to his wife and son, harassed his maid, and was a bigoted, social-climbing snob who did not understand the social code of the class he was attempting to enter. Even the huge business and financial success he achieved with his dry-cleaning business did not change George Jefferson. He remained short-tempered, bigoted, pompous, and a know-it-all. One critic noted that George Jefferson was an African-American version of Archie Bunker, except that George had money while Archie was struggling to make ends meet.

The public responded to George, sensing that behind his blustery exterior there was insecurity and sadness. George had always believed that money was the key to the American dream. Once he had acquired money, it was devastating to him that he still could not find acceptance.

Sherman Hemsley, who played George, had grown up as a member of a street gang in Philadelphia. Four years in the Air Force gave him discipline and direction in life and, on his discharge, he attended the Philadelphia Academy of Dramatic Arts. In 1967, he went to New York City to perform on Broadway. Norman Lear saw Hemsley in a performance and recalled him years later when he was casting for *All in the Family.*

Isabel Sanford played Louise, the wife of George. The function of her character was to smooth out the feathers George ruffled and to remind him of his roots. Whenever George engaged in delusions of grandeur and narcissistic self-involvement, Louise would prick his bubble and put his feet solidly back on earth. Even in their high-rise luxury apartment, Louise was a very down-to-earth person. She had known hard work and economy before their marriage, and she retained a practical outlook on life.

Sanford grew up in New York City and was so enamored of acting that she began doing nightclub acts without her mother's knowledge or permission. She joined the American Negro Theatre and acted whenever and wherever she could. Her goal was to become a black comedienne, and she pursued that goal by moving to Hollywood.

Marla Gibbs played Florence, the Jeffersons' maid. Her ambition long had been to become a television star. She studied singing and acting in Hollywood before appearing on the *Barney Miller* show. From there she became a regular on *The Jeffersons*. Although some critics thought her portrayal of Florence perpetuated stereotypes about lazy black workers, Gibbs rejected this criticism by saying that she worked against such stereotypes by talking back to her employers and insisting that they do some of their own menial work. In her view, Florence was the representative of a common black heritage, that of the servant.

It is requisite of sitcoms that there be eccentric neighbors for the major characters to react to. Paul Benedict played such a character with his role of Harry Bentley. Occasionally, the character would suffer from back problems. On those occasions, Bentley would lie on the floor and ask George Jefferson to walk on him—symbolism carried to its ultimate degree. The microcosm inhabited by the characters on *The Jeffersons* gave Americans of the mid-1970's to the mid-1980's a chance to laugh at themselves and at the racial tensions of the time.

Impact of Event

The Jeffersons was part of the new wave of socially relevant situation comedies that began to come on the air in the 1970's. These can be attributed to Norman Lear, with assistance from Mary Tyler Moore. These relevance shows all involved a degree of social consciousness and dealt with current issues of concern and controversy. By being a part of this line of approach, *The Jeffersons* helped change the face of television. Beginning in 1971, topics and even language that once had been taboo were made legitimate by the impact of these shows.

The Jeffersons broke ground beyond what already had been accomplished by *All in the Family* and *The Mary Tyler Moore Show*. *The Jeffersons* confronted its viewers with a black family and its problems. The family was far from typical and issues came up in comic ways, but they were nevertheless issues. Black characters had been slow to be accepted in serious roles on television. Exceptions to this rule include Diahann Carroll in *Julia* and Bill Cosby in *I Spy*, but most black characters prior to the 1970's were used to provide comic relief. *The Jeffersons* used several stock characteristics in this respect, but characters had more than one dimension to them. George Jefferson often portrayed a loud-mouthed, opinionated windbag; Florence was an "uppity" black woman even though she worked as a maid. In many ways, *The Jeffersons* was no more than another domestic comedy, one that happened to be about an African-American family. This in itself set a precedent, in that it showed that black actors could play mainstream roles and be accepted by viewers.

The serious side to the program came through because behind George Jefferson's bluster was a sensitive nature that was hurt and bewildered by the failure of the American dream to be fulfilled by his financial success. The program also presented to the public subjects not previously explored in great depth on entertainment television, subjects such as integrated neighborhoods and interracial marriage. Franklin Cover and Roxie Roker appeared on *The Jeffersons* as the Willises, prime time's first interracial married couple. To the extent that *The Jeffersons* helped open the way for racial tolerance, the show had social significance.

The secret to the success of Norman Lear, in this respect, was his suspicion that some people attracted by stupid situations might also be prejudiced. Lear used humor to attract their interest, then, once they had become involved in the show, stimulated them to think about their prejudices. It is impossible to say how effective this relevance approach was in changing attitudes and opinions. Many studies indicate that the initial reaction of viewers was reinforcement of the attitudes they held before they watched the show; in short, they saw what they wanted to see. The long-term impact was to wear down resistance to unfamiliar social situations such as integrated neighborhoods, although this does not mean that these viewers came to approve of these conditions. It is noteworthy, however, that the liberal social context of *The Jeffersons* met with little resistance from ultraconservative groups and no stations canceled their broadcast of the program.

Although set in radically different social conditions, *The Jeffersons* was a lineal descendant of *Amos 'n' Andy*. The picturesque characters of the old radio show, which made the transition to television, made their comedy work by tricking other black people and had only minimal contact with white society. George Jefferson tried to outwit all of society and integrate himself into white society when it suited his purposes. *Amos 'n' Andy* was about black people, but the intended audience was largely white. The heavily stereotyped characters appealed to the ignorance and prejudice of whites who lived in a segregated society, but the black community recognized the program for what it was. *The Jeffersons* was clearly about black people and targeted a black audience as well as the large white audience. Perhaps the major difference between *Amos 'n' Andy* and *The Jeffersons*, and a measure of the impact of relevance programming, can be seen in the roles of the two Georges. George "The Kingfish" Stevens on *Amos 'n' Andy* ducked his head, shuffled his feet, and said "Yas, Suh, Boss." On *The Jeffersons*, George Jefferson looked the world in the eye because he was the boss, a successful independent businessman.

The Jeffersons remained a hit well into the Ronald Reagan years, going off the air in 1985. By that time, socially conscious shows generally had lost their appeal. Their legacy, and the legacy of *The Jeffersons* in particular, can be seen in the shows that developed later.

Bibliography

Fiske, John. *Television Culture.* London: Routledge, 1989. A heavily sociological work that analyzes television through technical sociological research and studies.
Goldstein, Fred, and Stan Goldstein. *Prime-Time Television.* New York: Crown, 1983.

Combines text and pictures to present a vivid history of television from 1948 to 1983. Discusses most programs or series during this period.

Hefzallah, Ibrahim M. *Critical Viewing of Television: A Book for Parents and Teachers.* New York: University Press of America, 1987. A teacher of classes on critical viewing of television discusses how to understand television, how it affects viewers, and advice on becoming a critical viewer.

Mitz, Rick. *The Great TV Sitcom Book.* New York: Richard Marek, 1980. Covers virtually every situation comedy shown on television from 1949 to 1980. In addition to describing the shows, the author discusses social reference points and proposes reasons why the shows succeeded or failed. Good for placing *The Jeffersons* in the context of its time.

O'Connor, John, ed. *American History, American Television.* New York: Frederick Ungar, 1985. Discusses how television acts as a social force and why television deserves serious study. The essays included range over a broad variety of topics.

Rose, Brian G., ed. *TV Genres: A Handbook and Reference Guide.* Westport, Conn.: Greenwood Press, 1985. Explains how and why television shows fall into a limited number of formats. Cross-fertilization of genres sometimes occurs, as in the case of situation comedies that become issue oriented.

Michael R. Bradley

Cross-References

Stormy Weather Offers New Film Roles to African Americans (1940's), p. 1159; *I Spy* Debuts to Controversy (1965), p. 2044; Relevance Programs Change Entertainment Standards (1970's), p. 2197; *All in the Family* Introduces a New Style of Television Comedy (1971), p. 2234; *Roots* Dramatizes the African-American Experience (1977), p. 2397; *The Cosby Show* Makes Television History (1984), p. 2532.

MARLEY'S *NATTY DREAD* ESTABLISHES REGGAE'S POPULARITY

Category of event: Music
Time: February, 1975
Locale: Kingston, Jamaica

Natty Dread *was the first reggae album to achieve widespread popularity outside Jamaica, bringing a previously obscure musical form to the attention of a worldwide audience*

Principal personages:
BOB MARLEY (1945-1981), a Jamaican musician whose songs espoused social and political change and the Rastafarian way of life
RITA MARLEY, a member of the Wailers' backup singers, the I-Threes, and Bob Marley's wife
CHRIS BLACKWELL (1937-   ), a white Jamaican record producer and founder of Island Records
ASTON "FAMILY MAN" BARRETT (1946-   ), the Wailers' bass player from 1969 to 1981
CARLTON BARRETT (1950-   ), the Wailers' percussionist from 1969 to 1981
AL ANDERSON (1953-   ), a black American rock guitarist who joined the Wailers in 1974 and played on *Natty Dread*
BERNARD "TOUTER" HARVEY (1958-   ), the Wailers' organ player on *Natty Dread*
PETER TOSH (WINSTON HUBERT MCINTOSH, 1944-1987), an original member of the Wailers who went on to a successful solo career after leaving the group
NEVILLE "BUNNY" LIVINGSTON (1947-   ), a childhood friend of Bob Marley and original member of the Wailers who had a successful solo career after leaving the group

Summary of Event

The 1975 release of Bob Marley and the Wailers' *Natty Dread* and the tour that followed marked the first time that Jamaican reggae music achieved widespread international success and recognition. Although reggae enjoyed tremendous popularity in Jamaica, it had registered only an occasional hit, such as Jimmy Cliff's "Wonderful World, Beautiful People" (1969), Desmond Dekker's "Israelites" (1969), and Johnny Nash's "I Can See Clearly Now" (1972), on the European and American charts. Paul Simon's reggae-inspired "Mother and Child Reunion," recorded in Jamaica in 1971, and Eric Clapton's immensely successful 1974 cover version of Marley's "I Shot the Sheriff" also helped to bring reggae to the attention of a wider audience, but it was Marley's compelling aura of moral authority, social commitment, and personal charisma, coupled with the Wailers' masterful musicianship on *Natty Dread*, that inspired a worldwide interest in the music called reggae for the first time.

Reggae, like American blues, is "hard times" music that appeals directly to the downtrodden and disenfranchised. It is characterized by a distinctive, complex rhythm that emphasizes the first instead of the second beat; in reggae, the guitar functions mainly as a rhythm instrument, and the bass offers a melodic counterpart to the vocals. The tempo is slow, and the lyrics are often esoteric, containing references to Rastafarianism, African folktales, and Jamaican politics. Reggae's roots are in the traditional Jamaican folk music known as mento and American rhythm-and-blues and soul music, which reached Jamaica for the first time from Miami and New Orleans in the 1950's with the introduction of the transistor radio.

The radio, along with sound systems—huge speakers and generator-powered stereos mounted on the backs of flatbed trucks—brought the hottest new sounds, including the work of such favorite artists as Fats Domino, Johnny Ace, and Louis Jordan, to the Kingston slums. Competition for new hits was fierce; sound system disc jockeys scratched the labels off hit singles to obscure the records' origin, and violence was routine, as disc jockeys sent gangs of thugs out to steal hits from the competition. When the supply of hot rhythm-and-blues records began to dry up in the 1960's, Jamaican artists started to produce their own music to fuel the sound systems.

The first of this home-produced popular music was known as ska. Ska, bouncy music with the emphasis on the off beat, enjoyed a brief spurt of popularity in Britain and was popularized in America with Millie Small's recording of "My Boy Lollipop" in 1964. By 1965, ska had been replaced in Jamaica by "rock steady," which was slower and had a heavier rhythm. Rock steady evolved into reggae, which was heavily influenced by American soul music, particularly that of James Brown. The derivation of the word "reggae" is not known, although many believe the word is simply a description of the music's beat; it first appeared in the title of a 1968 Toots and the Maytals release, "Do the Reggay."

Bob Marley, whose music followed the course from ska to rock steady to reggae, was born in the isolated rural parish of St. Ann's on February 6, 1945, to nineteen-year-old Cedella Malcom Marley and Captain Norval Marley, a white Jamaican attached to the British West Indian Regiment. Captain Marley, bowing to family pressure, soon deserted his wife and son, and Cedella, tiring of country life, moved to the teeming slums of Kingston. Bob joined her there at age fourteen and, like most Kingston youths, became enthralled with the American music he heard throughout the slums. Introduced to record producer Leslie Kong by fellow musician Jimmy Cliff, Marley recorded his first single, "Judge Not," in 1962. It attracted little attention, but a year later, Marley and his friends Peter Tosh and Bunny Livingston, along with vocalist Junior Braithewaite and two female backup singers, recorded "Simmer

Down" for record producer Clement Dodd, and the record became a big hit in Jamaica. Known as the Wailing Wailers, Marley and his friends quickly became Jamaica's top group, addressing themselves directly to the "rude boys," tough ghetto youths who fashioned themselves after American gangsters.

For the next eight years, the Wailers recorded for nearly every producer in Kingston, turning out hits but making little money until they signed with Chris Blackwell of Island Records in 1972. Blackwell, a white Jamaican with aristocratic roots and a reputation for honesty and artistic integrity, advanced the group money and allowed them the freedom to create more sophisticated and political music. The result, _Catch a Fire_, the band's first album to be released in the United States, was critically well received but did not attract a popular audience. Later in 1973, _Burnin'_, considered by many the purest of Marley's music, was released but also received little popular recognition.

With the release of _Natty Dread_ in 1975, reggae found a wide international audience. Now billed as Bob Marley and the Wailers, the group no longer included Peter Tosh and Bunny Livingston, who had left to pursue solo careers. The Wailers in 1975 consisted of Marley, Aston "Family Man" Barrett on bass, his brother Carlton on percussion, Al Anderson on guitar, Bernard "Touter" Harvey on organ, and the backup singers the I-Threes, including Bob's wife, Rita. The album contained the Wailers' most sophisticated and political music to date, including "Them Belly Full (But We Hungry)," a warning to Jamaican Prime Minister Michael Manley that "a hungry crowd is an angry crowd"; "Revolution," a declaration of revolutionary struggle; "Rebel Music (Three O'Clock Roadblock)," a condemnation of random roadside searches by army troops; and the title track, an anthem glorifying the Rastafarian life.

Reggae became closely associated with Rastafarianism, a religious movement founded in Jamaica and based on the belief that the former Emperor Haile Selassie I of Ethiopia was god, or "Jah," on earth and that he would arrange for the return of all people of African ancestry to Africa. Rastas shun alcohol, tobacco, meat, and shellfish, outlaw the combing or cutting of their hair (thus the "dreadlocks," the long matted plaits of hair worn by most Rastas), and consider the smoking of marijuana, or "ganja," to be a religious rite.

From 1976 on, Marley's concerts were sellouts throughout the world; he toured Canada, the United States, France, England, Italy, West Germany, Spain, Scandinavia, Ireland, Holland, Belgium, Switzerland, Japan, Australia, New Zealand, and the Ivory Coast. He sold more than $240 million worth of albums, including _Bob Marley and the Wailers Live!_ (1975), _Rastaman Vibration_ (1976), _Exodus_ (1977), _Kaya_ (1978), _Survival_ (1979), and _Uprising_ (1980). Marley died from cancer in 1981 at the height of his popularity and influence, leaving an enormous legacy of music and political and social change.

Impact of Event

After the release of _Natty Dread_, reggae found an audience outside Jamaica, particularly in Europe, South America, and Africa, and became a powerful tool of social and political change in Third World countries. Bob Marley became an influential figure not only in the music world but in the realms of politics and religion as well. More than a rock star, Marley was a hero of almost mythic proportions in the Caribbean and Africa. Reporters from around the world made the trek to Kingston to interview Marley, who used the opportunity as a kind of ministry to expound upon his religion and philosophy and the plight of his country, bringing the tenets of a previously obscure religion and a small developing country to the attention of the world.

Marley's musical success allowed him to become an extremely successful spokesman for the Rastafarian faith. Largely as a result of the missionary zeal with which Marley and the Wailers spread the message through their music, Rastafarianism grew from a fringe cult in Jamaica to a widely practiced belief. Songs such as "Natty Dread" portrayed Rastas as cultural heroes rather than as dangerous "crazies" and did much to change the public perception of the religion. Marley himself was thought by many Jamaicans to be a "mylaman," or holy man, with the power to banish or destroy evil spirits.

Marley's political influence was equally great, although he often disavowed any interest in politics or politicians. He was sometimes aligned with Michael Manley's People's National Party (PNP), and his words were carefully heeded by Edward Seaga and the Jamaica Labour Party (JLP) as well, for both politicans were keenly aware oᶠ the massive sway Marley held over the Jamaican people. On December 3, 1976, Markt and his friends and family were targets of an assassination attempt only two day, before Marley was to give a free concert in Kingston in an attempt to bring warring factions together. Although injured, Marley performed the concert as planned, singing before fifty thousand people; Rita Marley performed in her hospital robe and bandages. The assassins were never apprehended or identified, but the attempt testifies to Marley's immense political and social influence in Jamaica.

Marley's reputation as a black freedom fighter and reggae's powerful message reached much farther than Jamaica. In 1980, he was invited to perform at the official Independence Day ceremonies of the new nation-state of Zimbabwe to celebrate the end of British rule. Marley's appearance created such hysteria that the ceremonies had to be stopped for forty-five minutes until the crowd could be controlled.

Reggae achieved its peak of worldwide popularity from 1975 to 1980. The success of *Natty Dread* paved the way for other Jamaican artists such as Jimmy Cliff and Toots and the Maytals to reach a wider audience. Former Wailers members Peter Tosh and Bunny Livingston, both of whom had successful solo careers in Jamaica, also began to reach a wider audience. Burning Spear (Winston Rodney, also born in St. Ann's Parish), whose music continues the Marley tradition of reggae concerned with political oppression and mystical transcendence, remained popular into the 1990's. Several of Marley's children performed and recorded as the Melody Makers, and Bob's son, Ziggy, went on to a successful solo career.

Many other bands were strongly influenced by reggae, including the English punk bands of the 1970's; in particular, the adventurous and critically praised band the Clash, who had several songs produced by Jamaican record producer Lee "Scratch" Perry, drew from reggae sources. The success of reggae also inspired a brief revival of ska in Britain, performed by such bands as the Specials and the English Beat. The most successful pop band to incorporate reggae was the Police, who used a reggae beat in such hit songs as "Roxanne" and "Can't Stand Losing You." Many other popular artists, including Paul Simon, Stevie Wonder, Blondie, the Grateful Dead, Jimmy Buffett, Elvis Costello, Ry Cooder, Joan Armatrading, the J. Geils Band, and the Rolling Stones, incorporated reggae influences into their music.

Bibliography

Davis, Stephen. *Bob Marley.* Garden City, N.Y.: Doubleday, 1985. An extremely thorough biography that covers in detail all aspects of Marley's life, including his childhood, his youth in the Trenchtown slums, and his career as a musician. Includes pictures, an excellent bibliography, and an index.

McCormack, Ed. "Bob Marley with a Bullet." *Rolling Stone* (August 12, 1976): 37-41. Article examines the Kingston scene after *Natty Dread*'s success. Author visits Kingston slums, spending some time with a group of Rastafarians, and informally interviews Marley.

Thomas, Michael. "The Wild Side of Paradise: Steaming with the Rude Boys, the Rastas and Reggae." *Rolling Stone* (July 19, 1973): 44-50. Article evokes the atmosphere of Kingston in the early 1970's, before reggae became an international phenomenon. Discusses the music scene, the life of the Rastas and the rude boys, and Jamaican politics. Discusses Marley at length, as well as other Jamaican musicians.

White, Timothy. "Bob Marley." In *Rock Lives.* New York: Henry Holt, 1990. Recounts a conversation the author had with Marley in September of 1975 at Marley's home in Kingston. Marley discusses his musical influences, his children, his religion, the future of reggae, and the history of the Wailers. Very helpful in understanding Jamaica, Marley, and his music.

_____. *Catch a Fire: The Life of Bob Marley.* New York: Holt, Rinehart and Winston, 1983. A valuable source for background material on the social, cultural, political, and religious milieu that shaped Bob Marley, as well as an engrossing biography. Contains pictures, a bibliography and index, and an extensive discography.

Mary Virginia Davis

Cross-References

Berry's "Maybellene" Popularizes Rock and Roll (1955), p. 1635; Presley Becomes a Rock-and-Roll Sensation (1956), p. 1705; Gordy Founds Motown Records (1959), p. 1790; The Beatles Revolutionize Popular Music (1963), p. 1944; The Rolling Stones Release *Out of Our Heads* (1965), p. 2027; Dylan Performs with Electric

Instruments (1965), p. 2038; Brown Wins a Grammy for "Papa's Got a Brand New Bag" (1966), p. 2059; Hendrix Releases *Are You Experienced?* (1967), p. 2092; Wonder Releases *Innervisions* (1973), p. 2294; Rap Goes Platinum with Run-D.M.C.'s *Raising Hell* (1986), p. 2582.

JOPLIN'S *TREEMONISHA* IS STAGED
BY THE HOUSTON OPERA

Category of event: Music
Time: May 23, 1975
Locale: Houston, Texas

Scott Joplin's long-neglected opera Treemonisha *received its first professional full-scale production, sixty-four years after its publication*

> *Principal personages:*
> SCOTT JOPLIN (1868-1917), an African-American composer of ragtime music who aspired to write art music
> LOTTIE JOPLIN (1873-1950), Scott Joplin's second wife, whose support enabled him to work on *Treemonisha*
> HARRY LAWRENCE FREEMAN (1869-1954), the first African-American composer to write an opera
> VERA BRODSKY LAWRENCE (1909-   ), the editor of the collected works of Scott Joplin
> JOSHUA RIFKIN (1944-   ), an American musicologist and pianist whose recordings sparked the Joplin revival
> GUNTHER SCHULLER (1925-   ), an American composer whose orchestration of *Treemonisha* was used for the Houston Opera production

Summary of Event

Scott Joplin had earned a reputation as a legendary performer and composer of ragtime piano music, yet he had ambitions toward enlarging and expanding the form. In 1897, he enrolled at the George R. Smith College for Negroes in Sedalia, Missouri, to study advanced composition. His "Ragtime Dance" of 1902 included words and dance steps and was virtually a ragtime ballet. In the fall of 1903, he made his first venture into opera with the "ragtime opera" entitled *A Guest of Honor*, which he took on an unsuccessful tour in Missouri and Iowa; the score and parts of this work have been lost. Joplin made ventures into composition more serious than ragtime with his concert waltz "Bethena" (1905) and "Solace, Mexican Serenade" (1909), which featured a Habanera rhythm.

All of these works laid the groundwork for *Treemonisha*, which Joplin began in 1908, after his move to New York, and completed in 1910. His attempts to find a publisher having been unsuccessful, he had the piano-vocal score of the opera published at his own expense in 1911.

On the strength of a glowing review of the opera in *The American Musician*, Joplin tried to get his work performed. He consulted with Harry Lawrence Freeman, the first African-American composer to write an opera (*The Martyr*, first performed in Denver in 1893), and made some revisions in the piano-vocal score.

An attempt to have *Treemonisha* performed at the Lafayette Theater in Harlem in

1913 proved unsuccessful. A run-through for prospective backers of the production, done without costumes, scenery, or orchestra, was given possibly as early as 1911 or as late as 1915. Joplin, whose pianistic skills had sharply declined, played the orchestral part on the piano.

The performance was a disaster. The audience may have been expecting a musical comedy on the order of those written by Will Marion Cook, a professionally trained musician who had studied at Oberlin College and in Europe and who had sometimes collaborated with the poet Paul Laurence Dunbar. Joplin had been isolated in New York from the black bourgeois musical establishment that Cook represented, perhaps because ragtime was regarded as a "low-class" music with associations of the saloon and the bordello.

Others may have been repelled by the plot of the opera, set in post-Reconstruction rural Arkansas. In the first act, conjurers try to sell magic potions to Ned and Monisha, but are driven away by the couple's daughter, Treemonisha. Monisha describes how she was found and educated and a parson preaches a sermon punctuated with choral responses. The conjurers return and kidnap Treemonisha. Remus dresses in a scarecrow suit and goes off with the field hands to rescue her.

In the second act, the conjurers sing of their superstitions. Treemonisha is brought in and is accused of trying to cut off the conjurers' source of income; the conjurers threaten to punish her by pushing her into a wasp's nest. Eight bears then enter and engage in a musical frolic. Remus, dressed in the scarecrow's suit, then frightens the conjurers, who think he is the devil. The scene changes to a cotton plantation; the plantation workers direct Remus and Treemonisha home and engage in a dance.

Treemonisha and Remus return to general rejoicing. The leaders of the conjurers are brought in and threatened with a beating, but Treemonisha asks that they be forgiven. After musical lectures by Remus and Ned, the conjurers are pardoned, the field hands ask Treemonisha to be their leader, and the opera ends with singing and dancing by Treemonisha and the assembled company. To many in the audience, the plot must have reminded them of the days of their grandparents, a period that the black bourgeoisie were doing their best to forget.

Joplin had been obsessed with *Treemonisha* since its completion, and he had neglected composition of piano rags and teaching in order to get the work performed. The message of his opera was that education would be the salvation of his race (there may also have been elements of the plot that had personal autobiographical significance for him). Joplin believed that the work would prove him a composer of substance and establish him as an artist. The work's failure sent him into a profound depression and probably triggered the dementia for which he was institutionalized in 1916; he died the following year.

Treemonisha and Joplin were forgotten after his death except among a few connoisseurs of ragtime music. In 1968, Joshua Rifkin recorded several of Joplin's piano rags (the "Maple Leaf Rag," his first successful work, had remained in the repertoire, albeit in jazz versions). Subsequently, Vera Brodsky Lawrence edited a two-volume collection of Joplin's music, including the piano-vocal score of *Treemonisha*;

twenty-four publishers rejected her proposal until the New York Public Library, with support from various foundations, published the set in 1971.

The first full-scale performance of *Treemonisha* was given at Morehouse College in Atlanta, Georgia, in 1972. Katherine Dunham did the choreography, and the African-American composer T. J. Anderson orchestrated the work. A more professional performance took place later that year near Washington, D.C., with a new orchestration by William Bolcom that one reviewer compared to the work of Hector Berlioz. Reviewers praised the work but found the productions uneven, with fine solo and choral singing and dancing but poor stage work that made the opera resemble a minstrel show.

The Houston Opera production of 1975 has since proven to be the definitive version of *Treemonisha*. Gunther Schuller, a jazz scholar as well as composer who had previously reconstructed contemporaneous orchestrations of Joplin's ragtime pieces, scored the opera in keeping with the pit orchestras of the early years of the century, avoiding such incongruities as jazz-era saxophones and echoes of the sophisticated scoring of Richard Strauss or Giacomo Puccini. The production, which attracted audiences of up to twenty-five thousand, was later taken to the Uris Theater on New York's Broadway, in keeping with its character as a vintage musical rather than as a grand opera, and was recorded by Deutsche Grammophon. Subsequently, the production was released on videocassette.

Impact of Event

The Houston Opera's production of *Treemonisha* came to be regarded as the definitive version, for staging, costumes, and sets (the painter Romare Bearden was a consultant) as well as for the music. Those concerned about the opera's representation of African-American stereotypes were silenced by Carmen Balthrop, the singer who performed the role of Treemonisha: "Mammy talk? Pickaninny costumes? It doesn't embarrass me at all. That's the way it was."

Comparisons were made with other musical dramatic works of the time. It is highly doubtful that Joplin knew of the work of his contemporary Henry F. Gilbert, a white composer who used African-inspired melodies in his compositions. In 1906, Gilbert began an opera inspired by Joel Chandler Harris' "Uncle Remus" tales; Chandler's estate, however, refused to release the copyright, and the opera was abandoned. Gilbert was able to salvage the overture as the *Comedy Overture on Negro Themes* (1912) and as various set-numbers for his *Negro Dances* for piano.

Joplin was also in all likelihood not aware of the opera *Koanga* (1897), by Frederick Delius, which was set in eighteenth century Florida and which featured miscegenation and a slave revolt; *Koanga* is remarkable for its mixture of characters, sympathetic blacks and villainous whites. Delius, an expatriate Englishman living in France, had spent two years of his young manhood in the American South and had absorbed the African-American idiom. The text of *Koanga* is highly stilted (neither the librettist who worked with Delius' scenario nor Delius' German wife, who finished and translated the libretto for the German production, had any conception of American life), and the musical idiom is replete with the lush post-Romantic harmony that was later to become a staple of the film scores of Technicolor musicals. The opera was performed, in German, in Elbersfeld, Germany, in 1903 but was not given again until after the composer's death; however, a wedding dance from *Koanga* became well known as an orchestral piece, "La Calinda."

It would be unreasonable to compare Joplin's opera with such contemporary European works of the second decade of the century as Giacomo Puccini's *Fanciulla* (1910), Richard Strauss's *Der Rosenkavalier* (1911), Igor Stravinsky's *The Nightingale* (1914), or Béla Bartók's *Duke Bluebeard's Castle* (1918). These are works in completely different musical idioms and for entirely different theaters. More apt comparisons can be made with the musicals of the time, especially Victor Herbert's *Sweethearts* (1913) and the productions of Will Marion Cook.

George Gershwin's *Porgy and Bess* (1935) is the work most often compared to *Treemonisha*. The similarities of the two works include an all-black cast, a Southern setting, and a structure of individual set-numbers linked by spoken dialogue (the dialogue of *Treemonisha*, however, is lost). The setting of *Porgy and Bess*, however, is different, as is the musical idiom, which incorporates the influence of jazz and the revolution in the musical theater around 1920. Moreover, some writers have complained that neither the book nor the score of *Porgy and Bess* fully reflects the African-American experience. The most important similarity between the two works is that each features an all-black cast; the works can thus effectively be done in alternation by black theater companies.

Treemonisha is not without its weaknesses. The characters are one-dimensional, and some of the smaller parts drift in and out of the action. Joplin's poetry (he wrote the scenario, the words to be sung, the stage directions, and even the choreography) reflects his haphazard formal education, and harmonic clichés are used to intensify the moments of dramatic tension. The weakest set-numbers are those seeking to impart a high tone to the opera, such as the chorus "We Want You for Our Leader," which is written in the style of a church anthem, or the lectures performed in drawing-room ballad style by Remus and Ned. More successful are the numbers in a popular idiom, such as the square dance in act 1 and a barbershop quartet performance by cotton pickers in act 2. The most effective numbers, such as the sermon with choral response in act 1, the finales of the second and third acts, and the "Frolic of the Bears" in act 2, a ragtime scherzo, reflect the African-American musical experience and Joplin's ragtime background. Though *Treemonisha* is an uneven work, its best numbers merit the opera's retention as a repertory item.

Foreign productions of *Treemonisha* soon followed. The first, given in Italy in a mainland suburb of Venice, was performed with two pianos, was sung in heavily accented English, and was given by performers without the faintest understanding of the ragtime idiom. A critic remarked that the show was like an animated production of "Little Black Sambo." Subsequent productions with orchestra were given in Turin in 1980 (in Italian), Helsinki in 1981 (in Finnish), and Giessen, West Germany, in 1984 (in English). The critics were for the most part unaware of the cultural background of *Treemonisha*; many praised its sincerity and the liveliness of the productions, but most found the work akin to operetta and thought the text naïve. *Treemonisha* is an important document in the history of American music. It represents the idealization of the African-American experience during a difficult period (the post-Reconstruction South) by someone who was closer to it than any of his musical colleagues. This idealization is largely achieved through the opera's music, which is successful in direct proportion to its reflection of its African-American roots, and through the message of education triumphing over ignorance. Joplin's misfortune lay in his being ahead of his time, before it became possible for an African-American to be accepted as a composer of art music and before the Harlem where Joplin lived had become a center of black culture. Justifiably, he received a posthumous Pulitzer Prize in 1976 for *Treemonisha*, sixty years after his mental illness caused by the work's failure had compelled him to be institutionalized.

Bibliography

Berlin, Edward. "Scott Joplin's *Treemonisha* Years." *American Music* 9 (Fall, 1991): 260-276. By far the best study of Joplin's life during his years in New York. Updates all previous biographies.

Blesh, Rudi, and Harriet Janis. *They All Played Ragtime.* 4th ed. New York: Oak Publishers, 1971. A pioneering study of ragtime music. Its laudatory and detailed description of *Treemonisha* undoubtedly sparked interest in reviving Joplin's opera.

Gammond, Peter. *Scott Joplin and the Ragtime Era.* New York: St. Martin's Press, 1975. A curious British book; its biographical information is mostly obsolete, but it contains some interesting social background and perspectives.

Haskins, James, with Kathleen Benson. *Scott Joplin.* Garden City, N.Y.: Doubleday, 1978. A more up-to-date biography than Gammond's. Contains facsimiles of a census and other documents and still gives the best picture of Joplin's early years and his stays in Sedalia and St. Louis.

Jones, Robert. "Treemonisha." *Opera News* 40 (September, 1975): 12-15. An extensive account of the Houston Opera production of Joplin's operatic masterpiece.

Joplin, Scott. *The Collected Works of Scott Joplin.* Edited by Vera B. Lawrence. 2 vols. New York: New York Public Library, 1971. Volume 2 contains the piano-vocal score of *Treemonisha*, with an introduction by Rudi Blesh and a preface by the singer Carman Moore.

Zimmermann, Christoph. "Giessen." *Opera* 35 (August, 1984): 906-907. An excellent illustration of the bewilderment and misunderstanding of the European critics of *Treemonisha*.

R. M. Longyear

Cross-References

Joplin Popularizes the Ragtime Style (1899), p. 13; Handy Ushers in the Commercial Blues Era (1910's), p. 252; The First Pulitzer Prizes Are Awarded (1915), p. 407; The Harlem Renaissance Celebrates African-American Culture (1920's), p. 480; Gershwin's *Porgy and Bess* Opens in New York (1935), p. 1016.

SATURDAY NIGHT LIVE IS FIRST BROADCAST

Category of event: Television and radio
Time: October 11, 1975
Locale: New York, New York

Saturday Night Live, *the first network comedy-variety series aimed at young viewers since* Rowan and Martin's Laugh-In, *proved an enduring success and launched the careers of a talented group of young actors and writers*

> *Principal personages:*
> LORNE MICHAELS (1945-   ), a comedy writer and the original producer of *Saturday Night Live*
> AL FRANKEN (1951-   ), a writer and occasional sketch performer for *Saturday Night Live*
> CHEVY CHASE (1943-   ), a writer and performer who left the show during its second season to pursue an acting career
> JOHN BELUSHI (1949-1982), one of the original cast members, who left the show after four seasons to work in Hollywood
> DAN AYKROYD (1952-   ), an original cast member who left the show in 1979
> GILDA RADNER (1946-1989), a talented member of the show's original cast whose career was cut short by cancer

Summary of Event

On April 22, 1975, Dick Ebersol, the director of late-night programming for the National Broadcasting Company (NBC), announced that a late-night comedy-variety series, *Saturday Night Live*, would premiere on the network that autumn. NBC had been broadcasting reruns of Johnny Carson's *The Tonight Show* in its 11:30 P.M. time slot, and Ebersol's idea of replacing the reruns with an hour and a half of live sketch comedy seemed a gamble at best. Lorne Michaels, who had written for *Rowan and Martin's Laugh-In*, was named as the new show's producer.

Michaels immediately recruited a stable of talented young writers, including Al Franken and Tom Davis from Los Angeles, Alan Zweibel from Queens, and Michael O'Donoghue and Anne Beatts from the staff of *National Lampoon*. Legend has it that Chevy Chase, originally employed as a writer (he had earlier written for *The Smothers Brothers Comedy Hour* and *Mad* magazine) and later included in the cast, signed on when Michaels met him while waiting in line at a theater. Next came the actors who made up the show's permanent cast, the Not Ready for Prime Time Players. From the beginning, two comedy club institutions served as the spawning grounds for many of the show's most successful performers: the Groundlings in Los Angeles provided such talents as Laraine Newman, Phil Hartman, and Jon Lovitz, and the Toronto and Chicago branches of Second City produced *Saturday Night Live* stars John Belushi, Dan Aykroyd, Gilda Radner, Bill Murray, Martin Short, and

Mike Myers. Along with Aykroyd, Belushi, Chase, Newman, and Radner, Garrett Morris and Jane Curtin filled out the original repertory cast.

When *Saturday Night Live* premiered on October 11, 1975, New York was sliding toward fiscal bankruptcy, Boston and Cincinnati were locked in an epic World Series battle, Gerald Ford had not long before pardoned Richard Nixon for all the latter's Watergate crimes, and NBC was solidly in second place among the three television networks. By general consent, the first show was not an entirely auspicious beginning, nor was its format typical of what was to come. Comedian George Carlin hosted, wearing a T-shirt and a three-piece suit, but he declined to act in the sketches (as would become the norm for subsequent hosts), preferring to do several stand-up routines instead. Carlin's material was not always original, and his one genuinely successful routine (satirizing religion) provoked outrage among some network executives and viewers. Musical guests Janis Ian and Billy Preston each performed two numbers, and the show was top-heavy with non-sketch acts, not all equally successful. Neither of the advertised regular features, a film by Albert Brooks and a sketch featuring Jim Henson's Muppets, was particularly funny. By contrast, Audy Kaufman's lip-synching of the theme song from *Mighty Mouse* was inspired.

The show began with a "cold opening," no announcements or credits—a daring move that would become a trademark. The opening sketch, "The Wolverines," featured Belushi as an immigrant come to the apartment of his English teacher (played by writer O'Donoghue) for a lesson. After teacher and pupil speak some absurd sentences about wolverines and badgers, O'Donoghue grabs his chest and keels over, presumably having suffered a fatal heart attack. Belushi is bemused at first, but soon he apes the attack and falls to the floor. Chevy Chase then enters as a stagehand and shouts the now-familiar opening line, "Live, from New York, it's *Saturday Night!*" Other goofy sketches included the introduction of the ongoing characters the Bees in a mock soap opera, "Bees Hospital," and a parody of human-interest interview shows called "Shark Attacks." The sketches were interspersed with numbers by guest performers, who dominated overall.

Untypical as this first format was, it nevertheless introduced some of the show's enduring features. "Weekend Update" spoofed the news and included the show's first jabs at President Ford. Several advertisement parodies were inserted after sketches; and it was not always easy for viewers to tell the joke from the real thing. (During the third show, an engineer at WNBC, the network's flagship station in New York City, mistook a parody for a real advertisement and substituted a local commercial for it. The mix-up sent Michaels into paroxysms, and he threatened to quit on the spot.) Most of all, the Not Ready for Prime Time Players displayed their talents as sketch artists, adept at character portrayal in the wacky situations dreamed up by the still largely untested writers. The sketches would improve, and the performers would mature, but the unbridled zaniness that Michaels had so much admired in the British television show *Monty Python's Flying Circus* was already evident in abundance. By midseason, *Saturday Night Live* would become a runaway hit, and the show would garner a raft of Emmy Awards the following May.

Impact of Event

On the occasion of *Saturday Night Live*'s fifteenth anniversary special, *Newsweek* would call it "a show that blew apart and redrew the boundaries of television comedy." That judgment seems only partly just, arguably less so in later years than in those first heady seasons when both writers and performers let their irreverence range over politics, popular culture, America's unbridled commodity fetishism, showbusiness icons—indeed, the very medium in which the show's creators made their living. From its opening season onward, the show's deadliest humor has emerged in its "Weekend Update" spoofs of network news and in its caricatures of famous people, from Gilda Radner's unforgettable Barbara Walters, Chevy Chase's Gerald Ford, and Dan Aykroyd's Richard Nixon and Jimmy Carter impersonations to Dana Carvey's send-ups of Johnny Carson, George Bush, Casey Kasem, and George Michael. For example, in 1992, "Weekend Update" host Kevin Nealon caught the absurdity of the moment precisely when he deadpanned that President George Bush "visited South-Central Los Angeles this week, and he was shocked when he actually had to see black people up close."

In an early, generally shrewd appreciation published in *The New Yorker*, Michael Arlen located *Saturday Night Live*'s roots in two principal developments of post-World War II comedy. The first was the emergence, in stand-up and improvisation, of biting topical satire, the kind of comedy perfected by Mike Nichols and Elaine May, Mort Sahl, Shelley Berman, and, most famously, Lenny Bruce. The second was what Arlen called "a comedy of surplus education," associated principally with such British creations as the radio program *The Goon Show* and *Monty Python's Flying Circus.* Arlen discerned in the original *Saturday Night Live* a product appealing to a well-educated, mostly youthful audience who were media-wise and thus receptive to the show's Brechtian knowingness. Yet Arlen also, if only in passing, put his finger on another aspect that remained a staple of *Saturday Night Live*'s comic spirit. He mentioned the historical precedent of *Your Show of Shows*, the Sid Caesar and Imogene Coca vehicle that set the early standard—seldom equaled—for television comedy-variety shows. The sheer zaniness of *Your Show of Shows* was recaptured in such *Saturday Night Live* staples as the skits about the Coneheads, the Killer Bees, and the Widettes and in Belushi's various samurai routines. Subsequent casts would rarely rise to this level of comic absurdity but tended instead to excel at parodies, such as Eddie Murphy's hilarious Buckwheat character or his takeoff on the children's television show *Misterogers' Neighborhood.* Over the years, *Saturday Night Live* evolved into a less manic, cooler, arguably more cynical comic vehicle, a development symbolized by Dennis Miller's five-year run from 1986 to 1991 as "Weekend Update" anchor. Unlike Chase's mostly deadpan delivery or Jane Curtin's super-serious approach, Miller's contemptuous, know-it-all sneer left no room for doubt about who the targets of the show's humor were.

From the first, however, *Saturday Night Live* exhibited a signal weakness in two areas: gender and race. Radner, Newman, and Curtin participated in some of the most famous sketches (including the Nerds, Coneheads, and Widettes segments), and Radner performed some of the show's most memorable characters (including Baba Wawa, Roseann Roseannadanna, and Emily Litella), but they were invariably overshadowed—in sheer numbers of parts and lines delivered, for one—by the men, first Chase, then Belushi and Aykroyd, and later Bill Murray. After their departure, no female performer even approached the centrality of the men on the show.

Saturday Night Live's racial imbalance has also been evident from the beginning. Garrett Morris had his career effectively ruined by his tenure there, and in later years, only Eddie Murphy emerged as a dominant black personality. *Saturday Night Live* writers have often aimed at political correctness, savaging white racism with some regularity; yet the sketches written for black actors and hosts have, for the most part, been embarrassing, as Cicely Tyson complained when she appeared during the first season. The differences between *Saturday Night Live* and *In Living Color*, a successful 1990's comedy show featuring a largely black cast and crew, illustrate the former show's questionable racial politics starkly.

Another of *Saturday Night Live*'s notable aspects has been its role as a showcase for contemporary music. From the reunion—temporary, to be sure—of Paul Simon and Art Garfunkel on the second show in 1975 to the 1992 appearance of Public Enemy, *Saturday Night Live* has proven an attractive venue for successful artists. Even Paul McCartney appeared on the show. Musical guests are admittedly no innovation to variety shows, but it was *Saturday Night Live*'s signal contribution to feature avant-garde groups and individual performers years before they would become a staple of cable viewing on Music Television (MTV).

It is difficult to know how late-night television—and television comedy generally—would have evolved if *Saturday Night Live* had never aired, but the show's satiric approach clearly helped to pave the way for such subsequent successes as *Late Night with David Letterman*, *The Simpsons*, *In Living Color*, and MTV's *Comedy Club*. MTV itself has even returned the compliment by airing reruns of *Saturday Night Live* shows. *Saturday Night Live* brought cutting-edge comedy from the comedy clubs into mass media, showcasing new talent and creating a mass audience for offbeat, satirical humor, particularly among the young.

Many of *Saturday Night Live*'s mainstays were launched into stardom as a result of their tenure with the show. Aykroyd, Murray, and Chase each went on to successful film careers, as did frequent *Saturday Night Live* host Steve Martin. Jane Curtin went on to star in the situation comedy *Kate and Allie*. Belushi's and Radner's untimely deaths cut short promising careers, however, and Morris all but dropped out of sight. Undoubtedly, the most successful *Saturday Night Live* alumnus has been Eddie Murphy. His reputation as a stand-up comic soared after he joined the show, and his films, for the most part, proved apt vehicles for his multiple talents.

Still, few of the subsequent efforts by the show's cast have equaled the comic genius and satirical brilliance of *Saturday Night Live*'s best sketches and characters. Perhaps, as many commentators have noted, later incarnations have lacked some of the daring and venom of the show's early years. If so, however, the program's appeal demonstrably broadened, as more women and more middle-aged adults began to watch. Beyond doubt, *Saturday Night Live* has made an indelible imprint on American mass-media culture and, arguably, on political consciousness.

Bibliography

Arlen, Michael. "A Crack in the Greasepaint." *The New Yorker* 51 (November 24, 1975): 159-166. A fine early appreciation emphasizing *Saturday Night Live*'s relationship to other kinds of postwar comedy.

Barol, Bill, and Jennifer Foote. "Saturday Night Lives!" *Newsweek* 114 (September 25, 1989): 40-45. An assessment on the occasion of the show's fifteenth anniversary.

Billard, Mary. "Live for Fifteen Years, It's . . . 'Saturday Night'!" *Rolling Stone* (October 5, 1989): 65-70, 150. A more informative, less puffy piece than Barol and Foote's, though still filled with admiration for *Saturday Night Live*'s achievements.

Hill, Doug, and Jeff Weingrad. *Saturday Night: A Backstage History of "Saturday Night Live."* New York: William Morrow, 1986. Probably the best single book on the show, chronicling its beginnings and early success, then its decline after the departure of Lorne Michaels. Leaves off at 1985 and is less interesting on the show's middle period.

Radner, Gilda. *It's Always Something.* New York: Simon & Schuster, 1989. An autobiography, by turns painful, moving, and funny, of Radner's last years. Focuses on her marriage to Gene Wilder and her fight against the ovarian cancer that killed her.

"Rolling Stone" Visits "Saturday Night Live." Garden City, N.Y.: Dolphin Books, 1979. A compilation of interviews and articles from *Saturday Night Live*'s premier early chronicler.

Waters, Harry F., and Janet Huck. "Laughing All the Way." *Newsweek* 86 (December, 1975): 73. A brief, generally favorable early assessment.

Woodward, Bob. *Wired: The Short Life and Fast Times of John Belushi.* A biography of Belushi that documents the comedian's drug use in great detail.

Zoglin, Richard. "At 15, *Saturday Night* Lives." *Time* 134 (September 25, 1989): 75. A short, somewhat critical notice for the show's fifteenth anniversary.

Michael Sprinker

Cross-References

Variety Shows Dominate Television Programming (1948), p. 1383; *The Tonight Show* Becomes an American Institution (1954), p. 1623; *Rowan and Martin's Laugh-In* Is the Top Show on Television (1968), p. 2115; *Monty Python's Flying Circus* Captures Audiences Worldwide (1969), p. 2174; *The Simpsons* Debuts, Anchoring the Fledgling Fox Network (1990), p. 2652.

THE SEX PISTOLS SPARK PUNK ROCK'S MUSICAL INSURRECTION

Category of event: Music
Time: November, 1975-January, 1978
Locale: London, England

Standing a complacent record industry on its ear, the Sex Pistols generated a new wave of excitement in popular music

Principal personages:
JOHNNY ROTTEN (JOHN LYDON, 1956-   ), the Sex Pistols' aggressively charismatic lead singer and front man
MALCOLM MCLAREN (1946-   ), the former student radical and boutique owner who conceived the idea for the band and who managed it
SID VICIOUS (JOHN SIMON RITCHIE, 1957-1979), the bassist who replaced Matlock and who later died of a drug overdose
PAUL COOK (1956-   ), the drummer for the Sex Pistols
STEVE JONES (1955-   ), the guitarist for the Sex Pistols
GLEN MATLOCK (1956-   ) the Sex Pistols' bassist until 1977

Summary of Event

In 1975, Malcolm McLaren, an anarchist veteran of the Paris riots of 1968 who had worked as the manager of the protopunk band the New York Dolls in the band's final days, was the owner of a trendy London boutique called Sex. With England in its worst economic straits since World War II and a rising tide of unemployed youth angry over the hypocrisies of British society, McLaren began to imagine forming a rock group that could capture that rage and turn it against a music industry that had long since harnessed the liberating potential of rock and roll and turned it into an engine for corporate profit.

Glen Matlock, a part-time employee of Sex who played bass with guitarist Steve Jones and drummer Paul Cook, told McLaren that the three were looking for a singer. McLaren approached John Lydon, a surly youth who often hung around the jukebox at Sex, and asked him if he wanted the job. Lydon—whose lack of personal hygiene allegedly led Jones to dub him Johnny Rotten—had no singing experience, but that hardly mattered. As Cook later explained, "We weren't really interested in that 'cos we were still learning to play at the time." McLaren dubbed his new act the Sex Pistols.

The Sex Pistols performed their first gig at a suburban art-school dance in November of 1975, only to have their amplifiers unplugged. Word of mouth quickly spread about this crude, bilious, but powerfully energetic band that purveyed a musical sensibility that was soon labeled "punk rock." By the fall of 1976, the British Electrical and Musical Industries (EMI) record label outbid rival Polydor and signed the group to a lucrative contract. The Sex Pistols' first single, "Anarchy in the U.K." was released in December. The song's snarling, even vicious vocal—"I am an Antichrist!" screamed Rotten—and the group's repeated cursing on a nationally broadcast television program led EMI to terminate its contract with the band.

In March of 1977, Matlock left the Sex Pistols and was replaced by Sid Vicious. A&M records was the next label to take on the band, only to terminate its contract the following week. The Sex Pistols then signed with Virgin Records, which released the group's second single, "God Save the Queen," just in time for the monarch's Silver Jubilee. "God Save the queen/ the facist regime/ made you a moron," snarled Rotten on this song, repeating the phrase "There's no future" like an incantation. The song was banned from the nation's official pop chart; it became England's best-selling record of the summer anyway.

In July, the band virtually fled Great Britain to tour Europe. Its first album, *Never Mind the Bollocks, Here's the Sex Pistols*, seized the top of the British charts despite a ban on airplay. That fall, the album was released in the United States by Warner Bros. Records to wide critical acclaim. Broad media attention and an appearance on *Saturday Night Live* in December of 1977 stirred anticipation on the American music scene, as did plans for a nationwide tour in 1978.

Yet the Sex Pistols never attained the level of success in America that they had reached in Great Britain. Radio stations were cool to the band's music, and while shows at relatively small venues were well attended, this cult following was never transformed into a national one. Meanwhile, Rotten grew progressively more disgusted with the hype surrounding the band—and with McLaren. On January 14, 1978, he announced the group was finished after a concert in San Francisco.

Rotten himself went on to form a new band, Public Image Ltd., while Jones and Cook formed the Professionals. Vicious went solo. In October of 1978, he was charged with the murder of his girlfriend, Nancy Spungen. Vicious claimed her death was intentional drug overdose; before he could be tried, Vicious too died of a heroin overdose. The following year, Virgin released a Sex Pistols movie, *The Great Rock and Roll Swindle*, with an accompanying soundtrack. In 1986, Australian filmmaker Alex Cox directed *Sid and Nancy*, an account of Vicious' life.

In the wake of the Sex Pistols' early success, a whole movement of punk rock bands sprang to life. The most prominent of these was the Clash, formed by guitarist Joe Strummer after seeing the Sex Pistols. The Clash would enjoy a longer life (and more American chart success) than the Sex Pistols well into the 1980's. Other important punk bands included Generation X, the Buzzcocks, and the Damned. In the United States, a somewhat less caustic punk sensibility was expressed by a group of bands in New York that included the Ramones (whose 1978 tour of England had helped inspire the British punk scene) and Television.

The original musical spark embodied by the Sex Pistols had dissipated by the early 1980's, but the punk movement inspired a whole new generation of performers who went by the label "New Wave." These acts often lacked the acidic edge of punk rock, but many still injected an often angry passion into their work that revitalized popular music. Elvis Costello, the Pretenders, and the Cars were among the most prominent New Wave musicians. More recently, the musical roots of the highly successful Irish rock band U2 can be traced to punk-rock antecedents. Traces of the form can also be detected in some heavy-metal and thrash bands.

Impact of Event

To many outside observers in England and the United States, the whole punk-rock phenomenon was at best a cynical variation on music industry hype. At worst, it was a mindlessly destructive cultural movement that brought out the ugliest elements in youth culture. There is some truth to both charges; Malcolm McLaren very consciously manipulated industry machinery at great profit to himself and his clients, and the Sex Pistols could descend to truly revolting depths, as the title to their song "Belsen Was a Gas," a mock tribute to the Nazi gas chambers, suggested.

For its partisans, however, punk rock was a profoundly liberating social and political movement that exposed the latent hypocrisies and overt failures of Western society in an age of diminishing expectations. From this standpoint, punk was a deeply felt intellectual construct with genuinely democratic impulses.

In order to understand, if not endorse, such a position, one must consider the cultural and economic climate of England in the late 1970's. By that point in the postwar era, Great Britain's enervated Labour Party had not yet surrendered to the coming Thatcherite government of the 1980's but was clearly in its death throes. Unemployment was at an all-time high (though only about half as high as it would be a decade later). Government and the private sector were paralyzed by strikes. Alienated British youth, among them the notorious "skinheads," espoused racial and ethnic hatred and commited acts of violence.

Rock music, which had traditionally provided a vehicle for expressing cultural rebellion, now seemed dessicated and irrelevant. Art-rock bands such as Yes and Emerson, Lake and Palmer performed pseudoclassical music that labored under its own grandiosity. Even former rock heroes such as Rod Stewart, whose early work captured a pub-rock feel that later performers would try to emulate, had sold out for the glitz and superficiality of Hollywood. For the disciples of the emerging aesthetic of punk, the coarse sound of the Velvet Underground and the New York Dolls provided useful musical antecedents.

This was the context for the formation of the Sex Pistols and the band's heirs. In such a climate, not being able to play an instrument competently was an artistic statement, a willful refusal to buy into a thoroughly corrupted system of musical values. By seeking to efface what had become an enormous gap between performers and audiences, bands such as the Sex Pistols offered listeners the closest thing many had ever heard to a true musical democracy founded on mutual cultural and political disfranchisement.

Indeed, a passionate embrace of nihilism seemed genuinely cathartic. For many members of the generation that came of age after the 1960's, the hopeful promises of unending prosperity and an unquestioned belief in capitalism had become a shopworn lie. So when Johnny Rotten sang "There's no future for YOU," as he did over and over again on "God Save the Queen," he was expressing what many of his fans considered a fundamental truth that for too long had been suppressed.

Yet a musical philosophy built on ignorance and frustration, however potent, is inherently limited. Some punk bands, most notably the Clash, recognized this and emerged as an alternative voice within the movement. Whereas the Sex Pistols were the voice of pure, undistilled venom, the Clash sought to focus youth anger into a coherent program of political protest that borrowed heavily from Third World ideology and musical styles. This combination was most successfully realized on *London Calling* (1980), widely cited along with *Never Mind the Bollocks, Here's the Sex Pistols* as among the greatest rock records of all time. It is even more evident on the Clash's sprawling three-album set *Sandinista!* (1981). The astounding commercial success of *Combat Rock* (1982), with its hit single "Rock the Casbah," seemed to expose the contradiction between radical protest and mass acceptance, however, and the group soon devolved into factional infighting and broke up.

The United States never proved as receptive to punk rock as Great Britain did, perhaps because social and economic conditions were not as severe. Yet an American punk scene did form around the clubs of downtown New York. One of the best-known bands from this scene was the Ramones, whose less overtly political songs (typified by "I Wanna Be Sedated") found enthusiastic audiences. By the early 1980's, a few of these performers, among them the Talking Heads and Blondie, would become major stars.

In the strictest sense, punk rock was a failed insurrection. The record industry did not implode, nor did more conventional big-name acts (Fleetwood Mac, the Eagles, Bob Seger and the Silver Bullet Band) change their ways. By the mid-1980's, punk itself was dissipated and diluted beyond recognition. Politically, the electoral success of Margaret Thatcher and Ronald Reagan amounted to an emphatic rejection of all that punk rock represented.

To many listeners and critics, however, punk has had a lasting, and salutary, effect on popular music. In the 1950's, Elvis Presley blazed a path across a bland, conformist culture and awakened a nation to the power of rock music. In the 1960's, the Beatles revived what had become a co-opted musical form and demonstrated its artistic possibilities. In a very different way, the Sex Pistols specifically and punk rock generally raised powerful challenges to the musical status quo in the 1970's and pointed toward a valuable cultural alternative for many performers (such as the rap artists of the 1980's) that followed.

Bibliography

Bangs, Lester. "The Clash." In *Psychotic Reactions and Carburetor Dung*, edited by Greil Marcus. New York: Alfred A. Knopf, 1987. An amusing and incisive appreciation of the Clash and punk rock generally written from a decisively American perspective. Bangs, who died in 1982, had one of the most distinctive voices in rock criticism.

Hebdige, Dick. *Subculture: The Meaning of Style.* London: Methuen, 1979. A sociological study of British youth culture that has special relevance for students of punk rock. Widely regarded as one of the finest studies of its kind.

Marcus, Greil. "Anarchy in the U.K." In *The Rolling Stone Illustrated History of Rock and Roll*, edited by Jim Miller. Rev. ed. New York: Rolling Stone Press, 1980. Perhaps the best short analysis of punk rock available. Emphatically partisan, Marcus nevertheless helps explain the appeal of what to many seems an unintelligible form.

_____. *Lipstick Traces: A Secret History of the Twentieth Century.* Cambridge, Mass.: Harvard University Press, 1989. In this tour de force of cultural criticism, Marcus uses the Sex Pistols as a point of departure for exploring a wide range of movements—including Dada, the Situationists, and others—and in so doing establishes the band as the latest manifestation of a long history of cultural subversion. Sprawling and mannered, but intriguing throughout.

Matlock, Glen, with Pete Silverton. *I Was a Teenage Sex Pistol.* London: Faber, 1991. The first Sex Pistols bassist gives his account of the rise of the band and his departure from it.

Monk, Noel E., and Jimmy Guterman. *Twelve Days on the Road: The Sex Pistols in America.* New York: William Morrow, 1990. A firsthand account of the band's ill-fated American tour in January of 1978 and of the Sex Pistol's impact on the musical scene of the time—and after.

Savage, Jon. *England's Dreaming: Anarchy, the Sex Pistols, Punk Rock, and Beyond.* New York: St. Martin's Press, 1992. Savage, one of Great Britain's most respected popular music critics, has written what will probably become the definitive account of the band, from its origins to its heirs.

Tucker, Ken. "All Shook Up: The Punk Rock Explosion" and "The Postpunk Implosion." In *Rock of Ages: The Rolling Stone History of Rock and Roll*, by Ed Ward, Geoffrey Stokes, and Ken Tucker. New York: Rolling Stone Press, 1986. These two chapters amount to a good narrative history of the rise and fall of punk, placing the music into the larger context of rock at the time.

Jim Cullen

Cross-References

Berry's "Maybellene" Popularizes Rock and Roll (1955), p. 1635; Presley Becomes a Rock-and-Roll Sensation (1956), p. 1705; The Beatles Revolutionize Popular Music (1963), p. 1944; The Rolling Stones Release *Out of Our Heads* (1965), p. 2027; Dylan Performs with Electric Instruments (1965), p. 2038; Punk's Antifashion Style First Appears (1974), p. 2299; Marley's *Natty Dread* Establishes Reggae's Popularity (1975), p. 2344; Rap Goes Platinum with Run-D.M.C.'s *Raising Hell* (1986), p. 2582.

WANTED: THE OUTLAWS REVITALIZES COUNTRY MUSIC

Category of event: Music
Time: January 12, 1976
Locale: Nashville, Tennessee

The release of Wanted: The Outlaws *in early 1976 brought mainstream recognition to a brand of country music at once more progressive and more authentically rooted than the Nashville norm*

Principal personages:

WAYLON JENNINGS (1937-   ), the singer who best embodied the spirit of artistic independence and return to basics of the "outlaw" movement

WILLIE NELSON (1933-   ), a songwriter, singer, and cultural guru who brought millions of new fans to his eclectic brand of country music

CHET ATKINS (1924-   ), a legendary guitarist who helped to develop the type of country music Jennings and Nelson rejected

KRIS KRISTOFFERSON (1936-   ), a songwriter and singer who helped to convince other young songwriters to handle new themes in country songs

BOBBY BARE (1935-   ), a successful country music figure in the 1960's who eschewed many of the trappings of stardom

JOHNNY CASH (1932-   ), a country music superstar who inspired the younger rebels

Summary of Event

With the January, 1976, release of the album *Wanted: The Outlaws* on RCA Records, the talents of Waylon Jennings and Willie Nelson became nationally recognized. The album went platinum, selling more than one million copies—a first for a country album. The record crossed over to the pop charts and reached number ten on the *Billboard* magazine chart, the music industry's standard reference. A new breed of "progressive" or "outlaw" country music had arrived, and the corporate music industry in country music's capital had to take notice. It did; dollars and sales spoke, and things were never quite the same again.

In part, the album represented a music industry co-optation of a movement within country music that had been gestating for quite some time. Most immediately obvious to country music buyers was the fact that all the cuts on the album were reissues. *Wanted: The Outlaws*, in fact, was a promotional and public-relations package meant to capitalize on the ferment within country music circles and in the Nashville scene itself.

The album's tracks included Jennings' "My Heroes Have Always Been Cowboys" and "Honky Tonk Heroes," Nelson's "Me and Paul" and "Yesterday's Wine," and duets by Jennings and Nelson, such as "Good Hearted Woman" and "Heaven or Hell." Tracks by less prominent outlaw musicians such as Tompall Glaser were also included. The repackaged album featured the stripped-down style and roots country the younger rebel songwriters and performers of the 1970's preferred over the assembly-line crossover product being turned out for pop appeal by the Nashville country mainstream. Back in 1972, when Jennings had recorded a tune called "Ladies Love Outlaws," some journalists had picked up on the idea of cementing the newer forces in country music together with the concept of their rebellion against record company politics and control of their music and recordings releases. In reality, the so-called outlaws were not a coherent group but rather a creation of record-company publicists and press agents who sensed—correctly, as it turned out—that something was blowing in the wind in the increasingly homogenized Nashville music industry. Even the liner notes to *Wanted: The Outlaws* picked up on this kind of promotion; in the notes, Chet Flippo, an associate editor of the hip music magazine *Rolling Stone*, conferred his approval. He wrote of the "progressive" music of Jennings and Nelson, their struggle over the years to control their recording careers in the face of record company intransigence, and their bold enunciation of basic country themes, a harking back to country music's earlier and more rural roots. According to Flippo, the outlaws were rejecting country music's accommodation to the bland sounds of mainstream pop music in the 1960's and 1970's.

Much of the outlaw rebellion stemmed from Nashville's long-term reaction to the advent of rock and roll in the mid-1950's. Trying to win back the younger audience attracted to such stars as Elvis Presley, Jerry Lee Lewis, Roy Orbison, Johnny Cash, and Chuck Berry, Nashville producers began to produce a blander type of country in which fiddles and steel guitars were omitted. Strings, woodwinds, and backing choruses were added so that country could sound more like standard pop music. Singers who had nasal voices or who wanted to stick to traditional sounds were put on hold. To many, the music was compromised, watered-down. From the late 1950's on, though, this trend accelerated. The "Nashville Sound" came to mean a well-polished studio sound made by a cadre of musicians who were heard on record after record. Among the chief architects of this production-line sound were Decca Records' Owen Bradley and RCA Records' Chet Atkins. Atkins, a brilliant guitarist himself, turned to producing most of RCA's country acts and in the process homogenized the sound. While the Nashville Sound and the highly centralized corporate system it spawned brought success in the marketplace, other segments of the music scene in Nashville and elsewhere were undergoing a sea change.

The advent of rockabilly—or country rock and roll—from Memphis with the success of Presley, Lewis, Carl Perkins, Cash, Orbison, and others actually represented the thrust of deep South and Southwest musical fusions into country music. The area from Memphis south and west into Texas had always been rich in musical traditions, most notably black blues and rhythm and blues. Nashville, on the Cumberland Plateau in middle Tennessee, had been a more conservative bastion of mountain music and older styles until the 1940's, when the influence of Southwest "Western swing" and Texas-bred honky-tonk styles, with electric guitars, a heavy bass, and drums, started to shake up the old order. In the mid-1950's, new fusions of black and white music again forced their way into country music. "Country boogie," or rockabilly, was hard for the Nashville establishment to accept even then, and with the exception of some token copying of the Memphis sound, Nashville opted for the smoother approach typified by the development of the Nashville Sound, with its overtures to the larger pop music audience.

Yet the guitar- and drum-based rockabilly stream could not in the long run be held in check. In West Texas, where Waylon Jennings and his friend Buddy Holly grew up, the sounds and styles of rockabilly were more readily accepted. In the late 1950's, Jennings had played bass in Holly's band. With the tragic death of Holly in a plane crash in February, 1959, Jennings started a solo career as singer, and he arrived in Nashville to record for RCA in 1965. Chet Atkins tried to incorporate Jennings into the Nashville Sound system in the hope that some of his rough Texas edges could be smoothed over and that he could be marketed as a "folk-country" artist to cash in on the fad for folk-like versions of pop music then in vogue. While Atkins' effort was on one level strictly a marketing ploy, it did reveal that Jennings was different and had succeeded in developing a fusion of folk-derived musical influences.

Jennings was determined not to be taken over by the neat studio system Atkins and others had perfected. He wanted his own road band as his backup in the studio, whereas RCA wanted him to record with its cadre of studio men. In the early 1970's, Jenning forced a renegotiation of his contract by enlisting the services of a tough manager, and he won the right to supervise his own sessions.

Two other forces played a part. One was Texan Willie Nelson. Like Jennings, Nelson had been frustrated by the control over his music exerted by Nashville when he went there in the 1960's. Successful as a songwriter, he found his eclectic style— nourished, like Jennings', in the fusion of musics common in Texas—unacceptable when he recorded his own songs. Moving to Austin, Texas, in 1972, he suddenly found a new live audience waiting. Many young fans were interested in returning to country roots, and there was a burgeoning interest in bringing rock influences into the music. A group of country songwriters influenced by the more experimental rock and folk-inspired music of Bob Dylan and Gram Parsons were determined to go their own way. Nelson organized a series of open-air music festivals in Texas to highlight this music and his own singing and songwriting. He invited kindred spirits, including Jennings, to participate, and a movement was born.

At the same time, Nashville was being invaded by a new breed of songwriters who reflected the same influences. Kris Kristofferson is the best example. Well-educated and eclectic, Kristofferson opposed the rigid Nashville system. Encouraged by Johnny Cash, Kristofferson got his songs recorded and fought for the freedom to bring stronger lyric material into country music. Young rebels gathered around independent producers such as Tompall Glaser and demanded a say. Unconventional in behavior and dress and determined to buck the system, they finally had some of their way, and by 1976 they had broken through.

Impact of Event

The years that followed saw the media impact of the rebellion and saw the more authentic, less-produced brand of country music win a new pop audience. Willie Nelson became a guru for those wanting an open style of country in which rock and folk-like influences were acceptable. Nelson adopted a counterculture dress style, shunned the sequined costumes and supper-club dress of other country artists, and struck a chord among millions. His charismatic personality went over well on television; in live shows, his laid-back personality and informal music-making carried the day. He wrote concept albums, covered old pop songs such as "Stardust," and sold in markets not usually favorable to a country performer. His albums and his duets with Jennings and others sold to pop audiences. As an actor in films, he managed to spread his fame even wider. Both he and Jennings stressed stripped-down instrumentation and the new songs being turned out by writers such as Kristofferson, Billy Joe Shaver, Guy Clark, and others who favored new, unhackneyed themes.

A new sophistication in songwriting had invaded Nashville. Singer-songwriters such as Bobby Bare and Tom T. Hall exposed society's hypocrisies and handled such issues as adultery and social problems in a manner not common during the heyday of the Nashville Sound, when courting pop success had meant making blander music.

Nelson and Jennings took their material from where they wanted and were able to convince a large public that country music did not have to be well-mannered pap. Jennings, dressed in black and letting his hair grow long, conveyed an unconventional stance and a deep conviction in his songs that was a fresh breeze in the business. Like Cash and Bobby Bare had done earlier, Jennings avoided many of the trappings of stardom and went his own way. By expanding the styles and repertoire of country music, Nelson and Jennings in their different ways managed in the 1970's and 1980's to return much of country music to its real roots. They honored their creative predecessors such as Hank Williams and absorbed songs and styles outside the rigid boundaries of mainstream, pop-oriented country. Authentic country artists, they could take rock and even popular songs and infuse them with a country feel, a kind of process endemic to the music from the start.

Bibliography

Bane, Michael. *The Outlaws: Revolution in Country Music.* New York: Doubleday, 1978. A good overview of the outlaw scene, with many photographs. While not scholarly, Bane does capture the spirit of the movement. Popular in intent, the book does not have an index or discography.

Denisoff, R. Serge. *Waylon: A Biography.* Knoxville: University of Tennessee Press, 1983. Denisoff, a former rock journalist, knows his subject. This always readable and entertaining book conveys well the whole scene and origins of the music. Illustrated, with notes and sources, index, and discography by Jennings expert John L. Smith.

Malone, Bill C. *Country Music, U.S.A.* Rev. ed. Austin: University of Texas Press, 1985. A scholarly study of country music. Useful for the whole background and history of the music and incisive on the outlaw movement. Illustrated; fully annotated bibliography, brief discography, index.

Nelson, Willie, with Bud Shrake. *Willie: An Autobiography.* New York: Simon & Schuster, 1988. Nelson's own story; gives useful insight to the sources of his own rebellion and style. A firsthand account that helps to explain the reasons for Nelson's and Jennings' disatisfaction. Illustrated, index.

Pareles, Jon, and Patricia Romanowski, eds. *The Rolling Stone Encyclopedia of Rock and Roll.* New York: Rolling Stone Press, 1983. Useful brief recaps of the careers of Jennings and Nelson. Helpful in placing the outlaw movement in a broader musical context. Discographies.

Frederick E. Danker

Cross-References

WSM Launches *The Grand Ole Opry* (1925), p. 675; Rodgers Cuts His First Record for RCA Victor (1927), p. 729; Guthrie's Populist Songs Reflect the Depression-Era United States (1930's), p. 810; Bill Monroe and the Blue Grass Boys Define Bluegrass Music (1939), p. 1121; Hank Williams Performs on *The Grand Ole Opry* (1949), p. 1415; Presley Becomes a Rock-and-Roll Sensation (1956), p. 1705.

SHANGE'S *FOR COLORED GIRLS* . . . IS A LANDMARK

Category of event: Theater
Time: April-May, 1976; June 1, 1976
Locale: The New Federal Theater, New York, New York, and the Public/Anspacher Theater, New York, New York

Ntozake Shange's "choreopoem" dramatically increased public awareness of the black female search for self-identity

Principal personages:
NTOZAKE SHANGE (PAULETTE WILLIAMS, 1948-   ), a poet, playwright, and actress who designed *for colored girls* as a choreopoem, a multidisciplinary expression of the black female experience
PAULA MOSS, an actress and choreographer who was instrumental in the "choreo" aspect of the choreopoem
OZ SCOTT, the director who developed the staging for the New York productions
JUDY GRAHN (1940-   ), a poet whose poetry provided the model for the development of the seven female characters
HALIFU OSUMARE, a dancer and choreographer with whose troupe Shange danced
AMIRI BARAKA (LEROI JONES, 1934-   ), a poet and playwright whose work influenced Shange
ADRIENNE KENNEDY (1931-   ), a poet and playwright instrumental in Shange's development of a female aesthetic

Summary of Event

Following a two-month run at Off-Off Broadway's Henry Street Settlement New Federal Theater, Ntozake Shange's first play, *for colored girls who have considered suicide/ when the rainbow is enuf,* opened Off-Broadway on June 1, 1976, at Joseph Papp's New York Shakespeare Festival Public/Anspacher Theater. After 120 performances, *for colored girls* closed on August 29, 1976, to open September 15, 1976, on Broadway for 746 shows at the Booth Theatre. Ntozake Shange's choreographed poetry, or "choreopoem," broke barriers in both content and form by sharing the experiences and emotional lives of seven women of color through language, music, and motion.

Shange began to develop her choreopoem in San Francisco's coffeehouses, bars, and studios, improvising with five female poets and dancers, seeking first to explore their unique and communal identities and then to communicate their discoveries. Sonoma State College's women's studies program provided her with a historical context, and Shange's study of dance gave her a pervasive sense of familiarity and comfort with her body as an instrument of communication.

After seeing the group's typically informal presentation during a summer music festival, Oz Scott recognized the inherent quality of the production and proposed to give the show a more polished staging. Shange credits the moment of her relinquishing directorial control to Scott as the first time that she could see the twenty individual poems as an integrated whole, a choreopoem. Even so, the show's evolution in content and in form continued until, seven years after its inception, *for colored girls* overwhelmed the Broadway stage and its audience's hearts at the Booth Theatre.

On a stage bare of a traditional set or props, seven female characters are identified simply by the colors they wear as "Lady in Brown," "Lady in Yellow," "Lady in Red," "Lady in Green," "Lady in Purple," "Lady in Blue," and "Lady in Orange." These colors are reinforced by the set's lighting scheme. The only additional distinguishing descriptors are the entrances and exits unique to each character.

Absent also is the traditional three-act linear plot, as well as the classic dramatic monologue. No one character holds center stage or her own character boundaries. Instead, in a pulsating series of vignettes in which the women relinquish their own identities to play whatever role best supports the spotlighted figure's tale, stereotypes are demolished. The internal anguish of living in a world where both being black and being female seem to negate a character's right to exist is revealed, and the will to survive is celebrated.

With humor, music, dance, black dialects, and movement, the characters explore themselves and their relationships. They acknowledge their complicity through passive subjugation in destructive relationships. They reveal their profound sense of emptiness, anguish, and loss. Yet, as they and their audience embrace and move through the mutual pain, the sharing gradually transmutes grief and rage into a vital strength, a resilience. Acceptance of self as powerful and recognition of the crucial significance of female bonding in a relentlessly antipathetic world transcend the learned behaviors of silent, suffering subjugation and open the way of the heart to rebirth, to actualization.

Audience members, female and male, involved in *for colored girls* leave the theater viscerally moved by their experience, perhaps without the consolation of the classic catharsis, but infinitely more aware of themselves, of others, of the hope of transcendence. Dramatic production of Shange's choreopoem reaches beyond gender, beyond race, to sound a universal human chord.

For colored girls was nominated for a Tony Award and a Grammy Award. The choreopoem won Obie Awards for playwriting, directing, and ensemble acting. It also won the Outer Critics' Circle Award and four AUDELCO Awards. Acknowledgment that invisible, perhaps unconscious, barriers had been shattered was instantaneous.

Despite the awards, the critical acclaim, and the overwhelming audience response, Shange moved toward performance-art pieces as her stated dramatic preference. As a performance artist, she prefers alternative spaces, intimate audiences, and experimental theater pieces. Nevertheless, after having been a playwright, actor, dancer, and director, she still considers herself a poet first.

Impact of Event

Although a few critics see Shange's *for colored girls* as underdeveloped and label any positive reviews as pandering, the impact of the choreopoem is both immediate and continuing. The most immediate impact is that, for the first time, a black female playwright was successful in rendering an accurate dramatic portrayal of the black female psyche: her grief, her rage, her loss of self, her endurance, and her infinite capacity to love. This capacity to love, turned inward, is her saving grace; turned outward, it is the healing laying on of hands for others.

Shange believes that women can best understand and depict other women. Even though she may have alienated some by her lack of focus on male characters in *for colored girls*, she would have belied her own beliefs in attempting to draw as accurate a depiction of men. Shange's message is clear: The black female is worthy of as much dramatic attention as the black male. The message is an explosive suspension of the widespread notion that the black woman should sacrifice herself if necessary for the well-being of her family.

Similarly, Shange's smashing of the traditional fourth wall that distances the audience emotionally from the action facilitated the expression of the idea that the female is as worthy of dramatic attention as is the male. In 1976, that women could experience and suppress such traumata was eye-opening to the general public and evoked an emotional bonding among those who chose to heal themselves through sharing and forgiveness.

Shange's rhythms and verbal patterns are reminiscent of those of Amiri Baraka. As such, the choreopoem, while shattering black cultural myths, also has its roots in the Black Arts movement inspired by Baraka in the 1960's and 1970's. Thus, the complexities of being black and female are unavoidably conjoined with the seeming contradictions of being a black feminist dramatic experimentalist. Shange's work is a balancing act to which women of all races can relate.

When Shange successfully broke with traditional dramatic form to create a form (the choreopoem) more reflective of her black heritage in its integration of language and movement, she also helped to free other playwrights from the obligation to adhere to Aristotelian conventions. Playwright and director Emily Mann has used the versatility of performance art and juxtaposed monologues to create in her audiences intense emotional responses. She, too, smashes through the fourth wall. Mann has credited Shange as having had a significant influence on her dramatic style.

The liberating effects of Shange's impact extend beyond sexual preference and racial and cultural boundaries. Poet and playwright Alexis De Veaux maximizes the shattering experiences of black lesbians with a dramatic structure similar to that of Shange. David Hwang, is a Chinese-American playwright whose plays invariably reflect explorations into self-identity and the conflicts that inevitably arise with society, tradition, and loved ones. His characterizations, influenced by *for colored girls*, are nonlinear; his action is rhythmic and freeflowing. His attempts to draw his characters well enough that they become universal rather than sociocultural figures is one result of his fascination with the performances of Shange's choreopoem.

With the emergence of Shange and other female playwrights, many male playwrights have become more aware of their female characters and have become less likely to subvert their humanity into plasticity. As a result, some male playwrights have become more concerned with female speech patterns, subtext, and motivation. Additionally, some male playwrights have become more conscious of their facilitation or violation of the male aesthetic. These facets have enriched contemporary dramatic productions, from the traditional to the nontraditional.

Beyond her influence upon American theater, Shange has enhanced awareness of the mutual human condition across genders and races. She has helped to bring down cultural barriers between people by creating an environment that unites people in the struggle toward higher consciousness. In *for colored girls who have considered suicide/ when the rainbow is enuf*, Ntozake Shange demonstrated that through sharing comes healing, and that with healing, "the rainbow" is indeed enough.

Bibliography

Betsko, Kathleen, and Rachel Koenig. "Ntozake Shange." In *Interviews with Contemporary Women Playwrights*. New York: Beech Tree Books, 1987. Shange reflects upon her performance-art pieces and her multidisciplinary approach to life and art. Covers childhood experiences, theories of writing, the creative process, feminism, American and non-American audience response. An excellent and enlightening interview.

Brown-Guillory, Elizabeth. "Black Women Playwrights: Exorcising Myths." *Phylon: The Atlanta University Review of Race and Culture* 48 (Fall, 1987): 229-239. Discusses the dramatic works of Alice Childress, Lorraine Hansberry, and Ntozake Shange in terms of their unique contributions as black female playwrights. Brown-Guillory makes the point that the black female dramatist's perspective of black life is integral to an undistorted view of the black community: its struggles, its joys, its movement toward epiphany. Clearly written and well presented.

Elliot, Jeffrey. "Ntozake Shange: Genesis of a Choreopoem." *Negro History Bulletin* 41 (January, 1978): 797-800. After a glowing one-column introduction regarding *for colored girls*, Elliot reprints Shange's own introduction to the play. Valuable for the individual without access to Shange's first-person narrative on the development of the play.

Lester, Neal A. "At the Heart of Shange's Feminism: An Interview." *Black American Literature Forum* 24 (Winter, 1990): 717-730. An in-depth discussion of Shange's feminist philosophy. Includes her reflections on the spiritual growth of both males and females in contemporary American society as well as on language as a determinant of behavior. An excellent interview that also gives Shange's recommendations for additional study.

Peters, Erskine. "Commentary: Some Tragic Propensities of Ourselves: The Occasion of Ntozake Shange's *for colored girls who have considered suicide/ when the rainbow is enuf*." *The Journal of Ethnic Studies* 6 (Spring, 1978): 79-85. Peters' negative review of Shange's play centers on his dissatisfaction with the playwright's portrayal of black males, a portrayal he perceives at best as immature and at worst as appallingly destructive. A solid review with valid cross-references. Worth reading for an opposing viewpoint.

Peterson, Bernard L., Jr. *Contemporary Black American Playwrights and Their Plays: A Biographical Directory and Dramatic Index.* New York: Greenwood Press, 1988. A comprehensive listing of Shange's interests, activities (literary and nonliterary), and publications. An excellent resource base for research. Also provides brief synopses of representative works.

Richards, Sandra L. "Conflicting Impulses in the Plays of Ntozake Shange." *Black American Literature Forum* 17 (Summer, 1983): 73-78. Discusses Shange's dualistic approach to the development of a female aesthetic: the struggle against violence and oppression and the struggle toward transcendence. Difficult to follow; geared to collegiate audiences.

Rushing, Andrea Benton. "For Colored Girls, Suicide or Struggle." *The Massachusetts Review: A Quarterly of Literature, the Arts and Public Affairs* 22 (Autumn, 1981): 539-550. Discusses the play's sociological import specifically in terms of rising black female suicide rates, increased isolation, lack of extended family support systems, and negative self-image. Analyzes autobiographical context. Mentions four elements of the play as distressing. Worthwhile reading for those interested in the sociological impact of the black cultural experience.

Shange, Ntozake. "Ntozake Shange Interviews Herself." *Ms.* 5 (December, 1977): 35, 70-72. Interesting insights into Shange and the questions she believes are important. Shange's characteristically nontraditional grammatical structure and spelling may be difficult for some readers.

Kathleen Mills

Cross-References

Billie Holiday Begins Her Recording Career (1933), p. 930; Davis' *Birth of the Cool* Recordings Spawn 1950's Cool Jazz (1949), p. 1438; Beauvoir's *The Second Sex* Anticipates the Women's Movement (1949), p. 1449; Grass Publishes *The Tin Drum* (1959), p. 1780; Hansberry's *A Raisin in the Sun* Debuts on Broadway (1959), p. 1795; Baldwin Voices Black Rage in *The Fire Next Time* (1963), p. 1929; Baraka's *Dutchman* Dramatizes Racial Hatred (1964), p. 2000; Mitchell Founds the Dance Theater of Harlem (1968), p. 2110; Festivals Mark a Peak in the Dance Created by Black Artists (1983), p. 2521.

EINSTEIN ON THE BEACH IS A TRIUMPH OF MINIMALISM

Category of event: Music
Time: July 25, 1976
Locale: Avignon, France

The nonnarrative theatrical piece Einstein on the Beach *had a triumphant premiere at the Avignon Summer Festival and helped to create a new and varied audience for minimalist music*

Principal personages:
PHILIP GLASS (1937-   ), an American composer and performer who wrote the music for *Einstein on the Beach*
ROBERT M. WILSON (1944-   ), a Texas-born theatrical artist who designed and directed *Einstein on the Beach*
ALBERT EINSTEIN (1879-1955), the physicist whose discoveries, life, and personality served as the inspiration for *Einstein on the Beach*

Summary of Event

The avant-garde opera *Einstein on the Beach* was a consequence of two people meeting at the right time in their artistic evolution. Both Philip Glass and Robert Wilson lived in New York City in the early 1970's, by which time Glass had developed a new musical language based on the hypnotic repetition of small groups of notes and Wilson had created such gargantuan theatrical spectacles as the twelve-hour account of the life of Joseph Stalin, which forced viewers to immerse themselves in a world of striking images rather than follow a plot with a climax and resolution. After an all-night performance of the Stalin piece, Glass met Wilson, and they decided then and there to investigate the possibility of creating something together.

During their initial meetings, they spent most of their time getting acquainted. Glass discovered that Wilson had been an architect and painter before he created the theatrical works that challenged audiences' ideas of dramatic time, progression, and structure. Wilson learned that Glass, after receiving a traditional education in classical music in Baltimore and Chicago and at the Juilliard School of Music in New York City, had rebelled against the modern music he had been taught, which he found "ugly and didactic," and had begun to search for his own style. This search was greatly aided by his studies in Paris with Nadia Boulanger, who showed him how to handle several rhythms simultaneously. His most important experience in Paris—indeed, the turning point in his musical life—occurred when he encountered the music of Ravi Shankar, a skilled sitar player from India. Glass had accepted the job of transcribing Shankar's raga improvisations into Western notation. Since all the music Glass had previously heard, from classical to modern to jazz, had been based on narrative structures, that is, on propulsive melodies and harmonies, he initially had difficulty in grasping Shankar's mode of musical thinking. He soon came to see that Eastern music substituted repetitive for narrative structures. For Glass, the essential difference between Eastern and Western music was that in the West, musical time is divided (from whole to half to quarter notes, for example), whereas in the East, small musical units are combined and cycles of different rhythms are constructed (similar to the wheels within wheels of a clockwork).

Glass used these ideas of basic building blocks of music and rhythmic cycles in creating a unique, personal style that continued to evolve. As he expected, he encountered difficulties in getting people to play his music, so he formed the Philip Glass Ensemble, for which, after much experimentation and effort, he was able to develop a characteristic sound, a blend of amplified keyboards, winds, and female voice. When this group first played Glass's music, audiences were dismayed, and the popular press labeled it "trance music," "solid-state music," "hypnotic music," and "minimal music"—terms disliked by Glass, who saw his work simply as a new musical language. Despite Glass's demurral, "minimalism" came to be widely used to describe this cyclic and meditative style. Many modern musicians at the time, who tended to espouse various dodecaphonic, atonal, and arhythmic styles, offered Glass neither approval nor support. On the other hand, people who listened to popular music supported the new music, and this pleased Glass, since one of his motives in developing his style was to bridge the gap between classical and popular music. Another group that formed an important part of Glass's audience was artists of various genres; for example, painters of the New York School found connections between their minimalism and Glass's. Robert Wilson, too, whose theatrical works had been characterized as analytic, reductive, and repetitive, was enchanted by Glass's music, and so he and Glass felt that they could create a musical theater piece for which they could comfortably share artistic responsibility.

Wilson and Glass began their venture by deciding on its general thematic content. In his theatrical productions, Wilson had been fascinated by such historical figures as Sigmund Freud and Joseph Stalin, and he and Glass first discussed Charlie Chaplin, Adolf Hitler, and Mahatma Gandhi as possible subjects. When they discovered that, from childhood, they had both been captivated by Albert Einstein, they knew they had found their subject, since Einstein could also be used to explore, in music and in theater spectacle, the themes of creativity, the nuclear age, and the theory of relativity. In its original form, their work was tentatively entitled *Einstein on the Beach on Wall Street*. Since there is only a single enigmatic reference to a beach in the libretto, some writers have hypothesized that the title derives from Nevil Shute's apocalyptic post-nuclear-war novel *On the Beach* (1956), an association that Glass has denied.

Neither Glass nor Wilson wanted to make *Einstein on the Beach* a conventional opera. They had no interest in telling a story or composing arias to display the vocal talents of well-known soloists. Instead of creating music based on the text of a play, Glass derived his musical inspiration from various images around which he and

Wilson had organized their opera. Even the words that were sung, chanted, or spoken were used more for their sound than their sense (indeed, Glass has said that he generally prefers that audiences not understand what is being said or sung). The texts for *Einstein on the Beach* were written mostly by Christopher Knowles, a young boy with some neurological impairment whom Wilson had met when working with disturbed children; he found the adolescent's way of viewing the world strikingly original and, in Wilson's mind, as visionary as Einstein's.

Einstein on the Beach was structured by Glass and Wilson into four acts, nine scenes, and five "knee plays." The knee plays served as prologue, interludes separating the acts, and epilogue ("knee" was Glass and Wilson's way of characterizing their joining function). Using the scenes and the timings for them as a base, Glass shaped and colored each scene musically by linking harmonies to rhythms. He scored the opera for solo violinist, the instruments of the Philip Glass Ensemble, and mostly untrained voices (a few texts required a trained singer). Although he eschewed the traditional opera orchestra, he chose a single violinist because Einstein was well known as an amateur player, and Glass and Wilson situated the Einstein character between the music ensemble and the singers and dancers. Glass found the music, which he wrote during the spring, summer, and fall of 1975, surprisingly easy to compose. The music was clearly related to his preoperatic instrumental compositions, especially the music accompanying the dances and other stage activities. What was new was how he used sung, chanted, and spoken words, numbers, and phrases that sometimes complemented, other times mocked the rhythmic structure of the music.

By November of 1975, Glass had completed the score and helped Wilson to assemble a cast. The main problem left was financing. They did not think that *Einstein on the Beach* would find support from any American opera company. Fortunately, in France, a new minister of culture wanted a challenging work for the Avignon Festival, and Glass and Wilson's opera, whose subject, structure, and approach were out of the ordinary, suited his desires. Glass and Wilson's agent in Europe was also able to book a tour of *Einstein on the Beach* starting in Paris and continuing through theaters in Belgium, Holland, Germany, Italy, and Yugoslavia. Before 1976, the festival at Avignon had occasionally sponsored avant-garde works, and in the summer of 1976 reports about *Einstein on the Beach* attracted young audience members from all over Europe. As Glass and Wilson gathered their musicians, singers, and dancers together at Avignon for a final few weeks of rehearsal, a mood of intense energy and expectation saturated the company.

At the premiere on July 25, 1976, the audience encountered a radically new theatrical presentation and music. The opera began with two women sitting at tables in the front of the stage, counting aloud while their fingers performed a slow ballet. Like the other cast members, they were dressed in the Einstein costume—short-sleeved white shirts, baggy pants, suspenders, and sneakers. During the course of the opera, the audience witnessed many other elements drawn from the great scientist's life and work, for example, a train (an image often used by Einstein in "thought experiments" to explain his special theory of relativity). Some associations probably passed by most members of the premiere audience; Wilson, for example, had made the stage furniture out of plumbing pipes because he had read Einstein's remark that, if he had his life to live over again, he would have been a plumber. Between the early image of the train and the late image of a futuristic spaceship, various events occur on stage—a trial, a prison scene, and dances. After the curtain, upon which was written "E = mc²," the opera concluded with an epilogue in which the two female players who initiated the work talk of love on a park bench while a backstage chorus chants numbers. Gradually, the words and music cease.

The Avignon premiere of *Einstein on the Beach* generated a wide spectrum of opinion, from acclamation to condemnation. Glass and Wilson expected controversy, since they viewed their work as a piece for the audience to complete for themselves. They could not predict how audiences would interpret the opera, so the only thing they could do was present their subject as clearly as possible. Those audience members who expected a traditional opera were either shocked or outraged. The highly amplified music sounded more like a rock band than a traditional opera orchestra. Even the singing was not operatic, since Glass had used what he called "naïve voices." Those audience members who came expecting a narrative account of Einstein's life were also surprised, but Glass and Wilson had tried to make clear their intent of presenting their artistic vision of Einstein rather than Einstein himself. On the other hand, many audience members, especially those drawn from the European student population, found *Einstein on the Beach* beautiful, stimulating, and entrancing. Their response was so enthusiastic that large numbers of them became "Einstein groupies," traveling to many of the other performances that Glass's company gave throughout Europe.

Impact of Event

At the opening, Wilson and Glass had been so caught up in the performance of *Einstein on the Beach* that they paid little attention to the reaction of the audience, but it soon became clear to them and everyone else that their theatrical piece was the event of the festival. All the remaining performances rapidly sold out, and so eager were people to see the opera that they found ingenious ways of sneaking into the theater. This is not to say that everyone found the opera praiseworthy. Critics from the established musical avant-garde felt that Glass's repetitive music was boring and that Einstein's accomplishments required music of greater variety, development, and expressiveness. Others, including listeners accustomed to traditional Western classical music, found Glass's music uneventful and bizarre and Wilson's staging plodding and obscure. Glass himself noticed a strong dualism in audience reactions—outrage or delight, with few temperate opinions.

As the opera toured Europe, news of the excitement it was causing reached the United States. Jerome Robbins, who saw the opera in Paris, was instrumental in convincing people at the Metropolitan Opera to book the work. The American premiere of *Einstein on the Beach* occurred on November 21, 1976. As in Europe, the audience response was divided. Many found the new work exhilarating, whereas others, in shock and rage, stormed out of the theater—only to be met by hordes of young people outside the Met eager for ticket stubs. Critical reactions to *Einstein on the Beach* were more analytic than the audience responses. Some writers interpreted the opera as a mantra designed to lull the audience into a meditative state. John Rockwell, in *The New York Times*, described the postnarrative theatrical work as a mixture of "mathematical clarity and mystical allure." Andrew Porter, writing in *The New Yorker*, characterized Glass's score as "incantatory," though he admitted that the music's "needle-in-groove" nature might cause the mind to wander.

Despite the great success of *Einstein on the Beach*, Glass and his collaborators were left with a debt of about $90,000, and he was forced to return to making his living as a taxi driver. To raise money to retire what they called "The Einstein Debt," Wilson had exhibitions and sold drawings, and Glass performed with his ensemble and sold the original score of *Einstein on the Beach* to a private collector.

Einstein on the Beach certainly caused problems, but it created opportunities as well. As a result of *Einstein on the Beach*'s success, Glass received a Rockefeller Foundation grant of $30,000 a year for three years. With this financial support, he was able to complete another opera, *Satyagraha*, which premiered in Rotterdam in 1980. Another Glass portrait opera, *Akhnaten*, about a revolutionary Egyptian pharaoh, premiered in Stuttgart in 1984. Both *Satyagraha* and *Akhnaten* used themes from *Einstein on the Beach*, so these three minimalist operas—Glass's trilogy—possess a certain cohesiveness both musically and thematically.

As a result of the popularity of these operas, Glass acquired the largest audience of any living composer of serious music. With the many productions of his theatrical works, Glass has had to decide how they should be presented. In 1984, he completed a video documentation of the revival of *Einstein on the Beach* at the Brooklyn Academy of Music. He saw this video record as one way of guiding future productions, even though he realized that other directors would reinterpret his operas.

Since its first presentation, *Einstein on the Beach* has come to be recognized as a landmark in contemporary music and theater. Many critics still regard it as Glass's most significant work. Glass's minimalist music, first given a wide hearing through *Einstein on the Beach*, has influenced composers all over the world. This minimalist style and Glass's use of highly amplified electronic instruments have influenced such rock artists as David Bowie and Brian Eno and such rock groups as Pink Floyd and Tangerine Dream. Glass has approved of these developments, since he has sought to diminish the distance between serious and popular music. He sees himself primarily as a composer of liberation, freeing both himself and his listeners. Others may have a more jaundiced view of his contributions, but little doubt exists that many composers and listeners of both serious and popular music owe much to his creations.

Bibliography

Antokoletz, Elliott. *Twentieth-Century Music*. Englewood Cliffs, N.J.: Prentice-Hall, 1992. Organized in two sections, the first of which deals with the reaction against nineteenth century Romanticism during the first four decades of the twentieth century and the second of which analyzes the musical styles that developed after World War II. Glass's work is discussed in a chapter entitled "Chance, Improvisation, Open Form, and Minimalism." The text contains many musical examples, and each chapter ends with a list of suggested readings. Index.

Glass, Philip. *Music by Philip Glass.* Edited by Robert T. Jones. New York: Harper & Row, 1987. This autobiography presents Glass's view of his evolution from a child prodigy on the flute to a world-famous composer. He writes insightfully about his teachers, his work with Nadia Boulanger and Ravi Shankar, and the composition of his operatic trilogy. The librettos of *Einstein on the Beach, Satyagraha,* and *Akhnaten* are included. Illustrated with color and black-and-white photographs; contains a catalog of Glass's music, a discography, and an index.

Hamm, Charles. *Music in the New World.* New York: W. W. Norton, 1983. Treats American music not simply as an imitation of what was happening in Europe but in terms of achievements that can serve as a model for composers in other countries. Discusses Glass's work in a chapter on the American avant-garde. Copiously illustrated with musical examples and pictures. A bibliography, discography, and index.

Kingman, Daniel. *American Music: A Panorama.* 2d ed. New York: Schirmer Books, 1990. Gives the novice reader with an interest in American music a clear and systematic presentation of its evolution from the colonial period to the present. Analyzes Philip Glass's work in a chapter on the impact of technology and new aesthetic concepts on modern American music. Each chapter has an annotated reading list and a list of recordings for listening projects. A comprehensive index.

Mertens, Wim. *American Minimal Music: La Monte Young, Terry Riley, Steve Reich, and Philip Glass.* Translated by J. Hautekiet. New York: Alexander Broude, 1983. This brief account of American minimalism emphasizes the basic aesthetic interconnections among the minimalists and their roots in African and Asian music. Mertens also shows how certain avant-garde composers contributed to the evolution of some American minimalists. Illustrated, with a three-page bibliography.

Rockwell, John. *All American Music: Composition in the Late Twentieth Century.* New York: Alfred A. Knopf, 1983. Contains twenty essays, each of which centers on an American composer. Neither a chronological survey nor a systematic guide, Rockwell's book tries to communicate the great diversity of contemporary American classical music. His chapter on Philip Glass contains a good critical commentary. Bibliography, discography, and index.

Robert J. Paradowski

Cross-References

Boulanger Takes Copland as a Student (1921), p. 508; Gershwin's *Porgy and Bess* Opens in New York (1935), p. 1016; Minimalism Emphasizes Objects as Art (1963), p. 1949; Laurie Anderson's *United States* Popularizes Performance Art (1983), p. 2517; Adams' *Nixon in China* Premieres (1987), p. 2599.

ALLEN'S *ANNIE HALL* CAPTURES COMPLEXITIES OF 1970'S LIFE

Category of event: Motion pictures
Time: 1977
Locale: The United States

Woody Allen's film Annie Hall *depicted important aspects of American life in the 1970's, winning critical acclaim, large audiences, and a series of Academy Awards for its creator*

Principal personages:

WOODY ALLEN (ALLEN STEWART KONIGSBERG, 1935-   ), a leading New York cultural figure whose books, plays, and films developed an avid following around the country

MARSHALL BRICKMAN (1941-   ), Allen's cowriter on *Annie Hall*

CHARLES JOFFE (1929-   ), the producer of *Annie Hall*

DIANE KEATON (DIANE HALL, 1946-   ), the female lead in *Annie Hall*, whose off-screen relationship with Allen reputedly formed the basis for the movie

RALPH ROSENBLUM (1925-   ) the film editor who convinced Allen to focus *Annie Hall* on romance

GORDON WILLIS (1931-   ), Allen's cinematographer for *Annie Hall*

Summary of Event

By the mid-1970's, Woody Allen had consolidated his position as one of the most popular comedic personas in American culture. Born Allen Stewart Konigsberg in the Flatbush section of Brooklyn in 1935, the son of Orthodox Jews, Allen imbibed the vibrant working-class culture of New York City, even though he was something of a loner. An indifferent student—he would eventually be expelled from the City College of New York for his poor performance—the future comedian nevertheless showed an early aptitude for writing and a fascination with the stage shows he attended at a local theater. At age fifteen, he began sending humorous quips to newspaper gossip columnists under the name Woody Allen and soon found more regular work writing jokes, most notably as a staff member of Sid Caesar's television show.

Allen began the next phase of his career in the early 1960's, when he left television to begin working on his own as a stand-up comedian and writer. It was during this time that he began to cultivate an image as a neurotic, easily depressed, but always funny "schlemiel"—a personality he has insisted is not really like his own but that was adopted for comedic purposes. During this time, too, he first became involved in the film business, writing and acting in *What's New Pussycat?* (1965), *What's Up Tiger Lily?* (1966), and the James Bond spoof *Casino Royale* (1967). He also made his debut as a playwright with *Don't Drink the Water* (1967), followed by

Play It Again Sam (1969), which would be made into a film in 1972. Allen also gained some repute as a writer of humorous articles and books, including *Getting Even* (1971), *Without Feathers* (1975), and *Side Effects* (1980).

Yet it was as a screenwriter (with longtime partner Marshall Brickman), actor, and director for his own movies that Allen would finally come into his own. The first such film was *Take the Money and Run* (1969), a mock documentary about a bumbling, would-be criminal. Allen followed it with *Bananas* (1971), *Everything You Always Wanted to Know About Sex but Were Afraid to Ask* (1972), *Sleeper* (1973), and *Love and Death* (1975). These works had varied themes ranging from science fiction to a satire of Leo Tolstoy by way of Sigmund Freud, but all were topical, humorous, and eagerly embraced by sophisticated urban audiences. In something of a departure, he also acted in Martin Ritt's *The Front* (1976), a politically charged statement about the impact of the Joseph McCarthy witch hunts on Hollywood.

Yet Allen was feeling restless. He was tired of making movies in places far from his beloved New York (*Love and Death* was shot in Yugoslavia), and he was increasingly interested in making more serious statements, even if they were laced with comedy. It was with this mindset that he began working on a project he called "Anhedonia"—a psychiatric term connoting the inability to experience pleasure.

Originally, "Anhedonia" was supposed to be a murder mystery that would star Allen and then-companion Diane Keaton. Yet consultations with cinematographer Gordon Willis, editor Ralph Rosenblum, cowriter Brickman, and producer Charles H. Joffe led the filmmakers to conclude that the focus should really be on Allen's character, Alvy Singer and Keaton's character, Annie Hall (Keaton's actual surname was Hall, one of many instances of a blurring of the line between art and life in Allen's films). Under pressure from United Artists, the studio releasing the film, Allen consented to change the title to *Annie Hall*. Thus did a murder mystery with an arcane title complete its transformation into a contemporary romance.

Annie Hall opened in the spring of 1977 to excellent reviews that signaled a willingness on the part of critics and audiences to regard Allen with a new level of seriousness. The film's critical and commercial momentum was so strong, in fact, that it was nominated for a host of Academy Awards, including awards for best picture, best director, and best screenplay. Suddenly, Allen was catapulted into the ranks of Orson Welles and Charlie Chaplin, *auteurs* who decisively shaped their own personas and their work into distinctive cinematic art.

Yet Allen was deeply uncomfortable with the hype that surrounded Hollywood in general and the Oscars in particular, and he resisted conventional efforts to promote the film (such as the quoting of rave reviews in advertisements). On the night of the Academy Awards ceremony in Southern California, he remained in New York, playing clarinet with the Dixieland band he had performed with every Monday night for many years. It was only the next morning that he learned the *Annie Hall* had swept the Oscars, taking not only the picture, director, and screenplay awards but also capturing best actress honors for Diane Keaton.

Annie Hall was a turning point in Allen's career, bringing him to new heights of prestige and giving him opportunities to pursue his highly personal vision. He followed that vision in 1978 with *Interiors*, a serious (to the point of humorless) drama that paid homage to Ingmar Bergman; *Manhattan* (1979), widely viewed as his best film; and *Stardust Memories* (1980), another dark comedy with dour overtones. His work in the 1980's was more varied, reaching high points in the comically moving *The Purple Rose of Cairo* (1985), the emotionally rich *Hannah and Her Sisters* (1986), and the morally compelling *Crimes and Misdemeanors* (1989). While his audience has never been vast compared to that of such writer/directors as Steven Spielberg and George Lucas, Allen has developed a loyal following. The 1992 controversy surrounding his relationship with longtime companion Mia Farrow and Farrow's daughter Soon-Yi Previn may have cost him some fans and hurt his personal reputation, but it is not likely to substantially affect lasting opinions of his work.

Impact of Event

As many contemporaries recognized, *Annie Hall* was, in some hard-to-define but very real way, a quintessential film of its time. This perception only grew stronger in the decades that followed the film's release. In its use of unconventional narrative strategies in storytelling; in its drawing on psychoanalytic (especially Freudian) theory, in its depiction of New York and attitudes toward Middle America and California, and in its attitudes about contemporary romance, the film embraces and challenges a series of assumptions and prevalent beliefs distinctive to the late 1970's and the years that followed.

The 1970's, especially the early 1970's, was a time in film history when many Hollywood conventions were reconfigured and even subverted. While Woody Allen did not overtly challenge dominant assumptions the way iconoclastic directors such as Robert Altman and Martin Scorsese did, *Annie Hall* is characterized by a series of techniques (borrowed from filmmakers such as Federico Fellini and Jean-Luc Godard) that mark it as an unconventional film: split screens, subtitles to reveal what characters are thinking, cartoons, asides to the audience, and a nonchronological plot line. Indeed, by the standards of many Hollywood films, there was hardly a plot at all. In telling the story of a contemporary romance between two relatively ordinary people, there was a kind of willfully small-scale, even antiheroic cast to *Annie Hall* that was consonant with many films of the time.

This antiheroic dimension (typified by hilarious sequences in which Keaton and Allen struggle to master lobsters and insects) is augmented by the powerful grip that psychoanalysis has over the main characters and that hovers over the film as a whole. While Allen plays a far more assured character than he did in *Take the Money and Run* or *Sleeper*, he seems to imply that any normal person in the 1970's had to be a little neurotic. And people who think of themselves as well adjusted—especially Midwestern WASPs and fun-loving Californians—are particularly singled out for ridicule.

Such scenes underline the degree to which *Annie Hall* is a film about and for New York. While it is generally assumed that this theme reaches its fullest expression in

Manhattan, in _Annie Hall_, too, the city is a virtual character in the film, especially in shots of the waterfront, Coney Island, and the Manhattan skyline. New York's fiscal crisis is referred to in a scene with the irate Max (Tony Roberts), who wants to leave the city for Los Angeles, and is a metaphor for the decay decried by a number of the characters. If Allen's Los Angeles is sunny and comfortable, though, it is also superficial. (The film marked perhaps one of the last times Los Angeles could be depicted as an alternative to a city such as New York instead of as a financially troubled, fractious, and crime-ridden metropolis in its own right.) _Annie Hall_ is meant to show that New York has a sense of richness and sophistication that the homogeneous Midwest—savagely depicted in a sequence on Annie's family—and the vacuous West can never match. This cleverly made cinematic argument is one of the most striking impressions the film makes.

Annie Hall is also useful as a lasting document of changing social mores in the United States. Many Americans responded to the movie because it captured the awkwardness and uncertainty of a nation in transition from the post-World War II traditional family to the alternative arrangements that were becoming increasingly common in American life. Alvy and Annie's matter-of-fact rejection of marriage and casual embrace of sexuality makes for a striking contrast from movies of the previous generation. The film also embodies values that would provoke bitter opposition from conservatives in the 1980's and 1990's.

In fact, Allen's widely publicized relationship with companion Mia Farrow's daughter—headlined in the media during the Republican National Convention in 1992—led some critics to call Allen the very embodiment of the nation's lost family values. Regardless of its validity, such an assertion illustrates the extent to which Allen's work touched some of the most vital issues in contemporary American life.

In retrospect, _Annie Hall_ appears to mark the high-water point of Allen's popularity. His subsequent work's failure to reach the same commercial heights, however, may be the result of conscious choice as much as of public taste. In any case, it is clear that _Annie Hall_ represented a landmark in the artistic development of a major cultural figure in the late twentieth century United States.

Bibliography

Allen, Woody. _Four Films of Woody Allen._ New York: Random House, 1982. Consisting of the screenplays for _Annie Hall, Interiors, Manhattan,_ and _Stardust Memories,_ this collection offers the reader direct access to Allen's genius. See also the screenplay for _Hannah and Her Sisters_ (1987). For a look at Allen's literary gifts, see _Getting Even_ (1971), _Without Feathers_ (1975), and _Side Effects_ (1980).

Brode, Douglas. _The Films of Woody Allen._ New York: Carol, 1991. This oversized book offers a scholarly film-by-film analysis of Allen's work from the 1960's on (and has been periodically updated). Comprehensive, intelligent, and lavishly illustrated, it is perhaps the best study of its kind.

Hirsch, Foster. _Love, Sex, Death, and the Meaning of Life: Woody Allen's Comedy._ New York: McGraw-Hill, 1981. A bio-critique of Allen's career. Readable, but like so many books on the subject, it lacks critical distance. Perhaps most useful as a document of how and why Allen's fans felt as they did.

Jacobs, Diane. *But We Need the Eggs: The Magic of Woody Allen.* New York: St. Martin's Press, 1982. Another bio-critique along the same lines as Hirsch's. Jacob's book, though, has an unusually good filmography and an appendix of citations of Allen's plays and books.

Lax, Eric. *Woody Allen: A Biography.* New York: Alfred A. Knopf, 1991. This bestselling biography of Allen received a good deal of media attention (an excerpt was published in *The New York Times Sunday Magazine*) and may well remain the standard study of Allen's life. What it lacks in detachment is compensated for by the access Lax gained to his normally reticent subject.

McCann, Graham. *Woody Allen: New Yorker.* Cambridge, England: Polity Press, 1990. A scholarly British perspective of the filmmaker that blends biography and textual analysis. The excellent bibliography makes it a good point of departure for students who wish to place Allen's work in a larger theoretical and historical perspective.

Yacowar, Maurice. *Loser Take All: The Comic Art of Woody Allen.* New York: Ungar, 1979. A readable, if dated, compendium of Allen's various activities through the 1970's. As the title suggests, the book uses humor as its organizing theme.

Jim Cullen

Cross-References

Chaplin Produces His Masterpiece *The Gold Rush* (1925), p. 659; The Classic Screwball Comedy Reaches Its Height in Popularity (1934), p. 951; Welles's *Citizen Kane* Breaks with Traditional Filmmaking (1941), p. 1200; Ealing Comedies Mark a High Point in British Film (1949), p. 1427; *La Strada* Solidifies Fellini's Renown as a Brilliant Director (1954), p. 1596; Godard's Expressionistic *À bout de souffle* Revolutionizes Film (1960), p. 1845.

SATURDAY NIGHT FEVER EPITOMIZES THE DISCO CRAZE

Categories of event: Music and motion pictures
Time: 1977
Locale: The United States

Disco, a cultural form rooted in black and gay musical subcultures, became a national fad in the United States in the 1970's, culminating in the sound track for the 1977 film Saturday Night Fever

Principal personages:
BARRY GIBB (1947-),
ROBIN GIBB (1949-), and
MAURICE GIBB (1949-), the members of the successful musical group the Bee Gees
BERNARD EDWARDS (1952-) and
NILE RODGERS (1952-), the founders of the premier disco group Chic, who went on to have distinguished careers as writers and producers for other acts
DONNA SUMMER (LADONNA GAINES, 1948-), a popular disco singer, the only disco performer to have a successful career lasting into the 1980's
GIORGIO MORODER (c. 1941-), the record producer who rose to fame on the strength of Donna Summer's "Love to Love You Baby"
HARRY WAYNE CASEY (1951-), the leader of K.C. and the Sunshine Band, a highly successful disco group
GRACE JONES (1952-), a singer who continued to represent disco's core constituency after the music had gone mainstream
THE VILLAGE PEOPLE, a gay singing and dance group that enjoyed a series of hits in the late 1970's

Summary of Event

Seeming to emerge from nowhere in the mid-1970's, disco came to dominate popular music, a phenomenon that crested with the release of the film *Saturday Night Fever* and its sound track in 1977. A fierce backlash ensued, and by the early 1980's, disco had become a target of ridicule and had disappeared from the charts.

According to legend, disco originated in gay discotheques in the New York summertime resort of Fire Island and nearby Manhattan. Homosexuals who could not find live acts to perform for them at parties turned to professional disc jockeys to put together musical sequences suitable for dancing. The compilation of such sequences became an art form in itself and explains the prominent role that disc jockeys would play as disco began to reach wider audiences.

Disco's musical origins were in African-American traditions. James Brown boasted that he was the father of disco, and given the rhythmic and percussive elements that dominated his work in the 1960's, many would assent to the claim. The work of Sly and the Family Stone in the late 1960's and early 1970's is also widely considered a precursor of the form. More directly, soul groups such as the O'Jays and seductive singers such as Barry White developed styles that would be widely adopted by a variety of disco performers.

Disco emerged as a presence on the pop charts around 1974, when the Hues Corporation's "Rock the Boat" and Gloria Gaynor's "Never Can Say Goodbye" reached the top ten on *Billboard* magazine's pop chart. The Jackson Five's success with their hit "Dancin' Machine" that year suggested disco's potential for established acts willing to extend or adapt their style to reach a burgeoning audience.

In its first few years, however, disco was primarily a vehicle for new performers to find national recognition. Among them were K.C. and the Sunshine Band, who enjoyed a string of hits including "Get Down Tonight," "That's the Way (I Like It)," and "(Shake, Shake, Shake) Shake Your Booty." Also notable was the group Chic, which virtually defined the disco aesthetic with their hits "Dance, Dance, Dance (Yowsah, Yowsah, Yowsah)" and "Le Freak." At the heart of that aesthetic was a fascination with repetition, technology, and seamless musical transitions that often gave producers a prominent role in the making of disco records. Among the more famous disco producers were Jacques Morali, who helped the gay musical group the Village People enjoy a series of tongue-in-cheek hits that included "Macho Man," "Y.M.C.A.," and "In the Navy," and Giorgio Moroder, who produced Donna Summer's records.

Summer, dubbed the "queen of disco," proved to be its most durable performer. Her 1975 single "Love to Love You Baby," which featured a long orgasmic interlude, created a sensation in the musical world. For the rest of the 1970's, she would be the premier female singer on the pop charts, best known for her hits "I Feel Love" (1976), "MacArthur Park" (1978), and "Hot Stuff" (1979).

Disco's greatest success story, though, was the Bee Gees. A Beatlesque pop group who had known some success in the late 1960's, Maurice, Barry, and Robin Gibb (the name Bee Gees stands for "Brothers Gibb") had released a string of flops in the early 1970's. In 1975, after working with a new producer, the group returned to form with their infectious disco hits "Jive Talkin'" and "Nights on Broadway," which were followed in 1976 by "You Should Be Dancing." It was in this context, as the comeback group of the decade, that the Bee Gees were asked to contribute a few songs for a forthcoming motion picture that would feature disco acts.

That film, *Saturday Night Fever*, traced the life of a working-class Brooklynite (played by John Travolta) and his struggle to find release from his mundane existence. Though the film had a gritty, realistic edge that won praise from some critics, it was the dance sequences—buoyed by the sound track—that attracted audiences. *Saturday Night Fever* became one of the most celebrated films of the 1970's, and the sound track became the best-selling album of its time, with sales in excess of thirty million. It was followed in 1978 by *Thank God It's Friday*, another disco film sound track that spawned Donna Summer's Grammy Award-winning "Last Dance."

Saturday Night Fever inaugurated disco's utter dominance of popular music in 1977 and 1978. Leading the charge were the Bee Gees, whose "How Deep Is Your Love," "Stayin' Alive," and "Night Fever" each topped the *Billboard* magazine pop chart. At one point in 1978, the group had either performed or written five songs in the top ten, a feat surpassed only by the Beatles (to whom the Bee Gees were frequently compared). Bee Gees protégés Yvonne Elliman and Samantha Sang were among those to ride the tide.

Meanwhile, nondisco acts began to climb aboard the bandwagon. David Bowie, ever sensitive to musical trends, had released his disco-inflected single "Fame" back in 1975. Rod Stewart underwent a musical facelift with his 1979 smash "Do Ya Think I'm Sexy." Blondie combined its New Wave sensibility with a disco beat in "Heart of Glass," which topped the pop music chart later the same year. Even bastions of the rock aristocracy got into the act; the Rolling Stones's 1978 hit "Miss You" had unmistakable disco accents, while Queen unabashedly embraced the form with "Another One Bites the Dust," which became an instant classic in 1980.

A backlash had been building against disco however, and the reaction began gathering momentum at the end of the decade. The most obvious example of antidisco sentiment was a record burning hosted by a Chicago disc jockey at a baseball stadium in 1979. For many rock traditionalists, the popular slogan "disco sucks" became a rallying cry and the phrase appeared on T-shirts, stickers, and posters. More articulate listeners decried the musical and emotional superficiality that disco often uncritically purveyed and celebrated.

Meanwhile, other musical movements, including punk and New Wave, began seizing the musical spotlight. By 1982, disco had virtually disappeared from the charts. To many, in retrospect, it was an amusing (or irritating) fad. Yet disco defined a moment in popular musical history, and it continued to have an influence long after that moment passed.

Impact of Event

For its critics, and even for many of its fans, disco was little more than fluff, a form of entertainment devoid of any larger meaning. Indeed, to a great extent, this was the source of its appeal to some (and a source of unease to others). In retrospect, however, some observers have noted a series of cultural and intellectual influences that led disco to appear when it did. In this view, disco worked because it provided some compelling answers for Americans facing confusing questions in the social climate of the 1970's.

It was not the best of times. The Vietnam War, Watergate, and the energy crisis had engendered grave doubts among many Americans about the ability—or even the willingness—of government to solve some of the major problems facing the country. The idealism of the 1960's, epitomized by the enthusiasm surrounding the Civil Rights movement, had disintegrated amid the factional infighting and political defeats of the late 1960's and early 1970's. Under such circumstances, many young people sought diversions free of the false hopes and broken promises of the previous decade.

Popular music reflected this state of enervation. Some of the major acts of the 1960's—the Beatles, the Doors, Jimi Hendrix, Janis Joplin—had either broken up or died. Rock and roll, which had once seemed a vehicle for political liberation, now seemed little more than a vehicle for commercial gain. In England, which was suffering even more than the United States from economic malaise, the state of affairs helped to produce punk rock, which would have a notable, if less pervasive, impact on the United States. In a very different—but related—way, disco represented another response to cultural frustration among young people.

Like many forms of expression in the nation's history, disco was a product of subcultures working at the margins of the mainstream. Drawing on the symbols and strategies of the Civil Rights movement, gays in the United States had won a modicum of acceptance and freedom by the 1970's, but they were still largely considered outsiders. Similarly, black Americans had achieved some important social and political gains, yet blacks and whites were still largely segregated in revealing ways (such as FM radio formats). With its pulsating beat and emphasis on public display, disco began as a means to foster community among people alienated from the culture at large.

To a great extent, disco's growing appeal to a mainstream audience can be explained by the musical innovations of practitioners such as Donna Summer, K.C. and the Sunshine Band, and Chic. Disco, though, was also increasingly attractive for its celebration of the moment, the sense of release it offered from the workaday world, and the central role that expression—especially sexual expression—played in its world of costume, dance, and, in some cases, drugs. This was not music for changing the world; that had proved too difficult. This was music for having a good time.

Like most cultural movements, disco had many facets. Groups such as the Bee Gees—and movies such as *Saturday Night Fever*—made the music attractive to mainstream, heterosexual audiences. Overseas, a variant on the form called Eurodisco further emphasized technology and the role of the producer. Meanwhile, performers such as Grace Jones kept the unorthodox, sexually aggressive aspects of disco alive for its original audience.

Indeed, disco never altogether lost its early racial and sexual accents, and one can make a case that hostility to disco was often a veiled form of racism or homophobia. While the Chicago record-burning of 1979 was widely seen as a joke, others saw a much darker subtext. In any case, the more conservative social climate symbolized by Ronald Reagan's election to the presidency in 1980 may have been a factor in disco's precipitous decline.

Nevertheless, disco continued to influence the direction of popular music throughout the 1980's. Michael Jackson's dominance of popular music in that decade was to a great degree built on a disco foundation. Similarly, Prince would fuse dance rhythms with traditional rock to produce an innovative sound that attracted a wide variety of adherents; and in the mid- and late 1980's, too, Madonna essentially captured much of disco's old constituency. Even into the 1990's, British acts such as Lisa Stansfield demonstrated the continuing mass appeal of the form. Disco elements, particularly the prominent use of percussion and repetition, were also incorporated into rap.

A good deal of the disco music produced in the 1970's was instantly—and sometimes intentionally—forgettable. In subtle and sometimes lasting ways, however, the music epitomized its time and became part of a usable past drawn on by subsequent generations of performers.

Bibliography

Dannen, Frederic. "Casablanca." In *Hit Men: A True Tale of Power, Money, and Mayhem in the World of Rock and Roll.* New York: Times Books, 1990. Dannen's book is primarily a study of the contemporary music industry, but this chapter, a profile of Casablanca Records founder Neil Bogart, offers a revealing picture of an archetypal disco life-style. Casablanca was largely a disco label, and its collapse illustrates what some of the music's harshest critics were talking about.

Dyer, Richard. "In Defense of Disco." In *On Record: Rock, Pop, and the Written Word*, edited by Simon Frith and Andrew Goodwin. New York: Pantheon Books, 1990. An intelligent partisan reading of disco by a gay man. Dyer makes an unorthodox, but compelling, case for the music from a socialist perspective.

Shaw, Arnold. *Black Popular Music in America: From the Spirituals, Minstrels, and Ragtime to Soul, Disco, and Hip-Hop.* New York: Schirmer Books, 1986. A useful source for understanding disco's origins. Carries the discussion forward from the disco age into the rap-music era.

Smucker, Tom. "Disco." In *The Rolling Stone Illustrated History of Rock and Roll*, edited by Jim Miller. New York: Rolling Stone Press, 1980. The most incisive and readable piece ever written about disco. Smucker writes as one who participated in the disco subculture, and he makes its appeal intelligible to outsiders.

Tucker, Ken. "Outsider Art: Disco and Funk." In *Rock of Ages: The Rolling Stone History of Rock and Roll*, by Ed Ward, Geoffrey Stokes, and Ken Tucker. New York: Rolling Stone Press, 1986. A good brief discussion of the musical origins of disco. As usual, Tucker places the form within the wider context of the popular music of the time.

Jim Cullen

Cross-References

Gordy Founds Motown Records (1959), p. 1790; Brown Wins a Grammy for "Papa's Got a Brand New Bag" (1966), p. 2059; Wonder Releases *Innervisions* (1973), p. 2294; The Sex Pistols Spark Punk Rock's Musical Insurrection (1975), p. 2360; *Thriller* Marks Michael Jackson's Musical Coming-of-Age (1982), p. 2512; Rap Goes Platinum with Run-D.M.C.'s *Raising Hell* (1986), p. 2582.

THE *STAR WARS* TRILOGY
REDEFINES SPECIAL EFFECTS

Category of event: Motion pictures
Time: 1977-1983
Locale: The United States

George Lucas created a blockbuster science-fiction series with special effects that set the standard for an entire industry

Principal personages:

GEORGE LUCAS (1945-   ), the filmmaker who created the *Star Wars* trilogy

IRVIN KERSHNER (1923-   ), the director of *The Empire Strikes Back*, the second film in the series

RICHARD MARQUAND (1938-1987), the director of *Return of the Jedi*, the series' final installment

MARK HAMILL (1952-   ), the actor who rose to stardom as Luke Skywalker in the *Star Wars* trilogy

HARRISON FORD (1942-   ), the actor who starred as Han Solo in the trilogy

ALEC GUINNESS (1914-   ), the renowned British actor who played Obi Wan Kenobi in the trilogy

Summary of Event

George Lucas earned enough money from his critically successful film *American Graffiti* (1973) to produce *Star Wars*, the first installment of his science-fiction trilogy, in 1977. *Star Wars*, in turn, was such a phenomenally successful film at the box offices that Lucas had the money to expand the fantasy into *The Empire Strikes Back* in 1980 and *Return of the Jedi* in 1983. Extraordinary as the first movie was, the second and third were even more so; in making the sequels, Lucas could concentrate huge financial resources through his subsidiary company devoted to special-effects production, Industrial Light and Magic. Located north of San Francisco, Industrial Light and Magic was the material origin of the three motion pictures that extended the limits of sound and visual effects.

Star Wars captures attention with its mixture of several film genres, including Westerns and romances as well as science fiction. It honors America's search for new frontiers as Luke Skywalker searches through galaxies to save a beautiful princess and find his father. The fantasy of the story suggests mythic themes of the widest dimensions, from political to religious levels of significance. Pitting powers of rebellious light and imperial darkness against each other, *Star Wars* echoes medieval European stories of knights learning to fulfill divine destinies: thus, Luke Skywalker learns to control the mysterious "Force" because he learns to subordinate his will to it. The film is filled with adventures of flight and pursuit, near-disaster and triumphant escape, leading to cosmic celebration with a triumvirate of heroes who have saved the universe.

Like the weekend serials of earlier decades, the *Star Wars* trilogy was built upon episodes in which the heroes are nearly destroyed before achieving miraculous triumphs. Instead of cliff-hanging perils, however, there are astronomical dangers and asteroidal threats; spaceships and star-scooters replace stagecoaches and horses, as characters zoom through space at light speed. By location shooting on deserts and frozen wastes, the films create bizarre scenic effects to suggest alien worlds for cosmic battles. Most effective, however, are studio-shot episodes, remarkably constructed sets, and scenes created by computer-assisted electronic and photographic technology.

For an appreciation of what huge profits could do to elaborate visionary experience in movies, consider the transformation of the "Cantina" scene in *Star Wars* into the "Monster Rally" scene in *Return of the Jedi*. In the earlier scene, which evoked barroom settings from countless Western films, there were only a few monstrous creatures to view; in the later one, there were more than eighty creatures that took fifteen artists more than a year to construct. These monster creatures were made with painstaking detail, as molded masks for human actors or puppets for single hands or several persons. Indeed, some ten puppeteers, several mime artists, more than forty-two extras, eighteen principals, and ninety crew members were required to produce this one scene.

Shooting the scene took a month, but more impressive was the making of the figure of the chief monster, Jabba the Hut. This giant puppet was a complex machine requiring several operators for its various bodily parts. The puppet of Jabba took three months to build, weighed more than two thousand pounds, and cost half a million dollars. Equally impressive are the figures associated with the short episode of the barge battle in which the power of Jabba is destroyed. Constructed in an Arizona desert by a hundred workers, the two-hundred-foot-long, eighty-foot-high barge took four months to build—and less than five minutes to blow apart.

To make the scene work, however, live-action shots were mixed with special electronic and photographic effects, which are the glory of the trilogy. *Return of the Jedi* alone included more than five hundred shots of special effects; such scenes made up fifteen percent of the film. From laser swords to electric charges, these films mix flashing, glowing lights of brilliant coloring with buzzing, crackling sounds to create high-energy effects. The overwhelming presence of machinery extends to robots and to human beings who depend on machines; most intriguing is the breathing device that sustains the life of arch-villain Darth Vader. Some effects, such as the breathing of Vader and the richly resonating voice of actor James Earl Jones, are sound tricks, and some are visual achievements of state-of-the-art computers and highly trained technicians.

Using techniques long established—some since as far back as the turn-of-the-century silent films of George Méliès—the artists and technicians of Industrial Light and Magic choreographed intricately composed space battles, such as the attack on the nuclear reactor at the center of the colossal Death Star spacecraft, and they arranged layers of illusion to produce the richly textured celebration scenes in the edenic Valley of the Ewoks. The attack on the Death Star required hours of drawings for the scene's storyboard, followed by careful designing of meticulously detailed models; the models were then photographed by computer-controlled robot cameras programmed according to the storyboard sketches. The effects supervisor at Industrial Light and Magic, Ken Ralston, directed the work of many technicians to bring all the elements together for the complex space battles in *Return of the Jedi*; the film's battle scenes involved more than sixty separate spaceships photographed on 170 rolls of film.

The lush Ewok planet, where the last battle to destroy the armies of the empire is fought, had its origin in a high-speed scooter race through a real redwood forest in Northern California. Combining photography of models with live action against blue-screen backgrounds, the scene gives a thrilling introduction to the world of the Ewoks, small bearlike creatures. There followed the visit to the Valley of the Ewoks, which was created from matte paintings, electronically driven optical printers, forest location shooting, and a studio set in London, where dwarf actors donned Ewok costumes. The Ewok language was the special creation of Ben Burtt, the film's sound designer, and the musical scores of the trilogy were composed by John Williams.

These features combined to serve a simple tale of good triumphant over evil. While there were sinister implications of political, racial, and sexual ambiguities, the basic story of the trilogy is clear and forceful for a generation that grew up with video games and home robotics. Equally forceful was the trilogy's theme of family. The hero, deprived of a father and sister, finds both; he never, though, shows much interest in his mother. Indeed, feminist themes go a-begging; they had to await the successes of Sigourney Weaver as the star of *Alien* in 1979.

Impact of Event

The *Star Wars* trilogy had multiple impacts on popular culture, including an increase in the number of science-fiction films. In addition, the title of the first film was appropriated by the political debate over high-technology defense systems, and various directors utilized science-fiction vehicles to engage in religious and political debates that echoed 1950's film propaganda. In 1982, John Carpenter remade the classic 1952 horror film *The Thing*, which contains a message about the threat of Communism. Carpenter's film shows the impact of high-technology special effects in its monster's ability to mutate before the audience's very eyes (an effect not possible for the earlier film). This same kind of horrifying experience was still more effectively done in the *Alien* trilogy (1979-1992).

Embedded in the science-fiction genre is a general debate over the uses and abuses of scientific and technological power. Nowhere could the differences be more noticeable than in a comparison of the *Star Wars* films with a film such as *Blade Runner* (1982), a combination of detective thriller and science-fiction film that provides a cerebral answer to the Western romance of *Star Wars*. In addition, *Blade Runner* provides a religious dimension of ambiguous complexity to challenge the simpler religious fantasy of Lucas' films. Ironically, if not deliberately, *Blade Runner* showcases a troubled hero played by Harrison Ford, the same actor who played Han Solo in the *Star Wars* trilogy.

It would not be accurate to say that the *Star Wars* trilogy commenced the renewal of mass interest in science-fiction films or high-tech special effects; such credit should be reserved for *2001: A Space Odyssey* (1968) or *Silent Running* (1972). It would, though, be accurate to note that Lucas' trilogy established a threshold of cinematic intensity and economic prosperity stemming from huge investments in the production of special-effects movies in the science-fiction genre. To compare earlier versions of *Star Trek*, either the television shows or the motion pictures, with later ones is to notice the increasing use of special effects. Other films that show the *Star Wars* influence include the *Terminator* series, the *Superman* movies, and even the horror films of the *Nightmare on Elm Street* series, since special effects dominate all, even when such films are not particularly scientific in their fictions.

In 1971, Lucas was the writer and director of *THX-1138*, a science-fiction story of drug-controlled life underground in a future society in which robots police human behavior. Lucas was inspired by the success of Stanley Kubrick's *2001*, and he was supported by his association with Francis Ford Coppola at the American Zoetrope Studio in San Francisco. After the series of artistic and commercial successes that began for him with *American Graffiti*, Lucas' career has been oriented toward special-effects and adventure films. He produced *Raiders of the Lost Ark* (1981) and thus has played a role in the promotion of another successful series of motion pictures.

Whether he advanced, stimulated, or indeed shaped popular taste for films in the 1970's and 1980's, Lucas has made his mark on the industry, the technology, and the subjects of American motion pictures. The setting and theme of *THX-1138* anticipate those of *The Terminator* (1984) as well as *Back to the Future* (1985), with its mixture of science fiction and the domestic nostalgia of *American Graffiti*. Most emphatically, though, Lucas' high-tech expression of romance, adventure, cosmic curiosity, and religious yearning in the *Star Wars* trilogy energized popular taste for fast-paced story action propelled by light and sound effects. Perhaps Lucas' success also had something to do with the direction Steven Spielberg took when he made *Close Encounters of the Third Kind* (1977) and *E.T. The Extraterrestrial* (1982), although the timing of *Close Encounters* suggests it was more coeval with than a consequence of *Star Wars*. Without Lucas' creations, however, the distance from *The Thing* to *E.T.* would have been greater for all extraterrestrials in science-fiction films.

Bibliography

Braudy, Leo. "Genre and the Resurrection of the Past." In *Shadows of the Magic Lamp: Fantasy and Science Fiction in Film*, edited by George Slusser and Eric S.

Rabkin. Carbondale: Southern Illinois University Press, 1985. Emphasizing horror as making audiences aware of genre, Braudy cites *Star Wars* as a film dependent on familiarity with tradition. Other films, though, are given more attention than Lucas' trilogy.

Ellis, Jack C. "Here and Now: US, 1977—." In *A History of Film.* 3d ed. Englewood Cliffs, N.J.: Prentice-Hall, 1990. Making the point that economics and technology have driven the industry toward spectacular special-effect films, Ellis focuses on social themes in post-Vietnam American movies and speculates on the artistry of directors such as Lucas. Contains a list of films of the period and a brief bibliography.

La Valley, Albert J. "Traditions of Trickery: The Role of Special Effects in the Science Fiction Film." In *Shadows of the Magic Lamp: Fantasy and Science Fiction in Film,* edited by George Slusser and Eric S. Rabkin. Carbondale: Southern Illinois University Press, 1985. Approaching the subject historically, La Valley focuses on *Metropolis* (1926) and *Woman in the Moon* (1929) as dialectical in uses of special effects. *Forbidden Planet* (1956) is used as a more recent model for understanding special effects before *2001.* The *Star Wars* trilogy is used as an example of blockbuster films more optimistic in attitudes toward science.

Mast, Gerald. "The New Hollywood: 1966-1978." In *A Short History of the Movies.* 3d ed. Indianapolis, Ind.: Bobbs-Merrill, 1981. Mast explains the success of contemporary films as the result of competition with television, influence from European and underground directors, expansion of themes and subjects, and reflection of current social values. He identifies George Lucas as one of the younger directors who learned from Coppola and Kubrick. Contains a bibliography and filmography.

Ryan, Michael, and Douglas Kellner. *Camera Politica: The Politics and Ideology of Contemporary Hollywood Film.* Bloomington: Indiana University Press, 1988. A long, dense book with an introduction, ten chapters, and conclusion. Approaching the subject of politics in film, the authors examine films according to such characteristics as feminism, racism, genre, individualism, and technology. The *Star Wars* trilogy is examined in the context of an argument that genres have been transformed by the failure of liberal political causes.

Wood, Robin. "Papering the Cracks: Fantasy and Ideology in the Reagan Era." In *Hollywood from Vietnam to Reagan.* New York: Columbia University Press, 1986. Harshly critical of what he calls the "syndrome" of Lucas and Spielberg, Wood analyzes the *Star Wars* trilogy as a successful appeal to childishness. Wood also presses his favorite points about nuclear anxiety and homophobic elements under the category of searching for the father. The provocative thesis is sometimes shrill, but the analysis produces interesting insights into the trilogy.

Richard D. McGhee

Cross-References

Le Voyage dans la lune Introduces Special Effects (1902), p. 57; Lang Expands the Limits of Filmmaking with *Metropolis* (1927), p. 707; American Science Fiction Enjoys Its Golden Age (1938), p. 1094; Kubrick Becomes a Film-Industry Leader (1964), p. 1989; Syndication Turns *Star Trek* into a Cult Classic (1972), p. 2260; Scott's *Blade Runner* Is a Visual Masterpiece (1982), p. 2486; *E.T.: The Extraterrestrial* Breaks Box-Office Records (1982), p. 2491.

ROOTS DRAMATIZES THE AFRICAN-AMERICAN EXPERIENCE

Category of event: Television and radio
Time: January 23-January 30, 1977
Locale: The United States

Roots, *the history of an African-American family from freedom in Africa to slavery in the United States to emancipation, captivated the attention of the nation*

Principal personages:

ALEX HALEY (1921-1992), a writer who produced the best-selling book on which the miniseries was based

DAVID WOLPER (1928-   ), the producer of *Roots*

FRED SILVERMAN (1937-   ), the president of the American Broadcasting Company (ABC), who made the decision to broadcast *Roots* as a miniseries

LEVAR BURTON (1957-   ), the actor who played the role of Kunta Kinte

BEN VEREEN (1946-   ), the actor who played the role of Chicken George

Summary of Event

Alex Haley, an established writer who previously had authored *The Autobiography of Malcolm X* (1965) and who had done numerous interviews with well-known figures for *Playboy* magazine, published *Roots: The Saga of an American Family* on October 1, 1976. Within a month, the book was a best-seller. It was a mix of careful historical research and imagined fictional detail that began with Haley's ancestors in the village of Juffure in Gambia, West Africa, and ended with the former slaves gaining their freedom and moving to a farm—still in the Haley family possession—in Henning, Tennessee. Even before the book was published, the American Broadcasting Company (ABC), under its president, Fred Silverman, had made a decision to produce a made-for-television special based on the book. It soon became obvious that a movie of the usual two to three hours could not encompass the length and content of Haley's book. Because the book was so popular, ABC did not want to disappoint viewers by overcondensation in its presentation, so a decision was made to film twelve hours of material.

In many ways, the book was well suited for adaptation to television. It was not an academic history but instead a somewhat fictionalized account in which actual lives were re-created. Events were telescoped and sometimes fictionalized while being cast against a mosaic that was factual. At the time of its publication, various historians commented that there were numerous inaccuracies in *Roots*, yet Haley himself said that the book, and the series based on it, were not so much history as a study in mythmaking. Haley commented that "what *Roots* gets at in whatever form, is that it touches the pulse of how alike we human beings are when you get down to the bottom, beneath these man-imposed differences."

In its book form, *Roots* won the National Book Award for 1977 and also received a special Pulitzer Prize. The book sold more than one million copies during 1977. Its popularity was reinforced by the television miniseries—on the third day of the broadcast, the book sold sixty-seven thousand copies.

The success of the book heightened expectations but did not guarantee the success of a miniseries based on the published work. No one knew that *Roots* would be the most-watched dramatic show in the history of television. Instead, there were many unanswered questions.

British television had pioneered the miniseries, but the idea had not been used widely in the United States except on public television. ABC, however, had experienced success in the 1975-1976 season with *Rich Man, Poor Man*. This success encouraged the network to finance additional miniseries, including *Roots*.

As the filming was completed, network president Fred Silverman began to plan the price of commercials on the programs. He projected this cost on the basis of a rather modest share of the national audience. He expected thirty of every hundred television sets in the nation to be tuned to *Roots*. As the time for the broadcast drew closer, more problems were raised. The series was about a black family and had only black heroes. Would this subject attract a large audience? Would network affiliates all carry the show, or would sensitivity to racial questions cause some stations to bypass the broadcast? In the face of these types of questions, Silverman made a decision that was risky but seemed the best way to handle the matter. He decided to run *Roots* for eight consecutive nights, an hour or two each night, rather than broadcasting the show once a week. If the program was a failure, the damage would be confined to a single week rather than spread across the rest of the season. By parceling out *Roots* in short segments following already-popular shows, ABC hoped to minimize the impact of potential failure.

On the positive side for planning purposes, the series was well written. Each episode was complete within itself, yet each show led into the next. In addition, each episode, except the sixth and seventh, ended on a positive, hopeful note.

ABC need not have been worried. *Roots* proved to be the supreme example of a miniseries. Seven of its eight segments placed on the top ten list of most-watched television programs of all time, and the remaining segment was thirteenth on the list. The final episode was the most highly watched program ever broadcast on television to that time. In all, more than 130 million Americans watched at least some of *Roots*. Dozens of cities declared the eight-day broadcast period to be "*Roots* Week," more than twenty of these being in the South. More than two hundred fifty colleges and universities offered courses based on the telecast and the book.

Roots demonstrated that white Americans would respond positively to a show about black people in a socially and historically significant situation. The miniseries was basically conservative, presenting a family as a major source of stability in the midst of stress. The central element of *Roots* was the favorite American theme of family and family values.

Impact of Event

Although *Roots* was not the first television miniseries, its sweeping success established that genre as a permanent part of the American television industry. In so doing, *Roots* provided a valuable service to television in the United States. The miniseries, as a new form of programming, allowed television to achieve the thematic power and sweep of narrative that previously had been reserved for films. The extended narrative form provides an opportunity for actors to become a part of their characters and also allows the characters to take hold of the imagination of the viewer. *Roots* lengthened the attention span of its viewers and helped prepare the way for other extended, in-depth treatments of significant subjects. The twelve hours of viewing time was analogous to the time necessary to read a book of medium length. The detail that the miniseries achieved was much greater than the normal thirty-minute or one-hour television program length permits. Although no network would choose to have a miniseries of one kind or another constantly in broadcast, *Roots* determined that there would always be a place for such shows.

Roots also gave historical subjects a prominent place on television. Historic sites are popular vacation destinations in the United States among a significant part of the population, but the study of history is not popular. *Roots* helped create a taste for history that has been pursued by later miniseries, the best example being the 1990 public television broadcast of Ken Burns's *The Civil War.*

The relationship between commercial television and historians was uneasy at the time of the broadcast of *Roots*, and it has remained so. The presentation of historical subjects on television is not accurate enough to satisfy most academic historians. Many insist that programs such as *Roots* be labeled as "docudramas" and not as documentaries. Some television critics and producers agree with this point of view. As a docudrama, *Roots* was a melodrama with stereotypes that sometimes disclosed the point of view of those who, historically, have been victims. David Wolper, the producer of *Roots*, recognized this fact when he commented that *Roots* was not intended to be a reference work for historical information. The focus of *Roots* was to be emotional impact; it was intended to show how it felt to be a slave. Because of its vivid historical imagination and its careful attention to re-creation, *Roots* became a powerful tool to achieve this end. The miniseries was, after all, the first television program to address the issue of slavery from the point of view of slaves.

Roots directly challenged what was, in 1977, a major academic theory in the interpretation of slavery. In 1959, historian Stanley M. Elkins had published an important book entitled *Slavery: A Problem in American Institutional and Intellectual Life.* In this book, Elkins argued that slavery was a highly coercive, closed system with a modern analogy in the Nazi concentration camps. In the camps of the Nazi era, it was observed that some inmates identified with their guards and adopted the type of behavior the guards wanted. Elkins argued that this was a means of accommodation through role playing that allowed the inmates to deal psychologically with being oppressed. Elkins then argued that slaves did the same thing—they dealt with oppression by psychologically identifying with the masters. The psychological characteristic that developed from this Elkins called the "Sambo" role. Black slaves were like children; "docile but irresponsible, loyal but lazy, humble but chronic liars and thieves." In 1977, this was a widespread view of slavery.

Roots directly challenged this view of black history and helped open the way for another evaluation of the black experience of slavery. Kunta Kinte, the single most important character, never became docile despite several severe punishments and eventual amputation of a foot for his repeated attempts to run away. None of the descendants of Kunta Kinte looked at their owners as "good fathers"; indeed, Chicken George had to be restrained from killing the white man who was his biological father when the man made it clear that Chicken George was only a valuable piece of property and not a son.

Neither is it the case, as Elkins contends, that black people were so shocked and traumatized by the experience of enslavement that they gave up all ties to their African culture to become white people with black skins. *Roots* showed that the African heritage was not wiped out during the first generation of slaves and that aspects of tribal culture endured even into the twentieth century. Kunta Kinte, Chicken George, and Tom all functioned, even in slavery, as traditional African patriarchs. African humor, songs, dances, words, speech patterns, tales, games, folk beliefs, and sayings all were shown surviving the process of enslavement and transportation. One of the most powerful visual images of these African cultural survivals shown in *Roots* was the practice of naming a newborn child by lifting it upward toward a full moon, a symbol of renewing the link to Africa.

Another important impact of *Roots* was that the miniseries provided a source of national unity by keeping blacks and whites tuned in to acts of moral witness, of compassion, and of expiation. In short, *Roots* was a learning experience and seems to have had a positive impact on race relations. A nationwide survey by the National Association for the Advancement of Colored People (NAACP) reported that, except for a few isolated incidents, the showing of *Roots* strengthened black history offerings in schools and colleges and enlightened whites about the black heritage in both the United States and Africa. In this sense, critic Karl Meyer commented that *Roots* was like a medieval morality play, neither fact nor fiction but serving a didactic purpose.

Bibliography

Baye, Betty Winston. "Alex Haley's Roots Revisited." *Essence* 22 (February, 1992): 88. Discusses Haley's work just before his death as well as his connection with Malcolm X.

"Family Ties." *The New Yorker* 68 (October 26, 1992): 33-34. William Haley, the author's son, describes why he sees the auction of notes and proofs of his father's work as inappropriate. One scholar says that the auction of the deceased author's memorabilia is part of an ongoing fragmentation of the black literary legacy.

Fiske, John. *Television Culture*. London: Methuen, 1987. Describes how television creates a fantasy culture that is accepted in some ways by viewers as true and valid. The key to this process is that some elements of reality are incorporated into programming. *Roots*, with its fictionalized genealogy, is an example of this process.

O'Connor, John E., ed. *American History, American Television.* New York: Frederick Ungar, 1983. These collected essays present television as a powerful social force in American culture. Useful background on how television affects and mirrors American society; many topics are covered.

Podolsky, J. D. "Torn Up by the Roots." *People Weekly* 38 (October 5, 1992): 71-72. Describes the upcoming auction of Alex Haley's estate and conflicts concerning proper disposition of Haley's assets and literary legacy.

Michael R. Bradley

Cross-References

The Harlem Renaissance Celebrates African-American Culture (1920's), p. 480; Wright's *Native Son* Depicts Racism in America (1940), p. 1185; Ellison's *Invisible Man* Is Published (1952), p. 1541; Hansberry's *A Raisin in the Sun* Debuts on Broadway (1959), p. 1795; Baldwin Voices Black Rage in *The Fire Next Time* (1963), p. 1929; Baraka's *Dutchman* Dramatizes Racial Hatred (1964), p. 2000; *The Autobiography of Malcolm X* Is Published (1965), p. 2022; Marley's *Natty Dread* Establishes Reggae's Popularity (1975), p. 2344; Innovative Black Filmmakers Achieve Success (Late 1980's), p. 2565; *Do the Right Thing* Establishes Lee as a World-Class Director (1989), p. 2641; *The Civil War* Rivets the Attention of the United States (1990), p. 2657.

THE POMPIDOU CENTER OPENS IN PARIS

Categories of event: Architecture and art
Time: January 31, 1977
Locale: Paris, France

The Pompidou Center in Paris provoked controversy because of its innovative architecture, but its museum of modern art and culture proved popular

Principal personages:
RENZO PIANO (1937-   ), an Italian architect who helped to design the Pompidou Center
RICHARD ROGERS (1933-   ), an English architect who designed the Pompidou Center along with Piano
GEORGES POMPIDOU (1911-1974), the president of France who proposed that a new museum of modern art and culture be built in the Beaubourg section of Paris
PHILIP JOHNSON (1906-   ), an eminent American architect who served on the committee that selected Piano and Rogers as the architects for the Pompidou Center

Summary of Event

In December, 1969, only six months after his election to the presidency of France, Georges Pompidou proposed that a new museum of modern art and culture be constructed in the Beaubourg section of Paris. He selected as the site for the museum an undeveloped area that had been used as a parking lot for several decades. Although Pompidou would have preferred for political reasons that this very expensive museum be designed by French architects, he willingly accepted the recommendation of his committee that the proposal submitted by Renzo Piano and Richard Rogers, two relatively young foreign architects, be accepted over all the designs submitted by French architects.

The design presented by Piano and Rogers for the construction of the proposed museum was highly original. The plan called for all the structural supports, duct works, heating and air-conditioning equipment, and electrical boxes to be left clearly visible in the Pompidou Center. Visitors enter the museum by means of enclosed escalators, which take visitors halfway up the outside of the center. Unlike almost all other museums, the Pompidou Center does not have a traditional entrance on the ground floor. Huge transparent panes of glass form the exterior walls of the museum, and nothing is hidden inside or outside. Each of the museum's five floors is a vast open space. Piano and Rogers suggested that temporary partitions, and not permanent walls, be used to divide the various exhibition areas in the museum. Piano and Rogers wanted the Pompidou Center to be as flexible as possible so that it could accommodate the ever-changing needs of the museum's curators. Piano and Rogers decided to use four bright colors on the outside of the museum; red was used for escalators and elevators, blue for heating and air-conditioning ducts, yellow for electrical ducts, and green for water pipes. Colors indicated usage; this facilitated the job of workers, but it also created a very effective contrast both with the fairly drab nineteenth century buildings that surround the Pompidou Center and with more traditional Parisian museums such as the Louvre, the exterior walls of which are made of solid and imposing marble.

The vast open spaces on each floor and the extremely unconventional use of bright colors and huge, transparent panes of glass displeased many architects and public officials in France. The eminent American architect Philip Johnson, who had served on the committee that chose Piano and Rogers to design the museum, reacted with disbelief when Piano and Rogers assured him that they had no intention of installing permanent interior walls in the public areas on any of the five identical floors. The controversy concerning the Pompidou Center did not end with its official opening in January, 1977. The February, 1977, issue of *Architectural Design* magazine included several articles by influential architects who severely criticized the aesthetic choices made by Piano and Rogers.

The lively political and artistic controversy surrounding the Pompidou Center only served to attract huge crowds to the new museum, which proved immensely popular with French and foreign tourists. In a 1987 book, Rogers noted with real pride that the Pompidou Center consistently attracted more visitors than even the Louvre.

Renzo Piano and Richard Rogers designed a museum which has proved itself to be much more flexible than traditional museums. Exhibitions can be moved with ease to any of the five identical floors. The Pompidou Center contains not only an art museum but also an open-stack library with books and videocassettes, numerous restaurants and cafés, an architectural museum, and, underground, the Institute for Research and Coordination in Acoustics and Music (IRCAM). Piano and Rogers decided to build IRCAM completely underground in order not to destroy the aesthetic effect of the superstructure of the Pompidou Center.

In April, 1974, Georges Pompidou died and the next month Giscard d'Estaing was elected president of France. At first, d'Estaing was not sure that he wanted his government to continue funding the expensive and controversial project. He finally decided, however, not only to permit the completion of the museum but to change its name from the Beaubourg Center to the Georges Pompidou National Center of Modern Art and Culture. Since its opening in early 1977, the Pompidou Center has acquired numerous important works of modern art for its permanent collection and has also organized many influential historical and comparative exhibitions.

Impact of Event

Georges Pompidou was an unusual politician, and it is not surprising that the museum that now bears his name is so imaginative and controversial. While he served in the 1960's as the prime minister in the government of Charles de Gaulle, Pompidou participated in several conferences on French literature, and he also produced a highly respected anthology of French poetry. Although his academic training was in classical languages, he was interested in modern art from France and from other countries as well. Pompidou recognized the value of multiculturalism in France. While the selection committee was deciding which proposal should be accepted for the construction of the Beaubourg Center, Pompidou had a long discussion with Philip Johnson. Pompidou wanted to know what the French government could do in order to reestablish Paris as a major international center for the exhibition of modern art; Pompidou sensed that New York City, with its Museum of Modern Art and its Guggenheim Museum, had eclipsed Paris as the major artistic center for the exhibition of modern art. When he proposed in late 1969 the construction of the Beaubourg Center, though, he likely did not imagine that the museum would become so immensely popular that it would attract more visitors than any other Parisian museum.

The reaction to Pompidou's initial proposal was predictable. The French opposition parties, especially the Socialists, denounced the Beaubourg project as unnecessary, and their displeasure increased when the selection committee chose two foreign architects, who refused to hire exclusively French contractors and suppliers for the museum's construction. Rogers and Piano were not happy when many French construction companies submitted bids that the designers judged to be excessively high. They wanted to deal with both French and foreign companies so that the vast project could be completed on time and under budget; Piano and Rogers demanded and obtained the right to have complete control over the planning and construction of the Beaubourg Center.

Piano and Rogers understood that Paris already had a large number of formal museums built in imposing marble, and many critics believed that such museums appealed largely to a social or artistic elite. Piano and Rogers made a conscious effort to create a flexible museum in which people of all nationalities and social classes would feel comfortable. The exterior walls of the Pompidou Center are composed purely of panes of transparent glass, and this created an impression of openness. The bright colors used throughout the Pompidou Center strike visitors as playful and seem to convey the idea that one can have fun while admiring the magnificent works of art displayed. A vast plaza was preserved in front of the Pompidou Center, and magicians and street artists are allowed to perform there; such popular artists are not permitted in the vicinity of the more traditional Parisian museums. When the French government asked Piano and Rogers to include the IRCAM facilities in the Pompidou Center, the architects added a witty touch. IRCAM was constructed under an adjoining plaza, and Rogers and Piano designed a shallow rectangular fountain for the plaza; brightly colored mechanical statues of hearts, lips, musical symbols, and smiling human faces were placed in the fountain. These imaginative sculptures and the many water spouts in the fountain bring much aesthetic pleasure to visitors and to those working at IRCAM. Although the numerous innovative elements in the Pompidou Center provoked controversy, this only served to increase popular interest in the new center of modern art and culture. The controversy quickly abated, and the

Pompidou Center soon became an integral part of the landscape of Paris.

Although the Pompidou Center possesses an impressive permanent collection of paintings and sculptures by eminent artists, the Pompidou Center has become especially famous for its special historical exhibitions, which have illustrated the myriad artistic connections between France and other countries. In 1977, a major exhibition at the Pompidou Center dealt with the many links between the artistic centers of Paris and New York. This exhibition made visitors understand more completely both the profound influence of French artists on their American colleagues and the equally strong influence of American art, music, and cinema on the cultural life of France. Cooperative agreements between the Pompidou Center and many American museums made this special exhibition possible. The curators of the Pompidou Center wanted people to appreciate the fully international nature of the work displayed at the Pompidou Center. Priority would not be given to French artists. Artistic quality, and not the nationality of an artist, would determine whether a work of art should be shown in the Pompidou Center.

The New York-Paris exhibition of 1977 was followed by many other equally successful historical exhibitions that explored the artistic, musical, and even cinematographic links between Paris and Moscow and between Paris and Berlin. In addition to such massive historical and comparative exhibitions, the Pompidou Center has also organized many excellent exhibitions to examine the work of individual artists. One of the most successful exhibitions of this type was the museum's superb 1982 retrospective showing of selected masterpieces by the American abstract painter Jackson Pollock. Although it would be incorrect to say that Pollock's work was not held in high esteem in 1982, this retrospective exhibition at the Pompidou Center enabled a new generation of museumgoers to see for themselves his stunning masterpieces of abstract art.

Bibliography

Architectural Design 47 (February, 1977). A special issue devoted to discussion of the Pompidou Center. Contains several essays by prominent architects who comment on the significance of the Pompidou Center in relation to other museums of modern art. Includes a brief statement by Piano and Rogers, highly complimentary essays by Andrew Rabeneck and Dennis Crompton, and very negative essays by Alan Colquhoun and Ted Happold.

Centre National d'Art et de Culture Georges Pompidou. *Centre Pompidou.* New York: Rizzoli, 1977. Contains detailed plans of the original and revised designs prepared by Piano and Rogers for the construction of the Pompidou and clearly explains how Piano and Rogers solved the many practical problems involved in building the center.

Davis, Douglas. "Paris: The Palace of Pleasure." In *The Museum Transformed: Design and Culture in the Post-Pompidou Age.* New York: Abbeville Press, 1990. Contains a thoughtful analysis of the architectural importance of the Pompidou Center and describes very well the influence of Piano and Rogers on architects who have designed museums since the completion of the Pompidou Center in 1977. Includes an excellent bibliography.

Lucie-Smith, Edward, ed. *Masterpieces from the Pompidou Center.* Translated by Simon Watson Taylor. London: Thames and Hudson, 1983. Contains color photographs of 120 major paintings and sculptures in the permanent collection of the Pompidou Center. Critical commentaries are given for each masterpiece included in the book.

Steegmuller, Francis. "Paris Celebrates." *The Atlantic Monthly* 239 (June, 1977): 88-90. Steegmuller declares the Pompidou Center to be a sanctimonious flop. He asserts that the Duchamp brothers, artists whose work was displayed at the opening of the center, would have loved it—but that they would have thought of it as a gigantic joke.

Edmund J. Campion

Cross-References

New York's Museum of Modern Art Is Founded (1929), p. 782; The Guggenheim Museum Opens in a Building Designed by Wright (1959), p. 1806; Breuer Designs a Building for the Whitney Museum (1966), p. 2064; Expo 67 Presents Innovative Architectural Concepts (1967), p. 2081; The Musée d'Orsay Opens (1986), p. 2588; Deconstructivists Exhibit at the Museum of Modern Art (1988), p. 2614; Pei Creates a New Entrance to the Louvre (1988), p. 2619.

THE AT&T BUILDING EXEMPLIFIES POSTMODERNISM

Category of event: Architecture
Time: 1978
Locale: New York, New York

Philip Johnson's ironic, neoclassical design for a corporate headquarters made an avant-garde alternative to modernism a new path for American architecture

Principal personages:

PHILIP JOHNSON (1906-   ), an architect with a long history of bringing historical awareness and avant-garde ideas into the design establishment

JOHN BURGEE (1933-   ), an architect who was Johnson's partner in designing the AT&T Building and other buildings for corporations and developers

JOHN DULANY DE BUTTS (1915-1986), the AT&T chairman who commissioned Johnson and Burgee to design a new headquarters tower

Summary of Event

The American Telephone and Telegraph (AT&T) building in New York was the breakthrough project of architect Philip Johnson. Despite a long career, Johnson had become an architect of corporate skyscrapers only after he formed his partnership with John Burgee in 1968. In 1978, he was one of America's most influential architects; his prominence resulted from his prestigious clients (which included the Museum of Modern Art and the Pennzoil Corporation) and from his articulateness about the history and problems of modern architecture.

Johnson had begun proselytizing for modernism in 1932, when he curated the Museum of Modern Art's "International Style" exhibition of radical architecture. He made Ludwig Mies van der Rohe's steel-and-glass architecture the style of corporate America. Yet from the mid-1950's on, Johnson raised the possibility that modernism was not the mandatory, universal style he had once believed it to be. In 1960, he said that architects should feel free "to choose from history whatever forms, shapes, or directions" they wished. Johnson's own work was modernist, but he became an enthusiastic supporter of rebels against modernist orthodoxy.

AT&T commissioned Johnson and Burgee to design its new headquarters because their recent designs had tried to find a new aesthetic treatment for the skyscraper through such means as faceted corners and slanting roofs. John D. De Butts, AT&T's chairman, urged Johnson to make its new headquarters tower express the dignity of one of the most powerful corporations in America and to make the building instantly recognizable as the company's symbol.

At the time, Johnson was interested in the designs and ideas of a few younger architects who were committed to the use of historical references in architecture.

These designers—Michael Graves, Robert Stern, Robert Venturi, Charles Moore, and others—used bits of past styles to tie the building to its local context and to acknowledge the complexity of modernism's historical roots. Simple faith in functionalist methods was no longer possible. The ideas of these largely unknown "postmodernists" were uppermost in Johnson's mind when AT&T ordered him to break the glass box.

Johnson had to design for a narrow two-hundred-foot lot at Madison Avenue and Fifty-fifth Street. He placed the building at the front of the site, facing Madison, locating the required public space in an arcade behind the building and in open arcades that took up the entire first floor except the lobby. The building itself remained a thirty-seven-story box on a ninety-by-two-hundred-foot base. To keep the structure from being a modernist slab, Johnson put Postmodern ideas to use. He gave the building the monumentality of the great skyscrapers of the 1920's by making its curtain wall not of glass but of pinkish-gray granite. Instead of metal or concrete stilts, the supports to create the public space beneath the building would be in the form of a sixty-foot-high classical colonnade with a 110-foot arch in the center. The building's façade would follow the old-fashioned layout of base, shaft, and crown—that is, arcade, windows in vertical strips with stone mullions, and top—instead of being a single steel-and-glass wall.

The average office tower had a "functional" flat roof. Johnson and Burgee made the top of the AT&T Building a pitched roof with a twenty-foot-diameter circular void where the sides of the roof met, turning the crown into a huge version of another Renaissance motif, the broken pediment. As a design solution, the pediment was a tour de force. Its proportions just fit the narrow slab, and its overscaled simplicity matched the plainness that the project's budget required for the stone casing. For the company, it was an instantly recognizable image on the skyline, with dignified classical connotations. The roof also turned an office slab into an enormous Chippendale box. It could be read as a serious reference to eighteenth century Utopian architecture (Johnson's favorite subject) or as a cartoon version of a grandfather clock to amuse the public. In any case, it denied the rule "form follows function."

The concept of a stone-clad, historicist office tower owed much to Johnson's young protégé Robert Stern, who admired the New York skyscrapers of the 1920's. The Chippendale-style top derived from Robert Venturi's ironic, billboard-like variations on classicism. Johnson had long wanted to return a sense of history to architecture, but for many years he could look for classical elegance and proportions only in modernist guise, as in Mies van der Rohe's glass boxes. The postmodernists gave Johnson the courage to use the style explicitly. The AT&T Building was a flat-out attack on two "rules" of modernism: that architecture must honestly reveal its structure (without hiding a steel frame behind Renaissance stone, for example) and must never look backward for artistic solutions.

Johnson's design was announced on the front page of *The New York Times* for March 31, 1978, and instantly became controversial. The postmodernists' avant-garde design approach was suddenly being applied to an establishment job at huge scale and expense. Johnson was criticized for being shallow, for borrowing unknown innovators' ideas instead of thinking the problem through himself. Critics noted that postmodernism's amusing, over-scaled classical elements became oppressive in the AT&T project's huge dimensions. Johnson pointed out in response that he had met all his client's needs efficiently and that many people agreed that the older historicist skyscrapers worked better than functionalist ones. His "radical" building was really a gift to New York. By the time it was finished in 1984, the AT&T Building was generally accepted as a respite from the bleak architecture of the 1960's and 1970's. Historicism had found an entertaining solution to design problems to which modernists had produced only rote answers. AT&T's and Johnson's prestige made the building a milestone.

Impact of Event

Johnson designed the AT&T Building at a time of widespread dissatisfaction with the ways modern architecture had been used. The urban rebuilding projects of the 1950's and 1960's were condemned for having produced anonymous buildings, empty spaces, and alienating scale. The AT&T Building demonstrated that postmodern styling could deflect much criticism leveled at new structures. Granite facings, setbacks, human-scale arcades, and ornament that referred to older buildings could give even the bulkiest skyscrapers an aura of history and sensitivity.

Real-estate investors, especially Gerald R. Hines of Houston, commissioned Johnson to apply his new style to their buildings. Johnson's Republic Bank Building in Houston and PPG Industries Building in Pittsburgh were widely publicized. Previously, he had had a reputation as an artist with a limited clientele; he now made Johnson/Burgee the leading commercial architectural firm of the 1980's. Always articulate and media-conscious, Johnson became a celebrity who could explain the virtues of historicism to the public.

The AT&T Building's notoriety had a great impact on the architectural profession. The designers who inspired Johnson, especially Robert Stern and Michael Graves, received large commissions for the first time; Graves's Portland, Oregon, municipal office tower (1982) was as important to making the postmodern style respectable as the AT&T project was. Stern's and Graves's work for the Walt Disney Corporation cemented the idea that "serious" architecture could be popular and entertaining. By the end of the 1980's, such previously modernist architects and firms as Kevin Lynch, Kohn Pedersen Fox, and Skidmore, Owings, and Merrill had adopted traditional ornament and art deco profiles in their buildings. The large role developers gave postmodern architects in urban development made their theories news, and their colorful, recognizable designs became fashionable. (Both Graves and Robert Venturi designed tableware and furniture.)

The new buildings of the 1980's generally did not replicate past styles exactly. Building budgets and lack of traditional craftsmen made this impossible. Fortunately, the obvious fakeness of postmodernism's historicism was part of its theory. When in 1966 Robert Venturi had praised "complexity and contradiction" in architecture in defiance of Mies van der Rohe's dictum "less is more," he meant that the styles of the past were richer than modernism was. Architects could never unlearn modernist functionalism and simplicity, however; the two design approaches would have to coexist, although they denied each other's premises. In addition, a truly popular style would be more flashy and eclectic than either classicism or modernism. In a pluralist society, architecture's quest for beauty meant less to people than did the images they absorbed from shopping strips, billboards, and television.

Venturi saw that people understood buildings as visual clichés, not as unified works of art, and said that the postmodernist architect's job was to assemble images that could be consumed by the greatest number of people in the largest number of contexts. The contradictions involved would come out in the building, but only the architect would appreciate them. This ironic, relativist attitude denied the entire mindset of modernism, which was functional, serious, forward-looking, and committed to finding the one best way to design. The idea of an architecture of images let postmodernists tackle problems of human context in their buildings while remaining honest about the shortcuts such an approach required.

This lesson could be applied with greater or lesser seriousness. Johnson was an admirer of pop art and its conceptual games as well as of classicism; he designed what he claimed were close copies of older buildings, but their differences from the originals could be easily read in their megabuilding size, odd proportions, and modernist detail. (The PPG Industries Building, for example, was a Gothic quadrangle covered with the corporation's own mirror glass.) In the average architect's work, pitched roofs, colonial windows, and colored stone veneers were simply added to standard modernist buildings. In many projects, it was too obvious that architects had been hired to put fashionably historicist fronts on profitable but mediocre designs by developers. Johnson offended other architects by admitting that this often happened, even in his own practice. Postmodernism's preoccupation with the image made the difference between a building's visual cues and its three-dimensional reality wider than ever before.

Yet the AT&T Building's example of applying ornaments in traditional materials without worrying about functionalist "honesty" also justified architects in deferring explicitly to the past. This fact, too, had many applications. Architects such as Kohn Pedersen Fox used a high-tech variation on the art deco style to fit into older cityscapes. Venturi's and Graves's cartoon-like classical motifs were attempts at a truly popular style, while Stern's eclectic copies of landmark buildings acted out a social conservatism. In many cities, postmodernism encouraged preservation efforts and fostered civic identity. Such planners as the firm Duany and Plater-Zyberk—influenced by the extreme antimodernists in European postmodernism such as Leon Krier—rethought urban design in terms of traditional pedestrian scale. Outside America, James Stirling and Arata Isozaki used postmodernism's collage technique to seek a genuine artistic synthesis. As a final result of the style's popularity, even architects who did not embrace it—and many did not—received new attention as artists who could influence public values.

The overall result of postmodernism, once Johnson's AT&T Building brought it into the mainstream, was to widen architects' sense of their design options and the contexts in which to apply them. Moreover, Johnson's work showed the public that architects could add color, humor, and a sense of heritage to the way the world looked.

Bibliography

Games, Stephen. *Behind the Façade*. New York: Universe Books, 1986. Breezy but incisive essays on postmodernist architects and events in the design world, based on the author's British Broadcasting Corporation (BBC) radio programs. The chapter on Philip Johnson ("The Best Hated Architect in the World") is based on a revealing personal interview. A good introduction to postmodernism's popular face. No illustrations or index.

Jencks, Charles. *Post-Modernism: The New Classicism in Art and Architecture*. New York: Rizzoli, 1987. The most encyclopedic of many descriptions and defenses of antimodernist movements, written by the critic who first applied the word "postmodern" to the new historicist architecture. Overextended, and irritating in its tendency to invent all-inclusive categories. Valuable photos and evaluations of all major postmodern buildings in America and elsewhere. Endnotes are more helpful than the bibliography or the index.

Johnson, Philip. *Writings*. New York: Oxford University Press, 1978. Dated, as it appeared just as the AT&T design was made public; as an intellectual autobiography, however, it makes clear why Johnson abandoned modernism. The arguments about style and history reprinted here were enormously influential in postmodern theory and practice. Accompanying texts by Peter Eisenman and Robert Stern are too mired in New York architectural feuds to be helpful. Contains unillustrated list of Johnson's building designs through 1978, partial bibliography, and index.

Philip Johnson/John Burgee: Architecture, 1979-1985. New York: Rizzoli, 1985. An oversize photo book of Johnson's postmodernist designs, including the AT&T Building. Beautiful drawings and photographs, but no technical documents or preliminary studies. Poorly written text, with short, uncritical prefaces on each building that describe Johnson's aims and sources. Contains complete, illustrated building list for 1966-1985, selected bibliography, no index.

Venturi, Robert. *Complexity and Contradiction in Architecture*. New York: Museum of Modern Art, 1966. The sourcebook for postmodern theory. Essentially a collection of photos of ornate and unusual buildings taken from Venturi's 1966 lectures at the Museum of Modern Art, and justified for their visual effect at modernist theory's expense. Many of the buildings shown here were sources for later postmodernist borrowings. A few of Venturi's own early projects at the end. No index.

Wolfe, Tom. *From Bauhaus to Our House*. New York: Farrar, Straus & Giroux, 1981. This humorous but hostile and thinly researched essay on how modern architecture took hold in America is important because its plea for ornate, eclectic "bad taste" architecture fed popular support for postmodernism. The last chapters mock the premises of the leading postmodernists themselves. Poor illustrations, no index.

M. David Samson

Cross-References

German Artists Found the Bauhaus (1919), p. 463; Le Corbusier's Villa Savoye Redefines Architecture (1931), p. 869; The Empire State Building Opens as the World's Tallest Building (1931), p. 880; Rockefeller Center Is Completed (1939), p. 1149; Deconstructivists Exhibit at the Museum of Modern Art (1988), p. 2614; Disney Emerges as an Architectural Patron (Early 1990's), p. 2646.

SHEPARD'S *BURIED CHILD* PROMOTES OFF-BROADWAY THEATER

Category of event: Theater
Time: 1978-1979
Locale: New York, New York, and San Francisco, California

The production of Buried Child *established a new realistic and minimalist direction in Sam Shepard's work as well as a new degree of popular success*

> *Principal personages:*
> SAM SHEPARD (SAMUEL SHEPARD ROGERS, 1943-   ), a writer, actor, musician, and director who combined critical success as an avantgarde playwright with popular success as a film star
> DAVID MAMET (1947-   ), a playwright with works in the alternative theater
> ROBERT WOODRUFF (1946?-   ), the director of *Buried Child*

Summary of Event

Sam Shepard has been called the first totally postmodern voice in American drama, largely because of the aggressively experimental nature of his early work, a series of short one-act plays relying on collage and fantasy rather than straightforward narrative or coherent characterizations. *Curse of the Starving Class* (pr. 1977) initiated a new direction in Shepard's work, inaugurating a series of plays, including *Buried Child*, *True West* (pr. 1980), *Fool for Love* (pr. 1983), and *A Lie of the Mind* (pr. 1985), concerned with explorations of domestic and family life, in contrast to his earlier focus on characters who were loners. Unlike the experimental variations on popular genres, such as science fiction, Westerns, or rock operas, that typified the earlier plays, these later works are, despite their sometimes expressionistic exaggerations, given realistic, even naturalistic settings and relatively realistic characters. Shepard had already confessed in 1974 that he would "like to try a whole different way of writing now, which is very stark and not so flashy and not full of a lot of mythic figures and everything, and try to scrape it down to the bone as much as possible."

The relatively tight focus on a small family in *Buried Child* certainly can be seen as an expression of Shepard's new realistic and minimalist impulses. The realistic framework, however, always incorporates heavily symbolic actions and properties and a mythic reach in themes, and the contrast between the early and later works often has been emphasized at the expense of ignoring important continuities. The archetypes and mythic figures of the earlier plays have been worked into more extended narrative structures—*Curse of the Starving Class* and *Buried Child* were three-act plays, expansive by comparison with Shepard's earlier work—without losing the several layers of symbolic meaning they carry. Although critics have sometimes disagreed about the relative merits of the work of these two stages, the awarding of the Pulitzer Prize for *Buried Child*—one of the first plays never produced on

Broadway to have won the prize—suggests a consensus of opinion that this play is the most completely successful of the later period.

Buried Child, in a production directed by Robert Woodruff, who had directed the premieres of two other Shepard plays, *The Curse of the Starving Class* and *Pecos Bill*, opened at the Magic Theater in San Francisco on June 27, 1978. It was later produced in New York City at the Theater for the New City, where the audience quickly spilled over into the aisle. Woodruff then moved the production to the somewhat larger, but still intimate, Off-Broadway Theater de Lys in Greenwich Village in December, 1978, where it ran for 152 performances, a record for a Shepard play. A separate production, directed by Adrian Hall, ran during the same period at the Yale Repertory Theater.

The play explores three generations of a grotesque and exaggerated, but also representative, American family. Beneath the elements of gothic horror—the father, Dodge, apparently has committed infanticide and the child he then buried may have been the result of incest between his son Tilden and wife, Halie—lies an exploration of archetypal family conflicts. At the realistic level, the plot is a story about the passing of the family farm, once barren but perhaps now revitalized, from the older to the younger generation, from Dodge to his grandson Vince (Tilden's son). At the mythic level, the subject is the inheritance of an emotional sterility that has crippled the younger generation but that they can recognize, unearth, and transcend. Shepard criticizes the disintegration of the family but also recognizes the inevitability of conflict. Bradley, Dodge's eldest son, symbolically dominates his father by cutting his hair, but then Vince displaces both Bradley and Dodge as he throws away Bradley's artificial leg and takes Dodge's place on the couch after Dodge has willed him the house, land, and tools. Each generation can progress only through such a displacement of the preceding one, and the losses in the play are similarly inevitable. Dodge loses a son, as does Tilden, and Vince loses his girlfriend, Shelly, as he comes into his inheritance.

That there is somehow progress despite such losses is suggested by the play's ending, which emphasizes fertility and the growth of crops even as Dodge lies dead on the stage. The language of the closing suggests, with its allusion to a miracle and the play on "sun" and "son" echoing the imagery of Christian resurrection myth, that a symbolic renewal has taken or is about to take place even as Tilden brings the buried child out of his grave. As horrible as the past has been, the dead son it has denied and hidden has been brought to light and faced during the course of the play, and the new generation, as represented by the living son, Vince, has taken the place of the old generation. The buried child may be the source of a family curse that had begun to infect even Vince, and its removal may signal the curse's end and an expiation of the sins of the previous generation. The coming fertility, however, is only suggested, not guaranteed, and when Vince assumes the exact posture of Dodge and Shelly decides to escape, the implication seems to be that any optimism at the ending must be cautious.

Although the setting is scrupulously realistic, Shepard relies on the symbolism of his props and actions as much as words to tell his stories. The burying of Dodge under corn husks by Tilden both reenacts Dodge's burying of the child and fore-shadows Tilden's exhumation of the child at the play's end. The buried child is itself a powerful visual symbol, especially for an unprepared audience of a realistic pro-duction, when Tilden carries in the rotten shroud covered with mud at the end. Halie's emotional estrangement from the rest of the family is as clear from her frequent delivery of her lines from offstage as it is from the lines themselves, and her entirely black mourning outfit further symbolizes the point that her family is dead to her, and perhaps has been since the sacrifice of the buried child. By extension, her appearance in the last act in bright yellow clothing with her arms full of yellow roses, emblems of passion, can be seen as an element of the movement toward hope at the end of the play. She does, however, leave the roses downstairs and finishes offstage (upstairs) where she began; the ending of the play is ambivalent.

Impact of Event

The origins of the Off-Broadway theater are difficult to fix with any precision, but the establishment in 1956 of the Obie Awards, given annually by *The Village Voice* for distinguished theatrical achievement Off-Broadway (and, since 1964, Off-Off-Broadway), provides a convenient starting point. Beginning with revivals of classic American and European drama, the Off-Broadway theater moved in the early 1960's to an emphasis on new experimental work by avant-garde playwrights such as Jack Gelber, Edward Albee, and Arthur Kopit. With some three dozen plays produced since *Cowboys* and *Rock Garden* were first performed in 1964, Shepard has been the most prolific and the most consistently successful, with both audiences and critics, of all the American dramatists who emerged on the Off-Broadway scene in the 1960's. The awarding of an Obie to *Buried Child* marked the tenth time one of Shepard's plays had been so distinguished; no other American playwright had won more than two Obies. His combination of longevity and popularity, terms not gener-ally applicable to experimental writers, has contributed significantly to the relative health and stability of the American alternative theater.

Buried Child helped to confirm the legitimacy of the alternative theater in the United States by winning the Pulitzer Prize, an award traditionally given only to Broadway productions. The play's Off-Broadway run was a record for a Shepard play and easily could have led to a Broadway production. Shepard instead challenged the commercial theatrical establishment by refusing to let the play be coopted for a Broadway production, arguing that the large audiences on Broadway would destroy the intimacy needed in the theater experience. Signs that his challenge was to be a successful one soon followed; once *Buried Child* had been awarded the Pulitzer Prize, the way was opened for other alternative playwrights to win mainstream awards. The Pulitzer awards for drama for both 1983 (Marsha Norman's *'night Mother*) and 1984 (David Mamet's *Glengarry Glen Ross*) went to plays on the basis of regional productions outside New York, continuing the trend toward decentralization in the American theater.

Shepard's theatrical success fed off his career as a film actor, which brought him a recognition factor generally denied to American playwrights and extended the audience for his work well beyond the usual theatergoing public. His string of critical successes in the theater probably had drawn less popular recognition than his nomination for an Academy Award for his portrayal of Chuck Yeager in *The Right Stuff* (1983). His screenplay for *Paris, Texas* (1984), voted Best Film at Cannes in 1984, also had given him name recognition to an audience outside the theatrical community. Shepard's play *Fool for Love*, which opened at the Magic Theater in 1983 in a production he also directed, was made into a film in 1985. The film version was directed by Robert Altman and starred Shepard, who also wrote the screenplay, appearing with established stars Kim Basinger, Randy Quaid, and Harry Dean Stanton. Although some critics thought that the film version lacked the edge of the performed play and revealed weaknesses in Shepard's acting ability, there is little doubt that the rapid adaptation, starring well-known artists, extended Shepard's name recognition to a new and larger audience.

Just as Shepard's success in the Off-Broadway theater helped to pave the way for greater recognition for other avant-garde playwrights, his seemingly effortless transition to success in films may have helped playwrights such as David Mamet make similar transitions. Mamet's *Sexual Perversity in Chicago* (pr. 1974) was made into the film *About Last Night* (1986), and he has since become one of the film industry's most respected writers and directors, achieving critical as well as popular acclaim for films including *House of Games* (1987).

The success of Shepard and other Off-Broadway and regional playwrights (Mamet's work, for example, is based in the Chicago theater) has been such that the formerly marginal "alternative" theater, sometimes thought of as a training ground from which actors, directors, and writers would graduate to Broadway, has in some respects come to dominate the Broadway theater. In part because of Broadway's high production costs and in part because of the antipathy toward Broadway held by Shepard and other playwrights, the traditional Broadway stage is no longer the major venue for serious contemporary drama. Many playwrights have found it advantageous to guide their plays through the more flexible and experimental Off-Broadway and regional theaters as part of their development process for a play, often revising scripts substantially while they are being performed, as Shepard did with *Buried Child*. Apart from Neil Simon, no major American playwrights of the 1980's had their new works regularly produced on Broadway, though some plays did go there after success Off-Broadway, and 1986 marked the first time that not-for-profit theaters provided more weeks of work for artists than all forms of commercial theater combined. The contemporary American theater, exemplified by Shepard's work, seemed to reflect the rapid cultural transitions occurring in America throughout the 1980's and to flourish as a result.

Bibliography

Auerbach, Doris. *Sam Shepard, Arthur Kopit, and the Off-Broadway Theater.* Boston: Twayne, 1982. An introduction to Shepard's life and work through 1979. Compares and contrasts Shepard's work with Kopit's and analyzes the "healthy reciprocity between playwright and theater" that has made Shepard's work so well-suited to the Off-Broadway theater. Bibliography, index.

Hart, Lynda. *Sam Shepard's Metaphorical Stages.* Westport, Conn.: Greenwood Press, 1987. A useful biographical sketch and relatively detailed analyses of ten plays, including *Buried Child.*

King, Kimball, ed. *Sam Shepard: A Casebook.* New York: Garland, 1988. A collection of twelve essays dealing with several aspects of Shepard's work through the mid-1980's. Two of the essays focus on *Buried Child*; several others mention it in passing.

Marranca, Bonnie, ed. *American Dreams: Imagination of Sam Shepard.* New York: Performing Arts Journal Publications, 1981. A wide range of essays by various critics, many of whom mention *Buried Child.* Includes three brief essays by Shepard as well as interviews with Shepard and with directors and actors who have worked on his plays.

Mottram, Ron. *Inner Landscapes: The Theater of Sam Shepard.* Columbia: University of Missouri Press, 1984. A general biographical and critical overview of Shepard's career, presented chronologically, with discussion of most of the plays.

Orr, John. *Tragicomedy and Contemporary Culture: Play and Performance from Beckett to Shepard.* New York: Macmillan, 1991. Locates Shepard's work in a contemporary tradition of the genre of tragicomedy that includes playwrights such as Luigi Pirandello, Samuel Beckett, Jean Genet, and Harold Pinter. Divides Shepard's career through 1986 into three stages, with commentary on most of the plays. Bibliography, index.

Oumano, Ellen. *Sam Shepard: The Life and Work of an American Dreamer.* New York: St. Martin's Press, 1986. Primarily a biographical treatment, covering Shepard's life and career up to 1985. Little critical discussion of the plays, but valuable, if usually brief and anecdotal, commentaries by Shepard and his intimates. Photographs, bibliography, list of productions (not entirely accurate or complete), and index.

William Nelles

Cross-References

The Ford Foundation Begins to Fund Nonprofit Theaters (1957), p. 1736; Esslin Publishes *The Theatre of the Absurd* (1961), p. 1871; *The American Dream* Establishes Albee as the Voice of Pessimism (1961), p. 1903; Guare's *The House of Blue Leaves* Combines Comedy with Horror (1971), p. 2239; Fierstein's *Torch Song Trilogy* Meets with Unexpected Success (1982), p. 2502; Simon's *Biloxi Blues* Emphasizes Serious Themes (1984), p. 2537.

DALLAS POPULARIZES THE PRIME-TIME SOAP OPERA

Category of event: Television and radio
Time: April 2, 1978-1991
Locale: The United States

The exploits and personal relationships of the fictional super-rich Ewing family enthralled millions of television viewers

Principal personages:
 LARRY HAGMAN (1931-   ), the actor who played the role of the villainous John Ross (J. R.) Ewing, Jr.
 BARBARA BEL GEDDES (1922-   ), the actress who played the matriarch of the Ewing clan
 JIM DAVIS (1916-1981), the actor who played the father of J. R. in the original cast
 PATRICK DUFFY (1949-   ), the actor who played Bobby Ewing, younger brother of J. R.
 VICTORIA PRINCIPAL (1944-   ), the actress who played Bobby Ewing's wife
 LINDA GRAY (1941-   ), the actress who played Sue Ellen, the long-suffering wife of J. R.

Summary of Event

During the 1977-1978 television season, the Columbia Broadcasting System (CBS) found itself late in the season needing a replacement for a show with low ratings. On a trial run, the network showed episodes of *Dallas.* The first season brought good but unspectacular results. The 1978-1979 season brought better results, and the 1980-1981 season saw the show rated number one in its regular Friday-night time slot. This was a triumph for prime-time soap opera because *Dallas* was only the second dramatic series to reach the number one rating in the history of television. The show was soon very popular in almost every foreign nation except Japan.

The show involved the struggle for power and revenge between two families. The Ewing family was at odds with the Barnes family, but the youngest Ewing son fell in love with and married the youngest Barnes daughter. The characters included numerous relatives in both families over two generations. Other story lines, especially about the Ewings themselves, were woven into the series. The program became famous for introducing a cliff-hanger ending each season.

The genre to which *Dallas* belonged is quite old. During the last half of the nineteenth century, newspapers began to run serial stories, continued day by day or week to week, that dealt with the lives of characters in a melodramatic fashion. In the 1920's, as radio became popular, this type of story began to be broadcast in the late mornings and early afternoons by stations nationwide. These programs were sponsored by companies manufacturing detergents, leading to their designation as "soap operas." By 1955, these soap operas were making the move to television as that medium of entertainment began to supplant radio in popularity. *Peyton Place*, which went on the air in 1964, is the best-remembered nighttime soap opera of the period. As the decade of the 1970's began, there were seventeen soap operas being broadcast daily by the three television networks for a total of five hundred ten minutes a day. It seemed, however, that the move from print to radio to daytime television had brought soap operas to their ultimate destination. *Dallas* was to prove that assumption wrong by bringing soap operas back to prime time.

American society was changing in ways that meant that the daytime audience for soap operas was shrinking. An increasing number of women were joining the work force outside the home. Also, the potential audience was becoming younger, more affluent, and better educated. The Lorimar Production Company decided that an audience existed for a soap opera shown on prime time, with characters drawn from the upper classes. This company had experienced success in producing *The Waltons* and *Eight Is Enough*, warm-hearted programs about the stereotypical traditional American family. Its change to portraying the nontraditional, amoral Ewing clan brought even greater success.

Dallas featured the large Ewing family, centered around its ranch, Southfork, located not far from Dallas, Texas. The oldest son and later head of the family was John Ross Ewing, Jr., always known as J. R. Eleanor, his mother, was the matriarch of the family. J. R. was married to Sue Ellen, and Kristin Shepard was the sister of Sue Ellen and mistress of J. R. Numerous other relatives, business associates, and neighbors became involved in the plot, and the cast of recurring characters numbered in the dozens. The constant theme of the program was scheming to make money, to gain power, to achieve sexual domination, and to achieve all of these without regard for conventional moral concerns or the law.

The success of *Dallas* was phenomenal. It quickly became obvious that any show running opposite *Dallas* was in a suicide slot. In part, this success was achieved by making the major character, J. R. Ewing, a villain who grew meaner by the minute, becoming the man the audience loved to hate. This was a curious role for Larry Hagman, who played the character J. R. Hagman in real life was a middle-aged grandfather who had been married happily to the same woman since 1954. Hagman grew up around show business; his mother was the "Grand Dame" of Broadway musicals, Mary Martin. Hagman became an actor in the 1950's and achieved his first starring television role as astronaut Tony Nelson in *I Dream of Jeannie*.

The appeal of J. R. as villain was obvious when, on November 21, 1980, the *Dallas* episode "Who Shot J. R.?" was broadcast. At the end of the 1979-1980 season, in a classic cliff-hanger episode, J. R. was shot while working in his office. The mystery of who shot J. R. created enormous expectations for the 1980-1981 season and drew millions of dollars into betting parlors. The mystery was solved only five weeks into the season. This episode of *Dallas* became the most highly watched telecast in the history of television up to that time.

In typical *Dallas* fashion, J. R. had been shot by Kristin, his mistress and younger sister of Sue Ellen. Kristin had used Sue Ellen's pistol to shoot J. R. in an attempt to put suspicion on Sue Ellen. Kristin shot J. R. because she had become pregnant by him but he was attempting to frame her for prostitution. J. R. was not killed, only crippled, and became nastier than ever. Kristin later drowned herself in J. R.'s swimming pool. Such standards of behavior caused *Dallas* to be the television show that the fundamentalist "religious Right" opposed most vehemently.

The popularity of the show was such that in the 1979-1980 season CBS introduced a *Dallas* spin-off, *Knots Landing*, featuring the outcasts of the Ewing clan, Val and Gary Ewing. The location used as the Southfork ranch became the ninth most popular tourist attraction in the entire state of Texas and frequently was rented out for wedding receptions and parties when filming was not going on. The turnover of characters, as cast members tired of their roles, caused *Dallas* to decline in popularity. The show left the air in 1991.

Impact of Event

On a long-term basis, *Dallas* demonstrated that the television viewing audience in the United States was willing and able to support a drama program. Most television programs with a successful long run prior to *Dallas* had been situation comedies or variety shows. *I Love Lucy* and *The Ed Sullivan Show* are examples of these genres. Only one dramatic show, *Marcus Welby, M.D.*, had attained widespread popularity. *Dallas* broke new ground by identifying an audience for televised drama. Critics might argue that *Dallas* was more melodrama than drama, but the show still represents a major change of direction for television entertainment.

Dallas also provided a mirror in which the audience could view itself, both in the United States and abroad. This was the case because the program presented a network of characters. These characters had to be understood in relationship to each other—they could not stand alone. This network then became a microcosm of the society, as viewers understood and reacted to that society. For example, the characters in *Dallas* exceeded the moral standards of behavior of those who viewed the program. In most cases, viewers simultaneously reinforced and questioned their own norms while also accepting the actions of the actors as stereotypical of the super-rich. Many viewers found vicarious satisfaction in the misdeeds of the characters, knowing that they would never behave that way but wondering how it would feel to be that evil and immoral.

In this way, *Dallas* became part of an oral folk culture. This was an oral tradition because the feelings, comments, and information about the characters were not written down. It was part of the process of millions of people watching the program and then discussing it. The characters became readily identified elements of American culture.

Part of the impact of *Dallas* resulted from its diverse audience. In the United States, the appeal of the show was not limited by region of the country, education level of the viewer, or economic status. Furthermore, the program was enormously popular all over the world. Only in Japan did the show fail to gain a sizable following. An academic study done in the United States in 1984 showed that during and after the broadcast of an episode, audiences of different ethnic backgrounds would discuss the program and come to a collective understanding of what they had seen based on their ethnic culture.

This same phenomenon was present among people who brought a strong ideological point of view to the program. One feminist wrote, in response to an academic questionnaire, that she liked *Dallas* because it released deep primitive feelings in her, even though she knew that these feelings were at odds with her conscious beliefs. Those who supported capitalism saw in *Dallas* a depiction of the rewards of this economic system; critics of capitalism pointed out that the program rarely depicted productive labor. Money seemed to follow family, good looks, or social position. Physical beauty and wealth were presented as one. If the rewards of capitalism were on display, so were its excesses.

Dallas was also an international hit. Abroad, there was the same reinforcing of personal values as was present in the United States. A Moroccan Jew noted that he saw in *Dallas* a reason to be glad that he and his family were not like those portrayed. Arab viewers, however, saw in the program a confirmation of their own culture. When Sue Ellen took her baby and ran away from J. R., Arab viewers saw her as returning to her father, a typically Arab action under such circumstances.

Many of the regular viewers of the program believed that the characters were genuine or real, that they knew people who were like the characters. In casual talk and in gossip, regular viewers often referred to the program to explain situations they had encountered. For these viewers, life imitated art.

Any television broadcast always contains more meanings, more possible interpretations, than the broadcaster can control. *Dallas* made an unusually large impact in this respect because of the number of its characters and also because of the length of its broadcast run. As do all successful television shows, it produced numerous imitators. Audiences proved willing to follow ongoing plot lines, and soap operas became an established part of prime-time television.

Bibliography

Brooks, Tim, and Earle Marsh. *The Complete Directory to Prime Time Network TV Shows, 1946-Present.* 4th ed. New York: Ballantine Books, 1988. Summarizes the story line of all recurring programs aired during the time period covered. Useful for comparing shows and putting them into context. Lists major cast members for each show, has grids showing prime-time programming, and lists Emmy Awards year by year.

Fiske, John. *Television Culture.* New York: Methuen, 1987. An interesting analysis of the fantasy culture that television creates and the ways in which that culture is accepted as true and valid by people who are viewers. The key to this process is that television uses some elements from real life to enhance its imaginary lifestyles.

Gitlin, Todd. *Inside Prime Time.* New York: Pantheon Books, 1983. The author interviewed more than two hundred people who work in television and who described for him their search for a hit show. This book provides a good description and analysis of how television functions. This book also deals with the impact of the "religious Right" on programming.

Goldstein, Fred, and Stan Goldstein. *Prime-Time Television.* New York: Crown, 1983. The history of television from 1946 to 1983 is presented on a year-by-year basis. One of the major themes of the book is the way in which major film actors and actresses began to enter the medium as the technology of television broadcasting improved and television sets became more affordable, expanding the audience.

Rose, Brian G., ed. *TV Genres: A Handbook and Reference Guide.* Westport, Conn.: Greenwood Press, 1985. This useful guide discusses various genres, or types, of television programs. Specific shows are discussed and analyzed, as are the differences between types of programs. The ways in which lines between various genres have been blurred are also discussed.

Michael R. Bradley

Cross-References

Peyton Place Brings Serial Drama to Nighttime Television (1964), p. 2017; *The Forsyte Saga* Is a Hit on Public Television (1969), p. 2168; *M*A*S*H* Reflects 1970's Sentiments (1972), p. 2271; *The Cosby Show* Makes Television History (1984), p. 2532; The Decline of the Big Three Networks Becomes a Fall (Late 1980's), p. 2554.

SINGER WINS THE NOBEL PRIZE IN LITERATURE

Category of event: Literature
Time: December 10, 1978
Locale: Stockholm, Sweden

Isaac Bashevis Singer won the Nobel Prize in Literature, an award that honored not only the author but also the Yiddish language with which he had captured the pre-World War II culture of European Jewry

Principal personages:
ISAAC BASHEVIS SINGER (1904-1991), a noted Yiddish author and translator
ALMA SINGER, Isaac's second wife and chief supporter, who helped to support their family while he was still establishing his literary career
ISRAEL JOSHUA SINGER (1893-1944), Isaac's older brother and mentor
CARL XVI GUSTAF (1946-   ), the king of Sweden in 1978
ALFRED NOBEL (1833-1896), the Swedish inventor of dynamite, a philanthropist whose considerable fortune endowed the Nobel Prizes

Summary of Event

Isaac Bashevis Singer, a nonjudgmental lover of life who maintained that contentment can be found only on the personal level, was a major contributor to modern Yiddish literature and to humanism. Famed as a witty and wise storyteller, translator, novelist, playwright, literary critic, and children's author, he considered himself to be an entertainer and spiced his fiction with a unique exuberance and a peculiar blend of innocence and sophistication. Much of his writing was set in the Jewish shtetlach of Poland as well as in metropolitan areas of the United States. He published a considerable body of work before receiving from Sweden's King Carl XVI Gustaf a much-deserved Nobel Prize in Literature in 1978, a prize that included a gold medal, ornate certificate, trip to Sweden, and monetary award of approximately $163,000. The Nobel committee cited the author for his depiction of the universal human condition, which he drew from his Polish-Jewish roots. Singer, surrounded by friends and colleagues, serenaded by the Stockholm Philharmonic Orchestra playing *Trumpet Voluntary*, and escorted to the glittering ceremony by Princess Christina of Sweden, responded with thanks on his own behalf and on behalf of the dying Yiddish language, which he exalted with a lifetime's work.

The grandson of holy men and the third son of Rabbi Pinchas Mendel Singer and Jewish intellectual Bathsheba Zylberman Singer, Isaac Bashevis Singer was born in Leoncin, Poland, on July 14, 1904. He moved with his parents and two brothers to Radzymin at the age of three. His father, director of a yeshiva, secretary to the rabbi, and later judge of an ecclesiastical court, relocated in 1908 to Warsaw, where Isaac came into contact with a community full of Jewish tradition and a sense of place.

Deeply influenced by Fyodor Dostoevski, Baruch Spinoza, Anton Chekhov, and Leo Tolstoy, Singer, who was enrolled in Warsaw's Tachkemoni Rabbinical Seminary from 1921 to 1922 and was groomed for a religious life, studied the Torah, Talmud, and Kabala. Because he preferred secular literature, he antagonized his fanatical father, who never acknowledged his son's literary talents.

Singer's elder brother, Israel, followed the family's rabbinical bent, then opted for a secular writing career. From 1923 to 1933, Isaac, mimicking his brother's emancipation, abandoned his family's orthodox beliefs and chose worldly work as author, editor, proofreader, and translator for his brother's literary magazine, *Literarische Bletter*, in which he published his first short fiction. During this period he met his common-law wife, Runya, a fiery Communist with whom he frequently quarreled. Singer's only child, Israel Zamir, was born in 1929. Runya left Singer in 1934 and emigrated to Russia. Later, she settled in Palestine. Israel, a kibbutz farmer and journalist, remained apart from his father until their reunion in 1955. Singer rarely spoke of their relationship or of his first wife.

In pursuit of his literary career, Singer wrote first in Hebrew, then switched to Yiddish, into which he translated Erich Remarque's *All Quiet on the Western Front* (1929) and Thomas Mann's *The Magic Mountain* (1927). He edited *Globus* in 1932 and prepared the manuscript of his first novel, *Sotan in Goray* (1935; *Satan in Goray*, 1955), which was published in Yiddish and translated by his nephew, Joseph Singer, with whom Singer trusted much of his later work. Like his brother Israel, who emigrated to New York in 1934 to escape the growing menace of Nazism and virulent anti-Semitism, Singer, haunted by the terror that stalked European Jews, fled by rail to Paris and by steamer to the United States at the age of thirty-one. His exodus preceded a tense, fearful time when unreliable news from Eastern Europe concealed the fact that his mother and his brother Moishe, a devout rabbi, froze to death after being transported from their homes in Russian cattle cars.

Singer settled in New York City's Upper West Side and eight years later became a naturalized citizen. After divorcing Runya, he met Alma Haimann Wassermann, a well-traveled, well-read native of Munich, Bavaria, while on vacation in the Catskills in 1937. Despite the fact that she was married and had two small children, the couple maintained a relationship for two years before she decided to leave her husband. Following her marriage to Singer on February 14, 1940, Alma worked in a hat factory sewing sweatbands, while Singer, still a struggling writer during this period, tended her young son and daughter, Klaus and Inga. Later, until her retirement in the 1970's, she worked as a buyer for Saks and Lord and Taylor.

As a journalist and fiction writer for *Jewish Daily Forward*, Singer developed his considerable writing talents and published serialized novels, short stories, children's books, and plays, which he sometimes wrote under the pen names Isaac Bashevis and Isaac Warshofsky. He contributed short fiction to *Harper's*, *The New Yorker*, *Playboy*, *The Saturday Evening Post*, *Chicago Review*, *Die Yiddische Welt*, *Holiday*, *Commentary*, *Redbook*, *Esquire*, and *Partisan Review* and published critical essays, among them "Realism and Truth" in *Reconstructionist* and "What It Takes to Be a

Jewish Writer" in the *National Jewish Monthly.* He was active in the Jewish Academy of Arts and Sciences, the Polish Institute of Arts and Sciences in America, the American Academy of Arts and Sciences, and the National Institute of Arts and Letters, of which he was for a time the only foreign-language member.

Singer achieved sophistication with the English idiom yet clung to his native tongue, remarking that writers must write in their native language. In 1950, beginning with the publication of his second novel, *Di Familie Muskat* (1950; *The Family Moskat,* 1950), Singer involved himself wholeheartedly in the translation process and published in English, producing his greatest achievements: the novels *The Magician of Lublin* (1960), *The Slave* (1962), *The Manor* (1967), and *The Estate* (1969); the story collections *Gimpel the Fool and Other Stories* (1963), *The Spinoza of Market Street* (1961), *Short Friday and Other Stories* (1964), *The Séance and Other Stories* (1968), *A Friend of Kafka and Other Stories* (1970), and *A Crown of Feathers and Other Stories* (1973); and the nonfiction *In My Father's Court* (1966). When he was in his sixties, he acceded to his publisher's advice and began writing children's works, beginning with *Zlateh the Goat and Other Stories* (1966). For these works, Singer received a long list of awards, including the Agnon Gold Medal, a National Book Award for children's literature, a grant from the National Endowment for the Arts, the Newbery Honor Book Award, a fiction award from *Playboy,* the Bancarella Prize for translation, the Maggid Award for contributions to Jewish journalism, and honorary doctorates from Texas Christian University, Hebrew University in Jerusalem, and Bard College. More to his liking was Columbia University's creation of the I. B. Singer award, given to students of Yiddish and Yiddish literature.

Often courted by theatrical and cinema producers, Singer held little hope of seeing his work onstage until the production of *Yentl, the Yeshiva Boy* (1974), the story of a young Polish woman who conceals her sex so that she can follow her father's example and study the Torah. The popular stage version, scripted by Leah Napolin, starring Tovah Feldshuh, and produced in Brooklyn's Chelsea Theater in 1974, was expanded into a musical and filmed by Metro-Goldwyn-Mayer/United Artists as *Yentl* in 1983. Written by Jack Rosenthal and Barbra Streisand, the film starred Streisand, Mandy Patinkin, and Amy Irving in a poignant, colorful rendering of Polish family life and scholarship. These achievements, part of a large body of work, led to his winning the Nobel Prize in Literature in 1978.

Impact of Event

A major part of Singer's success was his appreciation for what his audience liked and needed. Avoiding the irritatingly knowing tone of the pseudopsychologist, the didacticism of the proselytizer, or the self-pitying whine of the modern narcissist, he concentrated on telling a good story, one that disarmed readers with a wise simplicity far more complex than surface details would admit. Grounded in a pervasive belief in God and respect for humanity, he filled his stories with bizarre and engaging characters—Gimpel the fool, Yentl the yeshiva boy, Max Persky the womanizer of Warsaw, Yoneh Meir the animal slaughterer, the semiautobiographical proofreader Aaron

Greidinger, and Yaboner the Yiddish New Yorker. The exotic atmospheres and exuberance and conviction of his characters never failed to find an audience or spark debate in critics.

Stunned by the Nobel committee's selection, Singer, who considered himself to be a humble storyteller, at first doubted that the announcement was genuine. Within hours, his quiet life with Alma was interrupted by interviewers, reporters, a reception hosted by New York Mayor Ed Koch, and phone calls from notables including President Jimmy Carter and Israel's Menachem Begin, who lauded the author's support of the Yiddish language. To preserve some privacy while he worked on his acceptance speech, Singer took a hotel room and unplugged his telephone but failed to elude persistent well-wishers.

Singer's readers, vindicated in their belief that he had been too long passed over, praised his piquant blend of mysticism, gossipy folk humor, family uproar, eroticism, and uplifting, humanistic rhythms. His critics, who decried his emphasis on sensuality and lambasted him for withdrawing from the prevailing attitudes toward Judaism and Yiddish tradition, made no inroads on his individuality. Refusing to be drawn into the idealism and self-absorption of his contemporaries, he remained adamant in his view of a world that was about as good as it would ever be and professed that love, in whatever form, was a gift from God. Compared to William Shakespeare, Nikos Kazantzakis, and Nathaniel Hawthorne for his absorption with religion, philosophy, and the occult, he maintained a focus on demons and possession, love and lust, faith and doubt, trust and betrayal.

Contrasting Singer's somber belief that life, no matter what the writer did to better it, would remain tragic, a jubilant Jewish community, particularly the pro-Yiddish segment, hosted numerous receptions in his honor. Jewish publishers, heartened by Singer's selection, predicted a rise in sales and greater recognition of Jewish themes. Producer Moshe Mizrahi inaugurated plans to film *The Slave*. Geria/Golan/Globus released a costly film version of *The Magician of Lublin* (1979), starring Alan Arkin, Louise Fletcher, Valerie Perrine, Shelley Winters, and Lou Jacobi.

The Nobel Prize came at a difficult time for Singer, who had undergone prostate surgery at the same time that Alma was suffering from circulatory problems in her legs. Although the preponderance of his achievements occurred before the award, Singer, resisting public acclaim so that he could write in peace, continued publishing. He produced, among other works, the novel *Shosha* (1978), a best-seller and Book-of-the-Month Club selection; two memoirs, *A Young Man in Search of Love* (1978) and *Lost in America* (1980); several collections of children's fiction; and a collection of short fiction, *Old Love* (1979). He continued probing the life of the isolated Jew, whether a denizen of European ghettos or a refugee lost in the meaningless tangle of New World metropolises. He refused to desert the idiosyncrasies of Yiddish, and much of his canon remained untranslated.

As his frail health continued its decline, Singer began spending more time in bed rather than at his desk. On doctor's orders, he declined most lecture invitations, and rejecting notions that he should run for political office, concentrated on writing.

Accompanied by Alma, he spent winter months in Surfside, Florida, where he died on July 24, 1991.

Bibliography

Alexander, Edward. *Isaac Bashevis Singer.* Twayne's World Authors Series. Boston: Twayne, 1980. A readable, scholarly critique, complete with timeline, notes, and bibliography. Perhaps too advanced for high-school students but more than adequate for the literary historian, teacher, or critic.

Kresh, Paul. *Isaac Bashevis Singer: The Magician of West Eighty-sixth Street.* New York: Dial Press, 1979. A ponderous biography, complete with introduction, photographs, and detailed index. Kresh unfortunately overburdens the reader with cumbersome minutiae and forgettable quotations but presents a faithful recounting of Singer's response to the Nobel Prize.

Malin, Irving. *Isaac Bashevis Singer.* New York: Ungar, 1972. A slim, well-documented volume of pre-Nobel criticism, complete with footnotes, critical bibliography, canon, timeline, and thorough index. This factual, forthright work suits the needs of the scholar, literary historian, and critic more than those of the general reader.

Miller, David N. *Recovering the Canon: Essays on Isaac Bashevis Singer.* Studies in Judaism in Modern Times. Leiden, The Netherlands: E. J. Brill, 1986. A useful compendium of commentary covering a variety of points of view. Although primarily intended for scholars and literary historians, this work meets the needs of the student who is willing to delve for insights.

Ripp, Allan. "Nobel Prize Winner Isaac Bashevis Singer on Life, Sex, and the Storyteller's Art." *People* 17 (May 17, 1982): 88-92. A candid glimpse of the author, including memorable photos and quotations.

Siegel, Ben. *Isaac Bashevis Singer.* Pamphlets on American Writers Series. Minneapolis: University of Minnesota Press, 1969. A worthy overview for high school and college students. Containing a balance of biographical and critical data, this volume is an excellent starting place.

Mary Ellen Snodgrass

Cross-References

The First Nobel Prizes Are Awarded (1901), p. 45; Wiesel's *Night* Recalls the Holocaust (1956), p. 1700; Kawabata Wins the Nobel Prize in Literature (1968), p. 2147; Mahfouz Wins the Nobel Prize in Literature (1988), p. 2625; Gordimer Wins the Nobel Prize in Literature (1991), p. 2668.

APOCALYPSE NOW IS HAILED AS THE ULTIMATE VIETNAM WAR FILM

Category of event: Motion pictures
Time: 1979
Locale: The United States

Apocalypse Now *helped to establish the themes and narrative structure of Vietnam War films*

> *Principal personages:*
> FRANCIS FORD COPPOLA (1939-   ), the filmmaker who produced, directed, and cowrote *Apocalypse Now*
> JOHN MILIUS (1945-   ), a screenwriter who cowrote *Apocalypse Now*
> MICHAEL HERR (1940?-   ), a journalist and the author of the Vietnam War memoir *Dispatches* (1977), who wrote the narration for *Apocalypse Now*

Summary of Event

The Vietnam War made it necessary to create a new kind of war film. World War II films assumed that the United States was exceptional—that the United States always won its wars and embodied freedom and virtue. Defeat in Vietnam, charges that the United States acted as an imperialist power there, and atrocities committed by U.S. soldiers—burning of villages, torture and assassination of suspected Viet Cong, the massacre of civilians at My Lai—undermined such assumptions. After Vietnam, war films made according to the old formula were not credible, while films that might make audiences feel guilty about Vietnam were financially risky. Given these problems, filmmakers avoided the subject.

In 1975, however, Francis Ford Coppola, the director of *The Godfather* films, announced that he intended to make a film about the war. A poll commissioned by Coppola had found that Americans would accept a "nondidactic" film about Vietnam.

Coppola had difficulty making his film. The military refused to assist (Pentagon officials objected to the script), a typhoon hit the Philippines, where the film was being shot, and one of the principal actors suffered a heart attack. The film ran millions of dollars over budget and took four years to complete; *Apocalypse Now* was not released until 1979.

The film tells the story of Captain Willard (Martin Sheen), a Central Intelligence Agency (CIA) assassin ordered to find Colonel Walter Kurtz (Marlon Brando), a Green Beret accused of murdering four suspected Viet Cong agents. Kurtz has escaped, gathered a force of natives, and moved into Cambodia, where he is waging a private war, "operating," an American general says, "without any decent restraint, totally beyond the pale of any acceptable human conduct." Kurtz's superiors have concluded that Kurtz is insane, and they order Willard to "terminate" Kurtz "with extreme prejudice." A Navy patrol boat carries Willard upriver into Cambodia. Along the way, he and the crew experience adventures that become more and more surreal: a helicopter assault on a village, an encounter with a tiger in the jungle, a United Service Organizations (USO) Playboy bunny show, the killing of civilians in a sampan, a battle at an isolated bridge, and an attack by natives with arrows and spears. Eventually, Willard finds Kurtz and assassinates him.

To appeal to the broadest possible audience, *Apocalypse Now* takes no moral or political stand; the film is so ambiguous it can be understood as antiwar or prowar. *Apocalypse Now* does call attention to American atrocities in Vietnam. Kurtz's crime suggests the actual case of Robert Rheault, a Green Beret colonel charged in 1969 with murdering a suspected North Vietnamese spy, and critics have argued that both the helicopter assault on the village and the brutal killing of civilians in the sampan allude to the massacre at My Lai. The film also implies that America was engaged in an imperialist adventure in Vietnam. *Apocalypse Now* is based in part on Joseph Conrad's *Heart of Darkness* (1902), a story of European imperialism in Africa. The film also makes reference to the Philippine "insurrection," in which the United States brutally suppressed a Filipino independence movement and made the Philippines an American colony, and contains scenes of Americans imposing themselves on the Vietnamese (as when, for example, waterskiing American sailors swamp a Vietnamese ferry).

These antiwar elements in *Apocalypse Now* are offset by a prowar message in the film's narrative. The narrative structure of *Apocalypse Now* is based on the classical myth of the visit to the underworld; in such myths, a hero descends into the land of the dead, encounters supernatural marvels, acquires wisdom, and returns to the surface to bring what he has learned to his fellow human beings. Willard, at the beginning of *Apocalypse Now*, waits in a hotel room in Saigon. Soldiers arrive with his orders, but he is too drunk to understand. One soldier characterizes him as "dead." The film cuts to a shot of a helicopter, in which Willard rides, descending. The sequence indicates Willard's descent into the underworld. As Willard travels upriver (a journey that recalls the crossing of the river of the dead in the underworld), he moves further from the realm of conventional morality represented by the officials who have sent him on his mission and further into the supernatural realm of Kurtz. The film implies that Kurtz is a wise man; he is photographed so as to resemble the Buddha. Kurtz teaches that the United States, hampered by conventional rules of war and conventional morality, lacks the will to do what is necessary to win, and that the war must be fought savagely, without restraint. When Willard reaches Kurtz's stronghold, he is captured but allowed to live because Kurtz wishes Willard to go back and tell Kurtz's story. After Willard kills Kurtz, Willard picks up a manuscript Kurtz has written that contains Kurtz's message: "Drop the bomb. Exterminate them all!" Willard takes the manuscript, boards the patrol boat, and heads downriver, beginning his return from the underworld to the surface. The wisdom he brings back is clearly a prowar message, one also found in the film's title, which reverses the peace movement's "Peace Now" slogan.

Initial reviews of *Apocalypse Now* were mixed. Critic Stanley Kauffmann hailed the film as the ultimate Vietnam War movie. The film won praise for its cinematography and for individual scenes, especially the helicopter assault (acclaimed as one of the greatest battle scenes ever filmed). Some critics, however, charged that the film lacked well-defined characters; critics especially disliked the performances of Sheen and Brando. Others criticized the film for its self-contradiction and political emptiness. Almost all regarded as a failure Coppola's attempt to use myth and allegory. Regardless of the response of critics, though, *Apocalypse Now* had an important effect on Vietnam War films.

Impact of Event

Even before its release, *Apocalypse Now* inspired the making of other Vietnam War pictures. When other filmmakers heard that Coppola planned to make a picture about the war, they followed his lead and rushed to get their films out first. The result was a series of Vietnam War films that appeared before *Apocalypse Now* including *Go Tell the Spartans*, *The Boys in Company C*, *Coming Home*, and *The Deer Hunter*, all released in 1978. None of those films, however, covered the range of issues that *Apocalypse Now* did. *Apocalypse Now* helped establish the themes and narrative structure that would appear in Vietnam War movies that came after it.

Platoon (1986), for example, uses the same narrative structure as *Apocalypse Now*— the story of the adventurer descending to the underworld and bringing back wisdom. *Platoon* opens with a group of soldiers, including Chris Taylor (Charlie Sheen), emerging from a military transport plane that has just landed. The first thing the soldiers see are body bags filled with corpses. This scene establishes the metaphor of Vietnam as the land of the dead, into which the troops have descended ("What are you doing in the underworld, Taylor?" a soldier asks later in the film). The plot of *Platoon* follows the plot of *Apocalypse Now* by depicting a struggle for Taylor's soul between two sergeants, Elias (Willem Dafoe), who fights within the prescribed rules of warfare, and Barnes (Tom Berenger), who, like Kurtz, fights without restraint. In the end, much as Willard murders Kurtz in a kind of sacrificial killing, so Taylor murders Barnes. Taylor then ascends in a helicopter in the film's final scene, leaving the underworld of Vietnam and beginning his return to the surface. He takes with him the knowledge he has gained from both sergeants (he is "a child born of those two fathers") and promises to teach what he has learned.

Casualties of War (1989) has a similar narrative structure. The film literally begins underground: Eriksson (Michael J. Fox), a Vietnam veteran, is sleeping on a subway; in his dreams, he relives his Vietnam experience (this scene, too, sets up the metaphor of Vietnam as the underworld). The film tells the story of Eriksson's squad members, who kidnap and repeatedly rape a Vietnamese girl. Eriksson refuses to participate. There follows the same kind of struggle found in *Apocalypse Now* between conventional morality, represented by Eriksson, and the morality of Vietnam, where soldiers operate without restraint. At the end of the film, Eriksson returns from the underworld to the surface; he awakes as the subway emerges from underground into the light.

A major theme of *Apocalypse Now* is Kurtz's identification with the enemy. Kurtz admires the will of the Viet Cong to do what is necessary without judgment or restraint. He adopts the enemy's tactics, engaging in guerilla warfare. This kind of identification with the enemy becomes the major theme of *First Blood* (1982). In that film, John Rambo (Sylvester Stallone), a Vietnam veteran, is unjustly arrested by the sheriff of a small town. Rambo escapes and fights a guerilla war in the forest against the police and the National Guard. Rambo's war is a miniature Vietnam War in which Rambo acts as the Viet Cong: He defeats soldiers who have helicopters and superior firepower, he vanishes into a cave that calls to mind the tunnels used by the Viet Cong, and he takes his war from the forest into the town in a way that recalls the Tet Offensive of 1968, in which the North Vietnamese army and the Viet Cong moved from the jungles to attack the cities of Vietnam.

Apocalypse Now implies that the United States could have won the Vietnam War had it possessed the will and had American power not been restrained by bureaucrats. *Rambo: First Blood Part II* (1985) develops this theme. Rambo is sent back to Vietnam to search for American prisoners of war left behind when the war ended ("Do we get to win this time?" Rambo asks). The bureaucrat in charge of the operation wants Rambo to fail; it would be politically embarrassing to admit that the United States had left soldiers behind. When Rambo finds a prisoner and escapes with him to a rendezvous point, the bureaucrat recalls the helicopter sent to pick them up, leaving them stranded. This scene, in which a bureaucrat arranges for defeat at the moment of victory, calls to mind the conservative interpretation of the Tet Offensive: Conservatives argued that the campaign was a great military victory for the United States but that, at that moment when victory in the war was in sight, bureaucrats lost their nerve and began the pullout that led to defeat. In the film, Rambo, through his will, overcomes all obstacles and achieves the victory that eluded the United States on the battlefield.

Another theme in *Apocalypse Now* emerges in the scene involving the USO show that features the Playboy bunnies. The show takes place in an amphitheater decorated with missiles, which appear to be huge phallic symbols. The troops scream obscenities at the women and finally storm the stage, disrupting the show. The scene conveys the messages that war is a male ritual and excludes women and that there is a connection between war and the domination and humiliation of women by men in American society. That theme is developed further in *Full Metal Jacket* (1987), which shows U.S. Marine recruits being indoctrinated in hatred of women during basic training (Michael Herr, who wrote the narration for *Apocalypse Now*, helped write the script of *Full Metal Jacket*). The theme is also prominent in *Casualties of War*, in which the rape of the Vietnamese girl is used as a male-bonding ritual to hold members of the squad together.

Francis Ford Coppola has said that when he began working on *Apocalypse Now*, he wrote down a list of about two hundred things about Vietnam that he wanted to include in his movie. The result was an extraordinarily rich film that did a great deal to establish the way in which American filmmakers have told the story of the Vietnam War.

Bibliography

Auster, Albert, and Leonard Quart. *How the War Was Remembered: Hollywood and Vietnam.* New York: Praeger, 1988. A history of Vietnam War movies. Critically evaluates films, classifies them according to type, and places Vietnam War movies in the context of the history of the war movie genre. 171 pages. Index, photographs.

Davidson, James West, and Mark Hamilton Lytle. "Where Trouble Comes." In *After the Fact: The Art of Historical Detection.* 3d ed. Vol. 2. New York: McGraw-Hill, 1992. An essay evaluating the historical authenticity of Vietnam movies and the role of movies in creating myths about the Vietnam War. Photographs, suggestions for additional reading.

Dittmar, Linda, and Gene Michaud, eds. *From Hanoi to Hollywood: The Vietnam War in American Film.* New Brunswick, N.J.: Rutgers University Press, 1990. A collection of essays on Vietnam War movies, including documentaries. See especially Frank P. Tomasulo's essay on the political ambiguity of *Apocalypse Now.* 387 pages. Index, photographs, chronology, and filmography.

Herr, Michael. *Dispatches.* New York: Alfred A. Knopf, 1977. An excellent personal memoir of the Vietnam War written by a journalist who covered the war for *Esquire* magazine. Concentrates on events of 1968, including the Tet Offensive and the battle for Khe Sanh, and on the experience of the ordinary soldier. Especially good at capturing the kind of surreal perception of the war also found in *Apocalypse Now.* 260 pages.

Literature/Film Quarterly 16, no. 4 (1988), and 20, no. 3 (1992). Special issues on Vietnam War movies. The first issue concentrates on *Full Metal Jacket.* The second issue deals with the narrative structure of Vietnam War movies, especially the use of classical mythology, and includes two essays on *Apocalypse Now.*

Sheehan, Neil. *A Bright Shining Lie: John Paul Vann and America in Vietnam.* New York: Vintage Books, 1988. An excellent study of the Vietnam War that uses the career of John Paul Vann, an American military officer, as a starting point from which to explore the entire American experience in Vietnam. Winner of the National Book Award and the Pulitzer Prize. 861 pages. Index, maps, photographs, and bibliography.

Donald M. Whaley

Cross-References

Heart of Darkness Reveals the Consequences of Imperialism (1902), p. 51; *Casablanca* Marks the Artistic Apex of 1940's War-Themed Films (1942), p. 1245; Coppola Revives Gangster Films with *The Godfather* Trilogy (1972), p. 2265; *Dog Soldiers* Portrays Vietnam in Fiction (1974), p. 2315; *Platoon* Explores the Vietnam Experience (1986), p. 2576.

SONDHEIM USES OPERATIC TECHNIQUES
IN *SWEENEY TODD*

Categories of event: Theater and music
Time: 1979
Locale: New York, New York

In Sweeney Todd, *Stephen Sondheim explored both a darker side and an operatic side of the musical theater*

Principal personages:
STEPHEN SONDHEIM (1930-   ), a composer/lyricist, a leading force in American musical theater
HAL PRINCE (1928-   ), a producer/director who produced many of Sondheim's musicals

Summary of Event

In the decade from 1969 to 1979, the team of Stephen Sondheim and Hal Prince essentially defined the American musical theater. Both had made significant contributions prior to this time and both continued to work afterward, but that decade belonged to Sondheim and Prince. Usually, when one refers to a team in the musical theater, the partnership includes a composer, lyricist, and librettist, sometimes with one partner taking on two of the roles. Famous teams have included Richard Rodgers and Lorenz Hart, Richard Rodgers and Oscar Hammerstein II, and Alan Jay Lerner and Frederick Loewe. Sondheim and Prince, however, took the idea of the musical theater team in a new direction. Sondheim worked as a composer/lyricist, and Prince as a producer/director.

Stephen Sondheim was born in 1930. When he was ten years old, his parents were divorced and his mother, with Stephen, moved to Doylestown, Pennsylvania, where they had as a neighbor Oscar Hammerstein II. Hammerstein became almost a surrogate father for Sondheim, and Sondheim was allowed to watch the development of some of the truly great American musicals. As Sondheim grew and expressed interest in the field, Hammerstein took to teaching him how to write a musical. The "course" had four parts and took six years. Sondheim was to write four musicals. First, he was to take a play he admired and turn it into a musical. Next, he was to attempt to improve a play with music. Third, he was to take nondramatic material (a novel or short story) and turn it into a musical. Finally, he was to write a completely original musical. Each of these efforts was evaluated by Hammerstein. Sondheim learned very specific things, such as the problems of dramatic structure.

This was not the full extent of Sondheim's education. He was also a student at Williams College, where he majored in music. Upon his graduation and the winning of the Hutchinson Prize at Princeton University, Sondheim went to New York to study for two years with Milton Babbitt, an avant-garde composer. Sondheim had no aspirations to be a "serious" classical composer. His clearly stated goal was to be a serious composer for the musical theater. With that goal, it is ironic that Sondheim's first professional job was decidedly nonmusical. Through friends, he was hired as a television writer for the *Topper* series. Although he did a good job, he was quite unhappy, and he quit when he had enough money to return to New York. He made some contacts and was hired to write the score for a project called *Saturday Night*. The project ended with the untimely death of the producer.

Sondheim, however, had made an impression with his work and soon was hired to write the lyrics for Leonard Bernstein's *West Side Story* (1957). The producers were Robert Griffith and Hal Prince. This was not Sondheim's first meeting with Prince. They originally met at the opening night party for *South Pacific* (1949). When Prince was released from the Army in 1952, he went to work for George Abbott as an assistant stage manager. Sondheim and Prince would meet for lunch and discuss plans for taking the theater in new directions. *West Side Story* was a first step in that direction.

Sondheim did not see it quite that way. He wanted to be a composer, not a lyricist, so he was torn when he was asked to write the lyrics to Jule Styne's music for *Gypsy* (1959). Although Sondheim wanted to write the complete score, he was rather proud of *Gypsy*. He thought it was the last good show written in the form his mentor, Hammerstein, had developed. In 1962, Sondheim got his chance. He composed the entire score for a Broadway musical, *A Funny Thing Happened on the Way to the Forum* (1962). Burt Shevelove and Larry Gelbart wrote the book. George Abbott directed, Prince produced, and Jerome Robbins came in to doctor the show. The show was a success in its original run and continued to be a success in revival.

Not everything Sondheim touched turned to gold, of course. His next show was the avant-garde *Anyone Can Whistle* (1964). Although the show only lasted six performances, the score showed a complexity that would appear in later works. It also featured Angela Lansbury in her first major appearance in a stage musical. Sondheim's collaborator on that show, Arthur Laurents, then began to turn his play, *The Time of the Cuckoo*, into a musical. Richard Rodgers was asked to compose and, since Hammerstein was dead, Sondheim was approached to write the lyrics. Not wanting to write just lyrics, Sondheim was hesitant. Rodgers' daughter, Mary, and Laurents were friends of Sondheim, and they prevailed on him to accept. It was not a happy collaboration, and the show, *Do I Hear a Waltz?* (1965), was not particularly successful.

His next shows were more of a collaboration with Hal Prince. By this time, Prince had decided to direct as well as produce. *Company* (1970) was the first production. George Furth had written a series of short plays that Prince and Sondheim believed could make a good, if different, musical. Rather than the conventional plot, *Company* showed a contemporary view of marriage in New York City. Because of its structure, many view Sondheim's *Company* as the first "concept" musical. This term means that the musical was driven more by ideas than by plot. Since the show was different, the audience had a difficult time understanding it. Those who understood it and appreciated the skill involved in the creation were left cold by a perceived lack of feeling. It was respected, made a profit as a result of low-cost production, and won several awards.

The next shows were *Follies* (1971), *A Little Night Music* (1973)—probably their most conventional and successful production—and *Pacific Overtures* (1976). The last of those was a musical about America's relations with Japan since 1852. It ran for 193 performances but lost $650,000 because of its lavish staging and effects. The Sondheim-Prince collaborations were artistically ambitious, to be sure. They experimented with new forms. Even *A Little Night Music*, which followed a conventional plot line, had an entire score of waltz music. It also had a book by Hugh Wheeler.

When the project of *Sweeney Todd* was first conceived, Sondheim planned to do all the writing. He saw the show as an opera. It had started as a melodrama in London. The original was written in 1847 as *The String of Pearls: Or, The Fiend of Fleet Street*, and there have been several versions. Sondheim saw a version written by Christopher Bond. It tells the familiar story of Benjamin Barker, wrongfully imprisoned by the evil Judge Turpin. Turpin then rapes Barker's wife and takes custody of Johanna, Barker's child. Barker returns as Sweeney Todd, bent on revenge. He opens a barber shop over the meat-pie shop of Mrs. Lovett. Todd is rather indiscriminate in his vengeance and begins to slit the throats of his customers. At a loss as to what to do with the bodies, Todd donates them to Mrs. Lovett as the material for meat pies. Todd continues to wield his razor until his vengeance is complete.

Sondheim was immediately intrigued by the idea of telling Todd's tale as a musical or an opera. Prince, on the other hand, was more difficult to interest. Prince did not share Sondheim's interest in farce (the story is a bit over the top) and melodrama. He, at first, could not form an approach. Then Prince discovered that the whole plot was about revenge, the Industrial Age, and the way man becomes a soulless machine. The set, by Eugene Lee, was a real iron foundry from Rhode Island. Every time there was a murder, Prince inserted a piercing steam whistle. One of Sondheim's songs, *A Little Priest*, was a comic representation of how the big fish eat the little fish, but are in turn eaten by bigger fish.

Sondheim realized early on that he was going to need help in the writing process, so Hugh Wheeler was brought in to write the book for the show. A libretto was constructed, but this was far from a conventional musical. It opened with Len Cariou and Angela Lansbury in the leads on March 1, 1979, in the Uris Theater. The show ran for roughly a year, then toured. It won various awards but lost money.

Impact of Event

Sweeney Todd can be looked at in two ways. First, it can be seen as an individual show, and second, it can be seen as the culmination of a partnership. Both views are valid. As a show, it continued what George Gershwin, with *Porgy and Bess* (1935), and Frank Loesser, with *The Most Happy Fella* (1956), had started. It continued to blur the line between musical theater and opera. There were more spoken words in *Sweeney Todd* than in most operas. There was almost constant music, and Sondheim made use of many recurrent themes and musical ideas to express character. The theme of blood and vengeance was also very operatic, as was the scale of the original production. In fact, the size was one of the economic problems. As a result of the size of the set (a real factory), the production was limited to larger theaters, and larger theaters require larger audiences to break even. There was a production done by the York Theater, which completely rethought the concept of the production. Instead of capturing the sweep of the Industrial Age and humanity's place in society, the revival focused on the individual characters. *Sweeney Todd* always did have operatic ambitions and, at the insistence of Beverly Sills, the production became a part of the New York City Opera repertoire. Later productions, such as *Les Misérables* (1980), had it as a predecessor for their operatic ambitions.

Sweeney Todd is also important as a high point of a truly important partnership. It was not the last show by Sondheim and Prince; *Merrily We Roll Along* (1981) followed. This show reflects a very conventional, though talented, score by Sondheim and rather muddled directing; it was not Prince/Sondheim at their best. Whether *Sweeney Todd* showed their best work is a judgment call, but *Sweeney Todd* did represent the team at its most ambitious. The intricacy of Sondheim's music and lyrics and the high production values of Prince's directing and producing were never more evident. As was evident in their other work, such ambitions rarely made room for romance or warmth. *Sweeney Todd* was difficult to care for, but many were impressed.

On their own, Sondheim and Prince continued with important projects. Prince directed the very successful *The Phantom of the Opera* (1986) by Andrew Lloyd Webber. Sondheim, in collaboration with James Lapine, wrote *Sunday in the Park with George* (1984), a musical about Georges Seurat's creation of a painting. Prince and Sondheim thus continued to influence the American musical.

Bibliography

Engel, Lehman. *The American Musical Theater.* New York: Macmillan, 1975. Not a source dealing specifically with *Sweeney Todd.* Engel has created a very useful sourcebook for the study of musical theater in general. He examines Sondheim's early work and critically evaluates trends. Contains several appendices.

Kislan, Richard. *The Musical.* Englewood Cliffs, N.J.: Prentice-Hall, 1980. A textbook for a general course in musical theater. Includes a philosophy, a brief but thorough history, and a study of the various crafts and artists in the musical theater. Features a chapter on Sondheim that is brief but deep.

Smith, Cecil, and Glenn Litton. *Musical Comedy in America.* New York: Theatre Arts Books, 1981. An excellent overall history. The pictures are adequate, and the text is thorough and literate. Smith and Litton go beyond the expected chronology and discuss technique. Litton, who wrote the more contemporary part, gives a view of the audience response to Sondheim's work. His discussion of *Sweeney Todd* emphasizes the conflict between art and audience expectations.

Wilk, Max. *They're Playing Our Song.* Kingsport, Tenn.: Kingsport Press, 1973. A book for popular use, though not much help in research. Wilk shows how sources other than Hammerstein influenced Sondheim as a young writer. No pictures. The writing style is very conversational.

Zadan, Craig. *Sondheim and Company.* New York: Harper & Row, 1989. A large book, written and designed for popular consumption. For research on Sondheim, this is clearly the source with which to start. Notes on the start of Sondheim's career, the abundant photos, and the countless interviews are all helpful. It is a very positive and thorough book. Zadan is especially interested in the process that gets a show to the stage.

William B. Kennedy

Cross-References

Show Boat Introduces American Musical Theater (1927), p. 745; Gershwin's *Porgy and Bess* Opens in New York (1935), p. 1016; *Oklahoma!* Opens on Broadway (1943), p. 1256; Bernstein Joins Symphonic and Jazz Elements in *West Side Story* (1957), p. 1731; Sondheim's *Company* Is Broadway's First "Concept" Musical (1970), p. 2213.

SCHNABEL EMERGES AS A CELEBRITY ARTIST

Category of event: Art
Time: The early 1980's
Locale: New York, New York

Self-confidence, extravagance, aggressive marketing and publicity, and finally talent made Julian Schnabel one of the first superstars of the art world in the 1980's

Principal personages:
JULIAN SCHNABEL (1951-), an American artist ranked in the forefront of the New Wave or neoexpressionist style
MARY BOONE (1951-), a prominent New York City art dealer who took an aggressive role in promoting Schnabel's work
LEO CASTELLI (1907-), the most prominent New York City dealer in contemporary art, who jointly was responsible for showing and promoting Schnabel's work

Summary of Event

Before 1980, almost no one outside Manhattan had heard of Julian Schnabel. In the decade of the 1980's, he became a household name in art circles extending far beyond the SoHo art district. His often vast neoexpressionist paintings captured the imagination of an art public that seemed weary of the cool look of minimalism or just confused by the multitude of trends in the pluralistic 1970's.

Schnabel's paintings were ambitious, inhabited by unusual, mysterious images and figures that evoked a broad range of references, from traditional religious art to pop culture. The picture plane was broken by gouges or jutting panels and a heavily built-up surface of encaustic (a kind of painting in which, by heating or burning in wax, the colors are rendered permanent) and paint. The artist used materials that ranged from pony hide to velvet, from smashed plates to real antlers. The works grew in scale as time passed. On one side of the spectrum, critics have stated that Schnabel reinvented the art world; others have stated that his work is fashionable with collectors for reasons the work does not make clear and that he is a symbol of regression. In any event, critics could ignore neither the personality of the man nor his work.

Schnabel's joint show at the galleries of Mary Boone and Leo Castelli in the spring of 1981 was one of the most talked-about events of the season. He showed thirteen paintings, dating from 1976 to 1981, that combined materials and objects—including wood, gold leaf, and real antlers—more boldly than ever. They were packed with religious imagery and resonated of sources as disparate as abstract expressionism and motion pictures. There were more plate paintings, which one critic referred to as "macho." Only much later did critics point out the significance of the plate paintings in Schnabel's view of the relations between the self and history, specifically his view of the fragmentation of a postmodern culture. Schnabel's work, in fact, was later seen as a mingling of modernism (progress and continuity) and postmodernism (fragmentation and discontinuity).

The show also included a series of huge (up to 150 square feet) works painted on velvet, one of which, called *Death*, was termed "quite unforgettable." The show grabbed attention in other respects. It was completely sold out before it opened, according to Boone, and the labels posted beside each of the thirteen works gave not only the title but the name of the collector who had bought it. This unorthodox display was the target of much criticism. Boone defended the labeling, contending that the paintings were already in private collections and that those collectors were gracious enough to lend them and should receive credit. They were collectors whose names could hardly hurt an artist's career: Morton Neumann of Chicago, Peter Ludwig, and Philip Niarchos among them. The prices ranged from $9,000 to $35,000, for the massive velvet *Understanding Self-Hate*.

Beginning with that first major show in 1981, Schnabel enjoyed a rapid commercial success, engineered in part by a shrewd young dealer, Mary Boone. Then came the patriarch of New York dealers, Leo Castelli, who took on Schnabel as his first new artist in a decade. Schnabel's paintings were bought by some of the most prestigious American and European collectors of contemporary art.

Although there are a number of artists of Schnabel's generation (or slightly older) who also were successful, including Susan Rothenberg, Neil Jenney, Jonathan Borofsky, Judy Pfaff, Bryan Hunt, Robert Longo, and Cindy Sherman, the focus on Schnabel has been unusually acute. A tidal wave of publicity attended his emergence— and, some say, helped to foster it. A feverish sense of scarcity of Schnabel's work was created by reports that his shows sold out before they opened and that collectors were waiting in line to purchase his work. His prices skyrocketed. The top price for a painting in 1981 was $40,000, up from $3,000 three years earlier. Schnabel was covered not only by the usual New York critics but by *The New Yorker* and *Newsweek*. Even *Rolling Stone* assigned an article on him. When the later defunct *SoHo News* ran a story on emerging New York artists, Schnabel's picture graced the cover, a portrait of an artist of serious demeanor, whose dark eyes met the camera with a direct gaze.

In the early 1980's, Schnabel rode the crest of popular attention and believed that he could use the recognition as poetic license to do whatever he chose. As the decade wore on, however, he increasingly complained about his celebrity status and the lack of attention paid to his paintings. He began to retreat from the press and attempted to focus on his art rather than on the critical controversies surrounding him.

Impact of Event

Julian Schnabel is an artist who helped to shape the climate and terms in which art in the 1980's was discussed. When "success" and attention come early, as they did for Schnabel, it is sometimes overlooked that the very paintings that have changed the vision of twentieth century art were born of a mood of opposition to established ways of seeing.

In the early 1970's, the studios of many young painters of Schnabel's generation were filled with canvases that paid homage to Barnett Newman and Ad Reinhardt and reflected the examples of Robert Ryman or Brice Marden. Schnabel was innovative in that he sought other models and, although for a short period the surface quality of his paintings owed something to the use of oil and encaustic by Brice Marden, he began to look to Europe rather than to the United States as a grounding for his work.

This distinct shift, many years ahead of the critics and the art market of which he is so often regarded as being merely the product, is one of the main strengths of his art. It continued to distinguish his work from that of other American artists of his generation. Early in his career, Schnabel had been interested in the work of the German expatriate Richard Lindner. Later, in seeking out a European approach, he took a characteristically singular course. Rather than choose the German expressionists, Schnabel decided to follow the example of Cy Twombly in Italy and, slightly later, of Joseph Beuys in Düsseldorf. From the viewpoint of New York in the mid-1970's, such choices must have seemed eccentric, yet in Europe Schnabel had discovered an art in which allusion could play a significant role.

The art market's adulation of him and the critics' frequent hostility toward him can be viewed as two sides of the same coin. He has been received as a champion of the resurgence of modernism, highly regarded by the art market, and implicitly as a destroyer of postmodernism, highly regarded by many art critics.

The year 1980 signaled a resurgence of modernism. In the art world, this resurgence centered around so-called neoexpressionist painting, which was received as the polar opposite of postmodern art. Schnabel in particular received attention as a neoexpressionist. The extreme intensity of feeling about him as an individual, or rather about his conspicuously successful career, derives from an exaggerated sense that his status as a celebrity actually endangers history, or that it is an expression of a real danger to history, by reestablishing the notion of artistic heroism from which the art world had so recently escaped. This feeling is encapsulated in the common critical comparison of Schnabel with Jackson Pollock, an artist who, along with Pablo Picasso, Schnabel has acknowledged as an important influence on his work. Most of the journalistic treatment of this relationship has focused not on the artwork but on the person of the artist. It is implied that Schnabel, as a marketing posture, is falsely aspiring to the "world-historical" role of Pollock. Thus, the critical use of the connection with Pollock has focused not on art historical elements but on the idea, antithetical to a postmodern attitude, of the artist as Romantic visionary hero.

In the brief age of the ascendancy of conceptual art, the death of painting was widely proclaimed. Painting brought with it the burden of modernism and its failure. To paint was to be regressive, yet the culture showed a profound and intense need for painting, perhaps in part because the upheavals of American culture had articulated themselves visually through painting for at least five centuries. It is, therefore, in painting that they can be immediately confronted. The function of painting, however, changed. Postmodern painting evolved types of works with a conceptual deconstructive force that revealed itself in various ways, including the prominent incorporation of verbal elements and, less frequently, elements of performance and the inclusion of a variety of contents that signified social involvement and a critical stance toward classical modernist myths such as the heroic self. Schnabel's work demonstrates something like an old-style enthusiasm for painting. His first New York show in 1979 was perceived as instrumental in what was called, apocalyptically, "The Return of Painting"—that is, of painting that wished to continue the modernist line instead of deconstructing it. As modernism resurged, Schnabel was seen as the enemy of female artists, of conceptual artists in whatever form, and of critical rather than visionary art. He was tossed about by the waves of the moment.

The resurgence of modernism was seen by some as brought about not by artistic but instead by market forces. The market success of Schnabel and others suggested to some that these artists were childishly complicit; that is, that they were being used and were going along with it. To this way of thinking, the neoexpressionists of the 1980's, hopelessly corrupted by money and the media, feigned the products of a totally direct, unmediated apprehension of things.

Despite the controversies surrounding him, Schnabel's work speaks for itself. Vibrant and often violent, Schnabel's work is both narrative and emotive. Bold, expressionistic, narrative, and melodramatic, his works often have religious overtones and a sense of destruction. By leaving his imagery unclear, he mystifies and opens up the possibility of many interpretations. He has stated that his paintings are about a state of mind, a state of what he has called "mindedness"; for him, "painting is a synonym for truth, where all the mistakes are visible."

Schnabel's rapid and controversial rise to critical focus—if not acclaim—has sometimes been regarded as a symptom of the art world's constant search for new form-givers, the equal of those who arose in earlier decades. His self-conscious attempt to present both his art and his persona as mythic may be symptomatic of the unstable nature of avant-gardist visual culture, a culture subject to media exploitation and itself quite willing to manipulate its image for the purposes of commerce under the guise of promulgation of an authentic aesthetic discovery.

Bibliography

Kramer, Hilton. "The New Expressionism: Signs of Passion." *The New Criterion* (November, 1982): 40-45. In this well-written article, the author discusses Schnabel's work in the context of neoexpressionism and its reawakening of the emotions in art.

Kuspit, Donald. *The New Subjectivism: Art in the 1980's.* Ann Arbor, Mich.: UMI Research Press, 1988. The first comprehensive survey of European and American art in the decade of the 1980's, this volume is an extensive collection of essays written by Kuspit focusing on three primary topics: "European Self-Assertion," "The Subjectivity of American Artists," and "Toward a Subjectivist Criticism."

The unifying thesis of Kuspit's argument is that the significant art of the 1980's places a new or renewed emphasis on subject and identity. Contains numerous reproductions.

Lucie-Smith, Edward. *Movements in Art Since 1945.* Rev. ed. London: Thames and Hudson, 1984. A classic account of the history of the visual arts since World War II, substantially revised and updated to include the trends in the 1980's. Clear, general survey for the nonspecialist. Contains a discussion of Schnabel's work in its historical context. Numerous color and black-and-white illustrations.

McGuigan, Cathleen. "Julian Schnabel." *Artnews* 81 (Summer, 1982): 88-94. Provides an insightful view of Schnabel's personal and professional life. Discussed are the artist's meteoric rise to fame, commercial success, collaboration with Mary Boone and Leo Castelli, and views on his own work.

Pincus-Witten, Robert. *Postminimalism into Maximalism: American Art, 1966-1986.* Ann Arbor, Mich.: UMI Research Press, 1987. An art critic's history of two decades of avant-garde American art. The book concentrates on major figures such as Richard Serra, Eva Hesse, and Mel Bochner, and it includes several significant essays on Schnabel. Contains numerous black-and-white reproductions.

Schnabel, Julian. *C.V.J.: Nicknames of Maître d's and Other Excerpts from Life.* New York: Random House, 1987. Schnabel provides an inside view of his life, work, and influences, as well as his travels. He comments on his philosophy of art and the growth and development of his life as well as his work from the early days to the mid-1980's. Also includes numerous color reproductions of his work.

Genevieve Slomski

Cross-References

Rosenberg Defines "Action Painting" (1952), p. 1557; Minimalism Emphasizes Objects as Art (1963), p. 1949; Warhol's *The Chelsea Girls* Becomes a Commercial Success (1966), p. 2053; New York's SoHo Develops into a Center for Contemporary Art (1970's), p. 2191; Four Modern Masters Affirm Germany's Place in the Art World (1980), p. 2464.

FEMALE DIRECTORS ATTAIN PROMINENCE

Category of event: Motion pictures
Time: The 1980's
Locale: Hollywood, California

Unnoticed and few in number for decades, female motion-picture directors began to enter the Hollywood mainstream

Principal personages:
> PENNY MARSHALL (1942-　　), the director of *Jumpin' Jack Flash* (1986), *Big* (1988), *Awakenings* (1990), and *A League of Their Own* (1992)
> BARBRA STREISAND (1942-　　), the director of *Yentl* (1983) and *The Prince of Tides* (1991)
> SUSAN SEIDELMAN (1952-　　), the director of *Desperately Seeking Susan* (1985), *Making Mr. Right* (1987), *Cookie* (1989), and *She-Devil* (1989)
> MARTHA COOLIDGE (1946-　　), the director of *Valley Girl* (1983), *Joy of Sex* (1984), *Real Genius* (1985), *Plain Clothes* (1988), and *Rambling Rose* (1991)
> AMY HECKERLING (1954-　　), the director of *Fast Times at Ridgemont High* (1982), *Johnny Dangerously* (1984), *National Lampoon's European Vacation* (1985), *Look Who's Talking* (1989), and *Look Who's Talking Too* (1990)
> RANDA HAINES (1945-　　), the director of *Children of a Lesser God* (1986) and *The Doctor* (1991)

Summary of Event

Before the 1980's, there were very few female directors working within the mainstream of the American film industry. Most women who were interested in directing motion pictures were able to do so only within the fringe of the motion-picture industry, primarily in independent, feminist, documentary, experimental, industrial, and educational filmmaking. Ironically, women flourished as directors during the beginnings of motion-picture production but found it difficult to find work in the industry after the 1950's. Not until the 1980's did female directors reemerge as a powerful presence in Hollywood.

Among the women directors in the period, six stand out as successful figures: Penny Marshall, Barbra Streisand, Susan Seidelman, Martha Coolidge, Amy Heckerling, and Randa Haines. This survey concentrates on films made in the 1980's and 1990's. By no means does it encompasses every woman director or include every film made by the directors discussed; it does, however, indicate the powerful presence of female directors during the time period.

Penny Marshall made her motion-picture directing debut with *Jumpin' Jack Flash* (1986). Marshall then directed *Big* (1988), the first film directed by a woman to gross more than $100 million. *Awakenings* (1990) achieved Best Picture, Best Screenplay, and Best Actor (for Robert De Niro) nominations from the Academy of Motion Picture Arts and Sciences. Film critics and talk-show hosts criticized Marshall's omission from the Best Director category as unfair, as did some of her colleagues. Marshall took a more objective approach, insisting that the same thing has happened to male directors such as Steven Spielberg. She denied that gender bias played a part in her omission from the list of nominees.

A *League of Their Own* (1992) boasts a cast including Tom Hanks, Madonna, and Geena Davis. That Marshall was able to assemble the impressive cast for the film is testimony to the impact of women directors. Rarely before the 1980's could a female director hire such bankable stars. Dorothy Arzner, among the women directors who gained great respect in the entertainment industry, succeeded in directing many of Hollywood's leading actresses between 1927 and 1943, including Clara Bow, Ruth Chatterton, Claudette Colbert, Katharine Hepburn, Rosalind Russell, Joan Crawford, and Merle Oberon. Although Marshall and her counterparts are impressive, they certainly are not the first women in the history of filmmaking to sit successfully in the director's chair.

Barbra Streisand's achievements include being an accomplished recording artist as well as a film producer, director, writer, and performer. She is one of few artists to win awards in all four major fields of performance art: an Oscar (motion pictures), Tony (New York stage), Grammy (music recording), and Emmy (television). It took more than fifteen years for Streisand to get enough backing to produce *Yentl* (1983), which she directed, coproduced, and cowrote and in which she starred. *The Prince of Tides* (1991), which she directed, produced, and starred in with Nick Nolte, was a huge box-office success. Even though Streisand is a powerful presence in the entertainment industry, women directors individually and collectively are still struggling for acknowledgment. Streisand, as Penny Marshall before her, was overlooked by the Academy for her work directing both *Yentl* and *The Prince of Tides*, even though *The Prince of Tides* was nominated for Best Picture and Nolte received a nomination in the Best Actor category. There were mentions of her omission in the press as well as personal jabs aimed at members of the Academy made at the televised 1991 Oscar presentations.

Susan Seidelman started her directing career as an independent feminist film-maker. *Smithereens* (1982) was the first American independent film accepted for competition in the history of the Cannes Film Festival. Her second film, *Desperately Seeking Susan* (1985), is, in a sense, an extension of *Smithereens* but is targeted toward a more mainstream audience. *Desperately Seeking Susan* stars Madonna as Susan, a wild and exotic woman, and Rosanna Arquette as Roberta, a suburban wife. Their lives and identities end up being crucially intertwined. In *Smithereens*, sex is treated offhandedly, and the central character is left adrift at the film's conclusion, as opposed to the romantic portrayal of sex and the domestication of Susan in *Desperately Seeking Susan*. Orion Pictures, which Seidelman praised for giving her tremendous freedom in making *Desperately Seeking Susan*, did not give her a final cut and required compromises between her original ideas for the film and the final product it chose to distribute.

Making Mr. Right (1987) also deals with questions of gender. The main character, a woman named Frankie Stone, is an image consultant who is assigned the job of forming an android into a successful social being. Seidelman's next film, *Cookie* (1989), was mostly panned by the critics. Then came *She-Devil* (1989), with Rose-anne (Barr) Arnold and Meryl Streep. This comedy was more successful at the box office but still lagged behind Seidelman's early success with *Desperately Seeking Susan.*

Martha Coolidge began her directing career with a feminist documentary about her grandmother, *Old Fashioned Woman* (1974), and then directed a film about rape, *Not a Pretty Picture* (1976). Turning to Hollywood, she directed *Valley Girl* (1983) and *Joy of Sex* (1984). *Valley Girl* earned $17 million from an initial investment of $350,000. It was an immediate hit with the teen market. *Real Genius* (1985) was another box-office success and pushed the teen formula to even greater extremes. The plot involved a male whiz kid recruited for a college think tank. He finds that other employees are being exploited and plots revenge. Coolidge said she was at-tracted to the idea of having the opportunity to work with men and men dealing with each other. She hoped she could bring some fresh perspectives into male character portrayals and show men as more vulnerable than would a male director.

Coolidge's *Rambling Rose* (1991) won Laura Dern an Oscar nomination for Best Actress and her mother, Diane Ladd, a nomination for Best Supporting Actress. This was the first time in the history of the Academy Awards that a mother and daughter were nominated simultaneously. *Rambling Rose* won critical acclaim but did not fare well financially. It is a period picture revolving around a sensual young woman and her involvement with a family and especially their son; risky themes in Hollywood rarely result in blockbusters at the box office.

Amy Heckerling found her niche in Hollywood by catering to the youth market. *Fast Times at Ridgemont High* (1982) initiated her into the genre. The plot follows the basic youth/high school comedy formula but treats sex, pregnancy, abortion, and relationships with much more sympathy than do many male-directed films of the same genre.

National Lampoon's European Vacation (1985) is one in the long line of National Lampoon films starring Chevy Chase as the bumbling head of a family who gets himself and everyone else into trouble while on vacation. Although successful at the box office, it was not notable directorially.

Look Who's Talking (1989) was written and directed by Heckerling. It is a comedy set within the framework of a 1980's subgenre of films about adults dealing with parenthood. Heckerling, as writer and director, takes a unique look at the complex-ities of being a successful woman in the late 1980's as well as being a single parent. The film took in more than $12 million its first weekend and $14 million the next. The success of the film is particularly interesting in that it was released in the fall, which is usually a slow season for movies. It was so popular that it played well into the Christmas season. Heckerling quickly made a sequel, *Look Who's Talking Too* (1990). The sequel was successful but not as profitable as the original.

Randa Haines began as an actor, then directed many television programs, including episodes of *Knots Landing* and *Hill Street Blues. Children of a Lesser God* (1986) pushed her into the Hollywood spotlight. The film won critical acclaim and box-office success, garnering five Academy Award nominations—for Best Picture, Best Actor (William Hurt), Best Actress (Marlee Matlin), Best Supporting Actress (Piper Laurie), and Best Adapted Screenplay (Hesper Anderson and Mark Medoff). Marlee Matlin came away with the Oscar for Best Actress. In 1991, *The Doctor,* starring William Hurt, was a critical and financial success. Haines put her mark on this film that deals with death, medical ethics, and personal relationships.

Impact of Event

These six women are the biggest moneymakers of the period, but there were countless other notable women directors working within the Hollywood system, including Joyce Chopra *(Smooth Talk,* 1985), Claudia Weill *(Girlfriends,* 1978), Elaine May *(The Heartbreak Kid,* 1972; *Mikey and Nicky,* 1976; *Ishtar,* 1987), Lisa Gottlieb *(Just One of the Guys,* 1985), Gillian Armstrong *(My Brilliant Career,* 1979), and Joan Micklin Silver *(Hester Street,* 1975; *Crossing Delancey,* 1988).

In the late 1980's and early 1990's, many more female directors were making bankable Hollywood features, among them Kathryn Bigelow *(Near Dark,* 1987; *Blue Steel,* 1990), Dyan Cannon *(The End of Innocence,* 1990), Jodie Foster *(Little Man Tate,* 1991), Penelope Spheeris *(Wayne's World,* 1992), Nora Ephron *(This Is My Life,* 1992), Nancy Savoca *(Dogfight,* 1991), Mary Lambert *(Pet Sematary,* 1989), Mary Agnes Donoghue *(Paradise,* 1991), Mira Nair *(Mississippi Masala,* 1992), Lizzie Borden *(Working Girls,* 1986), and Julie Dash *(Daughters of the Dust,* 1992). Many women from other countries have been able to market their films with moderate success at the American box office. Notable among such directors are Agnes Varda *(Vagabond,* 1985), Euzhan Palcy *(A Dry White Season,* 1989), Lina Wertmuller *(Swept Away . . . by an unusual destiny in the blue sea of August,* 1975), Jane Campion *(Sweetie,* 1988; *An Angel at My Table,* 1991), and Margarethe von Trotta *(Rosa Luxemburg,* 1986).

Lillian Gish once said that directing is not a job for a lady, and many female directors still believe that Hollywood agrees. Women directors still face barriers that range from the most blatant forms of discrimination, including the extreme salary gap between male and female directors, to more subtle and often more pervasive forms. The central conflict concerning hiring women directors, from Hollywood's point of view, is that the film industry envisions the ideal director as the tough and omniscient father figure who shouts orders and takes firm control of the picture-making process. Women directors, for the most part, undermine that ideal. They demonstrate their abilities in different but equally effective ways. There seems to be great resistance to giving up the traditional and narrowly defined role of the director. No American woman had ever been nominated for an Academy Award for best director by 1993. According to the Directors Guild of America, although women accounted for nearly twenty percent of Guild membership from January to November, 1990, only five percent had been hired to direct a feature film.

Women directors have to prove themselves on several fronts. Many times their ideas about what makes a good film and what constitutes a good director are in direct conflict with what is expected of them as Hollywood directors responsible for high-budget projects. Many female directors have expressed a desire to initiate a change in what is deemed marketable within the Hollywood system, while others wish only to be treated equally with their male colleagues. The latter would like to be seen as viable directors for action pictures and other genres traditionally identified with male directors, while the former wish to expand the potential for presenting more feminist-oriented subjects and delete some of the pervasive formulas that persist as staples of Hollywood filmmaking.

Bibliography

Brunsdon, Charlotte, ed. *Films for Women.* London: British Film Institute, 1986. Collection of articles traces representation of women in cinema since the late 1960's. Looks at treatment of women in films and deals with films by and for women. Includes sections exploring documentary, fiction, and Hollywood filmmaking. Also discusses exhibition and distribution, film content, theory, criticism, and feminist perspectives.

Haskell, Molly. *From Reverence to Rape: The Treatment of Women in the Movies.* New York: Holt, Rinehart and Winston, 1974. Intriguing analysis of women on both sides of the camera, as actresses, directors, producers, and writers. Separated by decade, with an introduction and a chapter on Europeans. Deals with sexism in the film industry from its advent through the 1960's. Dated, as all information ends at 1970. Interesting photographs.

Kay, Karyn, and Gerald Peary, eds. *Women and the Cinema: A Critical Anthology.* New York: E. P. Dutton, 1977. Fascinating sourcebook with essays of an incredible variety. Interviews with Dorothy Arzner, Ida Lupino, and Lina Wertmuller. Discusses feminist film theory, experimentalists and independents, and women and political films. Greta Garbo writes "Why I'm Called a Recluse." Each section contains a bibliography; an appendix includes selected filmographies.

Quart, Barbara Koenig. *Women Directors: The Emergence of a New Cinema.* New York: Praeger, 1988. Excellent source that includes American, Western European, Eastern European, and Third World women directors. The author provides coherent historical contexts in which to view the development of women in the film industry, as well as a useful bibliography. Includes sections about each director, her work, and biographical information when appropriate. Useful for seeing the progression of a director's work and her training and background.

Rosen, Marjorie. *Popcorn Venus: Women, Movies, and the American Dream.* New York: Coward, McCann & Geoghegan, 1973. Contains information about women in film, mostly how they were represented in films of the 1920's through the 1970's.

Epilogue deals with feminist footholds in filmmaking. Includes references, bibliography, and index. Good selection of photographs.

Felicia Bender

Cross-References

Beauvoir's *The Second Sex* Anticipates the Women's Movement (1949), p. 1449; Hansberry's *A Raisin in the Sun* Debuts on Broadway (1959), p. 1795; Plath's *The Colossus* Voices Women's Experience (1960), p. 1850; *The Mary Tyler Moore Show* Examines Women's Roles (1970), p. 2218; Laurie Anderson's *United States* Popularizes Performance Art (1983), p. 2517; Innovative Black Filmmakers Achieve Success (Late 1980's), p. 2565.

MADONNA REVOLUTIONIZES POPULAR FASHION

Category of event: Fashion and design
Time: The 1980's
Locale: The United States

Many music fans and cultural critics were outraged when rock star Madonna, wearing visible black lacy brassieres and other undergarments, popularized the wearing of such items as outerwear

Principal personages:
MADONNA (MADONNA LOUISE VERONICA CICCONE, 1958-   ), a singer, dancer, and drummer who brought back the notion of the "blonde bombshell"
JEAN-PAUL GAULTIER (1952-   ), a designer who influenced Madonna's fashion sense

Summary of Event

Even her use of a single name illustrates rock star Madonna's irreverent reaction to the traditional. After recording her debut album *Madonna* in 1983, she came out with *Like a Virgin* in 1984, and a string of successful albums followed. Singles from her albums hit the top of the charts, contributing to worldwide sales of more than sixty million albums by 1990. Yet many of her songs, though popular, offended broad segments of the public. Detractors objected to her frank statements about such topics as virginity, abortion, out-of-wedlock births, and materialism as well as to her overall image of open sexuality, expressed both through her songs and through her choices of clothing.

The "material girl," as Madonna referred to herself in one song, contributed significantly to the world of fashion through her choice of clothing to wear onstage during live performances and in her widely popular music videos. She chose clothing that was aggressively provocative, including brassieres and other undergarments worn in plain sight. In many ways, she updated the "blonde bombshell" image projected in the 1950's by actress Marilyn Monroe, creating a 1980's version of a shrewd, calculating, determined, and daring sex symbol. The music video for Madonna's hit "Material Girl," in fact, was a homage to Monroe that mimicked her performance of the song "Diamonds Are a Girl's Best Friend" in the 1953 film *Gentlemen Prefer Blondes.* Madonna's onstage persona made her a natural to be cast in a starring role in Warren Beatty's *Dick Tracy* (1990), in which she portrayed a glamorous singer who was simultaneously sexy and villainous.

On stage, Madonna dressed in various types of fashions. Some costumes resembled the gear of a female warrior, with bodices that suggested breastplates. Others were outrageously sexual, featuring lingerie. Still others mixed messages by including prominent crucifixes as religious symbols while at the same time expressing rebellious or sexual messages.

Madonna attended Catholic schools as a child. Part of her adult fashion nonconformity can be traced to her school career, during which she was forced to wear uniforms that she thought were drab, boring, and confining. She maintained high grades but rebelled by adding wild knee socks and small hair bows to her school uniform. Rebelliousness and flashy clothes perhaps were her means of gaining attention in a family that included eight children, two of them stepsiblings.

Madonna sought attention and the spotlight even as a child. She signed up to perform in virtually all her school plays and musicals, was a baton twirler and cheerleader, and took every dance lesson available to her. She won a four-year dance scholarship to the University of Michigan but left that school to study at New York's Alvin Ailey School, again on a scholarship. The burgeoning punk scene of 1970's New York contributed a number of influences to Madonna's fashion sense. In punk style, she dyed her hair in bright colors, ripped her leotards and pinned them back together with safety pins, double-pierced her ears, and began collecting and wearing quantities of beads and dangling earrings. She also began wearing vintage hats and clothes. A young jewelry designer named Maripol (also known as Mary Paul) assisted in developing Madonna's early look, designing jewelry including crucifixes and rubber bracelets. The look included ripped leotards, black T-shirts, net tops, massive amounts of jewelry, a bare midriff, and net stockings with lace-up boots.

Madonna took up residence with musician Dan Gilroy and began studying guitar, drums, and other instruments, along with voice. Dan and his brother Ed started a band called Breakfast Club, with Madonna on drums and Angie Smit on bass. Madonna, though, soon left that band and founded her own band in Manhattan. At the time, she sported a punk "Mohawk" haircut with blonde ends and black roots, wore white T-shirts with black jumpers, and accented her wardrobe with leather bracelets with wide stainless-steel bands and rhinestones.

By the time her *Like a Virgin* album was released, Madonna was successful enough to hire prominent aides, including Michael Jackson's manager, Freddy DeMann, and David Bowie's album producer, Nile Rodgers. The album reached the top position on the charts barely a month after its release. By the mid-1980's, the Music Television (MTV) network had attained widespread popularity. Madonna seemed made for music videos, with her training as a dancer and her good looks to support her tremendously popular music. She dressed for her music videos in the types of clothing, including visible white-lace undergarments, that she had worn for the cover illustration of *Like a Virgin*. These videos brought her visual presence and style to the attention of a much larger audience than had seen her in live performances, allowing her fashion statements to reach, directly or indirectly, most of the American public.

Impact of Event

Madonna's sexpot image angered the parents of teenagers who watched her music videos, but that was part of the point of her rebelliousness. Her image also angered feminists, who abhorred Madonna's retrogression into the status of sex object. Despite—or perhaps because of—such protests, fashion items associated with her style became the rage. Lace bras and bodices, lace gloves, microminiskirts, and spiked heels soon were prominent items in the closets of the trendy. One designer was able to sell $25 million worth of lacy strapless dresses in a single season. By choosing a black slip, a white wedding dress and a crucifix on a chain around her neck, or a white bra-bodice, Madonna could and did change her image in her many music videos. In every case, however, the image was one of glamour and sexuality. Many women, especially young ones, wanted to emulate Madonna, in large part because she projected an image of independence and of being unafraid to ask for what she wanted. Many men, of course, appreciated her open displays of sexuality and her "bad girl" image.

In 1985, Madonna played a prominent role in the film *Desperately Seeking Susan.* Madonna's character, Susan, was much like Madonna herself in being self-assured, bold, and shameless, and Madonna supplied much of her own wardrobe for the film. Rosanna Arquette played a staid housewife who attempted to substitute herself into Susan's life after losing her memory, a plot line that appealed to many women who wanted their own taste of being like Madonna. The film offered reinforcement of that goal and presented more of Madonna's fashion taste to the public.

By 1987, Madonna was sporting vinyl tops that laced up in the back, polka-dotted short skirts, fingerless black net gloves, and tattoos, contributing to an increase in the popularity of tattoos for women. Her tour in support of the 1987 *Who's That Girl?* album was another fashion show, featuring seven costumes and role-playing to accompany them. Dressed in a black bustier that did a world of good for the lingerie industry, Madonna began the show by appearing as a seductress. She later parodied that role, appearing as a clown with a silly hat and glasses. Later, she was surrounded by images of the pope, the president of the United States, and the White House. Perhaps realizing the influence she had on her public, Madonna also made her opinions known on social issues ranging from a woman's right to control her own body to the use of condoms.

The music video for "Like a Prayer" (1989) continued Madonna's trend toward mixing sexuality with religious symbols. The video offended many viewers, and the PepsiCo company dropped an advertising campaign connected to the song and video after observing the public's reaction to what many saw as Madonna's latest outrage. The song itself, though, reached the top position on the music charts.

Jean-Paul Gaultier, the French couturier who designed Madonna's clothes for her tour in support of the 1990 *Blonde Ambition* album, continued Madonna's theme of using underwear as outerwear. Dish bras with points on them were modeled into belted bodysuits. At one point in the show performed on that tour, two men appeared with fake pointed breasts attached to their chests. One of Madonna's costumes was a man's pinstriped suit with cutouts for her breasts. This mixture of femininity and masculinity inspired many clothing designers, who began to produce women's fashions expressing androgyny. Her movement toward androgyny certainly did not go as far as that of singer Annie Lennox, and Madonna's continued wearing of lingerie left no doubt that she was still sexy and in control. She also projected a stronger image. At one point in the show, while she was dressed like an Amazon warrior, she knocked down a chorus line of men.

Because of her success as a rock music star, Madonna's choice of fashions was bound to influence her fans. She was able to parlay her success in music to music videos and films, both of which displayed her fashion tastes to wide audiences. Her style caught on with many women, changing the definitions of clothing and allowing freer expression of sexuality for those who dared to emulate her.

Bibliography

Brown, Jane D., and Laurie Schulze. "The Effects of Race, Gender, and Fandom on Audience Interpretations of Madonna's Music Videos." *Journal of Communication* 40 (Spring, 1990): 88-102. By 1990, androgyny was reappearing in fashion and style, reflecting sexually integrated workplaces and a reaction to exaggerations in clothing such as that of Madonna. Madonna herself changed her fashion style in response to the new trend.

Cahill, Marie. *Madonna.* New York: Gallery Books, 1991. Deals extensively with Madonna's early years as well as her time as a superstar. Largely a photographic appreciation, but the text is useful and to the point. Index; no bibliography. A discography (covering dates of recording sessions, concert tours, films, and plays) is also helpful.

Christgau, Robert. "Madonnathinking, Madonnabout Madonnamusic." *Village Voice* 36 (May 28, 1991): 31-33. Discusses the various academic deconstructions of the Madonna phenomenon, ranging from postmodern to minimalist to feminist. Christgau sees Madonna as a pop cultural symbol but discusses the idea that she transcends popular culture.

Conniff, Ruth. "Politics in a Post-Feminist Age." *The Progressive* 55 (July, 1991): 17-18. Conniff sees Madonna as a "postfeminist" woman, controlling fashion rather than acting only as a buyer of fashion or employee in the fashion industry.

Gimelson, Deborah. "*Architectural Digest* Visits: Madonna." *Architectural Digest* 48 (November, 1991): 198-209. A photographic visit to Madonna's low-key yet glamorous Art Deco apartment home in New York City. Works of art and room arrangements are highlighted, and the singer's fondness for certain colors and textures in her clothes can be usefully understood in the context of these decorations.

Howell, Georgina. "The Maestro of Mayhem." *Vogue* 181 (March, 1991): 392-410. Concerns fashion designer Jean-Paul Gaultier, whose shows always shock and entertain his fans; his customers include Madonna. Gaultier played a significant role in influencing Madonna's fashion choices, though she has also used other design sources, particularly for her androgynous look.

Kelly, Michael. "Playgirl of the Western World." *Playboy* 38 (March, 1991): 82-84.

A profile of the singer and actress that discusses her "slut feminism." Surprisingly moralistic considering the magazine in which it appears.

Madonna. *Sex.* New York: Warner Books, 1992. A highly publicized, controversial, largely pictorial look at what the author considers to be erotic. Though Madonna dismisses the book's contents as "fantasy," the volume nevertheless offers a glimpse into the motivations behind her fashion choices. Decried by many as pornographic, but less lurid than its reputation; much of the writing and many of the photographs, in fact, seem more silly than anything else.

Matthews, Gordon. *Madonna.* New York: Simon & Schuster, 1985. This relatively early full-length biography is dated, but it has much useful material. No index, bibliography, or discography, although there are many photographs. The first serious book-length study of the subject, it remains valuable for quotations and anecdotes about Madonna's early years.

Shields, Jody. "Inside Out." *Vogue* 180 (November, 1990): 342-347. The provocative look of lingerie worn outside of clothing to express hyperfemininity is examined, with Madonna discussed as provocateur of the look. This is perhaps the best article on the subject.

Merrilee Cunningham

Cross-References

Poiret's "Hobble Skirts" Become the Rage (1910), p. 263; Chanel Defines Modern Women's Fashion (1920's), p. 474; Jantzen Popularizes the One-Piece Bathing Suit (1920), p. 491; Quant Introduces the Miniskirt (Early 1960's), p. 1824; Punk's Antifashion Style First Appears (1974), p. 2299.

WYNTON MARSALIS REVIVES ACOUSTIC JAZZ

Category of event: Music
Time: The 1980's
Locale: New Orleans, Louisiana, and New York, New York

Trumpeter Wynton Marsalis galvanized the jazz world with an acoustic approach to improvisation that explored new directions while drawing on jazzdom's great stylistic traditions

Principal personages:
WYNTON MARSALIS (1961-   ), an extraordinary jazz and classical trumpeter, leader of pivotal jazz groups, and indefatigable jazz advocate and educator
BRANFORD MARSALIS (1960-   ), an excellent jazz saxophonist and Wynton's brother
ELLIS MARSALIS (1934-   ), a highly regarded mainstream jazz pianist and jazz educator, the father of Wynton and Branford Marsalis
ART BLAKEY (1919-1991), a legendary jazz drummer who introduced numerous young players, including Wynton and Branford Marsalis, to the jazz world

Summary of Event

In 1980, jazzdom was in crisis. Having been marginalized by the commercial dominance of rock and roll, funk, and fusion (a hybrid musical form combining the rhythms of rock with mostly tepid and clichéd improvisations), jazz seemed to exist only at the fringes of the music world.

Yet 1980 also saw the emergence of a bright young man with a horn, a seemingly mild-mannered youngster who studied at the Juilliard School of Music during the day and then blew up a storm with jazz legend Art Blakey and his Jazz Messengers at night. That young man, trumpet virtuoso Wynton Marsalis, though only eighteen at the time, was destined to become one of the most important voices in American music. He was also destined to become the single most influential figure in jazz during the 1980's and, arguably, the 1990's as well.

Marsalis' central place in the contemporary jazz pantheon stems from several interrelated sources: his extraordinarily virtuosic playing; his outspoken efforts to position jazz as America's most profound and significant musical art form; his tireless and wide-ranging activities as a jazz educator; and his rapid rise to the status of celebrity through his early career achievements in jazz and classical music, a feat all the more astounding in light of Marsalis' youth. In 1984, Marsalis became the first musician to win Grammy Awards for both a classical album (1983's *Haydn, Hummel, Leopold Mozart Trumpet Concertos*) and a jazz album (*Think of One*, 1982), both recorded when he was twenty-two years old. In 1985, he repeated the feat. In the process, the young trumpeter had become a star. He also became a jazz icon; suddenly, there were hordes of young people all over the country—indeed, the world— pursuing jazz with a passion that would have been inconceivable had it not been for the phenomenon called Wynton Marsalis.

The story of Wynton Marsalis starts in New Orleans, Louisiana, where the jazz-star-to-be was born on October 18, 1961. Nurtured by the city's jazz tradition and a loving and musically gifted family, Wynton received his first musical training from his father, noted New Orleans jazz pianist Ellis Marsalis. Stressing the importance of learning to play both jazz and classical music, Ellis instilled in Wynton and his brother Branford (later an eminent saxophonist and the leader of *The Tonight Show* band) the urge to excel.

Wynton responded to the challenge with diligent studies that led to numerous honors, including the chance to perform Franz Joseph Haydn's demanding *Trumpet Concerto* with the New Orleans Philharmonic Orchestra when he was only fourteen. At seventeen, he was selected to attend the elite Berkshire Music Center at Tanglewood (near Lenox, Massachusetts), where he received the Harvey Shapiro Award as outstanding brass player. Next was Juilliard and Blakey's Jazz Messengers.

The stint with Blakey, part of which saw Wynton sharing the front-line horn-section duties with brother Branford on alto saxophone, gave the young trumpeter his first important exposure to the jazz world. Critics, fans, and musicians were impressed—the young Wynton Marsalis was someone quite special, indeed, a *wunderkind*. In mid-1981, Marsalis took a sabbatical from Blakey's Jazz Messengers to tour and record with pianist Herbie Hancock, bassist Ron Carter, and drummer Tony Williams, the all-star rhythm section that had propelled the great 1960's groups of celebrated jazz trumpeter Miles Davis, one of Marsalis' idols. This proved to be the trumpeter's big break.

In the wake of the news of the tour with Hancock, Carter, and Williams came an announcement that Columbia Records had signed Marsalis to an exclusive contract. It was an event that gave immediate rise to speculation that the major labels, which had mostly ignored jazz during the 1970's and early 1980's, might be ready to renew at least a token commitment to jazz, "America's classical music." It was no surprise, then, that Marsalis' recording debut as a leader for Columbia became a greatly anticipated event.

The young man from New Orleans did not disappoint. Indeed, his debut album for Columbia, *Wynton Marsalis* (1982) was astonishing in both its range and depth. Teaming with brother Branford, Wynton produced neo-bebop solos that soared over two contrasting rhythm sections, the Hancock-Carter-Williams tandem and a younger though no less provocative group consisting of pianist Kenny Kirkland, bassist Charles Fambrough, and drummer Jeff Watts. Though the Marsalis brothers returned to Blakey for one last stint, by the end of 1982, on the strength of his startling Columbia debut, Wynton Marsalis was jazzdom's new young lion and leader of its hottest new group. "Wynton's Decade"—the title of a 1992 retrospective *Down Beat* magazine cover story that charted the trumpeter's transcendent influence during the 1980's—had only just begun.

Impact of Event

One of the keys to Marsalis' mercurial rise to prominence was his capacity for excelling in both jazz and classical music. In many ways, the first decade of Marsalis' career paralleled that of fabled jazz clarinetist Benny Goodman, who in the 1930's wowed classical audiences with exquisite performances of "serious" works such as Wolfgang Amadeus Mozart's *Clarinet Concerto in A*. For Goodman, such demonstrations of classical musicianship served to legitimize, as well as to publicize, the jazzman's already highly successful swing band and combo projects, the latter with pianist Teddy Wilson, vibraphonist Lionel Hampton, and drummer Gene Krupa.

For Marsalis, the back-to-back Grammys as best classical soloist of 1983 and 1984 provided dramatic proof, even for classical purists, that the young trumpeter was a special, even singular, talent. His simultaneous lionization by the classical and jazz worlds as well as by the popular press provided a level of public visibility unprecedented for a jazz musician.

By 1984, however, the pressures of maintaining simultaneous classical and jazz careers had become a burden, largely because of Marsalis' self-imposed demands for excellence. Stating that he was essentially a jazz musician who could also play classical music, Marsalis concluded: "It takes a lot to develop as a jazz musician, and I couldn't find the time to keep my classical technique up. Finally, given the choice, I had to take jazz, because it's what attracted me to music in the first place."

It was a sanguine decision, and one that allowed Marsalis to intensify his focus on resurrecting and revitalizing the great traditions of jazz, from the New Orleans styles of trumpet masters Louis Armstrong and Rex Stewart to the bebop of Charlie Parker and Dizzy Gillespie, and from the rich harmonic densities of Duke Ellington to the brooding modal approach of modernists Miles Davis and tenor saxophonist John Coltrane.

Indeed, Marsalis' 1980's recordings reveal the trumpeter's commitment to honoring the still-living legacies of jazzdom's pioneers. In projects such as *Black Codes from the Underground* (1985), *J Mood* (1986), and *The Majesty of the Blues* (1989), the great traditions of jazz are brought to vivid life by Marsalis' ability to invoke and yet reconfigure the past simultaneously. Also significant is the trumpeter's angular and poignant reframing of songs from the repertory of such classic American popular composers as George Gershwin, Cole Porter, Jerome Kern, Fats Waller, and Duke Ellington. In *Marsalis Standard Time* (1987), for example, the trumpeter offers burnished and bracing renditions of such evergreens as "April in Paris," "Autumn Leaves," and "Foggy Day."

Throughout the 1980's, Marsalis was often described as a neoclassicist. Writing in 1983, critic Gary Giddins, after decrying the sterility of the so-called avant-garde and fusion mercenaries, pointed out that "musicians such as Marsalis are needed to restore order, replenish melody, revitalize the beat, loot the tradition for whatever works, and expand the audience." That is precisely what Marsalis accomplished through his own work, and through the work of the many young players who followed in his path. By the late 1980's, glowing stories in the popular press chronicling the burgeoning "Jazz Renaissance" all positioned Marsalis as the movement's central and galvanizing figure.

The Marsalis phenomenon affected the jazz world in several salutary ways. First is the example of his music. As a player, he demonstrated a virtuosic capacity distinguished by a sweeping range, an incisive edge, a ringing tone, and remarkable inventive flights. His expanding catalog of recordings stands as an ever-enlarging landmark and a continuing source of inspiration. Indeed, that so many young musicians in the 1980's and 1990's have been seriously pursuing jazz as a vibrant mode of self-expression is a tribute to Marsalis' influence. Like the groups of Art Blakey and Miles Davis, moreover, Marsalis' units have nurtured an array of young talents, including the pianists Kenny Kirk and Marcus Roberts. In fact, the signing and promotion of budding young jazz talents by major recording companies is itself a part of the Marsalis phenomenon.

By insisting that jazz be presented with the same dignity and preparation as classical music, Marsalis has also helped immensely in improving the conditions under which jazz is produced and presented, whether in concert halls, recording studios, or nightclubs. He has even influenced other neo-bebop players by the example of his dress and serious demeanor. The crop of young jazz lions Marsalis inspired have typically been attired in crisply pressed double-breasted suits; they have also tended to disdain the kind of antics and clowning that have long been a part of the business of playing jazz. Most significant, Marsalis has influenced younger players by stressing the importance—indeed the necessity—of knowing the history of jazz, its great styles and its great innovators. Thanks to Marsalis, too, acoustic jazz—without the buzz of electronic processing and thump of rock—has regained a pivotal place in the contemporary jazz pantheon.

In the program notes for a 1993 Marsalis concert tour, the trumpeter summed up his overall intentions: "My ultimate goal is to see the whole of American public education transformed and to see the arts in America, specifically the musical arts, achieve the place of prominence in our education that they deserve, because culture is the identity of the people, and one of the centerpieces of American culture is jazz music."

Bibliography

Berg, Chuck. "Wynton Marsalis." In *The Facts on File Encyclopedia of the Twentieth Century*, edited by John Drexel. New York: Facts on File, 1991. A brief summary of Marsalis' rise to prominence during the 1980's.

Cook, Richard, and Brian Morton. "Wynton Marsalis." In *The Penguin Guide to Jazz on CD, LP, and Cassette*. New York: Penguin Books, 1992. An excellent overview of Marsalis' career, with incisive reviews of his major recording projects of the 1980's. Includes detailed discographic information.

Giddins, Gary. "Wynton Marsalis and Other Neoclassical Lions." In *Rhythm-a-ning: Jazz Tradition and Improvisation in the 80s*. New York: Oxford University Press,

1985. *Village Voice* critic Giddins describes Marsalis as a "conscientious neo-classicist" who has taken on the task of restoring order to bebop and the other great traditions of jazz.

Jeske, Lee. "Wynton Marsalis." In *The New Grove Dictionary of Jazz*, edited by Barry Kernfeld. Vol. 2. New York: Grove's Dictionaries of Music, 1988. A brief but informative essay by a noted American jazz critic. Bibliography.

Reich, Howard. "Wynton Marsalis: 'It's Time for Jazz.'" *Down Beat* 59 (December, 1992): 16-21. Excellent interview in which Marsalis talks about his career, his hopes, and his concept of jazz as a means of transcending such social-cultural barriers as racism, educational sloth, and artistic mediocrity.

Stokes, W. Royal. *The Jazz Scene: An Informal History from New Orleans to 1990.* New York: Oxford University Press, 1991. Stokes, a former editor of *Jazz Times* magazine, lets the musicians, including Marsalis, speak for themselves on the history, sociology, and techniques of jazz. Compiled from hundreds of interviews conducted by the perceptive Stokes, whose commentaries frame the subject for laymen and experts alike.

Charles Merrell Berg

Cross-References

Joplin Popularizes the Ragtime Style (1899), p. 13; Handy Ushers in the Commercial Blues Era (1910's), p. 252; Bessie Smith Records "Downhearted Blues" (1923), p. 572; Armstrong First Records with His Hot Five Group (1925), p. 670; Ellington Begins an Influential Engagement at the Cotton Club (1927), p. 739; Billie Holiday Begins Her Recording Career (1933), p. 930; Goodman Begins His *Let's Dance* Broadcasts (1934), p. 968; Parker's Playing Epitomizes Bebop (1946), p. 1318; Davis' *Birth of the Cool* Recordings Spawn 1950's Cool Jazz (1949), p. 1438; The First Newport Jazz Festival Is Held (1954), p. 1617; Davis' *Bitches Brew* Vitalizes Jazz-Rock Fusion (1969), p. 2153.

BARYSHNIKOV BECOMES ARTISTIC DIRECTOR
OF AMERICAN BALLET THEATRE

Category of event: Dance
Time: 1980
Locale: New York, New York

Mikhail Baryshnikov's defection from the Soviet Union in 1974 gave American ballet its second superstar, but his subsequent tenure as artistic director of American Ballet Theatre from 1980 to 1990 proved less than fruitful

Principal personages:
MIKHAIL BARYSHNIKOV (1948-   ), a dancer who defected from the Soviet Union in 1974
GEORGE BALANCHINE (GEORGI MELITONOVITCH BALANCHIVADZE, 1904-1983), a brilliant choreographer whose company, the New York City Ballet, pioneered his revolutionary style of modern ballet
GELSEY KIRKLAND (1952-   ), the Balanchine-trained ballerina whose extraordinary grace and emotional expressiveness brought her international acclaim and an opportunity to dance with Baryshnikov after his defection

Summary of Event

Mikhail Baryshnikov took over as the artistic director of American Ballet Theatre (popularly known as ABT, in contrast to Balanchine's rival New York City Ballet, or NYCB) in 1980. A supremely brilliant and inspiring technical dancer, he might have welded ABT into the finest ballet company in the world, but his lack of skill as an administrator weakened the company to the point where many thought it would close altogether.

As a boy, Baryshnikov had been trained at the Riga School of ballet and already was recognized as a "future genius" by the time he danced with his visiting Latvian company in Leningrad in 1964. Three years had passed since Rudolf Nureyev's defection to the West in Paris, and Leningrad audiences were eager to find a star to fill the void Nureyev had left behind. They were to find him in Mikhail Baryshnikov, then almost sixteen years old.

Leningrad had been the birthplace of Russian ballet and was the home of the Kirov Ballet. Baryshnikov thought he had arrived at the hub of his world. He was accepted quickly into the prestigious Vaganova School, and at the end of his training in 1967 he moved directly into the Kirov Ballet as a soloist. In 1969, he won the gold medal at the First International Ballet Competition in Moscow and the Nijinsky Prize in Paris, and he danced his first leading role as Basil in *Don Quixote*. His beloved Natalia Makarova had defected to the West the year before, but Baryshnikov, who was on tour with her, contented himself with an unofficial visit to Nureyev's home and an evening watching the Royal Ballet and American Ballet Theatre. He returned to the Soviet Union.

Creation of the World (1971) made a star of Baryshnikov, and in 1972 he made his debut as Count Albrecht in the great classical ballet *Giselle.* Yet the tightly controlled world of Russian classical ballet was beginning to chafe. In June, 1974, during a tour with a Bolshoi company in Toronto, Baryshnikov defected, following in the footsteps of Makarova and Nureyev.

Nureyev on his defection specifically had asked to dance with Margot Fonteyn; Baryshnikov informed Gelsey Kirkland of the New York City Ballet that he wanted to dance with her—if she would leave George Balanchine's NYCB for American Ballet Theatre. Kirkland had been finding the NYCB unsatisfactory, and she staged her own smaller defection to ABT.

Baryshnikov, now widely known to the world as Misha, debuted in the West as Albrecht to Makarova's Giselle, winning twenty-four curtain calls and a half-hour standing ovation. It was the challenge of learning other, nonclassical dance styles that fascinated him as he rehearsed Frederick Ashton's *Les Patineurs* and Balanchine's *Theme and Variations.* His partner Kirkland, trained in the abstract style of Balanchine, was equally intent on learning the classical story-ballet style for her performances with him in *Coppelia.*

Between them, Baryshnikov and Kirkland represented two styles of ballet that were as different in their way as classical music is from jazz, and each wanted to learn the other's skills. Just as Baryshnikov's Kirov and Bolshoi companies had never attempted the more modern abstract style, so Kirkland's NYCB had eschewed the classical style in favor of abstract, geometrical ballets with no story line.

In many ways—and despite the undoubted brilliance of Balanchine—this was a false start. From its inception, classical ballet had told stories. Dancers had been actors performing roles that called for dramatic presence in addition to technical skills. Because the stories were told in wordless gesture and mime, only the simplest stories survived, stories with an almost mythic intensity. Baryshnikov, then, was learning to abandon his dramatic origins and adopt a more purely technical approach, while Kirkland was flowering into a dancer of great dramatic presence and emotion.

American Ballet Theatre was the right place for their two worlds to meet, and his next four years with ABT confirmed Baryshnikov's stature as both a genius and a megastar. Baryshnikov, however, wanted to delve ever more deeply into the modern abstract world: He wanted to dance for Balanchine. He turned his back on stardom and $200,000 a year with ABT to join NYCB at $700 a week. It was in some ways an unexpected choice, since Balanchine was known for an attitude summed up in his remark "ballet is woman" and his refusal to encourage star status within his troupe. To the still-Russian Baryshnikov, the choice made sense. He would dance for the great master, as he had danced for Alexander Pushkin at the Kirov, and he would be immersed in the abstract modern style that so fascinated him.

Baryshnikov debuted with NYCB in 1978 in Balanchine's speeded-up version of

Coppelia, one of the few classical ballets in NYCB's repertoire. He began systematically to retrain his body in the Balanchine manner, with sudden, unprepared leaps and contorted body positions. His New York debut with NYCB was in Balanchine's abstract *Rubies*. Jerome Robbins choreographed *Four Seasons* for him, premiering in 1979. That year, Baryshnikov danced Balanchine's *Apollo*, and by June he had learned twenty-two new ballets by Balanchine and Robbins.

The strain of retraining his body in the Balanchine manner was telling on Baryshnikov. Many critics thought he was unsuited to Balanchine's style. Balanchine himself was in serious ill-health. When Herman Krawitz, the executive director of ABT, offered Baryshnikov the post of artistic director, he accepted. Baryshnikov would become an administrator. In addition to his own dancing, he would henceforth be responsible for a repertoire of 75 ballets, a company of 90 dancers, and a $10 million annual budget. He left NYCB in 1979 and took his position with ABT in 1980.

He could continue to dance as a highly paid guest artist with other companies and on occasion at ABT, but his first duty would be to the company itself. All dancers, even the most skilled, reach a time when it is wise for them to cut back on the rigors of a heavy dancing schedule, and the move to an administrative post often facilitates this transition. If his tenure at ABT was anything to judge by, company administration would not be, for Baryshnikov, the path out of performance it has been for so many others.

Impact of Event

During more than three decades of Lucia Chase's direction, American Ballet Theatre had been like a family—occasionally a dysfunctional family with its own jealousies and pettiness, but a family nevertheless. The ABT star system, with its hierarchy of experience, was part of that family's stability.

Baryshnikov wanted to make ABT into a very different kind of company. He instituted a system of computerized rehearsal schedules, worksheets for individual dancers, and warning letters to let them know when they were coming close to being fired. He expected every one of his dancers to appear for company class every day instead of allowing them to take morning class with their own teachers or coaches, as is usually the case. This was a much more impersonal and businesslike arrangement than the company was used to. He also canceled the regular fall season in New York, giving his dancers the longest rehearsal period in ABT history.

On the night before opening night of the 1980 winter tour, Gelsey Kirkland and Patrick Bissell were fired. The next day, their roles were taken by Susan Jaffe, an eighteen-year-old member of the corps de ballet, and Alexander Godunov. The ABT star system was dead, and Baryshnikov's alternative—giving principal roles to young dancers—was under way. Some of the young dancers Baryshnikov promoted, such as Jaffe, Robert LaFosse, and Gil Boggs, were extremely talented, but the overall effect on the company was unsettling.

Baryshnikov had begun teaching ABT the great story ballets, using more recent Kirov versions in place of Nicholas Sergeyev's Royal Ballet versions of 1912, which had long been standards in ABT's repertoire. He produced "streamlined" versions of his own, cutting scenes from *Swan Lake* or *Sleeping Beauty* that he thought were boring, hoping to take ballet further into the entertainment mainstream. The critics were not impressed, seeing his changes as trivializing a great art, or worse, Sovietizing it. His willingness to cut the classics was viewed as cynical.

The fact that he also had streamlined the company into a fundamentally impersonal business-style organization did not help. One dancer referred to Baryshnikov as American Ballet Theatre's "KGB." Older stars were fired or left the company. Young dancers missed the inspiration they received during Chase's regime by dancing with these older, more mature dancers, stars with a historical knowledge of the interpretations of great roles such as Giselle that they could pass on. Dancing at ABT no longer seemed to be an art; it had become no more than a job.

Baryshnikov himself, by this time, was seldom in evidence. He had attended company class daily at the beginning of his tenure as artistic director, teaching, dropping in on rehearsals, and dancing alongside the company on stage. In February of 1982, he had sustained a knee injury, and his ensuing absence made an already impersonal company seem even more so. One dance writer noted that when Baryshnikov was not around, the dancing suffered. In the fall of 1983, Herman Krawitz was fired and various members of the board of directors quit.

After streamlining the classics, Baryshnikov had turned to more modern choreographers such as Merce Cunningham, Paul Taylor, George Balanchine, and Twyla Tharp. In 1985, he saw a performance by the "punk princess" Karole Armitage and commissioned her to write a work for ABT. The result was Armitage's portrait of Baryshnikov himself, *The Mollino Room*. While five couples waltzed around the stage, the Baryshnikov character danced by himself. He was the sullen loner who could not connect with the dancing couples. His movements were cut short, turned in upon themselves.

While Baryshnikov had been acting out in real life this role of a loner who could not connect with the dancers, he also had lent his name to a perfume and a line of clothing, appeared on film, and become co-owner of a fashionable Manhattan restaurant. Baryshnikov was hip, postmodern, an undoubted media star, and an entertainer. But what had happened to the dance?

Gelsey Kirkland's memoir, *Dancing on My Grave*, appeared in 1986, painting a less than ideal portrait of Baryshnikov, who had been both her lover and her partner in the days of her stardom but who seemed utterly unable to cope with her gradual slide—under intense pressure—into drug addiction and suicidal depression. The book is an intensely moving and human document, radiant with Kirkland's love for her art, transfused with the agonies that a young star dancer inevitably faces, entirely honest about her own failings, and insightful in its descriptions of the human qualities of those she worked with. In it, Baryshnikov figures as a man of intense charm and talent who was all too willing to throw his talents away on the whim of a moment, supremely self-obsessed, and frequently devastating to work with. It is not a flattering portrait, and it raises the question of whether Baryshnikov really ever felt the passion for the dance that so clearly possessed Nureyev—and for that matter, Kirkland herself.

American Ballet Theatre never became the world's greatest ballet company under the ten years of Baryshnikov's direction, as he clearly had hoped that it would. This may have been because he attempted a style of administration that did not suit the American temperament or simply because he lost interest.

Bibliography

Aria, Barbara. *Misha: The Mikhail Baryshnikov Story.* New York: St. Martin's Press, 1989. Interesting account of Baryshnikov's early training, defection from the Soviet Union, and work in the West, including his time as artistic director of the American Ballet Theatre. Black-and-white photo section, no index.

France, Charles Engell. *Baryshnikov at Work.* London: Adam and Charles Black, 1977. In this oversized book with numerous photos by Martha Swope, Baryshnikov discusses his most famous roles.

Fraser, John. *Private View: Inside Baryshnikov's American Ballet Theatre.* New York: Bantam Books, 1988. Superb black-and-white photo essay (photos by Eve Arnold) on the American Ballet Theatre under Baryshnikov's direction, with some textual commentary. Features both Baryshnikov and the company, mostly in rehearsal.

Kirkland, Gelsey, and Greg Lawrence. *Dancing on My Grave.* Garden City, N.Y.: Doubleday, 1986. Lyrical and intensely moving account of the aspirations of a young and brilliant dancer and the pressures of life in a contemporary ballet company, including a candid but unflattering portrait of Baryshnikov as lover and dance partner. Black-and-white photo section, no index.

Mazo, Joseph H. *Dance Is a Contact Sport.* New York: E. P. Dutton, 1974. Chronicles day-to-day life in the New York City Ballet, showing up close the dedication and discipline of the dancers, the risks of injury and stress they face, the gossamer illusions of stagecraft, and the joys of performing. Well written and fascinating. Black-and-white photo section, index.

Anne Atwell-Zoll

Cross-References

Balanchine's *Serenade* Inaugurates American Ballet (1934), p. 974; Balanchine and Kirstein Make New York a World Center for Ballet (1946), p. 1301; Nureyev and Fonteyn Debut Ashton's *Marguerite and Armand* (1963), p. 1962; Multiculturalism Dominates the Dance World (Late 1980's), p. 2559; Baryshnikov's White Oak Dance Project Debuts (1990), p. 2663.

FOUR MODERN MASTERS AFFIRM GERMANY'S PLACE IN THE ART WORLD

Category of event: Art
Time: 1980
Locale: Venice, Italy

By accepting and integrating their art into the greater German artistic tradition, four modern artists gained international recognition for contemporary German art

Principal personages:
> GEORG BASELITZ (1938-   ), an artist who through inversion of his subject matter gave greater meaning and depth to the strong representational quality of German art
> JOSEPH BEUYS (1921-1986), a pioneer in modern German art
> ANSELM KIEFER (1945-   ), the contemporary artist most willing to probe deeply into Germany's past
> A. R. PENCK (1939-   ), an artist whose use of symbolism served to give added impact to the conceptual tradition of German art
> ALBRECHT DÜRER (1471-1528), the German Renaissance master whose use of the visual and conceptual established the pattern for the subsequent development of German art
> ERNST LUDWIG KIRCHNER (1880-1938), the greatest of the German expressionists, whose works served as a source of inspiration for many contemporary German artists
> FRIEDRICH WILHELM NIETZSCHE (1844-1900), the controversial German philosopher whose theories on art confirmed and strengthened an existing tradition

Summary of Event

The almost unanimous condemnation by German art critics of the exhibit "Burning, Deforestation, Sinking, Silting," which Anselm Kiefer and Georg Baselitz mounted at the 1980 Biennale in Venice, ironically served to confirm what the international art community had recognized for some time—that Kiefer and Baselitz, together with Joseph Beuys and A. R. Penck, were the masters of German contemporary art. Indeed, some considered Kiefer, a student of Beuys, to be the most gifted and most promising of all contemporary artists. Baselitz and Penck were contemporaries, both having been born in what was to become the totalitarian state of East Germany. To escape persecution, both changed their names, to no avail. Both were accused by East German authorities of "incorrect thinking" and were forced to move to West Germany in order to continue their work.

What Baselitz, Kiefer, and Penck had in common were childhood memories of a national breakdown almost without parallel and an awareness of having to live not only with the sins of their fathers and mothers but also with a vast international reprobation likely to go on forever. Beuys, older than the rest, had experienced the nightmare of Nazism and the horrors of World War II firsthand. As a fighter pilot during the war, he was shot down over the Russian Crimea. Badly burned, he was almost literally brought back from the dead by the ministrations of tribal Tatars, who healed him by wrapping him in felt and fat.

What critics objected to in Kiefer's work was what they saw as excessive "Teutonization": the use of poses and symbols from the past, especially those related to the Nazi period. What many German critics did not see was that Kiefer and his colleagues were great precisely because they had come to terms with the German past. In so doing, they had reestablished contact with and had become part of the great German artistic tradition that extended back to the Renaissance master Albrecht Dürer and included the work of artists such as Caspar David Friedrich, a nineteenth century German Romantic painter whose landscapes were a source of inspiration for Kiefer.

The German artistic tradition basically involved a dualism between visual manifestation and expressed thought. Thought might be lofty idealism; more often, though, it was biting social criticism. German artists would deliberately distort line and composition, employ color or caricature, or even select a certain medium such as woodcut to give greater meaning and impact to the visual and thus achieve a didactic objective. The masters of this approach were the German expressionists active in the years before World War I. As if by premonition, they graphically portrayed the malaise of their time, a malaise that in succeeding decades would result in the near-destruction of European civilization. The greatest of the German expressionists, and a source of inspiration for Beuys, Kiefer, Baselitz, and Penck, was Ernst Ludwig Kirchner.

The nineteenth century philosopher Friedrich Nietzsche had intellectualized German artistic tradition when he declared that underlying all artistic creations are two principles, one, the "Apollonian," representing beauty, harmony, and clarity; the other, the "Dionysian," representing vitality, intoxication, and ecstasy. German artists embraced Nietzsche's philosophy with enthusiasim. German art, for the most part, is strongly figurative or representational, and seldom abstract.

Beuys stressed thought, or the emotional, in his artistic creations. What is important is the impression left with the viewer, even if the work of art is nontraditional or transitory. Materials used ideally should have personal emotional association: felt for warmth, fat and honey for food, wax and a flashlight for direction. Thought, for Beuys, is three-dimensional; therefore, the most memorable art is sculpture. Some of Beuys's most startling creations were his own actions; for example, wrapped in a huge cloak made of felt and with a live coyote as a companion, he would sit all day in a gallery. In becoming a living work of art in the round, Beuys broke the traditional barrier between art and life.

Of the four, Baselitz was probably the most strongly influenced by the expressionists, especially in the use of strong colors. Baselitz enhances the emotional aspects of his work and the sense of alienation it produces by the deliberate inversion of his subject matter. In so doing, he diverts the viewer from rational analysis to emotional uncertainty. Baselitz also divides or cuts up his representational object into strips, the gaps being filled by extraneous bits of reality. He thus makes the viewer aware of how fragile reality actually is.

Where Baselitz uses inversion to heighten emotional understanding, Penck reverts to a form of symbolism that verges on abstraction. To emphasize thought, the visual is reduced to the barest outlines, often to pictographs or stick figures, or likened to graffiti or the drawings of children. On the surface simplistic, the figures when combined become complex and disturbing. Even though they seem easily comprehensible, in the end they resolutely defy interpretation, a fact that does not detract from their power.

The most "German" of the four artists, Kiefer fills his works with references to the German past, from prehistoric myths to the Nazi years. What disturbs many of Kiefer's critics is his lack of automatic condemnation of this past. For Kiefer, however, the purpose of the artist is not to dictate thought—the methodology of the Nazis—but rather to stimulate thought, which he does in a masterful manner. His painting *To the Unknown Painter* depicts a grandiose, empty fascist palace. Using a military symbol as an example, he graphically portrays the death of German art at the hands of the Nazis.

Like his teacher Beuys, Kiefer also utilized nontraditional materials and techniques in his artworks—combining, for example, painting with photographs or embedding surface objects such as straw, sand, or ashes in the paint. One of Kiefer's more memorable paintings is *Operation Sealion*, which refers to the contemplated German invasion of England during World War II. The battle is staged in an enormous bathtub set in a desolate, burned landscape. The ships shown are toys, but the ensuing disaster is real. Kiefer exploits every device and technique to superimpose one level of meaning upon another, leaving scope for multiple interpretations. Another of his famous works, *Nero Paints*, shows the outline of an artist's palette superimposed again on a burned, exhausted landscape. In the background, the buildings of a postcard German village, not Nero's Rome, are in flames. The reference to Adolf Hitler as the failed artist but the monstrous destroyer becomes obvious.

Impact of Event

The effect of Beuys, Kiefer, Baselitz, and Penck on German art can be understood only in the context of the development of German art after World War II. The collapse of 1945 left a stunned, demoralized Germany whose immediate objective was to divorce itself as completely as possible from the Nazi heritage responsible for the unprecedented catastrophe. Two developments ensued. On the official level, especially after the establishment of the German Federal Republic (West Germany) in 1949, efforts were made to rehabilitate both the art of the pre-Nazi period and the artists who had been driven into exile or underground. The effort failed. The few artists who had remained were, for the most part, past their artistic prime. Others who had fled abroad remembered with bitterness how their art had been ridiculed, denigrated, and labeled "degenerate." Kirchner, for example, had been driven to suicide. These artists had no desire to return, and indeed many had tried to shed their German identity altogether.

The artistic community attempted to find an identity for German art on an international level. What was to be avoided at all costs was the realistic official style of Nazi-approved art, which could best be described as monumental kitsch. Therefore, despite the strong representational and figurative tradition of German art, the emphasis shifted toward the abstract, toward experiments with what was called minimal art, and toward a new movement called *Tachisme* that employed irregular dabs or spots of color, each regarded as an element in its own right and an emotional projection. It was with some consternation that German artists increasingly became aware that their artistic efforts had only a limited effect in Germany and none outside Germany. The new West German capital of Bonn was regarded as a city of philistines, an artistic wasteland.

The change came when divided and isolated Berlin again became the center of German art; there was then, an art historian noted, "a hunger for pictures." Both Baselitz and Penck lived and worked for a time in Berlin, and the Berlin galleries became the most enthusiastic supporters and promoters of the works of all four artists.

Beuys was the pioneer in the new art movement, primarily because he was among the first to reestablish artistic ties with the past and reawaken memories, no matter how painful. In fact it can be said that he is the only contemporary German artist of stature who unreservedly has come to terms with the war. Second was Kiefer, to be followed by Baselitz and Penck. It was said that these four artists helped to demolish two walls. Since both Baselitz and Penck came from East Germany, their acceptance in the West represented a triumph over the physical wall dividing East and West Berlin (a wall soon to be demolished in actuality); the second was the symbolic wall of German history between 1933 and 1945. There was now, as the German poet Paul Celan succinctly phrased it, a reconstituted "gash of fire" spanning Germany's cultural heritage.

What ensued was a new art movement called "neoexpressionism" that began to coalesce in the 1970's and reached maturity by 1980. Like the old expressionism, the new was born in a period of turmoil; also like the old, an integral part of neoexpressionism was social criticism. The basis, however, had broadened. Empathy had replaced abstract thought. The objective was attacking universal problems such as violence, bigotry, corruption, and hunger. Overpopulation and an endangered environment loomed large. Beuys was a cofounder of the Green Party, one of Europe's pioneer environmental groups. The art movement, at first essentially German, soon spread to other countries, including Italy, France, England, and the United States. The Germans, once again, had become a respected and productive part of the international art community.

Bibliography

Gordon, Donald E. *Expressionism, Art, and Idea.* New Haven, Conn.: Yale University Press, 1987. Donald Gordon is generally considered to be the leading American authority on German expressionism. This book is of interest because it details both the original expressionism and the neoexpressionism of Beuys, Kiefer, Baselitz, and Penck. Many fine illustrations, both black-and-white and color.

Joachimides, Christos M., Norman Rosenthal, and Wieland Schmied, eds. *German Art in the Twentieth Century: Painting and Sculpture, 1905-1985.* New York: Neues Publishing, 1985. Based on an exhibition of twentieth century German art held at the Royal Academy of Art in London in 1985 and the Staatsgalerie Stuttgart in 1986, this profusely illustrated volume details the new international interest in German art. This is probably also the best work available in English on contemporary German art. In addition to 299 full-color plates, the book contains a number of excellent essays on subjects ranging from the philosophy of Nietzsche to a monograph on Beuys. Also contains short but detailed biographies of forty-eight modern German artists.

Kiefer, Anselm. *A Book by Anselm Kiefer.* New York: George Braziller, 1988. Some of Kiefer's outstanding artistic works are in the form of books. This one is an interesting demonstration of his use of color, ranging from the cool blues and greens to the warm oranges and hot reds. Both the foreword and introduction give a great deal of personal and professional information on this extraordinary artist.

McShine, Kynaston, ed. *Berlinart, 1961-1987.* New York: Museum of Modern Art, 1987. Published in connection with a major exhibit of art associated with Berlin mounted by the Museum of Modern Art in New York. All the artworks in the exhibit, including those by Beuys and Baselitz, are reproduced in color. Interesting essays by authorities such as René Block, Laurence Kardish, Kynaston McShine, Karl Ruhrberg, and Wieland Schmied give valuable information on the development of modern German art, including the rejection of abstraction, the return to roots, and the reemergence of Berlin as a major international art center.

Ritchie, Andrew Carnduff, ed. *German Art in the Twentieth Century.* New York: Simon & Schuster, 1957. Although dated, this is still the best and most readable introduction to German art in the twentieth century. It is interesting to see the inertia affecting German art at the time of the book's publication.

Russell, John. *The Meanings of Modern Art.* Rev. ed. New York: Harper and Row, 1981. The modern art of any country cannot be fully understood without an understanding of how it relates to a broader international pattern. John Russell, the eminent art critic for *The New York Times*, explains such relationships in an understandable manner. He devotes considerable space to Beuys, whom he considers to be one of the leading artists of the time.

Nis Petersen

Cross-References

Avant-Garde Artists in Dresden Form Die Brücke (1905), p. 134; Der Blaue Reiter

Abandons Representation in Art (1911), p. 275; German Artists Found the Bauhaus (1919), p. 463; The New Objectivity Movement Is Introduced (1925), p. 631; Hitler Organizes an Exhibition Denouncing Modern Art (1937), p. 1083; The Nazis Ban Nolde's Paintings (1941), p. 1217.

HILL STREET BLUES DEFINES
HARD-REALITY TELEVISION

Category of event: Television and radio
Time: January 15, 1981-May 19, 1987
Locale: The United States

The success of Hill Street Blues' *hard-edged realism and groundbreaking structure would change the face of television drama and inspire several popular series cast in its image*

Principal personages:

STEVEN BOCHCO (1943-   ), the television writer and producer who developed the show and remained the guiding force behind it until 1985

MICHAEL KOZOLL (1940-   ), Bochco's longtime partner and the co-producer of the show

MARK FROST (1953-   ), one of the show's original writers, who would go on to develop other successful series

FRED SILVERMAN (1937-   ), the head of NBC who originated the idea for the show and supported it despite poor ratings in its first year

GRANT TINKER (1926-   ), the former head of MTM Enterprises, which produced the show, and later head of programming at NBC

DANIEL J. TRAVANTI (1940-   ), the actor who portrayed Captain Frank Furillo throughout the show's seven-season run

Summary of Event

When *Hill Street Blues* premiered on January 15, 1981, at ten o'clock on a Thursday night, *Variety* noted in its review that the National Broadcasting Company (NBC) "has obviously come up with the best-crafted series of the 1980-81 season to date. The question is 'do they know what to do with it?' " The show, produced and written by Steven Bochco and Michael Kozoll under the aegis of Grant Tinker's MTM Enterprises Productions, was a groundbreaking departure from formulaic television drama, and NBC seemed for several months to be at a loss regarding the series' place in its prime-time schedule. Although it garnered immediate, widespread critical praise, *Hill Street Blues* failed at first to connect with television viewers, and the show's initial ratings cast doubt over its future as the network moved it from Thursday to Saturday to Tuesday and back again to Thursday.

As *The New York Times* speculated on cancellation rumors and *Time* wondered if the series was "Too Good for Television?," the 1981 Emmy Awards solidified *Hill Street Blues'* uncertain future. The show won eight of the twenty-one awards for which it was nominated, a record for a weekly series. (It would receive a total of twenty-six Emmys during the course of its network run.) With the show suddenly thrust into a position of high visibility, NBC settled on Thursday nights at ten as a steady time slot, and *Hill Street Blues* began a rapid climb in the ratings as it attracted new viewers to its already loyal first-season audience. By the time it left the air on May 19, 1987, it had become one of the most honored and influential series in television history.

The idea for *Hill Street Blues* originated with NBC president Fred Silverman. To develop the series, Silverman sought out Steven Bochco and his partner, Michael Kozoll, who between them had worked on such notable police and detective shows as *McMillan and Wife, Columbo,* and *Kojak.* Although the two had hoped to leave the genre, they were intrigued by the possibility of producing a documentary-style dramatic series that could break free of the clichéd structure and plotting of traditional crime shows. Inspired by the documentary *The Police Tapes,* the pair set about creating a show that would combine complex stories, gritty realism, and a large ensemble cast of relatively unknown performers.

The pilot episode that resulted from Bochco and Kozoll's efforts was quickly judged by NBC's Department of Standards and Practices to be both too violent and too sexually provocative in its content, but Silverman backed the partners and gave them a free hand with the show. Handheld cameras, overlapping dialogue, and densely populated scenes in which extras continually walked between the camera and the lead actors gave the show a startling verisimilitude, a quality that reached its peak near the conclusion of the pilot episode when two engaging young officers stumbled upon a crime and were suddenly and brutally shot to death. The murder served notice that *Hill Street Blues* would not be playing by the conventional rules of television drama; a new era in television had begun. (Ironically, the two characters proved to be so popular that they were mysteriously restored to life and incorporated into the cast when the show was picked up by NBC.)

Impact of Event

Although Michael Kozoll would leave the series midway through its second season, Steven Bochco remained with the show until the end of its fifth season, when disagreements with MTM Enterprises led to his departure. Throughout most of *Hill Street Blues'* seven-season run, it was Bochco who shaped and guided the series, becoming in the process one of the best-known and most powerful producers in television. Known for his willingness to take risks and for his determination to take on subjects generally considered too controversial for television, Bochco charted a course for the show's development that saw plotlines drawn from real-life headlines and character developments that sometimes paralleled the actors' own lives. Black humor became a hallmark of the show's style, and the episodes regularly walked a fine line between comedy and the grotesque, evoking laughter with depictions of occasionally bizarre crimes and the vagaries of urban life.

Even among shows with large ensemble casts, *Hill Street Blues'* extensive roster of recurring characters was impressive, with episodes regularly juggling plots and subplots featuring more than a dozen individuals. At their center was Frank Furillo

(Daniel J. Travanti), the precinct's overworked captain. A decent and deeply committed man, Furillo was also divorced and—like the actor who played him—a recovering alcoholic. His relationship and eventual marriage to public defender Joyce Davenport (Veronica Hamel) was the show's primary romantic plotline, and many of the episodes ended with a scene showing the pair in bed together. Their complicated, sometimes troubled two-career relationship set the tone for the adult level on which the series operated, and the ongoing development of all the characters' emotional lives was one of *Hill Street Blues'* most impressive accomplishments. Throughout the course of the show, the men and women of Hill Street Station fell in love, married, and divorced, lost parents and became parents themselves, and dealt with the deaths of colleagues and friends.

What made this level of complexity possible was the show's groundbreaking dramatic structure. Unlike traditional television dramas, which typically deal with a single plot and subplot per episode and wrap both up by the show's conclusion, and unlike daytime and nighttime soap operas, which string out melodramatic story lines over entire seasons, *Hill Street Blues* adopted a format that resembled the ebb and flow of daily life. Each episode covered one day in the life of the precinct and combined both stories that were resolved by the show's end and segments of stories that played out over several weeks' time. Indeed, it was not unusual for the series to return to emotional issues in its characters' lives that had first arisen a season or two earlier, and no development within the series occurred in a vacuum. Unlike conventional dramas in which each new episode finds the characters exactly as they had been the week before, events in *Hill Street Blues* had repercussions that were felt permanently in its characters' emotional lives.

Hill Street Blues was also uncompromising in the themes it tackled. Over the course of its run, the series dealt with drugs, gangs, street violence, police brutality, political corruption, homosexuality, unwed mothers, rape, racism, transsexuality, and the sometimes blurry line separating those who uphold the law from those who break it. The show's sophisticated, intelligent handling of such sensitive issues opened thematic doors that had previously been tightly closed on commercial television, paving the way for other shows that would take their cue from the series.

The first show to follow successfully in *Hill Street Blues'* footsteps was *St. Elsewhere*, which made its appearance in 1983. (Bochco himself attempted an unsuccessful *Hill Street Blues* clone called *Bay City Blues* that same year.) Also produced by MTM Enterprises, *St. Elsewhere* transferred its predecessor's format to an inner-city hospital, where a group of doctors and residents coped with a wide variety of social and personal issues in addition to their patients' illnesses. Like *Hill Street Blues*, *St. Elsewhere* featured an ensemble cast, black humor, and a willingness to take risks. As the series progressed, however, it began to develop its own remarkably original style, undertaking experimental episodes that played with the medium of television itself and offering alert viewers numerous inside jokes and references in its witty, often outrageous scripts.

Bochco's own successful *Hill Street Blues* follow-up came in 1986, after his departure from the series. Collaborating with Terry Louise Fisher, he created the popular *L.A. Law*, which again featured an ensemble cast, controversial issues, and a structure based on the earlier show. Focusing on the lives and careers of the members of a Los Angeles law firm, the show—like its subject—was slicker than its predecessor, trading *Hill Street Blues'* gritty urban realism for the upscale gloss of successful West Coast attorneys. *L.A. Law* was an immediate and enduring hit, winning ratings that neither *Hill Street Blues* nor *St. Elsewhere* had ever achieved.

Another important, although less direct, descendant of *Hill Street Blues* was the much-debated *thirtysomething*. Both critically acclaimed and frequently villified, the show lasted for four seasons and managed to inspire a host of imitators after its demise. With an ensemble cast and a sophisticated approach to complex issues that would not have been possible without the groundwork laid by *Hill Street Blues*, the show focused on a group of friends and the events, both large and small, of their daily lives. While its detractors labeled it a series devoted to yuppie angst, its admirers praised the show's intelligent, witty writing and believably human story lines. Although vastly different from *Hill Street Blues* in tone and style, *thirtysomething* shared the earlier show's devotion to emotional truth in its characters' lives and made that the center of its focus to a degree rarely attempted in television drama.

Hill Street Blues also proved influential as the series that catapulted Steven Bochco to a position of power within the television industry. Bochco would go on to produce such series as *Hooperman*, *Doogie Howser, M.D.* and the short-lived, experimental *Cop Rock*, a weekly crime-drama/musical that was cancelled after only a few episodes. Even Bochco's failures generate publicity, however, and he has remained a shaping influence on television in the years since *Hill Street Blues'* inception.

Hill Street Blues' most remarkable legacy has been the level of realism it injected into television drama, an area seemingly limited by its very nature to stories that could be wrapped up neatly within an hour-long format in a medium where controversial subject matter can make a show the subject of boycotts and vocal criticism. That it was able to break free of the clichés and restraints that had defined earlier series would be enough to guarantee *Hill Street Blues* a place in the pantheon of television drama; that it did so with intelligence, complexity, and originality marks it as one of the best and most innovative dramas in the medium's history.

Bibliography

Freeman, David. "Television's Real A-Team." *Esquire* (January, 1985): 77-80. An indepth look at the series' principal writers and producers during its early years, and an examination of the process behind the writing of each episode.

"Hill Street Blues—A Hit with Problems." *The New York Times*, May 10, 1981, p. D19. An analysis of the series and the problems it faced during its first season.

"The Hill Street Blues Lesson." *The New York Times*, December 13, 1981. An examination of the show's post-Emmy Awards success.

"Hill Street Joys." *New York*, December 21, 1981, p. 20. An examination of the show's inception and its impact during its first season.

Lindsey, Robert. "From *Hill Street* to *L.A. Law.*" *The New York Times Magazine*, August 24, 1986, p. 30. An in-depth profile of Steven Bochco, written shortly before the premiere of *L.A. Law.*

Span, Paula. "Bochco on the Edge." *Esquire* (May, 1990): 158-166. A lengthy and informative profile of Steven Bochco.

"Too Good for Television?" *Time* (September 14, 1981). A look at the series during its first months.

Zoglin, Richard. "Changing the Face of Prime Time." *Time* (May 2, 1988): 75-76. A profile of Steven Bochco chronicling his emergence as an influential force in television drama.

Janet Lorenz

Cross-References

The Maltese Falcon Establishes a New Style for Crime Films (1941), p. 1223; *Dragnet* Is the First Widely Popular Police Show (1951), p. 1531; *Peyton Place* Brings Serial Drama to Nighttime Television (1964), p. 2017; Relevance Programs Change Entertainment Standards (1970's), p. 2197; *Dallas* Popularizes the Prime-Time Soap Opera (1978), p. 2418; *The Cosby Show* Makes Television History (1984), p. 2532.

MTV CHANGES THE LOOK
OF AMERICAN POPULAR CULTURE

Categories of event: Music; television and radio
Time: August 1, 1981
Locale: New York, New York

*MTV and other music-video broadcasts had a dramatic effect on the music busi-
ness and television and generated repercussions in a broad range of popular culture*

Principal personages:
ROBERT PITTMAN (1954-   ), the television executive responsible for
bringing MTV to life in 1981
MICHAEL JACKSON (1958-   ), a singer and dancer who created some
of the most complex and popular music videos ever made
MADONNA (MADONNA LOUISE CICCONE, 1958-   ), a singer, dancer, and
media figure who used MTV as a major vehicle to launch her career
MICHAEL NESMITH (1942-   ), a former member of the pop band the
Monkees and the creator of the show *Popclips*, the immediate precur-
sor of and inspiration for MTV
JOHN LACK, the Warner-Amex-Satellite Entertainment vice president who
approved the development of MTV

Summary of Event

In the 1950's, the most important site for rock-and-roll music was Memphis, home
of Elvis Presley and the legendary stars of Sun Records. In the 1960's, it was Liver-
pool, England, the point of departure for the Beatles and the other bands of the
British Invasion. In the 1970's, it was London, which spawned punk rock and the
New Wave that followed. In the 1980's, however, the most important place in rock
music was a television studio in Queens, New York; it was there that Music Television (MTV) was born.

The concept of pairing popular music with television imagery is a relatively old
one, dating back to the 1930's and 1940's, when cartoons were synchronized to the
songs of such performers as Cab Calloway and Louis Armstrong. In the 1960's, a
device called the Scopitone offered viewers something resembling music videos, but
it never attained widespread popularity, probably because it featured European singers rather than far more popular American performers. More directly, Beatles films
such as *A Hard Day's Night* (1964) and long-running British television shows such as
Top of the Pops, which featured long segments of musical performance and arresting
imagery, can be seen as the inspiration for what became MTV.

The new form began modestly enough. The immediate precursor of MTV was *Popclips*, a music and video show developed by Michael Nesmith, a former member of
the pop group the Monkees. *Popclips*, which featured video clips of music and im-

ages, was hosted by stand-up comedian Howie Mandel and appeared on the Warner-Amex-Satellite Entertainment company's Nickelodeon network in 1980. Recognizing the potential of such a show, Warner executive John Lack backed the creation of an entire channel to be devoted solely to music videos, twenty-four hours a day. The execution of this idea was entrusted to Robert Pittman, a twenty-seven-year-old television and radio executive who already had a long track record of successful programming (he would later be responsible for the talk show hosted by the abrasive Morton Downey, Jr.). The new project was a relatively low-risk proposition, because the programming would be provided by record companies to the network at no cost in the hope that the videos would serve as advertising. Expectations for MTV were modest; even its strongest proponents said profits would be years away. When the network made its debut on August 1, 1981, MTV had a mere 125 videos, thirteen advertisers, and a relatively meager access to 2.1 million households. It was not even carried in New York City or Los Angeles.

It soon became clear, however, that the new format had a number of assets: engaging video disc jockeys (or "veejays," as they came to be known), hip sets, and often-astounding graphics that ran between videos and commercials. The very first video shown was the Buggles' "Video Killed the Radio Star," an audacious statement that would prove in some ways prophetic. In 1982, the network introduced its famous slogan "I Want My MTV," uttered by a variety of rock stars incessantly throughout the day and night. By 1984, Warner had spun MTV into a separate company that was showing a profit and claiming more than twenty-four million viewers. Radio had not been killed, but it was now a poor relation to the video colossus.

Among the earliest beneficiaries of MTV were such foreign acts as Australia's Men at Work and England's Culture Club, which were familiar with video production from British television and which were thus ready with material on hand to add to MTV's small initial library. The result was a 1980's version of the British Invasion, as new acts such as Duran Duran and more established performers such as David Bowie and Elton John quickly seized the music-video spotlight.

Conspicuously absent from MTV, at first, were videos starring black artists. MTV programmers initially believed that the network's viewers, who were predominantly white, middle-class adolescents, would wish to see only white performers. Media critics claimed that the network was racist; more profit-minded record-company executives were angry at the lack of access to the channel for black performers who ranked among the most creative acts of the day. When Michael Jackson's *Thriller* topped the charts in early 1983 without the benefit of video, his label, CBS Records, reputedly threatened to stop providing videos for any of its artists if MTV did not start playing Jackson's work. The network complied, and the shortsightedness of its former policy quickly became apparent as Jackson and other black acts brought new excitement—and new audiences—to the form.

Indeed, the fabulous success of MTV spawned a wave of imitators on cable television, local stations, and even the major networks, which began producing television shows such as *Night Tracks* and *Friday Night Videos* to compete with the new channel. Some of these shows did reasonably well, but none achieved success on a similar scale. Perhaps the greatest potential challenge was posed by media mogul Ted Turner, who started a rival network, VH-1, that offered more family-oriented videos. Bad ratings, however, led Turner to abandon the attempt, and he sold VH-1 to MTV, where it thrived as a more adult-oriented version of the original network.

One important reason that MTV was able to thrive amid such challenges was the almost relentless pace of innovation that characterized it. For example, when rap music achieved broad popularity in the late 1980's, the network did not repeat its earlier mistake of marginalizing the work of black performers; instead, it achieved a high profile in rap culture with *Yo! MTV Raps*, a show devoted to the form. As its audience widened, MTV added news service, and the network was widely seen as playing an influential role in registering young voters and interesting them in the presidential election of 1992 (both Bill Clinton and George Bush appeared on the network during the campaign). Moreover, innovative programs such as *Liquid Television* offered showcases for the latest technological and visual developments in video culture.

MTV's audience declined—by nearly half, according to some estimates—following the heady days of the early 1980's, as the novelty of the format wore off. Yet the network continued to be profitable, because the youth market it targeted remained attractive to advertisers and because MTV continued to offer the best programming of its kind. Even in the trend-following and constantly changing popular-music business, it was clear that MTV had arrived to stay.

Impact of Event

Music Television was one of the most important cultural developments of the 1980's. Its influence on popular music was immense. It also, however, had a tremendous impact on American society at large, shaping television, advertising, and other areas of popular culture.

MTV's impact on popular music was manifold. On the most obvious level, it became a new outlet for performers to reach audiences, and as a result it developed unprecedented power in its ability to make or break careers. By the 1990's, the network's decision to show a video clip would represent a major break for fledgling artists, and a clip shown every few hours ("on heavy rotation") represented the kind of exposure no radio station or advertiser could hope to match in impact. In a highly segmented—even fragmented—market, MTV and its sister network VH-1 became the nearest approximation of a musical center, where diverse styles received representation and could influence a variety of performers and audiences alike.

The rise of music video also brought with it a new emphasis on the visual component of musical performance. This had always been important in rock, from Elvis Presley's hip thrusts through the Beatles' stylish haircuts and beyond. MTV, though, created a new showcase for charismatic, visually appealing acts, a development that outlandish performers such as Boy George of Culture Club and artistic innovators such as Peter Gabriel exploited to the fullest extent. The more dubious aspects of this development would become obvious in 1990, when it was revealed that the stars of the Grammy Award-winning group Milli Vanilli were nothing more than lip-synching impostors.

A subtler but nevertheless significant aspect of MTV's impact on music was the last push it gave to individual hit records, before compact discs and MTV's own decline in influence brought about the demise of the vinyl single. By the late 1970's, the single had long lost influence to the long-playing album, and some of the most successful artists never actually had hit records. Thanks to MTV, however, singles enjoyed a renaissance, and album-oriented performers enjoyed unprecedented strings of hits from the same album. Billy Joel's 1983 album *An Innocent Man* spawned six top-forty hits; Bruce Springsteen's 1984 album *Born in the U.S.A.* contained seven. Performers such as Lionel Ritchie and Michael Jackson who were widely familiar to hit-radio listeners got an even bigger boost. Jackson's 1982 release *Thriller* shattered sales records and became the first album in pop-music history to yield six top-ten singles.

Yet if MTV helped Michael Jackson to reach a vast new audience, it was Jackson who brought MTV to new heights of excitement and influence. His "Billie Jean," "Beat It," and "Thriller" were not merely videos that were eagerly anticipated and watched by millions of viewers; they were cultural events that demonstrated the artistic potential of the video form.

Another major figure who can be mentioned in the same breath as Jackson is Madonna. Trained as a dancer and singularly adept at manipulating images to generate interest in her work, Madonna used video to build a media empire that included music, film, and even books. Videos such as "Lucky Star," "Material World" (with its evocation of Marilyn Monroe), and "Vogue" have extended the form—and flirted with taboos that have only brought Madonna more notoriety. One wonders if there could have been a star such as Madonna without MTV—or, at the very least, whether she could have become so famous so quickly without the new medium.

Perhaps the most striking dimension of the MTV phenomenon, though, has been its impact on other cultural forms. What might be called the "MTV aesthetic"— bright images, rapid-fire editing, repeated motifs, and dreamlike imagery, among other techniques—has been widely appropriated. It was often noted that the hit television shows *Miami Vice* and *Pee Wee's Playhouse* owed much to MTV, as did television and magazine advertising.

Not all observers saw such developments as positive. Some critics argued that the MTV aesthetic was a superficial one that short-circuited sustained analysis and accelerated the movement away from traditional forms of literacy necessary for a truly educated citizenry. Others argued that MTV and its related forms represented the beginnings of a new visual order that would itself become the norm, much in the way the written word supplanted oral traditions. In either case, few would dispute the enormous impact MTV has had on American culture at the end of the twentieth century.

Bibliography

Aufderheide, Pat. "Music Videos: The Look of Sound." In *Watching Television: A Pantheon Guide to Popular Culture*, edited by Todd Gitlin. New York: Pantheon Books, 1987. An incisive and readable analysis of music video and MTV that emphasizes the highly postmodern nature of the form and both its intellectually liberating and constricting qualities. Slightly dated, but still highly relevant.

Frith, Simon. "Making Sense of Video: Pop into the Nineties." In *Music for Pleasure: Essays in the Sociology of Pop.* New York: Routledge, 1988. Like "Video Pop," this essay (the afterword for *Music for Pleasure*) looks at video's role in the music industry. Discusses MTV specifically.

_____. "Video Pop: Picking Up the Pieces." In *Facing the Music: A Pantheon Guide to Popular Culture.* New York: Pantheon Books, 1988. An important article by the most influential British rock critic and sociologist. Frith situates video within the larger reorganization of the music industry to argue that rock and roll, as it has been conventionally understood, has come to an end.

Rubey, Dan. "Voguing at the Carnival: Desire and Pleasure on MTV." *South Atlantic Quarterly* 90 (Fall, 1991): 871-906. A scholarly, postmodern reading of music video. Emphasizes the degree to which MTV represents a new kind of literacy that opens forms of expression that counter those of the dominant culture.

Tucker, Ken. "Rock in the Video Age." In *Rock of Ages: The Rolling Stone History of Rock and Roll*, by Ed Ward, Geoffrey Stokes, and Ken Tucker. New York: Rolling Stone Press, 1986. Good narrative summary of the rise of MTV and the immediate musical context of the form. Particularly good on the Michael Jackson controversy of 1982 and 1983.

Jim Cullen

Cross-References

Nam June Paik Exhibits Video and Television as Art (1963), p. 1955; *Rowan and Martin's Laugh-In* Is the Top Show on Television (1968), p. 2115; Madonna Revolutionizes Popular Fashion (1980's), p. 2449; *Thriller* Marks Michael Jackson's Musical Coming-of-Age (1982), p. 2512; Live Aid Generates Millions for Famine Relief (1985), p. 2543; The Decline of the Big Three Networks Becomes a Fall (Late 1980's), p. 2554.

THE NEW DANCE U.S.A. FESTIVAL CELEBRATES CONTEMPORARY DANCE

Category of event: Dance
Time: October 4-10, 1981
Locale: Walker Art Center, Minneapolis, Minnesota

The United States' largest performance of experimental dance took place when twenty-seven choreographers belonging to the postmodern dance field performed as part of a week-long festival

Principal personages:
CHARLES MOULTON (1954-   ), a former member of the Merce Cunningham Dance Company who performed in the first program at the festival
TRISHA BROWN (1936-   ), a postmodern choreographer and founding member of Judson Dance Theater who performed in the first program at the festival
DAVID GORDON (1936-   ), a postmodern dancer and choreographer who performed on the same program with Moulton and Brown
KEI TAKEI (1946-   ), a Japanese choreographer working in the United States who performed on the second program of the festival
ROSALIND NEWMAN (1946-   ), a choreographer who performed as part of the festival's second program
JIM SELF (1954-   ), a dancer who presented works on the same program with Takei and Newman
DOUGLAS DUNN (1942-   ), a dancer who presented works on the third program of the festival
DANA REITZ (1948-   ), an avant-garde choreographer who presented dances on the third program of the festival
LUCINDA CHILDS (1940-   ), a dancer and choreographer who presented dances at the festival
ANNA KISSELGOFF (1938-   ), the dance critic for *The New York Times* who reported on the festival

Summary of Event

The New Dance U.S.A. Festival, a seven-day celebration of experimental and postmodern dance, opened at the Walker Art Center in Minneapolis, Minnesota, on the evening of Sunday, October 4, 1981. A total of twenty-seven choreographers convened to exhibit their work in three different theaters, making the event the largest concentration of postmodern dance the nation had seen.

Dancers, choreographers, and dance critics gathered at the festival to view, lecture, and discuss the burgeoning field of "new dance." The assemblage was international in scope and included representatives from the United States, West Germany, and New Zealand. Three distinct programs made up the festival, each program featuring a trio of choreographers, all renowned exponents of postmodern dance. In addition to the nightly dance performances, the festival offered panel discussions and lectures on future trends in dance.

The origin of postmodern dance is generally traced to the Judson Dance Theater of the early 1960's. Regarded as a seminal group in the development of contemporary dance, the Judson Dance Theater included dancers, visual artists, and musicians who worked at the Judson Memorial Church on Washington Square in New York City. The Judson group experimented with many nontraditional concepts such as minimalism and pedestrian movement in its choreography and utilized nondancers as well as professionals.

Three of the early members of Judson Dance Theater, Trisha Brown, David Gordon, and Lucinda Childs, were featured as part of the New Dance U.S.A. Festival. During the first program, Brown offered a solo that was a combination of two separate pieces from her repertoire: *Accumulation* and *With Talking*. Brown originally choreographed these dances in the 1970's and presented them in a different configuration in order to endow the movement with new context. This deliberate change of perspective is an integral part of the postmodern movement.

In *Accumulation*, Brown gradually added motions together until she created an entire sequence of movement. Beginning with a simple movement motif in which the dancer pronated the forearms from a "thumbs-up" to a "thumbs-down" position, Brown expanded the dance sequence until an entire piece was "accumulated." *With Talking* included a verbalization of the choreographer's creative process recited while the dancer performed a short, virtuosic solo. Critics hailed Brown as combining humor with a formalistic approach to dance.

The blending of humor with an exposition of formal concerns was also achieved by postmodern choreographer David Gordon. In *Close Up*, performed by Gordon and his wife Valda Setterfield, the couple executed a duet that was juxtaposed with slides of themselves wearing both dance tights and conservative apparel. The duet acquired new meaning when seen in conjunction with the slides. In another duet, *Dorothy and Eileen*, Setterfield and dancer Margaret Hoeffel simultaneously danced and discussed their individual relationships with their mothers. Gordon's dance *Double Identity Part I* was a work in which the choreographer also experimented with movement and speech.

The work of Charles Moulton, a former dancer with the Merce Cunningham Dance Company, was also featured on the first program of the Minneapolis festival. Moulton, who was born in Minneapolis, premiered a pure-movement piece entitled *Arch Extract*. Whereas most of the other dances presented in the festival's first program combined speech with movement, Moulton's work consisted of a rhythmic athleticism. Hand-clapping, foot-stomping and head-rolling motifs enriched the theme and structure of the dance. Moulton's choreography was representative of the postmodern tendency to accentuate athletic prowess through the exploration of movement possibilities and problems. In contrast to the early postmodern work of the 1960's, postmodern dance in the 1980's and 1990's began to accentuate technical skill and bravura. During the New Dance U.S.A. Festival, the work of choreographers such as Moulton, Jim Self, and Dana Reitz exemplified this new emphasis on virtuosity.

Included in the second and third programs of the festival were postmodern choreographers such as Kei Takei, Rosalind Newman, Douglas Dunn, and Karole Armitage. Most of the festival's choreographers were based in New York, although a few worked in other regions of the country. A large number of the choreographers had studied or danced with Merce Cunningham: Moulton, Newman, Self, Dunn, Armitage, and Childs had all worked at some point with the experimental choreographer.

On the second program of the series, Rosalind Newman premiered a dance entitled *Shifting Divides/Inside Out* that consisted of a trio of dancers manipulating three ropes. The ropes were used to create diverse configurations within the stage space. Newman's choreography involved complex spatial patterns and movement sequences that illustrated her concern with form and visual design. Although critics lauded the dancers' performances, the choreography itself did not win praise. Anna Kisselgoff of *The New York Times* remarked that Newman seemed to utilize postmodern ideas as formulas for the choreography rather than as integrated elements of the dance.

Choreographer Jim Self also presented a trio on the second program. *Marking Time* was a piece in which the three dancers performed individual movement sequences. Self achieved a humorous effect when the different movement phrases were seen in juxtaposition to one another. The element of humor evident in the choreography was similar to that found in the work of both Brown and Gordon. Self received very favorable reviews from the dance critics who attended the festival.

Other choreographers trained in the Cunningham School presented dances that were not as favorably received. Douglas Dunn, for example, staged a dance entitled *Skid* as part of the festival's third program. Although the work included a duet for Dunn and dancer Susan Blankensop that steadily increased in tempo and dynamic, the overall effect did not elicit much response from critics. Karole Armitage, who recapitulated her dance entitled *Drastic Classicism*, collaborated with the composer Rhys Chatham. Only the first section of the work was presented, and although Armitage's choreography had been well received in New York, the Minneapolis audience remained reserved.

Impact of Event

The New Dance U.S.A. Festival was significant in its presentation of innovative and experimental approaches to modern dance choreography. Never before had so many choreographers congregated in order to present new works, thereby offering the viewer an opportunity to observe the prominent figures of postmodern dance in a single festival. The presentation of so much modern dance in one event helped to give some definition to the term "new dance" and pioneered new trends in modern and postmodern choreography.

At least six different elements of postmodern dance emerged as part of the New Dance U.S.A. Festival. The avant-garde mode that was derived from the era of the Judson Dance Theater evolved into new compositional techniques. Whereas the postmodern dance of the 1960's was largely concerned with pedestrian and nondance movement often performed by untrained dancers, the "new dance" of the 1981 festival exhibited much technical virtuosity. This emphasis on technical skill resulted directly from the explorations of choreographers; the dancers' training became specific to each choreographer's style. Although a certain amount of minimalism remained, such as the use of repetition and diverse manipulations of simple movement phrases, the choreographers at the 1981 festival relied more on athletic dance sequences.

New trends in movement exploration and the solving of choreographic problems resulted from the New Dance U.S.A. Festival. An element of humor was evident in many of the dances. Choreographers such as Childs and Reitz presented complex structures of movement that were in contrast to the more simple configurations of the 1960's. Also in contrast to the work of the 1960's was the anonymity of the dancers. Whereas the postmodern dancers of the 1960's were all individually recognizable, the dancers of the 1981 festival remained largely anonymous.

The influence of visual art and music was evident in the festival and invested the work of several choreographers. For example, the visual art manifestoes of the 1960's and 1970's influenced the work of Lucinda Childs and Yvonne Rainer. Postmodern trends developed by visual artists such as Marcel Duchamp and composers such as John Cage permeated the work of postmodern choreographers. A renewed focus on interdisciplinary collaboration evolved from both the New Dance U.S.A. Festival and resultant dance festivals patterned after it. For example, Lucinda Childs collaborated with lighting designers, composers, and visual artists in the creation of her work. This collaborative process was reminiscent of the work of modern dance choreographer Merce Cunningham during the 1960's and 1970's.

The success of the New Dance U.S.A. Festival inspired the sponsorship of other modern dance festivals. One major dance event spawned by the New Dance U.S.A. Festival was the "Next Wave Festival" hosted by the Brooklyn Academy of Music. Choreographer Lucinda Childs, who had appeared in the New Dance U.S.A. Festival, premiered her work entitled *Relative Calm* as part of the series. The piece, presented December 18, 1981, was an evening-length work danced by Childs and her nine-member company. As part of her creative process, Childs collaborated with set designer Robert Wilson and composer Jon Gibson. The result was a quintessential example of postmodern dance.

Childs, who was labeled a minimalist during the 1970's, continued to pursue formalist concerns in *Relative Calm*. She constructed simple, repetitive movement phrases that gradually evolved in complexity. Childs manipulated movements and phrases by incorporating changes in direction, tempo, and dynamics, thus varying the original dance phrase. Critics such as Kisselgoff and *The New York Times* contributor Jennifer Dunning responded favorably to the piece. As part of the Next Wave Festival,

Childs' choreography was chosen to bring the avant-garde dance series to a close.

Relative Calm exemplified several different aspects of postmodern dance. Childs utilized complex movement structures that originated from simple, repetitive dance phrases. Elements of humor were evident in the work. The choreographer also incorporated ideas from the visual arts and music within her dance. The interdisciplinary collaboration of visual art, music, and dance yielded a work representative of postmodern dance. As a result of events such as the Next Wave Festival and its progenitor, the New Dance U.S.A. Festival, postmodern dance flourished during the early 1980's.

Bibliography

Anderson, Jack. "The Ever-Modern" and "Images in Action." In *Choreography Observed*. Iowa City: University of Iowa Press, 1987. Anderson expounds on the phenomenon of new dance by presenting a collection of his dance reviews from 1967 to 1985. Choreographers are discussed, including Kei Takei, Trisha Brown, and Dana Reitz. The Judson Dance Theater is discussed in chapter 5. No photographs or bibliography. Index.

Banes, Sally. *Terpsichore in Sneakers.* Boston: Houghton Mifflin, 1980. A definitive book on postmodern dance and aesthetics. Banes includes extensive accounts dealing with the work of Trisha Brown, David Gordon, Lucinda Childs, and Douglas Dunn. Chronology of choreography, extensive notes, and index. Bibliography is conveniently arranged according to sources that deal with each individual choreographer. Excellent black-and-white photographs.

Jowitt, Deborah. *The Dance in Mind.* Boston: David R. Godine, 1985. A collection of Jowitt's dance reviews that includes significant information on the choreographers involved in the 1981 New Dance U.S.A. Festival. Jowitt discusses the choreography of Karole Armitage, Lucinda Childs, Dana Reitz, Douglas Dunn, and Trisha Brown, among others. Included are reviews of choreography presented at the New Dance U.S.A. Festival. Index.

Matheson, Katy. "Breaking Boundaries." In *Dance as a Theatre Art*, edited by Selma Jeanne Cohen. 2d ed. Princeton, N.J.: Princeton Book Company, 1992. Overview of the new generation of modern dance choreographers. Includes interviews with such choreographers as Twyla Tharp, Mark Morris, and Steve Paxton. Matheson includes some discussion of the choreographic process. Limited photographs. Excellent bibliography of sources.

Siegel, Marcia B. *The Tail of the Dragon: New Dance, 1976-1982.* Durham, N.C.: Duke University Press, 1991. A compilation of Siegel's dance reviews and observations. Provides information on new dance and the aesthetics of the avant-garde. All major choreographers involved in the New Dance U.S.A. Festival are included. Extensive information on the dances of Trisha Brown, David Gordon, and Douglas Dunn. Siegel includes a selected filmography of the late 1970's and early 1980's. Excellent photographs. Index.

John R. Crawford

Cross-References

Taylor Establishes His Own Dance Company (1954), p. 1602; Ailey Founds His Dance Company (1958), p. 1774; Cunningham Stages His First Dance "Event" (1964), p. 2011; Tharp Stages *Deuce Coupe* for the Joffrey Ballet (1973), p. 2288; Festivals Mark a Peak in the Dance Created by Black Artists (1983), p. 2521; Multiculturalism Dominates the Dance World (Late 1980's), p. 2559; Baryshnikov's White Oak Dance Project Debuts (1990), p. 2663.

SCOTT'S *BLADE RUNNER* IS A VISUAL MASTERPIECE

Category of event: Motion pictures
Time: 1982
Locale: The United States

Though poorly received on its release in 1982, Blade Runner *became a cult classic and demonstrated director Ridley Scott's technical perfection and mastery of the visual medium*

Principal personages:
RIDLEY SCOTT (1939-   ), the British director of *Blade Runner,* who moved into motion pictures after a background in directing television advertisements
SYD MEAD, an industrial design consultant who worked on *Blade Runner*
LAWRENCE G. PAULL, the production designer for *Blade Runner*
DOUGLAS TRUMBULL (1942-   ), and RICHARD YURICICH, the special-effects creators for *Blade Runner*
JORDAN CRONENWETH (1935-   ), the cinematographer for *Blade Runner*
HAMPTON FANCHER (1938-   ), and
DAVID PEOPLES, the scriptwriters for *Blade Runner*
PHILIP K. DICK (1928-1982), the author of *Do Androids Dream of Electric Sheep?,* the novel upon which *Blade Runner* is based

Summary of Event

When director Ridley Scott started work on the science-fiction film *Blade Runner* in 1980, his 1979 film *Alien* had made him as hot a director as almost any in Hollywood. Set on a giant spaceship, *Alien* combined elements of the horror and science-fiction genres to terrify and enthrall audiences at the same time. Some critics carped at the derivative story line, but none had anything but praise for the sets and the visual splendor. Though *Alien* was a straightforward commercial production, Scott demonstrated his willingness to take risks in the film, as in his tracking shot of the interior of a spaceship—a sequence that most Hollywood directors would consider overly "arty" for such a film.

Alien promoted Scott's reputation as a master craftsman in visual detail and in atmospherics. It also underlined his ability to utilize the genius of others to produce a desired effect (in this case, the designs of Swiss artist H. R. Giger). Scott's first film, *The Duellists* (1977), set in the early 1800's, had also drenched the eye with scenes of breathtaking beauty. He made it after learning his craft in television commercials (a path taken by many modern British directors) and after winning numerous awards for the many commercials in which he participated.

Taking on *Blade Runner* meant two science-fiction films in a row for Scott, though he claimed not to have any particular leaning to science fiction. The film's plot concerns a revolt in the year 2019 by "replicants"—living beings designed and assembled in the form of humans. After murdering several people, a group of replicants escapes to Earth from a space colony in order to find out how to prolong their limited lifespan. A bounty hunter (the "blade runner") is assigned to kill them. He reluctantly proceeds to do so, despite his distaste for killing beings with whom he increasingly feels empathy and with one of whom he eventually falls in love. As he "retires" them, one by one, they desperately search for information on their origins and their makers. Eventually, the replicants' leader tracks down the head of the Tyrell Corporation, manufacturers of the replicants, only to discover that their four-year life span cannot be altered. The leader kills the corporate head and returns to the group's hideaway for a final confrontation with the blade runner, who has in the meantime shot the only other remaining member of the escaped group. In a moving finale, the replicant spares the blade runner's life even as he himself dies.

Perhaps the most astonishing achievement of the film is the creation of a totally believable cityscape of the future. The opening shots place the viewer in an urban environment that is both familiar and nightmarish. Rain falls interminably from overcast skies onto polluted streets groaning with detritus. Giant video screens advertise the attractiveness of living "off-world." At ground level, an overcrowded, multiethnic population frantically ekes out an existence as gigantic skyscrapers overhead play host to the powerful and the rich.

Scott and his main visual collaborators—production designer Lawrence Paull, special-effects supervisors Douglas Trumbull and Richard Yuricich, and "visual futurist" Syd Mead—used all their combined creativity to make this future world seem real, both in particular detail and overall effect. They used the old Warner Brothers "New York" set and added high-tech machinery of every kind, including $100,000 worth of neon signs (many borrowed from another 1982 film, *One From the Heart*). For models, they borrowed skyscrapers from *Escape from New York* (1981) and even converted a spaceship from *Star Wars* (1977) into another building.

Harrison Ford played the blade runner. Some critics thought him too cold, though emotionally repressed and brutal are probably nearer the mark. Rutger Hauer gave a haunting portrayal of the replicant leader who gains viewers' sympathy despite his commission of numerous atrocities. Sean Young, as a replicant who thinks she is human, is beautiful and vulnerable and perhaps the most sympathetic character in the film. Darryl Hannah plays a "Standard Pleasure Model" replicant who is simultaneously alluring and chilling.

On *Blade Runner*'s release, most critics lavished praise on the film for its visual texture and look but found the characters poorly drawn. Roger Ebert's view was typical: "a stunningly interesting visual achievement, but a failure as a story." Audiences seemed to agree—the film lost money at the box office. Despite a narrative voice-over by Ford's character, viewers had difficulty following the plot. Yet Philip K. Dick, the author of the novel on which the film was based, was stunned by his first viewing and remarked that the film's creators had done "sight simulation on my brain . . . this is a new art form." The film did gain some recognition with Academy Award nominations for its visual effects and its set direction and decoration. Science-fiction fans gave it the 1982 Hugo Award as the year's best science-fiction film.

Ridley Scott took four years to complete and release his next film, *Legend* (1985). Like his *Someone to Watch Over Me* (1987), *Legend* was not a box-office success. In 1984, Scott directed a commercial for the Macintosh Computer Company and treated Super Bowl viewers to dazzling imagery. The advertisement was shown just once, but it had a great impact and was shown in reviews of the history of advertising. Scott's only other 1980's film, *Black Rain* (1989), again failed to make money, though critics liked it, particularly for its visual presentation of a foreign culture.

Scott's reputation, though, continued to grow with film buffs. A September, 1989, article in *The New York Times* referred to his "extraordinary eye," while a November, 1990, article in the same newspaper spoke of his "legendary visual style." Success finally returned with *Thelma and Louise* (1991), a sleeper hit that earned Scott an Academy Award nomination as best director.

Impact of Event

Blade Runner recovered from the dismal initial reception to become a minor classic over time. It is hard to think of any other film that repudiated its critics so squarely. If *Thelma and Louise* was a sleeper that gained momentum over the summer of 1991, then *Blade Runner* was the sleeper of the entire 1980's. All through the decade, its reputation grew. The film eventually went into the black through huge video sales and rentals.

With hindsight, *Blade Runner* was a film slightly before its time. By 1985, an illustrated history of science fiction, *Future Visions: The New Golden Age of the Science Fiction Film*, was calling it "among the most compelling and original of recent science-fiction pictures." *The New Encyclopedia of Science Fiction* (1988) forecast its possible future status as a masterpiece by comparing it to Stanley Kubrick's 1968 *2001: A Space Odyssey*. By 1990, *The New York Times* stated that *Blade Runner* was "regarded by many critics as a classic of science fiction."

Blade Runner needs to be placed in context before one can evaluate its importance. One of the great challenges of science fiction, both in literature and on the screen, is to create a plausible future (or alien) society with convincing textural detail. The first film to attempt this was Fritz Lang's masterpiece *Metropolis* (1926), a seminal influence on science-fiction film. If anything, Lang's future dystopia is even more nightmarish than *Blade Runner*'s. Such was the achievement of this classic that not until *2001* did any science-fiction film achieve anything like the same prominence. *2001* changed filmgoers' paradigms with regard to science fiction, but its action takes place aboard a spaceship; it made no detailed attempt to envisage the shape of societies to come. In the 1970's, the success of *Star Wars* spurred new Hollywood activity in science fiction and paved the way for the special effects that would be used so adroitly in *Blade Runner*. The two films, though, do not bear direct comparison; *Star Wars* is a space fantasy—its landscapes and architecture are the stuff of dreams, not of predictions.

In measuring the success of *Blade Runner*, therefore, the only comparable film is *Metropolis*. Other films such as *Soylent Green* (1973) and *Escape from New York*, while successful as action films, do not really attempt to detail the architecture and societal relationships of the future. Scott's creation of an alternative world can also be contrasted with David Lynch's failure in *Dune*, released in 1984.

Commentators have asserted that *Blade Runner* did for science-fiction film what editor John W. Campbell did for magazine science-fiction in the 1940's: made it totally realistic and reemphasized the possible consequences of new technology in the near future. The great science-fiction writer Robert Silverberg wrote that such realism in showing the way the future might look is the best thing that science-fiction film has to offer.

Blade Runner's direct and indirect influences are pervasive. Both *The Terminator* (1984) and *Terminator II: Judgment Day* (1991), which told stories about man-made men fighting human beings, were influenced by Scott's film. Commentators have also noted the film's influence on music videos, on the *Max Headroom* television show, and on the "cyberpunk" movement in science-fiction writing. In 1989, the Rolling Stones spent $18 million on a concert set that Mick Jagger said evoked *Blade Runner*. Around the same time, *The Wall Street Journal* said that the *Blade Runner* cityscape had become shorthand for describing conditions in urban America.

Sales of the fiction of Philip K. Dick increased greatly as a result of the burgeoning popularity of the film version of his novel (originally published in 1968 as *Do Androids Dream of Electric Sheep?*). Though respected by critics, Dick's books sold few copies until the novel's republication under the title *Blade Runner* introduced thousands to his unique brand of metaphysics and futurism. Though Dick died just before the film was released, he had enormous respect for it and felt that it supplemented his book.

Blade Runner had an impact beyond that generated by its visual splendor. Dozens of articles, many written by academics, continue to be written on its underlying meanings and iconography. In 1991, some of the best were collected and published under the title *Retrofitting Blade Runner: Issues in Ridley Scott's "Blade Runner" and Philip K. Dick's "Do Androids Dream of Electric Sheep?"* Reading these articles, it is hard to believe the early criticisms asserting shallow characterization and an uninspired plot. Some of the more academic, though, argue against Scott's early assertion that the film is basically entertainment.

Ridley Scott did not have the "final cut" in the first released version of the film. In early 1992, inspired by continuing interest in the film, he issued a "director's cut" and saw the film take in an amazing $80,000 in a single week in one San Francisco cinema. The updated version panders less to the mass audience; gone is the Ford voice-over and some dialogue that spells out the plot twists. *Variety* called the new film a classic and Warner Bros. planned a nationwide rerelease of the new version.

Bibliography

Dick, Philip K. *Blade Runner: Do Androids Dream of Electric Sheep?* Reprint.

New York: Ballantine Books, 1982. The novel upon which *Blade Runner* is based. Philip K. Dick refused to write a "novelization" of the film for Warner Bros., so the novel was retitled instead. A fascinating read; the book and film complement each other to a remarkable degree. The book has more metaphysical speculation and several more layers of plot, including some excellent plot twists.

Kael, Pauline. Review of *Blade Runner. The New Yorker* 58 (July 12, 1982): 82-85. Kael complains that all of Ridley Scott's creativity in the film went into the sets and not into the acting, dialogue, or plot. She generally praises the actors for doing what they could with what they were given; the exception is Rutger Hauer, who is criticized for a "scenery chewing" performance.

Kerman, Judith B, ed. *Retrofitting "Blade Runner": Issues in Ridley Scott's "Blade Runner" and Philip K. Dick's "Do Androids Dream of Electric Sheep?"* Bowling Green, Ohio: Bowling Green State University Popular Press, 1991. A book for those who want to know everything there is to consider and know about *Blade Runner.* The academic-sounding title conceals some fascinating and revealing articles. The first half of the book expounds theses and deals with issues in a scholarly fashion. The second half, which is probably of greater interest to the general reader, deals with the making of the film and with viewers' reactions to it.

Menville, Douglas, and R. Reginald. *Futurevisions: The New Golden Age of the Science Fiction Film.* Van Nuys, Calif.: Newcastle Publishing, 1985. An appreciative and well-written account of major science-fiction films, with particular emphasis on *Star Wars* and after. The book gives invaluable contextual information on the precursors to *Blade Runner.* The authors write in an undogmatic and knowledgeable style, without disdain for the merely commercial films.

Peary, Danny. *Cult Movies Three: Fifty More of the Classics, the Sleepers, the Weird, and the Wonderful.* New York: Simon & Schuster, 1988. Offbeat book discussing many films that, like *Blade Runner,* did not get much praise on first release. Includes a discussion of *Blade Runner,* with credits, synopsis, and six stills. The author is particularly indignant that critics said the film had no theme and that the characters were poorly drawn.

Philip Magnier

Cross-References

Le Voyage dans la lune Introduces Special Effects (1902), p. 57; Lang Expands the Limits of Filmmaking with *Metropolis* (1927), p. 707; *The Maltese Falcon* Establishes a New Style for Crime Films (1941), p. 1223; Kubrick Becomes a Film-Industry Leader (1964), p. 1989; The *Star Wars* Trilogy Redefines Special Effects (1977), p. 2391; *E.T.: The Extraterrestrial* Breaks Box-Office Records (1982), p. 2491.

E.T.: THE EXTRATERRESTRIAL
BREAKS BOX-OFFICE RECORDS

Category of event: Motion pictures
Time: 1982
Locale· The United States

Steven Spielberg became Hollywood's most sought-after director as a result of his science-fiction childhood fantasy, E.T.: The Extraterrestrial, *the most lucrative motion picture of the decade*

Principal personages:
STEVEN SPIELBERG (1947-   ), the director who made *E.T.*
MELISSA MATHISON (1950-   ), the screenwriter and associate producer
of *E.T.*
KATHLEEN KENNEDY (1953-   ), the coproducer of *E.T.* who encouraged Spielberg to assign the screenplay to Mathison

Summary of Event

Before 1982, Steven Spielberg was known mainly for two pictures, *Jaws* (1975), which made more than $100 million in its initial release and set a record as the highest-grossing film on record, and *Close Encounters of the Third Kind* (1977), which became a cult classic and established Spielberg's credentials in science fiction. *Raiders of the Lost Ark* (1981), which spoofed the conventions of the serial thriller, also gave evidence of Spielberg's ability to make action-adventure pictures that would appeal to mass audiences, but it was *E.T.: The Extraterrestrial* (1982) that made Spielberg Hollywood's most sought-after directing talent.

Spielberg originally intended to make a sequel to *Close Encounters*, which had earned him his first Academy Award nomination for direction. Though *E.T.* turned out to be more than simply a sequel to the earlier picture, both *Close Encounters* and *E.T.* have much in common, combining what Charles Derry has described as the typical components of Spielberg's work: "an Everyman protagonist has his conception of the world enlarged (often traumatically) as he comes face to face with some extraordinary and generally non-human antagonist who is often hidden from the rest of the world."

Spielberg first completed a story treatment entitled "Night Skies" that he assigned to John Sayles for further development in 1979. The story concerned an alien visitation to an isolated farmhouse, but the aliens as Sayles imagined them were hostile and dangerous. Production problems ensued, and Columbia Pictures eventually refused the picture because of the projected costs. Spielberg continued to rethink the idea.

The Sayles treatment involved a group of hostile aliens, but Spielberg eventually took a different approach that shifted the film's tone from terror to sentiment and that made *E.T.* a uniquely gentle monster film about a friendly alien stranded on another world. This was the conceptual stroke of genius that would enable Spielberg to create one of the best-loved pictures of all time. He had been moving toward fantasy with *Close Encounters* (which was also remarkable for its friendly aliens) and *Raiders of the Lost Ark*, but *E.T.* was to put him in a league with Walt Disney at a time when the Disney studio seemed to have lost touch with the tradition it had created.

Spielberg turned the story idea, now called "A Boy's Life," over to Melissa Mathison, who had written the screenplay for *The Black Stallion* (1979); by that time, Spielberg had shaped the idea into an encounter between children and a friendly, childlike alien stranded on earth. Kathleen Kennedy, who became his coproducer on the project, suggested that Mathison write the screenplay. Meanwhile, Universal Studios, which had backed *Jaws*, accepted the concept.

"I really wanted this movie to be about a world, a universe of children," Spielberg told his biographer Tony Crawley. "I wanted to become a child to make *E.T.*—not an adult speaking to children through adults." Given this strategy, Spielberg was fortunate to find the right cast for the picture. Ten-year-old Henry Thomas, who played Elliott, the central character, had made only one previous picture, *Raggedy Man* (1981). For Elliott's kid sister Gertie, Spielberg found six-year-old Drew Barrymore, the daughter of John Barrymore, Jr., and actress Ildiko Jaid. Sixteen-year-old Robert MacNaughton, who played Elliott's older brother, Michael, was the most experienced of the children, having had four years of work on stage. Dee Wallace played Mary, Elliott's mother, and Peter Coyote played the scientific investigator, a relatively sinister presence referred to in the credits only as "Keys."

Spielberg got composer John Williams, with whom he had worked on both *Jaws* and *Close Encounters*, to provide the music. The film's score won both an Oscar and a Grammy Award. Perhaps the most important artist in this creative collaboration, though, was the Italian sculptor Carlo Rambaldi, who had earlier worked with Spielberg on *Close Encounters*. Rambaldi had also created the monster for the remake of *King Kong* (1976), and he helped to give Spielberg's new picture its most distinctive touch. The appearance of the extraterrestrial was kept secret until the film's release, and no pictures of the creature were included in the press kits that were sent out to publicize the film.

Rambaldi worked with production designer Jim Bissell and cinematographer Allen Daviau, whose links with Spielberg went back to Spielberg's short feature *Amblin* (1968). Rounding out the creative team were Carol Littleton, the film editor, Dennis Muren, the visual effects supervisor, and Frank Marshall, the production supervisor. The film was shot at Laird International Studios in Culver City, California, and other locations in the Los Angeles area. Principal photography began on September 8, 1981, and the shooting was completed sixty-one days later.

Impact of Event

Before 1982, Spielberg had certainly established his credentials with *Jaws*, the action-adventure of *Raiders of the Lost Ark*, and the gentle metaphysics of *Close*

Encounters. He had already become a player and dealmaker in the industry. After *E.T.*, however, he became the most important director in Hollywood. He had demonstrated that he was a master of sentiment and, having made the most successful children's picture in decades, he came to be regarded as a sort of latter-day Disney. Tony Crawley and others who had studied Spielberg's career have likened *E.T.* to *Peter Pan*, and Spielberg obviously was drawn to the Peter Pan story. In 1985, Spielberg told *Time* magazine, "I have always felt like Peter Pan. It has been very hard for me to grow up." In 1992, he released *Hook*, his updating of the Peter Pan myth. *E.T.* not only opened up a new horizon of fantasy for Spielberg, but also turned him into a major celebrity.

When the film played at the Cannes Film Festival on May 26, 1982, coproducer Kathleen Kennedy told the press corps that the film had been made for $10.5 million (though in 1985 *Time* critic Richard Corliss estimated the cost at $19 million). *E.T.* went on to become an unqualified box-office success in America and took the country by storm. It set box-office records and earned Universal Studios an impressive $359,687,000 during its first run; the film was seen by an estimated two hundred million people worldwide. *E.T.* was nominated for nine Academy Awards, won four Oscars, and won the Golden Globe Award for best motion picture. The Los Angeles Film Critics named it the best film of the year and named Spielberg the year's best director. The secretary-general of the United Nations presented Spielberg with a special award, and the Writers Guild gave Melissa Mathison an award for her screenplay. *E.T.* was rereleased by Universal Pictures in 1985.

The film was a critical as well as a popular success and was hailed by many critics and reviewers as a masterpiece. The film was described variously as a "suburban psychodrama" and as a religious allegory. Critics responded to Spielberg's fable as a Christian allegory involving a ritual death, a resurrection, and an ascent into the heavens. Reviewing the film for *Commonweal*, Tom O'Brien called Spielberg a "suburban animist with a tinge of Manicheanism" and quoted Carl Jung on "The UFO as Religious Symbol." Reviewers, clearly, were generally enchanted by the picture and willing to take it seriously.

The film excelled in creating sympathy for an absurd, childlike alien visitor described by studio publicity as being "afraid, totally alone, and three million light years from home." William Kotzwinkel wrote the novelization of the *E.T.* screenplay, published by Berkley Books and G. P. Putnam's Sons, and in 1985 wrote *E.T.: The Book of the Green Planet*, which traced the creature's adventures on his trip home. The film's tag line, "E.T. phone home," immediately entered the vernacular of American popular culture.

The film made Spielberg the czar of the entertainment industry. Kathleen Kennedy and Frank Marshall, his production collaborators on the *E.T.* project, joined Spielberg to form the Amblin Entertainment enterprise, which later funded Robert Zemeckis' *Back to the Future* series. By 1992, Zemeckis, whose movies grossed more than $1 billion in North America, had even eclipsed Spielberg as a top director.

Partly, perhaps, to avoid being stereotyped as a director of fantasy films, Spielberg took on two "serious" projects after *E.T.*, adapting to cinema Alice Walker's *The Color Purple* (1985) and J. G. Ballard's *Empire of the Sun* (1987), which was named the best film of 1987 by the National Board of Review of Motion Pictures. Also in 1987, Spielberg received the Irving G. Thalberg Memorial Award from the Academy of Motion Picture Arts and Sciences, in part perhaps because the academy had snubbed *The Color Purple* but also in recognition of Spielberg's immense popular success with *E.T.*, *Jaws*, and *Raiders of the Lost Ark*. According to a 1992 survey, Spielberg's pictures produced between 1985 and 1990 had earned $726 million, indicating that his success with *E.T.* was not a fluke. Richard Corliss estimated that, before its 1985 rerelease, *E.T.* had earned $835 million on an investment of $19 million and had therefore made more money than any other film in history.

Bibliography

Corliss, Richard, et al. "I Dream for a Living." *Time*, July 15, 1985, 54-63. This cover story on the "Magician of the Movies" traces the career of "the world's most successful filmmaker." By 1985, *E.T.* had become the most successful film of all time. As a result, Spielberg remarked, people came to expect "a certain kind of film from me, a certain amount of screams and cheers and laughs and thrills." For that reason, he turned to *The Color Purple*, the "biggest challenge" of his career.

Crawley, Tony. *The Steven Spielberg Story*. London: Zomba Books, 1983. An excellent, lively, readable, and richly anecdotal survey of Spielberg's life and career through the production and popular success of *E.T.* The book provides the most complete treatment of Spielberg's early career in print, written by one who had direct access to his subject and the other talents with whom Spielberg was associated. The best source for information on *E.T.*

Derry, Charles. "Steven Spielberg." In *International Dictionary of Films and Filmmaking: Directors*, edited by Nicholas Thomas. 2d ed. Vol. 2. Chicago: St. James Press, 1991. Describes *E.T.* as a retelling of the Christ story. A perceptive digest and analysis of Spielberg's work.

Mott, Donald R., and Cheryl McAllister Saunders. *Steven Spielberg*. Boston: Twayne, 1986. The first book on Spielberg published in the United States is comprehensive but owes a great deal to Crawley's work, from which it borrows liberally. It is well researched, however, and follows Spielberg's fortunes as director and producer through 1985.

Sheehan, Henry. "The PANning of Steven Spielberg." *Film Comment* 28, no. 3 (May-June, 1992): 54-60. A critical reassessment of the "single most powerful and influential filmmaker in Hollywood," who is also criticized as being "artistically marginal." The *E.T.* creature is described as a "Pan figure reduced to an all-but-mute, walking nub." Spielberg exploits "every melancholy notion that drifts across Elliott's psyche—notably loneliness and the feeling of being abandoned—and pumps it up." Spielberg's whole career is surveyed in order to put *Hook* into perspective.

Spielberg, Steven. "Dialogue on Film." *American Film* 13 (June, 1988): 12-16. Spielberg claims that although he made *Close Encounters* and *Raiders of the Lost Ark* "to be popular," that was not the reason he made *E.T.* or *The Color Purple*. Putting his success into perspective, Spielberg notes that "*E.T.* is the biggest film of all time around the world, but the same number of people see two episodes of 'Cosby' over two weeks as have seen *E.T.* in the United States."

James M. Welsh

Cross-References

Le Voyage dans la lune Introduces Special Effects (1902), p. 57; The Classic *The Wizard of Oz* Opens (1939), p. 1109; Syndication Turns *Star Trek* into a Cult Classic (1972), p. 2260; The *Star Wars* Trilogy Redefines Special Effects (1977), p. 2391; Scott's *Blade Runner* Is a Visual Masterpiece (1982), p. 2486.

"MASTER HAROLD" . . . AND THE BOYS
EXAMINES APARTHEID

Category of event: Theater
Time: March 12, 1982
Locale: Yale Repertory Theater, New Haven, Connecticut

South African playwright Athol Fugard's play "MASTER HAROLD" . . . and the
boys *incisively probed the psychology of racism and the effects of apartheid*

Principal personages:
ATHOL FUGARD (1932-   ), a white South African playwright and di-
rector whose works have dramatized the impact of apartheid and the
psychology of racism
ZAKES MOKAE (1935-   ), a South African actor who originated the
role of Sam Semela at the Yale Repertory Theater and on Broadway
DANNY GLOVER (1947-   ), an American actor who played the role of
Willie in the original productions of the play at Yale and on Broadway
ŽELJKO IVANEK (1957-   ), an actor who originated the role of "Master
Harold" at Yale
LONNY PRICE (1959-   ), an actor who originated the role of "Master
Harold" on Broadway

Summary of Event

Set in the St. George's Park Tea Room in Port Elizabeth, South Africa, on a rainy
afternoon in 1950, *"MASTER HAROLD"* . . . *and the boys* begins as Sam Semela
and Willie Molopo, two black waiters, discuss the forthcoming ballroom dancing
championship, which Willie and his girlfriend Hilda Samuels have entered. They are
soon joined by Hally, the seventeen-year-old white boy whose mother runs the tea
room, though she is now at the hospital from which, to Hally's distress, his ill and
disabled father is soon to return home. After convincing himself that there must be
some mistake in that, Hally discusses with Sam his day at school. Soon they revert
to a long-established pattern, as Hally teaches Sam from his textbooks. A discussion
of moral reformers in history ensues, as they consider Napoleon Bonaparte, Charles
Darwin, Abraham Lincoln, William Shakespeare, Sir Alexander Fleming, Leo Tolstoy, and Jesus Christ as examples of a "man of Magnitude" in society, "intrepid
social reformer[s]" who are not "daunted by the magnitude of the task undertaken."
When Sam asks "Where's ours?," Hally can only answer that South Africa's may
not yet have been born.

Articulate and widely read, though he admits he has not understood such authors
as Darwin and Sigmund Freud, Hally is moderately precocious and clearly enjoys
his thoughtful exchanges with Sam. He is also quick-tempered, contemptuous toward
religion, and particularly disdainful toward his father, whose favorite reading mat-

ter—comic books—he dismisses as "rubbish" and "mental pollution." Hally recalls the first lesson that he and Sam shared, and Sam claims that Hally started passing his exams only in order to do better than Sam. Hally also recalls many happy times hanging around the servants' quarters. His happiest memory is a lyrically described incident in which Sam first taught Hally to make and fly a kite during an outing in a public park. Life, Hally says, has gotten "so bloody compli-- cated since then."

A telephone call from Hally's mother abruptly reveals another side of his character. Told that his father will be coming home from the hospital, Hally initially tries to assert adult-like control over the situation, disrespectfully telling his mother to order his father back to bed, since "if he's going to behave like a child, treat him like one." He is then quickly apologetic, acknowledging, childlike, his fear that she will "give in to him." Finding that he has no control over events at the hospital, he brusquely orders Willie and Sam to work.

Beginning his homework, Hally bitterly remarks on "the principle of perpetual disappointment" that he deems "a fundamental law of the universe." Assigned to write an essay on "an annual event of social or cultural significance," he is distracted by Sam and Willie's rehearsal for the dance competition. Reasserting his authority, he "gives Willie a vicious whack on the bum" with a ruler when, provoked by Sam's teasing, he disrupts Hally's concentration. After initially disdaining all dancing as unintellectual, Hally decides to write his essay about the dance competition, which Sam then describes, using its harmony and gracefulness as a metaphor for "the way we want life to be." The essay's title will be "A World Without Collisions."

With a second telephone call from the hospital, reality again intrudes, disrupting the vision of harmony and accord. Hally berates his mother, threatening to leave home and driving her to tears; when his father is put on the line, his tone changes again, offering genial encouragement to his "chum" whose release is supposedly welcome news. Emotionally distraught, Hally destroys the composition and launches into an embittered tirade on the dance floor as a shambles, "the All-Comers-How-To-Make-a-Fuckup-of-Life Championships." When Sam urges him to restrain the worst of his abuse, which cruelly derides his crippled father, Hally becomes more enraged, swearing, giving orders, and reminding Sam of his "place" as a servant and a black man. He threatens that Sam might lose his job and insists on being called "Master Harold"—not "Hally"—from now on. He then tells an ugly racist joke about "a nigger's arse"—a joke that is, he says, a favorite of his father's and his own. In response, Sam drops his pants and underpants, presenting his backside "for Hally's inspection"; after a pause, Hally spits in Sam's face. Calling Hally a coward, Sam angrily agrees to call Hally "Master Harold" and threatens to hit him, but he is restrained by Willie.

The threat of violence ebbs, though Sam tells "Master Harold" that he has been made to feel dirtier than ever in his life; it seems the lessons in compassion and common humanity that he tried to teach Hally over the years have failed. Hally confesses his love for his father, which Sam acknowledges as appropriate, notwithstanding the shame the boy also manifestly feels. Sam reveals the reason why he made Hally the kite years ago: to console the boy after an embarrassing incident involving the father's public drunkenness. He also discloses that their day in the park had to be curtailed because, under the laws of apartheid, the park bench was designated for whites' use only. Referring both to the kite and their disrupted relationship, Sam urges Hally to "try again," noting that much teaching and learning have been going on. After Hally leaves, the play ends with implicit promises of reconciliation. Willie and Sam rehearse another dance as the jukebox plays Sarah Vaughn's recording of "Little Man, You've Had a Busy Day."

Impact of Event

With the production of *"MASTER HAROLD"* . . . *and the boys*, Athol Fugard's twelfth play, the South African playwright and director offered his most personal dramatization to date of the impact of apartheid in his native land and, more broadly, of the psychology of racism in general. This three-character, one-act play was based on an autobiographical incident in which, in a moment of anger, the young white Fugard had deliberately spat in the face of Sam Semela, a black employee in his mother's boardinghouse and tea room. Semela had not only been Fugard's only friend throughout his school years but virtually a surrogate father to him, and their relationship had been one of mutual love, trust, and admiration. Fugard was instantly overcome with shame and guilt for his rash act, and the play is, on a personal level, a public act of atonement. Furthermore, it is a poignant, ironic, yet often humorous probing of the psychological impact and social underpinnings of racism, with a conclusion that offers hope for a more compassionate future.

First performed in 1982 amid mounting international pressures for political and economic sanctions against the South African government, Fugard's play provided a clear and widely accessible example of the insidious and destructive effects of apartheid in particular and of racism in general. Its seemingly simple plot belies the complexity of the relationships among the characters, and Fugard has painstakingly structured its multiple ironies, many of which are based on fundamental dualities. Thus, for example, Hally's allegiances are divided between his biological father and his spiritual father Sam, toward both of whom he feels both love and resentment. With Sam, he is both teacher and pupil; he shares his school lessons, but in many ways he learns from Sam important lessons in compassion and integrity that cannot be gleaned from books alone. Juxtaposed against Hally's relentless intellectuality, Sam's knowledge originates in the heart rather than the mind: Sam appreciates— and instructs Hally about—the beauty, emotion, and pleasure of the dance and of life itself.

Although Hally is said to be seventeen years old, he often seems prepubescent, particularly in his disavowal of any interest in the opposite sex and in some of his more immature outbursts. His character is poised between "man" and "boy," as he vacillates between expressions of fully adult authoritarianism and childlike intemperateness. The title "Master" is applicable in several ways: as a title befitting a young boy, as a synonym for "teacher," and as a term for a person in a position of politically or racially based authority. Fugard was himself considerably younger than seventeen when the actual incident took place. Presumably, the character was made older in order to cast more experienced actors in the role who would be better able to credibly convey the complexity of Hally's emotional conflicts and motivation.

The play's climactic act of violence is averted as Willie restrains Sam from striking Hally, but undercurrents of violence—much of which is socially sanctioned—pervade the play. Hally describes being beaten at school for drawing a caricature of his math teacher, but he seems eager to change the subject when Sam details the far more brutal beatings that the police routinely administer to blacks. Willie admits having beaten his erstwhile dance partner Hilda, the mother of his child; although at the end of the play he resolves not to do it again, his promise may not wholly reassure. As a black woman, Hilda—who is never seen in the play—remains its most marginalized character, doubly victimized on the basis of race and gender but having less recourse than any other victim of violence in the play.

The pervasiveness of such violence heightens the contrast between the beauty of the idealized world, which is symbolized by the dance, and the harshness of the real world, which is characterized by hostility, resentment, and racism. Similarly, the kite-flying incident lyrically evokes an idealized, idyllic world that was for Hally a time of innocence predating an awareness of racism and socially mandated injustice. That Hally will in fact grow up to be Athol Fugard (whose first name is, in fact, Harold and whose childhood nickname was Hally) is the primary basis of hope in the play's resolution, however tentative—its insistence that the climax is not an irrevocable moment of existential self-definition that it would otherwise seem to be, a portrait of the bigot as a young man.

This play, like Fugard's others, makes no overtly political or polemical statement, a fact that brought criticism from the ideological left in South Africa and elsewhere; at the same time, the South African government temporarily banned the play following its premiere in the United States. Notwithstanding such objections, *"MASTER HAROLD" . . . and the boys* stands alongside Eugene O'Neill's *Long Day's Journey into Night* (1956) as an intimately personal act of atonement, remarkable for its eloquent understatement, psychological insight, and emotional power.

Bibliography

Amato, Rob. "Fugard's Confessional Analysis: *'MASTER HAROLD' . . . and the boys.*" In *Momentum: On Recent South African Writing*, edited by M. J. Draymond, *et al.* Pietermaritzburg, South Africa: University of Natal Press, 1984. This essay begins with an account of the temporary ban on *"MASTER HAROLD" . . . and the boys* in South Africa, examines the play's climax and its autobiographical aspects, discusses the theme of hegemonic control of consciousnesses, and relates the play to Fugard's admiration of—and literary indebtedness to—Albert Camus.

Durbach, Errol. "*'MASTER HAROLD' . . . and the boys*: Athol Fugard and the Psychopathology of Apartheid." *Modern Drama* 30 (December, 1987): 505-513.

Durbach assesses the fundamental need for respect among Fugard's characters, both within the family units that typically shame his whites and within the culture that inherently humiliates blacks. He maintains that Fugard's "family history play" is not a drama of political protest per se and notes its oscillation between hope and despair.

Gussow, Mel. "Witness." *The New Yorker* 58 (December 20, 1982): 47-94. This insightful and extensive biographical profile of Fugard appeared shortly after *"MASTER HAROLD"* . . . *and the boys* was first produced on Broadway; it describes Fugard's family background, discusses the play's rehearsal process, and details the subsequent events in the relationship between Fugard and Sam Semela.

Post, Robert M. "Racism in Athol Fugard's *'MASTER HAROLD'* . . . *and the boys."* *World Literature Written in English* 30 (Spring, 1990): 97-102. This essay usefully establishes the play within the context of Fugard's other writings, South African history, and the development of apartheid. It also cites a number of reviews of the initial production.

_____. "Victims in the Writings of Athol Fugard." *Ariel: A Review of International English Literature* 16 (July, 1985): 3-17. This overview of Fugard's plays and his novel *Tsotsi* (1980) emphasizes that his characters are victims of the theory and practice of apartheid, with which they cope through dreaming and imagining. Dancing and flying birds are Fugard's recurrent symbols of escape, though madness and death provide escape for some.

Seidenspinner, Margarete. *Exploring the Labyrinth: Athol Fugard's Approach to South African Drama.* Essen: Blaue Eule, 1986. After providing chapter-length historical background on contemporary South African drama and on Fugard's career, this study focuses on his development from an "involved liberal writer" to a "courageous pessimist" and from "universalism to solitude." Appendix lists relevant historical dates and legislative measures from 1652 to 1986. Notes, list of first performances, bibliography.

Vandenbroucke, Russell. *Truths the Hand Can Touch: The Theatre of Athol Fugard.* New York: Theatre Communications Group, 1985. This excellent study of Fugard's works through *"MASTER HAROLD"* . . . *and the boys* examines the plays closely and comprehensively, paying particular attention to intellectual and historical contexts. Based on many conversations with Fugard and others, this book also includes analyses of influences, cross-currents, language, style, and critical reputation. Notes, index, bibliography.

Walder, Dennis. *Athol Fugard.* London: Macmillan, 1984. This brief introductory volume surveys Fugard's works through *"MASTER HAROLD"* . . . *and the boys* and draws on meetings, interviews, and correspondence with the playwright as well as performers, collaborators, and friends. Twelve photographs are included, with several from initial productions of the plays in South Africa and elsewhere. Notes, index.

Wells, Ronald A., ed. *Writer and Region: Athol Fugard.* Statements: Occasional Papers of the Phelps-Stokes Fund, No. 2. New York: Anson Phelps Stokes Institute for African, Afro-American, and American Indian Affairs, 1987. This forty-two page booklet contains Fugard's address to the Phelps-Stokes Institute on "Writer and Region." Essays by Karen K. Jambeck on "Images of the Land: The Drama of Athol Fugard" and by Ronald A. Wells on "Athol Fugard and South Africa" are also included.

William Hutchings

Cross-References

Heart of Darkness Reveals the Consequences of Imperialism (1902), p. 51; Wright's *Native Son* Depicts Racism in America (1940), p. 1185; *Things Fall Apart* Depicts Destruction of Ibo Culture (1958), p. 1763; Baldwin Voices Black Rage in *The Fire Next Time* (1963), p. 1929; Baraka's *Dutchman* Dramatizes Racial Hatred (1964), p. 2000.

FIERSTEIN'S *TORCH SONG TRILOGY* MEETS WITH UNEXPECTED SUCCESS

Category of event: Theater
Time: June 10, 1982
Locale: Little Theatre, New York, New York

Torch Song Trilogy, *a candid play about gay life, family mores, promiscuity, and commitment in the 1970's, received unexpected rave reviews*

Principal personages:
> HARVEY FIERSTEIN (1954-   ), a playwright and actor who unabashedly and unforgivingly brought mainstream homosexuality out of the closet in his writings
> JOHN GLINES (1933-   ), a producer and the founder of the Glines Theater, a theater dedicated to supporting works with homosexual themes
> ESTELLE GETTY (1923-   ), a stage and screen actress who played the role of Mrs. Beckoff in both the off-Broadway and Broadway versions of *Torch Song Trilogy*
> Court Miller (1952-   ), a stage actor who played the role of Ed in the Broadway version of *Torch Song Trilogy*

Summary of Event

In 1982, after four years of playing in Off- and Off-Off-Broadway houses, Harvey Fierstein's *Torch Song Trilogy* stepped onto the Broadway stage amidst thunderous applause and with two Tony Awards waiting in the wings. The playwright and lead actor Harvey Fierstein seemed to have begun his young life with a list of societal negatives; he was fat, he was Jewish, he was asthmatic, and, finally, he was gay. He had grown up in a lower-middle-class area of Brooklyn, the son of a handkerchief maker. At age thirteen, he told his parents that he was gay, but neither the revelation nor the reaction was particularly traumatic. He was what he was. At the age of sixteen, he started working as a drag queen in various East Village clubs. He had a voice like that of Tallulah Bankhead and wore costumes that rivaled Carmen Miranda's. After graduating in 1973 from Brooklyn's Pratt Institute, where he studied painting, Fierstein turned to playwriting and acting.

Fierstein strove to express himself honestly in the theater, and that included facing his sexuality head-on. Prior to Fierstein's work, realistic depictions of homosexuality on stage had been relegated to Off-Off-Broadway and drew only small audiences; mainstream portrayals of gays in the theater were typified by the abysmal stereotypes of the 1968 play *The Boys in the Band.* Gay plays often also seemed to have a soft-porn aspect to them. Fierstein longed to try something different; he wanted to write down his own life experiences, which he believed would strike a universal chord. He wanted to approach homosexuality in the theater in a brand-new way: He wanted to present homosexuals as human beings.

Torch Song Trilogy had its birth in 1978, when Ellen Stewart produced a new play by Fierstein called *International Stud* at La Mama, her Off-Off-Broadway theater. One year later, she produced his second play, *Fugue in a Nursery*. After Fierstein completed a third play, *Widows and Children First!*, John Glines, the founder of the Glines Theater, decided to produce the three plays as a trilogy with a running time of more than four hours. Fierstein would play the lead character, who would grow from a self-centered, promiscuous drag queen into a solid citizen and even an over-protective parent. The play gained momentum and found its way to the Little The-atre on Broadway, where straight as well as gay crowds flocked to see a play with universal themes. *Torch Song Trilogy* represented values that were no different than those of the heterosexual world; for gays who had been fed a diet of heterosexual movies, plays, and music, it was a particularly healthy instrument of identification.

Torch Song Trilogy unfolds at the beginning of the 1970's with *The International Stud*. Arnold Beckoff (Harvey Fierstein) is a drag performer who belts forth raspy renditions of torch songs. He becomes involved with a Brooklyn high school teacher, Ed (Court Miller), whom Arnold later learns is bisexual and who finally announces that he is marrying a woman. In *Fugue in a Nursery*, Ed's wife, Laurel (Diane Tar-leton), decides it would be very modern of her to have her husband's male ex-lover visit them at their new home in the country. Arnold arrives with a young model, Alan (Paul Joynt), and the play takes place in a giant surrealist bed in which Arnold, Ed, Laurel, and Arnold's new lover conduct a cross fire of debates, spats, and sexual intercourse enacted to a fugue. In the final part of the trilogy, *Widows and Children First!*, Arnold must fuse all the conflicts of the past five years into the present: Alan has been beaten to death by gay bashers; Arnold himself is in the process of adopting David (Fisher Stevens); Ed has left Laurel and is staying with Arnold; and, to top all this off, Arnold's mother, Mrs. Beckoff (Estelle Getty), enters the fold. Arnold is forced to balance the joys of rearing his adopted teenage boy against the torment of recycling the past with his mother, who cannot seem to accept the notion that her son's feelings for men could ever be likened to the love she had for her deceased husband. Yet, even as they quarrel, Fierstein's message is bursting forth loud and clear. While the two characters are polar opposites (mother/son, man/woman, straight/gay), they both want the same things out of life: a monogamous marriage, children, a good job, a life without prejudice and, most of all, respect.

Among the avowed homosexual playwrights, none has been more successful than Harvey Fierstein. He was the recipient of both Ford and Rockefeller playwriting grants. He has also won a Theater World Award and two Tony Awards, one for writing the year's best play, *Torch Song Trilogy*, and the other honoring him as best actor for his starring role in the play.

Fierstein's honesty and directness made *Torch Song Trilogy* a commercial success. He strove to take the pornography and the stereotypes out of the theatrical depiction of gay life. He wrote a play in which the gay hero does not commit suicide or turn away from what he comes to believe is an evil life-style. The basic themes are self-respect and the stunning realization that homosexuals can have the same moral fiber as heterosexuals.

Harvey Fierstein eventually left the role of Arnold Beckoff on Broadway to finish work on his 1983 musical version of *La Cage aux folles.* The role of Arnold Beckoff was taken over by David Garrison. Producers in more than half a dozen countries sought to purchase the film rights for *Torch Song Trilogy*; but Howard Gottfried of Hollywood won the bidding, and the film was released by New Line Cinema in 1988. The influence that Fierstein has had on homosexuality in the theater stemmed from the overwhelming success of the 1982 Broadway production of *Torch Song Trilogy.*

Impact of Event

When *Torch Song Trilogy* catapulted to success on Broadway a new trend began in gay theater and in theater in general. Producers initially had told Harvey Fierstein that audiences would never sit for more than four hours to watch the play, which they said was too homosexual. Yet Fierstein sought to prove a point: that gay writers could write from their own life experiences and still touch on universal truths. Never before had an out-of-the-closet play done so well with straight audiences.

Professional theater had always been largely composed of gay artists, but it would have been professional suicide for most to admit to their sexual preferences on the mainstream stage. In the evolving social climate of the 1970's and 1980's, though, Fierstein believed that there was no longer a need to hide sexual orientation or to find oblique ways of communicating such personal experiences in plays or films. *Torch Song Trilogy* served as a quantum leap, from the stereotyped gays in *The Boys in the Band* who strutted behind closed doors to the very outward and honest Arnold Beckoff. It ratified a new self-assertiveness of homosexuals in American pop culture. The play was so out of the closet that the producer of the play publicly thanked his coproducer, whom he also identified as his lover at the Tony Awards presentation ceremony.

Torch Song Trilogy was one of the first plays to present the homosexual life-style as unrepugnant. Values were no different in Arnold's world than they were in the heterosexual world; they simply happen to have been shared by lovers of the same sex.

Oddly enough, there had initially been a backlash from some homosexuals who were opposed to Arnold Beckoff's middle-class values such as monogamy and fidelity. With the onslaught of the Acquired Immune Deficiency Syndrome (AIDS) epidemic, however, dramatic attention was being drawn to the sexual relations among gays, and monogamy and fidelity were no longer sneered at by the homosexual community. Harvey Fierstein had a message not only for straights but for gays as well.

Fierstein's success made it easier for other gay plays and films to find backers. *Torch Song Trilogy* clearly taught that there was an audience for gay works that can cross sexual orientation barriers. When Fierstein had worked as a drag queen in his teens, he had been mocked, mugged, and arrested. He had watched his sequined peers overdose or commit suicide. The image of the drag queen, though, was about to change. While *Torch Song Trilogy* was still enjoying Broadway success, Fierstein bought the rights to the French play *La Cage aux Folles* and, after giving it a more human side, produced his second Broadway triumph: a five-million-dollar musical glorifying the drag queen. He had reworked the original French play to teach a Fierstein lesson. His George (Gene Barry) and Albin (George Hearn) were a happy, monogamous gay couple, while George's straight son, Jean-Michele (John Wiener), who sought to deny his father's life-style, and Jean-Michele's conspicuously moral prospective father-in-law were the villains. Fierstein's morality had the artistic elite in his corner. His musical gay extravaganza was composed by Jerry Herman, composer of *Hello, Dolly!* (1964) and directed by Arthur Laurents, librettist of *West Side Story* (1957). Although Fierstein was never bitter in his plays, he was finally getting his sweet revenge.

Even though *Torch Song Trilogy* had enjoyed rave Broadway reviews, Fierstein had to persevere another six years before he was able to adapt the play to the screen. It had been optioned in a number of foreign countries before Hollywood's New Line Cinema took on the project and granted Fierstein creative control. Fierstein then wrangled with a series of directors before settling on Paul Bogart. The final result from Bogart, who was best known for directing the television series *All in the Family*, was a blend of autobiography, situation comedy, and cabaret act. Ironically, in only ten years, the story had evolved into a period piece because of the absence of any mention of the AIDS epidemic. Soon, on the heels of *Torch Song Trilogy* came another gay film, *Longtime Companion* (1990), imbued with the suffering, grief, and loss of loved ones caused by the epidemic.

It was this noticeable absence of the AIDS issue, though, that was another way in which Fierstein was able to blur the lines between gay and straight. Fierstein had stated that he sought to present a picture in which homosexuals could see themselves as human beings and not as victims of a disease. By ignoring that dreaded cloud of the 1980's, he had been able to shed light on other issues rather than simply on the effect of a plague that had ravaged one of America's minority communities.

Even with the release of the film, Fierstein never backed away from the reality of gay life in the 1970's, but he did infuse the controversy with humor. A backroom bar scene in which Arnold is sodomized following his breakup with Ed is portrayed with a comic sensibility; in the scene, Arnold's only concern seems to be where to place his drink. The treatment is very much at odds with that of the English film *Prick Up Your Ears* (1987), which exposed the gritty sordidness of homosexual life in the 1950's. The contrast between the two productions reflects how much more tolerant society has become since the 1950's.

Since the success of *Torch Song Trilogy* on Broadway, many things have changed in the gay community. Harvey Fierstein, with his honesty and his humor, has shared his personal life-style with mainstream America. AIDS has also sharpened the focus on the gay community as a whole. In large cities where gay pride has become accepted since the debut of *Torch Song Trilogy*, the story seems in many ways a nostalgic period piece, something like a gay equivalent of the 1973 film *American Graffiti*.

Yet much of the contemporary honesty in film and theatrical presentations of homosexuality can be traced to the writings of Harvey Fierstein.

Bibliography

Clarke, Gerald. "Straight Talk." *Time* 119 (February 22, 1982): 70. A positive review of *Torch Song Trilogy* as it hit Broadway.

Gussow, Mel. "Fierstein's 'Torch Song.'" *New York Theatre Critics' Reviews* 44 (1983): 242. An early positive review of *Torch Song Trilogy*. Originally published in January, 1981, in *The New York Times* and reprinted in this magazine, a compilation of New York critics' reviews. Issue also includes a review by Edwin Wilson.

Kroll, Jack. "His Heart Is Young and Gay." *Newsweek* 101 (June 20, 1983): 71. Gives some background on Harvey Fierstein as a child and discusses some of his views on morality up to the time of the release of *La Cage aux Folles*.

_____. "Toujours Gay." *Newsweek* 99 (March 15, 1982): 63. Another positive review of "Torch Song Trilogy."

Wetzsteon, Ross. "*La Cage aux Folles* Comes to Broadway." *New York* 16 (August 22, 1983): 30-37. An article that traces Fierstein's life, from the early days of his career as a New York drag queen and an actor working with Andy Warhol up to the time of the release of his Broadway musical *La Cage aux Folles*.

Steven C. Kowall

Cross-References

Bernstein Joins Symphonic and Jazz Elements in *West Side Story* (1957), p. 1731; The Ford Foundation Begins to Fund Nonprofit Theaters (1957), p. 1736; Shepard's *Buried Child* Promotes Off-Broadway Theater (1978), p. 2413; Simon's *Biloxi Blues* Emphasizes Serious Themes (1984), p. 2537; Mapplethorpe's Photographs Provoke Controversy (1989), p. 2636.

USA TODAY IS LAUNCHED

Category of event: Journalism
Time: September 15, 1982
Locale: Washington, D.C.

After years of planning, Allen H. Neuharth began publication of a national general-interest daily newspaper that revolutionized newspaper design

> *Principal personages:*
> ALLEN H. NEUHARTH (1924-   ), the chairman of the Gannett newspaper chain, who was chiefly responsible for the creation of *USA Today*
> DOUGLAS MCCORKINDALE (1939-   ), the chief financial and legal officer at Gannett and a crucial adviser to Neuharth
> JOHN S. KNIGHT (1894-1981), the head of the Knight newspaper chain, who was responsible for starting Neuharth in newspaper management
> PAUL MILLER (1906-   ), the head of the Gannett newspaper chain who recruited Neuharth

Summary of Event

The ceremony for the launching of *USA Today* on September 15, 1982, reflected the vision and drive of the newspaper's founder, Allen H. Neuharth. At the ceremony, President Ronald Reagan, Speaker of the House of Representatives Tip O'Neill, and Senate Majority Leader Howard Baker were joined by hundreds of other dignitaries under a tent in view of the capitol building and the Washington Monument.

The event, celebrating the first day of publication for the national general-circulation daily newspaper, was monumental too. No publisher in the United States had attempted such a feat before, and Neuharth was determined to gain a circulation of one million for his newspaper within a year. Not only did he succeed in making *USA Today* the most widely read newspaper in the country, but he also in the process revolutionized newspaper design.

Neuharth's quest had begun in earnest thirty years earlier, during his first newspaper venture, but Neuharth's boyhood contained the seeds of his phenomenal success. Reared in rural South Dakota, Neuharth lost his father at age two; he, his brother, and their mother struggled to make ends meet. Neuharth's business education came from his early life of hardship.

Bitten in high school by the newspaper bug and trained in newswriting by a stint with Associated Press, Neuharth in 1952 started *SoDak Sports*, a statewide sports newspaper. By the time Neuharth was thirty, the under-capitalized paper had failed. He later considered this failure a stroke of luck; from it, he learned early that he must build gradually for any such venture in the future.

He next became a reporter at the *Miami Herald*, learning how to manage people and pass up short-term gains for long-term possibilities with the Knight newspaper chain.

Executives at the small Gannett newspaper chain lured Neuharth away, and soon he convinced top management to let him try opening a new paper in the rich Sun Coast market near Cape Canaveral, Florida, where the space race was under way.

Planning for *Florida Today* took place in secret; the bright layout and upbeat editorial approach would reflect the readership—well-educated, well-paid, forward-looking. If readers loved the paper, Neuharth reasoned, advertising would follow. Many of the design features he devised would reappear in *USA Today*. *Florida Today*, first published in 1966, was an immediate success that paved the way for Neuharth's ultimate goal: a new national-circulation daily.

During the 1970's, Neuharth became Gannett's chief executive officer, and the company acquired forty-six newspapers. The operating profits provided the foundation for *USA Today*. Using $1 million in company research money, Neuharth early in 1980 initiated the "Project NN" (for "new newspaper") task force in strict secrecy to assess the technical, financial, and editorial challenges. That autumn, his board of directors allocated $3.5 million for prototype production. Planning became more intense.

Neuharth used loaned reporters and other staff from Gannett papers for prototype production. This kept costs down, although start-up costs for *USA Today* ultimately ran to $300 million.

The scope of the project was huge, even before *USA Today* was ready to be unveiled to the Gannett board of directors pending their final approval. For Neuharth had to go beyond technical questions to philosophical considerations: He wanted a newspaper that would compete not only with other papers but also with television; he wanted a newspaper that would appeal to the mobile American public that considered the whole nation its home (Neuharth had in mind statistics showing that the United States had 850,000 air travelers daily, 1.75 million people staying in motels and hotels daily, and 100 million people who moved within a span of ten years).

New satellite and facsimile-transmission technology was crucial to the enterprise—and so was the far-flung Gannett empire, with its dozens of printing plants nationwide. Pages could be transmitted by satellite to local plants, where production and distribution could begin; distribution would require thousands of drivers to reach a hoped-for 105,000 outlets.

Details such as the new paper's vending boxes were important; *USA Today*'s vending boxes were designed to mimic a television screen in order to appeal to readers' viewing instincts. Color, not yet a newspaper staple, would be used lavishly—and this presented technical challenges. Perfect four-color alignment had to be identical at all printing outlets. Before Neuharth got his board's final approval of the project in December of 1981, two-week dry runs were conducted, including delivery, and 4,500 influential Americans were polled for their opinions of the new publication.

Between December, 1981, and the launch date the next fall, reporters had to learn a new writing style to conform to Neuharth's view that readers wanted short, upbeat, informative, and unopinionated stories. Almost all the paper's employees put in grueling twelve-to-fifteen hour days as they prepared for the paper's launch.

The first front page was controversial and signaled *USA Today*'s independence. Instead of leading with a story covering the death of Lebanese president Bashir Gemayel, as many establishment newspapers did that day, Neuharth's editors chose to feature stories about the death of Monaco's Princess Grace and an optimistic twist on an airline crash. These stories, the editors felt, had more reader appeal.

The first day's paper, distributed in the Washington-Baltimore area, sold out; within seven months, *USA Today* had reached the one-year goal of one million circulation. Over the next two years, production began at other Gannett plants; in 1986, the paper's production went international. At the fifth anniversary of the paper's launch, *USA Today* first turned a profit, although losses continued and reached some $800 million.

Impact of Event

Ten years after *USA Today* first appeared on newsstands, nearly every big-city newspaper in the United States—and many smaller papers—showed its influence, both in graphic design and in news coverage.

In a period when newspapers were rapidly going out of business, Allen H. Neuharth gambled that he could be successful with a new national newspaper. He succeeded by appealing to readers of the television generation on their own terms. Neuharth once described the approach that became so widely imitated: "It communicates with the reader on a personal level, very quickly, clearly, and directly in an upbeat, exciting, positive environment. It's giving the readers information that they want and need in order to form their own opinions."

That meant shorter articles than readers were used to; separate sections for news, business, sports, and entertainment; lots of graphs, charts, boxes, and other visual treats; color used lavishly, including in advertisements; and an upbeat slant on news and headlines. The *USA Today* approach meant that women and minorities were featured on every page if possible; after all, this was a paper for the whole nation, not merely for white males. Neuharth later wrote that he wanted "a newspaper so different, so advanced in design and appearance and content that it would pull the rest of the industry into the twenty-first century, albeit kicking and screaming."

Many in the news industry were quick to ridicule *USA Today*'s appearance. They called it "McPaper," implying that it was like junk food: attractive and tasty but without substance. However, after *USA Today*'s circulation shot up and some large papers began to suffer in consequence, newspaper executives all over the country began to imitate its style. *The Washington Post*, the *Pittsburgh Post-Gazette*, the *Miami Herald*, the *Chicago Sun-Times*, *Newsday*, the *Richmond Times-Dispatch*, the *Dallas Morning News*, the *San Francisco Examiner*, the *Baltimore Sun*, even *The New York Times*—all of these and more had to reexamine their treatment of news or risk a continued slide. In response, some newspapers improved their use of color and graphics, some shortened their stories and made better use of indexes to guide readers to the news, some imitated *USA Today*'s giant weather maps, some made their business coverage easier to follow, and some improved their sports reporting.

USA Today had made a giant leap in the reporting of sports scores and statistics. The immense investment that Gannett's many newspapers made in computer and cable technology just before *USA Today* was launched meant that *USA Today* was hooked directly into the databanks of major sports organizations. One commentator said that the depth of sports reporting in the new paper came from the accumulated effect of thousands of statistics together, rather than from several long stories.

Newspaper operations—not merely newspaper appearance—changed too once *USA Today* began publication. Neuharth had never forgotten the deep sense of injustice he had felt as a youngster when he saw women, including his mother, badly paid and badly treated. He knew the same treatment was often accorded to black and Hispanic workers, and he became an aggressive booster of affirmative action hiring and promotion, not only at *USA Today* but throughout the Gannet newspaper chain as well.

Although the newspaper industry as a whole had a poor record of minority hiring and of allowing women and minority group members to progress into management positions, Gannett was a beacon. Neuharth even tied executive pay raises to success in meeting equal employment opportunity goals ("Even the most chauvinistic of our male managers got the message when it hit their pocketbooks," he wrote). In 1988, *USA Today* had a workforce that was fifty-one percent female; forty-one percent of the paper's management positions were filled by women, and fourteen percent were filled by members of minority groups. In Gannett broadcast operations, nearly a third of general managers were women in 1988 and about twenty percent were minority group members. All this took place while some of the nation's most influential news organizations, including the Associated Press and *The New York Times*, were losing discrimination cases in court.

USA Today created a new class of reporter, the graphic journalist, who rushes to an event—even a rock concert—armed with a portable computer and sophisticated software to create visual images of the news. When Neuharth ordered Gannett printing plants around the country to upgrade their facilities to handle high-tech printing requirements, he knew that even if *USA Today* folded, the company would benefit from the investment. While the national paper did not turn out to be as immediately profitable as he hoped, the chain as a whole continued to perform well for stockholders.

Reception of *USA Today* and the changes it inspired has not, however, been wholly positive. Some critics, notably Ben Bagdikian, have argued that chain ownership of news outlets eats away at the vitality of a democratic society. Bagdikian has written that Gannett, the largest news chain in the United States, uses its monopoly position in many cities to strangle local reporting in favor of cheaper, centralized national coverage. As a consequence, he has alleged, Gannett profits continue even as voter participation falls.

Bibliography

Bagdikian, Ben. *The Media Monopoly.* Boston: Beacon Press, 1990 Classic study of the effects of concentrated media ownership on democracy. Discusses newspaper chain behavior, including that of Gannett. Lists inside sources of business information; index. Valuable counterpoint to Neuharth's book discussed below.

Emery, Edwin, and Michael Emery. *The Press and America: An Interpretative History of the Mass Media.* Englewood Cliffs, N.J.: Prentice-Hall, 1992. History of the news industry in America. Seven hundred densely written pages include charts and illustrations concerning dynamics of profits, technology, and news groups. Separate bibliography for each of twenty-one chapters.

Lee, Martin A., and Norman Solomon. *Unreliable Sources: A Guide to Detecting Bias in News Media.* New York: Carol, 1990. Highly critical, far-ranging work that discusses the dark side of the news industry. Appendices guide reader to media ownership groups, alternative media, and journalism organizations.

Moen, Daryl R. *Newspaper Layout and Design.* Ames: Iowa State University Press, 1984. Author shows how *USA Today* has changed assumptions about newspaper operations, particularly through its use of so-called graphic journalists.

Neuharth, Allen H. *Confessions of an S.O.B.* New York: Doubleday, 1989. Breezy, confidential tone reflects Neuharth's own gung-ho style. First-hand account of a lifetime spent working toward the launching of Neuharth's national newspaper.

Prichard, Peter. *The Making of McPaper.* Kansas City, Mo.: Andrews, McMeel & Parker, 1987. The definitive history of the founding of *USA Today*, this commissioned work describes the high-pressure atmosphere surrounding the paper's birth. Numerous photos of staff members, charts, and *USA Today* pages.

Nan K. Chase

Cross-References

The Christian Science Monitor Is Founded (1908), p. 209; Lippmann Helps to Establish *The New Republic* (1914), p. 385; Wallace Founds *Reader's Digest* (1922), p. 549; Luce Founds *Time* Magazine (1923), p. 577; Luce Launches *Life* Magazine (1936), p. 1031; McLuhan Probes the Impact of Mass Media on Society (1964), p. 1973; *60 Minutes* Becomes the First Televised Newsmagazine (1968), p. 2136.

THRILLER MARKS MICHAEL JACKSON'S
MUSICAL COMING-OF-AGE

Categories of event: Music; television and radio
Time: December, 1982
Locale: Los Angeles, California

With the release of his album Thriller, *Michael Jackson completed his transformation from a child prodigy into one of the most powerfully talented figures in American popular culture*

Principal personages:
MICHAEL JACKSON (1958-   ), the singer, songwriter, and dancer who dominated popular music in the early 1980's
QUINCY JONES (1933-   ), the trumpeter, bandleader, and songwriter who produced Jackson's most famous records
BERRY GORDY, JR. (1929-   ), the Motown Records founder who signed the Jackson Five and persuaded Michael Jackson to perform on a Motown television special
JACKIE (1951-   ), TITO (1953-   ), MARLON (1957-   ), and JERMAINE (1954-   ) JACKSON, the four other members of the hit-making Motown group the Jackson Five, who toured together in the wake of *Thriller's* massive success

Summary of Event

By the beginning of the 1980's, Michael Jackson had evolved from an instinctive child performer on Jackson Five songs such as "ABC" and "I Want You Back" into a highly self-conscious pop craftsman who had enjoyed considerable chart success with his 1979 album *Off the Wall*. That album, which spawned the hits "Don't Stop 'til You Get Enough" and "Rock With You," brought Jackson an entirely new audience, selling seven million copies and giving him the confidence and artistic freedom to pursue his next project.

In 1982, Jackson began assembling a production team in Los Angeles for a new album. Like *Off the Wall*, the record would be produced by Quincy Jones, with whom Jackson had begun working during the making of the 1978 film version of the Broadway musical *The Wiz*. Jackson, however, intended to have greater input this time around. In addition to acting as coproducer, he also wrote many of the songs, among them "Wanna Be Startin' Somethin'" and "Billie Jean." When Jones coaxed Jackson to round out the emerging collection with a solid rock and roll song, Jackson wrote "Beat It," a critique of gang violence. The two enlisted Eddie Van Halen, the virtuoso guitarist of the heavy-metal band Van Halen, to contribute a solo. Jackson was also able to draw on the talents of former Beatle Paul McCartney, who agreed to sing a duet with Jackson for "The Girl Is Mine."

Though it was not regarded as the strongest song on the album, Jackson released

"The Girl Is Mine" as the first single in late 1982, since the pairing of two major stars would attract radio attention. It was not until the release of "Billie Jean" in early 1983 that it became apparent to many that Jackson was offering more than mere pop pap. With its dark lyrics about illegitimate children and the sinuous rhythms of its bass line and percussion, "Billie Jean" catapulted *Thriller*—and Jackson—to new levels of critical attention.

Jackson then made the unorthodox decision of releasing "Beat It" with "Billie Jean" still on the charts. Despite concern that the two songs would cancel each other out, they ended up in the top ten at the same time. "The Girl Is Mine," "Billie Jean," and "Beat It" were followed in short order by "Wanna Be Startin' Somethin'," "Human Nature," "P.Y.T. (Pretty Young Thing)," and "Thriller." *Off the Wall* had been the first album in popular music history to generate four top-ten singles on *Billboard* magazine's charts; *Thriller* generated seven. The album spent twenty-one weeks on top of the album chart, went on to sell more than forty million copies worldwide, and became the best-selling album of all time.

Music, though, was only one part of the *Thriller* phenomenon. Another important component was video. In 1981, a new television network, Music Television (MTV), made its debut. MTV quickly established itself as an extraordinarily popular and influential medium for introducing new acts to the American public. Among the beneficiaries of this development were British performers, who were long familiar with video and who had product on hand to supply MTV's heavy demand. Acts such as Culture Club, Duran Duran, and Australia's Men at Work quickly became inhabitants of the American pop charts.

MTV, however, avoided music videos by African Americans. Some critics charged racism; MTV executives claimed that black music simply was not popular enough to justify airplay. Whatever the reason, the success of *Thriller* was simply too obvious to be ignored. Jackson's first video, for "Billie Jean," featured an arresting set and some electrifying dancing. "Beat It," which Jackson paid for himself, included elaborate choreography and a dramatic story line. With "Thriller," which Jackson again financed himself, he stretched the boundaries of the form. Shot on film rather than videotape, and directed by noted director John Landis, "Thriller" was less a music video than a short film. Packaged with a documentary about the production of the piece, *The Making of Thriller* became the best-selling music video of all time, and buoyed Jackson's musical success. At one point in 1984, he was selling a million records a week.

Other events kept the Jackson juggernaut rolling. On May 16, 1983, Motown Records celebrated its twenty-fifth anniversary with a television gala. Though Jackson had long since left behind the paternalistic strictures of the company, he agreed to perform on the show. His rendition of "Billie Jean," accompanied by a widely remarked-upon dance step called the "moonwalk," won accolades from Fred Astaire and Gene Kelly and introduced Jackson into the homes of millions of Americans previously unfamiliar with his work. The performance (which was soon sold on video) became part of television lore, comparable to Elvis Presley's and the Beatles' appearances on *The Ed Sullivan Show.*

With *Thriller* finally fading from the charts, Jackson turned to other projects. In the summer of 1984, he reunited with his brothers to record *Victory.* The album and subsequent tour proved to be a disappointment, however; the record sold below expectations, and the family came in for criticism in the black community for the high price of tickets, which effectively denied access to the tour to much of the Jacksons' most important constituency. In 1985, Jackson helped raise millions for famine relief in Africa when he and Lionel Richie cowrote "We Are the World," a benefit record on which dozens of famous pop stars appeared. The following year, he teamed up with directors George Lucas and Francis Ford Coppola to appear in *Captain EO*, a three-dimensional video shown at Walt Disney theme parks.

Jackson's follow-ups to *Thriller*, though impressive, did not match its success. His 1987 album *Bad* sold more than seventeen million copies and generated six hit singles—an impressive performance, but far from record-breaking. *Dangerous*, released in 1991 after Jackson signed a precedent-shattering contract with Sony Music, was widely viewed as a disappointment. It remained to be seen whether he—or anyone else—can again scale the heights of success attained by *Thriller.* In so raising the stakes, though, Jackson became the standard by which all performers, including himself, would be measured.

Impact of Event

In the 1980's, Michael Jackson played a role in popular music comparable to the one Elvis Presley played in the 1950's and the Beatles played in the 1960's. Like those figures, he sold unprecedented amounts of records and became an industry force in his own right; like them, he maintained a presence in other media, a presence that reinforced his musical supremacy and introduced him to other audiences; and like them, too, he influenced much of the music that followed, ranging from the lightweight pop of DeBarge to the more aggressive (and interesting) work of Jackson's own sister Janet.

Perhaps the most important trait Michael Jackson shared with Presley and the Beatles, however, was a powerful ability to synthesize varied strains in popular musical culture and present them in highly original ways. In rock-and-roll history, this has usually meant fusing black and white musical styles, and Jackson is no exception. While Presley and the Beatles translated and manipulated African American culture for largely white consumption, though, Jackson began his career immersed in black music and has largely shaped it on his own terms. To be sure, he has received criticism for pandering to white audiences, and he has—perhaps deservedly—lost some respect in the eyes of the black musical community for the saccharine qualities that have marred his work. Jackson's life-style choices, and the rumors that have surrounded them, have also raised questions about his judgment. Yet it would be difficult to question his mastery of gospel, rhythm-and-blues, or rock-and-roll idioms, or the often-astounding grace and charisma that have characterized his taped performances.

Thriller is a pivotal record in pop music history, because it both caused and reflected the racial convergence of American popular music in the 1980's. By the late 1970's, black urban music was largely segregated on its own radio stations, while white rock and roll, which drew much of its early vitality from African American music, was increasingly distanced from it. In restricting broadcasts of black performers, MTV was merely emulating the dominant assumptions governing the radio industry. Jackson's success in attracting listeners across race, class, and gender lines helped demonstrate the efficacy of a contemporary hit radio format that created a vast new center in popular music. The subsequent success of performers such as Prince, Tina Turner (who made a celebrated comeback in 1984-1985), and Tracy Chapman demonstrated the commercial and cultural potential for black performers interested in musically bridging the races.

Perhaps the best example of this in Jackson's own work is "Beat It." Marked by the hypnotic rhythmic grooves that have become Jackson's trademark, the song gained added heft from Eddie Van Halen's guitar work, which appealed to millions of white adolescents only vaguely aware of heavy-metal rock's debt to the blues. In so doing, Jackson enhanced white receptivity to other performers, including Prince, who recaptured the black flavor in rock and roll that had ebbed ever since Jimi Hendrix's death in 1970.

Thriller is also a compendium of popular cultural phenomena. Horror films (the title track); the pleasures and dangers of nightlife ("Wanna Be Startin' Somethin'" and "Billie Jean"); traditional romance ("Baby Be Mine" and "The Lady in My Life"); and philosophical meditation ("Human Nature") are among the themes, with influences ranging from James Brown to Vincent Price (who provides a voice-over for "Thriller"). Perhaps it was inevitable that Jackson would go on to make a video for Disney World; he so thoroughly imbibed American culture that in many ways he came to embody it.

Jackson's other major achievement stemming from *Thriller* concerns video. In addition to breaking the color barrier on MTV, he also demonstrated the visual possibilities of the form and raised it to new levels of artistry. By retaining financial control over his work, he retained creative control as well, and he was able to enlist some of the most important directors in the television and film industries to shoot his videos. "Billie Jean," "Beat It," and "Thriller" remain classics of the form and went a long way toward consolidating the legitimacy—and profitability—of MTV.

The years following the release of *Thriller* witnessed a slow but steady ebbing of Jackson's artistic and commercial power. Inevitably, success on the scale he achieved engendered some backlash, and his personal and social isolation made his work seem less in touch with musical currents. This is especially evident in the rise of rap into musical prominence, a form which makes *Thriller* seem dated and which Jackson does not seem able to perform with much conviction. Certainly, he has continued to write engaging songs, such as his 1988 hit "Smooth Criminal." Little of his work has had lasting thematic significance, however, and all too often Jackson lapses into banality in trying to write inspiring songs, as the titles of "Heal the World" and "Keep the Faith" suggest. Moreover, while he had his usual share of hits from

Dangerous (1991)—including "Black or White," "Remember the Time," and "In the Closet"—the almost frenetic collage of styles contained in those songs gave the impression that Jackson was trying to chase down an audience rather than lead (or better yet, create) one.

Yet none of this can erase *Thriller*. Without it, Jackson would be considered an important figure in contemporary popular music. Because of it, he has earned consideration as a major American artist of the late twentieth century.

Bibliography

Hirshey, Gerri. "Michael Jackson: Life in the Magic Kingdom." *Rolling Stone* 389 (February 17, 1983): 10-11. The only interview Jackson granted after the release of *Thriller*. Hirshey, the author of *Nowhere to Run: The Story of Soul Music* (1985) gets as close as anyone ever has to her notoriously reclusive subject. An excerpt from this interview was also published in *Rolling Stone* issue 632 (June 11, 1992).

Jackson, Michael. *Moonwalk*. New York: Doubleday, 1988. Hardly a candid, in-depth autobiography, but revealing in its own way. What Jackson does choose to say often reflects badly on him, suggesting a thin skin, questionable judgment, and a crass obsession with success measured by numbers. Most useful as an account of the making of Jackson's records and his other projects.

Taborelli, J. Randy. *Michael Jackson: The Music and the Madness*. New York: Ballantine, 1992. A little heavy on the gossip, and a little light on the music. A full-length critical biography of Jackson awaits; in the meantime, this tawdry book will have to do.

Tucker, Ken. "Rock in the Video Age." In *Rock of Ages: The Rolling Stone History of Rock and Roll* by Ed Ward, Geoffrey Stokes, and Ken Tucker. New York: Rolling Stone Press, 1986. A good brief account of the birth of video and Jackson's place in it. See also Tucker's chapter on what he calls the "Black Rock Revival," in which Jackson was a participant.

White, Timothy. "Michael Jackson." In *Rock Lives: Profiles and Interviews*. New York: Henry Holt, 1990. This interview, conducted in 1977, provides an interesting glimpse into Jackson's state of mind on the eve of his adulthood. White's introduction, written in 1989, helps place it, and Jackson's subsequent work, in perspective.

Jim Cullen

Cross-References

Berry's "Maybellene" Popularizes Rock and Roll (1955), p. 1635; Presley Becomes a Rock-and-Roll Sensation (1956), p. 1705; Gordy Founds Motown Records (1959), p. 1790; The Beatles Revolutionize Popular Music (1963), p. 1944; Brown Wins a Grammy for "Papa's Got a Brand New Bag" (1966), p. 2059; Wonder Releases *Innervisions* (1973), p. 2294; *The Wiz* Brings African-American Talent to Broadway (1975), p. 2334; *Saturday Night Fever* Epitomizes the Disco Craze (1977), p. 2386; Rap Goes Platinum with Run-D.M.C.'s *Raising Hell* (1986), p. 2582.

LAURIE ANDERSON'S *UNITED STATES* POPULARIZES PERFORMANCE ART

Category of music: Music
Time: 1983
Locale: New York, New York

Laurie Anderson performed her mixed-media song cycle United States I-IV, *an early example of performance art that featured sharp commentary on modern technology and American life .*

Principal personage:
>   LAURIE ANDERSON (1947-   ), a performer, poet, songwriter, and violinist from New York's SoHo arts community who helped to popularize performance art

Summary of Event

When she first emerged from the welter of minor instant celebrities in New York's SoHo artistic community to claim a national audience early in 1983, Laurie Anderson was greeted with enthusiasm by punk rockers and serious avant-garde musicians alike. Onstage for the performance of her mixed-media spectacular *United States I-IV*, Anderson cultivated a distinctly androgynous appearance. In an undersized black suit punctuated by an improbable spiky punk haircut, she might have passed for Stan Laurel on his lunch hour, a refugee from a Samuel Beckett play, or even a barely repressed anarchist about to detonate a bomb. Her first semiotic message to her audience was disturbing, sexually ambivalent, and highly complicated.

In her performance of *United States*, Anderson was cryptic, understated, and emotionally neutral as she dispassionately rattled off apocalyptic horrors in the lines of her songs while disturbing slide images were projected behind her. In the mixture of conservative exaltation and liberal frustration that characterized the early years of the Ronald Reagan presidency, Anderson's statements oddly captured the ambivalence of the American electorate: eager for conformity and control yet outraged and hungry for radical change. Amid the onstage clutter of instruments, she moved deftly from a Vocoder (a synthesizer that raised and lowered her voice by several octaves, allowing her to utter growls and birdlike squawks) to an electronic violin and some of her own inventions, such as a tape bow that emitted shrill and occasionally angelic sounds as it swept the strings of her violin.

The imagery of Anderson's poetry was despairing but was delivered in a deadpan, unprotesting manner. Her poetry was filled with pilotless planes about to crash, with shopping malls and drive-in banks covering the earth's surface, and with mothers who provide telephone answering machines as woefully inadequate substitutes for maternal warmth. Anderson reveals a world of vulgar materialism and a pointless obsession with technological development. Peopled by emotional cripples and ideological conformists, Anderson's poetic world is devoid of grand emotional gestures or sensitive interaction; it is appropriate that there are no soaring melodies in her songs, only shards and fragments.

Anderson became improbably popular on the basis of her hit "O Superman" and her subsequent full-length album, *Big Science* (1982). Her work had significant implications for rock and "minimalist" music. From rock, she took the beat that has been the invariable staple of popular music since the 1940's. From the politicized rock and folk music of the 1960's, she took a deep social concern. The clear message of her music, when combined with slides of human degradation and nuclear warfare, is a deeply pessimistic, apocalyptic view. She is also indebted to such musical minimalists as Terry Riley, Steve Reich, and Philip Glass, with their obsessive repetitions of harmonic triads in deliberate, unprogressive patterns. Like the minimalists, she preferred the repetitions of Javanese and African music for harmonic development or melodic interest. Her music for *United States* was a trancelike, hypnotic combination of theme and sound.

"O Superman" depicted America as a mad, heartless, plasticized mother eager to crush her children with destructive technology: "So hold me, Mom, in your long arms. Your petrochemical arms, your military arms. In your electronic arms." Ironically, "O Superman" is subtitled "For Massenet," presumably as a gesture of homage to Jules Massenet, the nineteenth century French composer of such operas as *Manon* (1884) and *Werther* (1892), distinguished by their arching, heartfelt melodic expressions of love and desire. "O Superman," though, like the songs of *United States* generally, gains its effect on the listener by its shocking inability to reach out or connect into healthy emotional wholes. It is as if Anderson were a battered child of a cruel culture. Her songs deal with failed gestures of communication: "I don't understand the languages. I hear only your sound." In the absence of love, political tyranny and impersonal maternal authority fill the vacuum created by the failure of love: "When love is gone, there's always justice. And when justice is gone, there's always force. And when force is gone, there's always Mom. Hi Mom!" Anderson's poetic America is presided over by a smiling, cruel, manipulative, plasticine mother. Anderson's future was not an Orwellian nightmare of ruthless bureaucratization but a horrific vision of the impersonalization that accompanies material prosperity and technological progress.

Impact of Event

Later performance artists, from the pop icon Madonna to the feminist protester Karen Finley, owe a major debt to Laurie Anderson, who rescued performance art from the lofts of the East Village in New York and found a national audience for her distinctive brand of social commentary. Although best remembered as a visual artist and creator of a striking stage persona, Anderson merged audacious visual and lighting techniques with a distinctive musical voice and poetic commentary and even briefly worked her way onto the popular music charts.

It would have been difficult for Anderson to keep a large audience for such a complicated work as *United States*. It would be difficult to describe the Anderson of *United States* as a feminist, since the women depicted by her songs are scarcely more caring or less obsessive than the male figures. In the "It Tango," a man and woman hurl crisp, truncated slogans at each other instead of needed, healing confessions: "He said: Isn't it. Isn't it just. Isn't it just like a woman. She said: It's hard. It's just hard. It's just kind of hard to say." Anderson's America was obsessed with meaningless commandments and prohibitions, and Anderson could thus be seen to concur with the popular will, as expressed in the Reagan mandate, to get government off people's backs. As an impersonal stewardess' voice explains in one of Anderson's songs, "We are about to attempt a crash landing. Please extinguish all cigarettes . . . Put your hands over your eyes. Jump out of the plane."

In his chapter on Anderson in *All American Music: Composition in the Late Twentieth Century* (1984), John Rockwell speaks admiringly of Anderson's roots in the loft-art community of New York's SoHo and the antecedents of Anderson's brand of performance art in Dada, surrealism, 1960's "happenings," and rock. Rockwell notes how Anderson first earned attention by performing familiar gestures in unusual situations—such as playing her violin while encased in a block of ice. Like many efficient mixed-media artists, she wrote poetry, recorded songs, and provided SoHo galleries with conceptual installations; Rockwell comments that Anderson "presents a landscape of the ordinary made extraordinary through unexpected juxtaposition."

The program notes for one of Anderson's performances described *United States* as "The *Ring of the Nibelungen* of our time." Even the most shameless of performance artists, which Anderson was not, would have been uncomfortable with such hype. For one thing, Anderson would have needed to display a wider range of human emotions before she could lay claim to the mantle of Richard Wagner as artist and social critic. Wagner, who was famed for his skill in composing soaring, expansive melody, would certainly not have been impressed by Anderson's stunted, malnourished fragments of tunes.

Like the pop artists Christo, Robert Rauschenberg, Andy Warhol, and Jeff Koon, Anderson clearly kept her eye on the flotsam and jetsam and trash of modern culture. When blown up to gigantic proportions, a simple three-pronged wall socket (used as the sleeve jacket photo for the *Big Science* album and as one of the slide projections in *United States*) looks like a despairing divine image from an abandoned temple.

Despite the exaggerated claims about the Wagnerian depth and complexity of Anderson's artistry, her material was characterized by a very narrow range and quality. It was hard, while admiring Anderson's work, to be certain whether her pessimism was deeply felt or merely a hip concession to her audience. Certainly, her suspicions about the cold, manipulative intentions of the maternal figures she depicts would not sit well with most 1990's feminists. In 1983, *United States I-IV* came as a breath of fresh air, as a distinctive and disturbing voice; from a longer perspective, though, Anderson seems like a figure in direct line of succession from 1960's happenings and the insular SoHo tradition of self-certifying avant-garde art.

Ironically, Anderson's own stage image—the apparently repressed, sardonic personality trapped out with Nordic good looks, a too-small black suit, and spiky haircut—rather than her visual, poetic, and musical skills, may have been her greatest contribution to performance art. Her image contributed to the public personae of such distinctive figures as Madonna and Pee Wee Herman. The ambiguity and fierce intelligence of Laurie Anderson made her a memorable figure in performance art for a small but loyal audience in the 1980's.

Bibliography

Goldberg, RoseLee. *Performance: Live Art 1909 to the Present.* New York: Harry N. Abrams, 1979. Surveys performance art of the twentieth century.

Kardon, Janet, ed. *Laurie Anderson: Works from 1969 to 1983.* Philadelphia: University of Pennsylvania Press, 1983. This catalog is an early collection of writings and information about Anderson.

Nelson, Byron. "A Disturbing Voice." *Pittsburgh Magazine* (December, 1982): 77-78. Responds to the excitement generated by Anderson's tour with *United States,* emphasizing her poetry and her stage manner.

Pareles, Jon, and Patricia Romanowski, eds. *The Rolling Stone Encyclopedia of Rock and Roll.* New York: Rolling Stone Press, 1983. Offers a useful brief recap of Anderson's career through *Big Science.* Helpful for placing her work in a broader pop-music context.

Rockwell, John. *All-American Music: Composition in the Late Twentieth Century.* New York: Vintage, 1984. Devotes a chapter to Anderson and the emerging performance art phenomenon. A generous survey of the varieties of serious American music, from academic serial composers to jazz, rock, and salsa bands. Provides a provocative snapshot of musical life in the early 1980's.

Byron Nelson

Cross-References

Duchamp's "Readymades" Challenge Concepts of Art (1913), p. 349; The Dada Movement Emerges at the Cabaret Voltaire (1916), p. 419; Minimalism Emphasizes Objects as Art (1963), p. 1949; Dylan Performs with Electric Instruments (1965), p. 2038; Warhol's *The Chelsea Girls* Becomes a Commercial Success (1966), p. 2053; New York's SoHo Develops into a Center for Contemporary Art (1970's), p. 2191; Christo Wraps the Pont Neuf (1985), p. 2548.

FESTIVALS MARK A PEAK IN THE DANCE CREATED BY BLACK ARTISTS

Category of event: Dance
Time: 1983-1984
Locale: The United States

A series of festivals on both the East and West coasts focused on black dance forms and black dance artists through films, seminars, lectures, and performances of choreography

Principal personages:

ALVIN AILEY (1931-1989), a leading exponent of American modern dance whose work was featured at the Dance Black America festival

TALLEY BEATTY (C. 1923-   ), an American modern dancer and choreographer whose work was performed at the Dance Black America festival

CHUCK DAVIS (1937-   ), a choreographer who staged the DanceAfrica festival and participated in Dance Black America in New York and the Festival Africa in North Carolina

ARTHUR HALL (1934-   ), an American dancer and choreographer whose work was performed as part of the Dance Black America festival

ARTHUR MITCHELL (1934-   ), the artistic director of the Dance Theater of Harlem, which performed at the Olympic Black Dance Festival in Los Angeles

GARTH FAGAN (1940-   ), a Jamaican-born dancer and choreographer who performed at the Dance Black America festival

CHARLES MOORE (1938-   ), an American modern and theatrical dancer who performed the work of Asadata Dafora at the Dance Black America festival

ASADATA DAFORA (1890-1965), a dancer and choreographer originally from Sierra Leone whose work was featured at the Dance Black America festival

ELEO POMARE (1937-   ), an American modern dancer and choreographer who was featured at the Dance Black America Festival

LULA WASHINGTON (1951-   ), the artistic director of the Los Angeles Contemporary Dance Theatre and the organizer of the Olympic Black Dance Festival

Summary of Event

The span of time from 1983 to 1984 marked a peak in the presentation of festivals, performances, and seminars that emphasized both black dance forms and the work created by black dance artists. The achievements of African American dancers gained more recognition by the general public during the 1980's, and dances that portrayed aspects of the black experience gained increasing acceptance. While scholars and artists concurred that no exact or concise definition of the term "black dance" existed, at least two distinctions within the field were made. Black dance was defined as dance forms that were developed by specific African, Caribbean, or African American cultural groups. The term also applied to the dances created by artists who happened to be black. In any event, the broad continuum of black dance continued to grow, and it was significant that the mid-1980's began to witness a long-overdue recognition of the achievements of African American choreographers and dancers.

In 1983, New York City's Brooklyn Academy of Music presented Dance Black America, a four-day event that featured performances, seminars, lectures, and historical films. Dance Black America was cosponsored by the State University of New York; those in attendance included not only dancers and choreographers but also historians, critics, anthropologists, musicologists, and folklorists.

The festival, which commenced on April 21 and continued through April 24, included six diverse programs of dance performances and was one of the major dance events of 1983. In addition to concert dance forms, the festival offered presentations of black street and social dance. Dance Black America celebrated nearly three hundred years of African American dance tradition and included virtually every prominent figure in the history of black dance.

On the first program, dancer and choreographer Charles Moore presented his reconstructions of two works by Asadata Dafora, a native of Sierra Leone who had staged concerts of African dance in New York during the 1930's. Dafora's work was dynamic and vivid, replete with spectacle and tribal heritage. Moore performed *Awassa Astrige* and *Kykunkor* to the accompaniment of African drums. In *Awassa Astrige*, a warrior metamorphosed into an ostrich, imitating the bird with arm and chest isolations. *Kykunkor* portrayed a courtship ritual of a warrior and a bevy of village maidens.

Jamaican-born Garth Fagan presented *From Before*, a dance that combined ethnic, modern, and ballet techniques to a score by Trinidad composer Ralph MacDonald. Fagan's Bucket Dance Theater performed the piece, which exhibited solid, low shifts of weight underneath lyrical upper bodies. In a manner reminiscent of an African tradition, each dancer performed a solo in turn. *From Before* revealed many of the influences on black American dance and was hailed by critics such as Jennifer Dunning of *The New York Times.* Fagan's choreography exhibited the syncretism of African dance traditions blended with contemporary dance stylizations.

The Alvin Ailey Repertory Ensemble performed *Road of the Phoebe Snow*, a dance choreographed by Talley Beatty that merged jazz and modern movement motifs. The senior company of the Alvin Ailey American Dance Theater presented excerpts from Ailey's signature work *Relevations*, considered by many to be a masterpiece of modern dance. Ailey's choreography evoked enthusiastic responses from the audience and reaffirmed his position as one of the most prominent figures in modern dance.

The Eleo Pomare Dance Company staged an interpretation of Federico García Lorca's play *The House of Bernarda Alba*. Pomare's retelling was entitled *Las Desenamoradas* and represented the choreographer's focus on social issues. Pomare also performed his solo *Junkie*, which offered a biting social commentary on drug abuse.

As part of the four-day series, the Dance Black America festival also presented an evening of street and social dance. Choreographers such as Chuck Davis and Arthur Hall were represented, as were performers such as Chuck Green, Leon Jackson, and Gloria and Sean Jones. *Lengen-Go/Mandiani* was a reconstruction of street games interpreted by the Chuck Davis Dance Company. Arthur Hall's Afro-American Ensemble performed *Marie Laveaux and Danse Congo Square*, which portrayed the location in nineteenth century New Orleans known as Congo Square; the Municipal Council of New Orleans had encouraged public performances by blacks in Congo Square as an attempt to curtail possible insurrection by the slaves. Hall's troupe also performed excerpts from *Fat Tuesday* accompanied by a New Orleans brass band. The choreography of both Davis and Hall illustrated the black dance tradition within historical frameworks.

These vernacular dance forms were supplemented by performances of jump-rope teams, roller skaters, drill teams, and break dancers. A group of young Brooklyn girls known as the Jazzy Jumpers jounced through intricate patterns that often featured two girls on a rope simultaneously. Roxy's Solar Rollers was a quartet of performers who danced on rollerskates, and Electric Boogie was one of two breakdancing groups that the festival featured. The performances of street dancing galvanized the audience, and dance critic Jennifer Dunning of *The New York Times* remarked that the dancing of the Magnificent Force-Breaking group was exciting as both ritual and spectacle.

Impact of Event

As a result of Dance Black America's success, and also since recognition of the contributions of black dance artists was long overdue, several other festivals of black dance occurred during 1983 and 1984. On Sunday, May 22, the Brooklyn Academy of Music sponsored an annual event called the DanceAfrica festival. Choreographer Chuck Davis staged the event, which featured ten different African-American dance companies. Davis centered the festival on an African lineage-based marriage ritual. After a wedding ceremony, which commenced with drum incantations to the earth and sky, a bride and groom were entertained by an assortment of dance companies.

An Ethiopian wedding song was performed by the Women of the Calabash, who were accompanied by traditional folk instruments. Dinizulu and His African Dancers, Drummers, and Singers staged a robust drum solo that was a highlight of the festival. The group's drummer played his instrument with both his hands and feet. Additional companies at the DanceAfrica festival included the multigenerational dance troupe called the Calabash Dance Company, the Izulu Dance Theater, the International African-American Ballet, and drummers from A Touch of Folklore and More. The Chuck Davis Dance Company, which had performed a month earlier at the Dance Black America festival, also danced as part of the celebration. Both the Dance Black America festival and the DanceAfrica festival marked a peak in the recognition of African-American dance artists during 1983.

A few months later, during the summer of 1983, Chuck Davis organized Festival Africa as part of the American Dance Festival in Durham, North Carolina. The festival consisted of three evenings of African dance and music and was the first festival of its kind in the Southeastern United States. Featured performers included Chuck Davis' company—the African-American Dance Ensemble—as well as the Calabash Dance Company, the Weaver Street Dancers, Dinizulu and His African Dancers, Drummers, and Singers, the Art of Black Dance and Music, the Cultural Movement, Kombo Omolara, and Olukose Wiles. Several of these troupes had previously participated at the Brooklyn Academy's DanceAfrica and Dance Black America festivals.

Another festival that occurred as a result of the 1983 events was the Olympic Black Dance Festival, held on June 16, 1984, at the Japan America Community Cultural Center in Los Angeles. The festival was significant in its presentation of prominent black dance artists such as Rod Rodgers and Cleo Parker Robinson. The event was a component of a larger ten-week parent festival that featured a variety of performing artists and companies. As part of this ten-week Olympic Arts Festival, the Dance Theater of Harlem staged seven performances under the artistic direction of Arthur Mitchell. The one-day black dance festival was organized by Lula Washington, the artistic director of the Los Angeles Contemporary Dance Theatre. Washington, with the assistance of a panel of adjudicators, chose black dance artists to perform at the festival. She also solicited private and corporate funding in order to sponsor films, workshops, and master classes prior to the actual performance date. In addition, panel discussions that addressed specific concerns of the black dance community were planned.

Panel discussions were also offered at a one-day seminar organized by Brenda Dixon-Stowell, Sally Banes, and Julinda Lewis and sponsored by the Dance Critics Association. The conference took place on November 5, 1983, in order to examine issues raised at the Dance Black America festival, which had occurred approximately six months before. The event was held at the Dance Theater Workshop/Bessie Schoenberg Theater in New York City and was entitled "You've Taken My Blues and Gone: A Seminar on Black Dance in White America." One purpose of the seminar was to attempt to define black dance in relationship to the entire dance field. Participants raised intriguing questions that prompted a discussion of the responsibilities of both white and black researchers, critics, and educators in regard to the subject of black dance. An additional conference was hosted by Joan Myers Brown, the artistic director of the Philadelphia-based dance company Philadanco.

In 1987, the American Dance Festival initiated a three-year project called "The Black Tradition in American Modern Dance." The project, which was cosponsored by the Ford Foundation and the National Endowment for the Humanities, included performances, seminars, and the publication of a collection of essays focused on black dance. The festival also commissioned archival recordings of the works of selected black choreographers.

In June, 1987, four black choreographers were featured at the American Dance Festival. The work of Talley Beatty, Eleo Pomare, Donald McKayle, and Pearl Primus was represented. The Joel Hall Dancers performed Beatty's "Congo Tango Palace," an excerpt from *Come and Get the Beauty of It Hot*. The Dayton Contemporary Dance Company performed *Las Desenamoradas*, originally choreographed by Pomare in 1967. A highlight of the concert was Donald McKayle's piece entitled *Games*, which the Chuck Davis African-American Dance Ensemble presented. Another program highlight consisted of three solos representative of the work of dancer and anthropologist Pearl Primus: *The Negro Speaks of Rivers*, *Strange Fruit*, and *Hard Times Blues*.

Bibliography

Adamczyk, Alice J. *Black Dance: An Annotated Bibliography*. New York: Garland, 1989. An annotated listing of books and articles relating to black dance. A good source that provides an overview of the vast scope of the subject, but lacking in cross-referencing and consistency of citations. The author includes sources from selected branches of the New York Public Library.

Aschenbrenner, Joyce. *Katherine Dunham: Reflections on the Social and Political Contexts of Afro-American Dance*. New York: Congress on Research in Dance, 1981. A well-researched book that presents the career of modern-dance pioneer Katherine Dunham through an anthropological perspective. Deals with the social and cultural climate of the United States in which African American dance developed and includes an analysis of critical responses to Dunham's work. A highlight of the book is the collection of appendices, including drawn notations of the Dunham method and technique. References, photographs.

Emery, Lynne Fauley. *Black Dance: From 1619 to Today*. 2d rev. ed. Princeton, N.J.: Princeton Book Company, 1988. A definitive work on the history of black dance in the United States. Text is informative and comprehensive. Both concert and vernacular forms are addressed, and a new chapter by Brenda Dixon-Stowell is included. Excellent endnotes supplement each chapter. Excellent bibliography. Photographs and index.

Haskins, James. *Black Dance in America: A History Through Its People*. New York: Thomas Y. Crowell, 1990. Although libraries classify this book under juvenile literature, it is nevertheless a good source that gives an overview of black dance in America. Brief biographies of prominent dancers and companies are included. Haskins provides an interesting videography of both concert and vernacular dance. Limited bibliography. Index and photographs.

Hazzard-Gordon, Katrina. *Jookin': The Rise of Social Dance Formations in African-American Culture*. Philadelphia: Temple University Press, 1990. An interesting study that focuses on the social dance phenomena of the black community from 1619 to the 1960's. Hazzard-Gordon's book is one of the few sources that addresses the institutions in which black social dance developed. Excellent and detailed endnotes. Photographs and index.

Kraus, Richard, Sarah Chapman Hilsendager, and Brenda Dixon. "Black Dance in America." In *History of the Dance in Art and Education.* Englewood Cliffs, N.J.: Prentice-Hall, 1991. An overview of black dance in America that provides an interesting chronology of black concert dance from 1931 to the late 1980's. Concerns in defining black dance are addressed, as are the exclusion of blacks from ballet. Contributions of African American choreographers and dancers are interspersed throughout the entire book. Excellent endnotes and bibliography. Appendices and index are provided. Photographs.

Thorpe, Edward. *Black Dance.* Woodstock, N.Y.: Overlook Press, 1990. Offers accounts of major black figures in the development of American concert dance. Thorpe provides a historical overview but does not offer an in-depth study of any one area; however, the text is informative and easy to read. Photographs are plentiful and excellent. Interesting chapter on black dance in Great Britain. Index.

John R. Crawford

Cross-References

Baker Dances in *La Revue nègre* (1925), p. 665; Ailey Founds His Dance Company (1958), p. 1774; Mitchell Founds the Dance Theater of Harlem (1968), p. 2110; The New Dance U.S.A. Festival Celebrates Contemporary Dance (1981), p. 2480; Multiculturalism Dominates the Dance World (Late 1980's), p. 2559; Baryshnikov's White Oak Dance Project Debuts (1990), p. 2663.

SIXTEEN CANDLES STARTS A WAVE OF TEEN FILMS

Category of event: Motion pictures
Time: 1984
Locale: Hollywood, California

Sixteen Candles, *John Hughes's directorial debut, marked the beginning of his remarkably successful career as a filmmaker known particularly for teenage films and comedies*

Principal personages:
JOHN HUGHES (1950-   ), one of the most successful and prolific film-makers of the 1980's
MOLLY RINGWALD (1968-   ), an actress who starred in three of Hughes's films and became identified with his work
ANTHONY MICHAEL HALL (1968-   ), an actor featured in several Hughes films
JOHN CANDY (1950-   ), a comic actor who has appeared as both bit player and star in many of Hughes's films.
CHRIS COLUMBUS (1959-   ), a film director who worked on Hughes's biggest hit, *Home Alone*

Summary of Event

With the release of *Sixteen Candles* in 1984, John Hughes began a remarkably prolific and successful career as a filmmaker best known for his teenage films. Although usually comedies, his films treat teenage problems and emotions seriously, without being exploitative or condescending. These films launched the careers of many young actors, spawned countless imitations, and established Hughes as the master of the genre.

John Hughes was born in Detroit, Michigan, in 1950 into a middle-class family whose frequent moves during his early childhood may have helped foster his identification with the "outsiders" featured in so many of his films. When he was in the seventh grade, his family settled in the North Shore suburbs of Chicago, where he would continue to live as an adult and where most of his films would be shot. As a student at Northbrook High School, Hughes, like many of his most memorable characters, was a self-described "geek," passionate about pop music (particularly John Lennon and Bob Dylan) and art. Hughes attended the University of Arizona at Tucson but left before graduating, returning to Chicago to work as a copywriter at one of the city's largest advertising agencies. While pursuing a successful career with the agency, he simultaneously wrote for comedians such as Rodney Dangerfield and Henny Youngman and published articles in the *National Lampoon*. He finally gave up his lucrative job as an adman for a less financially rewarding, but more creatively fulfilling, position on the *National Lampoon's* editorial board.

He began his career as a filmmaker by writing screenplays for the *National Lampoon*'s film division, including the screenplays for the 1983 release *National Lampoon's Vacation* (which featured Anthony Michael Hall and John Candy, who became two of Hughes's regular actors) and *National Lampoon's Class Reunion* (1982). He also wrote the commercially (though not critically) successful *Mr. Mom* (1983), based on his own years as a "house husband." Hughes found his experience as a screenwriter frustrating; the gap between his script and what finally appeared on the screen was too wide. Although he had never been on a film set, Hughes was determined to direct his next screenplay, *Sixteen Candles*, in order to exert more control over the finished product.

Sixteen Candles chronicles an eventful day in the life of Shermer High School sophomore, Samantha (Molly Ringwald), during which her parents forget her sixteenth birthday in the confusion of preparations for her sister's impending wedding, her bedroom (and telephone) is taken over by her obnoxious grandparents, a nerdy foreign-exchange student accompanies her to the school dance, and she pines for a seemingly unreachable senior (Michael Schoeffling) while at the same time being relentlessly pursued by a freshman geek (Anthony Michael Hall). As the story progresses, Samantha discovers that the geek is actually someone with whom she can share confidences, the "cool" senior is really a shy romantic, and her less-than-perfect parents really do care about her.

For a directorial debut, the film was generally well received. Pauline Kael of *The New Yorker*, calling it "less raucous in tone than most of the recent teen pictures," compared it to the "gentle English comedies of the forties and fifties," commenting that "John Hughes has a knack for making you like the high-school age characters better each time you hear them talk." Janet Maslin of *The New York Times* called it "cheerful and light, showcasing Mr. Hughes's knack for remembering all those aspects of middle-class American adolescent behavior that anyone else might want to forget."

Sixteen Candles can be seen as a template for many of Hughes's subsequent films, introducing the setting, plot devices, dialogue, characters, and themes that recur in subsequent films. The affluent, upper-middle-class Chicago suburb featured in the film appears throughout Hughes's work, and Shermer High School provides the background for *The Breakfast Club* (1985) and *Weird Science* (1985). Also appearing in several films is a lavish home, usually trashed during a wild, unchaperoned teen party.

The wonderfully authentic use of teenage slang in *Sixteen Candles* has since become a Hughes trademark. His dialogue always rings true, unlike the wooden slang adolescents mouthed in most rock-and-roll films of the 1950's and beach-party movies of the 1960's, and his use of cars, clothes, and popular music never hits a false note.

Sixteen Candles also introduces the kinds of characters that Hughes would continue to create in later films. His protagonists, usually middle- or upper-middle-class white teenagers, typically see themselves as outsiders, as does Samantha, who feels estranged not only from her family but also from the in crowd of sophisticated seniors at school. Also an outsider, and another of Hughes's favorite figures introduced in the film, is the Geek, whom Hughes described to one interviewer as "a guy who has everything going for him but he's just too young." Other stock Hughes characters appearing in the film are the foolish, out-of-it adults—teachers, parents, and grand-parents—and the wealthy in-crowd of handsome jocks and gorgeous prom queens who populate most Hughes movies.

Favorite Hughes themes such as the conflicts between outsiders and insiders, ap-pearance and reality, and adults and teenagers are also introduced in *Sixteen Candles*. As the chaos caused by the drunken party reveals, the difference between in-siders and outsiders is not great when the rigid adolescent social barriers are broken. The geek and the senior have a heart-to-heart talk, as do Samantha and the geek. Appearances prove to be deceiving as the prom queen, who is not so cool when she is drunk, finds herself sexually attracted to the geek, and the cool senior is shyly hesitant to approach Samantha. Adults are seen to be irrelevant at best, idiotic at worst, and exhibit only brief flashes of warmth and understanding.

Impact of Event

Sixteen Candles launched a remarkably prolific and successful career for Hughes as screenwriter, director, and producer. Most of his films were commercially suc-cessful, including *Home Alone* (1990), which became the biggest money-making comedy in Hollywood history. The fledgling careers of young actors Molly Ring-wald and Anthony Michael Hall were advanced by *Sixteen Candles*; in fact, the list of actors who have appeared in Hughes's films is a virtual who's who of young actors in the 1980's: Ally Sheedy, Judd Nelson, Emilio Estevez, Matthew Broderick, John and Joan Cusak, Eric Stolz, Mary Stuart Masterson, Lea Thompson, James Spader, and Andrew McCarthy all had parts in Hughes productions. The term "brat pack" was often applied to a group of popular young 1980's actors, many of whom worked with Hughes.

Hughes's career took off after the release of *Sixteen Candles. The Breakfast Club*, which he wrote and directed, was perhaps his most critically successful teenage film. Five teenagers forced to spend a day together in Saturday detention break down barriers to discover that, despite their outward differences, they are united by their feelings of alienation from their parents and teachers and their sense of being vic-tims of an elaborate social system. While criticized for stacking the deck against adults, the film still represents one of Hollywood's best portraits of the power of a high-school caste system.

In 1985, Hughes followed *The Breakfast Club* with *Weird Science*, a science-fiction take on his usual themes. The film was an entertaining diversion but was neither commercially nor critically successful. Hughes also wrote another film, *National Lampoon's European Vacation* (1985). In 1986, Hughes made *Pretty in Pink*, another critical and box-office success. Written and produced by Hughes but directed by Howard Deutch, the film starred Molly Ringwald as Andy, a girl from the wrong side of the tracks in love with Blaine (Andrew McCarthy), one of the rich in crowd.

Andy is adored by a geek (Jon Cryer). As in *Sixteen Candles*, a wild party scene provides an important plot device, and Andy finds strength in being different, the geek finds he can be attractive to women, and Blaine discovers that his friends can be jerks.

Still another Hughes success followed in 1986 with *Ferris Bueller's Day Off*. Once again, Hughes focuses on a day in the life of a teenage eccentric (Matthew Broderick), but this hero is a wildly popular, egocentric goof-off. The film celebrates the sheer joy of being young, as Ferris cuts school and celebrates a day of freedom. *Some Kind of Wonderful*, a mirror-image of *Pretty in Pink*, followed in 1987, with the protagonist, Keith (Eric Stolz) as a boy from the wrong side of the tracks and the geek (Mary Stuart Masterson) as a platonic girlfriend. Keith, like Andy, is in love with a member of the in crowd, while the geek pines away for him. Again a wild party scene provides the pivotal moment, when the hero stands up to the intimidating jocks, and the cool girl realizes her friends are fools.

Hughes then began to move away from the teenage film, writing, producing, and directing his first entirely "adult" comedy, 1987's *Trains, Planes, and Automobiles*. *She's Having a Baby* (1988) was Hughes's first (unsuccessful) attempt to follow his teenagers into young adulthood. He then wrote and coproduced three more comedies, all featuring John Candy, including *The Great Outdoors* (1988) and *Uncle Buck* (1989).

Ironically, Hughes's biggest success came with the phenomenal popularity of the family comedy *Home Alone* (1990). Written and produced by Hughes and directed by Chris Columbus, it appeared with little fanfare during the Christmas season of 1990 and became one of the most successful comedies of all time. Set in the affluent suburbs of his previous films, *Home Alone* revolves around perhaps the ultimate outsider, a child who is forgotten by his entire family, as he discovers his own strength of character (and trashes a lavish home along the way).

Hughes followed *Home Alone* in 1991 with *Career Opportunities*, *Only the Lonely* (which he coproduced and which was again directed by Chris Columbus), *Dutch*, and *Curly Sue* (in which he returned to the successful formula of *Home Alone*).

Teenage films can be traced from the Andy Hardy series of the 1940's through the rock-and-roll and juvenile-delinquent films of the 1950's and the beach-party films and teen melodramas of the 1960's. Those films, usually told from an adult point of view and often featuring an adult protagonist, usually failed to create a believable teenage milieu through use of slang, music, or characters. Hughes's greatest contribution to filmmaking has been to establish the teenage film as a genre to be taken seriously. An astute observer of teen culture, he refuses to condescend to his characters, treating their emotions and opinions with respect. There have been many imitations of Hughes' work, such as *Adventures in Babysitting* (1987), *Can't Buy Me Love* (1987), and *She's Out of Control* (1989), and many films that have successfully expanded the genre, such as *Heathers* (1989), *River's Edge* (1986), and *Edward Scissorhands* (1990), but Hughes can rightfully claim credit for making teen films a legitimate enterprise.

Bibliography
Barth, Jack. "Kinks of Comedy." *Film Comment* 20 (June, 1984): 44-47. Discusses film comedy trends of the early 1980's, with a brief paragraph on Hughes's films and a lengthier interview of the filmmaker.

Dworkin, Susan. "Beach Blanket Bingo Never Looked So Good." *Ms.* 10 (August, 1984): 14-15. Review from a feminist viewpoint of several teen movies of 1984, including *Sixteen Candles.*

Kael, Pauline. Review of *Sixteen Candles. The New Yorker* 60 (May 28, 1984): 101-103. Detailed and insightful film review.

Matousek, Mark. "John Hughes." *Interview* 14 (August, 1985): 60-61. Interview with Hughes discusses at length his own adolescence, working habits, and family life.

Mills, Bart. "Brat Movies." *Stills* (June-July, 1985): 10. Interview of Hughes discusses *Sixteen Candles, The Breakfast Club,* and *Mr. Mom,* his affinity for teen films, and why he prefers working in Chicago to working in Hollywood.

Mary Virginia Davis

Cross-References
The Classic Screwball Comedy Reaches Its Height in Popularity (1934), p. 951; Young Readers Embrace *The Catcher in the Rye* (1951), p. 1493; Dean Becomes a Legend in *Rebel Without a Cause* (1955), p. 1640; Female Directors Attain Prominence (1980's), p. 2443; *E.T.: The Extraterrestrial* Breaks Box-Office Records (1982), p. 2491.

THE COSBY SHOW MAKES TELEVISION HISTORY

Category of event: Television and radio
Time: September 20, 1984-May, 1992
Locale: The United States

Americans were introduced to a weekly television series that broke from standard black situation comedy and that starred an African American, Bill Cosby, who—as cocreator, coproducer, and executive consultant—had full artistic control

Principal personages:

BILL COSBY (1937-   ), an actor, writer, and stand-up comedian who, in the role of Cliff Huxtable, brought a gentle, educated, positive, and family-oriented humor to television

PHYLICIA RASHAD (1948-   ), an actress who costarred as Huxtable's wife, Clair

BRANDON TARTIKOFF (1949-   ), the president of the National Broadcasting Company (NBC), who supported the idea of presenting Cosby in a comedy about parenting

MARCY CARSEY (1944-   ), the executive producer of *The Cosby Show*

THOMAS WERNER, a producer of *The Cosby Show*

JOHN MARKUS, a writer who headed the successful writing-producing team for *The Cosby Show* during its peak seasons

CARMEN FINESTRA (1947-   ), an actor, writer, and producer for *The Cosby Show* during its years of greatest popularity

GARY KOTT (1945-   ), a writer and producer for *The Cosby Show* in its most popular seasons

MATT WILLIAMS (1952-   ), an actor, writer, and producer for *The Cosby Show* from 1984 to 1987

Summary of Event

By 1984, Bill Cosby was a major figure in American entertainment, especially on television. Although he had been a stage performer and popular nightclub comic in the early 1960's, Cosby became a national figure in the action-drama television series *I Spy*, costarring Robert Culp, which ran for three seasons from 1965 to 1968. For his *I Spy* performance, Cosby won three Emmy Awards and, as equal costar, dismantled the television stereotype of the African American as social and psychological subordinate. In 1969, Cosby had a television series created especially for him, *The Bill Cosby Show*, a situation comedy in which he played Chet Kincaid, a high school coach. The show remained on national television for two seasons. There followed the award-winning cartoon feature *Fat Albert and the Cosby Kids*, which ran for ten years (1972-1982) and which featured Cosby's stories about growing up in Philadelphia. A concert film, *Bill Cosby—Himself*, was distributed in 1982. By the 1980's, Cosby had become a national icon—with television series, films, audio tapes, stage shows, television specials, and guest appearances on television talk shows.

One story has it that it was an appearance on *The Tonight Show* that set in motion the creation of *The Cosby Show*. Brandon Tartikoff, president of the National Broadcasting Company (NBC), had been awakened by his young daughter. To pass time while he soothed his child, Tartikoff turned on *The Tonight Show*, on which Cosby was doing one of his monologues on the vicissitudes of rearing a family. Perhaps Tartikoff, a parent, was struck by the change that had been occurring in Cosby's material, for as Cosby's own family grew, Cosby had switched from creating humor about growing up to creating humor based on parenting. It could also be that Tartikoff was only reacting to an ongoing plea by Tom Werner and Marcy Carsey, whose production company, Carsey-Werner, had been promoting—perhaps for as long as two years—the idea of a new Cosby show. Whatever the case, Tartikoff became convinced that Bill Cosby should be featured in a comedy series based on parenthood.

The idea did not immediately produce positive response. Certainly, there was reason for network executives to be wary; Cosby was a forceful and determined personality. His celebrity status was significant enough to give him a powerful bargaining position. Moreover, what he was asking for was unprecedented: full artistic and content control. Such terms had led to the show's earlier being turned down by the American Broadcasting Company (ABC).

As discussion evolved, the concept of the show became bolder. First, in an echo of *I Spy*, Cosby was to play a detective. A later proposal was for him to play a chauffeur living in Brooklyn whose wife was a plumber. Cosby's final suggestion, Cliff Huxtable, M.D., prevailed with NBC.

Other series, notably *The Jeffersons* and *Julia*, had starred upwardly mobile African Americans in middle-class settings, but those shows featured blacks working their way into a white world. Moreover, every television series had always been controlled by established producers working with network executives.

Ultimately, negotiations led to an arrangement with the Carsey-Werner Company. Marcy Carsey was named executive producer, with Cosby as coproducer, cocreator, and executive consultant. In essence, Cosby had complete control, and he exercised his rights. He was involved in all artistic decisions—casting, directing, story, and dialogue. One of the principal staff writers characterized Cosby as "the emperor." Since he was a professional educator as well as a successful entertainer, Cosby intended that his show provide family education. He also intended that the show should reflect his own positive philosophy and life-style; he was known to reject unsuitable scripts even on the day before taping.

It is not surprising, then, that *The Cosby Show* paralleled Cosby's own life. Bill Cosby, a graduate of Temple University, had earned a doctor of education degree from the University of Massachusetts in 1977. His wife, Camille, was a professional woman, and the couple had four daughters and a son. They lived in an upscale neighborhood in Massachusetts. The television family was headed by Heathcliff Huxtable, a successful obstetrician who lives with his family above his office in an upscale neighborhood in New York City. Huxtable's wife, Clair, is a lawyer. Like the Cosbys, the Huxtables have five children, four daughters and a son.

The Cosby Show introduced important differences from other shows starring African Americans. First, there were no featured white performers. The show starred Cosby and Phylicia Rashad. The Huxtable's children, the other important continuing characters, were played by Lisa Bonet, Tempestt Bledsoe, Sabrina LeBeauf, Keshia Knight Pulliam, and Malcolm-Jamal Warner.

A second innovation was that the Huxtables were a black family without financial concern. Cliff and Clair were a physician and a lawyer—America's most prestigious occupations—whose children go to college. Their speech was not pretentious, but it was clearly educated.

Finally, the emphasis was on simple parenting problems, without tortured plot complications: a daughter wearing too much makeup, a son squandering his allowance, a pet goldfish whose death breaks the heart of the youngest child (the whole family, dressed in funeral attire, holds a burial next to the toilet).

From its September opening, the show was an immediate hit, and it quickly moved to the top position in the ratings, a place it held throughout the 1980's. As the show continued, the children matured, and the parents aged so that the Huxtable family was organic, living and changing with the families who watched them for eight years.

Impact of Event

The impact of *The Cosby Show* was immediate and long-lasting. First, it marked the revival of situation comedy as the basic form of television entertainment in prime time. Of the top ten shows in the A. C. Nielson ratings in the 1982-1983 season, only two were comedies; the 1983-1984 season featured only one comedy. Critics had begun to discuss the death of situation comedy. *The Cosby Show* proved such a discussion premature. Not only was it an immediate hit, but it also encouraged the development of other situation-comedy successes such as *Family Ties* (the NBC companion piece to *Cosby*) as well as the popular ABC series *Growing Pains* and *Valerie*.

Indeed, a new artistic-commercial vision was conceived out of the impetus of *The Cosby Show*. Each network now attempted to design whole evenings built around appeals to an aggregate market. For the early evening, when the whole family was viewing, there was *Cosby* followed by *Family Ties*. Later in the evening came *Cheers*, followed by adult fare such as *Night Court* and *Hill Street Blues*.

Yet nothing, not even the aggregate evening of shows, had the impact of Bill Cosby's program. One commentator observed that situation comedy as an art form can be divided into "BC" (before Cosby) and "AC" (after Cosby). During the late 1980's, *The Cosby Show* frequently attracted more than fifty percent of the total television audience. During its second year, thirteen of *The Cosby Show*'s episodes were among the fifteen most-watched shows of the entire year. The upshot of such unprecedented popularity was that NBC had a solid run as the number-one television network throughout the 1980's.

In the 1990's, *The Cosby Show* was challenged as the undisputed choice of American television viewers. The challenge came in part from *A Different World*, a spinoff series featuring Lisa Bonet as a Huxtable daughter gone off to college. A more significant challenge came from *Roseanne*, a series that was the artistic and spiritual child of *The Cosby Show. Roseanne* was created in 1987 by Matt Williams, a longtime writer and producer for Cosby, and was produced by the Carsey-Werner Company. Carsey-Werner went on to produce *Davis Rules*; Williams joined with Carmen Finestra, another writer from *Cosby*, to follow *Roseanne* with *Home Improvement.* All these shows are about parenting or the results of parenting. *Roseanne* is clearly a blue-collar version of *The Cosby Show. Home Improvement* probably possesses the closest affinity to Cosby's formula of straightforward, no-frills episodes, featuring simple, earnest language and gentle, positive humor. The outlandish predicaments of *I Love Lucy*, the overwrought emotions and self-conscious social significance of *All in the Family*, and the fatuousness of *Father Knows Best* are replaced by Roseanne's bluntness, by her overweight husband's cheerful acceptance of life as it is, and by the deadpan humor of the family in *Home Improvement.* "Bill is a genius," said Matt Williams. "We all learned from him and are applying those lessons." "Cosby is brilliant, a mind like a jazz musician," said Carmen Finestra.

Perhaps the most significant of Bill Cosby's lessons, Finestra has argued, is that earnest, positive humor is the funniest. When Clair asks why the Huxtables have five children and Cliff answers that it is because they did not want six, the only possible response is undiluted laughter. Another lesson concerning earnest humor has to do with the great store that the middle class puts in the process of thinking a problem through to a solution. Thinking, though, is hard work and meant to be done in private, with only the solution being made public. Thus, to think in public is a sort of embarrassment, a case of being caught with one's intellectual pants down. "We knew that they tuned in to watch Bill think," Matt Williams noted. "It was very funny when Bill thought."

Above all, the lesson of *The Cosby Show* was that Americans love the ideal of the family, especially a traditional family with a frequently present father and an omnipresent mother whose whole concern is the children. Here, the Huxtables were consummate: Cliff Huxtable's work place is downstairs; Clair Huxtable has a highly prestigious profession, but she apparently works only when all the children are asleep. Even so, she never discusses her work, never brings problems home. She represents complete achievement for the American woman: a satisfying profession equal to that of any man's, and the apparent time off from work to give entirely of herself to her children.

The Cosby Show made all of its featured players stars. Awards of all types—notably Emmy and Peabody Awards—were lavished on actors, writers, and directors. The reruns of the show from 1984 to 1990, consisting of 125 tapes of twenty-five minutes each, sold for $500 million.

In its last two seasons, *The Cosby Show* slipped steadily in the ratings but remained in the top ten. Most of the writing team had gone on to other shows. Still, the Cosby mystique drew fifty-four million viewers for the final episode. Cosby himself refused to accept Emmy Awards, but he was without doubt a superstar and a powerful force in American family life. His book, *Fatherhood* (1987), was a bestseller. He amassed great wealth; he was pictured on the cover of *Time* magazine and was the subject of a feature story. He has received honorary degrees, and he has returned the favor by giving twenty million dollars to Spelman College, a predominantly black, all-female institution in Atlanta.

Bibliography

Castleman, Harry, and Walter J. Podrazik. *Harry and Wally's Favorite TV Shows.* Englewood Cliffs, N.J.: Prentice-Hall, 1989. Fifty years of television shows in magazine format. Each show has a brief history, evaluation, photographs. A popular book, not intended to be used as a sociological or aesthetic document.

Crowther, Bruce, and Mike Pinfold. *Bring Me Laughter: Four Decades of TV Comedy.* London: Columbus Books, 1987. By British authors; compares American and English television comedies. Special viewpoint on *The Cosby Show* from a different culture. A work intended for a general-interest reader.

Fiske, John. *Television Culture.* New York: Methuen, 1987. A serious sociological study of television as a cultural and philosophic phenomenon. Offers methods of approaching the meaning of television as a mass medium.

Jauna, John. *The Best of the TV Sitcoms.* New York: Harmony Books, 1988. Review of situation comedies in a popular format. Photographs, encapsulation of shows, selected comments of critics, examples of dialogue.

Taylor, Ella. *Prime-Time Families: Television Culture in Postwar America.* Berkeley: University of California Press, 1989. Important and insightful study of the image of the American family as presented on nighttime television from *Father Knows Best* to *The Cosby Show.* Excellent final chapter explores Cosby's contributions, especially his positive, if idealized, approach.

Vande Berg, Leah R., and Nick Trujillo. *Organizational Life on Television.* New York: Ablex, 1989. Sociological study of the concepts of corporation organization as they are advanced on television, including entertainment series. Consideration given to *The Cosby Show,* among others, as demonstrating American corporate ideals.

August Staub

Cross-References

Television Family Comedy Becomes Extremely Popular (1950's), p. 1470; *The Dick Van Dyke Show* Popularizes Situation Comedy (1961), p. 1908; *I Spy* Debuts to Controversy (1965), p. 2044; *The Mary Tyler Moore Show* Examines Women's Roles (1970), p. 2218; *All in the Family* Introduces a New Style of Television Comedy (1971), p. 2234; *The Jeffersons* Signals Success of Black Situation Comedies (1975), p. 2339.

SIMON'S *BILOXI BLUES* EMPHASIZES SERIOUS THEMES

Category of event: Theater
Time: December 14, 1984
Locale: Ahmanson Theater, Los Angeles, California

Neil Simon's Biloxi Blues, *the second play of his autobiographical trilogy, established new serious themes in the comedy of America's most commercially successful playwright*

Principal personages:
NEIL SIMON (1927-   ), the most commercially successful playwright in the history of American theater
GENE SAKS (1921-   ), the director of many of Simon's plays, including *Brighton Beach Memoirs* (1983) and its sequel, *Biloxi Blues*
MATTHEW BRODERICK (1962-   ), the actor who originated the role of Eugene Jerome in both *Brighton Beach Memoirs* and *Biloxi Blues*

Summary of Event

Biloxi Blues opens as Eugene Jerome and four other soldiers are spending their third night aboard a train heading to basic training. Eugene describes the other soldiers to the audience as he reads from his journal, occasionally being interrupted by quarrels, crude humor, and insults as the other conscripts jostle each other while trying to sleep. Although Eugene already hates the army, he has resolved to accomplish three goals during the war: "Become a writer, not get killed, and lose my virginity."

First, he must survive basic training in Mississippi's sweltering heat, under the command of Sergeant Merwin J. Toomey, a gruff, battle-toughened Army man with a steel plate in his head. With a drill sergeant's typical toughness, he taunts and torments the recruits, arbitrarily imposing discipline by ordering them to perform push-ups for minor or imagined offenses and taking them on a fifteen-mile midnight hike through swamps. Though Eugene is arbitrarily exempted from doing push-ups to make him a target of the others' resentment, the most frequent object of Toomey's wrath and derision is Arnold Epstein, a sensitive, nervous, bookish, slightly built recruit who refuses to eat army food even when ordered to and who is punished with KP and latrine duty for days. Nevertheless, Eugene befriends him as a fellow "outsider," admiring his convictions and determination not to be dehumanized. At night, the recruits contemplate the possibility of dying in combat and compare fantasies of how they would spend their final week. Epstein wins by imagining making Toomey do push-ups in front of the platoon, while Eugene imagines the perfect girl. Amid recurrent ethnic insults against Epstein, Eugene feels guilty for preferring to remain neutral rather than defend a fellow Jew.

The first act concludes with Toomey's investigation of the theft of sixty-two dollars from recruit Joseph Wykowski. When Toomey threatens to cancel the entire squad's two-day leave unless the guilty party comes forward to accept punishment, Epstein replaces the money. When questioned, he explains that he chose to prevent five innocent people from suffering for one guilty one. Toomey then reveals that he took Wykowski's money, which had been carelessly left in his footlocker, unsecured. Intending to teach the platoon a lesson, he found himself "submarined" when Epstein confessed to a crime he did not commit. The recruit further admits that he saw Toomey take the money but deplores his inventing a crime in order to enforce discipline. Wykowski extends his hand, but Epstein declines a handshake, replying "Let's not be hypocritical. I did what I did for me, not for you." When Eugene privately expresses admiration for Epstein's principled actions, Epstein chides him for not getting "involved enough," for always watching others and jotting notes rather than taking sides on issues that he cares about. Another recruit, Don Carney, enters, wanting to ask Eugene's opinion on an unspecified subject; he then sings "Embraceable You" as Eugene "looks helplessly at the audience."

The second act opens in a cheap hotel, where Eugene, Carney, and another recruit wait their turns with a prostitute who is currently servicing Wykowski; Eugene is clearly inexperienced, naïve, and nervous about losing his virginity in this way. Carney leaves without taking his turn, not wanting to be unfaithful to his girlfriend, but Eugene goes in and meets Rowena. Giving a false name and family background, he gets in bed with her and quickly, with the lights off, accomplishes his goal.

Back in the barracks, Wykowski reads aloud from Eugene's "secret and private" journal, taken from his unsecured locker. The recruits are offended by his frank and unflattering remarks about them, while Eugene feels he should have been able to trust them to respect his privacy and property. Wykowski reads a passage describing his prodigious masturbatory capabilities but then finds a passage praising his earnestness and dependability in combat. Epstein reads the description of himself, including Eugene's "instinctive feeling" that Epstein "is homosexual, and it bothers me that it bothers me." He tosses the book on Eugene's bunk.

Sitting alone outside the barracks, near despair, Eugene is joined by Carney, who concedes that the characterization of him as not dependable or decisive was accurate. He then discusses his doubts about marrying his unfaithful girlfriend. Back inside, Toomey rouses the men from bed and announces that two soldiers were seen engaging in oral intercourse in a darkened latrine. One, who escaped through a window, was seen running into their barracks. After Toomey leaves, Wykowski implicates Epstein, referring again to Eugene's written remark. Eugene apologizes to Epstein and tears up the journal page; he has, he tells the audience, learned a lesson about responsibility. Another soldier, James Hennessey, is arrested shortly thereafter.

At a dance, Eugene falls in love with a Catholic student, Daisy Hannigan. In the barracks, Toomey has a drunken discussion with Epstein and points a loaded pistol at him, ordering him to drink and announcing plans to blow out the private's brains. He also says that the next morning he will enter a veterans' hospital, his army career having been terminated. Intending to make a disciplined soldier out of Eptsein, Toomey orders him to take the gun away forcibly and, after a struggle, allows him to do so. He then orders Epstein to arrest him and summon the platoon. Epstein offers to drop charges in exchange for two hundred push-ups, fulfilling his fantasy. Toomey is transferred out the next morning.

Basic training ends, as does Eugene's never-consummated infatuation with Daisy. On parting, she gives him a book to use to start another journal. The play ends as it began, on a troop train. In a final speech to the audience, Eugene summarizes what happened to the other characters and himself during the war. Wykowski loses a leg in combat and is cited for bravery; Epstein is missing in action and never found; Carney is hospitalized for neurological disorders and severe depression. Eugene injures his back in a jeep accident on his first day in England and sees no combat. Sent back stateside, he becomes a writer for *Stars and Stripes.*

Impact of Event

Biloxi Blues is the second play in Neil Simon's autobiographical "Eugene Jerome" trilogy, which began in 1983 with *Brighton Beach Memoirs* and concluded in 1986 with *Broadway Bound.* Whereas the earlier play had depicted the central character during early adolescence with his family in Brighton Beach, New York, the sequel presents his experience as a military inductee in Gulfport and Biloxi, Mississippi in 1943.

Theatergoers who had grown familiar with the comic style Simon had developed throughout his twenty-one previous Broadway comedies—the New York setting, the middle-class characters, the inoffensive language, the absence of challenging or controversial subject matter—were in for a surprise from *Biloxi Blues.* Unlike the earlier plays, *Biloxi Blues* occurs in multiple locations in Mississippi (including a train, the barracks, the mess hall, a hotel room, a church basement) and is made up of fourteen scenes in two acts, requiring a more flexible use of theatrical space than the standard single-set format of his other works. Although Eugene remains the same genial, thoughtful, wisecracking character that he was in the previous play, the other recruits are decidedly rowdier and lower-class than characters Simon had created before. Although the dialogue shows his usual craftsmanship and polished wit, his recruits speak in convincingly gritty language. From literally the first line and continually throughout the play, the dialogue is realistically profanity-laden. Each of the first six lines contains an oath or insult; when Eugene begins his first direct address to the audience, his tone and style set him clearly and immediately apart from his companions.

Much of the humor is also decidedly earthier than in Simon's previous plays: jokes about flatulence, foot odor, permanent erections, penis size, masturbation, sexual positions, and intimate fantasies abound, as do ethnic and sexual epithets. The centrality of sexual issues, frankly discussed, is also unprecedented in Simon's work, not only in the on-stage depiction of Eugene's loss of his virginity (even if in the dark) but also in the play's portrayal of homosexuality within the military and the explicit naming of the specific practice in which the apprehended soldiers were clandestinely engaged. Although *Biloxi Blues* is mild in comparison to such other contemporary plays as Harvey Fierstein's *Torch Song Trilogy* (1982) and David Rabe's *The Basic Training of Pavlo Hummel* (1971), its frankness is a significant innovation in Simon's style.

Like *Brighton Beach Memoirs, Biloxi Blues* tells a number of characters' stories simultaneously and creates more complex, well-rounded characters than there are in Simon's earlier plays, which tended to rely on deftly comic complications arising from a single-premise situation, as in *The Odd Couple* (1965) and *Barefoot in the Park* (1963). Such serious moral issues as ethnic persecution and Eugene's tacit complicity in not defending Epstein as a fellow Jew have obvious political ramifications. Such concerns consistently underlie the entertaining surface of the play, as does the question of the degree of commitment or disengagement required of the writer—a favorite theme of existentialist writers of a generation earlier as well.

Apart from the character of Eugene, who functions as a commentator on and participant in the action, as a sardonic narrator, and as a naïvely inexperienced conscript, several other roles require from their actors a complex characterization and emotional range surpassing that in most of Simon's earlier plays. Thus, for example, Sergeant Toomey's harshness and quasisadistic control must convincingly deteriorate into a drunken and nearly murderous abusiveness, though his insistence on the lifesaving value of discipline prevents him from being a mere caricature. Epstein embodies the counter-traits of logic, dignity, and compassion, but he is also the butt of jokes and scorn, markedly intellectual but occasionally priggish, as when he refuses Wykowski's proffered handshake. The female characters are less effectively developed and are in fact little more than stereotypes—literally a madonna (the chaste Catholic, Daisy) and a whore (Rowena).

Apart from Lanford Wilson's "Talley" plays—*Talley's Folly* (1980), *Fifth of July* (1981), and *Talley and Son* (1985)—and Eugene O'Neill's plays about the Tyrone family, *Long Day's Journey into Night* (1956) and *A Moon for the Misbegotten* (1957), there is no comparably developed set of interrelated plays in American drama. There are also few playwrights who have dealt as seriously—or as humorously—with the experience of becoming a writer. This theme is resumed in *Broadway Bound*, as Eugene returns home to his family, teams up with his brother, and begins his career as a comedy writer. The role of Eugene's mother is developed with particular poignancy in this final play of the trilogy.

Biloxi Blues won the Tony Award as best play of 1985, the first of Simon's plays to be thus recognized. He also wrote the screenplay for the 1988 film version, which was directed by Mike Nichols. Matthew Broderick reprised his role as Eugene in the film, and Sergeant Toomey was played, somewhat soft-spokenly, by Christopher Walken. Although the film version is, on the whole, a close and faithful adaptation of the play, it shows Toomey's final drunken confrontation taking place with Eugene rather than with Epstein. None of the recruits sees action in the film version, and the postwar lives detailed in Eugene's final speech are more benign.

Bibliography

Hirschhorn, Clive. "Make 'em Laugh: Neil Simon in Interview with Clive Hirschhorn." *Plays and Players* 24 (September, 1977): 12-15. Simon discusses his admiration for the plays of George Kaufman and Moss Hart and early silent-film comedies, in which he finds compassion that many plays lack. He also discusses his lesser-known but experimental works, including *God's Favorite* (1974) and *The Good Doctor* (1973), and contrasts the New York and London versions of his works.

Johnson, Robert K. *Neil Simon.* Boston: Twayne, 1983. Useful survey of Simon's work through *Only When I Laugh* (1981), including musicals and original screenplays. Emphasizes recurrent serious themes in Simon's comedy and his varied stylistic formats. Notes, index, annotated bibliography.

Kaufman, David. "Simon Says: A Conversation with Neil Simon." *Horizon* 28 (June, 1985): 55-60. In this interview, published shortly after *Biloxi Blues* opened, Simon notes the presence of serious themes in his previous plays but contends that *Brighton Beach Memoirs* and *Biloxi Blues* are his first "full-bodied" plays "dealing with a group of people as individuals and telling all their stories." Photographs.

Linderman, Lawrence. "Playboy Interview: Neil Simon." *Playboy* 26 (February, 1979): 58-78. In this extensive interview, Simon discusses his career as a playwright, his two marriages, and the casting of several of the films made from his plays.

McGovern, Edythe M. *Neil Simon: A Critical Study.* New York: Frederick Ungar, 1979. A play-by-play assessment of Simon's first twelve plays, through *Chapter Two* (1977), including cast lists, production data, many photographs, and drawings. Expands and updates a paperback version first published as *Not-So-Simple Neil Simon* (1978). Notes, index; preface contributed by Simon himself.

Richards, David. "The Last of the Red Hot Playwrights." *The New York Times Magazine*, February 17, 1991; 30-32, 36, 57, 64. In this biographical profile, Simon is described as the last "Broadway" playwright, a commercially successful but critically disdained hit-maker. Richards cites the trilogy that includes *Biloxi Blues* as Simon's turning point, as pain and sadness are increasingly present in his comic world. Simon also reflects on Broadway's bleak commercial prospects.

Simon, Neil, and David Rabe. "The Craft of the Playwright: A Conversation Between Neil Simon and David Rabe." *The New York Times Magazine*, May 26, 1985, 36-38, 52, 56-63. Published during the Broadway run of *Biloxi Blues*, this conversation includes Simon's most theoretical discussion of his art. Topics include writing for the theater, the distinction between comedy and drama, the role of the unconscious, misogyny and the writing of parts for women, the urge to direct, and the future of theatrical writing.

Zimmerman, Paul D. "Neil Simon: Up from Success." *Newsweek* 79 (February 2, 1970): 52-56. This portrait of the playwright as a young man includes much detail about Simon's childhood and his career as a writer for television. Simon also discusses his desire to develop more sophisticated plot structures and more complex characters.

William Hutchings

Cross-References

Hašek's *The Good Soldier Švejk* Reflects Postwar Disillusionment (1921), p. 523; Mailer Publishes *The Naked and the Dead* (1948), p. 1373; *Catch-22* Illustrates Antiwar Sentiment (1961), p. 1866; Mortimer's *A Voyage Round My Father* Is Embraced by Audiences (1971), p. 2249; Shepard's *Buried Child* Promotes Off-Broadway Theater (1978), p. 2413.

LIVE AID GENERATES MILLIONS FOR FAMINE RELIEF

Category of event: Music
Time: July 13, 1985
Locale: Philadelphia, Pennsylvania, and London, England

The biggest concert in history, Live Aid reached close to two billion television viewers in 150 countries and raised more than $72 million for African famine victims

Principal personages:

BOB GELDOF (1952-   ), the principal organizer of the Live Aid concerts and the leader of the rock band the Boomtown Rats

BILL GRAHAM (WOLFGANG GRAJONCA, 1931-1991), the legendary rock music impresario who coproduced the Philadelphia Live Aid concert

MICHAEL MITCHELL, the producer responsible for marketing the global television broadcast of Live Aid

HARVEY GOLDSMITH, a top music promoter in England who helped to assemble the London Live Aid concert

TATPARANANDAM ANANDA KRISHNAN (1938-   ), an oil executive who contributed money to the Live Aid project

Summary of Event

The Live Aid concerts were sixteen-hour musical benefits held simultaneously in Philadelphia, Pennsylvania, at John F. Kennedy Stadium and in London, England, at Wembley Stadium on July 13, 1985. More than sixty acts participated, including many of the biggest names in popular music. Long-established stars such as Eric Clapton, Bob Dylan, Crosby, Stills, and Nash, Joan Baez, Mick Jagger, Keith Richards, Led Zeppelin, Grace Slick, Elton John, Paul McCartney, Tina Turner, and the Who performed alongside a number of newer stars such as Madonna, Billy Idol, U2, Sting, and Run-D.M.C. All the artists performed without pay to help raise money for famine-stricken Ethiopians, victims of years of war, drought, and displacement.

The Live Aid concerts were the last in a series of events put on by Band Aid Trust, a British organization of people in the music business dedicated to drawing attention to world hunger and raising money to combat starvation. Band Aid was the name of a group of popular-music stars who in 1984 recorded the song "Do They Know It's Christmas" to raise money to help relieve the starvation and suffering occurring in Ethiopia. The band included British stars Bono of U2, Simon Le Bon, George Michael, Phil Collins, Sting, and Boy George, among others. The project was the brainchild of the musician Bob Geldof, leader of the Irish band the Boomtown Rats. Distressed by television images of malnourished Ethiopians, Geldof decided a large-scale project had to be undertaken to help them.

The concept of many big names joining forces for one recording to heighten social awareness and to raise money for famine relief was irresistible to the news media. The well-promoted song, written by Geldof and Midge Ure of Ultravox, was a number-one hit in England and sold one-and-a-half million copies in the United States. All profits went to Band Aid Trust and were donated to Ethiopian relief efforts. Geldof himself became a popular news item, and he was dubbed "St. Bob" by a slightly skeptical press.

Band Aid's success encouraged a number of American musicians to organize U.S.A. for Africa and to record the benefit single "We Are the World," produced by Quincy Jones and written by megastars Michael Jackson and Lionel Richie, in December, 1984. Bob Dylan, Paul Simon, Dionne Warwick, Ray Charles, Smokey Robinson, Diana Ross, and Bruce Springsteen were among the performers who sang on the record. Having attended this second recording session and seen the world-wide success of another benefit single, Geldof was encouraged. He took on the formidable responsibility of organizing the Live Aid concerts, which he hoped would further spotlight the problem of poverty and hunger in Africa and elsewhere.

About this time, a Malaysian oil baron named Tatparanandam Ananda Krishnan read about Geldof and decided that his efforts deserved the support of what Krishnan called his "social venture capital." A wealthy and altruistic Harvard University graduate, Krishnan believed that charity money should be invested in big projects capable of generating large amounts of money to help the world's underprivileged. Earlier that year, Krishnan had formed Worldwide Sports and Entertainment, a company intended to organize events on the same huge scale as Live Aid. He introduced Geldof to Michael Mitchell, who had helped to stage the spectacular 1984 Olympics in Los Angeles. Mitchell became responsible for marketing the concerts and coordinating the global television broadcast. Krishnan then provided Geldof with $1,750,000 in cash and credit. His donation got the massive concert rolling, according to Harvey Goldsmith, England's top music promoter and a coproducer of Live Aid.

For weeks, Geldof worked nonstop, contacting artists and their agents, giving interviews, and organizing the technical, financial, and marketing machinery needed to make the concerts a success. Most of the money would be raised through televised requests for call-in pledges; the planners adopted the video fund-raising method that entertainer Jerry Lewis had used for years in his telethons to raise money to combat muscular dystrophy.

The promoters for Live Aid at first presented the event as a 1980's version of the legendary Woodstock concert of 1969. As a media event, however, Live Aid became much bigger than Woodstock; it became both the biggest concert in history and the largest television broadcast ever made. Fourteen satellites were used to broadcast the concerts live to ninety-six countries; another sixty-five countries were provided with a televised four-hour taped version.

The twin concerts were at first expected to raise $10 million and reach an audience of one billion. The producers afterward estimated that from one-and-a-half billion to two billion people around the world watched the shows on television. Eventually, more than $72 million was raised for famine relief; the concerts cost about $5 million to mount.

Having visited Ethiopia after the success of "Do They Know It's Christmas," Bob Geldof was aware that distributing the funds generated by the project required careful planning. He was most interested in creating long-term improvements in Ethiopia's agricultural system. While some of the money was used to purchase food and supplies to distribute directly to people, Band Aid Trust donated most of the money to purchase trucks for transporting food and to support development projects: building bridges, installing irrigation systems, and drilling wells.

A few days after the shows aired, Geldof was nominated by high-level officials in England, Ireland, and Norway for the Nobel Peace Prize.

Impact of Event

Live Aid marked the first time that an event of such scale had incorporated television broadcasting and coverage as part of its basic planning. The global broadcast was crucial to accomplishing Live Aid's mission; television was actually a component of the event, rather than simply a means of sharing or reporting it.

Although the global broadcast was completed with relatively few hitches for so complex an undertaking, American television coverage of the Live Aid concerts was widely criticized. The cable channel Music Television (MTV) took the most criticism. Its "veejays" were panned by *The New York Times* for their apparent ignorance of rock music's history; *Variety* described them as "more intent on showing themselves than the performers." Nevertheless, MTV was praised for its decision to cover the full sixteen hours of the concerts.

One hundred and five independent stations aired a syndicated eleven-hour version of the event; the American Broadcasting Company (ABC) broadcast a three-hour prime-time special hosted by Dick Clark. These broadcasts, though, shared MTV's problems of bland hosts and video miscues. For example, on ABC's show, only a portion of the reunited group Led Zeppelin's performance of "Stairway to Heaven" was shown, even though it was one of the most eagerly anticipated events of the day.

Viewers were also overwhelmed by a steady barrage of commercials. Music promoter Bill Graham, who coproduced the Philadelphia concert, declared that he was appalled by what he saw on television. "The people at home were raped by television," he remarked. Moreover, the rock world was dismayed that the concerts and fund drive were not given serious news coverage. *Rolling Stone* magazine marveled that the show could have received so little responsible coverage even though it was the largest television broadcast in history and was designed to raise millions of dollars for the famine-stricken in Africa.

The Live Aid benefits marked what many considered a movement back toward a belief in music as an agent for social change, a belief that had seemed to wane since the early 1970's. Social concerns and causes were suddenly important again to musicians and audiences. Many felt that such 1970's trends as disco music and glamour rock had been frivolous, even empty, compared to the emotionally and politically daring songs of the 1960's and early 1970's that had decried the Vietnam War, demanded civil rights, and explored social changes of every kind.

The success of the Live Aid concerts may have shown that some fundamental reevaluation was taking place in popular music in the 1980's, just as it had in the early 1960's. Music critics have suggested that the 1980's revival of conscience in popular music is reflected in the lyrics of such socially committed performers as Tracy Chapman, Suzanne Vega, Natalie Merchant and the 10,000 Maniacs, and Bruce Hornsby and the Range. Their hits in the mid 1980's displayed their musical talent as well as their ability to study and respond to social problems. Live Aid certainly seemed in 1985 to herald a change of tone in the popular music world.

As a result of the Live Aid concerts, similar events blossomed to raise money for other stricken groups. Bob Dylan's comments during his Live Aid performance on the plight of the American farmer resulted in Farm Aid, a fourteen-hour concert on September 22, 1985, that raised ten million dollars. Farm Aid became an annual event. An antiapartheid album, *Sun City*, was released in 1985 under the direction of Little Steven Van Zandt, who had become famous as a guitarist for Bruce Spring-steen's E Street Band. Audiences, though, seemed less inclined to be moved by a human-rights issue such as apartheid than by the stark and horrifying film images of Ethiopian children wracked with starvation; the single "Sun City" barely entered the Top Forty.

On the other hand, further proof of popular music's renewed social conscience— and a more successful politically-oriented project—came with the human-rights or-ganization Amnesty International's series of tours and benefit concerts. The 1986 Conspiracy of Hope Tour of the United States and the worldwide Human Rights Now! tour of 1988 helped to boost the membership of Amnesty International from 200,000 in 1986 to more than 420,000 members worldwide in 1988. Amnesty Inter-national attracted high-caliber stars for its benefits; U2, Sting, Peter Gabriel, Joan Baez, Tracy Chapman, and Bruce Springsteen were among the tours' headliners.

Singer and songwriter Sting called the Amnesty International tours "the most satisfying thing I've ever done." Both Sting and Jackson Browne, well-known for his music's political commitment, praised the Amnesty tours for teaching interested people how to get involved in the process of pressing for social change. Jack Healy, the executive director of Amnesty International U.S.A., pointed out that people got involved in Live Aid only for long enough to call in a pledge. The Amnesty Interna-tional benefit concerts, on the other hand, provided a structure that permitted inter-ested concertgoers to join the organization. Still, Healy and others agreed that the Live Aid concerts had marked a turning point in popular music in the mid-1980's, making the subsequent benefits possible and encouraging artists whose work was fueled by social conscience.

Bob Geldof explained that being brought up in the 1960's, a heady period of radical change, had taught him that music was the driving force behind that change. Although many would disagree that popular music truly wields such power, during the Live Aid shows, music did manage to affect the way millions of people were thinking—and to translate that thought into humanitarian action.

Bibliography

Breskin, David. "Bob Geldof." *Rolling Stone* (December 5, 1985): 26-27, 30, 33-34, 60, 63-66. An in-depth interview with Geldof five months after the Live Aid concerts. Geldof discusses the project, his motivations, his band, his frustrations, and what he learned and saw during recent trips to Africa.

Coleman, Mark, and Rob Tannenbaum. "The Revival of Conscience." *Rolling Stone* 591 (November 15, 1990): 69-71, 76, 80. Coleman's article reviews the concert benefits that have been staged since Live Aid and offers comments from several singer-songwriters (Sting, Billy Bragg, Jackson Browne, Natalie Merchant) on the power of rock music to effect social change. Tannenbaum interviews Bob Geldof.

Geldof, Bob. *Is That It?* New York: Weidenfield & Nicholson, 1986. Geldof's auto-biography was written immediately after the Live Aid event; thus, even though the book begins conventionally with his boyhood, the momentum is really toward a full description of what it was like to organize Band Aid and the massive concert benefit. Includes index.

Goldberg, Michael. "The Day the World Rocked." *Rolling Stone* (August 15, 1985): 22-26, 32-34. Goldberg presents an entertaining on-the-scene account of the Live Aid concerts, beginning with a brief history of Geldof's charity efforts and how those behind the scenes put the shows together. Describes highlights of the shows and includes interviews with performers.

Szatmary, David P. *Rockin' in Time: A Social History of Rock and Roll.* Englewood Cliffs, N.J.: Prentice-Hall, 1987. This history of rock music from 1950 to 1986 uses music to illuminate the American experience. Szatmary does not mention Live Aid, but he explores topics the event raised: the impact of technological advances on rock music and the relationship between rock and business, economics, and politics. Includes bibliography, discography, and index.

Westley, Frances. "Bob Geldof and Live Aid: The Affective Side of Global Social Innovation." *Human Relations* 44 (October, 1991): 1011-1037. Westley discusses how Geldof used the strong affective power of music to create a bond between American youth and the starving people of Ethiopia. She explores how such vi- · sionary leadership is related to global social innovation.

JoAnn Balingit

Cross-References

The First Newport Jazz Festival Is Held (1954), p. 1617; Dylan Performs with Electric Instruments (1965), p. 2038; The Monterey Pop Festival Inaugurates the "Summer of Love" (1967), p. 2104; The Woodstock Music Festival Marks the Climax of the 1960's (1969), p. 2180; Led Zeppelin Merges Hard Rock and Folk Music (1971), p. 2228.

CHRISTO WRAPS THE PONT NEUF

Category of event: Art
Time: September 22-October 7, 1985
Locale: Paris, France

After more than ten years of planning and negotiations, Christo transformed the oldest bridge in Paris into a temporary art work

Principal personages:
CHRISTO (CHRISTO JAVACHEFF, 1935-   ), a Bulgarian artist who transforms objects and the environment to create his temporary works
JOHANNES SCHAUB, the project director for the *Pont Neuf Wrapped*

Summary of Event

For two weeks in 1985, the Pont Neuf, the oldest bridge in Paris, was draped and swathed in fabric, transforming the familiar tourist attraction into a personal statement by the artist Christo. Three million viewers swarmed to see the sight. Some reportedly sat on the bridge's stone benches, which Christo cushioned with foam rubber and covered with fabric. Some Parisians even slept there. More energetic viewers played musical instruments on the bridge or painted pictures, while photographers captured the light and shadows of the pleated fabric, appropriating Christo's work to make it their own. Some found the bridge, with all its viewers, a romantic place to steal a kiss. Others hired catering services and held dinner parties at the site, while others still, with more serious agendas, found the bridge a suitable place to demonstrate and air their grievances to a large, ready-made audience.

Reviewer John Howell, writing for *Artforum*, declared that Christo's latest art work would ensure him a "spot right up there in Cecil B. DeMille's class as a creator of dazzling spectacle." He likened the transformation of the old stone bridge, covered by 440,000 square feet of golden fabric, to a spectacular waterfall. Other reviewers, such as Thomas R. Matthews of *Progressive Architecture*, reminded readers that the spring collection fashion shows occurred at approximately the same time that Christo's temporary artwork was exhibited. He noted the even pleating of the fabric covering the bridge, made more regular by adjustment by specially hired professional rock climbers.

The physical wrapping of the Pont Neuf took seven days and eight thousand people-hours of effort. The removal of the work took an additional thirty-five hundred people-hours of work. While the work was exhibited, 660 people worked as monitors, answering questions and protecting the work from any vandalism. It is estimated that Christo spent $2.5 million American dollars on the project, which he financed personally through the sale of his preparatory drawings, collages, scale models, prints, and early work by the C.V.J. Corporation, of which his wife Jeanne-Claude and he are president and treasurer.

The Pont Neuf project, like all of Christo's large environmental works, offered unique challenges and problems. Christo respected the historic importance of the structure and designed an appropriate dignified treatment for it. Construction of the Pont Neuf (or "The New Bridge") was started in 1578 and completed in 1606. Joining the Left Bank of the Seine with the Right Bank, the Pont Neuf also transverses the Île de la Cité, the island in the Seine that has been the heart of Paris for more than two thousand years. From this bridge, one can see many sights of Paris—the Panthéon, where famous French people such as Victor Hugo and Émile Zola are entombed; the Eiffel Tower; the Académie Française; and the Louvre, the celebrated art museum that was once the palace of the French kings. One can also see La Samaritaine, one of the most famous department stores in France, displaying the best of Parisian high fashion.

Christo wanted to create the illusion that the fabric was supported by the bridge alone. In reality, though, such an approach could have damaged the fragile structure. Christo had to devise a method of suspending the fabric that would not entail driving nails or bolts into the limestone of the bridge. Working with architectural advisers, Christo's team tested and refined their methods by first experimenting on a trial bridge located in a town sixty miles southeast of Paris. The mayor of this town offered to let Christo use the twelfth century stone bridge in exchange for funds that were used for burying unsightly telephone lines.

The method that was devised and used on the Pont Neuf consisted of steel-tube construction created to keep the fabric and ropes away from the stone ledge. Wood protected the parapets of the bridge. Concrete beams held the piping to which the fabric was attached. Professional rock climbers scaled the bridge, placing rubber attachment points on the stone that were later removed without leaving a trace. The fabric was also secured three feet underwater at the base of the tower of each arch. This job required more than twelve tons of steel chains.

Christo promised that traffic on and around the bridge would not be hindered in any way at any stage of the project. That traffic included automobiles moving over the bridge and also under one of the twelve arches where the Georges Pompidou Expressway runs, pedestrian traffic that would move on fabric-covered sidewalks on the bridge and also on the point of an embankment surrounding a statue, and boat traffic under the arches of the bridge. Forty streetlights line the bridge, and four more illuminate the embankment. These were all personally covered by Christo. Originally, light was to shine through the cloth, and the fabric was treated with a flame retardant. For the safety of night traffic on the river, however, holes had to be made in the fabric so that the lights were more visible to boaters.

The project wound up costing one million dollars more than originally planned and took more than ten years in negotiations and preparations before its realization.

Impact of Event

To understand Christo, one must appreciate the fact that he was born in Nazi-occupied Bulgaria and was only nine years old when Soviet forces invaded to liberate his country. Christo lived behind the Iron Curtain in a world divided, and curtains and fabric are important to him in a symbolic way. Trained at the Academy of Fine Arts in Sofia, he was influenced by the ideas of the Russian constructivists, whose ideas officially were not to be taught but which in reality were. Christo was also introduced at this time to the value of art as propaganda and political statement. As students, he and his classmates spent weekends from 1952 to 1955 traveling the route of the luxurious Orient Express. Their task was to create, through art, the illusions of wealth and of a successful communist revolution for those who passed through Bulgaria on the rapidly moving train. Boxes and old objects were draped to give the illusion of new farm machinery or of mighty military equipment. In reality, very little of substance lay beneath the fabric.

This early experience greatly influenced Christo's later work. Christo is an artist who continuously creates illusions. His work is political in nature, and it is viewed by passersby rather than by regular museum or gallery attendees. He challenges political systems, governments, laws, and established mores and norms. Christo also challenges the art world and shies away from established art world procedures. He is allied with no gallery, and he owes no debt to art journals for any of his publicity. He prides himself on accepting no grants or public funding for any of his large, temporary projects. He is a capitalist from a communist country, completely embracing practices of entrepreneurship. He and his wife have created a corporation for the sale of his portable work. It is in this manner that they are able to raise the great amounts of money his projects demand.

Christo managed to leave Bulgaria, traveling first to Prague, then to Vienna, and then in 1958 to Paris, where he earned his living by meticulously painting realistic portraits in an academic style. In Paris, Christo was hired to paint a portrait by General and Comtesse Jacques de Guillebon. Their daughter was Jeanne-Claude, the woman who later became his wife and partner.

Christo lived in Paris for six years before moving to New York City with his wife and son in 1964. It was in the 1960's that Christo first envisioned his six plans for artwork in Paris in which he would wrap the Arc de Triomphe; shroud the crowns of trees along the Champs-Élysées; wrap the École Militaire, the Pont Neuf, and the Pont Alexander III; and barricade the Rue Visconti, the smallest street in Paris. In 1962, without a permit, he created a wall of stacked oil barrels two stories high on the Rue Visconti, obstructing traffic in this area of the city for eight evening hours. He called this work "Iron Curtain-Wall of Oil Barrels" and linked it thematically to two events in the politics of the time: the creation of the Berlin Wall in 1961, and an attack on British Petroleum in Oran that resulted in an explosion of ten million liters of oil. This risky work pushed the little-known refugee into the area of international renown.

Christo created photo collages and photo montages of his other intended art works for Paris, and in 1968 he made a formal proposal to wrap the trees on the Champs-Élysées, hiring an arborist to study the various side effects. In autumn of 1969, permission for this project was denied. During this same period, however, Christo had many other projects approved, including wrapping of the Museum of Contemporary Art in Chicago (1969), the Kunsthalle in Bern, Switzerland (1968), a sea coast in Little Bay, Australia (1969), and a wall in Rome (1974). With each successful project, he matured and became more knowledgeable about the procedures necessary to accomplish his goals. In 1974, he returned to his Paris project idea, concentrating on the Pont Neuf, making his first formal proposal for the *Pont Neuf Wrapped* project in 1976.

Using all the influence of Jeanne-Claude's family connections, Christo and his wife attended countless meetings with people such as the wife of former French president Georges Pompidou, Michel Boutinard Rouelle (the director of cultural affairs of the city of Paris), and Jacques Chirac (the mayor of Paris). Despite the influence, negotiations were at a standstill until Christo met Johannes Schaub, a Swiss management consultant. Schaub persuaded Christo and Jeanne-Claude to change their tactics and campaign like politicians for the Pont Neuf project. Rather than focusing on or obtaining approval from highly placed political figures, Schaub believed that the business community surrounding the Pont Neuf and the Parisian social establishment needed to be reached. Support at this grass-roots level had to be demonstrated before politicians would agree to anything.

In 1981, Schaub became the project director for the *Pont Neuf Wrapped* and immediately set up press conferences and a lecture series for Christo. Christo began speaking at major universities in the Paris area. A door-to-door lobbying campaign for the project was also conducted. Young women were hired, armed with thousands of postcards of Christo's drawings of the wrapped Pont Neuf to distribute to residences and business in the vicinity of the bridge. These women explained the project on a one-to-one basis and arranged for individuals and groups to meet with the artist. This aroused the interest of hundreds of people who started a letter-writing campaign to the mayor of Paris.

Schaub also got permission from the chief executive officer of the La Samaritaine department store to have Jeanne-Claude and Christo meet with the employees of the store during their luncheon and coffee breaks. The artist and his wife spent three days at the store speaking with employees. Because of this, store personnel spoke knowledgeably about the project to thousands of customers.

La Samaritaine also allowed a twenty-foot model of the *Pont Neuf Wrapped* to go on display in one of the store's windows facing the bridge. Information sheets on the project were posted on the department store on a heavily trafficked sidewalk. In this way, yet more people were mobilized, and an organization called "Parisians for the Pont Neuf Project" was formed. Members organized a series of dinner parties involving the art world, especially those connected with Paris' new Museum of Modern Art. It was apparent to everyone, except the politicians, that permission would be granted.

The mayor of Paris and his conservative advisers remained emphatically against the project. It was not until 1984 that the mayor finally gave his consent, only to have the chief of police of Paris block the final permit in 1985. Johannes Schaub persisted, and was able to reach France's president, François Mitterrand, who ordered that the final permit be granted.

The Pont Neuf was the most spectacular of Christo's work to date. He mobilized an entire city, gaining final approval from no less than the head of the country himself. He continued his work despite the lack of approval of Parisian officials. The refugee artist who had blocked city traffic with 240 oil barrels returned in triumph, spending millions of dollars of his own money to realize his dream. He involved millions of people in the same dream. No longer commenting on a specific political event, he created a political event.

With the *Pont Neuf Wrapped*, Christo linked art to other areas of existence. He negotiated and campaigned as if he were the head of a political movement. His budget was that of a film production, involving a cast of thousands. He created the fervor of a rock show, with people sleeping outside his office to be the first to register to become a monitor or a worker. Christo lectures that he does this to keep his sanity. Out of this frenetic energy and endless bureaucracy emerge his ideas, showing that the individual still has significance in the modern world. The fact that he accomplishes work such as the *Pont Neuf Wrapped* changes art and the concept of what art can be.

Bibliography

Christo. *Christo Prints and Objects, 1963-1987: A Catalogue Raisonné*. Edited by Jörg Schellmann and Josephine Benecke. New York: Abbeville Press, 1988. A catalog of Christo's work during this time period, with an introduction by Werner Spies.

Himmel, Eric, ed. *Christo: The Pont-Neuf, Wrapped: Paris, 1975-1985*. New York: Harry N. Abrams, 1990. An oversized book featuring in detail everything about the Pont Neuf project, including copies of the original correspondences and documents concerning the project. Also contains a history of the Pont Neuf, many reproductions of Christo's preliminary drawings and collages, and wonderful photographs of the completed *Pont Neuf Wrapped*.

Laporte, Dominique. *Christo*. New York: Pantheon Books, 1986. A translation from Laporte's original French text, this is an excellent, detailed discussion of the artist from political, historical, and artistic perspectives.

Satani Gallery. *Christo: The Pont Neuf Wrapped, Project for Paris*. Tokyo: Author, 1984. An exhibition catalog featuring text by Yusuke Nakahara and an interview by Masahiko Yanagi.

Vaizey, Marina. *Christo*. New York: Rizzoli International Publications, 1990. A coffee-table book with little text but with many pictures of the artist's work.

D. Tulla Lightfoot

Cross-References

Duchamp's "Readymades" Challenge Concepts of Art (1913), p. 349; The Dada

Movement Emes at the Cabaret Voltaire (1916), p. 419; Minimalism Emphasizes Objects as Art (1963), p. 1949; Nam June Paik Exhibits Video and Television as Art (1963), p. 1955; Warhol's *The Chelsea Girls* Becomes a Commercial Success (1966), p. 2053.

THE DECLINE OF THE BIG THREE NETWORKS BECOMES A FALL

Category of event: Television and radio
Time: The late 1980's
Locale: The United States

The "Big Three" networks—NBC, CBS, and ABC—dominated television for more than three decades, but during the latter half of the 1980's, this domination was increasingly challenged on a number of fronts

> *Principal personages:*
> TED TURNER (1938-   ), the owner of Turner Broadcast Systems (TBS), who repeatedly challenged the supremacy of the networks
> RUPERT MURDOCH (1931-   ), an Australian immigrant who became chairman of Twentieth Century-Fox

Summary of Event

The United States' three major networks, the American Broadcasting Company (ABC), the Columbia Broadcasting System (CBS), and the National Broadcasting Company (NBC), rose to power during the 1950's and for the next two decades dominated the American television industry. For much of that time, network shows attracted more than ninety percent of all U.S. television audiences. During the 1980's, though, the networks' dominance began to wane; by the 1990-1991 season, the "Big Three" networks' audience share had plummeted to sixty-one percent.

The networks ignored the early harbingers of trouble. The Public Broadcasting System (PBS) was launched in the early 1970's, but public television never succeeded in capturing more than five percent of the viewers in any major market. A more serious challenge arose in the 1970's with the Time-Life corporation's launch of Home Box Office (HBO), the first subscription-service channel. Its impact was minimal during the 1970's but HBO and other pay-television stations would make inroads against the Big Three during the 1980's. By 1990, pay-for-view stations had a combined total of just under forty million subscribers, with HBO alone accounting for seventeen million subscribers.

Flamboyant multimillionaire Ted Turner entered the foray against the networks' hegemony in the 1970's when he purchased an Atlanta-based independent television station. WTBS would become the first "superstation," beaming its signal into tens of millions of cable subscribers' homes. Turner's station, purchased for $2.5 million in 1970, would be estimated to be generating revenue of $75 million a year in 1989. Turner used such profits to purchase Metro-Goldwyn-Mayer (MGM), including MGM's library of film classics. With the acquisition of this extensive library, he was poised to launch another venture, Turner Network Television (TNT), which broadcast motion pictures around the clock.

Added to the growing number of pay-for-view stations and superstations was the phenomenal growth of specialized stations that offered programming nonexistent before the 1980's. Most of these new stations were geared toward a specific audience. Music Television (MTV) featured rock videos and was aimed at the twelve-to-twenty-three-year-old age group; other stations were geared toward specific presentation forms, such as the Entertainment and Sports Network, (ESPN), the Weather Channel, the Cable News Network (CNN), and many more. Specialized program channels and other widely viewed channels such as Lifetime, Arts and Entertainment (A&E), TNT, Black Entertainment Television (BET), and American Movie Classics (AMC) also entered the market. Many of these stations were typically available on basic cable systems; most had gained some following during the 1980's and had vastly extended their earlier limited format to twenty-four-hour a day broadcasts by the end of the decade.

In addition to the variety of channels widely available on cable for a relatively modest fee, the Big Three had to share the limelight with the upstart Fox Network beginning in 1986. Backed by media mogul Rupert Murdoch, Fox started slowly, introducing original programs only on Sunday evening, then branching out over the next few years to other nights. Within four years, Fox was broadcasting original programs five nights a week and children's shows on Saturday morning. By 1990, regular original television programming was no longer confined to the Big Three; now it was the Big Four.

The networks were also to be challenged by a revolution in viewing habits that began with the introduction of Sony's Betamax videocassette recorder in 1976. Like many other inventions, Sony's videocassette recorder (VCR) gained acceptance slowly at first. One reason for the slow initial reception was competitive confusion over which VCR format would have staying power, Betamax or the rival VHS system. (VHS would emerge the winner, accounting for ninety-one percent of all VCR sales by the end of the 1980's.) Another reason for the initial consumer hesitancy was the cost of each unit, which would drop dramatically during the decade. As prices dropped, sales soared; while less than one percent of American households owned a VCR prior to 1980 and sales remained lackluster through 1983, sales climbed rapidly through the rest of the decade. Thirty-six percent of American households had a VCR by 1986, a number that had risen to seventy percent by 1989. In less than ten years, the VCR had become an appendage to television sets across the country.

The VCR had a major effect on American viewing habits, giving rise to two new viewing phenomena, "time-shifting" and "zapping." The VCR freed people from the tyranny of network prime time. Programs could be taped and watched at other, more convenient hours. This time-shifting was a double-edged sword for the networks. On the one hand, VCRs increased program viewing by allowing people to tape shows they would not normally be home to watch. On the other hand, VCR playback typically occurred during prime-time evening hours, and viewers who were watching taped shows during prime time were obviously not watching current broadcasts. Time-shifting was naturally of concern to the networks, as was zapping, the ability of viewers to fast-forward past commercials, the lifeblood of the networks.

The loss of viewers during the 1980's to other programming formats and to the VCR had an enormous effect on the networks. CBS, the top-rated network in the 1990-1991 season, still lost $85.8 million. The pie that had once been shared three ways was sliced so thin during the 1980's that, by the end of the decade, the networks were having difficulty feeding themselves.

Impact of Event

The increased number of stations led to greater choices for viewers, but in the early 1980's, the material such stations could broadcast was largely limited to network reruns or recently released films, and there just were not enough of these programs to fill the available airtime. To vie with the networks, the new outlets had to move to create more original programming. By the close of the 1980's, many of the newer stations were producing made-for-television specials and films at a rate unprecedented in the history of the medium. These stations were also more progressive than the networks and provided some highly stimulating and controversial programming, since they were not under the same "public air" constraints that the networks were. For the first time in television history, there was indeed something for everyone.

The highly specialized market-segmented stations have also had their impact. MTV revolutionized the record industry. In MTV's wake, no record label could think of releasing a pop record without simultaneously releasing a video, so integral had video become to record sales. The high cost of video production made some labels more cautious in promoting new talent, since many executives hesitated to spend large sums of money on unknown artists.

Many critics initially scoffed at the notion of an all-news channel, but CNN revolutionized the news industry, making prime-time news almost an anachronism. The additional airtime available for its news broadcasts enabled CNN to devote more time to its stories, providing a depth of information unobtainable during the networks' thirty-minute nightly spots. Additionally, other news sources (including the networks) soon came to rely on CNN for up-to-the-minute worldwide coverage of events. Though not singlehandedly responsible for the decline of the once ubiquitous United Press International and Associated Press wire services, CNN made plain their obsolescence.

The VCR, too, had an impact beyond the simple freeing of viewers from network time constraints and commercials. The VCR also helped to revolutionize Hollywood and gave birth to a new multibillion-dollar industry, the home-video market. Film attendance dropped, but Hollywood studios made more money than ever.

The creation of the home-video market meant that films no longer had to make money primarily at the box office, as they traditionally had been expected to do. Instead, films could be made with an eye to the profit that could be generated through video sales and video rentals. Films began to make their way out of the theater faster than ever before and often bypassed the medium of television entirely to move directly into viewers' homes; consumer demand thus created the need for more new films than ever before.

Video sales and rentals created a boom for Hollywood; on the other hand, they were a major factor in the lack of growth for pay-subscription services. Such services were the primary outlet for non-theatrical showings of new films in the late 1970's and early 1980's, and viewer interest in such films was one of the major reasons for pay television's initial rapid growth. Poised with six percent of the market in 1982, subscription stations appeared about to take off; soon, though, the VCR began to make inroads, and subscription services started to lag behind. They have managed to succeed no better than public television, garnering only five percent of viewer subscriptions in 1990. The only profit-making subscription station at the outset of the 1990's was HBO, and this was largely the result of HBO's diversification to include the broadcast of original made-for-television movies, programs, and specials. The VCR, then, promoted the growth of the video-rental industry while casting a shadow over the continued existence of cable subscription stations that relied extensively on Hollywood releases.

The VCR and cable's growth had extraordinary impact on the once-powerful Big Three. The mass audience of the 1950's, 1960's, and 1970's no longer existed by the end of the 1980's but had been shattered into fragments courted by dozens of smaller broadcasters. The question posed at the end of the 1980's was whether the networks would survive the 1990's.

Certainly, the networks could not continue to exist as they once did; their days of total domination of mass viewership were clearly over. This was not their death knell, however; the networks showed an ability to adapt to new exigencies. Programming in the early 1990's indicated that the networks were more willing to take chances on programs that might not have been considered for broadcast in the Big Three's glory days. Competition shook up the networks and made them work harder, and the result was more dynamic programming.

The longstanding affiliate system also began changing. Affiliate stations had been the backbone of the networks since the creation of commercial television; networks had long required local stations to carry their programs during the stipulated time in exchange for the right to show network programming. The need to generate cash, however, altered this time-honored practice. In 1992, CBS announced that it would begin to charge its affiliates for the shows that they carried.

The 1980's were a decade of phenomenal change in the television industry, the first major changes since the network system became entrenched in the mid-1950's. More changes seemed in store for the 1990's, as the new technologies of high-resolution television and interactive television loomed on the horizon.

Bibliography

Dolan, Edward. *TV or CATV?: A Struggle for Power.* Port Washington, N.Y.: Associated Faculty Press, 1984. A detailed account of the early rise and initial challenge posed by cable television. The side for cable is strongly made, and the resistance of the networks is amply documented.

Geltner, Sharon. "Matching Set: Brian Lamb and C-SPAN." In *American Mass Media: Industries and Issues,* edited by Robert Atwan, Barry Orton, and William Vesterman. 3d ed. New York: Random House, 1986. The author traces the segmentation, or "narrow-casting," of programming. The educational aspect of C-SPAN, which carries live coverage of Congress, is shown to appeal to a growing viewership. The article includes a profile of C-SPAN's founder, Brian Lamb, and shows how one individual can still make a substantial impact in television.

Negrine, Ralph M., ed. *Cable Television and the Future of Broadcasting.* New York: St. Martin's Press, 1985. A collection of eight essays that treat the growth of cable television as a worldwide phenomenon. Includes a short glossary of technical terms.

Papazian, Ed, ed. *TV Dimensions '91.* New York: Media Dynamics, 1991. A statistical compilation of pertinent information, special reports on the state of the industry, and important trends. One of the few analyses that includes in the same text information on competitive stations and programs other than those carried by the major networks. Includes an in-depth section on the impact of cable and the influence of VCRs.

Pember, Don. "Television." In *Mass Media in America.* 6th ed. New York: Macmillan, 1992. A straightforward discussion of network television and alternative stations. The author clearly defines basic terms and sketches the rise of alternative formats. The often complex relationship between alternative stations and programs and their effect on the networks is presented. Numerous charts and graphs, key comparative industry statistics, pictures.

John Markert

Cross-References

NBC Launches American Television at the World's Fair (1939), p. 1143; NBC and CBS Launch Commercial Television (1941), p. 1211; NBC Broadcasts the World Series (1947), p. 1362; ABC Begins Its Own Network Television Service (1948), p. 1368; Television Enters Its Golden Age (1950's), p. 1465; ABC Makes a Landmark Deal with Disney (1954), p. 1612; MTV Changes the Look of American Popular Culture (1981), p. 2475; *The Simpsons* Debuts, Anchoring the Fledgling Fox Network (1990), p. 2652.

MULTICULTURALISM DOMINATES THE DANCE WORLD

Category of event: Dance
Time: The late 1980's
Locale: Worldwide

Multiculturalism in dance flourished when the cultural exchange between continents brought an influx of new ideas, performances, and teaching techniques

Principal personages:
MIKHAIL BARYSHNIKOV (1948-   ), the former artistic director of American Ballet Theatre who collaborated with Mark Morris to create the White Oak Dance Project in 1990
MARK MORRIS (1956-   ), an American modern dancer and choreographer who directed a company at the Théâtre Royal de la Monnaie in Brussels between 1988 and 1991
RUDOLF NUREYEV (1938-1993), a ballet defector from the Soviet Union who also performed in several works by modern-dance choreographer Martha Graham
NATALIA MAKAROVA (1940-   ), a former soloist with American Ballet Theatre who was the first Russian defector allowed to return and dance in the Soviet Union

Summary of Event

During the latter part of the 1980's, the term "multiculturalism," which denotes the coexistence of diverse groups that share different cultural and ideological backgrounds, began to be frequently used in the dance world. As a result of such coexistence, exchanges of dance ideas, methodologies, and performances took place.

As a result of a cultural exchange agreement with the Soviet Union, Russian dance companies have performed in the United States since 1985. These include companies such as the Kirov and Bolshoi Ballets, the Moiseyev Folk Dance Company, and Virsky's Ukrainian State Dance Company. In the dance world, the *perestroika* (restructuring) and *glasnost* (openness) policies of former Soviet Union leader Mikhail Gorbachev took the form of 1988 performances by Bolshoi Ballet dancers Nina Ananiashvili and Andris Liepa with the New York City Ballet; two dancers from the Kirov also danced with American Ballet Theatre that same year.

Although the Dance Theatre of Harlem was the first American dance company invited to perform in the Soviet Union under *glasnost*, the New York City Ballet had enjoyed enormous success decades earlier when it toured the Soviet Union in 1962 and 1972. Not until 1984, though, did a Soviet ballet company produce a work by George Balanchine; the former director of the New York City Ballet had been excluded from his country's ballet history until the mid-1980's. Under Gorbachev's more liberal leadership, however, the Soviet Union recognized the artistic achievements of the Russian-born Balanchine.

Cultural exchanges with the Soviet Union continued in 1987 when the Bolshoi Ballet performed in four cities across the United States. The prestigious company completed another American tour in the summer of 1990. October, 1988, saw the U.S. debut of the Moscow Classical Ballet. In addition, in 1986 the Kirov Ballet performed in Canada and the United States for the first time since 1964. This Leningrad ballet troupe also danced in New York City during the summer of 1989 for the first time in twenty-five years.

The first full-scale collaboration between an American and a Soviet ballet company took place in Boston on May 3, 1990, when the Boston Ballet staged *Swan Lake*. Within the production, Soviet danseurs partnered American ballerinas, and American danseurs partnered Soviet ballerinas. Even the sets, designed by an American artist, were constructed in the Soviet Union.

In 1989, ballerina Natalia Makarova returned to Leningrad for the first time since her defection to the United States in 1970. The former soloist with American Ballet Theatre was invited to perform at the Kirov in two duets from John Cranko's *Onegin*. For nearly two decades, Makarova's name had been stricken from Soviet literature; however, in the liberal atmosphere of *perestroika* and *glasnost*, Makarova was allowed to return to her homeland. Although the names and achievements of Makarova and fellow expatriates Rudolf Nureyev and Mikhail Baryshnikov were returned to Soviet ballet encyclopedias in 1988, none of the three had ever returned to the Soviet Union to dance. Makarova's performance represented a new liberation for both Soviet and American ballet dancers.

In 1987, two Chinese festivals showcased Chinese dance companies as well as international groups. The Shanghai Festival and the China Arts Festival in Beijing attracted a large number of participants. In 1988, the Singapore Festival of the Arts and the Hong Kong Arts Festival were examples of the cultural exchange of ideas occurring throughout Asia and the Pacific.

A pre-Olympics Korean Dance Festival took place in Seoul, South Korea, during the summer of 1988. The roster of guests included nine Korean dance companies, two modern dance groups from France, two Butoh groups from Japan, and one American modern-dance troupe. Audiences in 1988 also witnessed a three-week tour of the United States by the Finnish National Ballet. Other examples of multiculturalism in the late 1980's included an influx of teachers to South Africa. Modern and jazz dancers, choreographers, and teachers who had trained in the United States and Europe brought their experience to South Africa in order to expose students to contemporary dance styles.

American Ballet Theatre performed in Japan in 1989; the New York City Ballet also toured works in Japan during the late 1980's. On another continent, after a respite of fourteen years, the Australian Ballet performed in Washington, D.C., New York City, and Costa Mesa, California, during July and August, 1990. Two years earlier, the company had toured the Soviet Union, England, and Greece.

Another example of multiculturalism in dance was a festival of Indonesian dance that toured the United States for sixteen months during 1990 and 1991. Also in 1991, Delhi, India, sponsored the India International Dance Festival. Twenty-three countries were represented at the event during an eighteen-day period.

The worlds of modern dance and ballet were combined in 1987 when Rudolf Nureyev and Mikhail Baryshnikov performed in Martha Graham's *Appalachian Spring* at the opening of the Graham company's season. During the same year, Baryshnikov also performed in Graham's *El Penitente*. Two years later, Baryshnikov danced in a reconstruction of Graham's *American Document*, first created in 1938. The 1990 season of the American Ballet Theatre included Graham's 1948 group piece *Diversion of Angels*.

American modern dance also flourished in Europe. Between 1988 and 1991, American modern-dance choreographer Mark Morris directed a company at the Théâtre Royal de la Monnaie in Brussels, replacing Maurice Bejart's Ballet of the Twentieth Century. The French government declared the year 1988 the "year of dance" in the country. In order to fund sixty-six companies and nineteen choreographic centers, the French ministry of culture's dance budget increased by thirty-five percent. Especially in the field of modern dance, collaborations among artists, dancers, and designers emerged in galleries and performing spaces throughout the country. One year after France's declaration of a "year of dance," eight French dance companies performed in the United States as part of the bicentennial celebration of the French Revolution. In the fall of 1990, the Lyon Biennale de la Danse presented "An American Story: A Century of Dance in the United States." Held two years after the French government's proclamation, this French festival presented a comprehensive collection of American dance.

Impact of Event

As an art form, dance has broadened to embrace cultural diversity and an expansive spectrum of ideas. A growing trend that emerged in the 1980's has been the internationalization of concert dance forms. America, for example, had long been the hub of modern-dance activity; during the late 1980's, however, an increasing number of foreign dance companies have toured the United States. Dance companies from Europe, Asia, and Africa have toured the North American continent. The International Choreographer's Workshop based at the American Dance Festival in Durham, North Carolina, is one institution that has enabled dancers and choreographers from England, France, Germany, Russia, China, and Japan to visit and work in the United States; the workshop began in 1984 under the auspices of the U.S. Information Agency.

In addition, many American dancers and choreographers work in European countries. The 1980's witnessed an international exchange of ideas among dancers from all nations. For example, in 1988 the first New York International Festival of the Arts hosted dancers and companies from Germany, Japan, and the United States. Eleven premieres were staged that included performances by companies such as the Frankfurt Ballet, Pina Bausch Tanztheater, the Dance Theater of Harlem, and the New York City Ballet. Works by Merce Cunningham, Jean-Pierre Perreault, and Kazuo Ohno were also performed. In 1990, the American Mark Morris, who directed a company in Brussels, began to choreograph for the White Oak Dance Project, a touring ensemble established by Mikhail Baryshnikov.

In ballet as well as modern dance, multiculturalism has influenced the repertory, style, and standards of many companies. Ballet superstars such as Baryshnikov, Makarova, and Nureyev have appeared as guest artists with companies around the globe. The parameters of different dance forms and styles expand when contributions from outside influences occur.

In part because of the contributions of dancers and choreographers such as Baryshnikov and Morris, the chasm that once existed between ballet and modern dance has been bridged. Modern-dance choreographers such as Twyla Tharp, Laura Dean, Paul Taylor, and Molissa Fenley, among others, have accepted commissions to create works for major ballet companies. America dominated the genre of modern dance for nearly seventy-five years, yet several companies from Germany, France, and Japan have emerged as burgeoning forces in the art form. For example, the French have continued to create their own modern-dance aesthetic rather than depending solely on American influences. As a result of the 1988 "year of dance" in France, the French ministry of education decided to introduce dance at the primary-school level. That same year, forty French companies toured the globe in a promotion of contemporary dance.

As a result of dance-company exchanges with the Soviet Union, higher standards of dance education emerged in the United States. The support system for the arts that operated in the former Soviet Union also served as a model for dance enthusiasts hoping for a more financially secure future for the art form.

As a result of *perestroika*, Soviet dancers and choreographers were able to study at the American Dance Festival in 1989. During the summer of 1992, another exchange took place. Two modern dance companies, the Dayton Contemporary Dance Company and the Pilobolus Dance Company, traveled to Russia to perform; it was the first time either company had danced in Russia. Even more important, master teachers such as Betty Jones, Jeanne Ruddy, Stuart Hodes, and Martha Myers taught modern-dance technique and dance composition to the Russian students. Charles and Stephanie Reinhart of the American Dance Festival organized the event. For the first time, the spirit and content of the American Dance Festival was presented in Moscow. One year earlier, the Reinharts had organized classes in dance technique, improvisation, and dance composition that were offered to more than one hundred young dancers from across the Indian subcontinent as part of the India International Dance Festival.

A Soviet-American exchange program also occurred between Leningrad and Boston in 1988. Natalia Dudinskaya, a noted teacher from the Vaganova Institute in Leningrad, coached the Boston Ballet in its production of *Giselle*. Bruce Marks, artistic director of the Boston Ballet, planned the event in order to instigate classes in the Vaganova method, a teaching system developed by Soviet pedagogue Agrippina Vaganova, at the Boston Ballet School.

From March 16 to April 3, 1988, the Opera Company of Boston sponsored the appearance of Bolshoi ballerina Maya Plisetskaya in Boston. Plisetskaya and more than one hundred Soviet performers danced. Baryshnikov appeared at the 1988 gala concert with Plisetskaya, marking the first time the Soviet government had allowed a ballet defector to participate actively within the Soviet cultural arena. A year earlier, Baryshnikov had received an invitation to dance in a Moscow gala, although he was unable to accept. In 1989, the second part of the Soviet-American exchange took place when Boston performers traveled to Moscow.

During the summer of 1992, Bolshoi Ballet dancers Nina Ananiashvili and Andris Liepa appeared in the United States in the Kirov Ballet's production of *Romeo and Juliet*. Four years earlier, the two had been the first Bolshoi dancers to perform George Balanchine's works with the New York City Ballet. Ananiashvili and Liepa were allowed by the Soviet government to travel to the United States without the remainder of the Bolshoi company.

During the 1990's, the dance world has continued to witness multicultural exchanges of ideas and choreography. Since all dance stems from some kind of ethnic base, dance scholars consider an anthropological perspective of the art form to be appropriate. Dance performances, festivals, and teaching methodologies have been part of the cultural exchange between countries in the late 1980's and early 1990's.

Bibliography

Cohen, Selma Jeanne, ed. *Dance As a Theatre Art*. Princeton, N.J.: Princeton Book Company, 1992. Presents source readings in dance history from 1581 to the 1990's; has been updated to include contemporary modern dance. Interviews with George Balanchine, Meredith Monk, and Twyla Tharp are insightful. Essays on Mikhail Baryshnikov, Pina Bausch, and Mark Morris are highlights of the book. An excellent bibliography is included. Photographs; no index.

Highwater, Jamake. *Dance: Rituals of Experience*. Pennington, N.J.: Princeton Book Company, 1992. A fascinating book that presents stages of dance history within a multicultural perspective. Aspects of Native American, Asian, and African-American cultures are examined by the author. Excellent photographs supplement the text. Indexed, although the author provides only a limited bibliography.

Kraus, Richard, Sarah Hilsendager, and Brenda Dixon. *History of the Dance in Art and Education*. Englewood Cliffs, N.J.: Prentice-Hall, 1991. A definitive work on dance history and the cultural implications of selected events. Sections on international trends in concert dance are most informative. Chapters on black dance and dance education provide information not easily found in other sources. Excellent endnotes augment each chapter. Bibliography and appendix listing dance periodicals and organizations. Index, photographs.

Royce, Anya Peterson. *The Anthropology of Dance*. Bloomington: Indiana University Press, 1977. Anthropologist Anya Peterson Royce presents ways in which to view dance through an anthropological perspective; multicultural examples are abundant throughout. The author draws relationships between dance and society and presents ways in which to infer meaning from dances of different cultures. Excellent bibliography, endnotes, and index. Illustrations.

Willis, Margaret. "Kiroviana: The Glasnost Difference." *Dance Magazine* 63 (July, 1989): 36-41. An article in the mainstream publication *Dance Magazine* addressing the Soviet-American dance exchanges that began in the late 1980's. Willis discusses performances by Soviet companies in the United States. This article is one of several in a series describing the Soviet-American cultural exchanges that occurred under *glasnost*. Other *Dance Magazine* articles of the late 1980's and early 1990's frequently present multicultural views of dance.

John R. Crawford

Cross-References

Duncan Interprets Chopin in Her Russian Debut (1904), p. 113; Balanchine and Kirstein Make New York a World Center for Ballet (1946), p. 1301; Ailey Founds His Dance Company (1958), p. 1774; Mitchell Founds the Dance Theater of Harlem (1968), p. 2110; Baryshnikov Becomes Artistic Director of American Ballet Theatre (1980), p. 2459; The New Dance U.S.A. Festival Celebrates Contemporary Dance (1981), p. 2480; Festivals Mark a Peak in the Dance Created by Black Artists (1983), p. 2521; Baryshnikov's White Oak Dance Project Debuts (1990), p. 2663.

INNOVATIVE BLACK FILMMAKERS ACHIEVE SUCCESS

Category of event: Motion pictures
Time: The late 1980's and early 1990's
Locale: Hollywood, California

After a number of gifted black actors had established during the 1980's that a crossover audience existed for films dealing with black subjects, a renaissance of black films and directors emerged

Principal personages:

SPIKE LEE (1957-   ), a young black film director, one of the most popular of the era

JOHN SINGLETON (1968-   ), a director who astonished the film industry with the quality of his first feature film, *Boyz 'N the Hood* (1991)

MARIO VAN PEEBLES (1957-   ), a director and actor, the son of filmmaker Melvin Van Peebles

ROBERT TOWNSEND (1957-   ), an actor and comedian who went on to direct *Hollywood Shuffle* (1987), an ethnic comedy playing on black stereotypes

CHARLES BURNETT (1944-   ), a graduate of the UCLA film school who had to wait fifteen years before breaking into major league filmmaking with *To Sleep with Anger* (1990)

BILL DUKE (1943-   ), an actor and television director who directed *A Rage in Harlem* (1991)

MATTY RICH (1970-   ), the youngest of the new wave of black filmmakers

DENZEL WASHINGTON (1954-   ), a stage actor and Academy Award winner

MORGAN FREEMAN (1937-   ), a stage and film actor

WHOOPI GOLDBERG (CARYN JOHNSON, 1949-   ), one of the most recognizable black actresses of the era

Summary of Event

During the late 1980's and early 1990's, a substantial wave of serious black films entered the mainstream of American filmmaking, utilizing a growing number of African-American talents—actors, writers, directors, and composers who managed to redefine the American cinema and expand its horizons to pay closer attention to black culture. The catalyst for this revolution—it was more than simply a trend—was the controversial success of Spike Lee's *Do the Right Thing* (1989), following the more marginal success of his earlier films, *School Daze* (1988) and *She's Gotta Have It* (1986). By 1990, Lee had become both a national celebrity, appearing in television commercials for Nike Shoes, and a respected major filmmaker, creating opportunities for other African-American talents such as Mario Van Peebles, whose *New Jack City* was released early in 1991, and John Singleton, whose semiautobiographical *Boyz 'N the Hood* was released later in the year to high critical acclaim.

These films grew out of the black urban experience and reflected the concerns and culture of African Americans in new and vital ways. What was especially significant was the mainstreaming of those concerns and the development of a substantial cross-over audience. There had always been an ethnic audience for films treating African Americans, who earlier in the century had their own film industry that produced pictures outside the mainstream, starring black actors, made for black audiences in segregated theaters. That industry was separate but unequal, serving a limited market.

On occasion, Hollywood had experimented with novelty pictures starring African Americans, such as King Vidor's *Hallelujah* (1929); Andrew L. Stone's *Stormy Weather* (1943), noteworthy for the vitality of a cast that included Lena Horne, Bill Robinson, Fats Waller, Cab Calloway, and the Nicholas brothers; and Otto Preminger's *Carmen Jones* (1954), adapting the opera as a musical starring Dorothy Dandridge, Pearl Bailey, and Harry Belafonte. In addition, there were occasional pictures that attempted to treat significant racial issues, ranging from Elia Kazan's *Pinky* (1949), starring Jeanne Crain as a black girl passing for white in the South, to Stanley Kramer's *Guess Who's Coming to Dinner* (1967), with Sidney Poitier supporting Spencer Tracy and Katharine Hepburn; Poitier played the fiancé of their daughter in this film exploring interracial relationships. In 1961, Daniel Petrie adapted Lorraine Hansberry's *A Raisin in the Sun*, providing starring roles for Sidney Poitier and Ruby Dee, and in 1964 Michael Roemer's *Nothing but a Man* dramatized the struggle of a black worker (Ivan Dixon) to protect his family against racial inequality. Such efforts as these were few and far between.

During the early 1970's, a trend for black films developed, led by Ossie Davis, Gordon Parks, Sr., and Melvin Van Peebles. *Cotton Comes to Harlem* (1970), directed by Davis from a story developed by Chester Himes, and *Shaft* (1971), directed by Parks, presented black policemen as hero figures. In a television interview aired November 9, 1971, in New York City, Davis noted that "the choice of materials and employees is determined by those who have no direct knowledge of the black experience." Melvin Van Peebles, the director of *Watermelon Man* (1970) and *Sweet Sweetback's Baadasssss Song* (1971), asserted that black films "should all work toward the decolonization of black minds and the reclaiming of black spirit," a goal that was not to be widely achieved for another twenty years. The most lucrative films of the 1970's trend were Parks' *Shaft* and, later, the drug drama *Super Fly* (1972), directed by his son, Gordon Parks, Jr. The number of films directed by African Americans increased in the early 1970's, but each year brought only a few dozen. Clearly, a market was developing, but the audience was largely ethnic and the films produced were by and large regarded as "blaxploitation" pictures, sexually oriented films with a focus on action and violence. A substantial crossover audience was needed, and that was not to come until the end of the 1980's, when the content of black films had developed. Film critics of the mid-1970's were unsure of where black filmmaking would go or whether black directors would ever reach more than an ethnic audience.

The widening of the crossover audience took place during the 1980's, thanks to the efforts of white filmmakers determined to make films that would treat the black experience honestly and willing to risk experimenting with predominantly black casts. Leading the way was Norman Jewison with *A Soldier's Story* (1984), adapted by the African-American playwright Charles Fuller from his own play and featuring an amazing cast that included Howard E. Rollins, Jr., Denzel Washington, Robert Townsend, and Adolph Caesar. Steven Spielberg directed *The Color Purple* (1985), adapted from Alice Walker's novel but not scripted by the novelist herself. Spielberg's film made the story less grim and ornamented it with sentimentality, but the Spielberg touch also made it a popular success and turned Whoopi Goldberg into a major star. These two films opened the mainstream market to stories about the black experience.

Another significant development was the rise of an increasingly large pool of gifted black actors with drawing power at the box office. Denzel Washington shot into prominence as a consequence of *A Soldier's Story*, for example, as did Robert Townsend. Howard E. Rollins established his credentials forcefully in *Ragtime* (1981), directed by Miloš Forman. Danny Glover gave a memorable performance as a loyal black farmworker in *Places in the Heart* (1984) and went on to star in *Grand Canyon* (1991) and with Mel Gibson in *Lethal Weapon* (1987). Whoopi Goldberg proved her acting abilities in *The Color Purple*, as did Morgan Freeman in *Driving Miss Daisy* (1989). Eddie Murphy became a major star during the 1980's in such films as *Beverly Hills Cop* (1984), *Beverly Hills Cop II* (1987), and *Trading Places* (1983), arguably his best film. Gregory Hines made his film debut in *Wolfen* (1981), a supernatural thriller, and was transformed into a leading actor by Francis Ford Coppola's *The Cotton Club* (1984), in a role appropriate for a dancer who began performing at the Apollo Theater at the age of six. Television talk-show host Arsenio Hall's career received a tremendous boost when he appeared as Eddie Murphy's comic sidekick in *Coming to America* (1988) and in a smaller part in *Harlem Nights* (1989). Oprah Winfrey, a local talk-show host, became a national celebrity after co-starring with Whoopi Goldberg in *The Color Purple*.

Many of the popular stars of the 1980's, both in film and on television, were black, reflecting mainstream acceptance. *The Cosby Show* completed an eight-year television run in 1992 after frequent appearances at the top of the ratings. Bill Cosby's earlier work with Robert Culp in the *I Spy* television series established the black-white buddy formula in the 1960's. The black renaissance of the 1980's and 1990's represented a culmination of audience acceptance by both black and white audiences and an outpouring of African-American artists capable of doing original, entertaining work.

Impact of Event

The transition from be-bop to hip-hop culture could be dated to *Beat Street* (1984), the first film to popularize rap culture. The success of that film might suggest that

American culture had become less racist and more willing to accept, or at least examine, black culture. Spike Lee explored racial tensions, however, in *Do the Right Thing* and *Jungle Fever* (1991), showing that tensions and racism still existed. Certainly the films of the 1990's were far different from such black exploitation features as *Super Fly*, less superfluous and ephemeral, more realistic, original, and inventive. This was particularly true of the films of Spike Lee, John Singleton, and Matty Rich, which examined social problems and attitudes in depth from a distinctly black perspective.

The black renaissance hit full force in 1990 in two separate but related ways, in films directed by mainstream directors who used black actors and in films directed by African Americans. One of the very best films of 1989, for example, was *Driving Miss Daisy*, directed by Australian Bruce Baresford from Alfred Uhry's Pulitzer Prize-winning play, starring Morgan Freeman as Hoke Colburn, Miss Daisy's compassionate chauffeur, and Esther Rolle as Idella, her sardonic cook. The same year saw *Glory*, directed by Edward Zwick, a film that told the story of a black regiment that fought against the Confederacy during the Civil War, starring Morgan Freeman and Denzel Washington, with Matthew Broderick as Robert Gould Shaw, the white colonel who organized and led the regiment. Washington won the Academy Award for Best Supporting Actor for his portrayal of a runaway slave turned soldier in *Glory*. In 1991, he starred with Ice T in the police drama *Ricochet*. *Driving Miss Daisy* got Academy Award nominations for best actor, best actress, and best picture, but at the same time the Academy of Motion Picture Arts and Sciences virtually ignored Spike Lee's *Do the Right Thing*. With a new generation of African-American directors in place by the 1990's, it became less likely that films dealing with black topics would be made by white directors.

Spike Lee continued to stabilize his reputation with *Mo' Better Blues* (1990), which featured strong performances from Denzel Washington and Wesley Snipes, followed by *Jungle Fever* (1991) and the controversial *Malcolm X* (1992), which went over budget and resulted in a public argument between Lee and the studio over funding to complete the picture. Although still the most visible of black directing talents, Spike Lee faced strong competition by 1991. The first to challenge Lee was Mario Van Peebles, whose *New Jack City* (1991), a film about a police crackdown on drug dealers starring the director himself, got nationwide attention when riots broke out in theaters where it opened. John Singleton's *Boyz 'N the Hood* eclipsed both *New Jack City* and *Jungle Fever* when it was released at midyear and was the consensus pick of critics around the nation for the top film of 1991. Singleton, for that film, became the youngest person and the first African American to be nominated for an Oscar as Best Director.

The impact of the black renaissance was obvious in the other major black films released in the early 1990's: Matty Rich's *Straight Out of Brooklyn* (1991), Bill Duke's *A Rage in Harlem* (1991), followed by *Deep Cover*, starring Larry Fishburne and released in early 1992, Robert Townsend's *The Five Heartbeats* (1991), and Topper Carew's *Talkin' Dirty After Dark* (1991). Other films in production in 1991 were released in 1992, such as Ernest R. Dickerson's *Juice*, extending interest in the problems of black urban neighborhoods, and Reginald Hudlin's *Boomerang*, which undertook to reinvigorate Eddie Murphy's sagging career by starring him in a comedy-romance with Robin Givens, Halle Berry, Grace Jones, and Eartha Kitt, a film dominated by black talent, coproduced by Warrington Hudlin, the director's brother and cofounder of the Black Filmmakers Foundation. These films, to a greater or lesser degree, focused on black themes and issues. They promised to reach mainstream audiences with something more than standard Hollywood blockbuster fare, showing that African-American artists were providing many of the new ideas in American film.

Bibliography

Bogle, Donald. *Toms, Coons, Mulattoes, Mammies, and Bucks: An Interpretive History of Blacks in American Films.* New York: Viking Press, 1973. Bogle is a black critic. Chapter 1 defines the types, such as the "Tom," the "Coon," and the "Mammy." Subsequent chapters progress by decade. Bogle concludes that even in the 1970's, "Black films often still use degrading myths and clichés as well as the five basic stereotypes to define the black experience" and that American black movies "remain distorted and far from satisfying."

Corliss, Richard. "Boyz of New Black City." *Time* 137 (June 17, 1991): 64-68. Corliss evaluates the explosion of black films in 1991 and credits Spike Lee for creating "the market for the black-movie rage." Besides summarizing Lee's career, Corliss profiles John Singleton, Matty Rich, Charles Burnett, and Bill Duke, as well as other talents. The main focus, however, is upon Lee's *Jungle Fever.*

Cripps, Thomas. *Black Film as Genre.* Bloomington: Indiana University Press, 1978. A thorough and scholarly treatment of the earliest films made by African Americans for black audiences, with black creative roots in the persons of producer, director, writer, or performers. Cripps traces the "genre" from the silent period to the 1970's to develop his thesis that such a genre exists. After the field has been surveyed, six films are singled out for representative treatment.

Friedman, Lester D., ed. *Unspeakable Images: Ethnicity and the American Cinema.* Urbana: University of Illinois Press, 1991. Mark Winokur's essay "Black Is White/ White Is Black" considers the "strategy of racial compatibility in contemporary Hollywood comedy." Robyn Wiegman discusses "gender, race, and the bourgeois ideal" in an essay entitled "Black Bodies/American Commodities." Paul S. Cowen's "Social-Cognitive Approach" offers a taxonomy of films involving ethnicity.

Kroll, Jack. "How Hot Is Too Hot? The Fuse Has Been Lit." *Newsweek* 114 (July 3, 1989): 64-65. Kroll examines the controversial nature of *Do the Right Thing* and the riot that Lee dramatizes in the film. Lee functions as both "ironic humanist" and as "black nationalist with a movie camera," as he describes himself. In attempting to be "both ingratiating and militant," Kroll states, "Lee has done the wrong thing."

Leab, Daniel J. *From Sambo to Superspade: The Black Experience in Motion Pictures.* Boston: Houghton Mifflin, 1975. Traces black stereotyping from the origins of the motion picture to the popularity of the so-called "blaxploitation" films of the 1970's. Concludes that up to the mid-1970's, except for a few exceptions such as *Sounder* (1972), *The Learning Tree* (1969), and *Nothing but a Man* (1964), "the film image of the black is as condescending and defamatory as it has ever been."

Leland, John, and Donna Foote. "A Bad Omen for Black Movies?" *Newsweek* 118 (July 29, 1991): 64-65. This reaction to the concern about violent outbreaks at theaters showing *Boyz 'N the Hood*, despite the film's strong antiviolence message, discusses the problem in the context of similar outbreaks of violence at the release of *New Jack City* four months earlier.

Murray, James. *To Find an Image: Black Films from Uncle Tom to Super Fly.* Indianapolis: Bobbs-Merrill, 1973. Murray, the first black critic to join the New York Film Critics Circle, traces the evolution of black cinema up to the early 1970's, devoting separate chapters to Sidney Poitier ("The Black Superstar Finally Arrives") and Ossie Davis, as well as to directors Gordon Parks, Sr., and Melvin Van Peebles.

James M. Welsh

Cross-References

The Harlem Renaissance Celebrates African-American Culture (1920's), p. 480; *Hallelujah* Is the First Important Black Musical (1929), p. 772; *Stormy Weather* Offers New Film Roles to African Americans (1940's), p. 1159; Poitier Emerges as a Film Star in *The Blackboard Jungle* (1955), p. 1650; Hansberry's *A Raisin in the Sun* Debuts on Broadway (1959), p. 1795; Baldwin Voices Black Rage in *The Fire Next Time* (1963), p. 1929; Baraka's *Dutchman* Dramatizes Racial Hatred (1964), p. 2000; *The Autobiography of Malcolm X* Is Published (1965), p. 2022; *I Spy* Debuts to Controversy (1965), p. 2044; *The Wiz* Brings African-American Talent to Broadway (1975), p. 2334; *The Jeffersons* Signals Success of Black Situation Comedies (1975), p. 2339; *Roots* Dramatizes the African-American Experience (1977), p. 2397; *Do the Right Thing* Establishes Lee as a World-Class Director (1989), p. 2641.

AKALAITIS' *GREEN CARD* CONFRONTS AUDIENCES WITH HARSH REALITIES

Category of event: Theater
Time: 1986
Locale: Mark Taper Forum, Los Angeles, California

JoAnne Akalaitis' play Green Card *is an outgrowth of her early experiences in performance art, which showed her how to bring the harsh realities of life to the stage*

Principal personages:

JoANNE AKALAITIS (1937-   ), a theatrical performer, director, writer, and designer

RUTH MALECZECH (1938-   ), an actress who, with Akalaitis and Lee Breuer, founded Mabou Mines

LEE BREUER (1937-   ), an actor and playwright who, with Akalaitis and Maleczech, founded Mabou Mines

PHILIP GLASS (1937-   ), a composer and theater artist who worked with Akalaitis during her early years in the theater, the father of her two children

JOSEPH PAPP (YOSL PAPIROFSKY, 1921-1991), a stage producer and director who was instrumental in Akalaitis becoming artistic director of the New York Shakespeare Festival

Summary of Event

JoAnne Akalaitis' play *Green Card*, produced in 1986 at the Mark Taper Forum in Los Angeles, California, is an interesting and complex mingling of Akalaitis' prior experiences as a performer, writer, director, and designer. The play is set in Los Angeles, which Akalaitis has referred to as the new Ellis Island because more immigrants have come to Los Angeles than to any other city in the United States in recent years. The play juxtaposes the stories of many immigrants ranging from those arriving in the nineteenth century at Ellis Island, through war refugees from Southeast Asia and Central America, to those held at the El Centro Detention Center in California's Imperial Valley. Both of the two acts are separated into sections under different headings. The first act consists of a prologue, "L.A. Woman," "Success Story," "Customs and Costumes," "Work," "English," "Natives," "Immigration," and "California." Act 2 contains a prologue, "Religion," "Colonialism," "Culture," "CIA," "A Glossary," "Testimony," "Dead Letters," "Dying in Your Arms," and "Waiting."

Akalaitis' method of theatrical art does not settle for easy answers or traditional approaches but instead strives for a stark and revealing honesty so that the most subtle shades of meaning are felt and heard. The way Akalaitis achieves this balance of the visual and the emotional is through an intertwining of her training and experiences within the theater since the early 1960's. A distinctive compilation of her artistic travels within her craft can be seen in her production of *Green Card*.

Akalaitis left Stanford University in 1963 for the Actor's Workshop in San Francisco. There she met Lee Breuer, Ruth Maleczech, and Bill Raymond. These three actors would be instrumental in the founding of Mabou Mines, an acting company in New York. Also during this period, Akalaitis spent time with the San Francisco Mime Troupe during its ardent political phase. The mime troupe expressed controversial current sociopolitical messages through presentational techniques derived from the *commedia dell'arte*, circus and carnival acts, minstrel shows, vaudeville, comic strips, and nineteenth century melodrama. The later plays and theoretical writings of Bertolt Brecht added to the troupe's awareness of a theatrical aesthetic involving social analysis. The troupe gradually transformed its style from performances in presentational styles, such as utilizing traditional masked characters and exaggerated movement and voice, to a more subtle style that might more readily provoke empathy from the audience. In 1970, the troupe declared its members as "art workers" with a common goal of bringing about social change. They still used theatrical techniques to reach their goals, but they employed a different set of stock characters, taken from American life rather than from European life (as in the *commedia dell'arte*), in hopes that they would reach working-class people with their message. They tried to achieve a heightened sense of realism with their style of presentation.

After their involvement with the San Francisco Mime Troupe, Akalaitis, Breuer, and Maleczech became members of the San Francisco Tape Music Center. There they worked intensely with visual artists and avant-garde musicians. In 1964, Akalaitis and soon-to-be-husband Philip Glass left for Paris. She met two actors, David Warrilow and Fred Neumann, in Paris. The three of them became involved in dubbing films, which expanded their knowledge of the cinematic techniques they eventually would use in their theater productions. In Paris, Akalaitis worked with Breuer, Maleczech, Glass, and Neumann on Samuel Beckett's *Play*, which was first produced in 1963 in German. She then left Paris for a short time to study acting in New York, but she returned to attend workshops held by Polish director Jerzy Grotowski.

Akalaitis studied with Grotowski for about a month in 1969. His methods completely changed her ideas about work. She witnessed a development of the Stanislavsky method that involved not only the body but also her own personal history and her value as an artist. She was particularly impressed with Grotowski's idea that an actor is as much an artist as is a writer, painter, or a playwright; the actor is not simply an interpreter. Excited by Grotowski's teachings and his vision of a "poor" theater, a theater driven by the actor rather than by the elements of makeup, costume, scenery, and lighting, Akalaitis returned to New York to engage her friends in the prospect of starting a troupe. Their first endeavor, Breuer's *The Red Horse Animation* (1970), incorporated elements of techniques learned from Joseph Chaikin's Open Theatre workshops, the Berliner Ensemble, and Grotowski.

Ellen Stewart of LaMama Experimental Theatre Club supported the troupe's endeavors by inviting it to perform. The company named itself Mabou Mines after an old mining village near Glass's beach house in Nova Scotia where the company had spent time rehearsing. During the 1970's, Mabou Mines was an important member of the New York avant-garde. The troupe started out performing in galleries and museums in collaboration with visual artists. After leaving LaMama in 1973, the company received a grant that made it possible to move from museums to theaters. It soon aligned itself with A Bunch of Experimental Theatres of New York, Inc., where it worked with an assortment of avant-garde groups. By the early 1980's, Mabou Mines was in the forefront of the genre known as "performance art," the merging of theater, music and dance, cinema and video, painting, and sculpture.

The work Akalaitis and Mabou Mines engaged in synthesized motivational acting in the tradition of Konstantin Stanislavsky with techniques borrowed from Grotowski's more presentational acting style. Along with these varied techniques, the company used choral monologues in the Brechtian mode, narrative dance taken from Japanese Kabuki theater, and abstract musical accompaniment and visual imagery. Mabou Mines was a deciding force in the attempt to extend the possibilities of theater into wider arenas of visual arts.

From 1970 to 1979, Akalaitis worked on two other plays by Breuer, won a Village Voice Obie (an award for excellence in the Off-Broadway theater) for her direction of Beckett's *Cascando* (originally a 1963 radio play), and designed, directed, and performed in *Dressed Like An Egg* (1977), for which she was awarded an Obie as well as the American Theatre Wing's Joseph Mahrem Award for scenic design. She then won another Obie for *Southern Exposure* (1979), a work she wrote, directed, and designed.

During the 1980's, Akalaitis began her ongoing relationship with producer and director Joseph Papp. She wrote and directed *Dead End Kids: A History of Nuclear Power* (1980), which Papp presented at the Public Theatre in New York City. She directed *Request Concert* in 1981, garnering good reviews by critics. Michael Hurson's *Red and Blue* (1982) was directed by Akalaitis and produced by Joe Papp. In 1983, Akalaitis directed *The Photographer*, a play about one of the inventors of motion pictures. She directed *Through the Leaves*, featuring friends Ruth Maleczech and Fred Neumann, in 1984. Also in 1984 was her controversial direction of Samuel Beckett's *Endgame: A Play in One Act* (first produced in 1957 as *Fin de partie: Suivi de Acte sans paroles*) for the American Repertory Theatre in Cambridge, Massachusetts. In this unorthodox production, Akalaitis ignored Beckett's stage directions and added an overture and other music. Her concept spurred Beckett to seek legal assistance in order to bar Akalaitis' version of the play from being seen. This action brought the issue of directorial license to national attention.

Akalaitis did more work for the American Repertory Theatre in 1985 and 1986 by directing Jean Genet's *The Balcony* (1957; published as *Le Balcon* in 1956). Returning to Mabou Mines in February of 1986, she directed herself and Ruth Maleczech in Franz Xaver Kroetz's *Help Wanted*. While working on these two projects, Akalaitis wrote and directed her play *Green Card*.

Impact of Event

Green Card originally was produced by Center Theatre Group of Los Angeles at the Mark Taper Forum in 1986. It later was produced at the Joyce Theatre as part of the first New York International Festival of the Arts in June of 1988. Akalaitis wrote the play and directed on both occasions. *Green Card* is about refugees and other immigrants and their struggle to adapt to and assimilate into American life while keeping some sense of themselves and their traditions.

Akalaitis' connection with performance art is evident throughout the play. The entire piece is an intermingling of an array of performance art media. Music by such artists as David Byrne, Brian Eno, Sid Vicious, Terry Allen, Jimmy Cliff, the Doors, and Frank Sinatra is used to emphasize the theme of each section. Taped dialogue and live voices are interspersed within the play. Akalaitis also employs a mixture of realism with symbolism, expressionism, cinematic montage devices, and dream sequences to achieve an intensified feeling of emotion.

One distinctive element of the *Green Card* performances was that the actors would go into the audience and address its members personally. The names of the characters in the play are the real names of the actors performing their parts. The importance of the ensemble is manifest. The cast of *Green Card* is multiethnic, with the actors often playing characters of ethnic origins other than their own. Akalaitis gives a blueprint for actors, directors, and designers with her text, leaving room for personal interpretation of her words and stage directions.

The Brechtian influence on *Green Card* can be seen in her use of enormous slide projections as an integral part of the performance. The projections are used to punctuate events and actions as well as to display pictures serving as stories and action by themselves. The projections also are stationed on the floor, transforming it into many locations; for example, a jungle is represented by faces, maps, icons, and monuments. Stanislavsky's influence can be seen in moments of "realistic" dialogue, particularly in the telling of the atrocities of the immigrants' treatment. These moments also are conscious retreats to a more conventional narrative structure, giving the audience a rest from the bombardment of images. Realistic dialogue is used to contrast with the heavily stereotyped accents Akalaitis employs. Characters often change accents in mid-speech to make a point of the large influence of language and accents in the lives of immigrants.

Jerzy Grotowski's influence on Akalaitis' play is seen in her use of the actors. They are not ordered to act in a realistic manner; rather, the choreography and stylized movement requires the actors to be more abstract and sculptural than an actor would be if performing in a thoroughly "realistic" play. The three large Vietnamese water puppets that are used throughout the second act are reminiscent of the San Francisco Mime Troupe. The puppets are used as participants in the action as well as spectators of it.

There were many responses to *Green Card*. Few objected to its message, but Akalaitis did draw criticism from some by drawing parallels between nineteenth century Jews and twentieth century Southeast Asians. Some observers objected strongly to her criticism of the influence that the foreign policy of the United States has on immigration. In the play, Akalaitis suggests that America's foreign policy has forced immigrants to come to the country in recent years, although she does seem to keep a sense of objectivity, refraining from forcing a conclusion in her telling of the story.

Akalaitis continued her unique and innovative work in the theater in the 1990's. As artistic director of the New York Shakespeare Festival, she had a tremendous influence in the world of theater as well as a greater arena for her work. She directed William Shakespeare's *Cymbeline* (c. 1609-1610) and John Ford's *'Tis Pity She's a Whore* (c. 1629) during the late 1980's and early 1990's, continuing to be a creative force in the world of theater.

Bibliography

Akalaitis, JoAnne. *Green Card.* New York: Broadway Play Publishing Inc., 1991. This is the primary source for anyone looking at Akalaitis' work. The play is difficult to find in libraries.

Grotowski, Jerzy. *Towards a Poor Theatre.* New York: Simon & Schuster, 1968. This book, with a preface by Peter Brook, is a firsthand look at Grotowski. Includes portions written by him along with essays by other actors about their experiences with specific techniques. Also contains interviews with Grotowski. Invaluable for those wanting to know directly from the source what his methods were. Gives a wonderful foundation for understanding what Akalaitis experienced under Grotowski's tutelage.

Kirby, Michael. *Happenings.* New York: E. P. Dutton, 1965. This illustrated anthology offers a valuable introduction to "Happenings" and gives a history of the beginnings of the Happenings movement. Chapters consist of statements about specific artists' work. Also gives explanations concerning certain works by those involved, including Allan Kaprow, Red Grooms, Robert Whitman, Jim Dine, and Claes Oldenburg.

Shank, Theodore. *American Alternative Theatre.* New York: Grove Press, 1982. Deals with all types of alternative theater organizations and personalities. Interesting explanations and commentary about the Living Theatre, the Open Theatre, Richard Schechner and the Performance Group, the Bread and Puppet Theatre, Spaulding Gray, Elizabeth LeCompte, and many others.

Sommer, Sally R. "JoAnne Akalaitis of Mabou Mines." *The Drama Review* 20 (September, 1976): 3-16. An interview interspersed with biographical information about Akalaitis. Useful for revealing Akalaitis' thoughts about her acting process at that time in her career. Also elaborates on her training and background.

Felicia Bender

Cross-References

Brecht and Weill Collaborate on *Mahagonny Songspiel* (1927), p. 724; Brecht Founds the Berliner Ensemble (1949), p. 1410; Esslin Publishes *The Theatre of the Absurd* (1961), p. 1871; Shange's *for colored girls . . .* Is a Landmark (1976), p. 2370; Laurie Anderson's *United States* Popularizes Performance Art (1983), p. 2517.

PLATOON EXPLORES THE VIETNAM EXPERIENCE

Category of event: Motion pictures
Time: 1986
Locale: The United States

Drawing from his own personal experience as a combat veteran, film director Oliver Stone created the most powerfully realistic Vietnam film ever made with Platoon, *which set the standard for all such films*

> *Principal personages:*
> OLIVER STONE (1946-   ), the writer and director of *Platoon*
> DALE A. DYE (1945-   ), the military adviser to the film
> JOHN DALY (1940-   ), a film executive who arranged financing for *Platoon*

Summary of Event

The Vietnam War became a topic for Hollywood films soon after the United States began its military commitment of men and material to Southeast Asia in the mid-1960's. As *The Green Berets* (1968) soon demonstrated, this was not the sort of war that could be treated with the enthusiasm and patriotism that had typified Hollywood films concerning World War I, World War II, or even the Korean War. The purpose of the American commitment was ambiguous and seemed potentially imperialistic; the justification for the war was seriously and hotly debated by the Senate Foreign Relations Committee, headed by Senator J. William Fulbright; a protest movement grew and flourished; draft evaders were openly contemptuous of the federal government and burned their draft cards gleefully in public; and many questioned the wisdom of getting involved in a civil war in Southeast Asia. The temperament of the country was divisive and hostile. President Lyndon Baines Johnson became a victim of his own faltering foreign policy and mendacious military advisers. He ultimately chose not to run for a second term in 1968; meanwhile, the body count kept increasing. Reports of genocide, the My Lai massacre, the suffering of Vietnamese citizens indiscriminately shot and bombed, and the determination of the Vietcong, as demonstrated by the Tet Offensive, made many Americans ashamed of what their government was doing in the name of democracy to prop up despots in what appeared to be the American colonial enclave of South Vietnam. This was not, in short, a popular war of conventional heroism to be celebrated superficially on film. It was more like a bad dream that became a national nightmare.

Apocalypse Now (1979), directed by Francis Ford Coppola, had been praised by critic Stanley Kauffmann of *The New Republic* as an ultimate expression of an unsavory war, "the definitive Vietnam War epic." Coppola's strategy was literary, borrowing plot and structure from Joseph Conrad's *Heart of Darkness* (1899), and mythic. The film's political strategy was apparently nondidactic and presumably neutral, other than demonstrating that "war is hell." The characters of both *Apocalypse Now* and Michael Cimino's *The Deer Hunter* (1978) made symbolic descents into the hell of Vietnam and were transformed by the experience, without necessarily being made better. Neither Coppola nor Cimino had really experienced the war at first hand. Their mythic approaches became merely a dodge, a means of "treating" the war without really coming to grips with it in the manner of journalistic narratives such as Michael Herr's *Dispatches* (1977) and Philip Caputo's *A Rumor of War* (1977) or oral histories such as Mark Baker's *Nam: The Vietnam War in the Words of the Men and Women Who Fought There* (1981) or Wallace Terry's *Bloods: An Oral History of the Vietnam War* (1984).

Oliver Stone's *Platoon* was the first film that attempted to treat the Vietnam War realistically. At the age of twenty-one, Stone reported for duty in Vietnam on September 15, 1967, assigned to the Second Platoon of Bravo Company, Third Battalion, Twenty-fifth Infantry. The film follows what he saw and experienced. Although still potentially mythic in its structure, the framework was essentially autobiographical, deriving from the writer-director's firsthand combat experience as a "grunt" in the Infantry during 1967 and 1968. "I wanted to explore the everyday realities of what it was like to be a nineteen-year-old boy in the bush for the first time," Stone explained in a publicity statement when the film was released: "The story is based on experiences I had over there in three different combat units, and the characters of people I knew during the war."

It took Stone ten years to get his screenplay produced, and this was not because he was a newcomer to the film industry. He had won an Academy Award for his screenplay for *Midnight Express* (1978), along with the Writers Guild of America Award. He wrote and directed *The Hand*, a psychological thriller, in 1981. He was one of the collaborators on the screenplay for *Conan the Barbarian* (1982) and wrote screenplays for the remake of *Scarface* (1983) and *Year of the Dragon* (1985).

Stone was not, therefore, simply a beginner, but his *Platoon* script "was rejected everywhere," Stone noted, because "it was too harsh a look at the war—too grim and realistic." Perhaps the first draft of his screenplay was ahead of its time, following too closely on the embarrassed evacuation of Saigon. Perhaps America was not ready to concede that thousands of young men had bled and died in vain in an essentially pointless war.

Stone's "realistic" approach was both risky and controversial, but after making his equally controversial film *Salvador* (1986) for the Hemdale Film Corporation, Stone got the attention of Hemdale chairman John Daly. "When I read the script, I was struck by its shattering insight into Vietnam and all the cruelty and insanity that war brings," Daly explained. "I felt that this was a movie that had to be made." The film was scheduled to be shot on location in the jungles of the Philippines, and the crew arrived at about the time of the civil war that removed President Ferdinand Marcos from power and set up a new government under Corazon Aquino. The film was shot in seven weeks on a budget of $6 million.

Stone had seen hard duty in Vietnam. Born in New York, he had spent two years teaching English to students in the Chinese district of Saigon before enlisting for duty. He was wounded in 1967 during a night ambush and again in 1968, just before the Tet Offensive, earning the Bronze Star for combat valor and the Purple Heart before being transferred to the First Cavalry Division. Before the cameras started rolling for *Platoon*, he recruited retired Marine captain Dale Dye to give his cast two weeks of basic training in the jungle. "The idea of the cram course was to immerse the actors into the infantryman's life," Stone explained. He wanted the actors to be angry, frustrated, and tired. Stone remembered being "so tired that I wished the N.V.A. [North Vietnam Army] would come up and shoot me and get this thing over with." The filming began immediately after thirteen days of this rigorous jungle training.

The plot follows a new recruit, Chris Taylor (Charlie Sheen), on his rite-of-passage tour of duty in Vietnam, under the influence of two strong and battle-weary sergeants, Barnes (Tom Berenger), a potential psychopath killer who has no respect for civilians, and Elias (Willem Dafoe), who is more compassionate and still has a sense of morality and decency. In Barnes, Richard Corliss wrote in *Time*, "the grunts find everything worth admiring and hating about the war." The action is set in 1967, near the Cambodian border, where Stone served. The main conflict is between Barnes and Elias and climaxes when the platoon enters a village and nearly commits a massacre. Although the memory of My Lai may be recalled here, Stone works from his own experience: "We did shoot livestock," he told *The New York Times* (December 21, 1986). "We burned hooches. One of my comrades did kill a woman. I did save two girls from being raped and killed. It was madness."

Platoon follows a mythic structure similar to *Apocalypse Now*, involving a journey into the underworld, a knight's quest (with Sheen as the voyager and crusader), and iconography recalling both Oedipus and Christ, in both a symbolic crucifixion and a resurrection. The resemblance to *Apocalypse Now* is even more striking when one considers that the two Sheens, father Martin and son Charlie, play similar symbolic roles in the films. Stone's film is not as surreal as Coppola's, and the you-are-there first-person perspective of the voice-over narration gives *Platoon* a much stronger sense of realism. Upon its release, *Platoon* was praised by many as one of the greatest war films ever made.

Impact of Event

After the release of *Platoon*, *Apocalypse Now* was quickly demoted to the penultimate Vietnam War film, as Stone's uncompromising screen realism sent shock waves through the film industry. It set a new standard for the genre and perhaps changed the way people thought not only about Vietnam films but also about the Vietnam crisis in general. *Platoon* served notice that a radical reassessment of the American legacy in Vietnam was long overdue. In his *Time* magazine review (December 14, 1986), Richard Corliss called *Apocalypse Now* "by comparison, all machismo and mysticism; Stone's film is a document written in blood that after almost 20 years refuses to dry." For Corliss, it was "the most impressive movie to deal with the fighting in Viet Nam." David Ansen of *Newsweek* (January 5, 1987) found earlier films on Vietnam wanting in comparison: *The Deer Hunter, Coming Home* (1978), and *Apocalypse Now*, he wrote, merely "used the war as a metaphor to explore the American psyche, metaphysics or personal relationships."

Some journalists took umbrage with the film. Syndicated columnist Tom Tiede, for example, rejected the notion that Vietnam veterans were "ticking bombs" and resented the way Stone showed American soldiers as "murderers, rapists, and terrorists, which is to say simply and completely evil." He scoffed at the *Time* reviewer's claim that *Platoon* showed "Vietnam as it really was." If *Platoon* was rejected by right-wing Americans, it also was denounced by left-wing Germans at the Berlin Film Festival of 1987, who considered it "imperialistic maundering." A right-winger from Scottsdale, Arizona, wrote to *The New York Times* (April 12, 1987) to deplore the film's portrayal of the "moral vacuum" of soldiers "whose chief concerns were to shirk duty, blame the next fellow for one's own dereliction, get high, assassinate and rape the innocent, disobey orders and murder either one's fellow soldier or one's superior." For some, then, *Platoon* was both disturbing and controversial, but then Vietnam was hardly a comforting war experience. Stone's film spat in the face of many Americans who wanted to forget about Vietnam and feel good about their country.

Platoon broke with traditional war films in its graphic and psychological realism. Vincent Canby remarked that he had never seen "in a war movie such a harrowing evocation of fear." The film was disturbing not only in its vivid dramatization of the ordeal of combat but also in what it suggested about the behavior of American soldiers abroad. It is doubtful that any motion picture could tell the entire truth about Vietnam, since there were so many facets to the war, but Stone's film told a truth, personally realized. David Halberstam, the Pulitzer Prize-winning correspondent who covered Vietnam for *The New York Times*, wrote (March 8, 1987) that Stone struck "an enormous blow for reality, for what happens when we do not understand what we are doing and what our limits are." The film was nominated for eight Oscars and won four, including those for best director and best picture. It also earned Golden Globe Awards for best director and best dramatic movie of 1986.

The issue of Vietnam remained an obsession for Oliver Stone, who later filmed the bitter story of Ron Kovic in *Born on the Fourth of July* (1989). Kovic's story paralleled Stone's with one crucial difference: Oliver Stone did not return from Southeast Asia as a paraplegic. Stone's background, however, was similar to Kovic's. He described his father as a very patriotic right-winger: "I believed the John Wayne movies," Stone said in an interview after *Platoon* was released. "I believed the Audie Murphy movies. I thought war was . . . the most difficult thing a young man could go through." With *Born on the Fourth of July*, Stone broke with the conventional mythic structure, but that film was as much about the aftermath of the war on the homefront as about the war itself. Perhaps even more controversial was Stone's *JFK* (1991), which, among other things, attempted to answer the question: "Why were we in Vietnam?"

Oliver Stone understood Vietnam because he had lived it. David Halberstam praised *Platoon* as "the ultimate work of witness, something which has the authenticity of documentary and yet the vibrancy and originality of art." He asserted that Stone "has done something more important than all the war's historians; he has given us something which is not only real, but which lives." This is perhaps the strongest tribute to one of the most important films of the 1980's.

Bibliography

Adair, Gilbert. *Hollywood's Vietnam.* London: Heinemann, 1989. Chapter 8, "I Am Reality," devotes nearly twenty pages to *Platoon*, examining the alleged "realism." Adair criticizes the film's "scenes of paroxysmatic physical violence" as being "basically as gratuitous and exploitative as those of any other film." Adair delights in his attempt to be iconoclastic.

Anderegg, Michael A., ed. *Inventing Vietnam: The War in Film and Television.* Philadelphia: Temple University Press, 1991. Several essays in this collection, but notably Judy Lee Kinney's "Ritual and Remembrance," comment on *Platoon*, its realism and mythic structure, its voice-over narration, and its Christian iconography.

Auster, Albert, and Leonard Quart. *How the War Was Remembered: Hollywood and Vietnam.* New York: Praeger, 1988. Part 4, "Confronting Vietnam," deals with *Platoon* as "part of the healing process." The film's greatest strength "lies in its social realism" and "its feeling of verisimilitude." *Platoon* is praised as offsetting the dangerous patriotism of the Rambo films. Well researched, sensibly written, and readable.

Dittmar, Linda, and Gene Michaud, eds. *From Hanoi to Hollywood: The Vietnam War in American Film.* New Brunswick, N.J.: Rutgers University Press, 1990. Includes essays that treat the film substantially, generally from a left-wing perspective. Also includes a chronology listing both films and historical events along with a "Selected Filmography."

Dye, Dale A. *Platoon.* New York: Charter Books, 1986. Dye, a retired Marine captain who served in Vietnam and later as Stone's military adviser, wrote this novelization based on Oliver Stone's screenplay.

Jeffords, Susan. *The Remasculinization of America: Gender and the Vietnam War.* Bloomington: Indiana University Press, 1989. This feminist approach to the "gendered structure of representation of the Vietnam War in America" indulges in jargon to build its thesis concerning a "renegotiation of masculinity." *Platoon* is used as an example of the "regeneration of American masculinity" and is linked with the Rambo series.

Sklar, Robert, et al. "PLATOON on Inspection: A Critical Symposium." *Cineaste* 15, no. 4 (1987): 4-11. The editors invited five writers to respond to *Platoon*, and, according to Sklar, each responded in a very different way.

Welsh, James M., ed. *Literature/Film Quarterly* 16, no. 44 (1988). The lead essay in the "Vietnam Issue," Michael Pursell's "*Full Metal Jacket*: The Unravelling of

Patriarchy," compares Stanley Kubrick's 1987 film to *Platoon.* David Whillock's "Defining the Fictive American Vietnam Film" also uses Stone's film as a major example.

Whaley, Donald M., ed. *Literature/Film Quarterly* 20, no. 3 (1992). Michael Selig's lead essay in the "Vietnam Revisited" issue sets the tone that defines Vietnam films as "talking cures" for the anguish of the Vietnam generation. *Platoon* is discussed specifically in Donald Whaley's "The Hero-Adventurer in the Land of Nam" and in Avent Beck's "The Christian Allegorical Structure of *Platoon.* "

James M. Welsh

Cross-References

All Quiet on the Western Front Stresses the Futility of War (1929), p. 767; Mailer Publishes *The Naked and the Dead* (1948), p. 1373; *Catch-22* Illustrates Antiwar Sentiment (1961), p. 1866; *Dog Soldiers* Portrays Vietnam in Fiction (1974), p. 2315; *Apocalypse Now* Is Hailed as the Ultimate Vietnam War Film (1979), p. 2428.

RAP GOES PLATINUM WITH RUN-D.M.C.'S *RAISING HELL*

Category of event: Music
Time: July, 1986
Locale: Los Angeles, California

Run-D.M.C. confirmed rap's place in multicultural pop music when its album Raising Hell *sold more than one million copies*

> *Principal personages:*
> JOSEPH SIMMONS (1965-   ), the rapper nicknamed "Run" whose popularity crossed racial lines, bringing the black urban sound to pop music
> RUSSELL SIMMONS (1958-   ), Joseph Simmons' elder brother who managed and produced many top rap groups, including Run-D.M.C.
> DARRYL MCDANIELS (1964-   ), the "D.M.C." of Run-D.M.C. and Joseph Simmons' best friend since kindergarten

Summary of Event

Rap music originated in the inner cities of America as a new voice for the frustration and hopelessness of ghetto life. A continuation of African-American musical culture, rap drew from oral traditions and the rhythmic drumming and syncopation of black music. It was also influenced by the Jamaican "sound system" disc jockeys of the 1960's and the political jazz of Gil Scott-Heron and the Last Poets. Emerging in New York City during the mid-1970's, early rap was performed almost exclusively for black audiences in Brooklyn, Queens, Manhattan, and the South Bronx. Rap remained a predominantly race- and class-specific form of expression until 1986, when two young rappers known as Run-D.M.C. released the album *Raising Hell*. This platinum hit crossed cultural boundaries and firmly established rap as part of popular music.

Raising Hell combined metallic rock, rhythm and blues, and rap into a popular mixture that jumped up the charts to number three. The album included a collaboration with the heavy metal band Aerosmith on a remake of its classic "Walk This Way," also released as a music video that received heavy play on the Music Television (MTV) network. "Walk This Way" was the first rap hit to cross over the racial barriers that previously had made rap the domain of black musicians. *Raising Hell's* success opened the door to Caucasian, Hispanic, American Indian, and Samoan rappers, and encouraged collaborations between rappers and musicians best known for other genres. Rap diversified, branching off from the violent and controversial "gangster" or "hard-core" genre. The late 1980's and early 1990's saw the emergence of "pop" or "bubblegum," "countercultural" or "hippie-hop," and "party" rap, as well as feminist rappers such as Salt-N-Pepa and Queen Latifah.

Prior to 1986, rap was not completely unknown to the music world. In 1979, songwriter Sylvia Robinson released "Rapper's Delight" by Harlem's Sugarhill Gang. This rap hit was the first to make a mark on national charts. It was soon followed by "The Breaks" and "125th Street" by Kurtis Blow and by Grandmaster Flash and the Furious Five's graphic protest "The Message." Rap concerts drew larger crowds, and the record industry began to take notice.

It was at this time that a young man named Joseph Simmons began developing his own rap style. The son of a civil rights activist and poet, Joseph grew up in the middle-class neighborhood of Hollis, Queens. His elder brother Russell managed Kurtis Blow and would allow Joseph, a glib fifteen-year-old, a few minutes on stage to do his own thing. Nicknamed "Run" at the age of twelve because of his tendency to run off at the mouth, Joseph was enrolled in college studying mortuary science when he teamed up with his friend Darryl McDaniels to form Run-D.M.C.

Run-D.M.C.'s first album, *It's Like That*, was released by Profile Records in 1983. Interesting for its dramatic, tense lyrics and the juxtaposition of Run's higher, smoother voice and McDaniel's rougher tone, *It's Like That* sold 250,000 copies and went to number fifteen on the black charts. By 1985, Run-D.M.C. had two gold albums and was headlining concerts. It added Jason Mizell as D.J. and developed a gangster-style look: black hats and suits and white Adidas shoes. Run-D.M.C.'s major breakthrough came in July, 1986, when the album *Raising Hell* was simultaneously certified gold and platinum.

Run-D.M.C. followed up on the record's success with the Raising Hell national tour. The group sold out 20,000-seat arenas across the country, but the tour was devastated by violence in at least six cities. There was rioting in Pittsburgh, New York, and St. Louis. In Long Beach, California, gangs tore through the arena before the concert, injuring more than forty people. Although rowdiness at concerts was nothing new, the magnitude of the violence attracted the attention of the Parents Music Resource Center. Tipper Gore, wife of Senator Al Gore, criticized Run-D.M.C. for use of provocative lyrics, and many promoters reconsidered the decision to book rap groups.

Run argued that he acted as a role model to inner-city youth. "They listen to me *because* I act tough and cool. I got a lot of juice with them. . . . So when we say don't take drugs and stay in school, they listen." One music critic described *Raising Hell* as "highly moral," and Run-D.M.C. did have a history of social involvement, including an appearance at the Live Aid concert and public-service announcements against drugs and venereal disease. After the Long Beach riot, Run went on Los Angeles radio urging people to calm down. "I told the gangs," Run said, "if you're listening to me—you're stupid."

The next significant crossover hit was inspired when Russell Simmons teamed up with heavy metal producer Rick Rubin to form Def Jam Records. Def Jam managed more than a dozen rap acts, including Run-D.M.C. and the Beastie Boys, three white punkers turned rappers. The two groups collaborated on "Paul Revere," released in late 1986 on the Beastie Boys' *Licensed to Ill*. This hit album continued the musical direction started by Run-D.M.C. and appealed to black fans as well as white. In

1987, Run-D.M.C. and the Beastie Boys went on the road with the Together Forever tour, selling out major arenas despite bad press and attracting a mixed audience of blacks and whites. Rap had become the music of the youthful masses, a multicultural voice expressing anger, joy, political opinion, and idealism.

Impact of Event

When Run-D.M.C. went platinum with *Raising Hell* in 1986, rap became an undeniable force in the popular music industry. "Walk This Way," the hit collaboration with Aerosmith, broke the precedent that rap was created by black musicians for black youth. Increased popularity with a racially mixed audience provided incentive for artists of different ethnic backgrounds to experiment with rap. Rap diversified and flourished. Rap music's impact was not limited to the music world alone. Heated debates regarding the violence associated with concerts and the obscenity, sexism, and hostility prevalent in the lyrics of "gangster" or "hard-core" rap raged in the media, the courtroom, and the classroom.

Although "gangster" rap was the most visible because of its controversial nature, a variety of distinct approaches to the genre developed, each with its own stars and audience. "Pop" or "bubblegum" rap, pioneered by M.C. Hammer, was characterized by its repetitive musical samples and innocuous lyrics. Groups such as Hammer, Heavy D. and the Boyz, Sir Mix-a-Lot, and Kris Kross as well as white rappers Vanilla Ice and Marky Mark, were popular with the media because of their inoffensive style. Pop rap received air time on MTV, and advertising campaigns targeting teenagers utilized such hits as Hammer's "Can't Touch This" (1990), Vanilla Ice's "Ice Ice Baby" (1990), and Kris Kross's "Jump" (1992).

Female rappers assumed a more dominant role with the 1986 release of *Hot, Cool, and Vicious* by Salt-N-Pepa. Women had performed in rap since its inception but were usually labeled as novelty acts. Salt-N-Pepa's feminist attitude encouraged other women to respond aggressively to the misogyny of most male rappers. Queen Latifah delivered a powerful message on *All Hail the Queen* (1989) and *Nature of a Sista'* (1991) and created a niche for female fans in a genre known for its endorsement of violence against women.

Another female rapper, Sister Souljah, elicited Bill Clinton's criticism in response to her remarks on interracial violence. The militancy of her album *360 Degrees of Power* (1992) is expressive of the politicized rap for which Public Enemy is best known. That group's innovative albums *It Takes a Nation of Millions to Hold Us Back* (1988) and *Fear of a Black Planet* (1990) received the attention of musicologists, jazz musicians, and composers, and Spike Lee used "Fight the Power" as the theme song for his film *Do the Right Thing* (1989). Because of Public Enemy's association with the Nation of Islam, the media generalized political rap as nationalistic and anti-Semitic, obscuring the actual diversity of political opinions being expressed. Albums released in the late 1980's and early 1990's included the antiapartheid collaboration *Sun City*, the militant *Sleeping with the Enemy* by Paris, the spiritual Afrocentrism of X Clan's *To the East, Blackwards*, and Isis' *Rebel Soul*.

Criticized in the early days for nihilism and lack of utopian vision, rap experienced a resurgence of optimism and ethnic identity common to black music. Combining spiritual and mystical lyrics with the rhythmic textures sampled from 1960's music, P. M. Dawn's *Of the Heart, of the Soul, and of the Cross: The Utopian Experience* united those alienated by other forms of rap. Along with P. M. Dawn, De La Soul, Arrested Development, and A Tribe Called Quest met with great success in the mainstream, receiving acclaim for their work in *Rolling Stone, Spin, The New York Times,* and *The Village Voice.*

As early as 1980, rap was used by educators who took advantage of its retainability. Douglass "Jocko" Henderson, a radio personality of the 1950's and 1960's, formed Get Ready, Inc., an educational rap program with topics ranging from black history to career-preparation skills. Later, groups such as KRS-One (Knowledge Reigns Supreme Over Nearly Everyone), the Poor Righteous Teachers (PRT), and the Intellectual Hoodlum incorporated the message that knowledge is a crucial aspect of survival.

Rap music has flourished since Run-D.M.C. caught the public's attention in 1986. Many artists unique in music and message have come on the scene. Rap also has influenced American culture in a wider arena. The controversial nature of some rap music encouraged people who had never listened to it to hold strong opinions about it nevertheless. The effect of explicit rap on society (and vice versa) cannot be ignored, and rap music contributed to debates concerning censorship and restrictions on material that could be presented to children.

The controversy surrounding the graphically violent and sexist lyrics of 2 Live Crew's *As Nasty as They Wanna Be* came to a head on June 10, 1990, when the group, led by Luther Campbell, was charged with violating obscenity laws in an adults-only concert in Hollywood, Florida. After a two-week trial, 2 Live Crew was found innocent of all charges. Freedom of speech as guaranteed by the First Amendment and the limits of this right, if any, are issues critical to American society. When a rap musician expresses himself or herself freely and without censorship in the public eye, the content of rap cannot go unnoticed. One impact of controversial rap music has been to provoke examination and evaluation of the environmental conditions that foster antagonistic philosophies.

Rap continues the tradition of African-American music. It is the honest voice of a diverse set of people, espousing divergent viewpoints and encompassing many attitudes. Run-D.M.C., the first rap group to enter the limelight of popular music, opened the door for a segment of society shut out for too long.

Bibliography

Blauner, Peter. "The Rap on Run-D.M.C.: The Kids from Hollis Strike Gold." *New York* 19 (November 17, 1986): 62. Describes Run-D.M.C.'s rise to fame and for tune. Gives the background of Joseph ("Run") Simmons and follows the group's development under the management of elder brother Russell. Includes interviews with fans and criticism by old friend and fellow rapper Kurtis Blow.

Bruno, Vito. "Rap: a Positive Force for Social Change; Coralling the Violence."

Billboard Magazine 98 (November 8, 1986): 9. Commentary by a rap promoter opposing the argument that rap causes violence. Bruno views rap as the voice of frustrated inner-city kids whose aggression arises from complex social issues and not merely the excitement of a live concert.

Chin, Brian. "Rap Hits Home: The Biggest, Brashest, Freshest Breakthrough of the Decade." *Billboard Magazine* 98 (December 27, 1986): Y8. A brief history of rap from 1979 to 1986 by a music expert. Chin rejoices in rap's freshness and free expression, which he attributes to a lack of acknowledgment by the "over-ground" music industry.

Dyson, Michael Eric. "Rap Culture, the Church, and American Society." In *Sacred Music of the Secular City: From Blues to Rap*, edited by Jon Michael Spencer. Durham, N.C.: Duke University Press, 1992. Written by a professor at the Chicago Theological Seminary, this essay depicts rap as the continuation of black oral culture. Rap is analyzed for both its positive and its negative influences.

_____. "Rights and Responsibilities: 2 Live Crew and Rap's Moral Vision." In *Sacred Music of the Secular City: From Blues to Rap*, edited by Jon Michael Spencer. Durham, N.C.: Duke University Press, 1992. A thoughtful essay defending 2 Live Crew's right of expression according to the First Amendment and yet criticizing a society that produces such violent and sexist attitudes.

George, Nelson. "Rap and Hip Hop Are Here to Stay: Major Tours Bring Genres to Prominence." *Billboard Magazine* 99 (September 5, 1987): 24. Brief article listing the major rap tours of 1987. Notes the increase in crossover audiences and the teaming up of Run-D.M.C. with the Beastie Boys.

Manuel, Ruth Dolores. "The Three R's: Reading, 'Riting, Rapping." *Essence* 14 (April, 1984): 56. Profile of Douglass "Jocko" Henderson, radio personality turned educator, who created rap records on such subjects as black history, drug abuse, and career-preparation skills.

Tyre, Peg. "Rap Stars." *New York* 19 (August 11, 1986): 14. Profile of the owners of Profile Records, Steve Plotnicki and Cory Robbins. Rap music's most successful independent record label, Profile took a chance on Run-D.M.C. and got paid off in platinum with the 1986 release *Raising Hell*.

West, Cornel. "On Afro-American Popular Music: From Bebop to Rap." In *Sacred Music of the Secular City: From Blues to Rap*, edited by Jon Michael Spencer. Durham, N.C.: Duke University Press, 1992. Places rap in the broad historical context of African-American music. Chronicles development of bebop, gospel music, jazz, soul, Motown, technofunk, and rap. An interesting commentary on music's function in black society.

Susan Frischer

Cross-References

Gordy Founds Motown Records (1959), p. 1790; *The Autobiography of Malcolm X Is Published* (1965), p. 2022; Brown Wins a Grammy for "Papa's Got a

Brand New Bag" (1966), p. 2059; Innovative Black Filmmakers Achieve Success (Late 1980's), p. 2565; Mapplethorpe's Photographs Provoke Controversy (1989), p. 2636; *Do the Right Thing* Establishes Lee as a World-Class Director (1989), p. 2641.

THE MUSÉE D'ORSAY OPENS

Categories of event: Architecture and art
Time: December 9, 1986
Locale: Paris, France

The Musée d'Orsay officially opened to the general public, providing Paris with arguably the world's greatest museum dedicated to nineteenth century art and culture

Principal personages:

GAE AULENTI (1927-   ), an Italian architect who was commissioned to design the interior of the Musée d'Orsay

FRANÇOISE CACHIN, a prominent art historian who was appointed as the first director of the new museum

VICTOR LALOUX (1850-1937), the French architect who designed the original Orsay railroad station, which eventually was transformed into a modern museum

VALÉRY GISCARD D'ESTAING (1926-   ), the president of France who approved, funded, and enthusiastically supported the Orsay project

MADELEINE REBERIOUX (1920-   ), a prominent social historian who was appointed vice president of the Musée d'Orsay

Summary of Event

By the early 1970's, a pressing question in Paris was what to do with the old Gare d'Orsay, a huge abandoned railway station occupying a prime site along the Seine River, opposite the Tuileries Gardens and the Louvre. Originally constructed by Victor Laloux in 1900, it was an impressive building that included a luxury hotel and a flamboyant external façade. Its most dominating feature was the huge barrel-vaulted roof, constructed of iron and glass, having the impressive dimensions of 450 feet in length, 131 feet in width, and 103 feet in height. By 1970, the building was marked for demolition, most likely to be replaced by an ultramodern hotel and conference center. A pronounced public reaction had set in, however, against any further destruction of Paris' architectural legacy, spurred largely by the impending brutal demolition of the once colorful food-market pavilions in the historic Les Halles quarter.

Fortunately for the Orsay's future, Paris needed a new museum for nineteenth century art and culture, partly as a result of an explosion of interest in the painting and painters of that era, especially the Impressionists, who were riding a wave of unprecedented popularity. The old Musée du Jeu de Paume, which previously held the Impressionist collection, was simply too small to handle the enormous crowds, and there were increasing concerns about its security system. President Georges Pompidou issued the initial order to halt the demolition of the old Gare d'Orsay, but it was President Valéry Giscard d'Estaing who was primarily responsible for making the ultimate decision to transform the railway station into a museum. The inital plan called for the museum to cover the entire nineteenth century, but the Louvre refused to part with its magnificent collection of early nineteenth century Romantic paintings. Consequently, political rather than artistic dates were chosen: The museum would display works from 1848, the year of radical revolutions throughout Europe, to 1914, when World War I broke out.

The challenge of the transformation was enormous, since the railway station, with its huge bulk and vast open spaces, seemed to be the very antithesis of what one desired in a museum. In addition to restoration of the decaying station, entire new floors and rooms had to be constructed, thus making the project one of the largest renovation schemes in Parisian history. Eventually, after several discouraging early phases, it was decided to commission Gae Aulenti, an Italian modernist architect, to be responsible for designing the interior of the museum. Aulenti had worthy credentials, having already remodeled the Palazzo Grassi in Venice and designed showrooms for major corporations including Olivetti and Fiat. Some observers thought that her expertise was more in the field of interior design than in architecture.

Aulenti took firm grasp of the project and produced a bold, breathtaking plan that elicited strong reactions. Her final product was characterized by a central aisle or avenue that ran the length of the entire station, flanked on each side by imposing stone walls of tan burgundian limestone. The avenue was filled with numerous statues, thus creating a theatrical effect. Behind the stone walls on each side of the central aisle were exhibition rooms that held the museum's collection of paintings and art objects. The second level was largely devoted to sculpture, cinema, photography, and Art Nouveau. The crowning glory of the museum's collection, its Impressionist and Postimpressionist paintings, was wisely located on the top floor, where it could take advantage of the natural overhead lighting. Here was where the museum displayed its spectacular collection of works by Pierre-Auguste Renoir, Claude Monet, Edgar Degas, Paul Cézanne, Édouard Manet, Camille Pissarro, and Vincent van Gogh. In total, the Orsay's interior volume contained more than seventeen thousand square meters of permanent exhibition space. This exceeded the space in the enormous Pompidou Center and was approximately half of that in the old Louvre before its remodeling. All this space was devoted to only a half century of art.

No sooner had the museum opened in December, 1986, than it began to provoke extensive controversy. In general, critics focused upon two major areas: the interior architectural design and the manner in which the art was displayed. Aulenti's central avenue was condemned for being too imperial and majestic, leading some observers to say that it conjured up visions of ancient Egypt or Babylonia. Some caustic critics dubbed Aulenti's severe modernism as "neo-Mussolini," since it was reminiscent of the architectural style favored by former fascist dictators. Others made the reverse criticism. They believed that the central aisle was too successful in that it dominated the very art it was supposed to feature, a classic case of architecture overwhelming art. Aulenti also was censured for her dull stone walls, which allegedly formed a poor background for many of the paintings, and for her technique of drilling holes in the walls at seven-inch intervals. Although this allowed for flexibility in hanging pictures, it gave the unfortunate impression that some rooms had been sprayed by a machine gun.

Nevertheless, Aulenti had her admirers. They praised the Orsay's heavy stone avenue for imposing a sense of order and discipline upon the building's unwieldy spaces and the cleverness of the layout, which channeled crowds through the museum in a logical order. Admirers praised the design for making a visit one of architectural delight as well as artistic pleasure. It also was noted that little fault could be found with the manner in which Aulenti and the contractors had handled the acoustics, lighting, and air circulation of the building, easily meeting the high standards expected of modern museums.

The second major area of criticism focused upon the philosophy underlying the display of the Orsay's art. In general, critics complained that the museum contained too much mediocre art. They censured the curators in general and Françoise Cachin, the Orsay's director, in particular for adopting a neutral stance and allowing "bad" art to be displayed side by side with "good" art. Critics were particularly incensed over the inclusion of "academic" or "official" art. This was the art that had been approved by the despotic regime of Napoleon III or was commissioned by the aristocracy and businesspeople of the period, art that frequently was displayed in government buildings, public squares, and the salons of the rich and powerful. By and large, art historians have contemptuously dismissed the "academic" art of the nineteenth century as being pompous, unimaginative, and decidedly lacking in creativity. They were incensed that such art was allowed to be displayed along with works of great Romantic painters such as Eugène Delacroix or some of the talented realists such as Gustave Courbet and Henri Fantin-Latour. Because the curators' policy was so inclusive and democratic, they failed to educate visitors as to why some artists might rightfully be regarded as superior to other artists. A related criticism was that the museum also failed to inform visitors about the history of the nineteenth century, somewhat puzzling in that Madeleine Reberioux, a prominent social historian, was appointed as vice president of the Orsay. She apparently chose not to exert her authority in this area.

Those who defended the existing arrangement claimed that great art was separated subtly by various techniques from mediocre art, and that visitors who follow the exhibits in a chronological fashion can easily see why avant-garde art triumphed and how it is obviously superior to that which preceded it. This was one of the reasons why the Impressionists and Postimpressionists were given their own floor, separate from earlier schools of art. The full glory and genius of their work is self-evident and exposes the inferiority of the "academic" school. As for the criticism that one learns relatively little about nineteenth century history, it was argued that the Orsay is in the final analysis an art museum. It was never meant to be a history museum dedicated to re-creating an era and showing "how people lived back then."

Impact of Event

The most obvious impact of the renovation was that it gave Paris arguably the greatest museum in the world for nineteenth century art and culture. The Orsay allowed Paris to rationalize its artistic treasures and group them logically. Visitors and scholars go to the Louvre for great art from antiquity to the mid-nineteenth century, the Orsay for the remainder of the nineteenth century, and the Pompidou Center for the twentieth century. Unlike some museums of Paris, the Musée d'Orsay is multidimensional, including not only painting and sculpture but also furniture, porcelain, architecture, photography, and the early cinema. Moreover, renovating an existing building which in some respects epitomized the architectural and design forms of the nineteenth century obviously made more sense in this case than constructing a new edifice in the modern style or some pathetic imitation of the nineteenth century's Beaux-Arts tradition.

Renovation of the Gare d'Orsay also preserved the architectural integrity of the surrounding area in the very heart of Paris. Thus, this quarter was saved from the obliteration that Les Halles and the Beaubourg quarters suffered in order to make way for ultramodern projects such as the Forum and the Pompidou Center. Plans submitted by architects and urban planners for the significant public space that would have been created if the Orsay had been torn down included grotesque gargantuan structures of concrete, glass, and steel, some of them of skyscraper proportions, which would have overwhelmed the area and permanently disfigured the Parisian skyline. Although the original Gare d'Orsay had limitations, it offered a worthy counterpoint to the Louvre on the opposite bank of the Seine River, and its monumental and ornate character was in keeping with the city's architectural heritage. One of the more attractive features of the renovation was that part of the roof terrace was made accessible to visitors, thereby affording one of the more impressive views of this lovely area of Paris.

Another, more subtle, impact of the renovation and museum opening was that the museum reflected the growing importance of women in French society. The architect, director, and vice president were all women. The fact that few observers in the French media commented on this phenomenon suggests that these women were chosen for their unquestioned talent and ability and for no other reason. Although their decisions and actions prompted much controversy, debates were remarkably free of sexism. In general, criticism was seldom personalized or placed in a gender context but simply reflected the arguments that were going on in the contemporary worlds of art, culture, and architecture.

The Musée d'Orsay, as much as any museum opened at that time, encapsulated both the architectural style and the display techniques of the modern museum. Museums and art became democratized in the latter part of the twentieth century. This mandated that modern museums be built quite differently from in the past. Museums must now be able to accommodate huge crowds. Initial projections were for the Orsay to handle three million visitors a year. It can accommodate about five thousand people at any one time without painful overcrowding.

In a democratic age, the definition of art has had to be expanded to include popular culture as well as "high art." As a consequence of this redefinition, it is not unusual for academic and cultural elites to bemoan the alleged deterioration in the quality of exhibits. Since the public often pays for these new museums through taxes—the Orsay's renovation cost $250 million in public funds—it expects more in the way of amenities, such as cafés, restaurants, book stores, and easy access for the elderly and handicapped. In addition, modern museums impose new challenges upon those who run them. Architects and curators now realize that they must educate the public as well as passively display art; thus, the Musée d'Orsay has offered classes, lectures, and concerts; maintained an audiovisual center; conducted special programs and exhibitions; and catered to the unique needs of children and young people.

A particular challenge for both architects and curators is to incorporate the latest technology in running these museums. Scientific knowledge and technology are used to increase the security of museums, maintain accurate computerized records, restore deteriorating paintings and statues, determine the proper height and placement of exhibits for maximum enjoyment, and protect paintings from the ravages of heat, humidity, and excessive natural light. The Musée d'Orsay incorporated most of these new concepts into its building. Undoubtedly, controversy will continue to swirl about the Musée d'Orsay, but no one can say that visiting the museum is not a feast for the eyes; nor will a visitor come away bored or uninformed.

Bibliography

Davis, Douglas. *The Museum Transformed: Design and Culture in the Post-Pompidou Age.* New York: Abbeville Press, 1990. Davis, the former architectural critic for *Newsweek*, offers some valuable insights into the major differences between the traditional museum and the museums of the late twentieth century. Brief section on the Orsay.

"Gae Aulenti." *Architecture and Urbanism* 201 (June, 1987): 11-72. Focuses upon Aulenti and includes a rare discussion of her other major architectural projects. Contains an interesting "conversation" that Aulenti has with an imaginary visitor while walking through the Orsay. Photos, diagrams, and blueprints.

Guide to the Musée d'Orsay. Paris: Ministere de la Culture et de la Communication, 1987. Translated by Anthony Roberts. This official guidebook produced by the French government is an indispensable source offering expert commentary on the artistic treasures held by the museum. Contains hundreds of photographs, most in color.

"Musée d'Orsay." *Architecture Interieure Cree* 215 (December, 1986): 1-112. An outstanding article on the history of the building. Although a French publication, extensive portions of the article are in English, and all readers can benefit from the generous and impressive collection of sketches, photographs, and axonometric plates. Includes unusual photos of the old railway station and the new museum during their construction periods.

The Musée d'Orsay, Paris. New York: Harry Abrams, 1986. Translated by Jane Brenton. Compiled by a team of specialists from the museum's staff, this lavishly illustrated book contains more than 250 color reproductions of the building's artistic treasures.

Nochlin, Linda, et al. "The Musée d'Orsay: A Symposium." *Art in America* 76 (January, 1988): 84-107. A series of brief articles by established artists and academics, offering a variety of opinions on the architectural merit of the building and the quality of art displayed. For the advanced student. Photos included.

"Orsay." *Connaissance des Arts* (1987): 1-74. This special issue of a prestigious French magazine, translated into English, is perhaps the best single introduction to the museum. Outstanding collection of colored photographs. Valuable for both novices and advanced students.

David C. Lukowitz

Cross-References

Monet's *Water Lilies* Are Shown at the Musée de l'Orangerie (1927), p. 718; New York's Museum of Modern Art Is Founded (1929), p. 782; The Pompidou Center Opens in Paris (1977), p. 2402; Van Gogh's *Irises* Sells for $53.9 Million (1987), p. 2603; Pei Creates a New Entrance to the Louvre (1988), p. 2619.

SOYINKA WINS THE NOBEL PRIZE IN LITERATURE

Category of event: Literature
Time: December 10, 1986
Locale: Stockholm, Sweden

Wole Soyinka became the first African to receive the Nobel Prize in Literature, which he called a tribute to all African writers

> *Principal personages:*
> WOLE SOYINKA (1934-   ), a Nigerian-born writer whose courageous political stand and literary productivity brought him international acclaim
> ALFRED NOBEL (1833-1896), a Swedish engineer and chemist who established the annual Nobel Prizes
> OSTEN SJOSTRAND, a member of the Swedish Academy, who translated Soyinka's poems into Swedish

Summary of Event

When a reporter in Paris informed Wole Soyinka that he had been awarded the Nobel Prize in Literature, Soyinka replied that he did not consider the award his alone but rather an honor bestowed on Africa itself: "I'm a part of the whole literary tradition of Africa. The prize is for all my colleagues who are just as qualified to win it as I. I see myself as part of their collective reality."

An uninformed observer might think such self-proclaimed selflessness a pose, but an examination of Soyinka's career shows that the remarks accurately reflect the way he has lived his life. Born in Nigeria, Soyinka was educated in Ibadan, Nigeria, and at Leeds University in England. After spending several years in London writing and working with the British Broadcasting Corporation and in the theater, he returned to Nigeria in 1960, the year the country gained independence from Great Britain. There, amid the euphoria of independence, he plunged into the theatrical and political life of Nigeria. He wrote for the stage, television, and radio and helped to found a theater company in which he acted and directed. His involvement, however, was not purely literary in nature; he set out even to use art to work against racism and oppression. He also joined a human rights organization and spoke out on the critical issues the new nation of Nigeria faced. From the outset, he had little use for those black leaders he described as stepping "fast into the shoes of the departing whites" to gain wealth and to satisfy their lust for power.

By 1965, he had fallen afoul of the Nigerian government, and he was charged with stealing from a radio station tapes supposedly protesting a rigged election. Tried and acquitted on this charge, he was arrested again in August of 1967 during the Nigerian Civil War. Attempting to bring about a cease-fire with the rebels who had created the state of Biafra within Nigeria, he was charged with conspiracy and jailed for nearly two years.

While in prison, he continued to write; *Poems from Prison* (1969) and *The Man Died: Prison Notes of Wole Soyinka* (1972) reflect his time in jail. Recalling this experience, he said, "Whatever I believed in before I was locked up, I came out a fanatic in those things." In the years since his imprisonment, Soyinka has lived on the larger international stage, establishing himself as a playwright whose work has been staged in London and New York and gaining praise for his poetry, fiction, essays, and autobiographical writing. Considering himself "a man of the theater," he often directs or oversees productions of his own plays—sometimes in prestigious theaters, other times with obscure companies sponsored by the United Nations Educational, Scientific, and Cultural Organization (UNESCO). When he received the Nobel Prize, he was serving as president of UNESCO's International Theater Institute and working with a company from Martinique.

In spite of his worldwide acclaim, it was to Nigeria that Soyinka went immediately following the Nobel announcement, in order to celebrate and to share the honor with his African colleagues. Shortly after he arrived in the capital city of Lagos, an investigative journalist there was killed by a letter bomb. Soyinka immediately made use of his increased stature as a Nobel laureate to call for the government to conduct a thorough investigation of the murder. One critic has noted that Soyinka "often works in comparative obscurity in the theater and uses his renown to work for justice."

On a practical level, then, Soyinka has worked to fulfill one criterion that Alfred Nobel set for the award: to confer "the greatest benefit on mankind." His writing has conferred a like benefit. Most critics of Soyinka's work consider the twenty or so plays his outstanding achievement, even though they hardly disregard his considerable accomplishment in other genres. The Nobel citation speaks of how Soyinka "in a wide cultural perspective and with poetical overtones fashions the drama of existence." One significant aspect of Soyinka's dramatic writing lies in the way he melds his African inheritance—specifically the rich mythology of his Yoruba tribal background—with the Western tradition in which he was educated. A poetic drama such as *Death and the King's Horseman* (1975) has about it the cadence of Shakespearean verse and the structural purity of Greek drama. The play, though, is a hybrid at the same time; the story is based on Yoruba tribal mythology, and the overall effect suggests an ancient African ritual. While never denying Soyinka's Africanness, critics have often noted the impact on his work of Western writers, ranging from Euripides, whose *The Bacchae* he adapted and subtitled *A Communion Rite* (1973), to John Gay and Bertolt Brecht, whose techniques figure in *Opera Wonyosi* (1977).

Finally, it might be said that Soyinka's vision has its roots in the process of reconciliation: On the day-to-day level, he has worked to bring together, in equality, all peoples; on the artistic level, he has melded the literary traditions of his dual inheritance into a work marked by striking originality.

Impact of Event

Recalling Soyinka's experiences with the Nigerian rulers in the 1960's, reporters asked him if he thought his receipt of the Nobel Prize twenty years later might make life easier for those writers still persecuted by their governments. Soyinka's response was not encouraging: "Writers have lost their lives and are in prison because they have refused to compromise. I don't believe the prize will increase awareness of their plight." Unjust treatment of uncompromising artists has been common in postcolonial Africa, and it was probably foolhardy for anyone to suggest that a literary prize, no matter how distinguished, would make much difference. The broader impact of the award, then, may be a more symbolic one: It helps to validate African literature. Yet, as Soyinka pointed out when questioned on this point, "African literature is a concept and I don't know how you influence a concept." It is understandable that Soyinka would question the accuracy of the term "African literature" and its application to the vast field it allegedly describes. For the writing comes from a continent divided into a multitude of nations and peoples who vary in their cultural heritage, religion, social customs, and historical experience. It is written in a number of languages, both native and European—English, French, and Portuguese. While some might think African literature originated when the colonizers introduced their languages or created alphabets for the native languages, such a view ignores centuries of oral literature. This form still flourishes among a sizable part of the African population and plays an important role in religious ceremonies. Oral literature also strongly influences African written forms, whether in native or European languages.

As African nationalism has seeped into the arts, some critics insist that writing in English is not African at all. Soyinka himself thinks it ironic that a colonial language should bring linguistic cohesion to Nigeria. Some critics, though, go further than admitting and accepting the irony and call for a "decolonization" of African literature. Soyinka has been one of the main targets of such criticism, which has questioned his dual relationship with Africa and the West and accused him of pandering to overseas readers, of being a "colonial lackey," and of writing "tourist literature." This matter of language continues to cause debate among both writers and critics, as does the place of publication of African writers' works. Prior to receiving the Nobel award, Soyinka, like many prominent African authors, published his work for the most part through London publishers whose editions were imported into Africa. After 1986, he reversed that practice, and his writing began to appear first in Nigeria. Soyinka, though, continues to write in English—except for his poetry, which he composes in Yoruba and then renders into English.

To some Africans, therefore, Soyinka's Nobel award was just another form of colonization. Yet that seems an extreme view. An important document that helps to balance such a categorical position appeared in Ibadan, Nigeria, a year after Soyinka received the Nobel Prize: *Before Our Very Eyes: Tribute to Wole Soyinka, Winner of the Nobel Prize for Literature* (1987). This book includes tributes from African and overseas figures as well as personal recollections by Soyinka's colleagues. Its contributors do not engage in theoretical discussions or issue invectives on what African literature is or should be; rather, they take pride that an African had been recognized for his outstanding achievement, no matter what language he had used.

Despite the difficulty of defining the concept of African literature, the prestige the Nobel Prize carries cannot help but affect this concept positively. At the same time, African literature in English belongs to a larger body of writing that has emerged from the old British Commonwealth, including an impressive array of fiction, poetry, and drama from regions such as India, the West Indies, Canada, New Zealand, Australia, and Pakistan. Long relegated to the sidelines as a minor appendage to British literature, this writing has in the past few decades started to come into its own. Four of its writers have been named Nobel laureates: Patrick White from Australia in 1973, Soyinka in 1986, Nadine Gordimer from South Africa in 1991, and Derek Walcott from the West Indies in 1992. Their individual recognition enlarges into a collective one that helps to elevate international literature in English.

Bibliography

Black American Literature Forum 22 (1988). An issue devoted to Soyinka. Contains a variety of articles covering international responses to the Nobel Prize and Soyinka's Swedish reception, along with essays on Soyinka's sense of national responsibility and use of ritual and satire. Valuable source for specific discussions of various aspects of Soyinka's writing and career.

Gibbs, James, ed. *Critical Perspectives on Wole Soyinka*. Washington, D.C.: Three Continents, 1980. Contains an overview of Soyinka's work, along with essays by international critics focusing specifically on his poetry, drama, and fiction. Provides an extensive secondary bibliography. Excellent introductory resource.

_____. " 'Marrying earth to heaven': A Nobel Laureate at the End of the Eighties." In *International Literature in English: Essays on the Major Writers*, edited by Robert Ross. New York: Garland, 1991. Includes a biographical sketch, an essay, a primary bibliography, and an annotated secondary bibliography. Essay focuses on how Soyinka has tried always to "marry" his social concerns to his writing and examines the significance of the Nobel Prize in Soyinka's career. Contains an excellent discussion of Soyinka's poetic technique.

Jones, Eldred Durosimi. *The Writing of Wole Soyinka*. 2d ed. London: Heinemann, 1983. Provides a comprehensive introduction to Soyinka's dramatic, fictional, autobiographical, and poetic work, examining theme and technique. Attempts to show the development of his art over the years. Extensive secondary bibliography. Considered one of the standard books on Soyinka.

Katrak, Ketu H. *Wole Soyinka and Modern Tragedy: A Study of Dramatic Theory and Practice*. New York: Greenwood Press, 1986. Focuses specifically on Soyinka's dramatic writing and offers intelligent discussions of the work in the light of dramatic theory, incorporating both Soyinka's and others' views. An advanced study that sometimes relies too heavily on theoretical terminology.

Maduakor, Obi. *Wole Soyinka: An Introduction to His Writing*. New York: Garland, 1987. Contains a guide to Soyinka's work in all the genres; introductory in nature for the most part. The book's major contribution lies in its discussion of Soyinka's critical and theoretical writing about literature, which is often not covered. Extensive secondary bibliography.

Olney, James. "Wole Soyinka's Portrait of the Artist as a Very Young Man." *Southern Review* 23 (1987): 527-540. Focuses on Soyinka's *Aké: The Years of Childhood* (1981), an autobiographical account of his first eleven years. The issue also includes poetry by Soyinka and other articles on aspects of his work.

Robert L. Ross

Cross-References

The First Nobel Prizes Are Awarded (1901), p. 45; *Heart of Darkness* Reveals the Consequences of Imperialism (1902), p. 51; *Things Fall Apart* Depicts Destruction of Ibo Culture (1958), p. 1763; Kawabata Wins the Nobel Prize in Literature (1968), p. 2147; Singer Wins the Nobel Prize in Literature (1978), p. 2423; *"MASTER HAROLD" . . . and the boys* Examines Apartheid (1982), p. 2496; Mahfouz Wins the Nobel Prize in Literature (1988), p. 2625.

ADAMS' *NIXON IN CHINA* PREMIERES

Category of event: Music
Time: 1987
Locale: Houston, Texas

John Adams, a "postminimalist" working in traditional opera, completed the opera Nixon in China *in collaboration with director Peter Sellars and poet Alice Goodman*

Principal personages:

JOHN ADAMS (1947-   ), an American postminimalist composer who found an audience for a serious American opera on a contemporary historical theme

PETER SELLARS (1957-   ), a provocative American theater and opera director who creates anachronistic settings for historical operas and compelling styles for new operas

ALICE GOODMAN, a poet and librettist for the operas of John Adams

JOHN DEMAIN (1944-   ), the conductor of the Houston Grand Opera's premiere production of *Nixon in China*

Summary of Event

As a bold attempt to repoliticize the operatic tradition, John Adams' *Nixon in China* proved to be a successful artistic venture and a surprisingly popular effort; it was, one writer noted, a "stunning success." This was the first opera score by composer John Adams, and the first libretto by Alice Goodman. Peter Sellars had already earned success by staging operas by George Frideric Handel and Wolfgang Amadeus Mozart in anachronistic settings (a Handel opera set at Kennedy Space Center, for example). In recalling that Richard Nixon had shrewdly exploited a line from Mao Tse-tung's own poetry, "Seize the moment," in a banquet toast in Peking, Adams and Sellars pounced on popular images of this unique triumph of American diplomacy, the rapprochement of Nixon and Mao, to create a vivid stage work that quickly garnered attention seldom granted to a new American opera. The opera enjoyed successful productions in Houston and New York and was broadcast on public television.

In pondering a pivotal moment in recent American foreign policy, the collaborators offered a striking meditation on the collision of alien cultures, a surprisingly sympathetic psychological portrait of a disgraced American leader, and a vision of a recent historical episode as equal in importance to monumental historical episodes of the past. If earlier opera composers such as Handel could offer visions of the political triumphs of Xerxes and Julius Caesar, Adams determined to do the same for the finest moment of the only American president forced to resign. Adams' musical style builds on the technique of earlier minimalist composers such as Steven Reich and Philip Glass, placing simple, nonprogressive harmonies atop complex rhythmic patterns, but Adams shows a greater interest in soaring melodic lines. Adams' style is postminimalist in its renewed recognition of melodic power and of the powerful potential of the minimalist style in operatic storytelling.

Peter Sellars, who first conceived the opera, was correct in seeing media images as instant iconography in Nixon's visit to China in February, 1972. Nixon had hoped to be greeted by vast crowds of cheering Chinese when he arrived at Peking's airport on February 21, 1972; he sought to end China's estrangement from the United States and to boost his own popularity, which was plummeting from the Watergate revelations. As Jonathan Spence noted in *The Search for Modern China* (1990), the real diplomatic grist was refined by committees of Chinese and American negotiators, while Nixon visited the Great Wall of China and "endured an endless round of banquets." It was these banquets and public appearances that the operatic collaborators exploited to good effect.

As staged first at the Houston Grand Opera and then at the Brooklyn Academy of Music and elsewhere, the opera's production offered a succession of vivid images, rescued from the national memory but presented in surrealistic ways. Richard and Pat Nixon emerge onto the tarmac at Peking, where they are met by Chou En-lai; Chou later toasts his American guests in a soaring vision of human brotherhood. Mao Tse-tung himself emerges from a window in a gigantic wall poster of his face, and Chiang Ch'ing (Madame Mao), seated between the Nixons at a performance of "The Red Detachment of Women," prompts the dancers—one of whom, as a sadistic landlord, is none other than Henry Kissinger. In the closest thing to a show-stopper, Chiang Ching waves her "little red book" and sings, "I am the wife of Mao Tse-Tung . . . I speak according to the Book"; the scene reaches a frenzied climax, with the excesses of the Red Brigades swirling around the frightened Nixons.

The opera ends with a scene more lyrical than dramatic; the five leads of the opera engage in a series of interwoven personal musings on the historic events of the Nixons' week-long visit to China. Pat Nixon yearns forlornly, "Oh California, hold me close," while Richard retreats into memories of his experiences in World War II. Mao and Chiang remember their youthful courtship in a foxtrot, while the philosophical Chou En-lai ponders "Unto what end? Tell me." That the scene is more lyric and meditative than dramatic seems at first a major miscalculation. Did the creators find themselves unable to match the frenzied drama of the ballet scene, or did they simply wish to contrast the individual characters as they drifted off into their own dreams? The ending reinforces the impression that the opera's creators saw the visit to China as a significant political event with a potential for enormous good, despite the fallibility of the main actors.

Impact of Event

Nixon in China received its premiere at the Houston Grand Opera's new hall, the Wortham Center, in October, 1987, and the production was reprised the following month at the Next Wave Festival at the Brooklyn Academy of Music. The opera was the result of a joint commission by the Houston Grand Opera, the Brooklyn Academy, the Kennedy Center in Washington, D.C., and the Netherlands Opera. It found a wide audience when it appeared on the Public Broadcasting Systems' *Great Performances* series in 1988. Unlike most new American operas, *Nixon in China* seemed likely to achieve a modest foothold in the repertory and to enjoy new productions. Not until John Corigliano's *The Ghosts of Versailles* was produced in January, 1992, did a new American opera generate comparable enthusiasm.

Despite the widespread initial curiosity and a good deal of audience enthusiasm, the opera received mixed critical reviews. In a negative review in *New York* magazine, Peter G. Davis explained the rationale of the creators: "Like the heroes and heroines of any Classical or Romantic opera, these familiar public figures are initially presented as clichés who, the authors hope, are gradually transformed and perceived from a new, more elevated poetic perspective. It doesn't work." Davis placed the blame squarely on Adams, whom he berated for an inability to set the words dramatically or to allow them to project over the orchestra. Others more sympathetic to minimalism and postminimalism might point to the success of earlier minimalist operas on provocative historical subjects, such as the Philip Glass/Robert Wilson collaboration, *Einstein on the Beach* (1976) or Glass's *Akhnaten* (1984), both of which enjoyed successful productions.

Nixon in China has its musical and dramatic longueurs, but the effect of the first production was oddly moving. Inveterate Nixon-haters and liberals among the audience who may have come hoping for an evening of Nixon-bashing went home puzzling over the oddly sympathetic portrayal of the president as a fallible, frightened, sympathetic, and nostalgic man. One can admire the opera's creators for the sheer audacity of their choice of subject without affirming its complete success. Yet if the creators were unexpectedly sympathetic toward Nixon, they were unexpectedly hostile toward Henry Kissinger, who emerges in the opera as much the most reprehensible character, gleefully seizing the opportunity to enact sadistic fantasies in "The Red Detachment" ballet. Chiang Ch'ing is depicted as a fanatic, but she and Mao, like the Nixons, are partly redeemed by their sense of nostalgia for a lost past.

It would be hard to deduce the specific political stance of the creators, given their sympathy for Nixon and the Chinese male leaders and their hostility to Kissinger and Madame Mao, but the opera holds out hope for the future of humankind based on the kind of diplomatic rapprochement depicted. Mark Morris' choreography for the ballet sequence was a masterful combination of energy, grace, and violence. John DeMain, the vigorous conductor of the first performances, was a persuasive advocate for the provocative opera.

The original singers, many of whom served in effect as a repertory company for Peter Sellars, performed with uniform distinction. James Maddalena gave a disturbingly accurate impersonation of Nixon without degenerating into parody. As Chou En-lai, Sanford Sylvan remained weighty, eloquent, and serene throughout the production. Carolann Page was appealing as the vulnerable Pat Nixon, while Trudy Ellen Craney was impressive in the most demanding vocal role, that of Madame Mao.

Adams had offered a glimpse of the music for *Nixon in China* by releasing in advance of the opera's premiere a twelve-minute sample called "The Chairman Dances," which hints at the foxtrot that Mao and Chiang dance in their concluding reverie. This selection, which has become a popular concert piece, was premiered by Lukas Foss and the Milwaukee Symphony on January 31, 1986. The lyrical strategy of the final scene anticipated Adams' later successful setting to music of Walt Whitman's poem "The Wound-Dresser," Whitman's own nostalgic reverie of his finest moment of compassion and love.

The subsequent operatic collaboration of Adams, Goodman, and Sellars, *The Death of Klinghoffer* (1991), again conceived as an effort to turn a contemporary historical moment into a mythic event, was widely attacked for appearing to be sympathetic toward the murderers of an elderly, handicapped man, and the production garnered few positive reviews. The political repression of the Chinese leaders that resulted in the horrifying massacre on Tiananmen Square in August, 1989, temporarily damp-ened American enthusiasm for rapprochement with the Chinese and probably helped to limit the continuing appeal of *Nixon in China*, which treats the elderly leaders of the Chinese government with sympathy and respect. Ironically, the efforts of Adams and Goodman to appear to be sympathetic to all sides of a political conflict seemed likely to work against the continuing popularity of their operas, as American atti-tudes toward events in China and the Middle East remained volatile.

Bibliography

Adams, John. Interview by David McKee. *Opera Monthly* 5 (July, 1992): 3-9. The composer stresses the need for contemporary opera to speak directly to its au-dience.

Davis, Peter G. "Nixon—The Opera." *New York* 20 (November 9, 1987): 102-104. Davis offers some of the best arts criticism in current American journals.

Rockwell, John. *All American Music.* New York: Alfred A. Knopf, 1983. Attempts to survey the varieties of creators of serious American music, from serial composers and minimalists such as Philip Glass to computer composers and performance artists. Mentions Adams, then still early in his career, in passing.

Spence, Jonathan D. *The Search for Modern China.* New York: W. W. Norton, 1990. A great critical success, this book shows a superb command of its subject. Covers modern Chinese history to the period just before the Tiananmen massacre.

Strickland, Edward. *American Composers: Dialogues on Contemporary Music.* Bloom-ington: Indiana University Press, 1991. A collection of interviews of noted avant-garde American composers, including Adams.

Byron Nelson

Cross-References

Berg's *Wozzeck* Premieres in Berlin (1925), p. 680; Britten Completes *Peter Grimes* (1945), p. 1296; *Jesus Christ Superstar* Establishes the Rock Opera (1971), p. 2254; Joplin's *Treemonisha* Is Staged by the Houston Opera (1975), p. 2350; *Einstein on the Beach* Is a Triumph of Minimalism (1976), p. 2375.

VAN GOGH'S *IRISES* SELLS FOR $53.9 MILLION

Category of event: Art
Time: 1987
Locale: New York, New York

Vincent van Gogh's Irises *sold for $53.9 million at a New York auction, shocking the art world and reflecting economic changes that led to the use of art as a commodity traded by the rich*

Principal personages:

ALAN BOND (1938-   ), Australian beer magnate who bought *Irises* in 1987

RYOEI SAITO (1916-   ), a Japanese paper-manufacturing tycoon who bought the two most expensive paintings during the boom.

A. ALFRED TAUBMAN (1925-   ), an American real-estate magnate who bought Sotheby's in 1983 and instituted changes in the marketing of auctionable art that led to the boom

VINCENT VAN GOGH (1853-1890), the Dutch painter whose work brought record prices during the boom

Summary of Event

Like the stock market, the price of art began rising during the mid-1980's, reaching levels it had never reached before. Art became an investment, more prestigious than pork futures but, for many buyers, having the same ultimate reward—making money. Prices began to soar around 1983, with a few Renaissance and early modern paintings selling for around $10 million, but prices truly skyrocketed after changes were made in the United States tax code in 1986.

After the changes, U.S. citizens donating art to museums were allowed to deduct only the price paid for a work of art from their taxes, rather than the work's current market value. This removed much of the incentive for art donations, and with art prices moving higher, many higher-quality paintings that would previously have been donated were put on the auction block, driving prices higher still.

Stock markets around the world were reaching new record levels, and many of the newly wealthy put some of their money into art. Record prices for art were set regularly. Vincent van Gogh's *Bridge of Trinquetaille* sold for $20.2 million in early 1987. Just a few months later, that artist's *Sunflowers* went for $39.9 million, bringing gasps of astonishment. Then, in a supercharged atmosphere that *The New York Times* described as "half carnival, half casino," van Gogh's *Irises* went for $53.9 million on November 11, 1987, bought by Australian entrepreneur Alan Bond. The combined worldwide sales of the two largest auction houses, Sotheby's and Christie's, came to a record $2.6 billion for 1987. Art auctions, rarely a news item, were suddenly a hot topic, as the art world and the public struggled to figure out why prices were surging and how broad a spectrum of art the increase affected.

Pablo Picasso emerged as the other artist whose work broke records. A Picasso that went for $12,000 in 1957 sold for $2.6 million in 1988. *Motherhood*, a canvas from Picasso's "blue period," sold for $24.8 million in mid-1988. His *Acrobat and Young Harlequin* sold for $38.45 million, the highest price ever paid for a twentieth century painting, at a London auction in November, 1988. Critics said the painting was the best work from Picasso's "rose period" to go on the market in a long time. The buyer was Akio Nishino, manager of the fine-arts department of Tokyo's Mitsukoshi department store. Early Picasso paintings were greatly admired in Japan, from which much of the money entering the art market was coming, and Japanese buyers played an important role in the prices the paintings reached.

Also in 1988, sculptor Alberto Giacometti's *Walking Man* went for $6.9 million, Robert Rauschenberg's *Rebus* went for $6.3 million, and a Jasper Johns canvas sold for $17 million. Even the work of postwar artists was too expensive for most museums.

The twentieth century record was broken again in May, 1989, when a 1901 Picasso self-portrait sold for $47.9 million at Sotheby's New York. The seller was Wendell Cherry, the president of Humana Incorporated, a large hospital management corporation, who had bought the painting for $5.8 million in 1981. At the same sale, Paul Gauguin's *Mata Mua*, painted in Tahiti in 1892, sold for $24.2 million. The seller was Jaime Ortiz-Patiño, the heir to a Bolivian tin fortune, who had bought the painting in 1984 for $3.8 million.

Multimillionaires were not the only people who could afford to invest in art; prosperous professionals could also hope to make money through art investments. The market for prints, traditionally far more sluggish than that for painting and sculpture, was also bustling. Prints by brand-name artists such as Andy Warhol and James Rosenquist were put out in editions in the low hundreds at relatively affordable prices. Work by lesser-known but established contemporary artists could be had for prices in the low tens of thousands of dollars.

By the end of 1988, the speculation in art had reached such a feverish intensity that many investors became nervous, sensing that the art market might be a bubble about to burst. One indication that it might was the return to market of *Irises*. It had emerged that the buyer, Alan Bond, had made arrangements with Sotheby's before the auction to borrow up to half the purchase price, provoking a storm of controversy. Bond's own business was in trouble. He proved unable to pay for *Irises*, and it went back to the auction block. It was bought by one of the only museums with enough money to afford such expensive art—the J. Paul Getty Museum in Malibu, California, which had a $3.5 billion endowment.

Sales for the auction houses reached record levels in 1989. Sotheby's sales for the year stood at $2.93 billion and Christie's at $2.08 billion.

The greatest excess came in May, 1990, when van Gogh's *Portrait of Dr. Gachet*, considered one of his best works, sold for $82.5 million. Two days later, the same buyer, Ryoei Saito, head of the Daishowa paper manufacturing company, bought Jean Renoir's *Au Moulin de la Galette* for $78.1 million.

Despite the record prices for the Renoir and the van Gogh, prices were moving downward. A large percentage of works sold for twenty to thirty percent below their low estimate. More works were falling short of their minimums and not being sold at all. The downward trend grew stronger in the fall of 1990, when about half of contemporary art at auction did not sell, including a number of paintings by Andy Warhol, whose work had been considered a safe bet. The stock of the auction houses plummeted with the fall of the market; Sotheby's stock fell from thirty-seven dollars a share in 1988 to ten dollars a share in 1990.

Impact of Event

Until the 1980's, buying and selling art for a quick profit was looked down upon by many in the art world. It was also difficult, as finding buyers willing to pay a good price took time, and dealers' commissions often totaled a third of the price. Prices were driven up by a combination of factors, some of them long-term, some of them transitory. Short-term factors included the economic boom of the 1980's, which created vast pools of disposable income in the United States, Japan, and Europe, and the spreading belief that art was a smart investment with a value that would only increase. Medium-term factors included an expanding art audience around the world resulting from increased attention to art in schools and the media, and, perhaps reflecting this increased knowledge, an increasing appetite for art as a status symbol for new wealth. During the height of the boom, one dealer told *The New York Times* that "art comes right after the mink and the Mercedes."

The interlinking of world economies and information structures played an important role, as European, Japanese, and American buyers all quickly found out about art for sale and decided whether or not to bid. The decline of the American dollar in the mid-1980's, combined with the rapid growth of European and Japanese economies, made art bought in dollars very attractive. The most important long-term factor was the rarity of topnotch art for sale.

With most first-rate works of art in museums or long-held private collections, when the changes in the tax laws helped to push top-quality pieces onto the market, they became the object of intense competition, elevating prices throughout the market. This was particularly true of work by van Gogh, most of whose paintings had long been in museums. Van Gogh also had cachet because of his place in popular mythology as the quintessential tortured modern artist.

Aside from the vast concentrations of wealth generated during the 1980's, one of the precipitating factors was the purchase of Sotheby's auction house in 1983 by an American real-estate investor named Alfred Taubman. He began marketing art using more modern methods, sending lavishly illustrated catalogs to wealthy potential bidders and arranging credit terms in advance of the auctions.

Some analysts felt that the late 1980's recession in the U.S. economy was largely to blame for the price decline. Others blamed the greed of collectors, auction houses, and galleries and the resulting unrealistic price expectations, which could not be sustained. The prices of works widely regarded as masterpieces fell only a few percentage points, but prices of other work fell by forty percent and more. Prices were driven down even further in the fall of 1990, as the creditors of some art speculators forced them to put work on the market.

Prices were also lower because Japanese buyers had left the market. Economic difficulties and a stock-market plunge hit Japan, but equally important were scandals in which it emerged that some Japanese buyers were using art sales for money-laundering purposes.

Some art galleries were pleased by the rising market, which allowed them to raise the prices of the work they sold. Other galleries were unhappy, because high auction prices meant sellers brought resale material to the auction houses rather than to galleries. Since auctions were a resale market, however, art dealers still sold freshly minted art.

Like the speculators who bought much of the art during the 1980's boom, though, many established galleries overextended themselves, and a glut of new galleries opened. In 1986, there were close to a hundred galleries in New York City's SoHo art district; in 1988, there were about 250. In 1990, many of those galleries were closing. With auction prices tumbling and the U.S. economy in recession, buyers stayed away in droves.

The boom was devastating to museums, particularly in the United States. Museums were pinched between the tax laws that discouraged donations and acquisition funds that lost their purchasing power as prices inflated. With prices for work of such postwar artists as Rauschenberg and Johns selling for multiple millions, museums that collected contemporary art often chose to concentrate on younger, lesser-known artists. Other museums used the controversial practice of "deaccessioning," or selling off art from their collections, to pay for art that they wished to buy. Often, the work hanging on its walls was the only source of quick, substantial capital a museum had. Like the market itself, deaccessioning reached new heights in the 1980's.

Christie's reported that twenty-eight museums deaccessioned through its sales in 1984 and 1985; in 1988 and 1989, that number reached eighty-eight. When a museum sold a work, it usually went into private hands, often in a different city, and many critics felt that some museums were gutting their cities' cultural heritages. New York's Guggenheim Museum caused cries of outrage when it sold highly respected paintings by Wassily Kandinsky, Marc Chagall, and Amadeo Modigliani to buy less-respected work by minimalist painters. Many criticized museums for such moves, believing it to be a betrayal of a museum's mission to preserve art. The practice also cost some museums the very donations they were missing, since some donors refused to give work to museums that deaccessioned.

A longer-term question asked by many art critics was whether or not new collectors who bought for investment and prestige in the 1980's would eventually grow into a new generation of committed art patrons.

Bibliography
Hughes, Robert. "Sold!" *Time* 134 (November 27, 1989): 60-65. A witty look at the

price bubble just after it popped. Hughes argues that the average person lost during the boom because museums declined in quality, and he likens the commercialization of the art market to the strip-mining of culture. Hughes argues that art loses its inherent value when it is treated purely as a commodity. A far more cynical view of the practices described than that of Susan Lee.

Lee, Susan. "Greed is Not Just for Profit." *Forbes* 141 (April 18, 1988): 65-70. Examines changes in the art market itself for explanations of the price surges. The article cites increased liquidity, with lower transaction costs and better financing, as causes of the price surges and the quicker pace of art sales. Looks at the marketing strategies of major auction houses. The focus is limited to the financial and marketing end of the boom.

Rosenbaum, Lee. "The Anxious Acquisitors." *Art News* 88 (March, 1989): 144-151. Looks at the role of art museums during the price boom: essentially as spectators, unable to afford to participate. Entire areas of collecting were nearly impossible for museums, particularly Impressionism, Postimpressionism, and major old masters. Covers the donation crisis, focusing on its effect on a few museums and how the tax changes worked against them. Offers an in-depth understanding of the problems faced by museums, and their options, including deaccessioning.

Virshup, Amy, Jamie James, Brigid Grauman, et al. "Signs of the Time." *Art News* 87 (April, 1988): 101-123. A series of articles examining the changing roles of art and artists in society at a time when art was becoming more expensive and more popular. Not specifically an examination of the trend to art as a commodity; more a look at the effect of the trend on peripheral issues: the role of museums in people's lives, how the role of artists changes in a more monied and complex art world, and more. Also a look at Europe and how its art scene differed from that of the United States, especially regarding commercialism.

Walker, Richard W. "The Saatchi Factor." *Art News* 86 (January, 1987): 117-121. Focuses on the role of one influential collector just as the art market was going into overdrive. Powers not unlike those of a Renaissance patron are ascribed to billionaire advertising mogul Charles Saatchi, whose buying influenced market trends for contemporary art. Many investors followed his lead, speculating on artists whose work he was buying. When Saatchi bought six paintings by Sandro Chia, that artist's prices were driven up; when Saatchi decided to sell all six, Chia's prices plummeted.

Scott M. Lewis

Cross-References

Jasper Johns Paints the American Flag (1954), p. 1590; New York's SoHo Develops into a Center for Contemporary Art (1970's), p. 2191; The Pompidou Center Opens in Paris (1977), p. 2402; Schnabel Emerges as a Celebrity Artist (Early 1980's), p. 2438; The Musée d'Orsay Opens (1986), p. 2588.

THE NATIONAL MUSEUM OF WOMEN IN THE ARTS
OPENS AMID CONTROVERSY

Category of event: Art
Time: May, 1987
Locale: Washington, D.C.

The National Museum of Women in the Arts, founded to celebrate and recognize women's achievements in art, opened amid controversy over its role as a sex-segregated institution

Principal personages:

WILHELMINA (BILLIE) COLE HOLLADAY (1922-   ), the museum's founder and chief fund-raiser, who with her husband, Wallace Holladay, donated the museum's core collection of artworks

ANNE-IMELDA RADICE (1948-   ), an architectural historian and former chief curator at the U.S. Capitol who was made director of the museum in 1986

ELEANOR TUFTS (1927-   ), a curator and art historian hired to organize the museum's inaugural exhibition

JOHN RUSSELL (1919-   ), an art critic for *The New York Times* who was the first to criticize the museum and its philosophy

ROBERT ROSENBLUM (1927-   ) a professor of fine arts at New York University whose criticism of the museum attracted media attention.

LINDA NOCHLIN (1931-   ), a feminist art historian who criticized the museum for its lack of a feminist agenda

Summary of Event

The National Museum of Women in the Arts (NMWA) opened in May, 1987, six years after its founder, Wilhelmina Cole Holladay, began planning what was probably the first museum of its kind in the world. The NMWA was established to awaken the public to works by women artists and to serve as an educational center and inspiration to future generations of women. Holladay believed that women artists needed a separate museum to showcase their work and to celebrate unrecognized achievements.

For years, Holladay and her husband, Wallace Holladay, a Washington real estate broker and businessman, had been collecting works of art by women. The Holladays' interest began in the early 1960's, when they bought a painting by the seventeenth century Dutch still-life painter Clara Peeters. Their search for information about Peeters produced little, and they discovered that neither Peeters nor any other woman artist was discussed in the standard college art-history text, H. W. Janson's *History of Art* (1962). The Holladays' amazement at this exclusion led to their interest in women artists, especially those neglected by art establishments both past and present. Over the next twenty years, they acquired a collection of artworks by women that was international in scope and that spanned four centuries. The Holladays donated this collection, some four hundred items, to the National Museum of Women in the Arts to serve as its permanent core collection.

Holladay envisioned the museum as a national center for research on women artists and as a leader in scholarship on women artists. She believed that the obscurity of talented women artists was primarily the fault of an art establishment that had always favored male artists and given them more support. In an article on the NMWA, art historian Anne Higonnet recapped the statistics: In 1987, more than ninety-five percent of the works exhibited in American art museums were by men, although thirty-eight percent of all American artists were women. From 1981 to 1987, only twelve percent of the artists exhibited at the Museum of Modern Art were women. American women artists, Higonnet pointed out, earned thirty-three cents to every dollar earned by male artists. Holladay, who wanted to promote and publicize contemporary women artists, hoped the museum would give them the boost they needed to get noticed and established in the art world.

Holladay and her husband had the connections and clout to launch a major museum. She was director of Holladay-Tyler Printing Corporation (her husband was its president), which printed the magazines *Connoisseur, Smithsonian*, the *Metropolitan Museum of Art Quarterly*, and parts of *National Geographic.* Thus, Holladay had the money and business acumen needed to get a fund-raising campaign off the ground. She was also director of interior design for the real estate investment company owned by her husband and had served on several Washington boards, including that of the Corcoran Gallery of Art.

In 1981, Holladay began an independent, nonprofit corporation. Over the next six years, she drove her idea to success almost single-handedly. Using money, social influence, and her knowledge of business and finance, she headed a fund-raising campaign that drew an extraordinary number of members to the museum, which was not yet even opened. By 1988, the NMWA had 83,000 members, compared to the 3,500 members of the Corcoran Gallery of Art, an established museum roughly the same size.

Holladay was relentlessly vocal and enthusiastic about the importance of her project. Her personal contacts allowed her to attract prestigious supporters and much media attention. For example, Barbara Bush, then wife of the vice president of the United States, cut the ribbon at the museum's inaugural ceremony. First Lady Nancy Reagan served as titular head of three consecutive annual museum balls, and Caroline Hunt Scheolkopf, the richest woman in America, became a founding member and praised Holladay's drive and dedication.

Holladay, though, knew that establishing a museum in the nation's capital would be a risky undertaking. Using her understanding of the world of money, she launched a high-energy fund drive that targeted major corporations for big contributions. By July, 1988, a total of 128 corporations had donated $5000 or more. American Telephone and Telegraph donated $100,000 for the museum's library, and United Technologies contributed $500,000 to underwrite the museum's inaugural exhibition, "American Women Artists, 1830-1930," which opened in April, 1987. Corporations were unusually generous, explained Wilhelmina Holladay, because "I speak their language. And I'm not sure [museum] people always do." To house the museum, Holladay purchased a $4.8-million former Masonic temple two blocks from the White House and spent $10 million in renovations and redecoration.

Fund-raising was a success for Holladay, but she was criticized for the quality of the museum's collection and the credentials of its employees. Many critics argued that Holladay should have spent more time and money searching for an experienced director, top curators, and seasoned staff. According to some critics, the operation reflected great commercial appeal but little professionalism. The first show was assembled by a free-lance curator, Eleanor Tufts, and the museum's first permanent director, Anne-Imelda M. Radice, was considered by many to be too inexperienced to deal with major acquisitions and exhibitions.

The museum opened to mixed reviews in 1987. One senior Washington museum official called the collection "of marginal interest"; some critics declared it too uneven in quality. Others celebrated the museum as the first of its kind and noted that the Holladay collection was unusually adventurous. Among the most highly praised works were paintings by Lavinia Fontana, Rachel Ruysch, Angelica Kauffman, Suzanne Valadon, Lilla Cabot Perry, and Alice Neel.

Impact of Event

Holladay believed that, historically, women artists had never been well treated. She and her supporters maintained that, even in the United States, the idea persisted that art by women was necessarily second-rate. They held this belief even though growing numbers of women could be found working as museum curators, dealers, art critics, and corporate art advisers.

Therefore, the National Museum of Women in the Arts roused serious debate over whether a museum should focus on gender at all. Conservative critics argued that an art museum should emphasize quality first and disregard the gender of the artists. John Russell of *The New York Times*, the first art critic to criticize the museum, compared the segregation of women's art to the segregation of blacks in buses. Robert Rosenblum, a professor of fine arts at New York University, suggested that a separate museum of women's art represented a "ghettoizing" of women artists and added, "If I were a woman artist, I would prefer to be in the National Gallery and not there."

Others, however, supported Holladay's stance. Abram Lerner, director emeritus of the Hirshhorn Museum and Sculpture Garden, expressed his belief that the premise of a museum focused on gender was not really different from that of a museum dedicated to artists of a particular nationality, aesthetic movement, or period.

The debate continued. Feminist critics questioned not whether but how one should focus on gender. Norma Broude, a professor of art history at American University, represented the reservations of many feminists in the art world when she remarked that a separate museum for women's art "trivializes the position of women as artists, reinforcing their artificial separateness and second-class status in a culture to which they have made central but unrecognized contributions."

Miriam Schapiro, a leading feminist artist, added that a women's museum should include women's crafts as well as their fine arts; Holladay had frequently claimed that one of the museum's goals was to heighten awareness that "women have painted great paintings." This medium-specific bias, critics felt, was inherited from a history of art written largely by men. Furthermore, women painters had been taught the techniques of male masters, and for centuries had been judged by their standards.

Schapiro and others held that the female experience was distinctly and uniquely expressed in crafts as well as in painting; often, they argued, quilting, ceramics, weaving, and other crafts were the chief artistic mediums available to women. Schapiro explained that women "want to be recognized for what they make. They want a history of their own." A museum that displayed crafts alongside fine arts would address the social history and culture of women, and as such would be a true specialty museum.

Many feminists wanted the museum to support their agenda. "A women's museum of art that is not a strongly feminist project can only have a negative and conservative impact," said Linda Nochlin, a professor of art history at the City University of New York. Nochlin argued that a women's museum of art that did not actively challenge the male status quo and assert its intention to change the position of women artists would be nothing more than a "pleasuring ground for the socially prominent."

Holladay, meanwhile, insisted that the social context for women's art would be included only if it were historically significant. She stated that she intended to "accent the positive" and explained, "We are doing something else than the feminist art historians. We have not placed the emphasis on inequities but on achievements."

Ironically, the museum's most memorable achievement might have been its fundraising campaign. Holladay's funding drive was considered inspired and brilliant, and her successful membership drive for the NMWA seemed likely to influence how museums would do their fund-raising in the future. The museum's planning, from inception to opening, was carefully orchestrated to take advantage of its consumerist potential. Holladay used everything she knew about business and marketing and exploited the appeal of gender issues. Mass-mailing campaigns for membership targeted five main groups of women: museum-shop customers, female members of art organizations, supporters of cultural programming, feminists, and women who ordered from upscale mail-order catalogs.

In addition, the museum's lavish hall served as a sort of endowment; it could be rented for social functions for $7,500 per evening and was booked nearly every night. The focus on consumerist functions may have seemed foreign to art appreciation, but the fact that the group of women who launched the National Museum of Women in the Arts used the worlds of consumer culture and corporate finance to forward their cause seemed almost revolutionary. While these worlds might once have been an impediment to female self-expression, Holladay used their resources—and her own considerable ones—for female empowerment. The founder of the NMWA claimed to represent conservative women, but in her use of power organizing—mobilizing women for a cause—she owed debts to the women's movement and to the feminist left.

Bibliography

Chadwick, Whitney. *Women, Art, and Society.* World of Art Series. New York: Thames and Hudson, 1990. This medium-length illustrated study provides a general introduction to the history of women's involvement in the visual arts. Identifies major issues and new directions in the study of women artists and seeks to "reframe" many issues raised by feminist research. Good bibliography and index.

Comini, Alessandra. "Introduction: Why a National Museum of Women in the Arts?" In *National Museum of Women in the Arts*, edited by Margaret B. Rennolds. New York: Harry N. Abrams, 1987. Comini's essay provides an overview of the museum's collection and describes the institution's purpose. Includes a rebuttal to arguments against the "segregation" of women's art and queries how, if at all, women's art might be uniquely shaped by female experience.

Day, Sara. "A Museum for Women." *ARTnews* 85 (Summer, 1986): 111-118. Day reviews the genesis of the museum and the controversy that surrounded its opening, quoting critics, professors, and the feminist artist Miriam Schapiro. Day discusses the collection and looks at key women behind the scenes at various stages of planning.

Higonnet, Anne. "Woman's Place." *Art in America* 76 (July, 1988): 126-130, 149. A keen inquiry into the planning and purpose of the NMWA that explains the reasons for much of the controversy between feminist and conservative forces surrounding the project. Higonnet's evaluation of the museum's commercial structure is especially good. The notes contain references to several articles on the museum.

Nochlin, Linda. *Women, Art, and Power: And Other Essays.* Icon Editions Series. New York: Harper & Row, 1988. This illustrated collection of essays by the noted art historian includes her groundbreaking 1971 piece "Why Have There Been No Great Women Artists?" and six more recent essays exploring crucial questions in feminist art history, a field Nochlin's essay helped to launch.

Rosen, Randy, and Catherine C. Brawer, eds. *Making Their Mark: Women Artists Move into the Mainstream, 1970-1985.* New York: Abbeville Press, 1989. Reviews U.S. exhibitions held during a period of great political activity in the women's movement and discusses feminist principles of art theory and art criticism. The book is the catalog of an exhibition held at the Cincinnati Art Museum and other museums in 1989. Includes index and bibliography.

Tufts, Eleanor. *American Women Artists, 1830-1930.* Washington, D.C.: International Exhibitions Foundation for the National Museum of Women in the Arts, 1987. This catalog of the inaugural exhibition of the National Museum of Women in the

Arts discusses the painters and includes an index and bibliography. Introductory essays are by Gail Levin, Alessandra Comini, and Wanda M. Corn.

JoAnn Balingit

Cross-References

New York's Museum of Modern Art Is Founded (1929), p. 782; The Whitney Museum Is Inaugurated in New York (1931), p. 885; Peggy Guggenheim's Gallery Promotes New American Art (1942), p. 1239; Beauvoir's *The Second Sex* Anticipates the Women's Movement (1949), p. 1449; A Dalí Museum Opens in Figueras, Spain (1974), p. 2310; The Musée d'Orsay Opens (1986), p. 2588.

DECONSTRUCTIVISTS EXHIBIT AT
THE MUSEUM OF MODERN ART

Category of event: Architecture
Time: 1988
Locale: New York, New York

*The skewed, poetic distortions of modernism presented at MOMA enriched a plu-
ralistic design scene but revealed the confused politics and aims of avant-garde
architecture*

> *Principal personages:*
> PHILIP JOHNSON (1906-   ), an architect with a long history of bringing
> avant-garde architectural ideas into the design establishment
> MARK WIGLEY, a Princeton academic whom Johnson recruited to mount
> and write the catalogue text for "Deconstructivist Architecture"
> STUART WREDE (1944-   ), a design historian and curator who was
> acting director of MOMA's Department of Architecture during "De-
> constructivist Architecture"
> PETER D. EISENMAN (1932-   ), a New York architect and theorist who
> articulated most of the arguments in "Deconstructivist Architecture"
> FRANK GEHRY (1929-   ), a Canadian-born California architect whose
> personal experiments with common materials and disorganized forms
> were one of the most popular forms of deconstructivism

Summary of Event

"Deconstructivist Architecture" was the belated public debut of a tendency that
had been developing for several years. Postmodernism, using past styles to break
modernism's stifling insistence on logic and function, was the leading architectural
force of the 1980's. During the years in which postmodernism took shape, however,
some architects had used theoretical projects to advance a less simple approach.
Like the postmodernists, they denied modernism's simplistic "form follows function" rules, welcomed visual and conceptual complexity, and stressed architecture's
confused social situation. Yet they kept modernism's abstract forms, industrial materials, and visible structural elements. These were combined in unsettling, seemingly
chaotic ways—attacking just those qualities of stability, harmony, and intelligibility
that the public valued in postmodernism.

The approach was most intensely pursued at the Institute for Architecture and
Urban Studies (IAUS) in New York City, a study and exhibition center run by Peter
Eisenman. The IAUS had supported postmodernist architects as well, and Eisenman
was first linked with that movement, as were the unusual designs of Frank Gehry.
Postmodernism's turn toward literal historicism and cooperation with developers
made that label no longer fit.

Starting in 1985, several people—the Chicago architects Paul Florian and Stephen

Wierzbowski, an employee of Gehry's named Aaron Betsky, and *The New York Times* writer Joseph Giovannini—began separately to plan exhibitions or books on this destabilized modernism. The two Chicagoans eventually gave their material to Betsky. In the summer of 1987, Betsky and Giovannini each discussed their plans with Philip Johnson, a perennial and powerful enthusiast for radical architecture. Johnson had supported the IAUS financially and served as a mentor to Eisenman, which made him a kind of godfather to the "deconstructivist" tendency (Giovannini's term). Although he had designed postmodernism's landmark AT&T Building, Johnson had begun to lose interest in the style by 1987. Since his advocacy of modernism over historicism in the early 1930's, he had always delighted in attacking the architectural status quo. "Deconstructivism" appealed to him as an intellectually ambitious way to produce exciting forms while discrediting architectural order itself.

Johnson approached Stuart Wrede, the acting director of the Department of Architecture at the Museum of Modern Art (MOMA), and asked that he be allowed to mount a show on the deconstructivists at the museum. Johnson had set up the department in 1932 to propagandize for modernism and was now a museum trustee. It amused the eighty-one-year-old architect to end his career with a last statement at the museum department he had founded. He made it clear that Wrede's handling of the show might determine whether Johnson would support him for the post of permanent director of the department.

"Deconstructivist Architecture" ran at MOMA from June 23 until August 30, 1988. It presented works by Eisenman, Gehry, and five others—the Dutch architect Rem Koolhaas, the American Daniel Liebeskind, the Iraqi-born London architect Zaha Hadid, the Viennese firm Coop Himmelblau, and the Swiss-born Bernard Tschumi. (Tschumi and Koolhaas had been at the IAUS, and Hadid had worked for Koolhaas.) The mostly unbuilt projects differed widely in material and mood, from Gehry's unpretentious, cheap materials to Liebeskind's nightmarish explosions of lines and beams. They shared a distortion of modernism's right angles into broken, clashing trajectories; a deliberate confusion of modernism's "functional" parts, so that enclosures became ruptured cages and cantilevers held up too much or not at all; and a subversion of modernist abstract shapes into junk assemblages or violated masses.

Mark Wigley's exhibition text argued that this chaotic aesthetic came from a unified theory and a common art-historical source. "Deconstructivism" was a pun on both. Architects had always limited themselves by striving for purity and harmony in their work. Yet in deconstructionist literary criticism, a movement associated with the French thinker Jacques Derrida, supposedly monolithic terms of meaning (words and narratives themselves) were revealed as arbitrary impositions of stability, the writer's authoritarian inventions. The critic must distort and misuse the text's words until its true disorder was revealed. Likewise, deconstructivist architecture attacked the empty authority of architectural "rules," especially modernism's, by misusing its "words"—structure, abstract form, orderliness—in deliberately unresolved ways. The style was a Derridean transformation of the most exciting and utopian brand of modernism, the slashing diagonals and floating abstract forms of

Russian constructivism in the 1920's.

The show was widely publicized but almost universally condemned—less for the work than for Johnson's and Wigley's blanket arguments. Literary deconstruction was so fashionable among intellectuals that its use to justify a new style seemed cynical. The link to constructivism looked contrived to make deconstructivism palatable by giving it an art-historical pedigree. The idea of an architecture that spurned coherence and usefulness sounded like an extreme version of postmodernism's ironies and contradictions, without any of its attempts at human context. Finally, Johnson's own disruptive behavior—dropping his postmodernist allegiances and playing the MOMA show as a power game—looked like a surrender to nihilism.

Some of the show's designs, said critics, were exciting and important. Johnson's show infected them all with fashionmongering and the abuse of cultural power. MOMA's decision to make Wrede permanent director of architecture was almost the only positive result of the show.

Impact of Event

Despite poor responses to the deconstructivist show itself, many of the design approaches in it were welcomed as reactions against postmodernism. The building boom of the 1980's had seen many of postmodernism's gestures toward scale and context become trivialized. Although the deconstructivist tendencies seemed unnecessarily ugly next to postmodernism's more ingratiating shapes, they still represented an attempt to invent forms and think through their fundamentals instead of a manipulation of old ones to ironic intent. Reaction to particular designers in the exhibition varied. While Eisenman's unreadably complex abstract grids seemed to embrace futility and frustration too naïvely, Gehry's junky assemblages—owing much more to abstract sculpture and the everyday environment than to Derrida—looked like personal architectural poetry.

The deconstructivist show's failure was a sign that connections between avant-garde design and the architectural establishment had frayed beyond repair. Broadly speaking, the experiments in the show resisted the vision of modernism presented by Johnson and MOMA in 1932. Many of the great modernists of the 1920's had been poetic dreamers and utopians, not simply functionalists. In Johnson's first show, "Modern Architecture," their investigations into unornamented form, functional planning, and mass-produced elements were reduced to a single style that met building functions cheaply and intelligently. By 1960, this reduction of the modernist experiment to dead-serious utilitarianism had become the norm throughout the world. Johnson and other celebrity designers presented minor, more tasteful variations on functionalism as novelty items—avant-garde designs as part of the upper-class lifestyle.

One response was the postmodernist movement, which Johnson also boosted as a fashion. Yet as advanced art became increasingly difficult conceptually and unappealing visually, so that it could not easily become another beautiful plaything for collectors, many architects (notably the Italian collective Superstudio) argued that architecture must become just as difficult to co-opt. It was more important to critique the establishment's architect/client system than to be a successful practitioner. Sharing the cultural upheavals and renewed political utopianism of the 1960's, the architects later associated with deconstructivism took this route.

The personal visions that Johnson and Wigley lumped together in "Deconstructivist Architecture" were different ways of turning technology and abstraction into springboards for the imagination, keeping the individual freedom at the heart of modernism alive. Tschumi revived constructivism as a symbol of the lost hopes of the 1920's, and Eisenman quoted Derrida to defend his unintelligibly complex productions. Koolhaas was interested in the playfulness of the "low-culture," drive-in modernism of the 1950's. Gehry showed the egalitarian potential of technology in his anti-elegant style, an "architecture without architects." Liebeskind and Coop Himmelblau hoped their tangles of beams and lines would create liberating effects of taut, energized, ever-expanding space.

These approaches were difficult to bring into the mainstream because they were attempts to avoid the dead-end restrictions of a "style." At the IAUS, distortion of mainstream forms for distortion's sake could be appreciated as a critical statement. In actual buildings, how could such distortions be kept from looking like attention-grabbing stunts? One legacy of the 1960's art scene was the idea of bringing anti-art objects into the art world by attaching aesthetic manifestos to them. Eisenman's application of deconstructionist theory to his buildings, for example, let him be more avant-garde than "mainstream" figures such as Richard Meier, whose elegant grids actually looked much like Eisenman's. The peril of deconstructivism's avoidance of the status quo was that cultural proclamations would attract more attention than—or take the place of—thoughtful design.

This was the pitfall of "Deconstructivist Architecture." Philip Johnson based much of his influence on reconciling avant-gardism with conventional taste, explaining how forms with radical agendas could be safely appeciated as beautiful buildings. By 1988, after postmodernism's compromises, the design world was too self-conscious about theory's relation to practice to believe such claims. In MOMA's deconstructivist show, Johnson's showmanship became a posture of attack for its own sake, but without real faith in a style that had been invented, explained, and accepted by others. The angry reaction revealed a hunger for more serious explanations of radical architecture and kept deconstructivism from becoming the fad that postmodernism had been.

Deconstructivism fell short as the avant-garde statement it was meant to be. Yet it continued the questioning of architecture's cultural place that postmodernism began; it also echoed the growing acceptance of disorder in culture, seen in such other forms as appropriationist art and rap music. In the widening architectural pluralism of the 1990's, deconstructivism complemented Tod Williams and Billie Tsien's hard-edged investigations of materials and the dynamic, eccentric modernism of Arquitectonica. Frank Gehry, already respected for his interesting but low-budget buildings, was hired by richer and more influential clients such as Chiat-Day Advertising. The more visually difficult approaches, such as Liebeskind's German History Museum proposal for Berlin, had a wider audience in Europe. Tschumi's playful red-grid pavilions for the Parc de Villette in Paris were widely admired, and he was also named dean of Columbia University's School of Architecture.

It proved easier to move from imaginary projects to built work than critics had expected, but deconstructivism's rarefied appeal and the recession of the early 1990's kept its commissions at a generally "boutique" scale (single-family homes, cultural facilities, and interiors). Nevertheless, by moving away from the decorativeness of postmodernism and engaging with modernism's original hopes, however self-consciously, deconstructivism was evidence of a new search for the fundamentals of modern design.

Bibliography

Betsky, Aaron. *Violated Perfection: The Architectural Fragmentation of Modernism.* New York: Rizzoli, 1990. A brief illustrated essay that focuses on deconstructivist work as a variant of modernism. Much more wide-ranging in its categories than the deconstructivism show. Helpfully relates the work to postmodernist theory and downplays literary deconstruction. Index.

Broadbent, Geoffrey. *Deconstructivism: A Student Guide.* New York: St. Martin's Press, 1991. A short overview that sympathetically explains the Eisenman-Tschumi-Derrida wing of deconstructivism. Valuable for its inclusion of much European and Japanese work. References, no index.

Jencks, Charles, et al. *Deconstructivism.* New York: St. Martin's Press, 1988. Explanatory essay by the leading critic and historian of post-1970 radical architecture; also contains an interview with Peter Eisenman and a discussion of such related figures and firms as Emilio Ambasz and Morphosis. As wide-ranging as Betsky's book, with more depth on individual figures. No index.

Sorkin, Michael. *Exquisite Corpse: Writings on Buildings.* New York: Verso, 1991. Reviews of the 1980's New York architectural scene by a radical architect sympathetic to many of the deconstructivist designers but hostile to MOMA. Biased and journalistic, but valuable for its outside perspective on the deconstructivist architects and their show. Few illustrations, no index.

Wigley, Mark, and Philip Johnson. *Deconstructivist Architecture.* Boston: Little, Brown, 1988. The catalogue of the MOMA show. Beautiful drawings, but very selective in its choice of architects and poorly thought out as an explanation of the movement. Johnson's preface, in which he essentially dismisses the intentions of the architects and the show itself, is a revealing document. No references or index.

M. David Samson

Cross-References

German Artists Found the Bauhaus (1919), p. 463; New York's Museum of Modern Art Is Founded (1929), p. 782; Le Corbusier's Villa Savoye Redefines Architecture (1931), p. 869; The AT&T Building Exemplifies Postmodernism (1978), p. 2407; Disney Emerges as an Architectural Patron (Early 1990's), p. 2646.

PEI CREATES A NEW ENTRANCE TO THE LOUVRE

Category of event: Architecture
Time: March 4, 1988
Locale: Paris, France

I. M. Pei's controversial glass pyramid was officially dedicated by President François Mitterrand of France, thus providing the Louvre with an entrance that was modern, distinctive, and functional

Principal personages:
    I. M. PEI (1917-   ), the Chinese-American architect who was commissioned to undertake a fundamental renovation of the Louvre
    JACQUES CHIRAC (1932-   ), the mayor of Paris, who, significantly, did not oppose Pei's controversial plans
    FRANÇOIS MITTERRAND (1916-   ), the president of France, who arbitrarily appointed Pei as principal architect for the Louvre project and gave him unwavering support

Summary of Event

By the early 1980's, the Louvre, one of the world's most prestigious museums, was in a terrible state of disrepair. It lacked a dignified and visible entrance, was desperately short of gallery space, failed to provide visitors with decent amenities, lacked proper repair workshops and administrative offices, and possessed no coherent plan for displaying its vast treasures; moreover, the building's exterior facades were in need of substantial renovation. When François Mitterrand was elected as the first Socialist president of the Fifth Republic in 1981, he was determined to restore the Louvre to its former glory. A plan to renovate the museum was set in motion. In a controversial move, Mitterrand disdained an international competition and arbitrarily appointed I. M. Pei, a Chinese-American, as the project's principal architect.

Pei was already a respected figure with an international reputation, noted for his modernist designs characterized by stark, angular geometric shapes. Significantly, he had considerable experience in working on art museums; his east wing of the National Gallery in Washington, D.C., was widely regarded as a critical success. Pei quickly rejected the idea of remodeling any of the three existing entrances to the Louvre, and he decided rather to locate a totally new entrance in the geometric center of the Louvre complex. The new entrance would lead visitors into a vast underground complex, which would be not simply a reception hall but an area providing the offices, restoration rooms, conference centers, restaurants, bookstores, and other support facilities that the old Louvre lacked. What, though, would be the shape of the new entrance?

After serious reflection, Pei decided upon a glass pyramid. Pei believed that the pyramid was an inherently classical design and therefore would harmonize with the classical facades of the surrounding Louvre structure. A pyramid, moreover, would occupy less volume than a dome or a square and thereby be less intrusive. Pei would construct the pyramid of transparent glass that would allow people on the surface level to see through the structure and would also admit light into the museum's underground area—thus reducing any claustrophobic effect and avoiding giving the impression that visitors were descending into a subway station.

When Pei formally unveiled his plans on January 23, 1984, the design provoked an immediate storm of controversy. Fights broke out, and Pei himself was subjected to a vitriolic verbal assault. In the ensuing weeks and months, what the press dubbed "the battle of the pyramid" took place. Two important newspapers, *Le Figaro* and *Le Quotidien de Paris*, led the opposition, and even the prestigious *Le Monde* lent its columns to Pei's critics. Editors, journalists, and members of the cultural establishment derided the pyramid as a useless gadget, a postmodernist knickknack, an annex of Disneyland, and a cheap and gaudy diamond. A former French minister of culture, Michel Guy, founded a new association to fight the project and quickly enrolled fifteen thousand people, while a member of the French Academy went so far as to call for an insurrection. Three respected art historians published a book claiming that the project was a disaster, and the book sold thirty thousand copies the first month after publication. *Le Nouvel Observateur*, a periodical that defended Pei, found itself the victim of hate mail, some of it racist in nature.

Why the venomous reaction? One must first remember that the Louvre is not simply a museum; it is part of French history, culture, and heritage, and many French citizens did not want the Louvre to be defiled by foreigners or imported architects. Pei was resented because he was not French, and the fact that he was an American of Chinese birth made him even more suspect in some circles. More reasonably, the pyramid was regarded as incongruous, a modern edifice totally out of place in stately classical surroundings. The symbolism of the pyramid, it was also argued, was closely identified with death, while the Louvre stood for the life-giving forces of culture and civilization. Some critics, moreover, argued that the final project would result in a gigantic Louvre; it would be better, they said, to have multiple entrances that admitted the public into several smaller Louvres to avoid overwhelming visitors. Finally, it was obvious that politics played an unfortunate role. Mitterrand was a Socialist, while many of the project's critics were conservatives; the latter accused Mitterrand of wishing, like the ancient pharaohs, to build a grandiose monument to himself. More objective observers suggested that the argument was not really about a pyramid; it was about conservatives confronting progressives, the old against the new, a snobbish cultural elite being frightened by the democratic masses.

Pei, though, was not without friends. In an unusual statement, all seven curators of the Louvre publicly announced their support. Pierre Boulez, the orchestra conductor, gave his endorsement to the project, as did the widow of former French president Georges Pompidou. A particularly valuable ally was the mayor of Paris, Jacques Chirac. Chirac, though leader of one of France's major conservative parties, stated that he was not hostile to the project, but he did request that a full-scale model of the new entrance be erected at the proposed site. The model was built in early May, 1985, and no fewer than sixty thousand Parisians streamed by the site. Most were pleasantly surprised that the pyramid was not anywhere near as large or obtrusive as feared; indeed, many commented on its proportion and sedate placement. This event seemed to play a key role in defusing much of the criticism, and opposition to the project began to collapse. Not surprisingly, shortly thereafter public opinion polls began showing substantial support for the pyramid. The worst was over for Pei.

Finally, on March 4, 1988, Mitterrand officially dedicated the Crystal Pyramid, as it was now popularly known. The finished product was stunning, if nothing else. Exquisitely proportioned, it stood 71 feet high, measured 118 feet at the base, contained 793 diamond-shaped panes of the finest polished optical glass, and, although weighing some two hundred tons, looked like it floated slightly above ground. Surrounding it were three smaller glass pyramids as well as a series of triangular reflecting pools with fountains made of dark blue granite. Even critics could find no fault in the superb craftsmanship and the quality of the materials. At the time, though, visitors could not use the pyramid, since the underground portions of the project were still incomplete. In another ceremony on March 30, 1989, Mitterrand officially dedicated the finished project, thus allowing the general public finally to use the new entrance to the Louvre.

Impact of Event

The most obvious impact of Pei's work is that he essentially transformed the Louvre into a modern, efficient facility, bringing it up to the service and exhibition standards of a late twentieth century museum. He created a functional entrance in a spot where tourists would expect to find it, in the geometric center of the vast complex that constitutes the Louvre. The entrance was marked by a distinctive building that was recognizable but not overwhelming; the pyramid is actually only two-thirds the height of the surrounding buildings. Visitors can descend into the entrance hall by escalators, a beautiful helicoidal staircase, or in the case of the elderly or handicapped, in a modernistic circular hydraulic elevator. Visitors have easy access to tickets and information and are guided through a series of underground tunnels to the portion of the museum they wish to see.

Pei also dramatically enlarged the capacity of the Louvre. In modern museums, a fifty-fifty split is regarded as the optimal ratio between exhibition space and space devoted to support facilities; in the old Louvre, galleries had represented between eighty and ninety percent of the total space. Normally, an architect would add a modern wing to an existing museum, but of course such an addition was unthinkable in the case of the Louvre. Part of the new space was to come from the north wing of the Louvre, from which the Ministry of Finance was moved. Pei, in a brilliant stroke, found the solution for additional space by going underground, creating no fewer than twenty acres of museum space underneath the Louvre's courtyard. This presented some formidable engineering problems, since the nearby Seine River could possibly flood the new entrance. Special provisions had to be taken to create a drainage network and to ensure that pumps were ready should the Seine reach flood stage.

While excavating, another problem arose. Workers uncovered the remains of the fortress of Philip Augustus, erected around 1200, and also found portions of the palace of Charles V. The construction schedule was so arranged that progress could continue while teams of archaeologists were sent into the critical areas, working quickly and efficiently for several months in what was probably the largest archaeological expedition in French history. Not only were some twenty-five thousand artifacts found and preserved for posterity, but large segments of the fortress tower, wall, and moat were also restored, and Pei skillfully worked them into the exhibition spaces. Thus, visitors can view not only the artistic treasures of the Louvre but valuable archaeological remains if they are so inclined.

It was not simply the Louvre that Pei affected, however; his project also had a broader impact on the city of Paris. Previously, much of the Louvre's courtyard was disfigured during the day by serving as a parking lot, and after dark it tended to be deserted at best or used as a rather unsavory trysting area at worst. Since the construction of the pyramid, though, the area constantly teems with vibrant activity, thanks to the fact that the pyramid is lighted at night. Indeed, some argue that the pyramid is at its best either catching the rays of the setting sun or when it is illuminated. Thus, Pei played a key role in reinvigorating a significant public space, saving it from decay and underuse and transforming it into a safe, pleasant area for Parisians and tourists alike.

Other architects are also likely to benefit from Pei's contributions, in that he gave a renewed respectability to modern architecture. Parisians may be forgiven for having a negative attitude toward modern architecture. Several previous attempts at building skyscrapers or creating ultramodern urban projects in the city have been censured for their sterility and lack of taste and grace, among them the Pompidou Center and the Tour Montparnasse. Pei demonstrated that one can use modern architecture, materials, and engineering to create something functional and efficient while at the same time showing respect for the past and sensitivity to the needs of city dwellers.

The Louvre project was not entirely finished at the time of its opening; segments of it, such as a lengthy tunnel to connect with an underground parking area, were not expected to be completed until the turn of the century. Yet Pei provided an admirable start. Perhaps he should be commended for what he did not do as much as for what he actually built. He created new space without adding a disharmonious modern wing to the Louvre. He made it possible to move large numbers of visitors through the Louvre and provide them with decent amenities without ripping up historic rooms, staircases, and hallways. After the work was completed, a pyramid of restrained proportions and some lovely reflecting water basins were the only visible external signs of the vast renovation that had occurred. The full glory of the old Louvre stood intact, majestic, imperial, and beautiful as ever. Pei was fully aware that this commission was something special, that it had a unique and historical dimension to it. After all, not every architect is privileged to leave a mark upon what is arguably the world's greatest museum.

Bibliography

Biasini, Emile, Jean Lebrat, Dominique Bezombes, and Jean-Michel Vincent. *The Grand Louvre: A Museum Transfigured, 1981-1993.* Translated by Charlotte Ellis and Murray Wyllie. Paris: Electra Moniteur, 1989. This sophisticated study focuses upon the architectural and technical aspects of the construction, presenting highly detailed information in the form of a diary of the project. Contains an extensive and valuable collection of pictures, drawings, and plans. Biasini was the first director of the project.

Coignard, Jerome, Joel Girard, and Christophe Lagrange. *The Grand Louvre and the Pyramid.* Translated by Lois Grjebine. Paris: Beaux Arts Magazine, 1990. Perhaps the best brief introduction on the subject, written primarily for the novice. While the book does not discuss the controversy generated by Pei to any extent, it is valuable for its excellent colored photographs of both the pyramid and the vast complex underneath it.

Davis, Douglas. *The Museum Transformed: Design and Culture in the Post-Pompidou Age.* New York: Abbeville Press, 1990. Although containing only a brief section on the pyramid, the chief contribution of this impressive study is to place the transformation of the Louvre into the larger context of how modern museums are built and conceived in the late twentieth century. Written by the former architectural critic for *Newsweek,* who is also the author of several books on architecture and photography.

Lipstadt, Helene. "A Paris for the Twenty-first Century?" *Art in America* 72 (November, 1984): 104-113. Places the renovation project into the larger political and cultural context of other recent ultramodern projects in Paris. Argues that Mitterrand sought to represent his Socialist government as the patron of a new democratic culture and that the pyramid, with its easy access, is symbolic of his attempt to make culture accessible to the masses.

Stein, Susan. "French Ferociously Debate the Pei Pyramid at the Louvre." *Architecture* 74 (May, 1985): 25, 34, 40, 46. Written by the director of the American Institute of Architects' Octagon Museum, this article is a competent and balanced account of the controversy generated by the pyramid up to 1985. Limited but useful collection of photographs, including the famous mock-up that helped transform public opinion in Pei's favor.

Wiseman, Carter. *I. M. Pei: A Profile in American Architecture.* New York: Harry N. Abrams, 1990. An outstanding study of the man's life and work. Based upon solid scholarship, yet readable and filled with interesting anecdotes. An entire chapter is devoted to the Louvre project, and another chapter, entitled "An Orderly Enigma," gives a unique and penetrating insight into Pei's personality, character, and work habits. Contains hundreds of photographs and illustrations.

David C. Lukowitz

Cross-References

Monet's *Water Lilies* Are Shown at the Musée de l'Orangerie (1927), p. 718; New York's Museum of Modern Art Is Founded (1929), p. 782; The Pompidou Center Opens in Paris (1977), p. 2402; The Musée d'Orsay Opens (1986), p. 2588; Van Gogh's *Irises* Sells for $53.9 Million (1987), p. 2603.

MAHFOUZ WINS THE NOBEL PRIZE IN LITERATURE

Category of event: Literature
Time: October, 1988
Locale: Stockholm, Sweden

Recognition of the literary importance of Naguib Mahfouz's fifty-year career marked the first time a Nobel Prize in Literature was awarded to a writer in Arabic

Principal personages:
NAGUIB MAHFOUZ (1911-   ), a Nobel laureate in literature
TAHA HUSAYN (1889-1973), an Egyptian writer who provided inspiration to Mahfouz in his early years as an author
SALAMAH MUSA (1887-1958), the Egyptian writer and socialist thinker who published Mahfouz's earliest works in his literary journal
GAMAL ABDEL NASSER (1918-1970), the head of Egypt's governing military junta, under whom Mahfouz served in the ministry of culture
ANWAR EL-SADAT (1918-1981), the successor to Nasser

Summary of Event

The announcement in the fall of 1988 that the Nobel Prize in Literature was being awarded to the Egyptian writer Naguib Mahfouz may have appeared to be a turning point in the history of the Nobel Prize program, as very few literature laureates during the previous decades had come from non-Western countries. The earliest, in 1913, had been awarded to the Indian Rabindranath Tagore. In the period from 1918 to 1945, all literature prizes had gone either to Europeans or to Americans. The next quarter of a century saw awards to authors from South America, Israel, and Japan, but it was not until 1986 that the first African, Wole Soyinka, was so honored. Two years later, Naguib Mahfouz became the first author from the African continent writing in Arabic to become a Nobel laureate in literature.

For Mahfouz himself, however, international recognition of his work represented more than the culmination of several decades of personal literary application. It encouraged him and others in many different parts of the world to believe that recognition of the universality of human values and emotions had made intercontinental strides.

Mahfouz's own elaboration of the way in which his career developed, recorded in an interview on his fiftieth birthday, was a testimony of the interconnectedness of intellectual and cultural influences, from both the East and the West, that contributed to his writing career. Mahfouz noted in his experience as a youth something that was a key characteristic of how members of different cultures and nationalities learn about other cultures' existence: dependence on translated works. His own exposure to the literature of non-Arabic culture, and therefore a "window" on its values, began with enthusiastic consumption of Western detective stories as a youth. Once he was past the impressionistic phase of youth, there was a dual interplay of influences. One set of influences came from his rising interest in literary models of Europe, the other from his reading of classical Arabic literature and early twentieth century writers in Arabic. In the latter field, he readily acknowledged the early importance of Egyptian authors such as Taha Husayn as well as later influences stemming from his exposure to Tawfiq al-Hakim and Muhammad Haykal. It was the latter writer who, when he wrote *Zeinab* in 1914, was the earliest to win recognition for pioneering the literary form that would be most attractive to Mahfouz, the fictional novel. Others inspired him through their perfection of the short story as a literary art form. It was the Egyptian Fabian socialist Salamah Musa, however, who extended practical encouragement to Mahfouz by inviting him to publish his earliest short stories in *Al Majalla al Jadida*, the journal Musa edited.

By the time Mahfouz had reached university age, he realized that, even though his field of academic specialization would be philosophy, he was interested in combining literature and philosophy. His decision to write a master's thesis at Cairo University on aesthetics was intended to allow him to develop this connection. There is no doubt that Mahfouz's penchant toward philosophy left its mark on his literary career. What became most notable in his work was his concern for the deep philosophical significance of life experiences of quite ordinary personages. His fictional stories were almost always set in the heavily populated urban quarters of his own native Cairo, and his stories portrayed the lives of either the popular underprivileged classes or, in a number of cases, members of the modest bureaucratic milieu. The latter was a grouping he came to know at first hand during his years of service (during the 1950's and 1960's) in the ministry of culture.

In several of his works, beginning with the novel *Zuqāq al-Midaq q* (1947; *Midaq Alley*, 1966), Mahfouz combined his version of stark realism (something he cultivated after studying European writers including Franz Kafka) with an almost mystical aura that is magnified by a style inspired in some ways by James Joyce, in others by Marcel Proust. His focus on "the little man" in a society clearly beginning to experience tensions between traditional and modern forms of expression and action provided a way to portray images of the internal workings of minds that, because they were somewhat stereotypic of traditional societal types, could strike familiar notes with Egyptian readers. Juxtaposed with the familiar and presumably easily understood were the forces of "new" society that menaced the very existence— material as well as psychological and philosophical—of Mahfouz's simple characters.

This phenomenon is seen most clearly in Mahfouz's famous *Al-Thulāthiyya* (trilogy), published in 1956 and 1957, just at the beginning swing of Egypt's new military regime under Gamal Abdel Nasser toward radical, and then revolutionary, politics. Here again, using an entire family as the focus for his three novels, Mahfouz developed his reputation for delving deep into the psychological subconsciousness of ordinary people. In the trilogy, emphasis is laid on the frustrations of a father figure confronting rising clashes between traditional views of religion in society and alternative choices being made by a younger generation tempted by the "new truths" of science. The last volume, treating the third generation, portrays similar tensions in clashes in family values when grandchildren on one side enter the ultraconservative Muslim Brotherhood, while others adhere to the Communist party.

Mahfouz continued in the 1960's to build similar sociopsychological themes, some of them quite tragic. It became clear that he had become a spokesperson not only for Egypt but also for a number of non-Western cultures that demanded recognition of their need and capacity to express the frustrations of Third World "marginality" through the medium of fictional literature.

Impact of Event

Coming in the late 1980's, following a decade and a half of rapid, almost uncontrollable change in the Middle East and the rest of the Third World, recognition of Mahfouz's accomplishments suggested a number of indirectly related possibilities for wider impact. In some respects, for example, the culmination of so many years of persistence by an Egyptian writer who had lived through the effects of his own and neighboring countries' political instability, regional warfare on four separate occasions, and locally oppressive propagandistic mechanisms was something of a victory. Both locally in Egypt and elsewhere in the world, Mahfouz's Nobel award represented a spark of hope that freedom of cultural expression could survive despite overwhelming obstacles that seemed to divorce the creative intellectual mind from the massive realities of struggling, uncertain democracies, regional political conflict (specifically the Arab-Israeli dilemma), and widespread poverty.

Part of this spark of hope, but at the same time a lingering fear, was represented in the "new Egypt" of the post-Nasser years. Following some twenty years of inconclusive and quasirevolutionary upheaval, Nasser's successor, Anwar el-Sadat, had begun in the mid-1970's to move Egypt in the direction of "opening," by which he implied a reversal of controls that had stifled the country's political, economic, and intellectual aspirations. Sadat's accomplishments, as well as several notable failures (particularly in the political domain), ended in 1981 when he was gunned down by assassins' bullets. This precipitous event forced the immediate question of political succession (to the new president, Hosni Mubarak), but just as critically, it raised the question of the future social and intellectual climate of the country. In the wake of Sadat's reopening of Egypt's windows to the West, with a concurrent escalation of the country's dependence on the West for military and economic assistance, there were conflicting pressures to continue Sadat's liberalizing changes on one hand, or, on the other, to revert not to the pre-Sadat years of Nasserism but to an idealized conception of a "true" and timeless Egypt dedicated to traditional values. Clearly a quandary was posed for writers such as Mahfouz, who had tried to posit a literary and philosophical framework containing elements of both, and who now found themselves asked either to reconsider or to demonstrate the relevance of what they had written to a society that was again not at all clear which way it should turn.

According to Hayim Gordon, a non-Egyptian author who dedicated an entire monographic study to Mahfouz's Egypt in 1990, the widely recognized significance of Mahfouz's literary career, and in particular certain of the themes he had incorporated into his writings, cannot be separated from this quandary. In many ways, the rush of external events, whether these are seen as the events that occurred during the main period of Mahfouz's writing career or as the events affecting Egypt's destiny as the country entered the 1990's, can be seen according to some critics as a tide of blind forces that overwhelms that external world without actually penetrating and affecting the internal conciousness of the writer's otherwise inconsequential subjects. Because Mahfouz seems to be most interested in that domain of internal consciousness, the inconclusiveness of the sense of contact between events (the external) and psychological impressions (the internal) may have led some of Mahfouz's readers to attribute to him, through his subjects, an incapacity or unwillingness to confront and struggle to overcome "reality."

The full impact of Mahfouz's literary contribution, therefore, can be said to depend on two factors. One is the extent to which what he wrote will be read and understood outside the culture zone that was the focus of its microanalysis. A second, equally important, factor will be the receptivity of that same culture zone to the forms of introspection that Mahfouz offered to several generations who, although they understood the dilemmas represented by introspection, assumed that externally induced changes must necessarily "modernize" in terms that can benefit the old and the new alike.

Bibliography

Allen, Roger. "Some Recent Works of Najib Mahfuz: A Critical Analysis." *Journal of the American Research Center in Egypt* 14 (1974): 101-110. This contribution to criticism of works appearing in the era of Nasser's presidency and of Mahfouz's service in the ministry of culture had particularly timely significance since it appeared only shortly after Sadat's public declaration of the "opening" of Egyptian politics and society following twenty years of close control.

_____. "Najib Mahfuz." In *Nobel Laureates in Literature*, edited by Rado Pribic. New York: Garland, 1990. This is the most concise and objectively balanced review of Mahfouz's career. It deals with the literary and philosophical themes of his writings in terms that, although more descriptive than analytical, give a comprehensive impression of the evolution of his work.

Enani, M. M., ed. *Naguib Mahfouz, Nobel 1988: Egyptian Perspectives.* Cairo: General Egyptian Book Organization, 1989. A collection of essays written by Egyptians and translated into English. The scope of coverage of Mahfouz's work ranges from symbolism of literary themes (the significance of the alley, the tragedy of rebellion) to his personal political convictions.

Gordon, Hayim. *Naguib Mahfouz's Egypt.* New York: Greenwood Press, 1990. This monograph was written by an Israeli scholar who benefited from long-term personal contacts with Mahfouz during the 1980's. He combines analysis of the Egyptian writer's written works with insight into psychological and philosophical characteristics of Mahfouz.

Le Gassick, Trevor, ed. *Critical Perspectives on Naguib Mahfouz.* Washington, D.C.: Three Continents Press, 1991. The majority of contributions to this book are from Egyptian specialists, with two articles by Western scholars. The dominant theme involves analysis of symbolism in Mahfouz's works. One contributor raises the question of "Egyptian Women as Portrayed in the Social Novels of Najib Mahfuz."

Byron D. Cannon

Cross-References

The First Nobel Prizes Are Awarded (1901), p. 45; Tawfiq al-Hakim Introduces Absurdism to the Arab Stage (1961), p. 1893; Kawabata Wins the Nobel Prize in Literature (1968), p. 2147; Singer Wins the Nobel Prize in Literature (1978), p. 2423; Soyinka Wins the Nobel Prize in Literature (1986), p. 2594; Khomeini Calls for Rushdie's Death (1989), p. 2630; Gordimer Wins the Nobel Prize in Literature (1991), p. 2668.

KHOMEINI CALLS FOR RUSHDIE'S DEATH

Category of event: Literature
Time: February 14, 1989
Locale: London, England, and Tehran, Iran

Novelist Salman Rushdie's 1988 publication of The Satanic Verses *led Iran's Ayatollah Ruhollah Khomeini to sentence him to death, forcing the novelist into hiding and renewing debate over writers' freedom of speech*

Principal personages:

SALMAN RUSHDIE (1947-   ), a British-Indian novelist born of Muslim parents in Bombay, India, whose earlier writings established his reputation as a critic of both political establishments and religious orthodoxy

RUHOLLAH KHOMEINI (1902-1989), the all-powerful Iranian religious leader or *ayatollah*

MARIANNE WIGGINS (1947-   ), an American novelist who married Rushdie in January, 1988

HOJATOLESLAM ALI HOSEINI KHAMENEI (1940-   ), the successor to Ruhollah Khomeini as Iran's religious leader after the latter's death in 1989

Summary of Event

Although born into a Muslim family in India that later moved to Pakistan, Rushdie's encounters with Islamic orthodoxy, together with his prolonged stay in the West, led him to give up his faith. He thus came to have what he called a "God-shaped hole" inside him, one that he tried to fill with literature. Two of his novels, *Midnight's Children* (1981) and *Shame* (1983), brought him both fame and awards. They represented a secular, humanist critique of the role of religious forces in South Asia.

In *The Satanic Verses*, published in England in September, 1988, Rushdie continued his themes of migration, alienation, and criticism of Islamic orthodoxy. The novel begins with the blowing up of an Air India plane, en route from Bombay to London, over the English Channel. Two passengers—Gibreel Farishta, an Indian film star who was trying to flee from his life of fame and glamour after a severe illness during which he had lost his belief in God; and Saladin Chamcha, a performer in British television commercials who was returning to his adopted country after a nostalgic visit to Bombay—miraculously survive the descent. Strange things happen to them as they return to England, and Gibreel goes through a sequence of dreams.

One of the characters in Gibreel's dreams is Mahound, a businessman-turned-prophet who goes to preach to the city of Jahilia. Although Rushdie was using a fictional character, it was inevitable that readers, especially Muslims, would take him as a disguised representation of the prophet Muhammad. The title of the novel was a reference to an incident in the prophet Muhammad's life, when he accepted three pagan goddesses to help his cause but later repudiated his act as one that had been inspired by the devil.

Rushdie's fictional character Mahound goes through a similar experience. In the novel, Mahound's wives are shown as prostitutes. In Rushdie's narration, the whores of a local brothel assume "the identity of one of Mahound's wives" as a kind of business gimmick. For the Muslims, however, Prophet Muhammad's wives are considered as the "mothers of all believers."

Rushdie's novel also expresses doubt about the Koran as being the word of God. In Gibreel's dream, Salman, a fictional scribe, is shown writing down God's words as they are conveyed through the prophet Mahound. Salman takes liberties and makes changes on his own to see if Mahound will catch him. Mahound fails to do so even when Salman writes down "Jew" rather than "Christian." As Salman says in the novel, "when I read him the chapter he nodded and thanked me politely, and I went out of his tent with tears in my eyes. . . . There is no bitterness like that of a man who finds out he has been believing in the ghost."

It was inevitable that *The Satanic Verses* would be met with both criticism and praise, as had been the case with *Midnight's Children* and *Shame*. Although using a fictional character, the irreverent description of some of the incidents in Prophet Muhammad's life and the casting of doubt on the authenticity of the Koran as the word of God were bound to draw ire from the Islamic world.

What actually happened was something that Rushdie, or anyone else, could hardly have imagined. There were large-scale demonstrations organized by various Muslim groups against the book in such countries as India and Pakistan, and the book eventually was banned in most of the countries with large Muslim populations, with Rajiv Gandhi, the Indian prime minister, taking the initiative. Some of this could have been expected, but what changed the context of the debate and the life of the novelist was the fateful decision of Iran's Ayatollah Ruhollah Khomeini to announce a death sentence against Rushdie. In his *fatwa* of February 14, 1989, Khomeini said that the novel was "in opposition to Islam, the Prophet and Koran" and that the author must die. A day later, it was announced from Iran that anyone killing Rushdie would be rewarded handsomely—$2.6 million to an Iranian assassin or $1 million to a non-Iranian.

This not only made Rushdie cancel a planned tour of the United States to promote his book but also forced him to go underground for his physical safety. In the ensuing months, Rushdie defended his work as "a work of fiction, one that aspires to the condition of literature," as he wrote in a long essay, "In Good Faith." In an article written shortly after the publication of Khomeini's *fatwa*, he asserted that what he was trying to do was "to give a secular, humanist vision of the birth of a great world religion." In an open letter to Prime Minister Gandhi of India, he criticized the Indian leader for succumbing to the pressure of Indian Muslim extremists and fundamentalists in banning his book. In a challenge to the Indian leader, which he meant to be addressed to leaders of other countries in which his book had been banned, Rushdie asserted that the real question was "whether India, by behaving in this fashion, can any more lay claim to the title of a civilized society."

While Rushdie defended his book and criticized his critics, he also, in an attempt to avert a crisis and have the death sentence lifted, tried to mollify Muslim opinion by expressing his "profound" regret—as he did in a statement on February 18, 1989—for "the distress that publication has occasioned to sincere followers of Islam." He also decided to embrace Islam publicly, a decision that he later regretted and recanted. Early in 1993, two years after that decision, he tried to explain it in an interview with Irish journalist John Banville. He talked of his despair at the time and the pain he had felt because the people he had written about were the ones burning his book. He thought he could heal that rift by returning to the Islamic fold.

Rushdie's expressions of regret and espousal of Islam failed to evoke any positive response from Tehran. In February, 1993, on the fourth anniversary of Khomeini's *fatwa*, Iran's new religious leader, Ayatollah Hojatoleslam Ali Hoseini Khamenei, declared that the death sentence against Rushdie must be carried out.

Rushdie's personal life apparently was changed forever. Living under hiding and being forced to move from one place to another ended his marriage with Marianne Wiggins, an American novelist. They were separated in July, 1989, and granted a divorce in March, 1993. Rushdie longed for a return to normal life. Explaining his condition, he said after a year in hiding, "the things that are most difficult to take are not being able to walk down a street, not being able to browse in a bookshop, not being able to go to a movie."

Rushdie, however, refused to compromise his right to write freely. In a moving address to New York's Columbia University in December, 1991, for which he appeared unannounced and in great secrecy, he declared, "Free speech is life itself." Saying that he was ready to face the consequences of his use of this freedom, Rushdie said, "I must cling with all my might to my soul; must hold on to its mischievous, iconoclastic, out-of-step clown instincts, no matter how great the storm."

Impact of Event

Because Khomeini's *fatwa* had pronounced a death sentence not only for Rushdie but also for the novel's publishers, there was a widespread fear that many more individuals could become victims of Muslim retaliation against the book. As a result of a bomb threat, Viking Penguin, the novel's publishers, decided to evacuate their offices in New York City. They also decided to cancel Rushdie's planned U.S. tour. In England, after copies of the novel had been burned by Muslim demonstrators in Bolton and Bradford, the chain booksellers W. H. Smith decided to withdraw Rushdie's book from their bookstores. The plan to bring out an American paperback edition of the novel was cancelled, to be revived much later, after the outpouring of Muslim anger and rage had subsided. Many bookstores refused to sell the novel, and those that did sell it sometimes became victims of retaliation.

The international controversy surrounding the novel, together with Khomeini's death sentence against the author, raised anew questions concerning freedom of expression. This issue had been raised at the international level primarily in connection with writers in Communist countries—as in the celebrated cases of Soviet writers Boris Pasternak and Aleksandr Solzhenitsyn—but now a budding writer in the West had touched some sensitive nerves of Islamic orthodoxy and seemed prepared to face the consequences of his perceived heresy. Rushdie's novel elicited strong comments from writers, both Muslim and non-Muslim, from almost every part of the world. In general, Muslim writers criticized Rushdie, while Western intellectuals on both sides of the Atlantic came to the author's defense. There were exceptions in both cases.

Explaining why Muslims reacted so passionately and angrily against Rushdie, Amir Taheri, an Iranian journalist, wrote in *The Times* of London that Islam did not recognize "unlimited freedom of expression." He added, "The Western belief in human rights, which seems to lack limits, is alien to Islamic traditions." It was, therefore, no wonder that Syed Ali Ashraf, a Muslim professor at the University of Cambridge, accused Rushdie of "preaching an anti-Islamic theory in the guise of a novel."

There were a few exceptions in the reactions of Muslim intellectuals. Naguib Mahfouz, a famous Egyptian novelist and winner of the 1988 Nobel Prize in Literature, criticized Khomeini for "intellectual terrorism." In Syria, a group of writers issued a statement objecting to their government's ban on the novel. These were isolated cases. Even Mahfouz changed his view three years later when, in an interview published in *The Paris Review*, he said that Rushdie did not have "the right to insult anything, especially a prophet or anything considered holy."

Western intellectuals, as expected, mostly sided with Rushdie. In England, a group of writers led by Harold Pinter, a noted playwright, went to the British prime minister's residence expressing "outrage" at Khomeini's decree. In the United States, a public reading of the novel was sponsored by a coalition of the Authors Guild, American PEN, and Article 19, an international anticensorship organization. Those who participated included Susan Sontag, a prominent American novelist. Norman Mailer, another American writer, perhaps expressed the feelings of most when he said, "If he [Rushdie] is ever killed for a folly, we must be killed for the same folly." There were some who were critical of Rushdie. John le Carré, a best-selling author of spy novels, said, "Nobody has a God-given right to insult a great religion and be published with impunity."

The publication of *The Satanic Verses* also became a political event, and a number of governments were drawn into the controversy. This was especially true of the British government, as Rushdie was a British citizen. The government faced the dilemma of protecting the author while, at the same time, continuing meaningful relations with the Tehran regime. It decided to accord full protection to Rushdie and his wife. On the diplomatic front, the United Kingdom and other European Community nations decided to recall diplomats from Tehran without breaking diplomatic ties. Iran, in turn, recalled its own envoys from England, threatening that it would sever diplomatic relations unless the British government apologized for its actions. Relations between the two countries, therefore, became a victim of the Rushdie affair. Diplomatic relations were restored in September, 1990, but as British Foreign Secretary Douglas Hurd said in early 1993, full diplomatic relations would have to await the final resolution of the Rushdie case.

American official response has been more ambivalent, largely because Washington seemed reluctant to risk any unpleasant open crises in U.S.-Iran relations. The immediate reaction to Khomeini's death sentence was to express regret. After facing severe criticism from American writers and civil rights advocates, President George Bush finally characterized the Iranian action as "deeply offensive to the norms of civilized behavior." When Rushdie came to Washington to attend a conference on free speech in March, 1992, however, the Bush Administration failed to support him. Calling Rushdie just another author, Marlin Fitzwater, the presidential spokesman, said that "there's no reason to have any special interest in him."

The physical fate of the author of *The Satanic Verses* remained uncertain four years after the issuance of the death threat against him from Tehran. Iran had doubled the price on Rushdie's head and had refused to retract the Khomeini decree. On the other hand, Rushdie found it possible to travel abroad, attending conferences, meeting government leaders, and engaging in some writing. Whatever might be the outcome of his difficulties, the issue raised by his iconoclastic novel was not a new one. The question of whether a writer should have the freedom to write, even the freedom to offend, was settled long ago in the West with the emergence of democratic institutions. Rushdie's book has now forced other, especially Islamic, societies to face this major issue. How they deal with it will help determine and shape their political institutions.

Bibliography

Appignanesi, Lisa, and Sara Maitland, eds. *The Rushdie File*. Syracuse, N.Y.: Syracuse University Press, 1990. An invaluable resource that has most of the important documentary material on Rushdie dealing with the period 1988-1989.

"Declaration of Iranian Intellectuals and Artists in Defense of Salman Rushdie." *The New York Review of Books* 39 (May 14, 1992): 31. A courageous statement in defense of Rushdie issued by about fifty prominent Iranians living in exile. The statement characterized freedom of speech as "one of the greatest achievements of mankind" and quoted the prominent eighteenth century French writer Voltaire as saying that "this freedom would be meaningless unless human beings had the liberty to blaspheme."

Rushdie, Salman. "An Interview with Salman Rushdie." Interview by John Banville. *The New York Review of Books* 40 (March 4, 1993): 34-36. In a long interview with an Irish journalist, Rushdie explains his trials under Khomeini's *fatwa* as well as his reasons for espousing Islam and then recanting it.

_____. "In Good Faith." In *Imaginary Homelands: Essays and Criticism*

1981-1991, by Salman Rushdie. London: Granta Books, 1991. In this long essay, Rushdie made a serious effort to explain his book to his Muslim readers.

_____. "Lessons, Harsh and Difficult, from 1000 Days 'Trapped Inside a Metaphor.'" *The New York Times*, December 12, 1991, p. A4. Rushdie, in this speech delivered before an audience at Columbia University in New York, makes a passionate plea for freedom of thought, which he describes as "freedom from religious control, freedom from accusations of blasphemy."

_____. *The Satanic Verses*. New York: Viking Penguin, 1989. Because of the worldwide controversy generated by this novel, it may turn out to be one of the most important writings of the twentieth century.

Ruthven, Malise. *A Satanic Affair: Salman Rushdie and the Rage of Islam*. London: Chatto and Windus, 1990. One of the many studies on the Rushdie affair, Ruthven's book is especially useful for its discussion of the Muslim community in England and its reactions to *The Satanic Verses*.

Surendra K. Gupta

Cross-References

Huxley's *Brave New World* Reflects Fears About the Future (1932), p. 896; Socialist Realism Is Mandated in Soviet Literature (1932), p. 908; Miller's Notorious Novel *Tropic of Cancer* Is Published (1934), p. 963; Shostakovich's *Lady Macbeth of Mtsensk* Is Condemned (1936), p. 1042; The Nazis Ban Nolde's Paintings (1941), p. 1217; *Nineteen Eighty-Four* Portrays Totalitarianism and Mind Control (1949), p. 1421; Young Readers Embrace *The Catcher in the Rye* (1951), p. 1493; Pasternak's *Doctor Zhivago* Is Published (1957), p. 1747; Mahfouz Wins the Nobel Prize in Literature (1988), p. 2625.

MAPPLETHORPE'S PHOTOGRAPHS
PROVOKE CONTROVERSY

Category of event: Art
Time: June 14, 1989
Locale: Corcoran Gallery of Art, Washington, D.C.

> *Robert Mapplethorpe's photographic exhibition was canceled before its arrival at ·
> the Corcoran Gallery of Art by gallery officials who cited concerns that its presence
> would incite a backlash from Capitol Hill*

Principal personages:

ROBERT MAPPLETHORPE (1946-1989), an artist and photographer best known
for his sadomasochistic and homoerotic photographs

CHRISTINA ORR-CAHALL (1947-   ), the director of the Corcoran Gallery of Art who canceled the Mapplethorpe exhibition

JESSE HELMS (1921-   ), a North Carolina senator who led a crusade
against "obscene" work

SAM WAGSTAFF (1921-1987), a former museum curator and advertising
executive who helped to shape Mapplethorpe's art

Summary of Event

Although debate over federal funding of provocative art had been raging since
1982, a 1989 exhibition of erotic art by the late Robert Mapplethorpe had played in
Philadelphia and Chicago without arousing controversy. The uproar began when the
director of the Corcoran Gallery of Art, Christina Orr-Cahall, already engaged in a
battle over federal funding, decided to impose censorship on her own gallery; she
canceled the scheduled Mapplethorpe exhibition because it included a series of photographs depicting homoerotic and sadomasochistic themes.

Outraged by the museum's censorship, artists demonstrated in front of the Corcoran, and protestors gathered there the night before the show was scheduled to
open. Laser artist Rockne Krebs projected a gigantic image of the deceased artist
against the stately museum. Trouble continued for the Corcoran; an artist's boycott
followed on the heels of the protests. Six sculptors and a conceptual artist all canceled their exhibitions so as not to appear to endorse the museum's actions. Lowell
Nesbitt, a New York artist who had twice exhibited at the Corcoran, revoked a be-
quest of $1.5 million that was to go to the museum upon his death. One tenth of the
museum's members terminated their membership.

To offset this tide of emigration, Christina Orr-Cahall sent ten thousand letters to
artists and museum members beseeching them to fight Senator Jesse Helms's call for
a ban on federal funding of indecent art. Shifting the blame did not appear to have
any effect on the flight of patrons or artists, and finally, three months after the turmoil began, Orr-Cahall issued a meek apology. Most saw it as too little, too late.

The museum had done the unforgivable; it had caved in to legislative pressures.

Controversy continued to rage, as Helms proposed (and Congress rejected) broad restrictions on federal arts and humanities. The National Endowment for the Arts (NEA) also forced its grantees to give an antiobscenity pledge in order to ensure that none of the proceeds from the NEA would go to finance any project considered obscene. Several artists had already decided that the grant was not worth the price. The most famous vocal opponent of the pledge was Joseph Papp, then producer of the New York Shakespeare Festival in Manhattan, who turned down two grants, one for $57,500 and another for $371,000. Others such as performance artist Rachel Rosenthal and choreographer Bella Lewitzky also refused to take the pledge and consequently lost grants.

Another local gallery, the Washington Project for the Arts, did show the Mapplethorpe exhibit that summer; the exhibit went on to break attendance records at galleries in Chicago, Berkeley, and other U.S. cities. There were only two pieces deleted from the showing, and those were noncontroversial works withdrawn by their owner. The exhibit itself was a hodgepodge of influences. The work exhibited included fashion and magazine illustrations, theater and dance photography, and portraits of celebrities including William S. Burroughs, Donald Sutherland, Louise Nevelson, Cindy Sherman, Doris Saatchi, Francesco Clemente, Alice Neel, Sam Wagstaff, and Laurie Anderson. Lastly, there was the sadomasochistic and homoerotic art, which was all that Middle America knew of Robert Mapplethorpe.

Mapplethorpe used to refer to "S & M" as standing for "sex and magic," not "sadomasochism." His *Erotic Pictures* exhibit depicted photographs of men clad in leather, often with exposed genitalia, performing various sexual acts or posing with such paraphernalia as whips and chains. His models were not hired but were friends doing what they normally did.

What the Mapplethorpe vision sought to do was to instill dignity and beauty in subjects that were outside of the norms of accepted behavior. Although his subject matter had shock value, his photographic composition was symmetrical, his backdrops conventional, and his lighting precise. In that respect, he was a conservative artist. Yet such works as *Mark Stevens (Mr. 10-1/2)* (1976), in which a man arches over a ledge in order to display his genitals, or *Self Portrait* (1978), which showed Mapplethorpe bent over inserting a whip into his rectum, did not seem so conservative to the general public.

For Mapplethorpe, an interest in eroticism and homoeroticism was evident even in the early works. His *Untitled* (1972) features an image of two boys kissing, with a highlighted rectangle placed around their lips. *Portrait* (1973) depicts an early sadomasochistic image, with Mapplethorpe dressed in a leather vest without a shirt and with a clamp attached to his right nipple. Mapplethorpe was trying to project in these photographs the reaction he had experienced when he got his first glance at male pornographic magazines in Times Square in the late 1960's.

Mapplethorpe himself missed the NEA controversy surrounding his exhibition at the Corcoran. He died March 9, 1989, three months before the scheduled opening.

The controversy he sparked with his few photographs from the *Erotic Pictures* series will likely be Mapplethorpe's most memorable legacy to the art world; the debate about whether he was an artist or a pornographer will probably continue for decades.

Impact of Event

When the Mapplethorpe exhibition at the Corcoran was abruptly halted, the foundation of the art world rocked from the jolt. Protests raged in front of the Corcoran, artists canceled their exhibitions, the top curator, Jane Livingston, quit her affiliation of fifteen years, and the very existence of the Corcoran Gallery was thrown into question. Even an apology by the museum, which was considered muted by most, did little to stop the outbound flow of members or the erosion of donations.

For Jesse Helms and his supporters, the cancellation of the Mapplethorpe exhibit was deemed a victory. The NEA's funding of exhibitions containing provocative photographs by Mapplethorpe and Andres Serrano had ignited the controversy, and Helms continued to press for broader restrictions on federal arts and humanities funding. After hours of stormy debate on September 28 and 29, 1989, a House-Senate conference committee voted down the Helms proposal and instead adopted a compromise. The compromise legislation omitted the original Helms references to art that was indecent or that denigrated a religion, race, ethnic background, age group, or handicap, but the bill retained a ban on federal funding of obscene art. The compromise amendment forbade the use of NEA funds to "promote, disseminate or produce obscene materials, including but not limited to depictions of sadomasochism, homo-eroticism, the sexual exploitation of children, or individuals engaged in sex acts." The two institutions that organized the Serrano and Mapplethorpe exhibitions, Winston-Salem's Southeastern Center for Contemporary Art and Philadelphia's Institute of Contemporary Art, were both placed on one-year probation. Any NEA grants to either organization were to be brought to the attention of two congressional committees that oversaw the NEA.

The NEA also adopted a restriction that required all grant recipients to sign a no-obscenity pledge; artists unanimously saw the move as a threat to the principle of artistic freedom. Joseph Papp, who turned down two large grants, stated that he would continue to do so as long as the no-obscenity oath remained a requirement. Bella Lewitzky, a Los Angeles choreographer, refused a $72,000 NEA grant to her Lewitzky Dance Company, claiming that the episode reminded her of the McCarthyism of the 1950's, when she had refused to testify before the House Committee on Un-American Activities.

Cincinnati, Ohio, became the next battleground for the deceased Mapplethorpe. In advance of the exhibition's April 7, 1990, opening, Citizens for Community Values, a powerful and well-funded 16,000-member organization, sponsored full-page ads in local papers and an extensive letter-writing campaign opposing the use of taxpayers' money to fund obscene art. As a result of the pressure, the chairman of the Contemporary Arts Center, where the exhibit was scheduled to appear, stepped down from his post, and another board member quit outright.

Conservatism had deep roots in Cincinnati, which was the headquarters for the National Coalition Against Pornography and which had purged sex shops, peep shows, X-rated theaters, and nude-dance clubs from its neighborhoods. The Contemporary Arts Center had scheduled the Mapplethorpe exhibition two years prior to its arrival and long before the controversy at the Corcoran. Following the Citizens for Community Values' opposition of the upcoming show, law-enforcement officials urged the museum to cancel the exhibit, announcing that, if it opened, they would seize photographs they deemed obscene.

Dennis Barrie, the director for the Contemporary Arts Center, felt ethically and legally committed to the exhibit, but he made several concessions, including placing the sexually explicit photographs in a separate room with posted warnings about their content and not allowing children to view the works without an adult companion. On opening day, however, anonymous members of a grand jury toured the museum and ruled within a few hours that seven of the 175 photographs on exhibit were obscene, either because they showed sexual acts between men (such as one man urinating into another man's mouth) or showed children with their genitals exposed. Consequently, at 3:00 P.M. on opening day, police raided the gallery, ejected about five hundred viewers, closed the museum for ninety minutes, videotaped Mapplethorpe's work as evidence, and indicted Dennis Barrie. On the following day, the museum was successful in bringing its case to Federal District Court; law-enforcement officials were forbidden from seizing any pictures, ensuring that the exhibit would continue until its scheduled closing date.

Barrie faced a $2000 fine and up to a year in jail if convicted; the museum faced a $10,000 fine. An eight-member jury, however, returned a not-guilty verdict. The antiobscenity lobby had suffered an important setback, but the decision was viewed as good news for the NEA. The grant to the Mapplethorpe exhibit had been for $34,500, which would have made for bad publicity had the verdict been guilty. At the time of the Cincinnati trial, the NEA's mandate was under consideration for a three-year renewal from the federal government.

David A. Ross, the director of the Institute of Contemporary Art in Boston, maintained that the preoccupation with rooting out obscenity had much to do with a prevailing climate of homophobia in the country. In June, 1990, on a recommendation of the National Council on the Arts, a presidential advisory body, the NEA chose not to award grants to four performance artists, three of whom were gay. All four had received NEA funding in the past, and a panel of their peers had already approved the grants.

The controversy over "art versus pornography" will no doubt continue to rage. The debate involving the question of whether depicted homosexual acts are automatically pornographic resurfaced with particular vigor with the closing of the Mapplethorpe show at the Corcoran. The exhibition had played in other cities without much fanfare, but the media attention given to its closing in Washington, D.C., prompted heated congressional debates and angry protests on the street. Was it pornographic smut, as Jesse Helms and the Citizens for Community Values would insist? Or was it what Dennis Barrie declared it was at his trial? In reference to the five photographs alleged to be obscene, Barrie stated that they artistically illustrated the "homosexual subculture of New York City in the 1970's." Of Mapplethorpe, he claimed that his "intention was to take a sometimes tough, sometimes brutal subject matter and bring beauty to it."

Bibliography

Gwynne, S. C., and Barbara Dolan. "Eruptions in the Heartland." *Time* 135 (April 23, 1990): 26-32. Discusses controversy in Cincinnati over the exhibition of works by Mapplethorpe.

McGuigan, Cathleen. "Corcoran Showdown: The Thwarted Mapplethorpe Show Has Bedeviled Congress and Is Tearing Apart a Museum." *Newsweek* 114 (October 9, 1989): 111-112. Another article on the future of the Corcoran in the aftermath of the Mapplethorpe exhibition's cancellation.

Merkel, Jayne. "Art on Trial." *Art in America* 78 (December, 1990): 41-46. An article dealing with the acquittal of Dennis Barrie in the Mapplethorpe exhibition case.

Wallis, Brian. "Can Crippled Corcoran Survive?" *Art in America* 77 (November, 1989): 41-42. A discussion on the future of the Corcoran after its cancellation of the Mapplethorpe exhibit.

——————. "Museum Director Threatened in Mapplethorpe Brouhaha." *Art in America* 78 (September, 1990): 59-61. Discusses Dennis Barrie and the obscenity chrages over the Mapplethorpe exhibit.

Young, Pamela. "Art and Obscenity: The Anti-Obscenity Lobby Has Its Day in Court." *Maclean's* 103 (October 15, 1990): 74-82. Discusses the antiobscenity movement.

Steven C. Kowall

Cross-References

Rivera's Rockefeller Center Mural Is Destroyed (1934), p. 957; Hitler Organizes an Exhibition Denouncing Modern Art (1937), p. 1083; Jasper Johns Paints the American Flag (1954), p. 1590; The National Endowment for the Arts Is Established (1965), p. 2048; Fierstein's *Torch Song Trilogy* Meets with Unexpected Success (1982), p. 2502.

DO THE RIGHT THING ESTABLISHES LEE AS A WORLD-CLASS DIRECTOR

Category of event: Motion pictures
Time: June 30, 1989
Locale: The United States

Do the Right Thing, *Spike Lee's third feature-length film, confronted the existence of racial tension in the United States and confirmed Lee's reputation as a pioneering African-American artist*

> *Principal personages:*
> SPIKE LEE (1957-   ), the writer, director, coproducer, and star of *Do the Right Thing*
> ERNEST DICKERSON (1952-   ), the film's director of photography
> DANNY AIELLO (1933-   ), the actor who played the role of "Sal" in the film

Summary of Event

When *Do the Right Thing* went into production, Spike Lee had already established himself as a provocative filmmaker. He had not, however, completed a project on the scale of *Do the Right Thing*, nor had he shed the label of "promising" young director.

Born in Atlanta in 1957, Lee was reared in Brooklyn. He returned to Atlanta in 1975 to attend Morehouse College, as had his father and grandfather before him. At Morehouse, Lee met Monty Ross, who would become his longtime coproducer. Lee also wrote his first short film at Morehouse. Entitled *Black College: The Talented Tenth*, it examined the minority of African Americans who had entered the American economic mainstream.

After graduating from Morehouse, Lee studied film at New York University (NYU), where he met Ernest Dickerson, who would become the director of photography for Lee's feature films. Lee first attracted notice as a filmmaker while at NYU. After making such student projects as *The Answer*, a provocative retort to the open racism of D. W. Griffith's film classic *The Birth of a Nation* (1915), and *Sarah*, which focuses on a Harlem Thanksgiving Day celebration, Lee teamed up with Dickerson to complete *Joe's Bed-Stuy Barbershop: We Cut Heads* (1983), an hour-long film shot in color. *Joe's Bed-Stuy Barbershop*, which successfully portrayed nuances of black conversation and culture, won a student Academy Award from the Academy of Motion Picture Arts and Sciences and was shown on public television.

After Lee left NYU, his first attempts at making a feature film failed. Lee persisted, however, and began writing and raising funds for *She's Gotta Have It* (1986). Filmed in black and white for a modest $175,000, *She's Gotta Have It* required Lee to make his first contacts with Hollywood film companies. A candid exploration of a black woman's sexuality, the film was a critical and box-office success. It also established the character of Mars Blackmon (played by Lee himself), who would later appear in a popular series of television shoe advertisements made by Lee with basketball star Michael Jordan. Lee's next film, *School Daze* (1988), was shot in color and was completed for about $6 million; the size of the budget made it necessary for Lee to work with a major film company, Columbia Pictures. Though the film, an examination of life at a black college modeled on Morehouse, drew mixed reviews, it earned a profit.

Do the Right Thing constituted a major test for Lee. He arranged for his most substantial budget, $6.5 million, in a deal cut with Universal Pictures. The sum was less than Lee wanted and far less than some motion pictures received; Hollywood was not yet willing to take a major risk on Lee. Nevertheless, Lee was set to make an aggressive exploration of race relations in the United States.

The film revolves around a cast of characters that includes Sal (played by Danny Aiello) and his two sons (one of whom is a blatant racist), Italian-American proprietors of Sal's Famous Pizzeria; Mookie, played by Lee, who delivers pizzas for Sal; Buggin' Out, the neighborhood radical; Smiley, an awkward, stuttering devotee of both Martin Luther King, Jr., and Malcolm X; and Radio Raheem, a massive figure who traverses the neighborhood playing militant rap music on a huge portable cassette player.

Lee unfolds his plot slowly. Buggin' Out has had a conflict with Sal because the pizzeria's "wall of fame" features only photographs of Italian Americans. Buggin' Out believes that black people ought to be represented on the wall, since Sal's customers are nearly all black. He tries to organize a boycott against Sal, but he meets with no success until he gets together with Radio Raheem, who has clashed with Sal over the volume of his music, and Smiley. As Sal is about to close for the day, he good-naturedly decides to remain open at the request of some tardy customers. Buggin' Out and Radio Raheem enter and demand action on the wall of fame. Driven to distraction by Raheem's music, Sal begins to use racial epithets and then destroys Radio Raheem's cassette player.

With this first act of violence, the molehill of a dispute becomes a veritable mountain. Sal and his sons begin to fight with Radio Raheem and his friends, and the fight flows outside the store. Police officers arrive, and one pulls Radio Raheem off Sal by using a choke hold, which he releases only after Raheem is dead. The crowd is stunned and angry. The police leave with Raheem's body, and the crowd begins to turn on Sal and his sons. Mookie grabs a garbage can and throws it through the pizzeria's plate-glass window. The shop is gutted and burned by the crowd; Smiley puts pictures of his two heroes on the wall of fame just before it burns. The crowd then turns menacingly to a store across the way but stops when the store's Korean owner pleads that he, too, is "black." The next morning, Mookie and Sal have a reconciliation of sorts, and the film closes with the display of dueling quotations: one from Martin Luther King, Jr., expounding on the futility of violence, the other from Malcolm X arguing that the use of violence in self-defense is justifiable and intelligent.

Do the Right Thing was both a critical and a commercial success. Lee had created a compelling if somewhat surrealistic image of the Bedford-Stuyvesant neighborhood (where he filmed on location). Once again, Ernest Dickerson's cinematography had been riveting. Lee also had drawn a strong acting performance from Danny Aiello as Sal. Aiello was nominated for an Oscar for his performance, as was Lee for the film's screenplay. The film also made money, becoming Lee's most profitable venture up to that point.

Lee, however, also received criticism for *Do the Right Thing*. He was criticized for having made his Bedford-Stuyvesant block appear more like a stage set than a real urban street with real urban characters, for the film's absence of a clear story line, and for the contrived nature of the film's climax. Critics pointed out that police would not likely leave such a violent crowd unsupervised. Added to this aesthetic criticism were allegations of social irresponsibility. According to many observers, Lee's film was dangerous, since it seemed to encourage inner-city African Americans to look for violent solutions to their problems. For his part, Lee referred to the film's violent scenes as depicting an "uprising" rather than a riot.

Defenders of the film, including Lee himself, pointed out that Lee did not invent riots or the social conditions that fuel them. In addition, the film presents two sides of the issue; Malcolm X's statement is counterbalanced by King's. Moreover, it is not clear that the burning of Sal's pizzeria is an act of self-defense (Malcolm X's precondition for the intelligent use of violence). Buggin' Out is portrayed as silly and boorish; his cause is made to appear trivial, and the violence he inspires ends up being pointless. The film makes this last point by focusing on an elderly black woman during the riot scene; at first, she cheers the crowd on, but she later cries when she sees the result of the crowd's action. The sympathetic treatment of Sal (partly influenced by Aiello) also tempers Lee's message. Finally, it is possible to see Mookie's breaking of the window as an act of moderation, since it draws the crowd's attention away from Sal and his sons and substitutes damage to property for violence against people.

In sum, *Do the Right Thing* confirmed Lee's unique combination of artfulness and box-office appeal. It also made him a controversial figure on matters of race, bringing his talent and ideas to a broader audience.

Impact of Event

Do the Right Thing's box-office and critical success had a major effect both on Lee's own career and on the prospects for other African-American filmmakers in Hollywood. In the wake of his third straight box-office success, Lee was given opportunities to direct *Mo' Better Blues* (1990), about a jazz musician who learns the value of human commitments, *Jungle Fever* (1991), which concerned interracial sexual relations, and *Malcolm X* (1992). Although the first two of these films were successful, they earned Lee further criticism for the use of questionable plot structure and contrived conclusions. In *Malcolm X*, Lee benefited from the powerful nature of his subject matter. Moreover, Lee was at last allowed a big Hollywood budget (about $35 million) to make a film on a theme many white Americans were likely to find threatening, and the result was an intense, well-focused film. Had *Do the Right Thing* not succeeded in establishing both Lee's credentials as a major voice on racial issues as well as his box-office appeal, the opportunity to direct *Malcolm X* would probably not have been given to him. Lee's success created strong pressure on Warner Bros. to use a black director for the story of Malcolm X's life.

The success of *Do the Right Thing* and Lee's other films also opened doors for other young African-American filmmakers such as Matty Rich (*Straight Out of Brooklyn*, 1991), Mario Van Peebles (*New Jack City*, 1991), and John Singleton (*Boyz 'N the Hood*, 1991). These filmmakers did not imitate Lee's style, nor did they, by and large, show Lee's thematic range. They did, however, begin exploring black themes for black audiences with independence and individuality, and their films attracted substantial white audiences as well. Though modest about his influence on younger directors, Lee does see himself as a pioneer; in his book *By Any Means Necessary: The Trials and Tribulations of the Making of Malcolm X* (1992), Lee likened himself to baseball star Jackie Robinson, whose uniform number Lee's character Mookie wore in *Do the Right Thing*. Robinson was uniquely suited to the task of integrating major league baseball; Lee believes he was uniquely suited to the task of opening up Hollywood to a variety of black perspectives.

Though Lee has been a controversial figure, his films and those of other young black directors have encouraged fresh thought about racial equality and racial harmony in the United States. Black audiences for such films have been drawn by the validation of their hopes and concerns; at the same time, white audiences have been challenged to respond to rather than ignore the feelings of black Americans. Most notable, perhaps, is the way in which such films have led white viewers to a greater understanding of the centrality of anger to the experience of black Americans.

Moreover, Lee demonstrated that appealing films could still be made without blockbuster budgets and special effects. He showed that artfulness and serious ideas are compatible with profitability, a lesson of value to directors and producers of any race.

Bibliography

Bogle, Donald. *Blacks in American Film and Television: An Encyclopedia*. New York: Garland, 1988. Provides information on the contributions to and frustrations of African Americans in the film and television industries. Sets Lee's achievements into historical context by pointing out important predecessors. Also focuses on the dearth of film opportunities for African Americans, particularly in directorial roles, and discusses the limits of films in which black culture and perspectives are portrayed by white writers; directors, and producers.

Kendall, Steven D. *New Jack Cinema*. Silver Springs, Md.: J. L. Denser, 1992. Provides a lively introduction to the growth of African-American cinema in the late

1980's and early 1990's. Includes discussion of Lee as well as of younger directors who received a chance to make films aimed at African-American audiences in the wake of Lee's artistic and box-office success.

Lee, Spike, and Lisa Jones. *"Do the Right Thing" : The New Spike Lee Joint.* New York: Simon & Schuster, 1989. Lee has accompanied each of his films with the publication of a book providing background on the film's genesis and actual production. This volume is made especially interesting by the authors' account of dealings with Bedford-Stuyvesant residents during the course of filming on location. The book also discusses the difference of opinion between Lee and Danny Aiello over the film's treatment of Sal as a character.

Lee, Spike, with Ralph Wiley. *By Any Means Necessary: The Trials and Tribulations of the Making of Malcolm X.* New York: Hyperion, 1992. In addition to providing an account of how *Malcolm X* was made, this book fits the film into the context of Lee's previous work. Lee also seizes this opportunity to answer selected critics, including some who associated the 1992 Los Angeles riots with the influence of *Do the Right Thing.*

McMillan, Terry, et al. *Five for Five: The Films of Spike Lee.* New York: Stewart, Tabori & Chang, 1991. Features still photos by David Lee, Spike's brother, covering Spike's first five feature films (through *Jungle Fever*). Each film's photos are preceded by an analytic essay. The authors are all well-known African-American scholars or critics; Nelson George writes on *Do the Right Thing.* An impressive volume. The photos, in stark black and white, are well-chosen, haunting reminders of the films; the essays are insightful and well writtten.

Patterson, Alex. *Spike Lee.* New York: Avon Books, 1992. In this "unauthorized" work, Patterson provides a brief account of Lee's early years, focusing the bulk of attention on Lee's film career. Although critical of Lee's films and personal foibles, Patterson is also deeply impressed by Lee's talent and achievements. He even criticizes some of Lee's more vehement critics. Written in an accessible (if somewhat sketchy) style, this book presents a provocative, gossipy introduction to the Spike Lee phenomenon.

Ira Smolensky

Cross-References

The Harlem Renaissance Celebrates African-American Culture (1920's), p. 480; Wright's *Native Son* Depicts Racism in America (1940), p. 1185; Ellison's *Invisible Man* Is Published (1952), p. 1541; Poitier Emerges as a Film Star in *The Blackboard Jungle* (1955), p. 1650; Baldwin Voices Black Rage in *The Fire Next Time* (1963), p. 1929; *The Autobiography of Malcolm X* Is Published (1965), p. 2022; *The Wiz* Brings African-American Talent to Broadway (1975), p. 2334; *Roots* Dramatizes the African-American Experience (1977), p. 2397; *The Cosby Show* Makes Television History (1984), p. 2532; Innovative Black Filmmakers Achieve Success (Late 1980's), p. 2565.

DISNEY EMERGES AS AN ARCHITECTURAL PATRON

Category of event: Architecture
Time: The early 1990's
Locale: Burbank, California; Orlando, Florida; and Marne-la-Vallée, France

By commissioning world-renowned architects to design high-profile buildings around the world, the Walt Disney Company established an unprecedented system of corporate patronage

> *Principal personages:*
> MICHAEL EISNER (1942-   ), the chairman and chief executive officer of the Walt Disney Company
> MICHAEL GRAVES (1934-   ), a Princeton, New Jersey-based architect best known for his designs of classically inspired corporate buildings and whimsical tea kettles
> ROBERT A. M. STERN (1939-   ), a New York-based architect known for designing opulent private residences on Long Island
> ARATA ISOZAKI (1931-   ), a Tokyo-based architect known for designing museums and other cultural buildings
> FRANK GEHRY (1929-   ), a Los Angeles-based architect known for his use of industrial materials on corporate and cultural buildings
> ANTOINE PREDOCK (1932-   ), an Albuquerque, New Mexico-based architect known for his use of bold "desert colors" on residential and cultural buildings
> ANTOINE GRUMBACH (1935-   ), a Paris-based architect known for designing corporate and cultural buildings

Summary of Event

At a spring, 1990, press conference heralding the opening of the Swan Hotel at Walt Disney World in Orlando, Florida, Walt Disney Company chairman and chief executive officer Michael D. Eisner announced that the world was entering the "Disney Decade." Typical corporate hyperbole, perhaps, but Eisner's declaration may have been prophetic. The architectural world, at least, was entering a new era, one in which a single corporation would champion contemporary architects with an unprecedented vigor.

Between 1990 and 1992, eighteen buildings by nine respected, world-renowned architects were constructed at three different Disney locations, with dozens more in the planning stages. From hotels to shopping malls to corporate headquarters, these buildings signaled that the Disney organization had made the leap from architectural enthusiast to patron.

Disney's patronage began in 1984, when Eisner became chairman and chief executive officer after an eight-year stint as president of Paramount Pictures. Eisner had always been interested in architecture, and assuming the helm at Disney gave him corporate backing for his interest. In 1985, he established the Disney Development Company, a subsidiary designed to oversee all land development and planning outside the corporation's theme-park gates. Headed by president Peter Rummell, who came to Disney with a background in real estate and finance, and senior vice president Wing Chao, a Disney veteran with a degree in architecture from Harvard, the Disney Development Company set out to make Eisner's architectural dreams a reality.

Eisner was particularly fascinated by corporate architecture and the different images it could project. Insisting that Disney was in the entertainment business above all else, he began studying architects in order to decide just whom he trusted with his corporate message. After visiting buildings, reading books, and attending lectures, he knew what he wanted. In the late 1980's, he commissioned Michael Graves to design the Team Disney headquarters building on Disney's Burbank, California, lot and the Swan and Dolphin hotels at Walt Disney World in Orlando.

Graves was an obvious first choice. Known for colorful, classically inspired buildings, Graves was considered a big-name, serious architect, but one who could never be accused of being too serious. At the time, he was best known for the Humana Corporation Headquarters Building in Louisville, Kentucky (1983) and the Portland Civic Center Building in Portland, Oregon (1983). By the late 1980's, he was one of the country's best-known architects.

When the Team Disney building was built, it generated considerable controversy in the architectural press. How, many critics asked, could anyone take a building decorated with the Seven Dwarfs seriously? Other critics agreed with Graves that the name "Disney" meant fun, and nineteen-foot-tall dwarfs were certainly fun.

Eisner also agreed. Shortly after seeing the design for the Team Disney building, he commissioned Graves to design two hotels at Walt Disney World. The Swan and Dolphin Hotels opened in early 1990, with such features as two twenty-eight-ton turquoise swans in front of the Swan Hotel and winsome dolphins decorating every conceivable surface of the Dolphin Hotel. Distinctly nontraditional buildings, they also received significant publicity. Again, Eisner was pleased. The hotels projected his message: "We're not about safe-deposit boxes. We're in the entertainment business."

As Disney World expanded, so did Eisner's roster of big-name architects. Disney owned 28,000 acres at Disney World, and some of the world's best-known architects were given the task of turning that acreage into entertainment in three dimensions. Robert A. M. Stern, a New Yorker best known for designing opulent private residences on Long Island, designed the Yacht and Beach Clubs, twin resorts wrapped around a manmade lagoon. Stern was another obvious choice; his architectural style, both pre-Disney and for Disney, closely resembled the work of the company's in-house designers, Walt Disney Imagineering. The Imagineers, who were responsible for almost every Disney building and attraction until the Eisner era, were experts at themed architecture such as that found on Main Street U.S.A. and New Orleans Square at Disneyland. Stern's Disney World hotels followed the Imagineering lead:

They were nostalgic, storybook versions of the great East Coast resorts of the turn of the century. Eisner was satisfied; he continued giving Stern commissions, and in 1991, Stern became a member of the Disney board of directors.

The most unusual job at Walt Disney World went to Arata Isozaki, one of Japan's best-loved architects, who was known in the United States for having designed the Los Angeles Museum of Contemporary Art (1986). Eisner's mandate to Isozaki was to design a building that expressed the notion of time, one of Eisner's self-acknowledged obsessions. Isozaki responded with a combination of pure geometric forms, the centerpiece of which was a 120-foot tilted cone, open to the sky, with a sundial perched on its rim. An ambitious building, Team Disney was definitely not cast in the Imagineering mold, yet it was nevertheless a themed building.

Two years after Eisner announced his "Disney Decade," Euro Disney opened at Marne-la-Vallée, twenty miles east of Paris. The planning of Euro Disney's theme parks and hotels began in 1988, when a group of architects, including Eisner favorites Graves and Stern, redesigned the park's master plan. They then implemented it. When the $4.4 billion, 4,800-acre Euro Disney opened in the spring of 1992, six hotels, an entertainment center, a campground, and a theme park were in place.

The individual hotels at Euro Disney were themselves part of a larger theme: Each represented a region of the United States. Stern designed the Hotel Newport Bay Club; Antoine Predock of Albuquerque, New Mexico, was responsible for the Hotel Santa Fe; Hotel New York was designed by Michael Graves; the lone European, Antoine Grumbach of Paris, built the Sequoia Lodge; and Stern also designed the Hotel Cheyenne. By far the most innovative aspect of Euro Disney, and the only one not overtly themed, was Festival Disney, a collection of restaurants, shops, and theaters by Los Angeles architect Frank Gehry. Festival Disney was an amalgamation of jagged building forms with a central, angled midway. Stainless-steel pylons reached into the sky, with a canopy of tiny white lights topping the pylons.

In just two short years, Eisner's "Disney Decade" was well under way. He had buildings by some of the world's most famous architects, and through these buildings, the Walt Disney Company had a new, more adventurous corporate image.

Impact of Event

Patronage has been a part of architecture since the profession began. From Egyptian pyramids to Italian Renaissance palazzos to huge steel-and-glass towers on Madison Avenue, powerful leaders have cultivated illustrious architects whose talents have been used to express their patrons' position and influence. In that respect, Michael Eisner and the Walt Disney Company are part of an age-old tradition.

Yet there are differences between the Disney style of patronage and the way it traditionally has been practiced. Unlike conventional patrons, Eisner did not choose and cultivate a single architect. Instead, he enlisted the services of more than a dozen of the best-known contemporary architects, repeatedly commissioning them to design some of the world's most high-profile buildings.

The outcome of Disney's architectural patronage also has been different from that of traditional patronage. Rather than designing buildings intended to glorify the patron, the architects working for Disney designed buildings for the average citizen. First in Florida and then in France, anyone who entered the gates of the Magic Kingdom could experience and appreciate architecture by some of the world's best-known architects. Thanks to Eisner's efforts, high-art architecture became accessible to the masses.

Not everyone was pleased with this development. From the time Graves' Team Disney building in Burbank was announced, Eisner and his grand scheme for Disney architecture became a favorite controversy among architects and the architectural—and, in time, the general—press. With each new building, the controversy grew; by the time Euro Disney opened, French critics were calling the theme park a "cultural Chernobyl."

Some architects refused to join the new Disney populism. British architect James Stirling, the 1991 winner of the prestigious Pritzker architecture prize, turned down an offer from Eisner. "We're not very sympathetic to the theme idea," he explained. "To me, it seems demeaning and trivial and somehow not profound or important." Even Frank Gehry, who in fact took up Eisner's offer and designed Festival Disney at Euro Disney, had second thoughts about the idea of mixing architecture and entertainment. He acknowledged that "it's precarious to be co-opted by Mickey Mouse."

In reality, no architect had to be co-opted by Disney; all had the option of turning down Eisner's offers, yet the offers usually were too lucrative to refuse. In the worldwide economic downturn of the late 1980's and the early 1990's, the institutional and cultural commissions that traditionally have been the path to architectural fame and success began to disappear. Even the best-known architects had to compete more fiercely for the few plum projects, and Eisner's enthusiasm was most welcome. Arata Isozaki admitted that he was questioned quite strongly when he accepted Disney commissions, yet he accepted the challenge, and his Orlando Team Disney headquarters is one of the most interesting of the new Disney buildings.

Rather than overtly trying to co-opt anyone, in certain ways Eisner was trying to give the public what it wanted. In the 1980's, architecture began to become simultaneously more commercial and more accessible to the general public; more general-interest books on the subject were published than ever before, and major museums mounted more architecture and design shows than they ever had. Architects began designing everyday objects such as furniture, silverware, and scarves in unprecedented numbers, and the public kept buying them. Architecture and design became mainstream. Eisner read the public and used an emerging trend to Disney's advantage.

Which is exactly what Walt Disney himself had done fifty years earlier. He made his reputation and fortune by drawing flat cartoon images and setting them into motion. When his animation efforts became hugely popular in the mid-1950's, he made them three-dimensional and built a town for them in Anaheim, California. Then he invited the public to come visit.

Eisner's task was tougher: The generation he needed to attract to his new theme parks grew up watching Disney and visiting Disneyland. Consumers were more sophisticated in the 1990's than they were in the 1950's, and they needed more sophisticated entertainment. Eisner took a chance that world-class architecture could provide that sophistication. In bringing famous architects and their work to the general public, he established a system of corporate patronage that seemed likely to remain unrivaled.

Bibliography

Andersen, Kurt. "Look, Mickey, No Kitsch!" *Time* 138 (July 29, 1991): 66-69. A general-interest look at the Walt Disney Company's architectural patronage. Andersen takes a genial stance toward Eisner and his ambitions, characterizing him as an enlightened despot. The accompanying sidebars on some of the architects attempt, somewhat clumsily, to explain the new buildings to the general public.
Branch, Mark Alden. "Why (and How) Does Disney Do It?" *Progressive Architecture* 71 (October, 1990): 78-81. A critical article attempting to understand Disney's place in the world of contemporary architecture. Branch concludes that although Disney architecture is not serious architecture because it occurs in an artificial, controlled environment, the company should be commended for bringing buildings by famous architects to the general public.
Brown, Patricia Leigh. "Disney Deco." *The New York Times Magazine* (April 8, 1990): 28. A comprehensive general-interest article about Disney's architectural commissions, including descriptions of the buildings. The author interviewed Michael Eisner and many of his architects in her attempt to understand why Eisner is commissioning famous architects.
Goldberger, Paul. "And Now, an Architectural Kingdom." *The New York Times Magazine* (April 8, 1990): 44-45. A critical companion to Patricia Leigh Brown's article in the same issue. Goldberger, then *The New York Times'* architecture critic, attempts to understand how Disney and "big-time" architecture fit together. He concludes that in the last decade of the twentieth century, architecture and entertainment, which had been moving together for years, finally reached a powerful intersection.
Scully, Vincent. "Animal Spirits." *Progressive Architecture* 71 (October, 1990): 89-90. One of the country's best-known architectural historians and a former professor at Yale University, Scully is perplexed by Disney's new architectural agenda. He likes the Swan and Dolphin hotels but laments the loss of innocence they seem to signify, and he admits that he misses Mickey Mouse.
Stephens, Suzanne. "Manifest Disney." *Architectural Record* 180 (June, 1992): 54-59. A critical review of Euro Disney that asks some important questions about the future of "entertainment architecture." After describing the buildings by the "high-design" architects, Stephens concludes that the architectural efforts at Euro Disney ultimately fail to offer either an escape from everyday life or a serious intellectual challenge.
Tetlow, Karin, Justin Henderson, Jean Gorman, and Beverly Russell. *Interiors* 151

(May, 1992): 118-171. The entire issue is devoted to the Disney Development Company, which was the winner of the journal's fourth "Corporate America Design Award." The authors take a systematic, noncritical approach to Disney's architectural program, giving detailed descriptions of each new building at each location. A good, albeit somewhat superficial, overview of the buildings themselves.

Terri Hartman

Cross-References

German Artists Found the Bauhaus (1919), p. 463; Le Corbusier's Villa Savoye Redefines Architecture (1931), p. 869; Aalto Designs Villa Mairea (1937), p. 1067; The AT&T Building Exemplifies Postmodernism (1978), p. 2407; Deconstructivists Exhibit at the Museum of Modern Art (1988), p. 2614.

THE SIMPSONS DEBUTS, ANCHORING
THE FLEDGLING FOX NETWORK

Category of event: Television and radio
Time: January 14, 1990
Locale: The United States

The first prime-time cartoon on television in nearly two decades, The Simpsons *struck a nerve in American society and helped to launch a new network*

Principal personages:
MATT GROENING (1954-   ), an alternative comic-strip artist who created *The Simpsons* and became one of its executive producers
JAMES L. BROOKS (1940-   ), an award-winning producer-director and executive producer of the show
SAM SIMON, a television situation-comedy writer and one of the show's executive producers
BARRY DILLER (1942-   ), a former chief of Paramount Pictures and the head of Fox Studios when *The Simpsons* debuted
RUPERT MURDOCH (1931-   ), the Australian-born media mogul who owned Twentieth Century-Fox Studios and the Fox network when *The Simpsons* debuted

Summary of Event

When *The Simpsons* made its series debut on January 14, 1990, as the first prime-time, animated series on television since *The Flintstones* and *The Jetsons* of the early 1960's, it represented not only an enormously successful venture for the fledgling fourth network, Fox, but also a bona fide cultural phenomenon. This seemingly modest situation comedy had ramifications far beyond those caused by usual network fare.

The Simpsons was the brainchild of alternative cartoonist Matt Groening, who had previously been best known as the creator of *Life in Hell*, a weekly comic strip syndicated in more than two hundred alternative and college newspapers. Groening, the son of parents named Homer and Margaret, grew up in Portland, Oregon, and attended Evergreen State College in Olympia, Washington, a progressive institution that gave neither examinations nor grades. He thrived in this unstructured environment, working on the school newspaper and studying journalism, literature, philosophy, and filmmaking.

After graduating in 1977, Groening moved to Los Angeles to launch a writing career. His life there initially proved so miserable that he began sketching comic strips to express his anger and frustration. These strips eventually evolved into *Life in Hell*, which appeared for the first time in the *Los Angeles Reader* in April of 1980. By 1988, the cartoon strip had turned into a successful proposition, spawning calendars, greeting cards, T-shirts, posters, and the popular book collections *Work Is Hell*

(1986), *School Is Hell* (1987), and *Childhood Is Hell* (1988).

In 1987, James L. Brooks, the Emmy Award-winning creator of *The Mary Tyler Moore Show* and *Taxi* and the Oscar-winning director of *Terms of Endearment* (1983) and *Broadcast News* (1987), asked Groening to create a series of animated "bumpers" from his strip to air between skits on Fox Broadcasting's *The Tracey Ullman Show*, which his company produced. Instead, Groening created a new set of characters, who appeared in forty-nine fifteen-to-twenty-second segments on the show. From this modest beginning, the Simpson family was born. The segments proved so popular that Fox requested thirteen half-hour episodes to debut in 1989. Groening and Brooks, together with situation-comedy writer Sam Simon, became executive producers of Fox's newest show, *The Simpsons*.

The Simpsons actually debuted on December 17, 1989, with a Christmas special, which was repeated on December 23; the regular series debuted on January 14, 1990. The series became an almost immediate hit, zooming into the top fifteen of the A. C. Nielsen ratings within two months of its debut (at a time when the Fox network reached only four-fifths of the country). The Simpson family captured the national imagination, appealing particularly to America's youth, and it gave rise to a variety of commercial products, and was the topic of much commentary and editorializing. Fox moved the phenomenally popular show to Thursday night opposite *The Cosby Show*, an established, long-running National Broadcasting Company (NBC) hit, in a move calculated to bring even more publicity to the series and the brash new network. The programming move was discussed in terms of David and Goliath: the young, upstart network bravely challenging the establishment culture and doing very well indeed.

The Simpson family hails from the fictional all-American town of Springfield (not coincidentally, the name of the hometown of the Anderson family of *Father Knows Best*) and is headed by bald, overweight Homer, a dim bulb who is totally unqualified for his job as safety inspector at the local nuclear power plant. Fond of doughnuts and Duff beer (the local brew), Homer dispenses such bad advice to his children as "Never say anything until you're sure everyone feels exactly the same way" and "Being popular is the most important thing in the whole world." His wife, Marge, whose most distinctive features are her towering blue beehive hairdo and throaty voice, is more intelligent and sensitive than Homer (she was an ardent, although somewhat clueless, feminist when she met Homer in high school), but she too is overwhelmed by the world. Ten-year-old Bart (an anagram for brat) is an authority-flouting, wisecracking smart aleck whose favorite expressions, "Ay, caramba," "Don't have a cow, man," and "Eat my shorts," quickly became standards in the repartee of the young. His sister Lisa, an eight-year-old intellectual and virtuoso jazz saxophone player, is often the family's lone voice of reason. Maggie, the baby, merely observes the proceedings in silence, sucking her ever-present pacifier.

The show is populated with recurring characters, including Moe, the local bartender; Mr. Burns, Homer's Scrooge-like boss; the next-door neighbors, a perfect *Father Knows Best* family; the mayor of Springfield, a Kennedy look-and-sound-alike politician; Krusty the Klown, a local television celebrity; and Itchy and Scratchy, stars of the gruesomely violent cartoon within a cartoon. The show turns the usual television sitcom on its ear and is full of pointed cultural references, subtle irony, and satire clearly aimed at an intelligent adult audience.

Impact of Event

The Simpsons had an immediate impact on popular culture in early 1990. The characters appeared on the covers of *Rolling Stone* and *Newsweek*, among other magazines, and on the tongues of social and cultural commentators. Commercial spin-offs, including T-shirts, posters, talking Bart dolls, and watches, were omnipresent. College students threw Simpsons parties, Marge and Bart costumes appeared at Halloween, even the Los Angeles Lakers declared *The Simpsons* their favorite program. A New York research company announced that Bart ranked with sports stars Michael Jordan and Bo Jackson as the top hero of preteen boys. Clearly a more intelligent show than the average television fare, *The Simpsons* aimed simultaneously at an audience of children and adults, portraying the lowest common denominator while never pandering to it.

Many observers saw *The Simpsons* as an indication of the decline of American values; some educators banned Bart Simpson T-shirts, particularly those bearing the slogan "Underachiever and Proud of It." Many believed that Bart glorified all that was wrong with the youth of the 1990's; he was irreverent, undisciplined, and unmotivated, and they were horrified that he had become a folk hero. Even drug czar William Bennett denounced him, but Bennett retreated from his position when it caused public outcry.

To many, the state of the television situation comedy has come to reflect the state of the American family. One commentator has stated that television "has come to reflect its context in its content, becoming the ritual of and about the family. Everything's okay, it says: the most outrageous problems can all be resolved, with wit and mutual trust, within a half-hour of teleplay." In this context, *The Simpsons* falls into the tradition of "anti-situation comedy" that began with *The Life of Riley* and *The Honeymooners* in the 1950's and continued with *All in the Family* in the 1970's.

Groening himself describes *The Simpsons* as "a mutant *Ozzie and Harriet*" that joins such programs as *Roseanne* and *Married . . . with Children* in exposing the more squalid aspects of family life; each of these programs focuses on working-class families rather than on the upper-middle-class households portrayed in *Father Knows Best* and *Leave It to Beaver.* Some psychologists claim that these depictions of the "perfect" family induce feelings of guilt, because viewers cannot live up to the impossible ideal presented. The unidealized pictures presented in these "antifamily" comedies, on the other hand, induce feelings of sympathy and identification that are more comforting. Depending on the viewer, these depictions either signal the decline and fall of the American family or lend a welcome dose of reality to television.

Irreverent Bart Simpson is symbolic not only of the changing American family but also of the network that gave him a home. If Bart represents the family, then Fox represents the shifting sands of the network television industry. Like the staid sitcoms of the 1950's and 1960's, the "big three" networks—NBC, the American Broadcasting Company (ABC), and the Columbia Broadcasting System (CBS)—seemed an inevitable and invincible part of the American scene. Although constantly vying for supremacy, they ruled the airwaves virtually uncontested. With the advent of cable and videotape technology, however, the networks' monopoly began to crumble, and in 1986 another small chink was made in their armor when Rupert Murdoch, who had purchased Twentieth Century-Fox studios and a group of independent television stations, announced his plans for a fourth network. Led by chairman Barry Diller, Fox debuted with a single night of shows in the spring of 1987 and by 1990 had expanded to three nights of programming. While the network had modest success, *The Simpsons* brought Fox into direct competition with the major networks.

Fox succeeded as Bart did, by being brash and aggressive and appealing to the young and hip. Its strategy has been to appeal to the eighteen-to-thirty-four-year-old age group that advertisers prefer and to take more chances than the established networks. Shows such as *In Living Color, Married . . . with Children*, and such offbeat fare as *It's Garry Shandling's Show* and *Alien Nation* represented Fox's willingness to try something new. The network attempted to corner the teen market, first with *Twenty-one Jump Street* and later with the overwhelmingly popular *Beverly Hills 90210*. In self-defense, the other three networks were forced to follow suit, admitting that Fox had opened doors for them. Although Fox continued to run clearly behind the established networks, it encouraged in them a spirit of daring and experimentation.

Newsweek commentator Meg Greenfield, admitting her fondness for *The Simpsons*, called it a "faithful sendup of all that is pretentious, self-important, compulsive, absurd, two-faced, pitiful and deranged in our commonplace lives. They are realistic and funny and recognizable and thus easy to get interested in and eventually hooked on." Frank McConnell observed in *Commonweal* that the genius of *The Simpsons* "is that it deconstructs the myth of the happy family wisely and miraculously leaves what is real and valuable about the myth unscathed." Its most lasting impact on society is likely to be just this: It has revealed to viewers something about themselves and their society, which is what the best of any art form is meant to do.

Bibliography

Elder, Sean. "Is TV the Coolest Invention Ever Invented?" *Mother Jones* 14 (December, 1989): 28-31. Written on the eve of *The Simpsons'* success, interview with Groening explores his thoughts on *The Simpsons*, the success of *Life in Hell*, and biographical material.

Walters, Harry F. "Family Feuds." *Newsweek* 115 (April 23, 1990): 58-62. Offers an overview of the history of the show, its impact on society, and its influence on the fortunes of the Fox Network. Places *The Simpsons* in the context of the history of the television situation comedy.

Zehme, Bill. "The Only Real People on TV." *Rolling Stone* 581 (June 28, 1990): 41-47. Written as an "interview" of the Simpsons; the author takes a trip to Springfield to visit the family. Also includes a brief interview with Groening, Brooks, and Simon as themselves.

Zoglin, Richard. "The Fox Trots Faster." *Time* 146 (August 27, 1990): 64-66. Presents a history of the Fox Network and the show's effect on the network. Also discusses Fox's impact on the three major networks and the direction of television in the future.

_____. "Home Is Where the Venom Is." *Time* 135 (April 16, 1990): 85-86. Discusses the "antifamily" situation comedy, including *Roseanne*, *Married . . . with Children*, and *The Simpsons*. Compares these shows to more conventional sitcoms such as *Ozzie and Harriet* and *The Cosby Show*.

Mary Virginia Davis

Cross-References

NBC and CBS Launch Commercial Television (1941), p. 1211; Television Family Comedy Becomes Extremely Popular (1950's), p. 1470; Situation Comedies Dominate Television Programming (1960's), p. 1835; *The Flintstones* Popularizes Prime-Time Cartoons (1960), p. 1840; *All in the Family* Introduces a New Style of Television Comedy (1971), p. 2234; *The Cosby Show* Makes Television History (1984), p. 2532; The Decline of the Big Three Networks Becomes a Fall (Late 1980's), p. 2554.

THE CIVIL WAR RIVETS THE ATTENTION OF THE UNITED STATES

Category of event: Television and radio
Time: September 23-27, 1990
Locale: The United States

The broadcast, over five consecutive nights, of Ken Burns's eleven-hour documentary The Civil War *drew the largest audience in the history of public television to a masterful meditation on national identity*

Principal personages:
KEN BURNS (1954-   ), the producer, director, cowriter, and cocinematographer of *The Civil War*
SHELBY FOOTE (1916-   ), a novelist, the program's principal on-camera commentator
RIC BURNS (1956-   ), the brother of Ken, the program's coproducer and cowriter
GEOFFREY C. WARD (1940-   ), the program's principal writer
DAVID MCCULLOUGH (1933-   ), a historian, the program's narrator

Summary of Event

For five consecutive nights in September, 1990, an estimated thirty-nine million Americans were mesmerized by a television documentary broadcast by the Public Broadcasting Service (PBS). The project, culled from 150 hours of footage, was a marvel of filmmaking and a triumph of public broadcasting. It took director, coproducer, cowriter, and cocinematographer Ken Burns five years to make *The Civil War*, longer than it took the North and the South to begin and conclude the Civil War itself. Eleven hours is a sizable investment of time, but no viewer would wish the program one minute shorter. "Our *Iliad* has found its Homer," wrote critic George F. Will of thirty-six-year-old Burns. Though each had won considerable acclaim, Burns's earlier forays into American history—*Brooklyn Bridge* (1982), *The Shakers: Hands to Work, Hearts to God* (1984), *Huey Long* (1985), *The Statue of Liberty* (1986), *Thomas Hart Benton* (1988), and *The Congress* (1989)—seemed in retrospect but a rehearsal for his magisterial survey of and meditation on the nation's most traumatic episode.

More than a million photographs were taken during the Civil War, and rather than rely on specious reenactments, Burns constructed his film almost entirely out of photographs of the era, using not only familiar Mathew Brady stills but also thousands of other pictures assembled from archives and attics. Many, like a shot of Abraham Lincoln's Second Inaugural Address that was enlarged to reveal John Wilkes Booth as a face in the crowd, astonished even those who thought they knew the period. All lifted the Civil War out of mythic abstraction and into a dense historical moment. *The Civil War*'s viewers observed actual human beings, as though gazing at a family album.

The images on the screen—also including lithographs, headlines, and newsreel footage of military reunions—were accompanied by voiceover quotations from letters, diaries, and other written testimony. The journals of Southern belle Mary Chesnut and New York lawyer George Templeton Strong provided dramatically different vantage points. Burns recreated history from the bottom up, and though he offered engaging, and at times unexpected, portraits of political and military leaders such as Lincoln, Jefferson Davis, Ulysses S. Grant, Robert E. Lee, Frederick Douglass, Nathan Bedford Forrest, and William T. Sherman, he also followed the fortunes of more obscure figures—in particular, two foot soldiers, one in blue and one in gray. Excerpts from a diary enabled viewers to trace the trajectory of Elisha Hunt Rhodes, who left Rhode Island as a private in 1861 and returned as a colonel in 1865. The memoirs of Sam Watkins, a volunteer in Company H of the 1st Tennessee, bore witness to every major campaign fought in the Western theater.

Burns's choices of voices were especially inspired—not only professional actors Sam Waterston, Julie Harris, Jason Robards, Morgan Freeman, Derek Jacobi, Jeremy Irons, and Colleen Dewhurst, but also such odd but effective speakers as Garrison Keillor, Arthur Miller, Jody Powell, Studs Terkel, Kurt Vonnegut, and George Plimpton. Historian David McCullough provided running narration in a steady, patient, Tiresias-like voice that suggested hard-earned wisdom and inconsolable grief. Historians Shelby Foote, Barbara Fields, Stephen Oates, C. Vann Woodward, and others spoke into the camera and out of knowledge and passion.

The Civil War was attentive to the battlefield strategies of commanders who were at times brilliant, audacious, timorous, and stupid. The program, though, was not merely chessboard military history; viewers mingled in the ranks at Antietam, the bloodiest encounter in American history, when twice as many lives were lost as on D day. The program explored the political collisions that led to continental catastrophe, acknowledging the complexities of the confrontation in the fact that Unionists from every Southern state but South Carolina sent regiments to join the North and that the Union cause was bitterly reviled throughout the North; in the New York draft riots of July, 1863, angry mobs attacked and murdered blacks and their sympathizers.

Slavery, even more than sectional pride and prerogatives, was, according to *The Civil War*, central to the conflict. If abolition was not the major objective of the Lincoln Administration in 1861, when every seventh American was legal chattel, by 1865, when ten percent of the Union Army was black, the war had become a struggle over the meaning of freedom. It became, according to Oates, "a testament for the liberation of the human spirit for all time." Its legacy lingered in an incomplete agenda of social justice. This very uncivil war also, as Burns demonstrated, forever altered the role of women in American society.

A lonely cannon set against a radiant sunset was the program's signature image, and period music, performed plaintively on solo fiddle or piano, accompanied the entire experience. For many of the three million soldiers who marched off to defend their cause, the Civil War was, in McCullough's words, "the greatest adventure of their lives." The war inspired acts of transcendent valor, but it also enabled unscrupulous entrepreneurs to enrich themselves through sales of shoddy goods. It was a field of honor but also an occasion for selfish gain; two days after Manassas, a battle that cost five thousand casualties, speculators bought up the real estate as a tourist attraction. *The Civil War* documented wanton atrocities committed by armies from both sides of the Mason-Dixon line.

Though its nine episodes followed a loose chronology from 1861 through 1865, *The Civil War* paused occasionally from the inexorable course of conflict to examine the textures of life at mid-century. Episode 7, for example, studied such activities as espionage, prostitution, gambling, and profiteering. No viewer could help but profit from the rich experience. "Any understanding of this nation has to be based on an understanding of the Civil War," declared Foote. "It defines us." Not even eleven hours is sufficient for a national definition, but *The Civil War* brought viewers closer to an understanding of American dreams and nightmares than any other television project, except perhaps the ambitious venture that Burns began to work on next: a history of baseball.

Impact of Event

Episode 1 of *The Civil War*, which inaugurated the PBS fall season, received a rating of nine and an audience share of thirteen according to the A. C. Nielsen survey of the thirteen largest American media markets—figures that were records for a PBS broadcast. Episode 2 surpassed even that, and the entire series reached the kind of mass audience expected only of commercial networks. An investment of $2.8 million and five years was rewarded with popular and critical success. *The Civil War*, which was underwritten by General Motors, the National Endowment for the Humanities, the Corporation for Public Broadcasting, the Arthur Vining Davis Foundations, and the John D. and Catherine T. MacArthur Foundation, went on to win two Emmy Awards and the affection of millions.

A book—*The Civil War: An Illustrated History*, by Geoffrey C. Ward with Ric Burns and Ken Burns—designed as a companion to the series sold close to a million copies for publisher Alfred A. Knopf, and videocassettes of all nine episodes likewise did brisk business. So, too, did a recording, *Songs of the Civil War*, of music featured in the film. Union soldier Sullivan Ballou achieved belated, posthumous renown when the letter he wrote to his wife on the eve of the Battle of Bull Run was broadcast at the end of Episode 1; Ballou's letter was reprinted, recorded, and widely quoted. Ken Burns, the series' unprepossessing creator, became an unlikely celebrity and the recipient of eight honorary doctorates. *Empire of the Air*, a televised history of radio that Burns developed while working on a vast documentary about baseball, was eagerly anticipated and, when broadcast on PBS in early 1992, was well received.

The success of *The Civil War* demonstrated the continuing viability of the miniseries, a television form that had been languishing more than a decade after 1977's *Roots* had proved so compelling that audiences sat watching night after night. Burns also attracted uncustomary, if temporary, attention to nonfiction film, a genre largely neglected by programmers and audiences. Yet PBS remained one of the few institutions hospitable to both the production and exhibition of a work with the magnitude and purpose of *The Civil War*. Even with his post-*Civil War* prominence, Burns continued to work with public broadcasting, where his productions were not constrained by time or content or diluted and diverted by commercial breaks.

If PBS was the electronic benefactor of *The Civil War*, the series was a timely boon to public television, a system that depends financially on contributions from viewers, corporate underwriters, foundation grants, and government allocations. Despite a feeble economy, donations to PBS affiliates increased by 8.4 percent in 1991, and much of the increase could reasonably be attributed to the popularity of *The Civil War*, both in its initial run and in subsequent rebroadcasts. Presentation of the film was a powerful tool for local affiliates during periodic membership drives. Washington, D.C.'s WETA reported that viewers pledged $500,000 during breaks between a rebroadcast of *The Civil War*—the largest sum ever raised by any one program.

As important as the contributions of the broadcast to the fiscal fitness of PBS was the credibility that *The Civil War* provided for the beleaguered network. Two decades after its 1970 founding, PBS was under attack by angry and influential conservatives who questioned whether, after the proliferation of channels through cable technology, taxpayers needed to be subsidizing any television operation. Conservative critics, moreover, took particular exception to the left-wing political bias and subversion of mainstream American values that they insisted were characteristic of PBS. The attack on PBS was similar to that leveled against the National Endowment for the Humanities (NEH) and the National Endowment for the Arts as alleged patrons of cultural decadence. Congressional defenders of PBS's mission pointed to *The Civil War*, a project admired across the political spectrum, as a powerful—and successful—argument for reauthorization of the Corporation for Public Broadcasting. Likewise, the fact that it had provided partial support for *The Civil War* was an important factor in the victorious battle to sustain the NEH.

The Civil War was initially broadcast while the United States was again preparing for military battle. In August, 1990, Saddam Hussein's Iraqi troops had invaded Kuwait, and the United Nations Security Council, meeting in emergency session, had issued an ultimatum insisting on unconditional and complete withdrawal. As an inducement to comply, economic sanctions were imposed against Iraq, and, throughout the fall, while forces were massing in the Middle East, Americans debated the efficacy of the measures and when, or whether, to escalate the confrontation into open warfare. Burns's study of the causes and costs of organized carnage both reflected and helped shape the mood of America on the eve of the Persian Gulf War. An extraordinary session of Congress was convoked in order to determine whether to authorize President George Bush to take military action against Iraq. During the televised debate, in which almost every member of the Senate and the House of Representatives spoke, *The Civil War* was frequently mentioned and quoted, by both those supporting a strike against Iraq and those opposing one. The United States did go to war in January, 1991, and the memory of another conflict, as interpreted by Burns, was vivid in the minds of both those who prosecuted and those who protested the current one. After the shooting stopped, Burns told a reporter that, when he met General Norman Schwarzkopf, the commander of Operation Desert Storm had explained the influence that *The Civil War* had exerted on him: "I watched the show every night while I was planning the campaign. It made me understand that the arrows on my maps were real human lives."

Newspapers during the Civil War reported a curious phenomenon called "acoustic shadows." Often, the harrowing din of conflict thundered in the ears of listeners many miles away, while in the immediate vicinity of battle an eerie silence reigned. The United States' most traumatic ordeal, a bloody struggle that cost more than 600,000 lives—two percent of the nation's population—cast acoustic shadows over its weary survivors. Yet 125 years after Appomattox, the echoes of it all, broadcast throughout the United States and as far away as Australia, were thunderous.

Though the question is itself evidence of passions lingering from the distant debacle, it is impossible to say whether *The Civil War* was pro-Union or pro-Confederacy. Burns's documentary was, instead, profoundly respectful of the complexities of human entanglement. "Useless, useless" were John Wilkes Booth's dying words. "The greatest mistake of my life," declared Lee in later years, "was taking a military education." Full of sound and fury, and rueful compassion, *The Civil War* provided a military, political, and cultural education that, until the next conflict, seemed to inoculate viewers against future senseless carnage.

Bibliography

Catton, Bruce. *A Stillness at Appomattox.* Garden City, N.Y.: Doubleday, 1954. A gracefully literary narrative of the War in Virginia, with emphasis on the Army of the Potomac.

Chesnut, Mary Boykin Miller. *Mary Chesnut's Civil War.* Edited by Comer Vann Woodward. New Haven, Conn.: Yale University Press, 1981. A Southern aristocrat, Chesnut kept a revealing diary of civilian life during the war and was frequently quoted in the PBS film.

Foote, Shelby. *The Civil War: A Narrative.* New York: Random House, 1958-1974. Three volumes. A mammoth, magisterial account of the conflict by a novelist who also participated in the PBS project.

Lincoln, Abraham. *Speeches and Writings, 1859-1865.* New York: Literary Classics of the United States, 1989. A central figure in the conflict, Lincoln was also an author of considerable literary grace whose writings were quoted frequently in *The Civil War.*

McPherson, James M. *Ordeal by Fire: The Civil War and Reconstruction.* New York: Alfred A. Knopf, 1982. Contends that the Civil War produced revolutionary changes in American life and proceeds to examine how and why. Photographs and detailed maps, tables, and bibliographies.

Smith, Page. *Trial by Fire: A People's History of the Civil War and Reconstruction.*

New York: McGraw-Hill, 1982. Emphasizing ordinary life over battle scenarios and preoccupation with leaders, Smith provides an accessible account of how the general population of the Union and the Confederacy experienced the war.

Ward, Geoffrey C., with Ric Burns and Ken Burns. *The Civil War: An Illustrated History.* New York: Alfred A. Knopf, 1991. A companion to the PBS series, this sumptuous volume is abundantly illustrated with photographs, illustrations, maps, and newspaper excerpts. Narrative by Ward and essays by other historians attempt to convey the texture of the past.

Steven G. Kellman

Cross-References

Gone with the Wind Premieres (1939), p. 1154; *The Forsyte Saga* Is a Hit on Public Television (1969), p. 2168; *Monty Python's Flying Circus* Captures Audiences Worldwide (1969), p. 2174; *Roots* Dramatizes the African-American Experience (1977), p. 2397; The Decline of the Big Three Networks Becomes a Fall (Late 1980's), p. 2554.

BARYSHNIKOV'S WHITE OAK DANCE PROJECT DEBUTS

Category of event: Dance
Time: October 24, 1990
Locale: Wang Center for the Performing Arts, Boston, Massachusetts

Celebrated choreographer Mark Morris provided the repertory for the premiere performance of Mikhail Baryshnikov's White Oak Dance Project, which featured Baryshnikov and other stellar dancers

Principal personages:
MIKHAIL BARYSHNIKOV (1948-   ), a Russian-born dancer who electrified the Western ballet world in 1974 when he defected from the Kirov Ballet
MARK MORRIS (1956-   ), a dancer and choreographer of several significant ballet and modern dance works
HOWARD GILMAN (1924-   ), a wealthy New York dance enthusiast who provided financial support for the White Oak Project

Summary of Event

On October 24, 1990, audience members at the Wang Center for the Performing Arts in Boston, Massachusetts, eagerly awaited the premiere performance of a completely new dance ensemble, the White Oak Dance Project. Nearly thirty-six hundred dance enthusiasts were on hand to see ballet and film star Mikhail Baryshnikov perform in the choreography of the world-renowned Mark Morris. Baryshnikov was accompanied onstage by Morris and a superb ensemble of stellar dancers representing a veritable who's who of ballet and modern dance professionals.

Billed as a dance "project" rather than as a company, the White Oak dancers, many of them leading dancers in other companies, were a unique ensemble. Chosen by Baryshnikov and Morris, the dancers included Peggy Baker, Rob Besserer, and Nancy Colahan from the Lar Lubovitch Dance Company, Jamie Bishton and Kathleen Moore from American Ballet Theatre, Kate Johnson, who had recently retired from the Paul Taylor Dance Company, Denise Pons, a soloist with the Boston Ballet, and William Pizzuto, who left Boston Ballet in 1989.

Noteworthy for its emphasis on mature dancers, many of whom were in their thirties and forties, the ensemble was also unusual in that it made no distinction between ballet dancers and modern dancers; all were viewed first and foremost as dancers, with the primary emphasis on their extraordinary abilities and not on their status as representatives of ballet or modern dance. It was the first time that such disparate and accomplished individuals had combined forces to dance together not as guest soloists from other companies but as an ensemble of dancers.

In an interview with *Dance Magazine* writer Nancy Dalva, project manager Barry Alterman made clear the distinction between company and project ensemble members: "A Company is self-perpetuating, with long commitments, and goes on for a long time. *This* might not last beyond this town or might go on to another town. The personnel may change." Indeed, after the Boston premiere, the project's personnel did change, as Morris returned to Belgium and dancers such as David Parsons and Donald Mouton briefly joined the touring project.

Created for a single initial tour of seventeen cities in the United States, the White Oak Dance Project took its name from the White Oak Plantation, the 7,500-acre estate of philanthropist Howard Gilman. The New York paper manufacturer, ardent balletomane, and supporter of Baryshnikov provided the financial backing for the touring project, offered the use of his plantation for rehearsals, and had a state-of-the-art dance studio specially constructed on the property. Located on the Saint Mary's River near the Florida-Georgia border, the estate became home for the ensemble during July and August, 1990. There, the dancers were treated like royalty during the five weeks of preparation: rehearsing in near-idyllic conditions, boating, swimming, and enjoying the delights of Gilman's paradise when not rehearsing. It was, as one dancer involved dubbed it, "the greatest dance camp ever."

When Baryshnikov founded the White Oak Project, he intended it as a temporary vehicle for himself and others. After his tenure as artistic director of American Ballet Theatre, Baryshnikov had no interest in taking on the responsibilities of a permanent company, and he conceived of the White Oak Project as an opportunity to dance in pieces he enjoyed alongside dancers who were his peers in achievement, age, and experience. Baryshnikov chose Morris because of his admiration for Morris' choreographic skills, and he chose the all-Morris repertory for the initial tour because he felt that the dancers would profit by working with the phrasing, style, and demands of a single choreographer at first. A self-proclaimed fan of Morris, Baryshnikov has said that he never considered any other choreographer for the White Oak Project.

Baryshnikov's respect for Morris' choreography dates back to 1987, when, as director of American Ballet Theatre, he commissioned Morris to create "Drink to Me Only with Thine Eyes" for the company. After his resignation from American Ballet Theatre in 1989, Baryshnikov surprised the dance world by traveling to Belgium, where he appeared as a guest with Morris' company in "Wonderland" in December of 1989; he repeated the performance during the company's New York season at the Brooklyn Academy of Music. Baryshnikov found the camaraderie he experienced while working with Morris' company a welcome antidote to the tumultuous politics of American Ballet Theatre. "It was such a nice atmosphere," Baryshnikov remarked. "We thought, 'Why couldn't we find a project to stretch this lovely feeling?' "

Baryshnikov's formation of the White Oak Project may also have had its roots in sheer physical reality. At forty-two, Baryshnikov was no longer at the peak of his form; injuries, age, and the demands of a multifaceted career made the continuation of his famous classical roles uncertain. Although both Morris and Baryshnikov denied that Baryshnikov's switch to modern-dance-based choreography was a response to his diminished technical abilities, performing in other than classical roles allowed him greater freedom and evoked fewer unfavorable comparisons to his younger self.

The White Oak Project debut was a benefit preview fund-raiser for the Boston-based Dance Umbrella, an organization that had long supported Morris. The concert included Morris' signature solo *Ten Suggestions*, performed that evening by Baryshnikov; *Pas de Poisson*, a trio for Baryshnikov, Kate Johnson, and Morris; and two group works, *Going Away Party* and *Motorcade*.

While well received by the huge audience drawn by Baryshnikov's name and Morris' choreography, the concert elicited mixed responses from dance critics. In reviewing *Ten Suggestions*, critics were quick to point out the differences between Baryshnikov's fastidious execution of the movements and the vigorous, earthy abandon of Morris, often preferring Morris. *Pas de Poisson* drew praise for the sparkling performances of Baryshnikov, Johnson, and Morris but garnered mixed reviews choreographically. *Going Away Party*, a boisterous, tongue-in-cheek look at love and Americana, was set to the music of Bob Wills and His Texas Playboys. A definite hit, the piece nevertheless prompted performance comparisons between Morris and Baryshnikov, and between the White Oak dancers and Morris' own troupe. Choreographed specifically for White Oak dancers, *Motorcade* was emblematic of the strengths of the project: highly technical and virtuosic dancing and alternately humorous, stately, and irreverent choreography.

The Boston debut of "The Mark and Misha Show," as *Time* magazine and others nicknamed the White Oak Dance Project, announced the arrival and immediate departure of a unique enterprise, as it embarked on a seventeen-city tour across America. The company that was not a company headed for Minneapolis.

Impact of Event

When asked about his rationale for the ensemble, Baryshnikov replied, "In the time I have left, I just want to go on stage and dance for the fun of it. It's really great to go on stage in pieces that people never expected me to be in." The White Oak Project offered Baryshnikov marvelous new performing opportunities, and the experience seemed to be as fulfilling for him as it was financially successful. Because of Baryshnikov's celebrity, the White Oak Project played to full houses at every stop, and by the end of the first tour, plans were under way for subsequent tours.

The White Oak Project further glamorized the reputation of Baryshnikov and extended the recognition of Morris as a major choreographer. The tour's itinerary had snubbed the traditional dance centers of the United States, including New York City, and therefore the impact of the project was oddly minimal in New York. By the spring of 1992, the ensemble had finished four American and European tours without a single performance in New York City. Writing for *The New Yorker*, Alastair Macaulay commented upon a London performance of the White Oak Project: "How strange—to watch such dancers . . . all of whom the rest of the world associates with New York, and to know they are appearing in a program that there are as yet no plans to show here."

After the White Oak Project's first three tours, the personnel and repertory of the ensemble changed considerably. Although subsequent tours continued to feature Morris' choreography, the repertory was augmented with works by Paul Taylor, Martha Graham, Lar Lubovitch, and other contemporary choreographers. Works commissioned specifically for the ensemble included Taylor's *Oz*, Lubovitch's *Waiting for the Sunrise*, and David Gordon's *Punch and Judy*. Of the original dancers, only four remained with the ensemble: Baryshnikov, Johnson, Besserer, and Colahan.

How much the success of the project affected Morris is difficult to assess. He was already considered by many the foremost choreographer of his generation, and his reputation was neither significantly enhanced nor diminished by the new works he produced for Baryshnikov's ensemble. Much of the repertory either originated with Morris' own company or was performed by it subsequently, and except for the initial rehearsal process, his contact with the White Oak Project was minimal. In the spring of 1991, Morris' three-year contract as artistic director of the Theatre Royal de la Monnaie in Brussels expired, and he and his company returned to the United States. His role with the White Oak Project remained that of guest choreographer, and his primary commitment remained to his company, the Mark Morris Group.

As an entity, the White Oak Project is such a loosely connected enterprise that its full impact on the dance world is difficult to determine. Certainly, the initial vision of an ensemble of compatible dancers performing choreography they enjoyed without the burden of long-term commitments has proven successful. Yet the very ephemerality of the White Oak Project may be an inherently fatal flaw: Its future hinges on the interest and continued participation of Baryshnikov. Without his cachet, it is unlikely that the ensemble could continue to draw audiences or remain financially solvent. Another factor is that the White Oak Project has no exclusive repertory. It seems unlikely that audiences will sustain a purely repertory company without Baryshnikov if the works are also currently being performed by the choreographers' own companies.

For many reasons, the formation of the White Oak Project was a welcome addition to the dance world. The brilliant and eclectic choreography of Morris offered Baryshnikov and his colleagues the opportunity to shine collectively while at the same time celebrating their individual talents. The White Oak Project also reminded the dance world that excellent dancers should not be classified by genre and style or forced into retirement in their twenties. While its future may be uncertain, the rise of the White Oak Project was a luminous occurrence.

Bibliography

Alovert, Nina. *Baryshnikov in Russia*. Translated by Irene Huntoon. New York: Holt, Rinehart and Winston, 1984. Written by a Soviet friend of Baryshnikov who defected to the West in 1977. Lavishly illustrated with photographs that had to be smuggled out of the Soviet Union.

France, Charles Engell. *Baryshnikov at Work*. London: Adam and Charles Black, 1977. A beautiful oversized book with photographs by Martha Swope. Baryshnikov discusses his most famous roles in the Soviet Union, at the New York City

Ballet, with American Ballet Theatre, and on Broadway.

Fraser, John. *Private View: Inside Baryshnikov's American Ballet Theatre.* New York: Bantam, 1988. A large picture book with photographs by Eve Arnold and text by John Fraser. Gives a nice feel for the dancers in the company and for Baryshnikov as a person.

Morris, Mark. "The Hidden Soul of Harmony." In *Dance As a Theatre Art: Source Readings in Dance History from 1581 to the Present,* edited by Selma Jeanne Cohen. 2d ed. Princeton, N.J.: Princeton Book Company, 1992. A short article in which Morris talks about his choreography, his musicality, and his images used in his masterpiece *L'Allegro, Il Penseroso, Ed Il Moderato.*

Smakov, Gennady. *Baryshnikov: From Russia to the West.* London: Orbis, 1981. Major focus is the earlier stages of Baryshnikov's career, from his defection from the Soviet Union in 1974 through his acceptance of the directorship of American Ballet Theatre in 1980.

Cynthia J. Williams

Cross-References

Balanchine and Kirstein Make New York a World Center for Ballet (1946), p. 1301; Taylor Establishes His Own Dance Company (1954), p. 1602; Nureyev and Fonteyn Debut Ashton's *Marguerite and Armand* (1963), p. 1962; Tharp Stages *Deuce Coupe* for the Joffrey Ballet (1973), p. 2288; The New Dance U.S.A. Festival Celebrates Contemporary Dance (1981), p. 2480; Multiculturalism Dominates the Dance World (Late 1980's), p. 2559.

GORDIMER WINS THE NOBEL PRIZE IN LITERATURE

Category of event: Literature
Time: December 10, 1991
Locale: Stockholm, Sweden

Nadine Gordimer, whose fiction depicts South Africa's racial turmoil, received the Nobel Prize for her achievement as an artist and as a humanitarian

> *Principal personages:*
> NADINE GORDIMER (1923-   ), a novelist born in South Africa whose novels and stories chronicle the effects of racism on the individual consciousness
> ALFRED NOBEL (1833-1896), a Swedish engineer and chemist who established the annual Nobel Prizes
> STURE ALLEN, a literature professor and a lifetime member of the Nobel Academy who made the announcement of Gordimer's selection

Summary of Event

After being passed over several times because of disagreement among the Nobel Academy members who make the decision, Nadine Gordimer was named on October 3, 1991, as the year's recipient of the Nobel Prize in Literature. Interviewed in New York City on the day of the announcement, Gordimer commented: "I had been a possible candidate for so long that I had given up hope." As is the custom of the academy, the nature of the disagreement will remain secret for fifty years. The award, which carried a stipend of approximately $985,000, was presented in Stockholm on December 10, 1991.

While the academy may have taken several years to name Gordimer, her international audience greeted the announcement with immediate approval and genuine enthusiasm, considering the Nobel Prize an honor long overdue. News reports stressed that she was the first woman in twenty-five years to be named and only the seventh woman selected in the literature prize's ninety-year history. While such statistics are revealing, they in no way reflect the thrust of Gordimer's writing. Never considering herself a feminist writer and sometime even castigated by feminist critics, Gordimer has created a world of women and men—lovers, parents, children, husbands, wives, friends—who struggle most often to establish relationships in what the Nobel Academy called, in its statement on her work, "an insupportable society."

This "insupportable society" has always been South Africa, where Gordimer was born, the daughter of immigrant Jewish parents from Europe. That Gordimer received the Nobel Prize during the dismantling of South Africa's infamous apartheid system led some observers to call the award politically motivated. Sture Allen, the Nobel Academy member who announced Gordimer's selection, pointed out that the Nobel Peace Prize was given for outstanding political contributions. (South African Archbishop Desmond M. Tutu had received the Nobel Peace Prize in 1985.) Gordimer's award, Allen stressed, was "literary," adding that "her works have a political basis, but her writing is different."

What makes Gordimer's writing "different" may be explained in two ways: first, through its structure and style; second, through its universal concerns in spite of the specific time and place. During a period when many writers were experimenting with postmodern techniques such as unreliable narrators and unexplained shifts in time, ignoring the line that divides fantasy and realism, and taking language to sometimes incomprehensible limits, Gordimer has remained a traditional novelist, more similar to the great British and European writers of the nineteenth and early twentieth centuries than to many of her contemporaries. Gordimer's major works, such as *A Guest of Honor* (1970), *The Conservationist* (1974), *Burger's Daughter* (1979), and *A Sport of Nature* (1987), are all big novels, big in that they fully and faithfully realize the basic elements of fiction: plot, character, and setting. This realization comes about through a distinctive style, yet one that is in itself traditional.

The style bears resemblance to the diamonds for which South Africa is famous. Like them, it is tempered and durable, admirable in its clarity, varied in its facets. Again, like a diamond, the style draws no attention for its flashiness, but gains notice for its inexplicable beauty and perfection. At times the prose turns bright and lyrical in description of the landscape; at other points, it takes on a harsh, dark quality when depicting human cruelty in graphic detail or when describing the ugliness of poverty-striken South African townships. The style is also purely African in the way it makes use of nature—animals, sounds, plants, trees, the texture of the soil, the shape of rocks, the sky's colors. The integration of these natural elements into the narrative not only establishes setting but serves as well to formulate metaphors delineating the human condition.

The other aspect that makes Gordimer's fiction "different" from purely political writing lies in the way it handles the polarity created by a social system based on racial separation. Neither didactic nor outwardly censuring, the short stories and novels pit individuals against an ideology that intrudes upon their lives—in this case apartheid. Human relationships, though, are ultimately what matter in the fiction— relationships between white and white, black and black, black and white, male and female, young and old. On one hand, Gordimer's work records how the political ideology that controlled South Africa for almost half a century affected those who lived it. On the other hand, however, to label the work a mere history of what life was like during the apartheid era would be to limit its moral vision. Gordimer's fellow South African Nobel Laureate, Archbishop Tutu, commented when he learned of her award: "She's an outstanding artist . . . but more than anything else she has had this tremendous commitment and caring about people, caring about justice." Those are the qualities that imbue Gordimer's fiction and will continue to do so once the policies of apartheid are mere historical notes.

Impact of Event

Unlike some of the Nobel Prize winners before her, Gordimer had already established an international reputation. Therefore, although the prize certainly enhanced her standing, it seemed most likely to have a greater impact on other writers. In particular, the award's prestige seemed likely to carry over into the field generally called international literature in English—that is, writing from countries other than Great Britain and the United States. English-language literature coming from such places as the West Indies, Africa, Australia, India, Canada, and New Zealand was for long considered a minor appendage to the long-established literatures of Great Britain and the United States. This attitude changed in the late twentieth century, as the literary world began to look with greater interest and respect beyond the traditional boundaries. The publicity surrounding Gordimer's Nobel Prize definitely served to heighten awareness of such literature.

For this prestigious award brings recognition first to the writer, then to his or her country, then to the literature represented. So far two other writers of international literature in English have been so honored, Patrick White from Australia in 1973 and Wole Soyinka from Nigeria in 1986. In the wake of those awards, other writers from White's and Soyinka's respective countries, as well as those from the regions once composing the British Commonwealth, probably gained far more than did the Nobel Laureates themselves. White placed the money accompanying the Nobel honor into a trust fund that provides from its earnings a sizable cash award given each year to an Australian writer. Gordimer said that she plans to carry out a similar project with part of her stipend by assisting the Congress of South African Writers, a predominantly black organization. She explained that most of these black authors write in English, the imposed language of the colonizer, but she hoped that they could be encouraged to make use of African languages as well.

The establishment of a black literature in South Africa, whether in English or in native tongues, is long overdue. Many of the African countries that gained their independence after World War II have built an indigenous literary tradition both in English and in African languages, but the political climate of South Africa has not been conducive to such development. Publishing opportunities for black writers were either scant or nonexistent; in fact, government oppression and censorship often prevented black writers from even speaking to their fellow South Africans. A major figure such as Alex La Guma, for example, spent most of his life in exile, and his work was never published in South Africa.

Given the restrictive conditions of South African life since 1947, it seems contradictory that a literature of protest developed at all. Yet books critical of the system did appear—by white authors. The first such novel to receive international recognition was Alan Paton's *Cry, the Beloved Country* (1948). The novels of André Brink and J. M. Coetzee and the plays of Athol Fugard also found audiences overseas. Much of this work, along with Gordimer's, was long banned by the South African government, but its white authors were not jailed or exiled, perhaps because the government feared the diplomatic consequences of persecuting white writers with reputations abroad. Other observers concluded that books inveighing against the regime in truth did little good, since the words were not generally available in South

Africa. Nevertheless, the Nobel citation called Gordimer "the doyenne of South African letters" and praised her for a "continual involvement on behalf of literature and free speech in a police state where censorship and persecution of books and people exist."

In a country with a small population, the emergence of one writer who overshadows all the others creates both bad and good effects, no matter how generous the major writer may be with time, attention, and money. This has certainly been the case with Patrick White and Australia; even though White's Nobel award is long in the past and he is dead, younger writers still feel their work to be too often judged in light of his brilliant achievement. Soyinka has been both lionized and denigrated in Nigeria, called the voice of Africa in one breath and in the next called a panderer to the literary tastes of the white world overseas. Such could be the case with Gordimer. On a more positive note, though, the attention accorded Gordimer may help to validate her country's literature in the eyes of the rest of the world. From that validation, her contemporaries and successors, black and white, cannot help but gain.

Bibliography

Clingman, Stephen. *The Novels of Nadine Gordimer: History from the Inside.* London: Allen & Unwin, 1986. Covers Gordimer's work through *July's People* (1981). Focuses for the most part on the way Gordimer has created a historical chronicle of South Africa in her novels. Emphasizes the relationship between the fiction and political events. Provides valuable background on the political and legal events that help to shape the outward form of the fiction. Extensive secondary bibliography.

Cooke, John. *The Novels of Nadine Gordimer: Private Lives/Public Landscapes.* Baton Rouge: Louisiana University Press, 1985. Close readings of the texts emphasize how all the novels are essentially about the private concerns of individuals who live their lives in the shadow of a "public landscape" formed by political oppression and social injustice. Also addresses the recurrent theme of a daughter rebelling against an overbearing mother. Extensive secondary bibliography.

Gordimer, Nadine. *Conversations with Nadine Gordimer.* Edited by Nancy Topping Bazin and Marilyn Dallman Seymour. Jackson: University Press of Mississippi, 1990. Contains reprints of selected interviews with Gordimer over the preceding two decades. Although varying in quality, the interviews provide insights into Gordimer's work through her comments on South African politics, the place of the writer in society, and her own theory of writing. Extensive secondary bibliography.

Smith, Rowland, ed. *Critical Essays on Nadine Gordimer.* Boston: G. K. Hall, 1990. Contains previously published material, including articles, reviews, and book chapters. Offers a variety of approaches and a wide span of critical appraisal from 1953 to 1988. Provides discussions of Gordimer's novels and short stories through *A Sport of Nature.* An extremely helpful collection that contains material otherwise not easily available. Extensive secondary bibliography.

Smith, Rowland. "Truth, Irony, and Commitment." In *International Literature in English: Essays on the Major Writers*, edited by Robert L. Ross. New York: Garland, 1991. Contains a biographical sketch, a discussion of the work, and a primary and secondary bibliography. Examines how Gordimer's work constantly scrutinizes the peculiar role of whites in South Africa. Shows how Gordimer has always been truthful and committed in her fiction, while stressing the irony that dominates white South African life.

Wade, Michael. *Nadine Gordimer.* London: Evans Brothers, 1978. An introductory study that covers Gordimer's novels through *The Conservationist.* Each chapter provides a detailed analysis of individual novels, focusing on the "complexity of moral vision" and the "failure of human relationships" that dominate the fiction. Although an early study, it remains an intelligent and informed examination of Gordimer's fictional progress to 1975.

Robert L. Ross

Cross-References

The First Nobel Prizes Are Awarded (1901), p. 45; *Heart of Darkness* Reveals the Consequences of Imperialism (1902), p. 51; *Things Fall Apart* Depicts Destruction of Ibo Culture (1958), p. 1763; Kawabata Wins the Nobel Prize in Literature (1968), p. 2147; Singer Wins the Nobel Prize in Literature (1978), p. 2423; *"MASTER HAROLD". . . and the boys* Examines Apartheid (1982), p. 2496; Soyinka Wins the Nobel Prize in Literature (1986), p. 2594; Mahfouz Wins the Nobel Prize in Literature (1988), p. 2625.

COLUMBUS DAY DEBATES
REFLECT CULTURAL DIVERSITY

Categories of event: Art, literature, and journalism
Time: October 12, 1992
Locale: Worldwide

The five hundredth anniversary of Christopher Columbus' first voyage to America was celebrated and condemned as scholars, educators, ethnic groups, and the public attempted to interpret the world-altering events of 1492 with historical objectivity and multicultural sensitivity

Principal personages:
CHRISTOPHER COLUMBUS (1451-1506), the explorer who made the first important contact between Europe and America
CARLOS FUENTES (1928-), a prominent Mexican novelist who interpreted Columbus' significance in a television special and a book
JAY LEVENSON, the chief curator of a major exhibit of Columbus-era art
KIRKPATRICK SALE (1937-), the author of the celebrated—and controversial—revisionist text *The Conquest of Paradise*
JOAQUIN BALAGUER (1907-), the Dominican Republic president who oversaw the creation of a costly Columbus memorial

Summary of Event

On October 12, 1492, Christopher Columbus stepped off his ship and onto an island in the Caribbean. This encounter between Europe and the Americas launched a chain of events that literally remade the world. October 12, 1992 marked the five hundredth anniversary, or quincentennial, of Columbus' landing. The event was commemorated with speeches, parades, protests, and mourning; Columbus was both praised and villified.

Continuing tradition, many cities in the United States held parades, mock landings, and fireworks displays. The Smithsonian National Museum of Natural History in Washington, D.C., sponsored the "Seeds of Change" exhibit, focusing on five "seeds" that had been critical to the evolution of the New World: sugar, corn, the potato, the horse, and disease. In New York City, the New-York Historical Society held an exhibit of European art depicting the New World as seen by the Old. The Intrepid Sea Air Space Museum told the story of Columbus and other early explorers through displays and reenactments.

Perhaps the most ambitious of the Columbus-related exhibitions was "Circa 1492: Art in the Age of Exploration," a mammoth show mounted by the National Gallery of Art in Washington, D.C. The show's chief curator, Jay Levenson, spent more than three years assembling a massive collection of art from around the world, including works from fifteenth century Japan, China, India, Africa, the Middle East, and South America. Some critics alleged that the vast scope of the show was an ill-conceived effort to avoid charges of Eurocentrism; in broadening the exhibit's focus to include art from so many cultures, it was argued, the National had lost sight of the reason for mounting a 1492-centered show in the first place. The renowned Harvard University historian Simon Schama, for example, criticized "Circa 1492" for its "refusal to consider head-on the phenomenon of Columbus himself and the historical experience of his four voyages." Schama characterized the exhibit as "the Blockbuster That Lost Its Nerve" in choosing to act with "a sense of preemptive prudence."

Other exhibits unequivocally adopted the viewpoint of the conquered. The Caribbean Cultural Center in New York City sponsored events highlighting pre-Columbian cultures. In Virginia, an exhibition at the historic Jamestown settlement portrayed the many "discoverers" of America, including the Paleo-Indians who crossed the Bering Strait.

Many Native Americans mourn on Columbus Day. Contact between Europe and the American continent spelled disaster for their cultures. Diseases such as smallpox decimated Indian populations, and European invaders killed, enslaved, or dispossessed countless natives. American Indians thus used the Columbus quincentennial to call attention to past crimes and present inequalities. Choctaw Indians hiked the five-hundred-mile "Trail of Tears" first walked by the tribe during its forced resettlement from Mississippi to Oklahoma in the 1830's. In Boston, the Dance Umbrella organization sponsored a huge communal powwow. In California, the International Indian Treaty Council held a "Five Hundred Years of Indigenous Resistance" concert in San Francisco, while the neighboring city of Berkeley officially changed the holiday's name to Indigenous People's Day. In Pasadena, California, the naming of a Columbus descendant as grand marshal of the city's famous New Year's Day Rose Parade touched off a dispute that was settled only when an American Indian was named as a co-grand marshal.

Throughout Latin America and the Caribbean, Columbus Day was marked by official silence and increased security around Spanish embassies. Although many protests were peaceful, demonstrators in Mexico City, San Salvador, and Santo Domingo attacked statues, burned tires, and clashed with police. The Pan-American Highway in Ecuador and Colombia was blocked by sit-ins and closed at one location by a dynamite blast. Santo Domingo, the capital of the Dominican Republic, intended to hold an elaborate celebration, including a worldwide television extravaganza hosted by Bob Hope. The plans fizzled, however, in the wake of the controversy caused by President Joaquin Balaguer's white elephant of a Columbus memorial. The Faro a Colón (Columbus' Lighthouse) is ten stories tall and nearly half a mile long. Fifty thousand people were evicted from their homes to make way for the structure, which cost about $70 million to build. A high wall surrounds the Faro, shielding visitors from the sight of an adjacent slum. The lighthouse is designed to project 138 laser beams into the sky in the shape of a cross—in a city that suffers frequent blackouts.

Numerous other Columbus-centered projects were received with varying degrees of controversy. Two major Hollywood productions, *1492: Conquest of Paradise* and *Christopher Columbus: The Discovery*, received generally poor reviews; despite the fact that neither film was idolatrous, the works were decried by anti-Columbians. (Marlon Brando, who portrayed the notorious inquisitor Tomás de Torquemada in the latter film, insisted that his name be removed from the credits because the finished picture did not depict Columbus as "the true villain he was.") A public television special narrated by author Carlos Fuentes also stirred controversy; a revival of *Cristoforo Colombo*, an opera composed for the 1492 anniversary, proved less inflammatory.

The Columbus issue had become such a hot potato that the explorer was, ironically, largely ignored at the 1992 World's Fair held at Seville, Spain. In concert with the 1992 Barcelona Olympics, the fair was the centerpiece of the "Year of Spain," a celebration of the country and its history planned to coincide with the five hundredth anniversary of Columbus' voyage. October 12 was even chosen as the fair's closing date—yet by then, nervous organizers had decided to downplay the Columbus connection, to such an extent that, one reviewer wrote, "In the end he was an unwanted guest. . . . Whatever his merits, Spain concluded, Columbus should not be allowed to spoil the party."

Impact of Event

The commemoration of a historic event often tells more about the people doing the commemorating than it does about the event itself. The Columbus quincentennial was characterized by increased historical awareness and multicultural sensitivity. What, though, about Columbus Day celebrations of the past? How did Columbus attain the hero status that is now widely believed to be so undeserved?

Patriotic businessmen were largely responsible for Columbus' traditional image as a praiseworthy American hero. On October 12, 1792, the Tammany Society, a New York fraternal organization, held the first Columbian commemorative dinner. A symbolic monument representing Columbus' achievements was placed in the society's museum. Inspired by the festivities in New York, the Massachusetts Historical Society of Boston honored Columbus with a procession and a poem on October 23. The press praised these events, encouraging other towns to organize celebrations.

Enthusiasm for Columbus as a symbol of progress reached a peak in 1893, when the World's Columbian Exposition opened in Chicago. Bigger than any previous World's Fair, the exposition honored American technology, resources, power, and general superiority. Reigning over it all was a noble statue of Columbus, armored and bearing an upraised sword.

In 1934, President Franklin Delano Roosevelt proclaimed October 12 the official Columbus Day. He called on the public to observe the day with ceremonies in schools and churches. Columbus Day, the anniversary of the "discovery" of America, had become a symbol of nationalism and progress and a firmly entrenched American tradition.

The Columbus quincentennial countercelebrations and pluralistic exhibits, however, reflected a changing sensibility in the United States. As the twentieth century drew to a close, ethnic pride and multicultural awareness began to gain ground on Eurocentric domination of U.S. culture. As scholars attempted to paint a more realistic picture of the past, many educators fought to implement programs designed to support, rather than conflict with, minority students' sense of self. Debate raged between advocates of multicultural curricula and defenders of educational orthodoxy. Hollywood, too, produced a number of high-profile projects about minority groups, as evidenced by such films as *Dances with Wolves* (1990) and *The Last of the Mohicans* (1992). African-American filmmakers such as Spike Lee and John Singleton emerged as among the film industry's most popular. When did American society begin to heed the ethnic voice? Columbus' portrayal over the past century is a benchmark of popular opinion, evidence of a notable shift in attitude over the years.

In 1892, Columbus was popularly believed to have been a great hero who had brought civilization to a virgin land. The indigenous people he "discovered" were alternately thought to have been immoral cannibals or noble savages, with childlike minds suitable for Christian conversion. This viewpoint had been espoused by Washington Irving's *A History of the Life and Voyages of Christopher Columbus* (1828), a romanticized version of the explorer's life that was the first full-length biography of Columbus published in English. Irving portrayed the explorer as courageous, wise, and enterprising, the archetype of an early American hero. This image endured and was accepted even by Native Americans and African Americans.

During the 1892 celebration in New York, Indian students marched in the parade and were praised for their "civilized" regimentation. Others rode on horseback wearing war paint and feathers. The prevailing attitude was that Indians had benefited from their "discovery." The value of indigenous cultures was measured by their contributions to the society of their European conquerors.

At the time of the four hundredth anniversary, moreover, legal slavery had been abolished for less than thirty years. Even so, black citizens were enthusiastic about the World's Columbian Exposition in Chicago. Their efforts to be included, to portray African-American accomplishments as part of America's greatness, were, however, dismissed at every turn.

By 1992, ethnic groups had completely rejected the idea that they were entitled to recognition only by riding on Euro-Caucasian coattails. Newspapers and magazines of the day were filled with protestations condemning both Columbus' cruelties toward the indigenous population and the continued crimes and inequalities perpetrated against American minorities in succeeding centuries. Columbus was charged with everything from genocide to ecological devastation.

The public mudslinging was aided and abetted by revisionist historians who rewrote the past to suit the modern environment. The quincentennial evoked a flood of books that historian Arthur Schlesinger, Jr., claimed reflected the "end of European domination of the planet . . . the bad conscience of the West and the consequent reexamination of the Western impact on the rest of humanity." Among the most celebrated—and controversial—of these publications was Kirkpatrick Sale's *The Conquest of Paradise* (1990). Sale portrayed the pre-Columbian continent as an "Eden of astonishing plenitude" where people lived in "balanced and fruitful harmony" with nature and with one another. Other scholars, though, criticized Sale's and similar books as exercises in mythmaking that ignored historical realities of pre-Columbian America, such as the institutionalized slavery and ritual murder practiced by the Aztecs and other indigenous peoples.

Although Christopher Columbus did not "discover" the American continent, his arrival there certainly spurred monumental changes. Controversy concerning the impact of Columbus' landings will doubtless persist far beyond their five hundredth anniversary. The Columbus quincentennial reinvigorated debates concerning the rights and contributions of indigenous peoples and minority groups, both on the American continent and elsewhere. As the twentieth century drew to a close, the renewed interest in non-European cultures seemed likely to bring greater diversity into popular culture for years to come.

Bibliography

Bushman, Claudia L. *America Discovers Columbus: How an Italian Explorer Became an American Hero.* Hanover, N.H.: University Press of New England, 1992. A history of American commemoration of Columbus, emphasizing the effect that a popular image can have on the shaping of public consciousness. Contains many paintings of Columbus, none of which resembles another. Numerous references cited.

Fuentes, Carlos. *The Buried Mirror: Reflections on Spain and the New World.* New York: Houghton Mifflin, 1992. A wide-ranging discourse by Fuentes, one of Latin America's most celebrated writers, on the significance of Columbus' journey and its implications for the New World. An outgrowth of the author's public television series.

Harjo, Suzan Shown. "I Won't Be Celebrating Columbus Day." *Newsweek* 118 (Fall/Winter, 1991): 32. Diatribe by the national coordinator of the 1992 Alliance, a coalition of Native American groups. A call to arms in no uncertain terms, this article demands that both church and state act to make restitution for the past and resolutions for the future.

Koning, Hans. "We Can No Longer, in Good Faith, Celebrate Columbus." *USA Today Magazine* 120 (November, 1991): 53. Columbus-bashing article by the author of *Columbus, His Enterprise: Exploding the Myth* (1991). Paints the explorer in the blackest light, citing atrocities committed by Columbus personally. Denounces the United States for its "orgy of flag-waving" on Columbus Day.

Krauthammer, Charles. "Hail Columbus, Dead White Male." *Time* 137 (May 27, 1991): 74. A cool-headed attack on the politically correct opinions that Columbus was a villain and the indigenous people were noble savages. Briefly describes the totalitarian Incan civilization and justifies its destruction by stating that humankind is better off today.

Levenson, Jay, ed. *Circa 1492: Art in the Age of Exploration.* New Haven, Conn.:
    Yale University Press, 1991. The catalog for the massive (some would say bloated)
    exhibit of Columbus-era art at the National Gallery. Scholarly, impressive, and
    large.
Schama, Simon. "They All Laughed at Christopher Columbus—Circus 1492: Who
    the Admiral Was, and Who He Wasn't." *The New Republic* 205 (January 6, 1992):
    30-40. A penetrating review of the National Gallery's massive exhibit of Columbus-
    era art. Schama's acute discussion is a masterful overview of the cultural and
    artistic debates inspired by the quincentennial.
Schlesinger, Jr., Arthur M. "Was America a Mistake? Reflections on the Long His-
    tory of Efforts to Debunk Columbus and His Discovery." *The Atlantic* 270 (Sep-
    tember, 1992): 16-30. A comprehensive article by a noted historian. Schlesinger
    debunks the nineteenth century Columbus myth and criticizes twentieth century
    revisionist overkill. He describes the cruelties of pre-Columbian America and con-
    cludes that the Mexican and European civilizations of 1492 were not essentially
    different in moral terms. The brutality of conquest is not rationalized; however,
    Schlesinger notes that democratic freedoms are also part of Columbus' legacy.

Susan Frischer

Cross-References

Heart of Darkness Reveals the Consequences of Imperialism (1902), p. 51; The
"Boom" Captures Worldwide Attention (Late 1950's), p. 1689; *Things Fall Apart*
Depicts Destruction of Ibo Culture (1958), p. 1763; *Roots* Dramatizes the African-
American Experience (1977), p. 2397; Multiculturalism Dominates the Dance World
(Late 1980's), p. 2559; Innovative Black Filmmakers Achieve Success (Late 1980's),
p. 2565.

CHRONOLOGICAL LIST OF EVENTS

VOLUME I

1897-1904	Stanislavsky Helps to Establish the Moscow Art Theater	1
1897-1907	Mahler Revamps the Vienna Court Opera	7
1899-1914	Joplin Popularizes the Ragtime Style	13
1899	Freud Inaugurates a Fascination with the Unconscious	19
1900	Brooks Brothers Introduces Button-Down Shirts	24
1900	Puccini's *Tosca* Premieres in Rome	29
1900	Tiffany and Tiffany Studios Develop New Ideas in Design	34
1900	Dreiser's *Sister Carrie* Shatters Literary Taboos	39
1901	First Nobel Prizes Are Awarded, The	45
1902	*Heart of Darkness* Reveals the Consequences of Imperialism	51
1902	*Voyage dans la lune* Introduces Special Effects, *Le*	57
1902	Stieglitz Organizes the Photo-Secession	63
1902	Caruso Records for the Gramophone and Typewriter Company	69
1903	*Great Train Robbery* Introduces New Editing Techniques, *The*	74
1903	Hoffmann and Moser Found the Wiener Werkstätte	79
1903	Shaw Articulates His Philosophy in *Man and Superman*	85
1903-1957	Vaughan Williams Composes His Nine Symphonies	90
1903	Henry James's *The Ambassadors* Is Published	96
1904-1905	Bartók and Kodály Begin to Collect Hungarian Folk Songs . . .	102
1904	Cohan's *Little Johnny Jones* Premieres	108
1904	Duncan Interprets Chopin in Her Russian Debut	113
1904	Abbey Theatre Heralds the Celtic Revival, The	119
1905	Hoffmann Designs the Palais Stoclet	124
1905	Stein Holds Her First Paris Salons	129
1905	Avant-Garde Artists in Dresden Form Die Brücke	134
1905	Fauves Exhibit at the Salon d'Automne, Les	140
1905	Reinhardt Becomes Director of the Deutsches Theater	145
1905	Strauss's *Salome* Shocks Audiences	151
1906-1907	Artists Find Inspiration in African Tribal Art . . . . :	156
1907	Bergson's *Creative Evolution* Inspires Artists and Thinkers . . .	161
1907	Busoni's *Sketch for a New Aesthetic of Music* Is Published	166
1907	William James's *Pragmatism* Is Published	171
1907	*Playboy of the Western World* Offends Irish Audiences, *The*	176

1907	Deutscher Werkbund Combats Conservative Architecture, The	181
1907	Pavlova First Performs Her Legendary Solo *The Dying Swan*	187
1908-1909	Schoenberg Breaks with Tonality	193
1908	*Ghost Sonata* Influences Modern Theater and Drama, *The*	199
1908	Salon d'Automne Rejects Braque's Cubist Works, The	204
1908	*Christian Science Monitor* Is Founded, *The*	209
1908	Elgar's First Symphony Premieres to Acclaim	214
1909	Behrens Designs the AEG Turbine Factory	219
1909-1929	Pickford Becomes "America's Sweetheart"	224
1909-1933	Sennett Defines the Slapstick Comedy Genre	230
1909	Futurists Issue Their Manifesto, The	235
1909	Diaghilev's Ballets Russes Astounds Paris	241
1909	Fokine's *Les Sylphides* Introduces Abstract Ballet	247
1910's	Handy Ushers in the Commercial Blues Era	252
1910	Gaudí Completes the Casa Milá Apartment House in Barcelona	257
1910	Poiret's "Hobble Skirts" Become the Rage	263
1910	*Firebird* Premieres in Paris, *The*	269
1911	Blaue Reiter Abandons Representation in Art, Der	275
1911-1923	Rilke's *Duino Elegies* Depicts Art as a Transcendent Experience	281
1911	Scriabin's *Prometheus* Premieres in Moscow	286
1911	Sibelius Conducts the Premiere of His Fourth Symphony	292
1911	Mahler's Masterpiece *Das Lied von der Erde* Premieres Posthumously	298
1912	Grey's *Riders of the Purple Sage* Launches the Western Genre	304
1912	Jung Publishes *Psychology of the Unconscious*	309
1912	Harriet Monroe Founds *Poetry* Magazine	314
1912	Kandinsky Publishes His Views on Abstraction in Art	320
1912-1917	Imagist Movement Shakes Up Poetry, The	326
1912	*Après-midi d'un faune* Causes an Uproar, *L'*	332
1913	Apollinaire Defines Cubism in *The Cubist Painters*	337
1913	Baker Establishes the 47 Workshop at Harvard	343
1913	Duchamp's "Readymades" Challenge Concepts of Art	349
1913-1927	Proust's *Remembrance of Things Past* Is Published	355
1913	Avant-Garde Art in the Armory Show Shocks American Viewers	361
1913	Webern's *Six Pieces for Large Orchestra* Premieres in Vienna	367

1913	*Rite of Spring* Stuns Audiences, *The*	373
1914	ASCAP Is Founded to Protect Musicians' Rights	379
1914	Lippmann Helps to Establish *The New Republic*	385
1915	Denishawn School of Dance Opens in Los Angeles, The	390
1915	*Metamorphosis* Anticipates Modern Feelings of Alienation, *The*	396
1915	*Birth of a Nation* Popularizes New Film Techniques, *The*	402
1915	First Pulitzer Prizes Are Awarded, The	407
1915	Malevich Introduces Suprematism	413
1916	Dada Movement Emerges at the Cabaret Voltaire, The	419
1916	Ives Completes His Fourth Symphony	425
1917	*Stijl* Advocates Mondrian's Neoplasticism, *De*	429
1917	"Six" Begin Giving Concerts, "Les"	435
1917	Yeats Publishes *The Wild Swans at Coole*	440
1917-1970	Pound's *Cantos* Is Published	445
1918	Cather's *My Ántonia* Promotes Regional Literature	452
1918-1919	Rietveld Designs the Red-Blue Chair	458
1919	German Artists Found the Bauhaus	463
1920's	Art of Radio Develops from Early Broadcast Experience, The	469
1920's	Chanel Defines Modern Women's Fashion	474
1920's	Harlem Renaissance Celebrates African-American Culture, The	480
1920	*Cabinet of Dr. Caligari* Opens in Berlin, *The*	486
1920	Jantzen Popularizes the One-Piece Bathing Suit	491
1920	*Mysterious Affair at Styles* Introduces Hercule Poirot, *The* ...	496
1920-1924	Melville Is Rediscovered as a Major American Novelist	502
1921	Boulanger Takes Copland as a Student	508
1921	Man Ray Creates the Rayograph	513
1921	Wittgenstein Emerges as an Important Philosopher	518
1921-1923	Hašek's *The Good Soldier Švejk* Reflects Postwar Disillusionment	523
1921-1923	Schoenberg Develops His Twelve-Tone System	528
1921	Pirandello's *Six Characters in Search of an Author* Premieres	534

VOLUME II

1922	Eliot Publishes *The Waste Land*	539
1922-1934	Soviet Union Bans Abstract Art, The	544
1922	Wallace Founds *Reader's Digest*	549

1922	Joyce's *Ulysses* Epitomizes Modernism in Fiction	555
1923	Stravinsky Completes His Wind Octet	561
1923	*Ten Commandments* Establishes Silent-Film Spectacle, *The*	567
1923	Bessie Smith Records "Downhearted Blues"	572
1923	Luce Founds *Time* Magazine	577
1924	Formation of the Blue Four Advances Abstract Painting, The	583
1924	Mann's *The Magic Mountain* Reflects European Crisis	588
1924	Von Stroheim Films His Silent Masterpiece *Greed*	593
1924	Gershwin's *Rhapsody in Blue* Premieres in New York	598
1924	Surrealism Is Born	604
1925	Cranbrook Academy Begins a History of Design Excellence	610
1925	Eisenstein's *Potemkin* Introduces New Film Editing Techniques	615
1925	Gide's *The Counterfeiters* Questions Moral Absolutes	620
1925	*Great Gatsby* Captures the Essence of the Roaring Twenties, *The*	626
1925	New Objectivity Movement Is Introduced, The	631
1925	Woolf's *Mrs. Dalloway* Explores Women's Consciousness	637
1925-1927	Gance's *Napoléon* Revolutionizes Filmmaking Techniques ...	642
1925	Ross Founds *The New Yorker*	648
1925	Paris Exhibition Defines Art Deco, A	654
1925	Chaplin Produces His Masterpiece *The Gold Rush*	659
1925	Baker Dances in *La Revue nègre*	665
1925	Armstrong First Records with His Hot Five Group	670
1925	WSM Launches *The Grand Ole Opry*	675
1925	Berg's *Wozzeck* Premieres in Berlin	680
1926	Book-of-the-Month Club and the Literary Guild Are Founded, The	686
1926	Keaton's *The General* Is Released	691
1926	Hemingway's *The Sun Also Rises* Speaks for the Lost Generation	696
1927	Kuleshov and Pudovkin Introduce Montage to Filmmaking	701
1927	Lang Expands the Limits of Filmmaking with *Metropolis*	707
1927	British Broadcasting Corporation Is Chartered, The	712
1927	Monet's *Water Lilies* Are Shown at the Musée de l'Orangerie	718
1927	Brecht and Weill Collaborate on *Mahagonny Songspiel*	724
1927	Rodgers Cuts His First Record for RCA Victor	729
1927	*Jazz Singer* Premieres in New York, *The*	734

1927   Ellington Begins an Influential Engagement at the
            Cotton Club 739
1927   *Show Boat* Introduces American Musical Theater 745
1928   Buñuel and Dalí Champion Surrealism in *Un Chien
            andalou* 750
1928   *Amos 'n' Andy* Radio Show Goes on the Air, The 755
1928   Sound Technology Revolutionizes the Motion-Picture
            Industry 761
1929   *All Quiet on the Western Front* Stresses the Futility of War ... 767
1929   *Hallelujah* Is the First Important Black Musical 772
1929   Loewy Pioneers American Industrial Design 777
1929   New York's Museum of Modern Art Is Founded 782
1929-1930   *Bedbug* and *The Bathhouse* Exemplify Revolutionary
            Theater, *The* 787
1929-1930   *Maltese Falcon* Introduces the Hard-Boiled Detective
            Novel, *The* 793
1929   First Academy Awards Honor Film Achievement, The 799
1929   *Sound and the Fury* Launches Faulkner's Career, *The* 805

1930's   Guthrie's Populist Songs Reflect the Depression-Era
            United States 810
1930's   Hindemith Advances Ideas of Music for Use and
            for Amateurs 816
1930's   Hollywood Enters Its Golden Age 822
1930's-1940's Radio Programming Dominates Home Leisure 828
1930's-1940's Studio System Dominates Hollywood Filmmaking, The 833
1930-1932   *Little Caesar, Public Enemy,* and *Scarface* Launch the
            Gangster-Film Genre 839
1930-1935   Von Sternberg Makes Dietrich a Superstar 845
1930   Crane Publishes *The Bridge* 851
1930   *Poems* Establishes Auden as a Generational Spokesman 857
1931   Karloff and Lugosi Become Kings of Horror 863
1931   Corbusier's Villa Savoye Redefines Architecture, Le 869
1931-1941   Group Theatre Flourishes, The 874
1931   Empire State Building Opens as the World's Tallest
            Building, The 880
1931   Whitney Museum Is Inaugurated in New York, The 885
1932   Celine's *Journey to the End of the Night* Is Published 890
1932   Huxley's *Brave New World* Reflects Fears About the Future ... 896
1932   Wright Founds the Taliesin Fellowship 902
1932-1934   Socialist Realism Is Mandated in Soviet Literature 908
1932   Stalin Restricts Soviet Composers 914
1932   Jooss's Antiwar Dance *The Green Table* Premieres 920

1933   Berkeley's *42nd Street* Revolutionizes Film Musicals 925
1933   Billie Holiday Begins Her Recording Career 930
1933   Coward's *Design for Living* Epitomizes the 1930's 936
1934   Lubitsch's *The Merry Widow* Opens New Vistas for Film
            Musicals 941
1934-1935   Hitchcock Becomes England's Foremost Director 946
1934-1938   Classic Screwball Comedy Reaches Its Height in
            Popularity, The 951
1934   Rivera's Rockefeller Center Mural Is Destroyed 957
1934   Miller's Notorious Novel *Tropic of Cancer* Is Published 963
1934   Goodman Begins His *Let's Dance* Broadcasts 968
1934   Balanchine's *Serenade* Inaugurates American Ballet 974
1935   Schiaparelli's Boutique Mingles Art and Fashion 979
1935   *Top Hat* Establishes the Astaire-Rogers Dance Team 984
1935-1939   Federal Theatre Project Promotes Live Theater, The 989
1935-1943   Roosevelt Administration Creates the WPA/FAP, The 995
1935   *Abstract Painting in America* Opens in New York 1001
1935   Odets' *Awake and Sing* Becomes a Model for
            Protest Drama 1006
1935   Temple Receives a Special Academy Award 1011
1935   Gershwin's *Porgy and Bess* Opens in New York 1016
Late 1930's Prouvé Pioneers the Prefabrication of Buildings 1021
1936   *Diary of a Country Priest* Inspires Readers, *The* 1026
1936   Luce Launches *Life* Magazine 1031
1936   Tudor's *Jardin aux lilas* Premieres in London 1036
1936   Shostakovich's *Lady Macbeth of Mtsensk* Is Condemned 1042
1936   Carnegie Publishes His Self-Help Best-Seller 1048
1937   Disney Releases *Snow White and the Seven Dwarfs* 1053
1937   Dreyfuss Designs the Bell "300" Telephone 1057
1937   Picasso Paints *Guernica* 1062
1937-1938   Aalto Designs Villa Mairea 1067
1937-1939   Renoir Marks the High Point of Prewar Filmmaking 1073
1937   Berg's *Lulu* Opens in Zurich 1078

VOLUME III

1937   Hitler Organizes an Exhibition Denouncing Modern Art 1083
1938   Ballet Russe de Monte Carlo Finds New Leadership, The 1088
1938-1950   American Science Fiction Enjoys Its Golden Age 1094
1938   *Our Town* Opens on Broadway 1099
1938   Welles Broadcasts *The War of the Worlds* 1103
1939   Classic *The Wizard of Oz* Opens, The 1109

1939   Ford Defines the Western in *Stagecoach* 1115
1939-1949   Bill Monroe and the Blue Grass Boys Define
                    Bluegrass Music 1121
1939   Marian Anderson Is Barred from Constitution Hall 1126
1939   Sherlock Holmes Film Series Begins, The 1131
1939   *Grapes of Wrath* Portrays Depression-Era America, *The* 1138
1939   NBC Launches American Television at the World's Fair 1143
1939   Rockefeller Center Is Completed 1149
1939   *Gone with the Wind* Premieres 1154

1940's   *Stormy Weather* Offers New Film Roles to African
                    Americans 1159
1940's-1950's   Kazan Brings Naturalism to the Stage and Screen 1164
1940's-1950's   New Criticism Holds Sway, The 1169
1940's-1950's   Sartre and Camus Give Dramatic Voice to Existential
                    Philosophy 1174
1940   García Lorca's *Poet in New York* Is Published 1179
1940   Wright's *Native Son* Depicts Racism in America 1185
1940-1941   Henry Moore Is Inspired by Shapes in Subway Shelters 1190
1940   Disney's *Fantasia* Premieres and Redefines the Boundaries
                    of Animation 1195
1941   Welles's *Citizen Kane* Breaks with Traditional Filmmaking ... 1200
1941   Messiaen's *Quartet for the End of Time* Premieres 1206
1941   NBC and CBS Launch Commercial Television 1211
1941   Nazis Ban Nolde's Paintings, The 1217
1941   *Maltese Falcon* Establishes a New Style for Crime
                    Films, *The* 1223
1942-1961   Italian New Wave Gains Worldwide Acclaim, The 1228
1942   Agnes de Mille Choreographs *Rodeo* 1234
1942   Peggy Guggenheim's Gallery Promotes New
                    American Art 1239
1942   *Casablanca* Marks the Artistic Apex of 1940's
                    War-Themed Films 1245
1943   Sinatra Establishes Himself as a Solo Performer 1250
1943   *Oklahoma!* Opens on Broadway 1256
1943   Sartre's *Being and Nothingness* Expresses Existential
                    Philosophy 1262
1944   Borges' *Ficciones* Transcends Traditional Realism 1268
1944   Robbins' *Fancy Free* Premieres 1274
1944   *U.S. Highball* Premieres in New York 1279
1944   Graham Debuts *Appalachian Spring* with Copland Score 1284
1945   *Arts and Architecture* Magazine Initiates the Case Study
                    Program 1290

1945	Britten Completes *Peter Grimes*	1296
1946	Balanchine and Kirstein Make New York a World Center for Ballet	1301
1946-1960	Hollywood Studio System Is Transformed, The	1307
1946-1962	Westerns Dominate Postwar American Film	1313
1946	Parker's Playing Epitomizes Bebop	1318
1946	Bikini Swimsuit Is Introduced, The	1324
1946	Mahalia Jackson Begins Her Recording Career	1329
1946	Capra Releases *It's a Wonderful Life*	1335
1947-1951	Blacklisting Seriously Depletes Hollywood's Talent Pool	1340
1947	Dior's "New Look" Sweeps Europe and America	1346
1947	Great Books Foundation Is Established, The	1351
1947	German Writers Form Group 47	1357
1947	NBC Broadcasts the World Series	1362
1948	ABC Begins Its Own Network Television Service	1368
1948	Mailer Publishes *The Naked and the Dead*	1373
1948	Olivier's *Hamlet* Is Released to Acclaim and Controversy	1378
1948-1957	Variety Shows Dominate Television Programming	1383
1948	Zhdanov Denounces "Formalism" in Music	1388
1948-1951	"Mr. Television," Milton Berle, Has the Top-Rated Show	1394
1948-1957	*Kukla, Fran, and Ollie* Pioneers Children's Television Programming	1400
1948	Porter Creates an Integrated Score for *Kiss Me, Kate*	1404
1949	Brecht Founds the Berliner Ensemble	1410
1949	Hank Williams Performs on *The Grand Ole Opry*	1415
1949	*Nineteen Eighty-Four* Portrays Totalitarianism and Mind Control	1421
1949-1951	Ealing Comedies Mark a High Point in British Film	1427
1949-1952	Kelly Forges New Directions in Cinematic Dance	1432
1949-1950	Davis' *Birth of the Cool* Recordings Spawn 1950's Cool Jazz	1438
1949	Pound Wins the Bollingen Prize	1443
1949	Beauvoir's *The Second Sex* Anticipates the Women's Movement	1449
1950's	"Angry Young Men" Express Working-Class Views	1454
1950's	Beat Movement Rejects Mainstream Values, The	1460
1950's	Television Enters Its Golden Age	1465
1950's	Television Family Comedy Becomes Extremely Popular	1470
1951	Kurosawa's *Rashomon* Wins the Grand Prize at Venice	1476
1951	New Novel (*Le Nouveau Roman*) Emerges, The	1481
1951	*Streetcar Named Desire* Brings Method Acting to the Screen, A	1487

1951	Young Readers Embrace *The Catcher in the Rye*	1493
1951-1953	Beckett's Trilogy Pushes Against the Frontiers of Fiction	1498
1951-1963	Corbusier Designs and Builds Chandigarh, Le	1503
1951-1975	Powell Publishes the Epic *A Dance to the Music of Time*	1509
1951	Stravinsky's *The Rake's Progress* Premieres in Venice	1514
1951-1971	*Red Skelton Show* Becomes a Landmark on Network Television, *The*	1520
1951-1961	*I Love Lucy* Dominates Television Comedy	1525
1951	*Dragnet* Is the First Widely Popular Police Show	1531
1951	*Amahl and the Night Visitors* Premieres on American Television	1536
1952	Ellison's *Invisible Man* Is Published	1541
1952	Cage's *4' 33"* Premieres	1546
1952	*Mousetrap* Begins a Record-Breaking Run, The	1551
1952	Rosenberg Defines "Action Painting"	1557
1953	Laura Ashley and Her Husband Found a Fashion Company . . .	1562
1953-1955	Marilyn Monroe Climbs to Stardom	1567
1953	*Waiting for Godot* Expresses the Existential Theme of Absurdity	1573
1953	Fuller's First Industrial Geodesic Dome Is Erected	1579
1954	Golding's *Lord of the Flies* Spurs Examination of Human Nature	1585
1954	Jasper Johns Paints the American Flag	1590
1954	*Strada* Solidifies Fellini's Renown as a Brilliant Director, *La*	1596
1954	Taylor Establishes His Own Dance Company	1602
1954-1955	Tolkien Publishes *The Lord of the Rings*	1607
1954	ABC Makes a Landmark Deal with Disney	1612
1954	First Newport Jazz Festival Is Held, The	1617
1954	*Tonight Show* Becomes an American Institution, *The*	1623
1954	Varèse Premieres *Déserts*	1629

VOLUME IV

1955	Berry's "Maybellene" Popularizes Rock and Roll	1635
1955	Dean Becomes a Legend in *Rebel Without a Cause*	1640
1955	O'Connor's *A Good Man Is Hard to Find* Is Published	1645
1955	Poitier Emerges as a Film Star in *The Blackboard Jungle*	1650
1955	Boulez's *Le Marteau sans maître* Premieres in Baden-Baden	1656
1955	Dickinson's Poems Are Published in Full for the First Time . .	1662
1955	*Gunsmoke* Debuts, Launching a Popular Television Genre . . .	1668

1955-1971   *Honeymooners* Enchants Audiences of All Ages, *The* 1673
1955   *Captain Kangaroo* Debuts 1678
1955   Buckley Founds *National Review* 1683
Late 1950's-
1960's   "Boom" Captures Worldwide Attention, The 1689
1956   Joffrey Founds His Ballet Company 1694
1956   Wiesel's *Night* Recalls the Holocaust 1700
1956-1957   Presley Becomes a Rock-and-Roll Sensation 1705
1956-1960   French New Wave Ushers in a New Era of Cinema, The 1710
1956-1962   Saarinen Designs Kennedy Airport's TWA Terminal 1716
1956   Osborne's *Look Back in Anger* Opens in London 1721
1956   *Long Day's Journey into Night* Revives O'Neill's
             Reputation 1726
1957   Bernstein Joins Symphonic and Jazz Elements in *West
             Side Story* 1731
1957-1962   Ford Foundation Begins to Fund Nonprofit Theaters, The 1736
1957   Bergman Wins International Fame with *The Seventh Seal* 1742
1957   Pasternak's *Doctor Zhivago* Is Published 1747
1957   Willson's *The Music Man* Presents Musical Americana 1752
1958   Behan's *The Hostage* Is Presented by the Theatre Workshop ... 1757
1958   *Things Fall Apart* Depicts Destruction of Ibo Culture 1763
1958-1959   Seven of the Top Ten Television Series Are Westerns 1768
1958   Ailey Founds His Dance Company 1774
1959   Grass Publishes *The Tin Drum* 1780
1959   First Successful Synthesizer Is Completed, The 1785
1959   Gordy Founds Motown Records 1790
1959   Hansberry's *A Raisin in the Sun* Debuts on Broadway 1795
1959-1973   *Bonanza* Becomes an American Television Classic 1800
1959   Guggenheim Museum Opens in a Building Designed by
             Wright, The 1806
1959   Ionesco's *Rhinoceros* Receives a Resounding Worldwide
             Reception 1812
1959   Villa-Lobos' Death Marks the End of a Brilliant Musical
             Career 1818

Early 1960's Quant Introduces the Miniskirt 1824
1960's   Social Philosophers Rediscover the Works of Hesse 1829
1960's   Situation Comedies Dominate Television Programming 1835
1960   *Flintstones* Popularizes Prime-Time Cartoons, *The* 1840
1960   Godard's Expressionistic *À bout de souffle* Revolutionizes
             Film 1845
1960   Plath's *The Colossus* Voices Women's Experience 1850
1960   *Psycho* Becomes Hitchcock's Most Famous Film 1855

1960	Pinter's *The Caretaker* Opens in London	1861
1961	*Catch-22* Illustrates Antiwar Sentiment	1866
1961	Esslin Publishes *The Theatre of the Absurd*	1871
1961	Foucault's *Madness and Civilization* Is Published	1877
1961	Heinlein Publishes *Stranger in a Strange Land*	1883
1961	Royal Shakespeare Company Adopts a New Name and Focus, The	1888
1961	Tawfiq al-Hakim Introduces Absurdism to the Arab Stage	1893
1961	*Webster's Third New International Dictionary* Sparks Linguistic Controversy	1898
1961	*American Dream* Establishes Albee as the Voice of Pessimism, *The*	1903
1961-1966	*Dick Van Dyke Show* Popularizes Situation Comedy, *The*	1908
1962	*Dr. No* Launches the Hugely Popular James Bond Series	1913
1962-1974	Kahn Blends Architecture and Urban Planning in Dacca	1919
1962	Great Britain Establishes the Royal National Theatre	1924
1963	Baldwin Voices Black Rage in *The Fire Next Time*	1929
1963	Le Carré Rejects the Fantasy World of Secret Agents	1934
1963	Vonnegut's *Cat's Cradle* Expresses 1960's Alienation	1939
1963-1965	Beatles Revolutionize Popular Music, The	1944
1963-1968	Minimalism Emphasizes Objects as Art	1949
1963	Nam June Paik Exhibits Video and Television as Art	1955
1963	Nureyev and Fonteyn Debut Ashton's *Marguerite and Armand*	1962
1963	Havel's *The Garden Party* Satirizes Life Under Communism	1967
1964	McLuhan Probes the Impact of Mass Media on Society	1973
1964	Riley Completes *In C*	1979
1964-1969	Leone Renovates the Western Genre	1984
1964-1971	Kubrick Becomes a Film-Industry Leader	1989
1964-1971	Lévi-Strauss Explores Myth as a Key to Enlightenment	1995
1964	Baraka's *Dutchman* Dramatizes Racial Hatred	2000
1964	Weiss's Absurdist Drama *Marat/Sade* Is Produced	2005
1964	Cunningham Stages His First Dance "Event"	2011
1964-1969	*Peyton Place* Brings Serial Drama to Nighttime Television	2017
1965	*Autobiography of Malcolm X* Is Published, *The*	2022
1965	Rolling Stones Release *Out of Our Heads*, The	2027
1965	*Sound of Music* Captivates Audiences, *The*	2033
1965	Dylan Performs with Electric Instruments	2038
1965	*I Spy* Debuts to Controversy	2044
1965	National Endowment for the Arts Is Established, The	2048
1966	Warhol's *The Chelsea Girls* Becomes a Commercial Success	2053

1966	Brown Wins a Grammy for "Papa's Got a Brand New Bag"	2059
1966	Breuer Designs a Building for the Whitney Museum	2064
1967	Celan's Influential *Atemwende* Is Published	2070
1967	Derrida Enunciates the Principles of Deconstruction	2075
1967	Expo 67 Presents Innovative Architectural Concepts	2081
1967	García Márquez's *One Hundred Years of Solitude* Is Published	2086
1967	Hendrix Releases *Are You Experienced?*	2092
1967	Beatles Release *Sgt. Pepper's Lonely Hearts Club Band, The*	2098
1967	Monterey Pop Festival Inaugurates the "Summer of Love", The	2104
1968	Mitchell Founds the Dance Theater of Harlem	2110
1968-1973	*Rowan and Martin's Laugh-In* Is the Top Show on Television	2115
1968	Radical Musical *Hair* Opens on Broadway, The	2121
1968	Handke's *Kaspar* Dramatizes Language Theory	2126
1968	Theatres Act Ends Censorship of English Drama, The	2131
1968	*60 Minutes* Becomes the First Televised Newsmagazine	2136
1968	Lauren Creates the "Polo" Line	2141
1968	Kawabata Wins the Nobel Prize in Literature	2147
1969	Davis' *Bitches Brew* Vitalizes Jazz-Rock Fusion	2153
1969	*Easy Rider* Captures the Spirit of 1960's Youth	2158
1969	Roth Publishes *Portnoy's Complaint*	2163
1969-1970	*Forsyte Saga* Is a Hit on Public Television, *The*	2168
1969-1974	*Monty Python's Flying Circus* Captures Audiences Worldwide	2174
1969	Woodstock Music Festival Marks the Climax of the 1960's, The	2180

VOLUME V

1969	*Sesame Street* Revolutionizes Children's Programming	2185
1970's	New York's SoHo Develops into a Center for Contemporary Art	2191
1970's	Relevance Programs Change Entertainment Standards	2197
1970's	Spanish Art Explodes After Years of Suppression	2203
1970	*Design for the Real World* Reorients Industrial Design	2208
1970	Sondheim's *Company* Is Broadway's First "Concept" Musical	2213

1970-1977   *Mary Tyler Moore Show* Examines Women's Roles, *The* 2218
1970   Trudeau's *Doonesbury* Popularizes Topical Comic Strips 2223
1971   Led Zeppelin Merges Hard Rock and Folk Music 2228
1971-1976   *All in the Family* Introduces a New Style of Television
            Comedy 2234
1971   Guare's *The House of Blue Leaves* Combines Comedy with
            Horror 2239
1971-1977   *Sonny and Cher Comedy Hour* Brings Glitz to
            Television, *The* 2244
1971   Mortimer's *A Voyage Round My Father* Is Embraced by
            Audiences 2249
1971   *Jesus Christ Superstar* Establishes the Rock Opera 2254
1972   Syndication Turns *Star Trek* into a Cult Classic 2260
1972, 1974, Coppola Revives Gangster Films with *The Godfather*
1990   Trilogy 2265
1972   *M*A*S*H* Reflects 1970's Sentiments 2271
1973-1975   *Gulag Archipelago* Exposes Soviet Atrocities, *The* 2277
1973   Pynchon's *Gravity's Rainbow* Is Published 2283
1973   Tharp Stages *Deuce Coupe* for the Joffrey Ballet 2288
1973   Wonder Releases *Innervisions* 2294
1974-1976   Punk's Antifashion Style First Appears 2299
1974-1984   *Happy Days* Exemplifies Escapist Television 2305
1974   Dalí Museum Opens in Figueras, Spain, A 2310
1974   *Dog Soldiers* Portrays Vietnam in Fiction 2315
1975   Forman Adapts *One Flew Over the Cuckoo's Nest* for Film . . . 2320
1975   Springsteen's *Born to Run* Reinvigorates Mainstream Rock . . . 2325
1975-1979   Violent Action-Adventure Television Series Flourish 2330
1975   *Wiz* Brings African-American Talent to Broadway, *The* 2334
1975-1985   *Jeffersons* Signals Success of Black Situation
            Comedies, *The* 2339
1975   Marley's *Natty Dread* Establishes Reggae's Popularity 2344
1975   Joplin's *Treemonisha* Is Staged by the Houston Opera 2350
1975   *Saturday Night Live* Is First Broadcast 2355
1975-1978   Sex Pistols Spark Punk Rock's Musical Insurrection, The 2360
1976   *Wanted: The Outlaws* Revitalizes Country Music 2365
1976   Shange's *for colored girls* . . . Is a Landmark 2370
1976   *Einstein on the Beach* Is a Triumph of Minimalism 2375
1977   Allen's *Annie Hall* Captures Complexities of 1970's Life 2381
1977   *Saturday Night Fever* Epitomizes the Disco Craze 2386
1977-1983   *Star Wars* Trilogy Redefines Special Effects, The 2391
1977   *Roots* Dramatizes the African-American Experience 2397
1977   Pompidou Center Opens in Paris, The 2402
1978   AT&T Building Exemplifies Postmodernism, The 2407

1978-1979   Shepard's *Buried Child* Promotes Off-Broadway Theater 2413
1978-1991   *Dallas* Popularizes the Prime-Time Soap Opera 2418
1978   Singer Wins the Nobel Prize in Literature 2423
1979   *Apocalypse Now* Is Hailed as the Ultimate Vietnam
             War Film 2428
1979   Sondheim Uses Operatic Techniques in *Sweeney Todd* 2433

Early 1980's Schnabel Emerges as a Celebrity Artist 2438
1980's   Female Directors Attain Prominence 2443
1980's   Madonna Revolutionizes Popular Fashion 2449
1980's   Wynton Marsalis Revives Acoustic Jazz 2454
1980   Baryshnikov Becomes Artistic Director of American Ballet
             Theatre 2459
1980   Four Modern Masters Affirm Germany's Place in the Art
             World 2464
1981-1987   *Hill Street Blues* Defines Hard-Reality Television 2470
1981   MTV Changes the Look of American Popular Culture 2475
1981   New Dance U.S.A. Festival Celebrates Contemporary
             Dance, The 2480
1982   Scott's *Blade Runner* Is a Visual Masterpiece 2486
1982   *E.T.: The Extraterrestrial* Breaks Box-Office Records 2491
1982   *"MASTER HAROLD" . . . and the boys* Examines
             Apartheid 2496
1982   Fierstein's *Torch Song Trilogy* Meets with Unexpected
             Success 2502
1982   *USA Today* Is Launched 2507
1982   *Thriller* Marks Michael Jackson's Musical Coming-of-Age . . . 2512
1983   Laurie Anderson's *United States* Popularizes
             Performance Art 2517
1983-1984   Festivals Mark a Peak in the Dance Created by
             Black Artists 2521
1984   *Sixteen Candles* Starts a Wave of Teen Films 2527
1984-1992   *Cosby Show* Makes Television History, *The* 2532
1984   Simon's *Biloxi Blues* Emphasizes Serious Themes 2537
1985   Live Aid Generates Millions for Famine Relief 2543
1985   Christo Wraps the Pont Neuf 2548
Late 1980's Decline of the Big Three Networks Becomes a Fall, The 2554
Late 1980's Multiculturalism Dominates the Dance World 2559
Late 1980's-
early 1990's Innovative Black Filmmakers Achieve Success 2565
1986   Akalaitis' *Green Card* Confronts Audiences with Harsh
             Realities 2571
1986   *Platoon* Explores the Vietnam Experience 2576

1986	Rap Goes Platinum with Run-D.M.C.'s *Raising Hell*	2582
1986	Musée d'Orsay Opens, The	2588
1986	Soyinka Wins the Nobel Prize in Literature	2594
1987	Adams' *Nixon in China* Premieres	2599
1987	Van Gogh's *Irises* Sells for $53.9 Million	2603
1987	National Museum of Women in the Arts Opens Amid Controversy, The	2608
1988	Deconstructivists Exhibit at the Museum of Modern Art	2614
1988	Pei Creates a New Entrance to the Louvre	2619
1988	Mahfouz Wins the Nobel Prize in Literature	2625
1989	Khomeini Calls for Rushdie's Death	2630
1989	Mapplethorpe's Photographs Provoke Controversy	2636
1989	*Do the Right Thing* Establishes Lee as a World-Class Director	2641
Early 1990's	Disney Emerges as an Architectural Patron	2646
1990	*Simpsons* Debuts, Anchoring the Fledgling Fox Network, *The*	2652
1990	*Civil War* Rivets the Attention of the United States, *The*	2657
1990	Baryshnikov's White Oak Dance Project Debuts	2663
1991	Gordimer Wins the Nobel Prize in Literature	2668
1992	Columbus Day Debates Reflect Cultural Diversity	2673

ALPHABETICAL LIST OF EVENTS

Aalto Designs Villa Mairea, II-1067

Abbey Theatre Heralds the Celtic Revival, The, I-119

ABC Begins Its Own Network Television Service, III-1368

ABC Makes a Landmark Deal with Disney, III-1612

Abstract Painting in America Opens in New York, II-1001

Adams' *Nixon in China* Premieres, V-2599

Agnes de Mille Choreographs *Rodeo*, III-1234

Ailey Founds His Dance Company, IV-1774

Akalaitis' *Green Card* Confronts Audiences with Harsh Realities, V-2571

All in the Family Introduces a New Style of Television Comedy, V-2234

All Quiet on the Western Front Stresses the Futility of War, II-767

Allen's *Annie Hall* Captures Complexities of 1970's Life, V-2381

Amahl and the Night Visitors Premieres on American Television, III-1536

American Dream Establishes Albee as the Voice of Pessimism, *The*, IV-1903

American Science Fiction Enjoys Its Golden Age, III-1094

Amos 'n' Andy Radio Show Goes on the Air, The, II-755

"Angry Young Men" Express Working-Class Views, III-1454

Apocalypse Now Is Hailed as the Ultimate Vietnam War Film, V-2428

Apollinaire Defines Cubism in *The Cubist Painters*, I-337

Après-midi d'un faune Causes an Uproar, L', I-332

Armstrong First Records with His Hot Five Group, II-670

Art of Radio Develops from Early Broadcast Experience, The, I-469

Artists Find Inspiration in African Tribal Art, I-156

Arts and Architecture Magazine Initiates the Case Study Program, III-1290

ASCAP Is Founded to Protect Musicians' Rights, I-379

AT&T Building Exemplifies Postmodernism, The, V-2407

Autobiography of Malcolm X Is Published, The, IV-2022

Avant-Garde Art in the Armory Show Shocks American Viewers, I-361

Avant-Garde Artists in Dresden Form Die Brücke, I-134

Baker Dances in *La Revue nègre*, II-665

Baker Establishes the 47 Workshop at Harvard, I-343

Balanchine and Kirstein Make New York a World Center for Ballet, III-1301

Balanchine's *Serenade* Inaugurates American Ballet, II-974

Baldwin Voices Black Rage in *The Fire Next Time*, IV-1929

Ballet Russe de Monte Carlo Finds New Leadership, The, III-1088

Baraka's *Dutchman* Dramatizes Racial Hatred, IV-2000

Bartók and Kodály Begin to Collect Hungarian Folk Songs, I-102

Baryshnikov Becomes Artistic Director of American Ballet Theatre, V-2459

Baryshnikov's White Oak Dance Project Debuts, V-2663

Beat Movement Rejects Mainstream Values, The, III-1460

Beatles Release *Sgt. Pepper's Lonely Hearts Club Band*, The, IV-2098

Beatles Revolutionize Popular Music, The IV-1944

Beauvoir's *The Second Sex* Anticipates the Women's Movement, III-1449

Beckett's Trilogy Pushes Against the Frontiers of Fiction, III-1498

Bedbug and *The Bathhouse* Exemplify Revolutionary Theater, *The*, II-787

Behan's *The Hostage* Is Presented by the Theatre Workshop, IV-1757

Behrens Designs the AEG Turbine Factory, I-219

Berg's *Lulu* Opens in Zurich, II-1078

Berg's *Wozzeck* Premieres in Berlin, II-680

Bergman Wins International Fame with *The Seventh Seal*, IV-1742

Bergson's *Creative Evolution* Inspires Artists and Thinkers, I-161

Berkeley's *42nd Street* Revolutionizes Film Musicals, II-925

Bernstein Joins Symphonic and Jazz Elements in *West Side Story*, IV-1731

Berry's "Maybellene" Popularizes Rock and Roll, IV-1635

Bessie Smith Records "Downhearted Blues," II-572

Bikini Swimsuit Is Introduced, The, III-1324

Bill Monroe and the Blue Grass Boys Define Bluegrass Music, III-1121

Billie Holiday Begins Her Recording Career, II-930

Birth of a Nation Popularizes New Film Techniques, *The*, I-402

Blacklisting Seriously Depletes Hollywood's Talent Pool, III-1340

Blaue Reiter Abandons Representation in Art, Der, I-275

Bonanza Becomes an American Television Classic, IV-1800

Book-of-the-Month Club and the Literary Guild Are Founded, The, II-686

"Boom" Captures Worldwide Attention, The, IV-1689

Borges' *Ficciones* Transcends Traditional Realism, III-1268

Boulanger Takes Copland as a Student, I-508

Boulez's *Le Marteau sans maître* Premieres in Baden-Baden, IV-1656

Brecht and Weill Collaborate on *Mahagonny Songspiel*, II-724

Brecht Founds the Berliner Ensemble, III-1410

Breuer Designs a Building for the Whitney Museum, IV-2064

British Broadcasting Corporation Is Chartered, The, II-712

Britten Completes *Peter Grimes*, III-1296

Brooks Brothers Introduces Button-Down Shirts, I-24

Brown Wins a Grammy for "Papa's Got a Brand New Bag," IV-2059

Buckley Founds *National Review*, IV-1683

Buñuel and Dalí Champion Surrealism in *Un Chien andalou*, II-750

Busoni's *Sketch for a New Aesthetic of Music* Is Published, I-166

Cabinet of Dr. Caligari Opens in Berlin, *The*, I-486

Cage's *4' 33"* Premieres, III-1546

Capra Releases *It's a Wonderful Life*, III-1335

Captain Kangaroo Debuts, IV-1678

Carnegie Publishes His Self-Help Best-Seller, II-1048

Caruso Records for the Gramophone and Typewriter Company, I-69

Casablanca Marks the Artistic Apex of 1940's War-Themed Films, III-1245

Catch-22 Illustrates Antiwar Sentiment, IV-1866

Cather's *My Ántonia* Promotes Regional Literature, I-452

Celan's Influential *Atemwende* Is Published, IV-2070

Celine's *Journey to the End of the Night* Is Published, II-890

Chanel Defines Modern Women's Fashion, I-474

Chaplin Produces His Masterpiece *The Gold Rush*, II-659

Christian Science Monitor Is Founded, *The*, I-209

Christo Wraps the Pont Neuf, V-2548

Civil War Rivets the Attention of the United States, *The*, V-2657

Classic Screwball Comedy Reaches Its Height in Popularity, The, II-951

Classic *The Wizard of Oz* Opens, The, III-1109

Cohan's *Little Johnny Jones* Premieres, I-108

Columbus Day Debates Reflect Cultural Diversity, V-2673

Coppola Revives Gangster Films with *The Godfather* Trilogy, V-2265

Corbusier Designs and Builds Chandigarh, Le, III-1503

Corbusier's Villa Savoye Redefines Architecture, Le, II-869

Cosby Show Makes Television History, *The*, V-2532

Coward's *Design for Living* Epitomizes the 1930's, II-936

Cranbrook Academy Begins a History of Design Excellence, II-610

Crane Publishes *The Bridge*, II-851

Cunningham Stages His First Dance "Event," IV-2011

Dada Movement Emerges at the Cabaret Voltaire, The, I-419

Dalí Museum Opens in Figueras, Spain, A, V-2310

Dallas Popularizes the Prime-Time Soap Opera, V-2418

Davis' *Birth of the Cool* Recordings Spawn 1950's Cool Jazz, III-1438

Davis' *Bitches Brew* Vitalizes Jazz-Rock Fusion, IV-2153

Dean Becomes a Legend in *Rebel Without a Cause*, IV-1640

Decline of the Big Three Networks Becomes a Fall, The, V-2554

Deconstructivists Exhibit at the Museum of Modern Art, V-2614

Denishawn School of Dance Opens in Los Angeles, The, I-390

Derrida Enunciates the Principles of Deconstruction, IV-2075

Design for the Real World Reorients Industrial Design, V-2208

Deutscher Werkbund Combats Conservative Architecture, The, I-181

Diaghilev's Ballets Russes Astounds Paris, I-241

Diary of a Country Priest Inspires Readers, The, II-1026

Dick Van Dyke Show Popularizes Situation Comedy, The, IV-1908

Dickinson's Poems Are Published in Full for the First Time, IV-1662

Dior's "New Look" Sweeps Europe and America, III-1346

Disney Emerges as an Architectural Patron, V-2646

Disney Releases *Snow White and the Seven Dwarfs*, II-1053

Disney's *Fantasia* Premieres and Redefines the Boundaries of Animation, III-1195

Do the Right Thing Establishes Lee as a World-Class Director, V-2641

Dr. No Launches the Hugely Popular James Bond Series, IV-1913

Dog Soldiers Portrays Vietnam in Fiction, V-2315

Dragnet Is the First Widely Popular Police Show, III-1531

Dreiser's *Sister Carrie* Shatters Literary Taboos, I-39

Dreyfuss Designs the Bell "300" Telephone, II-1057

Duchamp's "Readymades" Challenge Concepts of Art, I-349

Duncan Interprets Chopin in Her Russian Debut, I-113

Dylan Performs with Electric Instruments, IV-2038

Ealing Comedies Mark a High Point in British Film, III-1427

Easy Rider Captures the Spirit of 1960's Youth, IV-2158

Einstein on the Beach Is a Triumph of Minimalism, V-2375

Eisenstein's *Potemkin* Introduces New Film Editing Techniques, II-615

Elgar's First Symphony Premieres to Acclaim, I-214

Eliot Publishes *The Waste Land*, II-539

Ellington Begins an Influential Engagement at the Cotton Club, II-739

Ellison's *Invisible Man* Is Published, III-1541

Empire State Building Opens as the World's Tallest Building, The, II-880

Esslin Publishes *The Theatre of the Absurd*, IV-1871

E.T.: The Extraterrestrial Breaks Box-Office Records, V-2491

Expo 67 Presents Innovative Architectural Concepts, IV-2081

Fauves Exhibit at the Salon d'Automne, Les, I-140

Federal Theatre Project Promotes Live Theater, The, II-989

Female Directors Attain Prominence, V-2443

Festivals Mark a Peak in the Dance Created by Black Artists, V-2521

Fierstein's *Torch Song Trilogy* Meets with Unexpected Success, V-2502

Firebird Premieres in Paris, The, I-269

First Academy Awards Honor Film Achievement, The, II-799

First Newport Jazz Festival Is Held, The, III-1617

First Nobel Prizes Are Awarded, The, I-45

First Pulitzer Prizes Are Awarded, The, I-407

First Successful Synthesizer Is Completed, The, IV-1785

Flintstones Popularizes Prime-Time Cartoons, *The*, IV-1840

Fokine's *Les Sylphides* Introduces Abstract Ballet, I-247

Ford Defines the Western in *Stagecoach*, III-1115

Ford Foundation Begins to Fund Nonprofit Theaters, The, IV-1736

Forman Adapts *One Flew Over the Cuckoo's Nest* for Film, V-2320

Formation of the Blue Four Advances Abstract Painting, The, II-583

Forsyte Saga Is a Hit on Public Television, *The*, IV-2168

Foucault's *Madness and Civilization* Is Published, IV-1877

Four Modern Masters Affirm Germany's Place in the Art World, V-2464

French New Wave Ushers in a New Era of Cinema, The, IV-1710

Freud Inaugurates a Fascination with the Unconscious, I-19

Fuller's First Industrial Geodesic Dome Is Erected, III-1579

Futurists Issue Their Manifesto, The, I-235

Gance's *Napoléon* Revolutionizes Filmmaking Techniques, II-642

García Lorca's *Poet in New York* Is Published, III-1179

García Márquez's *One Hundred Years of Solitude* Is Published, IV-2086

Gaudí Completes the Casa Milá Apartment House in Barcelona, I-257

German Artists Found the Bauhaus, I-463

German Writers Form Group 47, III-1357

Gershwin's *Porgy and Bess* Opens in New York, II-1016

Gershwin's *Rhapsody in Blue* Premieres in New York, II-598

Ghost Sonata Influences Modern Theater and Drama, *The*, I-199

Gide's *The Counterfeiters* Questions Moral Absolutes, II-620

Godard's Expressionistic *À bout de souffle* Revolutionizes Film, IV-1845

Golding's *Lord of the Flies* Spurs Examination of Human Nature, III-1585

Gone with the Wind Premieres, III-1154

Goodman Begins His *Let's Dance* Broadcasts, II-968

Gordimer Wins the Nobel Prize in Literature, V-2668

Gordy Founds Motown Records, IV-1790

Graham Debuts *Appalachian Spring* with Copland Score, III-1284

Grapes of Wrath Portrays Depression-Era America, *The*, III-1138

Grass Publishes *The Tin Drum*, IV-1780

Great Books Foundation Is Established, The, III-1351

Great Britain Establishes the Royal National Theatre, IV-1924

Great Gatsby Captures the Essence of the Roaring Twenties, *The*, II-626

Great Train Robbery Introduces New Editing Techniques, *The*, I-74

Grey's *Riders of the Purple Sage* Launches the Western Genre, I-304

Group Theatre Flourishes, The, II-874

Guare's *The House of Blue Leaves* Combines Comedy with Horror, V-2239

Guggenheim Museum Opens in a Building Designed by Wright, The, IV-1806

Gulag Archipelago Exposes Soviet Atrocities, *The*, V-2277

Gunsmoke Debuts, Launching a Popular Television Genre, IV-1668

Guthrie's Populist Songs Reflect the Depression-Era United States, II-810

Hallelujah Is the First Important Black Musical, II-772

Handke's *Kaspar* Dramatizes Language Theory, IV-2126

Handy Ushers in the Commercial Blues Era, I-252

Hank Williams Performs on *The Grand Ole Opry*, III-1415

Hansberry's *A Raisin in the Sun* Debuts on Broadway, IV-1795

Happy Days Exemplifies Escapist Television, V-2305

Harlem Renaissance Celebrates African-American Culture, The, I-480

Harriet Monroe Founds *Poetry* Magazine, I-314

Hašek's *The Good Soldier Švejk* Reflects Postwar Disillusionment, I-523

Havel's *The Garden Party* Satirizes Life Under Communism, IV-1967

Heart of Darkness Reveals the Consequences of Imperialism, I-51

Heinlein Publishes *Stranger in a Strange Land*, IV-1883

Hemingway's *The Sun Also Rises* Speaks for the Lost Generation, II-696

Hendrix Releases *Are You Experienced?*, IV-2092

Henry James's *The Ambassadors* Is Published, I-96

Henry Moore Is Inspired by Shapes in Subway Shelters, III-1190

Hill Street Blues Defines Hard-Reality Television, V-2470

Hindemith Advances Ideas of Music for Use and for Amateurs, II-816

Hitchcock Becomes England's Foremost Director, II-946

Hitler Organizes an Exhibition Denouncing Modern Art, III-1083

Hoffmann and Moser Found the Wiener Werkstätte, I-79

Hoffmann Designs the Palais Stoclet, I-124

Hollywood Enters Its Golden Age, II-822

Hollywood Studio System Is Transformed, The, III-1307

Honeymooners Enchants Audiences of All Ages, The, IV-1673

Huxley's *Brave New World* Reflects Fears About the Future, II-896

I Love Lucy Dominates Television Comedy, III-1525

I Spy Debuts to Controversy, IV-2044

Imagist Movement Shakes Up Poetry, The, I-326

Innovative Black Filmmakers Achieve Success, V-2565

Ionesco's *Rhinoceros* Receives a Resounding Worldwide Reception, IV-1812

Italian New Wave Gains Worldwide Acclaim, The, III-1228

Ives Completes His Fourth Symphony, I-425

Jantzen Popularizes the One-Piece Bathing Suit, I-491

Jasper Johns Paints the American Flag, III-1590

Jazz Singer Premieres in New York, The, II-734

Jeffersons Signals Success of Black Situation Comedies, The, V-2339

Jesus Christ Superstar Establishes the Rock Opera, V-2254

Joffrey Founds His Ballet Company, IV-1694

Jooss's Antiwar Dance *The Green Table* Premieres, II-920

Joplin Popularizes the Ragtime Style, I-13

Joplin's *Treemonisha* Is Staged by the Houston Opera, V-2350

Joyce's *Ulysses* Epitomizes Modernism in Fiction, II-555

Jung Publishes *Psychology of the Unconscious*, I-309

Kahn Blends Architecture and Urban Planning in Dacca, IV-1919

Kandinsky Publishes His Views on Abstraction in Art, I-320

Karloff and Lugosi Become Kings of Horror, II-863

Kawabata Wins the Nobel Prize in Literature, IV-2147

Kazan Brings Naturalism to the Stage and Screen, III-1164

Keaton's *The General* Is Released, II-691

Kelly Forges New Directions in Cinematic Dance, III-1432

Khomeini Calls for Rushdie's Death, V-2630

Kubrick Becomes a Film-Industry Leader, IV-1989

Kukla, Fran, and Ollie Pioneers Children's Television Programming, III-1400

Kuleshov and Pudovkin Introduce Montage to Filmmaking, II-701

Kurosawa's *Rashomon* Wins the Grand Prize at Venice, III-1476

Lang Expands the Limits of Filmmaking with *Metropolis*, II-707

Laura Ashley and Her Husband Found a Fashion Company, III-1562

Lauren Creates the "Polo" Line, IV-2141

Laurie Anderson's *United States* Popularizes Performance Art, V-2517

Le Carré Rejects the Fantasy World of Secret Agents, IV-1934

Led Zeppelin Merges Hard Rock and Folk Music, V-2228

Leone Renovates the Western Genre, IV-1984

Lévi-Strauss Explores Myth as a Key to Enlightenment, IV-1995

Lippmann Helps to Establish *The New Republic*, I-385

Little Caesar, Public Enemy, and *Scarface* Launch the Gangster-Film Genre, II-839

Live Aid Generates Millions for Famine Relief, V-2543

Loewy Pioneers American Industrial Design, II-777

Long Day's Journey into Night Revives O'Neill's Reputation, IV-1726

Lubitsch's *The Merry Widow* Opens New Vistas for Film Musicals, II-941

Luce Founds *Time* Magazine, II-577

Luce Launches *Life* Magazine, II-1031

McLuhan Probes the Impact of Mass Media on Society, IV-1973

Madonna Revolutionizes Popular Fashion, V-2449

Mahalia Jackson Begins Her Recording Career, III-1329

Mahfouz Wins the Nobel Prize in Literature, V-2625

Mahler Revamps the Vienna Court Opera, I-7

Mahler's Masterpiece *Das Lied von der Erde* Premieres Posthumously, I-298

Mailer Publishes *The Naked and the Dead*, III-1373

Malevich Introduces Suprematism, I-413

Maltese Falcon Establishes a New Style for Crime Films, The, III-1223

Maltese Falcon Introduces the Hard-Boiled Detective Novel, The, II-793

Man Ray Creates the Rayograph, I-513

Mann's *The Magic Mountain* Reflects European Crisis, II-588

Mapplethorpe's Photographs Provoke Controversy, V-2636

Marian Anderson Is Barred from Constitution Hall, III-1126

Marilyn Monroe Climbs to Stardom, III-1567

Marley's *Natty Dread* Establishes Reggae's Popularity, V-2344

Mary Tyler Moore Show Examines Women's Roles, The, V-2218

*M*A*S*H* Reflects 1970's Sentiments, V-2271

"MASTER HAROLD" . . . *and the boys* Examines Apartheid, V-2496

Melville Is Rediscovered as a Major American Novelist, I-502

Messiaen's *Quartet for the End of Time* Premieres, III-1206

Metamorphosis Anticipates Modern Feelings of Alienation, The, I-396

Miller's Notorious Novel *Tropic of Cancer* Is Published, II-963

Minimalism Emphasizes Objects as Art, IV-1949

"Mr. Television," Milton Berle, Has the Top-Rated Show, III-1394

Mitchell Founds the Dance Theater of Harlem, IV-2110

Monet's *Water Lilies* Are Shown at the Musée de l'Orangerie, II-718

Monterey Pop Festival Inaugurates the "Summer of Love," The, IV-2104

Monty Python's Flying Circus Captures Audiences Worldwide, IV-2174

Mortimer's *A Voyage Round My Father* Is Embraced by Audiences, V-2249

Mousetrap Begins a Record-Breaking Run, The, III-1551

MTV Changes the Look of American Popular Culture, V-2475

Multiculturalism Dominates the Dance World, V-2559

Musée d'Orsay Opens, The, V-2588

Mysterious Affair at Styles Introduces Hercule Poirot, The, I-496

Nam June Paik Exhibits Video and Television as Art, IV-1955

National Endowment for the Arts Is Established, The, IV-2048

National Museum of Women in the Arts Opens Amid Controversy, The, V-2608

Nazis Ban Nolde's Paintings, The, III-1217

NBC and CBS Launch Commercial Television, III-1211

NBC Broadcasts the World Series, III-1362

NBC Launches American Television at the World's Fair, III-1143

New Criticism Holds Sway, The, III-1169

New Dance U.S.A. Festival Celebrates Contemporary Dance, The, V-2480

New Novel (*Le Nouveau Roman*) Emerges, The, III-1481

GREAT EVENTS FROM HISTORY II

New Objectivity Movement Is Introduced,
The, II-631
New York's Museum of Modern Art Is
Founded, II-782
New York's SoHo Develops into a Center for
Contemporary Art, V-2191
Nineteen Eighty-Four Portrays
Totalitarianism and Mind Control, III-1421
Nureyev and Fonteyn Debut Ashton's
Marguerite and Armand, IV-1962

O'Connor's *A Good Man Is Hard to Find* Is
Published, IV-1645
Odets' *Awake and Sing* Becomes a Model
for Protest Drama, II-1006
Oklahoma! Opens on Broadway, III-1256
Olivier's *Hamlet* Is Released to Acclaim and
Controversy, III-1378
Osborne's *Look Back in Anger* Opens in
London, IV-1721
Our Town Opens on Broadway, III-1099

Paris Exhibition Defines Art Deco, A, II-654
Parker's Playing Epitomizes Bebop, III-1318
Pasternak's *Doctor Zhivago* Is Published,
IV-1747
Pavlova First Performs Her Legendary Solo
The Dying Swan, I-187
Peggy Guggenheim's Gallery Promotes New
American Art, III-1239
Pei Creates a New Entrance to the Louvre,
V-2619
Peyton Place Brings Serial Drama to
Nighttime Television, IV-2017
Picasso Paints *Guernica*, II-1062
Pickford Becomes "America's Sweetheart,"
I-224
Pinter's *The Caretaker* Opens in London,
IV-1861
Pirandello's *Six Characters in Search of an
Author* Premieres, I-534
Plath's *The Colossus* Voices Women's
Experience, IV-1850
Platoon Explores the Vietnam Experience,
V-2576
Playboy of the Western World Offends Irish
Audiences, The, I-176
Poems Establishes Auden as a Generational
Spokesman, II-857
Poiret's "Hobble Skirts" Become the Rage,
I-263

Poitier Emerges as a Film Star in *The
Blackboard Jungle*, IV-1650
Pompidou Center Opens in Paris, The,
V-2402
Porter Creates an Integrated Score for *Kiss
Me, Kate*, III-1404
Pound Wins the Bollingen Prize, III-1443
Pound's *Cantos* Is Published, I-445
Powell Publishes the Epic *A Dance to the
Music of Time*, III-1509
Presley Becomes a Rock-and-Roll Sensation,
IV-1705
Proust's *Remembrance of Things Past* Is
Published, I-355
Prouvé Pioneers the Prefabrication of
Buildings, II-1021
Psycho Becomes Hitchcock's Most Famous
Film, IV-1855
Puccini's *Tosca* Premieres in Rome, I-29
Punk's Antifashion Style First Appears,
V-2299
Pynchon's *Gravity's Rainbow* Is Published,
V-2283

Quant Introduces the Miniskirt, IV-1824

Radical Musical *Hair* Opens on Broadway,
The, IV-2121
Radio Programming Dominates Home
Leisure, II-828
Rap Goes Platinum with Run-D.M.C.'s
Raising Hell, V-2582
Red Skelton Show Becomes a Landmark on
Network Television, The, III-1520
Reinhardt Becomes Director of the
Deutsches Theater, I-145
Relevance Programs Change Entertainment
Standards, V-2197
Renoir Marks the High Point of Prewar
Filmmaking, II-1073
Rietveld Designs the Red-Blue Chair, I-458
Riley Completes *In C*, IV-1979
Rilke's *Duino Elegies* Depicts Art as a
Transcendent Experience, I-281
Rite of Spring Stuns Audiences, The, I-373
Rivera's Rockefeller Center Mural Is
Destroyed, II-957
Robbins' *Fancy Free* Premieres, III-1274
Rockefeller Center Is Completed, III-1149
Rodgers Cuts His First Record for RCA
Victor, II-729

XC

Rolling Stones Release *Out of Our Heads,* The, IV-2027

Roosevelt Administration Creates the WPA/ FAP, The, II-995

Roots Dramatizes the African-American Experience, V-2397

Rosenberg Defines "Action Painting," III-1557

Ross Founds *The New Yorker,* II-648

Roth Publishes *Portnoy's Complaint,* IV-2163

Rowan and Martin's Laugh-In Is the Top Show on Television, IV-2115

Royal Shakespeare Company Adopts a New Name and Focus, The, IV-1888

Saarinen Designs Kennedy Airport's TWA Terminal, IV-1716

Salon d'Automne Rejects Braque's Cubist Works, The, I-204

Sartre and Camus Give Dramatic Voice to Existential Philosophy, III-1174

Sartre's *Being and Nothingness* Expresses Existential Philosophy, III-1262

Saturday Night Fever Epitomizes the Disco Craze, V-2386

Saturday Night Live Is First Broadcast, V-2355

Schiaparelli's Boutique Mingles Art and Fashion, II-979

Schnabel Emerges as a Celebrity Artist, V-2438

Schoenberg Breaks with Tonality, I-193

Schoenberg Develops His Twelve-Tone System, I-528

Scott's *Blade Runner* Is a Visual Masterpiece, V-2486

Scriabin's *Prometheus* Premieres in Moscow, I-286

Sennett Defines the Slapstick Comedy Genre, I-230

Sesame Street Revolutionizes Children's Programming, V-2185

Seven of the Top Ten Television Series Are Westerns, IV-1768

Sex Pistols Spark Punk Rock's Musical Insurrection, The, V-2360

Shange's *for colored girls . . .* Is a Landmark, V-2370

Shaw Articulates His Philosophy in *Man and Superman,* I-85

Shepard's *Buried Child* Promotes Off-Broadway Theater, V-2413

Sherlock Holmes Film Series Begins, The, III-1131

Shostakovich's *Lady Macbeth of Mtsensk* Is Condemned, II-1042

Show Boat Introduces American Musical Theater, II-745

Sibelius Conducts the Premiere of His Fourth Symphony, I-292

Simon's *Biloxi Blues* Emphasizes Serious Themes, V-2537

Simpsons Debuts, Anchoring the Fledgling Fox Network, The, V-2652

Sinatra Establishes Himself as a Solo Performer, III-1250

Singer Wins the Nobel Prize in Literature, V-2423

Situation Comedies Dominate Television Programming, IV-1835

"Six" Begin Giving Concerts, "Les," I-435

Sixteen Candles Starts a Wave of Teen Films, V-2527

60 Minutes Becomes the First Televised Newsmagazine, IV-2136

Social Philosophers Rediscover the Works of Hesse, IV-1829

Socialist Realism Is Mandated in Soviet Literature, II-908

Sondheim Uses Operatic Techniques in *Sweeney Todd,* V-2433

Sondheim's *Company* Is Broadway's First "Concept" Musical, V-2213

Sonny and Cher Comedy Hour Brings Glitz to Television, The, V-2244

Sound and the Fury Launches Faulkner's Career, The, II-805

Sound of Music Captivates Audiences, The, IV-2033

Sound Technology Revolutionizes the Motion-Picture Industry, II-761

Soviet Union Bans Abstract Art, The, II-544

Soyinka Wins the Nobel Prize in Literature, V-2594

Spanish Art Explodes After Years of Suppression, V-2203

Springsteen's *Born to Run* Reinvigorates Mainstream Rock, V-2325

Stalin Restricts Soviet Composers, II-914

Stanislavsky Helps to Establish the Moscow Art Theater, I-1

Star Wars Trilogy Redefines Special Effects, The, V-2391

Stein Holds Her First Paris Salons, I-129

Stieglitz Organizes the Photo-Secession, I-63

Stijl Advocates Mondrian's Neoplasticism, *De*, I-429

Stormy Weather Offers New Film Roles to African Americans, III-1159

Strada Solidifies Fellini's Renown as a Brilliant Director, *La*, III-1596

Strauss's *Salome* Shocks Audiences, I-151

Stravinsky Completes His Wind Octet, II-561

Stravinsky's *The Rake's Progress* Premieres in Venice, III-1514

Streetcar Named Desire Brings Method Acting to the Screen, *A*, III-1487

Studio System Dominates Hollywood Filmmaking, The, II-833

Surrealism Is Born, II-604

Syndication Turns *Star Trek* into a Cult Classic, V-2260

Tawfiq al-Hakim Introduces Absurdism to the Arab Stage, IV-1893

Taylor Establishes His Own Dance Company, III-1602

Television Enters Its Golden Age, III-1465

Television Family Comedy Becomes Extremely Popular, III-1470

Temple Receives a Special Academy Award, II-1011

Ten Commandments Establishes Silent-Film Spectacle, *The*, II-567

Tharp Stages *Deuce Coupe* for the Joffrey Ballet, V-2288

Theatres Act Ends Censorship of English Drama, The, IV-2131

Things Fall Apart Depicts Destruction of Ibo Culture, IV-1763

Thriller Marks Michael Jackson's Musical Coming-of-Age, V-2512

Tiffany and Tiffany Studios Develop New Ideas in Design, I-34

Tolkien Publishes *The Lord of the Rings*, III-1607

Tonight Show Becomes an American Institution, The, III-1623

Top Hat Establishes the Astaire-Rogers Dance Team, II-984

Trudeau's *Doonesbury* Popularizes Topical Comic Strips, V-2223

Tudor's *Jardin aux lilas* Premieres in London, II-1036

U.S. Highball Premieres in New York, III-1279

USA Today Is Launched, V-2507

Van Gogh's *Irises* Sells for $53.9 Million, V-2603

Varèse Premieres *Déserts*, III-1629

Variety Shows Dominate Television Programming, III-1383

Vaughan Williams Composes His Nine Symphonies, I-90

Villa-Lobos' Death Marks the End of a Brilliant Musical Career, IV-1818

Violent Action-Adventure Television Series Flourish, V-2330

Von Sternberg Makes Dietrich a Superstar, II-845

Von Stroheim Films His Silent Masterpiece *Greed*, II-593

Vonnegut's *Cat's Cradle* Expresses 1960's Alienation, IV-1939

Voyage dans la lune Introduces Special Effects, *Le*, I-57

Waiting for Godot Expresses the Existential Theme of Absurdity, III-1573

Wallace Founds *Reader's Digest*, II-549

Wanted: The Outlaws Revitalizes Country Music, V-2365

Warhol's *The Chelsea Girls* Becomes a Commercial Success, IV-2053

Webern's *Six Pieces for Large Orchestra* Premieres in Vienna, I-367

Webster's Third New International Dictionary Sparks Linguistic Controversy, IV-1898

Weiss's Absurdist Drama *Marat/Sade* Is Produced, IV-2005

Welles Broadcasts *The War of the Worlds*, III-1103

Welles's *Citizen Kane* Breaks with Traditional Filmmaking, III-1200

Westerns Dominate Postwar American Film, III-1313

Whitney Museum Is Inaugurated in New York, The, II-885

ALPHABETICAL LIST OF EVENTS

Wiesel's *Night* Recalls the Holocaust,
IV-1700

William James's *Pragmatism* Is Published,
I-171

Willson's *The Music Man* Presents Musical
Americana, IV-1752

Wittgenstein Emerges as an Important
Philosopher, I-518

Wiz Brings African-American Talent to
Broadway, The, V-2334

Wonder Releases *Innervisions*, V-2294

Woodstock Music Festival Marks the Climax
of the 1960's, The, IV-2180

Woolf's *Mrs. Dalloway* Explores Women's
Consciousness, II-637

Wright Founds the Taliesin Fellowship,
II-902

Wright's *Native Son* Depicts Racism in
America, III-1185

WSM Launches *The Grand Ole Opry*, II-675

Wynton Marsalis Revives Acoustic Jazz,
V-2454

Yeats Publishes *The Wild Swans at Coole*,
I-440

Young Readers Embrace *The Catcher in the
Rye*, III-1493

Zhdanov Denounces "Formalism" in Music,
III-1388

SUBJECT / KEY WORD INDEX

Abbey Theatre, I-119-123

ABC. *See* American Broadcasting Company.

Abstract art, I-275-280, 320-325, 337-342,
349-354, 361-366, 413-418, 419-424,
429-434, 463-468; II-544-548, 583-587,
718-723, 782-786, 885-889, 1001-1005,
1062-1066; III-1083-1087, 1239-1244,
1557-1561

Abstract ballet, I-247-251; II-1036-1041

Abstract expressionism, III-1239-1244,
1557-1561

Abstract Painting in America, II-1001-1005

Absurdism, III-1573-1578; IV-1812-1817,
1871-1876, 1893-1897, 1903-1907,
2005-2010; V-2239-2243

Academy Awards, II-799-804, 1011-1015

Action/adventure shows, III-1531-1535;
V-2330-2333

Action painting, II-885-889; III-1239-1244,
1557-1561

Adventures of Sherlock Holmes, The,
III-1131-1137

AEG Turbine Factory, I-219-223

African Americans in film, II-772-776;
III-1159-1163; IV-1650-1655; V-2334-2338,
2641-2645

African Americans in television,
IV-2044-2047; V-2339-2344, 2397-2401,
2532-2536

African art, I-156-160

African literature, IV-1763-1767;
V-2496-2501, 2594-2598, 2668-2672

African-American art, I-480-485

African-American dance, IV-1774-1779,
2110-2114; V-2521-2527

African-American directors, V-2565-2570,
2641-2645

African-American literature, I-480-485;
III-1185-1189, 1541-1545; IV-1795-1799,
1929-1933, 2000-2004, 2022-2026;
V-2370-2374

*Afternoon of a Faun, The. See Après-midi
d' un faune, L'.*

All in the Family, V-2197-2202, 2234-2238

"All or Nothing at All," III-1250-1255

All Quiet on the Western Front (Remarque),
II-767-771

Allgemeine Elektrizitäts-Gesellschaft
Turbine Factory. *See* AEG Turbine
Factory.

Alvin Ailey American Dance Theater,
IV-1774-1779

Amahl and the Night Visitors (Menotti),
III-1536-1540

Ambassadors, The (H. James), I-96-101

American Ballet Theatre, V-2459-2463

American Broadcasting Company (ABC),
III-1368-1372, 1612-1616; V-2554-2558

American Dream, The (Albee), IV-1903-1907

American literature, I-39-44, 96-101,
502-505; III-1460-1464

American Society of Composers, Authors,
and Publishers (ASCAP), I-379-384

Amos 'n' Andy, II-755-760

"Angry Young Men," III-1454-1459;
IV-1721-1725

Animation, II-1053-1056; III-1195-1199;
IV-1840-1844; V-2652-2656

Annie Hall (Allen), V-2381-2385

Anti-Semitism, III-1083-1087, 1217-1222;
IV-1700-1704, 2163-2167

Antiwar novels, I-523-527; II-767-771;
III-1357-1361, 1373-1377; IV-1780-1784,
1866-1870

Apartheid, V-2496-2501, 2668-2672

Apocalypse Now (Coppola), V-2428-2432

Appalachian Spring, III-1284-1289

Après-midi d' un faune, L', I-332-336

Arabic literature, IV-1893-1897; V-2625-2629

Architecture, I-124-128, 181-186, 219-233,
463-468; II-654-658, 869-873, 880-884,
902-907, 1021-1025, 1067-1072;
III-1149-1153, 1290-1295, 1503-1508,
1579-1584; IV-1716-1720, 1806-1811,
1919-1923, 2064-2069, 2081-2085;
V-2407-2412, 2614-2618, 2619-2624,
2646-2651

Are You Experienced? (Hendrix),
IV-2092-2097

Armory Show, I-361-366

Art. *See* Abstract art, Abstract
expressionism, Action painting, African
art, African-American art, Cubism,
Dadaism, Expressionism, Fauvism,

Futurism, Modernism, Painting, Performance art, Photography, Primitive art, Readymades, Suprematism, Surrealism.
Art auctions, V-2603-2607
Art Deco, II-654-658
Art Nouveau, I-181-186
Art of This Century Gallery, III-1239-1244
Arts and Architecture, III-1290-1295
Arts and Crafts movement, I-34-38; II-610-614
ASCAP. *See* American Society of Composers, Authors, and Publishers.
Ash Can School, I-361-366
AT&T Building, V-2407-2412
Atemwende (Celan), IV-2070-2074
Atonality, I-151-155, 166-170, 193-198, 367-372, 528-533; II-680-685, 1078-1082; IV-1656-1661
Autobiography of Malcolm X, The, IV-2022-2026
Awake and Sing (Odets), II-1006-1010

Ballet, I-187-192, 241-246, 247-251, 269-274, 332-336, 373-378; II-920-924, 974-978, 1036-1041; III-1088-1093, 1234-1238, 1274-1278, 1301-1306; IV-1694-1699, 1962-1966, 2110-2114; V-2288-2293, 2459-2463, 2521-2527, 2559-2564, 2663-2667
Ballet Russe de Monte Carlo, III-1088-1093
Ballet Society, III-1301-1306
Ballets Russes, I-241-246, 247-251, 269-274, 332-336, 373-378; III-1088-1093
Bathhouse, The (Mayakovsky), II-787-792
Battleship Potemkin, The. See *Potemkin.*
Bauhaus, I-181-186, 463-468
BBC. *See* British Broadcasting Corporation.
Beat Movement, III-1460-1464
Beatles, the, IV-1944-1948, 2098-2103
Bebop, III-1318-1323
Bedbug, The (Mayakovsky), II-787-792
Being and Nothingness (Sartre), III-1262-1267
Bell "300" Telephone, II-1057-1061
Berliner Ensemble, III-1410-1414
Big-band music, II-739-744, 968-973; III-1250-1255
Bikini, III-1324-1328
Biloxi Blues (Simon), V-2537-2542
Birth of a Nation, The (Griffith), I-402-406

Birth of the Cool (Davis), III-1438-1442
Bitches Brew (Davis), IV-2153-2157
Black Muslims, IV-1929-1933, 2022-2026
Blackboard Jungle, The (Brooks), IV-1650-1655
Blacklisting, III-1340-1345
Blade Runner (Scott), V-2486-2490
Blaue Reiter, Der, I-275-280, 320-325
Blaue Vier, Der. *See* Blue Four.
Blue Four, II-583-587
Blue Rider. *See* Blaue Reiter, Der.
Blue yodels, II-729-733
Bluegrass music, III-1121-1125
Blues, I-252-256, 480-485; II-572-576, 729-733, 739-744, 810-815, 930-935; III-1329-1334; IV-1635-1639, 1705-1709
Bollingen Prize, III-1443-1448
Bonanza, IV-1768-1773, 1800-1805
Book-of-the-Month Club, II-686-690
"Boom," the, IV-1689-1693, 2086-2091
Born to Run (Springsteen), V-2325-2329
Bout de souffle, À (Godard), IV-1845-1849
Brave New World (Huxley), II-896-901
Brazilian music, IV-1818-1823
Bridge, The (Crane), II-851-856
Bringing Up Baby (Hawks), II-951-956
British Broadcasting Corporation (BBC), II-712-717; IV-2168-2173, 2174-2179
Brooks Brothers, I-24-28
Brücke, Die, I-134-139
Buch der hängenden Gärten, Das (Schoenberg), I-193-198
Buddenbrooks (Mann), II-588-592
Buried Child (Shepard), V-2413-2417

Cabaret Voltaire, I-419-424
Cabinet of Dr. Caligari, The (Wiene), I-486-490
Cannes Film Festival, IV-1742-1746
Cantos (Pound), I-445-451; III-1443-1448
Captain Kangaroo, IV-1678-1682
Caretaker, The (Pinter), IV-1861-1865
Cartoons, IV-1840-1844; V-2652-2656
Casa Milá, I-257-262
Casablanca (Curtiz), III-1245-1249
Case Study Program, III-1290-1295
Catcher in the Rye, The (Salinger), III-1493-1497
Catch-22 (Heller), IV-1866-1870
Cat's Cradle (Vonnegut), IV-1939-1943
CBS. *See* Columbia Broadcasting System.

Celtic Revival, I-119-123, 440-444
Censorship, art, II-544-548, 957-962;
    III-1083-1087, 1217-1222; V-2203-2207,
    2636-2640
Censorship, film, II-839-844, 941-945;
    III-1340-1345
Censorship, literature, I-39-44; II-555-560,
    908-913, 963-967; III-1138-1142;
    IV-1747-1751, 2163-2167; V-2277-2282,
    2630-2635, 2668-2672
Censorship, music, II-914-919, 1042-1047;
    III-1126-1130, 1388-1393
Censorship, theater, II-787-792; IV-1967-1972,
    2131-2135
Chamber music, II-561-566; III-1206-1210
Chandigarh, III-1503-1508
Chanel, House of, I-474-479
Chelsea Girls, The (Warhol), IV-2053-2058
Chien andalou, Un (Buñuel and Dalí),
    II-750-754
Children's television, III-1400-1403;
    IV-1678-1682, 1840-1844; V-2185-2190
Christian Science Monitor, The, I-209-213
Citizen Kane (Welles), III-1200-1205
Civil War, The (Burns), V-2657-2662
Clash, the, V-2360-2364
Clockwork Orange, A (Kubrick),
    IV-1989-1994
Clothing, I-14-28, 263-268, 474-479, 491-495;
    II-979-983; III-1346-1350, 1562-1566;
    IV-1824-1828, 2141-2146; V-2299-2304,
    2449-2452
Colossus, The (Plath), IV-1850-1854
Columbia Broadcasting System (CBS),
    III-1211-1216; V-2554-2558
Comic strips, V-2223-2227
Company (Sondheim), V-2213-2217
Concept musicals, V-2213-2217
Concerning the Spiritual in Art (Kandinsky),
    I-320-325
Constitution Hall, III-1126-1130
Constructivism (architecture), IV-2064-2069
Cool jazz, III-1438-1442
Cosby Show, The, V-2532-2536
Cotton Club, II-739-744
Counterfeiters, The (Gide), II-620-625
Country music, II-675-679, 729-733; 810-815;
    III-1121-1125, 1415- 1420; IV-1635-1639,
    1705-1709, V-2365-2369
Cranbrook Academy, II-610-614
Création du monde, Le (Milhaud), I-435-439

Creative Evolution (Bergson), I-161-165
Cubism, I-129-133, 204-208, 337-342,
    349-354, 361-366, 413-418; II-1062-1066
Cubist Painters, The (Apollinaire), I-337-342
Czech literature, I-523-527; IV-1967-1972

Dacca, IV-1919-1923
Dadaism, I-129-133, 235-240, 419-424,
    513-517; IV-1955-1961
Dallas, V-2418-2422
Dance. *See* Abstract ballet, Ballet, Ballets
    Russes, Dance festivals, Modern dance,
    Psychological ballet.
Dance festivals, V-2480-2485, 2521-2527,
    2559-2564
Dance Theater of Harlem, IV-2110-2114
Dance to the Music of Time, A (Powell),
    III-1509-1513
Daughters of the American Revolution,
    III-1126-1130
Deconstruction (literature), IV-2075-2080
Deconstructivism (architecture), V-2614-2618
Denishawn School of Dance, I-390-395
Déserts (Varèse), III-1629-1634
Design for Living (Coward), II-936-940
Design for the Real World (Papanek),
    V-2208-2212
Design, I-34-38, 79-84, 458-462, 463-468;
    II-610-614, 654-658, 777-781, 1057-1061;
    III-1324-1328, 1579-1584; V-2208-2212
Detective films, III-1131-1137, 1223-1227
Detective novels, I-496-501; II-793-798;
    III-1131-1137; IV-1934-1938
Detective shows, III-1531-1535
Deuce Coupe (Tharp), V-2288-2293
Deutscher Werkbund, I-181-186, 219-223
Deutsches Theater, I-145-150
Diary of a Country Priest, The (Bernanos),
    II-1026-1030
Dick Van Dyke Show, The, IV-1908-1912
Directors, African-American, V-2565-2570,
    2641-2645
Directors, female, V-2443-2448
Disco music, V-2386-2390, 2512-2516
Disneyland, III-1612-1616
Do the Right Thing (Lee), V-2641-2645
Dr. No, IV-1913-1918
Dr. Strangelove (Kubrick), IV-1989-1994
Doctor Zhivago (Pasternak), IV-1747-1751
Dog Soldiers (Stone), V-2315-2319
Doonesbury (Trudeau), V-2223-2227

"Downhearted Blues," II-572-576
Dragnet, III-1531-1535
Duino Elegies (Rilke), I-281-285
Dutchman (Baraka), IV-2000-2004
Dying Swan, The, I-187-192
Dynamism. *See* Futurism.

Ealing Studios, III-1427-1431
Easy Rider (Hopper), IV-2158-2162
Einstein on the Beach (Glass), V-2375-2380
Electronic music, III-1629-1634;
    IV-1785-1789, 2098-2103; V-2375-2380
Empire State Building, II-880-884
Empire Strikes Back (Lucas), V-2391-2396
Epic theater, II-724-728; III-1410-1414;
    V-2239-2243
Espionage novels, IV-1934-1938
Espionage shows, IV-2044-2047
E.T.: The Extraterrestrial (Spielberg),
    V-2491-2495
Existentialism, III-1174-1178, 1262-1267,
    1498-1502, 1573-1578; IV-1742-1746
Expo 67, IV-2081-2085
Exposition Internationale des Arts
    Décoratifs et Industriels Modernes,
    II-654-658
Expressionism, I-134-139, 275-280, 486-490;
    IV-1845-1849

Fallingwater, II-902-907
Fancy Free (Robbins), III-1274-1278
Fantasia (Disney), III-1195-1199
Fantasy literature, III-1607-1611; IV-1883-1887,
    1939-1943
FAP. *See* Federal Art Project.
Fashion, I-14-18, 263-268, 474-479, 491-495;
    II-979-983; III-1324-1328, 1346-1350,
    1562-1566; IV-1824-1828, 2141-2146;
    V-2299-2304, 2449-2452
Fauves, Les, I-140-144
Fauvism, I-129-133, 140-144, 156-160
Federal Art Project (FAP), II-995-1000
Federal Theatre Project, II-989-994
Feminist literature, III-1449-1453;
    IV-1850-1854
Ficciones (Borges), III-1268-1273
Film editing, I-57-62, 74-78, 402-406,
    486-490; II-615-619, 642-647, 691-695,
    701-706, 707-711, 750-754, 822-827,
    925-929, 1073-1077; III-1109-1114,
    1195-1199, 1200-1205, 1596-1601;

IV-1855-1860; V-2391-2396, 2486-2490,
    2491-2495
Film noir, III-1223-1227; IV-1710-1715
Film spectacles, II-567-571, 615-619,
    642-647, 707-711; III-1109-1114, 1154-1158
Films, animated, II-1053-1056; III-1195-1199
Films, comedy, I-224-229, 230-234;
    II-659-664, 691-695, 951-956;
    III-1427-1431, 1567-1572; V-2381-2385,
    2527-2531
Films, dance in, II-925-929, 984-988;
    III-1432-1437; V-2386-2390
Films, espionage, II-946-950; IV-1913-1918
Films, gangster, II-839-844; V-2265-2270
Films, horror, I-486-490; II-863-868,
    946-950; IV-1855-1860
Films, musical, II-734-738, 772-776, 845-850,
    925-929, 941-945, 984-988; III-1109-1114,
    1159-1163, 1432-1437, 1567-1572;
    IV-2033-2037
Films, mystery, II-946-950; III-1131-1137,
    1223-1227; IV-1855-1860
Films, science fiction, I-57-62; IV-1989-1994;
    V-2391-2396, 2486-2490, 2491-2495
Films, silent, I-57-62, 74-78, 224-229,
    230-234, 402-406, 486-490; II-567-571,
    593-597, 615-619, 642-647, 659-664,
    691-695, 701-706, 707-711
Films, teen, V-2527-2531
Films, war, III-1245-1249; V-2428-2432,
    2576-2581
Films, Western, III-1115-1120, 1313-1317;
    IV-1984-1988
Fire Next Time, The (Baldwin), IV-1929-1933
Firebird, The, I-269-274
First Symphony (Elgar), I-214-218
Flintstones, The, IV-1840-1844
Folk music, I-102-107, 252-256; II-729-733,
    810-815; III-1121-1125, 1329-1334,
    1415-1420; IV-1705-1709, 1818-1823,
    2038-2043, 2180-2184; V-2228-2233
*for colored girls who have considered
    suicide/ when the rainbow is enuf*
    (Shange), V-2370-2374
Ford Foundation, IV-1736-1741
Formalism, III-1388-1393
Forsyte Saga, The, IV-2168-2173
42nd Street (Berkeley), II-925-929
47 Workshop, I-343-348
4′ 33″ (Cage), III-1546-1550
Fourth Symphony (Ives), I-425-428

Fourth Symphony (Sibelius), I-292-297
Fox Network, V-2652-2656
French literature, I-355-360; II-1026-1030,
  620-625, 890-895; III-1174-1178,
  1262-1267, 1481-1486, 1498-1502,
  1573-1578; IV-1812-1817, 1877-1882,
  1995-1999, 2075-2080
Fusion music, IV-2153-2157
Futurism, I-129-133, 235-240, 413-418

Garden Party, The (Havel), IV-1967-1972
Gay rights, V-2502-2506, 2636-2640
Gebrauchsmusik, II-724-728, 816-821
General, The (Keaton), II-691-695
Gentlemen Prefer Blondes (Hawks),
  III-1567-1572
Geodesic domes, III-1579-1584;
  IV-2081-2085
German literature, I-281-285, 396-401;
  II-588-592, 767-771; III-1357-1361;
  IV-1700-1704, 1780-1784, 1829-1834,
  2070-2074, 2126-2130
German theater, I-145-150
Ghost Sonata, The (Strindberg), I-199-203
Godfather, The (Coppola), V-2265-2270
Gold Rush, The (Chaplin), II-659-664
Gone with the Wind, III-1154-1158
Good Man Is Hard to Find, A (O'Connor),
  IV-1645-1649
Good Soldier Švejk, The, (Hašek),
  I-523-527
Gospel music, III-1329-1334
Grand Illusion, The (Renoir), II-1073-1077
Grand Ole Opry, The, II-675-679;
  III-1415-1420
Grapes of Wrath, The (Steinbeck),
  III-1138-1142
Gravity's Rainbow (Pynchon), V-2283-2287
Great Books Foundation, III-1351-1356
Great Gatsby, The (Fitzgerald), II-626-630
Great Train Robbery, The (Porter), I-74-78
Greed (Von Stroheim), II-593-597
Green Card (Akalaitis), V-2571-2575
Green Table, The (Jooss), II-920-924
Group 47, III-1357-1361
Group Theatre, II-874-879, 1006-1010
Guernica (Picasso), II-1062-1066
Guggenheim Museum, IV-1806-1811
Gulag Archipelago, The (Solzhenitsyn),
  V-2277-2282
Gunsmoke, IV-1668-1672, 1768-1773

Habitat 67, IV-2081-2085
Hair, IV-2121-2125
Hallelujah (Vidor), II-772-776
Hamlet (Olivier), III-1378-1382
Happy Days, V-2305-2309
Harlem Renaissance, I-480-485
Hausmusik, II-816-821
Haute couture, I-474-479; II-979-983;
  III-1346-1350
Heart of Darkness (Conrad), I-51-56;
  V-2428-2432
Hill Street Blues, V-2470-2474
Hobble skirts, I-263-268
Hollywood, II-822-827, 833-838, 1011-1015;
  III-1159-1163, 1307-1312, 1340-1345,
  1567-1572; V-2443-2448, 2565-2570
Holocaust, IV-1700-1704
Honeymooners, The, IV-1673-1677
Hostage, The (Behan), IV-1757-1762
Hot Five, II-670-674
Hound of the Baskervilles, The, III-1131-1137
House Committee on Un-American
  Activities (HUAC), III-1340-1345
House of Blue Leaves, The (Guare),
  V-2239-2243
How to Marry a Millionaire (Negulesco),
  III-1567-1572
How to Win Friends and Influence People
  (Carnegie), II-1048-1052
Howl (Ginsberg), III-1460-1464
HUAC. See House Committee on
  Un-American Activities.

I Love Lucy, III-1525-1530
I Spy, IV-2044-2047
Imagism, I-314-319, 326-331
Imperialism, I-51-56; IV-1763-1767, 1861-1865
Impressionism, II-718-723; V-2588-2593,
  2603-2607
In C (Riley), IV-1979-1983
Industrial design, II-777-781, 1057-1061;
  III-1579-1584
Innervisions (Wonder), V-2294-2298
International Style, I-463-468; II-869-873
Interpretation of Dreams, The (Freud),
  I-19-23
Invisible Man (Ellison), III-1541-1545
Irises (Van Gogh), V-2603-2607
Irish literature, I-85-89, 119-123, 176-180,
  440-444; II-555-560
Irish theater, I-85-89, 119-123, 176-180

It Happened One Night (Capra), II-951-956
It's a Wonderful Life (Capra), III-1335-1339
Italian literature, I-534-538

James Bond films, IV-1913-1918
Jantzen Knitting Mills, I-491-495
Japanese literature, IV-2147-2152
Jardin aux lilas (Tudor), II-1036-1041
Jazz, I-13-18, 480-485; II-572-576, 598-603,
  670-674, 739-744, 930-935, 968-973,
  1016-1020; III-1318-1323, 1438-1442,
  1617-1622; IV-1731-1735, 2153-2157;
  V-2453-2458
Jazz Singer, The, II-734-738, 761-766, 822-827
Jeffersons, The, V-2339-2344
Jesus Christ Superstar, V-2254-2259
Joffrey Ballet, IV-1694-1699
Journals, I-209-213, 385-389, 429-434;
  II-549-554, 577-582, 648-653, 1031-1035;
  IV-1683-1688; V-2507-2511
Journey to the End of the Night (Celine),
  II-890-895
Jugendstil, I-181-186

Kabinett des Dr. Caligari, Das. See *Cabinet
  of Dr. Caligari, The.*
Kaspar (Handke), IV-2126-2130
King Kong, II-822-827
Kiss Me, Kate (Porter), III-1404-1409
Kukla, Fran, and Ollie, III-1400-1403

Lady Macbeth of Mtsensk (Shostakovich),
  II-1042-1047
Latin-American literature, III-1268-1273;
  IV-1689-1693, 2086-2091
Latin-American music, IV-1818-1823
Laugh-In. See *Rowan and Martin's Laugh-In.*
Led Zeppelin, V-2228-2233
Let's Dance, II-968-973
Lied von der Erde, Das (Mahler), I-298-303
Life, II-1031-1035
Literary criticism, III-1168-1173
Literary Guild, II-686-690
Literature. *See* American literature, Arabic
  literature, African literature, African-
  American literature, Antiwar novels,
  Czech literature, Deconstruction,
  Detective novels, Existentialism, Fantasy
  literature, Feminist literature, French
  literature, German literature, Imagism,
  Irish literature, Italian literature, Japanese

literature, Latin-American literature,
  Literary criticism, Modernism, Mystery
  novels, New Criticism, Philosophy,
  Realism, Regional Literature, Russian
  literature, Science fiction, South African
  literature, Soviet literature, Spanish
  literature, Western novels, Yiddish
  literature.
Little Caesar, II-839-844
Little Johnny Jones (Cohan), I-108-112
Live Aid, V-2543-2547
Long Day's Journey into Night (O'Neill),
  IV-1726-1730
Look Back in Anger (Osborne), IV-1721-1725
Lord of the Flies (Golding), III-1585-1589
Lord of the Rings, The (Tolkien),
  III-1607-1611
Lost generation, I-129-133; II-696-700
Louvre, the, V-2619-2624
Lulu (Berg), II-1078-1082

Madness and Civilization (Foucault),
  IV-1877-1882
Magic Mountain, The (Mann), II-588-592
Magical Realism, III-1268-1273;
  IV-1689-1693, 2086-2091
Mahagonny Songspiel (Brecht and Weill),
  II-724-728
Malone Dies (Beckett), III-1498-1502
Maltese Falcon, The (Hammett), II-793-798
Maltese Falcon, The (Huston), III-1223-1227
Man and Superman (Shaw), I-85-89
Man Who Knew Too Much, The (Hitchcock),
  II-946-950
Marat/Sade (Weiss), IV-2005-2010
Marguerite and Armand (Ashton),
  IV-1962-1966
Marteau sans maître, Le (Boulez),
  IV-1656-1661
Mary Tyler Moore Show, The, V-2218-2222
M*A*S*H, V-2271-2276
Mass production, I-34-38, 79-84; II-777-781,
  1021-1025, 1057-1061; V-2208-2212
"MASTER HAROLD" . . . *and the boys*
  (Fugard), V-2496-2501
"Maybellene" (Berry), IV-1635-1639
Melville revival, I-502-505
Merry Widow, The (Lubitsch), II-941-945
Metamorphosis, The (Kafka), I-396-401
Method acting, I-1-6; III-1164-1168, 1487-1492
Metropolis (Lang), II-707-711

Minimalism, IV-1949-1954
Minimalist art, IV-1949-1954
Minimalist music, III-1546-1550;
V-2375-2380
Miniskirts, IV-1824-1828
Mir Iskusstva, I-241-246
Mrs. Dalloway (Woolf), II-637-641
Moby Dick (Melville), I-502-505
Modern art, III-1590-1595; V-2191-2196
Modern dance, I-113-118, 390-395;
II-665-660; III-1284-1289, 1432-1437,
1602-1606; IV-1774-1779, 2011-2016;
V-2288-2293, 2480-2485, 2521-2527,
2559-2564, 2663-2667
Modernism, II-555-560, 851-856
Modernismo, I-257-262
Molloy (Beckett), III-1498-1502
Montage, II-615-619, 701-706, 750-754
Monterey Pop Festival, IV-2104-2109
Monty Python's Flying Circus, IV-2174-2179
Moscow Art Theater, I-1-6
Motion pictures. *See entries under* Film.
Motown Records, IV-1790-1794
Mousetrap, The (Christie), III-1551-1556
Movies. *See entries under* Film.
MTV (Music Television), V-2475-2479,
2512-2516, 2543-2547
Multiculturalism, V-2559-2564, 2673-2678
Musée d'Orsay, V-2588-2593
Musée de l'Orangerie, II-718-723
Museum of Modern Art (MOMA),
II-782-786; V-2614-2618
Museums and galleries, II-718-723, 782-786,
885-889; III-1239-1244; IV-1806-1811,
2064-2069; V-2310-2315, 2402-2406,
2588-2593, 2608-2613, 2614-2618
Music. *See* Atonality, Big-band music,
Bluegrass music, Blues, Chamber music,
Country music, Disco music, Electronic
music, Folk music, Formalism, Fusion,
Gebrauchsmusik, Gospel music, Jazz,
Minimalist music, Music videos,
Musicology, Neoclassicism, Opera, Punk
rock, Ragtime music, Rap music, Reggae
music, Rhythm and blues, Rock and roll,
Serialism, Sound recording, Symphonic
music.
Music festivals, III-1617-1622; IV-2038-2043,
2104-2109, 2180-2184; V-2543-2547
Music Man, The (Willson), IV-1752-1756
Music Television. *See* MTV.

Music videos, V-2475-2479, 2512-2516
Musical theater, I-108-112; II-598-603,
724-728, 745-749, 1016- 1020;
III-1256-1261, 1404-1409; IV-1731-1735,
1752-1756, 2121-2125; V-2213-2217,
2254-2259, 2334-2338. *See also* Opera.
Musicology, I-102-107, 166-170, 193-198,
286-291, 528-533; II-561-566, 816-821;
III-1546-1550
My Ántonia (Cather), I-452-457
Mysterious Affair at Styles, The (Christie),
I-496-501
Mystery novels, I-496-501; III-1131-1137;
IV-1934-1938
Mythology, IV-1995-1999

Naked and the Dead, The (Mailer),
III-1373-1377
Naked Lunch (Burroughs), III-1460-1464
Napoléon (Gance), II-642-647
Nation of Islam, IV-1929-1933, 2022-2026
National Broadcasting Company (NBC),
III-1143-1148, 1211-1216, 1362-1367;
V-2554-2558
National Endowment for the Arts (NEA),
IV-2048-2052; V-2636-2640
National Museum of Women in the Arts,
V-2608-2613
National Review, IV-1683-1688
Native Son (Wright), III-1185-1189
Natty Dread (Marley), V-2345-2349
Naturalism, III-1164-1168
Nazism, III-1083-1087, 1217-1222;
IV-1780-1784
NBC. *See* National Broadcasting Company.
NEA. *See* National Endowment for the Arts.
Neoclassicism, III-1514-1519
Neoplasticism, I-429-434
Networks, development of radio and
television, I-469-473; II-712- 717, 828-832;
III-1143-1148, 1362-1367, 1368-1372,
1465-1469, 1612-1616; V-2554-2558
Neve Sachlichkeit. See New Objectivity.
New Criticism, III-1168-1173
New Dance U.S.A. Festival, V-2480-2485
New Deal, II-995-1000
New Look, III-1346-1350
New Novel, III-1481-1486
New Objectivity, II-631-637
New Republic, The, I-385-389
New Wave, French, IV-1710-1715, 1845-1849

C

New Wave, Italian, III-1228-1233, 1596-1601
New York City Ballet, III-1301-1306
New Yorker, The, II-648-653
Newport Jazz Festival, III-1617-1622
Night (Wiesel), IV-1700-1704
Nineteen Eighty-Four (Orwell), III-1421-1426
Nixon in China (Adams), V-2599-2602
Nobel Prizes, I-45-50; IV-2147-2152;
   V-2423-2427, 2594-2598, 2625-2629,
   2668-2672
Nonprofit theaters, IV-1736-1741
Noveau roman. See New Novel.

Octet for Wind Instruments (Stravinsky),
   II-561-566
Of Grammatology (Derrida), IV-2075-2080
Oklahoma! (Rodgers and Hammerstein),
   III-1256-1261
On the Road (Kerouac), III-1460-1464
One Flew Over the Cuckoo's Nest (Forman),
   V-2320-2324
One Hundred Years of Solitude (García
   Márquez), IV-2086-2091
Opera, I-7-12, 29-33, 69-73, 151-155;
   II-680-685, 1042-1047, 1078-1082;
   III-1126-1130, 1296-1300, 1514-1519,
   1536-1540; V-2350-2354, 2375-2380,
   2433-2437, 2599-2602
Oscars, II-799-804, 1011-1015
Our Town (Wilder), III-1099-1102
Out of Our Heads (the Rolling Stones),
   IV-2027-2032

Painting, IV-1806-1811; V-2402-2406. *See
   also* Abstract art, Abstract expressionism,
   Action painting, Cubism, Dadaism,
   Expressionism, Fauvism, Futurism,
   Modern art, Suprematism, Surrealism.
Palais Stoclet, I-124-128
"Papa's Got a Brand New Bag,"
   IV-2059-2063
Parade (Cocteau), I-435-439
Performance art, I-419-424; V-2517-2520,
   2571-2575
Performance rights, I-379-384
Peter Grimes (Britten), III-1296-1300
Peyton Place, IV-2017-1021
Philosophy, I-85-89, 161-165, 171-175,
   309-313, 518-522; III-1262-1267;
   IV-1829-1834, 1877-1882, 1995-1999
Photo-Secession, I-63-68

Photography, I-63-68, 513-517; V-2636-2640
Photojournalism, II-1031-1035; IV-2136-2140;
   V-2507-2511
Platoon (Stone), V-2576-2581
Playboy of the Western World, The (Synge),
   I-176-180
Poems (Auden), II-857-862
Poet in New York (García Lorca),
   III-1179-1184
Poetry, I-129-133, 281-285, 314-319, 326-331,
   440-444, 445-451, 480-485; II-539-543,
   851-856, 857-862; III-1179-1184, 1443-1448,
   1460-1464; IV-1662-1667, 1850-1854,
   2070-2074
Poetry Magazine, I-314-319, 326-331
Poirot, Hercule, I-496-501
Police shows, III-1531-1535
"Polo" line, IV-2141-2146
Pompidou Center, V-2402-2406
Pont Neuf Wrapped (Christo),
   V-2548-2553
Porgy and Bess (Gershwin), II-1016-1020
Portnoy's Complaint (Roth), IV-2163-2167
Postmodern architecture, V-2407-2412,
   2646-2651
Potemkin (Eisenstein), II-615-619
Pragmatism (W. James), I-171-175
Prefabricated buildings, II-1021-1025;
   III-1579-1584
Primitive art, I-156-160
Prometheus: The Poem of Fire (Scriabin),
   I-286-291
Psycho (Hitchcock), IV-1855-1860
Psychoanalysis, I-19-23, 309-313;
   IV-1877-1882
Psychological ballet, II-1036-1041
Psychology of the Unconscious (Jung),
   I-309-313
Public Enemy, II-839-844
Public television, IV-2168-2173, 2174-2179;
   V-2185-2190, 2657-2662
Pulitzer Prizes, I-407-412
Pulp magazines, III-1094-1098
Punk rock, V-2299-2304, 2360-2364

Quartet for the End of Time (Messiaen),
   III-1206-1210

Race records, II-572-576, 930-935
Racism, III-1126-1130, 1185-1189;
   IV-1650-1655, 1763-1767, 2000-2004,

2022-2026, 2044-2047; V-2397-2401,
2496-2501, 2641-2645, 2668-2672
Radio, development of, I-469-473;
II-675-679, 712-717, 755-760, 828-832
Radio networks. *See* Networks, development
of radio and television.
Ragtime music, I-13-18; V-2350-2354
Raisin in the Sun, A (Hansberry),
IV-1795-1799
Raising Hell (Run-D.M.C.), V-2582-2587
Rake's Progress, The (Stravinsky),
III-1514-1519
Rap music, V-2582-2587
Rashomon (Kurosawa), III-1476-1480
Rayograph, I-513-517
RCA Victor, II-729-733
Reader's Digest, II-549-554
Readymades, I-349-354
Rebel Without a Cause (Ray), IV-1640-1644
Red Skelton Show, The, III-1520-1524
Red-Blue Chair, I-458-462
Reggae music, V-2345-2349
Regional literature, I-452-457; II-805-809;
IV-1645-1649
Relevance programming (television),
V-2197-2202, 2234-2238, 2470-2474
Remembrance of Things Past (Proust),
I-355-360
Return of the Jedi (Lucas), V-2391-2396
Revue nègre, La, II-665-669
Rhapsody in Blue (Gershwin), II-598-603
Rhinoceros (Ionesco), IV-1812-1817
Rhythm and blues, IV-1790-1794, 2027-2032,
2059-2063, 2092-2097, 2104-2109,
2180-2184; V-2294-2298, 2512-2516,
2582-2587
Riders of the Purple Sage (Grey), I-304-308
Rite of Spring, The, I-373-378
Roaring Twenties, II-626-630
Rock and roll, IV-1635-1639, 1705-1709,
1790-1794, 1944-1948, 2027-2032,
2038-2043, 2059-2063, 2092-2097,
2098-2103, 2104-2109, 2153-2157,
2180-2184; V-2228-2233, 2294-2298,
2325-2329, 2360-2364, 2475-2479,
2512-2516, 2517-2520, 2543-2547,
2582-2587
Rockefeller Center, II-957-962;
III-1149-1153
Rodeo (de Mille), III-1234-1238
Rolling Stones, the, IV-2027-2032

Roosevelt Administration, II-989-994,
995-1000
Roots, V-2397-2401
Rowan and Martin's Laugh-In, IV-2115-2120
Royal National Theatre, IV-1924-1928
Royal Shakespeare Company, IV-1888-1892
Rules of the Game, The (Renoir),
II-1073-1077
Run-D.M.C., V-2582-2587
Russian literature, II-787-792, 908-913;
IV-1747-1751

*Sacre du printemps, Le. See Rite of
Spring, The.*
"St. Louis Blues," I-252-256
Salome (Strauss), I-151-155
Salon d'Automne, I-140-144, 204-208
Salons, I-129-133
Satanic Verses, The (Rushdie), V-2630-2635
"Satisfaction," IV-2027-2032
Saturday Night Fever, V-2386-2390
Saturday Night Live, V-2355-2359
Scarface, II-839-844
Science fiction, I-57-62; III-1094-1098,
1103-1108, 1421-1426, 1607-1611;
IV-1883-1887, 1939-1943, 1989-1994;
V-2260-2264, 2391-2396, 2486-2490,
2491-2495
Screwball comedy, II-951-956
Sculpture, III-1190-1194; IV-1806-1811,
1949-1954, 2081-2085
Second Sex, The (Beauvoir), III-1449-1453
Second Viennese School, I-367-372,
528-533. *See also* Berg, Anton;
Schoenberg, Arnold; *and* Webern,
Anton von.
Serenade (Balanchine), II-974-978
Sgt. Pepper's Lonely Hearts Club Band (The
Beatles), IV-2098-2103
Serialism, I-193-198, 367-372, 528-533;
II-1078-1082, 680-685; IV-1656-1661
Sesame Street, V-2185-2190
Seven Year Itch, The (Wilder),
III-1567-1572
Seventh Seal, The (Bergman), IV-1742-1746
Sex Pistols, the, V-2360-2364
Show Boat, II-745-749
Simpsons, The, V-2652-2656
Sister Carrie (Dreiser), I-39-44
Situation comedy, III-1470-1475, 1525-1530;
IV-1673-1677, 1835-1839, 1908-1912;

V-2234-2238, 2271-2276, 2305-2309,
    2339-2344, 2532-2536, 2652-2656
Six Characters in Search of an Author
    (Pirandello), I-534-538
"Six, Les," I-435-439
Six Pieces for Large Orchestra (Webern),
    I-367-372
Sixteen Candles (Hughes), V-2527-2531
60 Minutes, IV-2136-2140
Sketch for a New Aesthetic of Music
    (Busoni), I-166-170
Slapstick comedy, I-230-234; II-659-664,
    691-695
Snow White (Disney), II-1053-1056
Socialist Realism, II-544-548, 787-792,
    908-913, 914-919, 1042-1047; III-1388-1393
SoHo, V-2191-2196, 2438-2442, 2517-2520
Sonny and Cher Comedy Hour, The,
    V-2244-2248
Sound and the Fury, The (Faulkner),
    II-805-809
Sound of Music, The (Wise), IV-2033-2037
Sound recording (motion pictures),
    II-734-738, 761-766, 822-827
Sound recording (music), I-69-73; II-572-576
South African literature, V-2496-2501,
    2668-2672
Soviet literature, II-787-792, 908-913;
    IV-1747-1751; V-2277-2282
Spaghetti Westerns, IV-1984-1988
Spanish art, II-1062-1066; V-2203-2207,
    2310-2315
Spanish Civil War, II-1062-1066;
    III-1179-1184
Spanish literature, III-1179-1184, 1268-1273;
    IV-1689-1693, 2086-2091
Special effects, I-57-62, 402-406, 486-490;
    II-615-619, 642-647, 691-695, 701-706,
    707-711, 750-754, 822-827, 863-868,
    925-929, 1053-1056; III-1109-1114,
    1195-1199; V-2391-2396, 2486-2490,
    2491-2495
Sports and television, III-1362-1367
Spy Who Came in from the Cold, The
    (le Carré), IV-1934-1938
Stagecoach (Ford), III-1115-1120
Stanislavsky method, I-1-6; III-1164-1168,
    1487-1492
Star Trek, V-2260-2264
Star Wars (Lucas), V-2391-2396
Steppenwolf (Hesse), IV-1829-1834

Stijl, De (magazine), I-429-434, 458-462
Stormy Weather, III-1159-1163
Strada, La (Fellini), III-1596-1601
Stranger in a Strange Land (Heinlein),
    IV-1883-1887
Streetcar Named Desire, A (Kazan),
    III-1487-1492
Structuralism, IV-1995-1999
Structures I (Boulez), IV-1656-1661
Studio system (Hollywood), II-833-838;
    III-1307-1312, 1340-1345
Sun Also Rises, The (Hemingway),
    II-696-700
Suprematism, I-413-418
Surrealism, I-257-262, 396-401; II-604-609,
    750-754, 979-983; V-2310-2315
Swedish literature, I-199-203
Sweeney Todd (Sondheim), V-2433-2437
Swimwear, I-491-495; III-1324-1328
Symphonic music, I-90-95, 214-218, 286-291,
    292-297, 298-303, 425-428, 435-439,
    508-512; III-1284-1289; IV-1818-1823
Synthesizers, IV-1785-1789

Taliesin Fellowship, II-902-907
Teatro-Museo Dalí, V-2310-2315
Television, African Americans in,
    IV-2044-2047; V-2339-2344, 2397-2401,
    2532-2536
Television, children's, III-1400-1403;
    IV-1678-1682, 1840-1844; V-2185-2190
Television, development of, III-1143-1148,
    1211-1216, 1362-1367, 1368-1372, 1465-1469,
    1612-1616; V-2554-2558
Television, public, IV-2168-2173, 2174-2179;
    V-2185-2190, 2657-2662
Television, violence in, V-2330-2333
Television, westerns on, IV-1668-1672,
    1768-1773, 1800-1805
Television, women in, V-2218-2222
Television and sports, III-1362-1367
Television comedy, III-1383-1387, 1394-1399,
    1470-1475, 1520-1524, 1525-1530,
    1623-1628; IV-1673-1677, 1835-1839,
    1840-1844, 1908-1912, 2115-2120,
    2174-2179; V-2218-2222, 2234-2238,
    2244-2248, 2271-2276, 2305-2309,
    2339-2344, 2355-2359, 2532-2536,
    2652-2656. *See also* Situation comedy.
Television drama, III-1531-1535;
    IV-1668-1672, 1768-1773, 1800-1805,

2017-1021, 2044-2047, 2168-2173;
V-2330-2333, 2397-2401, 2418-2422,
2470-2474
Television networks. *See* Networks,
development of radio and television.
Television variety shows, III-1383-1387,
1394-1399, 1520-1524, 1623-1628;
IV-2115-2120; V-2244-2248, 2355-2359
Ten Commandments, The (DeMille),
II-567-571
Texaco Star Theater, III-1394-1399
Theater. *See* Absurdism, "Angry Young
Men," Epic theater, Existential drama,
German theater, Group theater, Irish
theater, Method acting, Musical theater,
Theater of the Absurd, Vaudeville.
Theater of Cruelty, III-1410-1414
Theater of the Absurd, I-199-203, 534-538;
III-1174-1178, 1410-1414, 1573-1578;
IV-1812-1817, 1871-1876, 1903-1907,
2005-2010, 2126-2130
Theatre of the Absurd, The (Esslin),
IV-1871-1876
Theatre Workshop, IV-1757-1762
Theatres Act, IV-2131-2135
Things Fall Apart (Achebe), IV-1763-1767
Thirty-nine Steps, The (Hitchcock),
II-946-950
"300" Telephone, II-1057-1061
Thriller (Jackson), V-2512-2516
Tiffany Studios, I-34-38
Time (magazine), II-577-582
Tin Drum, The (Grass), IV-1780-1784
Tonight Show, The, III-1623-1628
Top Hat (Sandrich), II-984-988
Torch Song Trilogy (Fierstein), V-2502-2506
Tosca (Puccini), I-29-33
Tractatus Logico-Philosophicus
(Wittgenstein), I-518-522
Tree Climber, The (Hakim), IV-1893-1897
Treemonisha (Joplin), V-2350-2354
Tropic of Cancer (Miller), II-963-967
TWA Terminal, IV-1716-1720
Twelve-tone music, I-528-533; II-1078-1082;
IV-1656-1661
2001: A Space Odyssey (Kubrick),
IV-1989-1994

Ulysses (Joyce), II-555-560
Understanding Media (McLuhan),
IV-1973-1978
United States (Anderson), V-2517-2520
Unnamable, The (Beckett), III-1498-1502
U.S. Highball (Partch), III-1279-1283
USA Today, V-2507-2511

Variety shows, III-1383-1387, 1394-1399,
1520-1524, 1623-1628; IV-2115-2120;
V-2244-2248
Vaudeville, I-108-112
Video, IV-1955-1961
Vienna Court Opera, I-7-12
Vietnam War, V-2315-2319, 2428-2432,
2576-2581
Villa Mairea, II-1067-1072
Villa Savoye, II-869-873
Violence in television, V-2330-2333
Voyage dans la lune, Le (Méliès),
I-57-62
Voyage Round My Father, A (Mortimer),
V-2249-2253

Waiting for Godot (Beckett), III-1573-1578
Walt Disney Company, II-1053-1056;
III-1195-1199, 1612-1616; V-2646-2651
Wanted: The Outlaws, V-2365-2369
War of the Worlds, The (Welles), 1103-1108
Waste Land, The (Eliot), II-539-543
Water Lilies (Monet), II-718-723
*Webster's Third New International
Dictionary*, IV-1898-1902
West Side Story (Bernstein), IV-1731-1735
Western novels, I-304-308
White Oak Dance Project, V-2663-2667
Whitney Museum, II-885-889; IV-2064-2069
Wiener Werkstätte, I-79-84
Wild Swans at Coole, The (Yeats), I-440-444
Wiz, The, V-2334-2338
Wizard of Oz, The, III-1109-1114
Women in art, V-2608-2613
Woodstock Music and Art Fair, IV-2180-2184
Wozzeck (Berg), II-680-685
WPA/FAP. *See* Federal Art Project.

Yiddish literature, V-2423-2427

CATEGORY INDEX

ARCHITECTURE

Aalto Designs Villa Mairea, II-1067
Arts and Architecture Magazine Initiates the Case Study Program, III-1290
AT&T Building Exemplifies Postmodernism, The, V-2407
Behrens Designs the AEG Turbine Factory, I-219
Breuer Designs a Building for the Whitney Museum, IV-2064
Corbusier Designs and Builds Chandigarh, Le, III-1503
Corbusier's Villa Savoye Redefines Architecture, Le, II-869
Deconstructivists Exhibit at the Museum of Modern Art, V-2614
Design for the Real World Reorients Industrial Design, V-2208
Deutscher Werkbund Combats Conservative Architecture, The, I-181
Disney Emerges as an Architectural Patron, V-2646
Empire State Building Opens as the World's Tallest Building, The, II-880
Expo 67 Presents Innovative Architectural Concepts, IV-2081
Fuller's First Industrial Geodesic Dome Is Erected, III-1579
Gaudí Completes the Casa Milá Apartment House in Barcelona, I-257
German Artists Found the Bauhaus, I-463
Guggenheim Museum Opens in a Building Designed by Wright, The, IV-1806
Hoffmann Designs the Palais Stoclet, I-124
Kahn Blends Architecture and Urban Planning in Dacca, IV-1919
Musée d'Orsay Opens, The, V-2588
Paris Exhibition Defines Art Deco, A, II-654
Pei Creates a New Entrance to the Louvre, V-2619
Pompidou Center Opens in Paris, The, V-2402
Prouvé Pioneers the Prefabrication of Buildings, II-1021
Rockefeller Center Is Completed, III-1149
Saarinen Designs Kennedy Airport's TWA Terminal, IV-1716
Wright Founds the Taliesin Fellowship, II-902

ART

Abstract Painting in America Opens in New York, II-1001
Apollinaire Defines Cubism in The Cubist Painters, I-337
Artists Find Inspiration in African Tribal Art, I-156
Avant-Garde Art in the Armory Show Shocks American Viewers, I-361
Avant-Garde Artists in Dresden Form Die Brücke, I-134
Blaue Reiter Abandons Representation in Art, Der, I-275
Christo Wraps the Pont Neuf, V-2548
Columbus Day Debates Reflect Cultural Diversity, V-2673
Dada Movement Emerges at the Cabaret Voltaire, The, I-419
Dalí Museum Opens in Figueras, Spain, A, V-2310
Duchamp's "Readymades" Challenge Concepts of Art, I-349
Fauves Exhibit at the Salon d'Automne, Les I-140
Formation of the Blue Four Advances Abstract Painting, The, II-583
Four Modern Masters Affirm Germany's Place in the Art World, V-2464
Futurists Issue Their Manifesto, The, I-235
Henry Moore Is Inspired by Shapes in Subway Shelters, III-1190
Hitler Organizes an Exhibition Denouncing Modern Art, III-1083
Jasper Johns Paints the American Flag, III-1590
Kandinsky Publishes His Views on Abstraction in Art, I-320
Malevich Introduces Suprematism, I-413
Man Ray Creates the Rayograph, I-513
Mapplethorpe's Photographs Provoke Controversy, V-2636
Minimalism Emphasizes Objects as Art, IV-1949
Monet's Water Lilies Are Shown at the Musée de l'Orangerie, II-718
Musée d'Orsay Opens, The, V-2588
Nam June Paik Exhibits Video and Television as Art, IV-1955

National Endowment for the Arts Is
Established, The, IV-2048
National Museum of Women in the Arts
Opens Amid Controversy, The, V-2608
Nazis Ban Nolde's Paintings, The, III-1217
New Objectivity Movement Is Introduced,
The, II-631
New York's Museum of Modern Art Is
Founded, II-782
New York's SoHo Develops into a Center for
Contemporary Art, V-2191
Peggy Guggenheim's Gallery Promotes New
American Art, III-1239
Picasso Paints *Guernica* , II-1062
Pompidou Center Opens in Paris, The,
V-2402
Rivera's Rockefeller Center Mural Is
Destroyed, II-957
Roosevelt Administration Creates the WPA/
FAP, The, II-995
Rosenberg Defines "Action Painting,"
III-1557
Salon d'Automne Rejects Braque's Cubist
Works, The, I-204
Schnabel Emerges as a Celebrity Artist,
V-2438
Soviet Union Bans Abstract Art, The, II-544
Spanish Art Explodes After Years of
Suppression, V-2203
Stein Holds Her First Paris Salons, I-129
Stieglitz Organizes the Photo-Secession,
I-63
Stijl Advocates Mondrian's Neoplasticism,
De, I-429
Surrealism Is Born, II-604
Van Gogh's *Irises* Sells for $53.9 Million,
V-2603
Warhol's *The Chelsea Girls* Becomes a
Commercial Success, IV-2053
Whitney Museum Is Inaugurated in New
York, The, II-885

DANCE
Agnes de Mille Choreographs *Rodeo*,
III-1234
Ailey Founds His Dance Company, IV-1774
Après-midi d'un faune Causes an Uproar, *L'*,
I-332
Baker Dances in *La Revue nègre*, II-665
Balanchine and Kirstein Make New York a
World Center for Ballet, III-1301

Balanchine's *Serenade* Inaugurates
American Ballet, II-974
Ballet Russe de Monte Carlo Finds New
Leadership, The, III-1088
Baryshnikov Becomes Artistic Director of
American Ballet Theatre, V-2459
Baryshnikov's White Oak Dance Project
Debuts, V-2663
Cunningham Stages His First Dance
"Event," IV-2011
Denishawn School of Dance Opens in Los
Angeles, The, I-390
Diaghilev's Ballets Russes Astounds Paris,
I-241
Duncan Interprets Chopin in Her Russian
Debut, I-113
Festivals Mark a Peak in the Dance Created
by Black Artists, V-2521
Firebird Premieres in Paris, *The*, I-269
Fokine's *Les Sylphides* Introduces Abstract
Ballet, I-247
Graham Debuts *Appalachian Spring* with
Copland Score, III-1284
Joffrey Founds His Ballet Company, IV-1694
Jooss's Antiwar Dance *The Green Table*
Premieres, II-920
Kelly Forges New Directions in Cinematic
Dance, III-1432
Mitchell Founds the Dance Theater of
Harlem, IV-2110
Multiculturalism Dominates the Dance
World, V-2559
New Dance U.S.A. Festival Celebrates
Contemporary Dance, The, V-2480
Nureyev and Fonteyn Debut Ashton's
Marguerite and Armand, IV-1962
Pavlova First Performs Her Legendary Solo
The Dying Swan, I-187
Rite of Spring Stuns Audiences, *The*, I-373
Robbins' *Fancy Free* Premieres, III-1274
Taylor Establishes His Own Dance
Company, III-1602
Tharp Stages *Deuce Coupe* for the Joffrey
Ballet, V-2288
Top Hat Establishes the Astaire-Rogers
Dance Team, II-984
Tudor's *Jardin aux lilas* Premieres in
London, II-1036

FASHION AND DESIGN
Bikini Swimsuit Is Introduced, The, III-1324

Brooks Brothers Introduces Button-Down Shirts, I-24

Chanel Defines Modern Women's Fashion, I-474

Cranbrook Academy Begins a History of Design Excellence, II-610

Deutscher Werkbund Combats Conservative Architecture, The, I-181

Dior's "New Look" Sweeps Europe and America, III-1346

Dreyfuss Designs the Bell "300" Telephone, II-1057

Hoffmann and Moser Found the Wiener Werkstätte, I-79

Jantzen Popularizes the One-Piece Bathing Suit, I-491

Laura Ashley and Her Husband Found a Fashion Company, III-1562

Lauren Creates the "Polo" Line, IV-2141

Loewy Pioneers American Industrial Design, II-777

Madonna Revolutionizes Popular Fashion, V-2449

Paris Exhibition Defines Art Deco, A, II-654

Poiret's "Hobble Skirts" Become the Rage, I-263

Punk's Antifashion Style First Appears, V-2299

Quant Introduces the Miniskirt, IV-1824

Rietveld Designs the Red-Blue Chair, I-458

Schiaparelli's Boutique Mingles Art and Fashion, II-979

Tiffany and Tiffany Studios Develop New Ideas in Design, I-34

JOURNALISM

American Science Fiction Enjoys Its Golden Age, III-1094

Buckley Founds National Review, IV-1683

Christian Science Monitor Is Founded, The, I-209

Columbus Day Debates Reflect Cultural Diversity, V-2673

First Pulitzer Prizes Are Awarded, The, I-407

Harriet Monroe Founds Poetry Magazine, I-314

Lippmann Helps to Establish The New Republic, I-385

Luce Founds Time Magazine, II-577

Luce Launches Life Magazine, II-1031

McLuhan Probes the Impact of Mass Media on Society, IV-1973

Ross Founds The New Yorker, II-648

60 Minutes Becomes the First Televised Newsmagazine, IV-2136

Trudeau's Doonesbury Popularizes Topical Comic Strips, V-2223

USA Today Is Launched, V-2507

Wallace Founds Reader's Digest, II-549

LITERATURE

All Quiet on the Western Front Stresses the Futility of War, II-767

American Science Fiction Enjoys Its Golden Age, III-1094

"Angry Young Men" Express Working-Class Views, III-1454

Autobiography of Malcolm X Is Published, The, IV-2022

Baker Establishes the 47 Workshop at Harvard, I-343

Baldwin Voices Black Rage in The Fire Next Time, IV-1929

Beat Movement Rejects Mainstream Values, The, III-1460

Beauvoir's The Second Sex Anticipates the Women's Movement, III-1449

Beckett's Trilogy Pushes Against the Frontiers of Fiction, III-1498

Bergson's Creative Evolution Inspires Artists and Thinkers, I-161

Book-of-the-Month Club and the Literary Guild Are Founded, The, II-686

"Boom" Captures Worldwide Attention, The, IV-1689

Borges' Ficciones Transcends Traditional Realism, III-1268

Carnegie Publishes His Self-Help Best-Seller, II-1048

Catch-22 Illustrates Antiwar Sentiment, IV-1866

Cather's My Ántonia Promotes Regional Literature, I-452

Celan's Influential Atemwende Is Published, IV-2070

Celine's Journey to the End of the Night Is Published, II-890

Columbus Day Debates Reflect Cultural Diversity, V-2673

Crane Publishes The Bridge, II-851

Derrida Enunciates the Principles of
Deconstruction, IV-2075

Diary of a Country Priest Inspires Readers,
The, II-1026

Dickinson's Poems Are Published in Full for
the First Time, IV-1662

Dog Soldiers Portrays Vietnam in Fiction,
V-2315

Dreiser's *Sister Carrie* Shatters Literary
Taboos, I-39

Eliot Publishes *The Waste Land*, II-539

Ellison's *Invisible Man* Is Published, III-1541

Esslin Publishes *The Theatre of the Absurd*,
IV-1871

First Nobel Prizes Are Awarded, The, I-45

First Pulitzer Prizes Are Awarded, The,
I-407

Foucault's *Madness and Civilization* Is
Published, IV-1877

Freud Inaugurates a Fascination with the
Unconscious, I-19

García Lorca's *Poet in New York* Is
Published, III-1179

García Márquez's *One Hundred Years of
Solitude* Is Published, IV-2086

German Writers Form Group 47, III-1357

Ghost Sonata Influences Modern Theater
and Drama, *The*, I-199

Gide's *The Counterfeiters* Questions Moral
Absolutes, II-620

Golding's *Lord of the Flies* Spurs
Examination of Human Nature, III-1585

Gordimer Wins the Nobel Prize in
Literature, V-2668

Grapes of Wrath Portrays Depression-Era
America, *The*, III-1138

Grass Publishes *The Tin Drum*, IV-1780

Great Books Foundation Is Established, The,
III-1351

Great Gatsby Captures the Essence of the
Roaring Twenties, *The*, II-626

Grey's *Riders of the Purple Sage* Launches
the Western Genre, I-304

Gulag Archipelago Exposes Soviet
Atrocities, *The*, V-2277

Harlem Renaissance Celebrates African-
American Culture, The, I-480

Harriet Monroe Founds *Poetry* Magazine,
I-314

Hašek's *The Good Soldier Švejk* Reflects
Postwar Disillusionment, I-523

Heart of Darkness Reveals the Consequences
of Imperialism, I-51

Heinlein Publishes *Stranger in a Strange
Land*, IV-1883

Hemingway's *The Sun Also Rises* Speaks for
the Lost Generation, II-696

Henry James's *The Ambassadors* Is
Published, I-96

Huxley's *Brave New World* Reflects Fears
About the Future, II-896

Imagist Movement Shakes Up Poetry, The,
I-326

Joyce's *Ulysses* Epitomizes Modernism in
Fiction, II-555

Jung Publishes *Psychology of the
Unconscious*, I-309

Kawabata Wins the Nobel Prize in
Literature, IV-2147

Khomeini Calls for Rushdie's Death, V-2630

Le Carré Rejects the Fantasy World of Secret
Agents, IV-1934

Lévi-Strauss Explores Myth as a Key to
Enlightenment, IV-1995

McLuhan Probes the Impact of Mass Media
on Society, IV-1973

Mahfouz Wins the Nobel Prize in Literature,
V-2625

Mailer Publishes *The Naked and the Dead*,
III-1373

Maltese Falcon Introduces the Hard-Boiled
Detective Novel, *The*, II-793

Mann's *The Magic Mountain* Reflects
European Crisis, II-588

Melville Is Rediscovered as a Major
American Novelist, I-502

Metamorphosis Anticipates Modern Feelings
of Alienation, *The*, I-396

Miller's Notorious Novel *Tropic of Cancer* Is
Published, II-963

Mysterious Affair at Styles Introduces
Hercule Poirot, *The*, I-496

New Criticism Holds Sway, The, III-1169

New Novel (*Le Nouveau Roman*) Emerges,
The, III-1481

Nineteen Eighty-Four Portrays
Totalitarianism and Mind Control,
III-1421

O'Connor's *A Good Man Is Hard to Find* Is
Published, IV-1645

Pasternak's *Doctor Zhivago* Is Published,
IV-1747

Plath's *The Colossus* Voices Women's Experience, IV-1850

Poems Establishes Auden as a Generational Spokesman, II-857

Pound Wins the Bollingen Prize, III-1443

Pound's *Cantos* Is Published, I-445

Powell Publishes the Epic *A Dance to the Music of Time*, III-1509

Proust's *Remembrance of Things Past* Is Published, I-355

Pynchon's *Gravity's Rainbow* Is Published, V-2283

Rilke's *Duino Elegies* Depicts Art as a Transcendent Experience, I-281

Roth Publishes *Portnoy's Complaint*, IV-2163

Sartre's *Being and Nothingness* Expresses Existential Philosophy, III-1262

Shaw Articulates His Philosophy in *Man and Superman*, I-85

Singer Wins the Nobel Prize in Literature, V-2423

Social Philosophers Rediscover the Works of Hesse, IV-1829

Socialist Realism Is Mandated in Soviet Literature, II-908

Sound and the Fury Launches Faulkner's Career, The, II-805

Soyinka Wins the Nobel Prize in Literature, V-2594

Stein Holds Her First Paris Salons, I-129

Surrealism Is Born, II-604

Things Fall Apart Depicts Destruction of Ibo Culture, IV-1763

Tolkien Publishes *The Lord of the Rings*, III-1607

Trudeau's *Doonesbury* Popularizes Topical Comic Strips, V-2223

Vonnegut's *Cat's Cradle* Expresses 1960's Alienation, IV-1939

Webster's Third New International Dictionary Sparks Linguistic Controversy, IV-1898

Wiesel's *Night* Recalls the Holocaust, IV-1700

William James's *Pragmatism* Is Published, I-171

Wittgenstein Emerges as an Important Philosopher, I-518

Woolf's *Mrs. Dalloway* Explores Women's Consciousness, II-637

Wright's *Native Son* Depicts Racism in America, III-1185

Yeats Publishes *The Wild Swans at Coole*, I-440

Young Readers Embrace *The Catcher in the Rye*, III-1493

MOTION PICTURES

Allen's *Annie Hall* Captures Complexities of 1970's Life, V-2381

Apocalypse Now Is Hailed as the Ultimate Vietnam War Film, V-2428

Bergman Wins International Fame with *The Seventh Seal*, IV-1742

Berkeley's *42nd Street* Revolutionizes Film Musicals, II-925

Birth of a Nation Popularizes New Film Techniques, The, I-402

Blacklisting Seriously Depletes Hollywood's Talent Pool, III-1340

Buñuel and Dalí Champion Surrealism in *Un Chien andalou*, II-750

Cabinet of Dr. Caligari Opens in Berlin, The, I-486

Capra Releases *It's a Wonderful Life*, III-1335

Casablanca Marks the Artistic Apex of 1940's War-Themed Films, III-1245

Chaplin Produces His Masterpiece *The Gold Rush*, II-659

Classic Screwball Comedy Reaches Its Height in Popularity, The, II-951

Classic *The Wizard of Oz* Opens, The, III-1109

Coppola Revives Gangster Films with *The Godfather* Trilogy, V-2265

Dean Becomes a Legend in *Rebel Without a Cause*, IV-1640

Disney Releases *Snow White and the Seven Dwarfs*, II-1053

Disney's *Fantasia* Premieres and Redefines the Boundaries of Animation, III-1195

Do the Right Thing Establishes Lee as a World-Class Director, V-2641

Dr. No Launches the Hugely Popular James Bond Series, IV-1913

Ealing Comedies Mark a High Point in British Film, III-1427

Easy Rider Captures the Spirit of 1960's Youth, IV-2158

Eisenstein's *Potemkin* Introduces New Film Editing Techniques, II-615

E.T.: The Extraterrestrial Breaks Box-Office Records, V-2491

Female Directors Attain Prominence, V-2443

First Academy Awards Honor Film Achievement, The, II-799

Ford Defines the Western in *Stagecoach*, III-1115

Forman Adapts *One Flew Over the Cuckoo's Nest* for Film, V-2320

French New Wave Ushers in a New Era of Cinema, The, IV-1710

Gance's *Napoléon* Revolutionizes Filmmaking Techniques, II-642

Godard's Expressionistic *À bout de souffle* Revolutionizes Film, IV-1845

Gone with the Wind Premieres, III-1154

Great Train Robbery Introduces New Editing Techniques, The, I-74

Hallelujah Is the First Important Black Musical, II-772

Hitchcock Becomes England's Foremost Director, II-946

Hollywood Enters Its Golden Age, II-822

Hollywood Studio System Is Transformed, The, III-1307

Innovative Black Filmmakers Achieve Success, V-2565

Italian New Wave Gains Worldwide Acclaim, The, III-1228

Jazz Singer Premieres in New York, The, II-734

Karloff and Lugosi Become Kings of Horror, II-863

Kazan Brings Naturalism to the Stage and Screen, III-1164

Keaton's *The General* Is Released, II-691

Kubrick Becomes a Film-Industry Leader, IV-1989

Kuleshov and Pudovkin Introduce Montage to Filmmaking, II-701

Kurosawa's *Rashomon* Wins the Grand Prize at Venice, III-1476

Lang Expands the Limits of Filmmaking with *Metropolis*, II-707

Leone Renovates the Western Genre, IV-1984

Little Caesar, Public Enemy, and *Scarface* Launch the Gangster-Film Genre, II-839

Lubitsch's *The Merry Widow* Opens New Vistas for Film Musicals, II-941

Maltese Falcon Establishes a New Style for Crime Films, The, III-1223

Man Ray Creates the Rayograph, I-513

Marilyn Monroe Climbs to Stardom, III-1567

Olivier's *Hamlet* Is Released to Acclaim and Controversy, III-1378

Pickford Becomes "America's Sweetheart," I-224

Platoon Explores the Vietnam Experience, V-2576

Poitier Emerges as a Film Star in *The Blackboard Jungle*, IV-1650

Psycho Becomes Hitchcock's Most Famous Film, IV-1855

Renoir Marks the High Point of Prewar Filmmaking, II-1073

Saturday Night Fever Epitomizes the Disco Craze, V-2386

Scott's *Blade Runner* Is a Visual Masterpiece, V-2486

Sennett Defines the Slapstick Comedy Genre, I-230

Sherlock Holmes Film Series Begins, The, III-1131

Sixteen Candles Starts a Wave of Teen Films, V-2527

Sound of Music Captivates Audiences, The, IV-2033

Sound Technology Revolutionizes the Motion-Picture Industry, II-761

Star Wars Trilogy Redefines Special Effects, The, V-2391

Stormy Weather Offers New Film Roles to African Americans, III-1159

Strada Solidifies Fellini's Renown as a Brilliant Director, *La*, III-1596

Streetcar Named Desire Brings Method Acting to the Screen, *A*, III-1487

Studio System Dominates Hollywood Filmmaking, The, II-833

Temple Receives a Special Academy Award, II-1011

Ten Commandments Establishes Silent-Film Spectacle, The, II-567

Top Hat Establishes the Astaire-Rogers Dance Team, II-984

Von Sternberg Makes Dietrich a Superstar, II-845

Von Stroheim Films His Silent Masterpiece *Greed*, II-593

Voyage dans la lune Introduces Special Effects, *Le*, I-57

Warhol's *The Chelsea Girls* Becomes a Commercial Success, IV-2053

Welles's *Citizen Kane* Breaks with Traditional Filmmaking, III-1200

Westerns Dominate Postwar American Film, III-1313

MUSIC

Adams' *Nixon in China* Premieres, V-2599

Armstrong First Records with His Hot Five Group, II-670

ASCAP Is Founded to Protect Musicians' Rights, I-379

Bartók and Kodály Begin to Collect Hungarian Folk Songs, I-102

Beatles Release *Sgt. Pepper's Lonely Hearts Club Band*, The, IV-2098

Beatles Revolutionize Popular Music, The, IV-1944

Berg's *Lulu* Opens in Zurich, II-1078

Berg's *Wozzeck* Premieres in Berlin, II-680

Bernstein Joins Symphonic and Jazz Elements in *West Side Story*, IV-1731

Berry's "Maybellene" Popularizes Rock and Roll, IV-1635

Bessie Smith Records "Downhearted Blues," II-572

Bill Monroe and the Blue Grass Boys Define Bluegrass Music, III-1121

Billie Holiday Begins Her Recording Career, II-930

Boulanger Takes Copland as a Student, I-508

Boulez's *Le Marteau sans maître* Premieres in Baden-Baden, IV-1656

Brecht and Weill Collaborate on *Mahagonny Songspiel*, II-724

Britten Completes *Peter Grimes*, III-1296

Brown Wins a Grammy for "Papa's Got a Brand New Bag," IV-2059

Busoni's *Sketch for a New Aesthetic of Music* Is Published, I-166

Cage's *4′ 33″* Premieres, III-1546

Caruso Records for the Gramophone and Typewriter Company, I-69

Cohan's *Little Johnny Jones* Premieres, I-108

Davis' *Birth of the Cool* Recordings Spawn 1950's Cool Jazz, III-1438

Davis' *Bitches Brew* Vitalizes Jazz-Rock Fusion, IV-2153

Dylan Performs with Electric Instruments, IV-2038

Einstein on the Beach Is a Triumph of Minimalism, V-2375

Elgar's First Symphony Premieres to Acclaim, I-214

Ellington Begins an Influential Engagement at the Cotton Club, II-739

First Newport Jazz Festival Is Held, The, III-1617

First Successful Synthesizer Is Completed, The, IV-1785

Gershwin's *Porgy and Bess* Opens in New York, II-1016

Gershwin's *Rhapsody in Blue* Premieres in New York, II-598

Goodman Begins His *Let's Dance* Broadcasts, II-968

Gordy Founds Motown Records, IV-1790

Graham Debuts *Appalachian Spring* with Copland Score, III-1284

Guthrie's Populist Songs Reflect the Depression-Era United States, II-810

Handy Ushers in the Commercial Blues Era, I-252

Hank Williams Performs on *The Grand Ole Opry*, III-1415

Harlem Renaissance Celebrates African-American Culture, The, I-480

Hendrix Releases *Are You Experienced?*, IV-2092

Hindemith Advances Ideas of Music for Use and for Amateurs, II-816

Ives Completes His Fourth Symphony, I-425

Jesus Christ Superstar Establishes the Rock Opera, V-2254

Joplin Popularizes the Ragtime Style, I-13

Joplin's *Treemonisha* Is Staged by the Houston Opera, V-2350

Laurie Anderson's *United States* Popularizes Performance Art, V-2517

Led Zeppelin Merges Hard Rock and Folk Music, V-2228

Live Aid Generates Millions for Famine Relief, V-2543

Mahalia Jackson Begins Her Recording Career, III-1329

Mahler Revamps the Vienna Court Opera, I-7

Mahler's Masterpiece *Das Lied von der Erde* Premieres Posthumously, I-298

Marian Anderson Is Barred from
Constitution Hall, III-1126
Marley's *Natty Dread* Establishes Reggae's
Popularity, V-2344
Messiaen's *Quartet for the End of Time*
Premieres, III-1206
Monterey Pop Festival Inaugurates the
"Summer of Love," The, IV-2104
MTV Changes the Look of American
Popular Culture, V-2475
Oklahoma! Opens on Broadway, III-1256
Parker's Playing Epitomizes Bebop, III-1318
Porter Creates an Integrated Score for *Kiss
Me, Kate*, III-1404
Presley Becomes a Rock-and-Roll Sensation,
IV-1705
Puccini's *Tosca* Premieres in Rome, I-29
Radical Musical *Hair* Opens on Broadway,
The, IV-2121
Rap Goes Platinum with Run-D.M.C.'s
Raising Hell, V-2582
Riley Completes *In C*, IV-1979
Rite of Spring Stuns Audiences, The, I-373
Rodgers Cuts His First Record for RCA
Victor, II-729
Rolling Stones Release *Out of Our Heads*,
The, IV-2027
Saturday Night Fever Epitomizes the Disco
Craze, V-2386
Schoenberg Breaks with Tonality, I-193
Schoenberg Develops His Twelve-Tone
System, I-528
Scriabin's *Prometheus* Premieres in Moscow,
I-286
Sex Pistols Spark Punk Rock's Musical
Insurrection, The, V-2360
Shostakovich's *Lady Macbeth of Mtsensk* Is
Condemned, II-1042
Show Boat Introduces American Musical
Theater, II-745
Sibelius Conducts the Premiere of His
Fourth Symphony, I-292
Sinatra Establishes Himself as a Solo
Performer, III-1250
"Six" Begin Giving Concerts, "Les," I-435
Sondheim Uses Operatic Techniques in
Sweeney Todd, V-2433
Sondheim's *Company* Is Broadway's First
"Concept" Musical, V-2213
Springsteen's *Born to Run* Reinvigorates
Mainstream Rock, V-2325

Stalin Restricts Soviet Composers, II-914
Strauss's *Salome* Shocks Audiences, I-151
Stravinsky Completes His Wind Octet,
II-561
Stravinsky's *The Rake's Progress* Premieres
in Venice, III-1514
Thriller Marks Michael Jackson's Musical
Coming-of-Age, V-2512
U.S. Highball Premieres in New York,
III-1279
Varèse Premieres *Déserts*, III-1629
Vaughan Williams Composes His Nine
Symphonies, I-90
Villa-Lobos' Death Marks the End of a
Brilliant Musical Career, IV-1818
Wanted: The Outlaws Revitalizes Country
Music, V-2365
Webern's *Six Pieces for Large Orchestra*
Premieres in Vienna, I-367
Willson's *The Music Man* Presents Musical
Americana, IV-1752
Wonder Releases *Innervisions*, V-2294
Woodstock Music Festival Marks the Climax
of the 1960's, The, IV-2180
WSM Launches *The Grand Ole Opry*,
II-675
Wynton Marsalis Revives Acoustic Jazz,
V-2454
Zhdanov Denounces "Formalism" in Music,
III-1388

TELEVISION AND RADIO

ABC Begins Its Own Network Television
Service, III-1368
ABC Makes a Landmark Deal with Disney,
III-1612
All in the Family Introduces a New Style of
Television Comedy, V-2234
Amahl and the Night Visitors Premieres on
American Television, III-1536
Amos 'n' Andy Radio Show Goes on the Air,
The, II-755
Art of Radio Develops from Early Broadcast
Experience, The, I-469
Bonanza Becomes an American Television
Classic, IV-1800
British Broadcasting Corporation Is
Chartered, The, II-712
Captain Kangaroo Debuts, IV-1678
Civil War Rivets the Attention of the United
States, The, V-2657

Cosby Show Makes Television History, The, V-2532

Dallas Popularizes the Prime-Time Soap Opera, V-2418

Decline of the Big Three Networks Becomes a Fall, The, V-2554

Dick Van Dyke Show Popularizes Situation Comedy, The, IV-1908

Dragnet Is the First Widely Popular Police Show, III-1531

Flintstones Popularizes Prime-Time Cartoons, The, IV-1840

Forsyte Saga Is a Hit on Public Television, The, IV-2168

Gunsmoke Debuts, Launching a Popular Television Genre, IV-1668

Happy Days Exemplifies Escapist Television, V-2305

Hill Street Blues Defines Hard-Reality Television, V-2470

Honeymooners Enchants Audiences of All Ages, The, IV-1673

I Love Lucy Dominates Television Comedy, III-1525

I Spy Debuts to Controversy, IV-2044

Jeffersons Signals Success of Black Situation Comedies, The, V-2339

Kukla, Fran, and Ollie Pioneers Children's Television Programming, III-1400

McLuhan Probes the Impact of Mass Media on Society, IV-1973

Mary Tyler Moore Show Examines Women's Roles, The, V-2218

M*A*S*H Reflects 1970's Sentiments, V-2271

"Mr. Television," Milton Berle, Has the Top-Rated Show, III-1394

Monty Python's Flying Circus Captures Audiences Worldwide, IV-2174

MTV Changes the Look of American Popular Culture, V-2475

NBC and CBS Launch Commercial Television, III-1211

NBC Broadcasts the World Series, III-1362

NBC Launches American Television at the World's Fair, III-1143

Peyton Place Brings Serial Drama to Nighttime Television, IV-2017

Radio Programming Dominates Home Leisure, II-828

Red Skelton Show Becomes a Landmark on Network Television, The, III-1520

Relevance Programs Change Entertainment Standards, V-2197

Roots Dramatizes the African-American Experience, V-2397

Rowan and Martin's Laugh-In Is the Top Show on Television, IV-2115

Saturday Night Live Is First Broadcast, V-2355

Sesame Street Revolutionizes Children's Programming, V-2185

Seven of the Top Ten Television Series Are Westerns, IV-1768

Simpsons Debuts, Anchoring the Fledgling Fox Network, The, V-2652

Situation Comedies Dominate Television Programming, IV-1835

60 Minutes Becomes the First Televised Newsmagazine, IV-2136

Sonny and Cher Comedy Hour Brings Glitz to Television, The, V-2244

Syndication Turns *Star Trek* into a Cult Classic, V-2260

Television Enters Its Golden Age, III-1465

Television Family Comedy Becomes Extremely Popular, III-1470

Thriller Marks Michael Jackson's Musical Coming-of-Age, V-2512

Tonight Show Becomes an American Institution, The, III-1623

Variety Shows Dominate Television Programming, III-1383

Violent Action-Adventure Television Series Flourish, V-2330

Welles Broadcasts *The War of the Worlds*, III-1103

THEATER

Abbey Theatre Heralds the Celtic Revival, The, I-119

Akalaitis' *Green Card* Confronts Audiences with Harsh Realities, V-2571

American Dream Establishes Albee as the Voice of Pessimism, The, IV-1903

"Angry Young Men" Express Working-Class Views, III-1454

Baker Establishes the 47 Workshop at Harvard, I-343

Baraka's *Dutchman* Dramatizes Racial Hatred, IV-2000

Bedbug and *The Bathhouse* Exemplify Revolutionary Theater, *The*, II-787

Behan's *The Hostage* Is Presented by the Theatre Workshop, IV-1757

Brecht and Weill Collaborate on *Mahagonny Songspiel*, II-724

Brecht Founds the Berliner Ensemble, III-1410

Cohan's *Little Johnny Jones* Premieres, I-108

Coward's *Design for Living* Epitomizes the 1930's, II-936

Esslin Publishes *The Theatre of the Absurd*, IV-1871

Federal Theatre Project Promotes Live Theater, The, II-989

Fierstein's *Torch Song Trilogy* Meets with Unexpected Success, V-2502

Ford Foundation Begins to Fund Nonprofit Theaters, The, IV-1736

Gershwin's *Porgy and Bess* Opens in New York, II-1016

Ghost Sonata Influences Modern Theater and Drama, *The*, I-199

Great Britain Establishes the Royal National Theatre, IV-1924

Group Theatre Flourishes, The, II-874

Guare's *The House of Blue Leaves* Combines Comedy with Horror, V-2239

Handke's *Kaspar* Dramatizes Language Theory, IV-2126

Hansberry's *A Raisin in the Sun* Debuts on Broadway, IV-1795

Havel's *The Garden Party* Satirizes Life Under Communism, IV-1967

Ionesco's *Rhinoceros* Receives a Resounding Worldwide Reception, IV-1812

Jesus Christ Superstar Establishes the Rock Opera, V-2254

Kazan Brings Naturalism to the Stage and Screen, III-1164

Long Day's Journey into Night Revives O'Neill's Reputation, IV-1726

"MASTER HAROLD" . . . *and the boys* Examines Apartheid, V-2496

Mortimer's *A Voyage Round My Father* Is Embraced by Audiences, V-2249

Mousetrap Begins a Record-Breaking Run, *The*, III-1551

Odets' *Awake and Sing* Becomes a Model for Protest Drama, II-1006

Oklahoma! Opens on Broadway, III-1256

Osborne's *Look Back in Anger* Opens in London, IV-1721

Our Town Opens on Broadway, III-1099

Pinter's *The Caretaker* Opens in London, IV-1861

Pirandello's *Six Characters in Search of an Author* Premieres, I-534

Playboy of the Western World Offends Irish Audiences, *The*, I-176

Porter Creates an Integrated Score for *Kiss Me, Kate*, III-1404

Radical Musical *Hair* Opens on Broadway, The, IV-2121

Reinhardt Becomes Director of the Deutsches Theater, I-145

Royal Shakespeare Company Adopts a New Name and Focus, The, IV-1888

Sartre and Camus Give Dramatic Voice to Existential Philosophy, III-1174

Shange's *for colored girls* . . . Is a Landmark, V-2370

Shaw Articulates His Philosophy in *Man and Superman*, I-85

Shepard's *Buried Child* Promotes Off-Broadway Theater, V-2413

Show Boat Introduces American Musical Theater, II-745

Simon's *Biloxi Blues* Emphasizes Serious Themes, V-2537

Sondheim Uses Operatic Techniques in *Sweeney Todd*, V-2433

Stanislavsky Helps to Establish the Moscow Art Theater, I-1

Tawfiq al-Hakim Introduces Absurdism to the Arab Stage, IV-1893

Theatres Act Ends Censorship of English Drama, The, IV-2131

Waiting for Godot Expresses the Existential Theme of Absurdity, III-1573

Weiss's Absurdist Drama *Marat/Sade* Is Produced, IV-2005

Willson's *The Music Man* Presents Musical Americana, IV-1752

Wiz Brings African-American Talent to Broadway, *The*, V-2334

GEOGRAPHICAL INDEX

ARGENTINA

Borges' *Ficciones* Transcends Traditional Realism, III-1268

García Márquez's *One Hundred Years of Solitude* Is Published, IV-2086

Wiesel's *Night* Recalls the Holocaust, IV-1700

AUSTRIA

Cunningham Stages His First Dance "Event," IV-2011

Freud Inaugurates a Fascination with the Unconscious, I-19

Hoffmann and Moser Found the Wiener Werkstätte, I-79

Mahler Revamps the Vienna Court Opera, I-7

Schoenberg Breaks with Tonality, I-193

Schoenberg Develops His Twelve-Tone System, I-528

Webern's *Six Pieces for Large Orchestra* Premieres in Vienna, I-367

BELGIUM

Hoffmann Designs the Palais Stoclet, I-124

BRAZIL

Villa-Lobos' Death Marks the End of a Brilliant Musical Career, IV-1818

CANADA

Expo 67 Presents Innovative Architectural Concepts, IV-2081

McLuhan Probes the Impact of Mass Media on Society, IV-1973

CZECHOSLOVAKIA

Hašek's *The Good Soldier Švejk* Reflects Postwar Disillusionment, I-523

Havel's *The Garden Party* Satirizes Life Under Communism, IV-1967

Metamorphosis Anticipates Modern Feelings of Alienation, The, I-39

EAST GERMANY

Brecht Founds the Berliner Ensemble, III-1410

EGYPT

Tawfiq al-Hakim Introduces Absurdism to the Arab Stage, IV-1893

ENGLAND. *See* GREAT BRITAIN.

EUROPE (*see also individual countries*)

Diary of a Country Priest Inspires Readers, The, II-1026

Formation of the Blue Four Advances Abstract Painting, The, II-583

FINLAND

Aalto Designs Villa Mairea, II-1067

Design for the Real World Reorients Industrial Design, V-2208

Sibelius Conducts the Premiere of His Fourth Symphony, I-292

FRANCE

Apollinaire Defines Cubism in *The Cubist Painters*, I-337

Après-midi d' un faune Causes an Uproar, L', I-332

Artists Find Inspiration in African Tribal Art, I-156

Baker Dances in *La Revue nègre*, II-665

Beauvoir's *The Second Sex* Anticipates the Women's Movement, III-1449

Beckett's Trilogy Pushes Against the Frontiers of Fiction, III-1498

Bergman Wins International Fame with *The Seventh Seal*, IV-1742

Bergson's *Creative Evolution* Inspires Artists and Thinkers, I-161

Bikini Swimsuit Is Introduced, The, III-1324

Boulanger Takes Copland as a Student, I-508

Buñuel and Dalí Champion Surrealism in *Un Chien andalou*, II-750

Celan's Influential *Atemwende* Is Published, IV-2070

Celine's *Journey to the End of the Night* Is Published, II-890

Chanel Defines Modern Women's Fashion, I-474

Christo Wraps the Pont Neuf, V-2548

Corbusier Designs and Builds Chandigarh, Le, III-1503

Corbusier's Villa Savoye Redefines Architecture, Le, II-869

Derrida Enunciates the Principles of Deconstruction, IV-2075

Diaghilev's Ballets Russes Astounds Paris, I-241

Dior's "New Look" Sweeps Europe and America, III-1346

Disney Emerges as an Architectural Patron, V-2646

Duchamp's "Readymades" Challenge Concepts of Art, I-349

Einstein on the Beach Is a Triumph of Minimalism, V-2375

Fauves Exhibit at the Salon d'Automne, Les, I-140

Firebird Premieres in Paris, The, I-269

Fokine's Les Sylphides Introduces Abstract Ballet, I-247

Foucault's Madness and Civilization Is Published, IV-1877

French New Wave Ushers in a New Era of Cinema, The, IV-1710

Futurists Issue Their Manifesto, The, I-235

Gance's Napoléon Revolutionizes Filmmaking Techniques, II-642

Gide's The Counterfeiters Questions Moral Absolutes, II-620

Godard's Expressionistic À bout de souffle Revolutionizes Film, IV-1845

Hemingway's The Sun Also Rises Speaks for the Lost Generation, II-696

Jooss's Antiwar Dance The Green Table Premieres, II-920

Joyce's Ulysses Epitomizes Modernism in Fiction, II-555

Lévi-Strauss Explores Myth as a Key to Enlightenment, IV-1995

Man Ray Creates the Rayograph, I-513

Miller's Notorious Novel Tropic of Cancer Is Published, II-963

Monet's Water Lilies Are Shown at the Musée de l'Orangerie, II-718

Musée d'Orsay Opens, The, V-2588

New Novel (Le Nouveau Roman) Emerges, The, III-1481

Paris Exhibition Defines Art Deco, A, II-654

Pei Creates a New Entrance to the Louvre, V-2619

Picasso Paints Guernica , II-1062

Poiret's "Hobble Skirts" Become the Rage, I-263

Pompidou Center Opens in Paris, The, V-2402

Pound's Cantos Is Published, I-445

Proust's Remembrance of Things Past Is Published, I-355

Prouvé Pioneers the Prefabrication of Buildings, II-1021

Renoir Marks the High Point of Prewar Filmmaking, II-1073

Rite of Spring Stuns Audiences, The, I-373

Salon d'Automne Rejects Braque's Cubist Works, The, I-204

Sartre and Camus Give Dramatic Voice to Existential Philosophy, III-1174

Sartre's Being and Nothingness Expresses Existential Philosophy, III-1262

Schiaparelli's Boutique Mingles Art and Fashion, II-979

"Six" Begin Giving Concerts, "Les," I-435

Stein Holds Her First Paris Salons, I-129

Stravinsky Completes His Wind Octet, II-561

Surrealism Is Born, II-604

Varèse Premieres Déserts, III-1629

Voyage dans la lune Introduces Special Effects, Le, I-57

Waiting for Godot Expresses the Existential Theme of Absurdity, III-1573

Wiesel's Night Recalls the Holocaust, IV-1700

GERMANY. See also EAST GERMANY and WEST GERMANY.

All Quiet on the Western Front Stresses the Futility of War, II-767

Avant-Garde Artists in Dresden Form Die Brücke, I-134

Behrens Designs the AEG Turbine Factory, I-219

Berg's Wozzeck Premieres in Berlin, II-680

Blaue Reiter Abandons Representation in Art, Der, I-275

Brecht and Weill Collaborate on Mahagonny Songspiel, II-724

Busoni's Sketch for a New Aesthetic of Music Is Published, I-166

Cabinet of Dr. Caligari Opens in Berlin, The, I-486

Deutscher Werkbund Combats Conservative Architecture, The, I-181

German Artists Found the Bauhaus, I-463

German Writers Form Group 47, III-1357

Hindemith Advances Ideas of Music for Use and for Amateurs, II-816

Hitler Organizes an Exhibition Denouncing Modern Art, III-1083

Kandinsky Publishes His Views on Abstraction in Art, I-320

Lang Expands the Limits of Filmmaking with *Metropolis*, II-707

Mahler's Masterpiece *Das Lied von der Erde* Premieres Posthumously, I-298

Mann's *The Magic Mountain* Reflects European Crisis, II-588

Nazis Ban Nolde's Paintings, The, III-1217

New Objectivity Movement Is Introduced, The, II-631

Reinhardt Becomes Director of the Deutsches Theater, I-145

Strauss's *Salome* Shocks Audiences, I-151

GREAT BRITAIN

"Angry Young Men" Express Working-Class Views, III-1454

Beatles Release *Sgt. Pepper's Lonely Hearts Club Band*, The, IV-2098

Beatles Revolutionize Popular Music, The, IV-1944

Behan's *The Hostage* Is Presented by the Theatre Workshop, IV-1757

British Broadcasting Corporation Is Chartered, The, II-712

Britten Completes *Peter Grimes*, III-1296

Dr. No Launches the Hugely Popular James Bond Series, IV-1913

Ealing Comedies Mark a High Point in British Film, III-1427

Elgar's First Symphony Premieres to Acclaim, I-214

Eliot Publishes *The Waste Land*, II-539

Golding's *Lord of the Flies* Spurs Examination of Human Nature, III-1585

Great Britain Establishes the Royal National Theatre, IV-1924

Heart of Darkness Reveals the Consequences of Imperialism, I-51

Hendrix Releases *Are You Experienced?*, IV-2092

Henry Moore Is Inspired by Shapes in Subway Shelters, III-1190

Hitchcock Becomes England's Foremost Director, II-946

Huxley's *Brave New World* Reflects Fears About the Future, II-896

Imagist Movement Shakes Up Poetry, The, I-326

Khomeini Calls for Rushdie's Death, V-2630

Kubrick Becomes a Film-Industry Leader, IV-1989

Laura Ashley and Her Husband Found a Fashion Company, III-1562

Le Carré Rejects the Fantasy World of Secret Agents, IV-1934

Led Zeppelin Merges Hard Rock and Folk Music, V-2228

Live Aid Generates Millions for Famine Relief, V-2543

Melville Is Rediscovered as a Major American Novelist, I-502

Monty Python's Flying Circus Captures Audiences Worldwide, IV-2174

Mortimer's *A Voyage Round My Father* Is Embraced by Audiences, V-2249

Mousetrap Begins a Record-Breaking Run, The, III-1551

Mysterious Affair at Styles Introduces Hercule Poirot, The, I-496

Nineteen Eighty-Four Portrays Totalitarianism and Mind Control, III-1421

Nureyev and Fonteyn Debut Ashton's *Marguerite and Armand*, IV-1962

Olivier's *Hamlet* Is Released to Acclaim and Controversy, III-1378

Osborne's *Look Back in Anger* Opens in London, IV-1721

Plath's *The Colossus* Voices Women's Experience, IV-1850

Poems Establishes Auden as a Generational Spokesman, II-857

Pound's *Cantos* Is Published, I-445

Powell Publishes the Epic *A Dance to the Music of Time*, III-1509

Punk's Antifashion Style First Appears, V-2299

Quant Introduces the Miniskirt, IV-1824

Rolling Stones Release *Out of Our Heads*, The, IV-2027

Royal Shakespeare Company Adopts a New Name and Focus, The, IV-1888

Sex Pistols Spark Punk Rock's Musical Insurrection, The, V-2360

Shaw Articulates His Philosophy in *Man and Superman*, I-85

Theatres Act Ends Censorship of English Drama, The, IV-2131

Things Fall Apart Depicts Destruction of Ibo Culture, IV-1763

Tolkien Publishes *The Lord of the Rings*, III-1607

Tudor's *Jardin aux lilas* Premieres in London, II-1036

Vaughan Williams Composes His Nine Symphonies, I-90

Wittgenstein Emerges as an Important Philosopher, I-518

Woolf's *Mrs. Dalloway* Explores Women's Consciousness, II-637

HUNGARY
Bartók and Kodály Begin to Collect Hungarian Folk Songs, I-102

INDIA
Corbusier Designs and Builds Chandigarh, Le, III-1503

IRAN
Khomeini Calls for Rushdie's Death, V-2630

IRELAND
Abbey Theatre Heralds the Celtic Revival, The, I-119

Playboy of the Western World Offends Irish Audiences, *The*, I-176

Yeats Publishes *The Wild Swans at Coole*, I-440

ITALY
Caruso Records for the Gramophone and Typewriter Company, I-69

Four Modern Masters Affirm Germany's Place in the Art World, V-2464

Italian New Wave Gains Worldwide Acclaim, The, III-1228

Kurosawa's *Rashomon* Wins the Grand Prize at Venice, III-1476

Leone Renovates the Western Genre, IV-1984

Pasternak's *Doctor Zhivago* Is Published, IV-1747

Pirandello's *Six Characters in Search of an Author* Premieres, I-534

Pound's *Cantos* Is Published, I-445

Puccini's *Tosca* Premieres in Rome, I-29

Rilke's *Duino Elegies* Depicts Art as a Transcendent Experience, I-281

Strada Solidifies Fellini's Renown as a Brilliant Director, *La*, III-1596

Stravinsky's *The Rake's Progress* Premieres in Venice, III-1514

JAMAICA
Marley's *Natty Dread* Establishes Reggae's Popularity, V-2344

LATIN AMERICA (*see also individual countries*)
"Boom" Captures Worldwide Attention, The, IV-1689

MEXICO
Formation of the Blue Four Advances Abstract Painting, The, II-583

García Lorca's *Poet in New York* Is Published, III-1179

NETHERLANDS, THE
Rietveld Designs the Red-Blue Chair, I-458

Stijl Advocates Mondrian's Neoplasticism, *De*, I-429

NORWAY
First Nobel Prizes Are Awarded, The, I-45

PAKISTAN
Kahn Blends Architecture and Urban Planning in Dacca, IV-1919

POLAND
Messiaen's *Quartet for the End of Time* Premieres, III-1206

RUSSIA. *See also* SOVIET UNION.
Duncan Interprets Chopin in Her Russian Debut, I-113

Malevich Introduces Suprematism, I-413

Pavlova First Performs Her Legendary Solo *The Dying Swan*, I-187

Scriabin's *Prometheus* Premieres in Moscow, I-286

Stanislavsky Helps to Establish the Moscow Art Theater, I-1

SILESIA. *See* POLAND.

SOVIET UNION. *See also* RUSSIA.

Bedbug and *The Bathhouse* Exemplify Revolutionary Theater, *The*, II-787

Eisenstein's *Potemkin* Introduces New Film Editing Techniques, II-615

Gulag Archipelago Exposes Soviet Atrocities, *The*, V-2277

Kuleshov and Pudovkin Introduce Montage to Filmmaking, II-701

Pasternak's *Doctor Zhivago* Is Published, IV-1747

Shostakovich's *Lady Macbeth of Mtsensk* Is Condemned, II-1042

Socialist Realism Is Mandated in Soviet Literature, II-908

Soviet Union Bans Abstract Art, The, II-544

Stalin Restricts Soviet Composers, II-914

Zhdanov Denounces "Formalism" in Music, III-1388

SPAIN

Dalí Museum Opens in Figueras, Spain, A, V-2310

Gaudí Completes the Casa Milá Apartment House in Barcelona, I-257

Spanish Art Explodes After Years of Suppression, V-2203

SWEDEN

Design for the Real World Reorients Industrial Design, V-2208

First Nobel Prizes Are Awarded, The, I-45

Ghost Sonata Influences Modern Theater and Drama, *The*, I-199

Gordimer Wins the Nobel Prize in Literature, V-2668

Kawabata Wins the Nobel Prize in Literature, IV-2147

Mahfouz Wins the Nobel Prize in Literature, V-2625

Singer Wins the Nobel Prize in Literature, V-2423

Soyinka Wins the Nobel Prize in Literature, V-2594

SWITZERLAND

Berg's *Lulu* Opens in Zurich, II-1078

Dada Movement Emerges at the Cabaret Voltaire, The, I-419

Gulag Archipelago Exposes Soviet Atrocities, *The*, V-2277

Jung Publishes *Psychology of the Unconscious*, I-309

Rilke's *Duino Elegies* Depicts Art as a Transcendent Experience, I-281

UNITED STATES

ABC Begins Its Own Network Television Service, III-1368

ABC Makes a Landmark Deal with Disney, III-1612

Abstract Painting in America Opens in New York, II-1001

Adams' *Nixon in China* Premieres, V-2599

Agnes de Mille Choreographs *Rodeo*, III-1234

Ailey Founds His Dance Company, IV-1774

Akalaitis' *Green Card* Confronts Audiences with Harsh Realities, V-2571

All in the Family Introduces a New Style of Television Comedy, V-2234

Allen's *Annie Hall* Captures Complexities of 1970's Life, V-2381

Amahl and the Night Visitors Premieres on American Television, III-1536

American Dream Establishes Albee as the Voice of Pessimism, *The*, IV-1903

American Science Fiction Enjoys Its Golden Age, III-1094

Amos 'n' Andy Radio Show Goes on the Air, The, II-755

Apocalypse Now Is Hailed as the Ultimate Vietnam War Film, V-2428

Armstrong First Records with His Hot Five Group, II-670

Art of Radio Develops from Early Broadcast Experience, The, I-469

Arts and Architecture Magazine Initiates the Case Study Program, III-1290

ASCAP Is Founded to Protect Musicians' Rights, I-379

AT&T Building Exemplifies Postmodernism, The, V-2407

Autobiography of Malcolm X Is
Published, *The*, IV-2022

Avant-Garde Art in the Armory Show
Shocks American Viewers, I-361

Baker Establishes the 47 Workshop at
Harvard, I-343

Balanchine and Kirstein Make New York
a World Center for Ballet, III-1301

Balanchine's *Serenade* Inaugurates
American Ballet, II-974

Baldwin Voices Black Rage in *The Fire
Next Time*, IV-1929

Ballet Russe de Monte Carlo Finds New
Leadership, The, III-1088

Baraka's *Dutchman* Dramatizes Racial
Hatred, IV-2000

Baryshnikov Becomes Artistic Director
of American Ballet Theatre, V-2459

Baryshnikov's White Oak Dance Project
Debuts, V-2663

Beat Movement Rejects Mainstream
Values, The, III-1460

Beatles Release *Sgt. Pepper's Lonely
Hearts Club Band*, The, IV-2098

Beatles Revolutionize Popular Music,
The, IV-1944

Berkeley's *42nd Street* Revolutionizes
Film Musicals, II-925

Bernstein Joins Symphonic and Jazz
Elements in *West Side Story*, IV-1731

Berry's "Maybellene" Popularizes Rock
and Roll, IV-1635

Bessie Smith Records "Downhearted
Blues," II-572

Bill Monroe and the Blue Grass Boys
Define Bluegrass Music, III-1121

Billie Holiday Begins Her Recording
Career, II-930

Birth of a Nation Popularizes New Film
Techniques, *The*, I-402

Blacklisting Seriously Depletes
Hollywood's Talent Pool, III-1340

Bonanza Becomes an American
Television Classic, IV-1800

Book-of-the-Month Club and the
Literary Guild Are Founded, The,
II-686

Breuer Designs a Building for the
Whitney Museum, IV-2064

Brooks Brothers Introduces Button-
Down Shirts, I-24

Brown Wins a Grammy for "Papa's Got
a Brand New Bag," IV-2059

Buckley Founds *National Review*,
IV-1683

Cage's *4' 33"* Premieres, III-1546

Capra Releases *It's a Wonderful Life*,
III-1335

Captain Kangaroo Debuts, IV-1678

Carnegie Publishes His Self-Help Best-
Seller, II-1048

Casablanca Marks the Artistic Apex of
1940's War-Themed Films, III-1245

Catch-22 Illustrates Antiwar Sentiment,
IV-1866

Cather's *My Ántonia* Promotes Regional
Literature, I-452

Chaplin Produces His Masterpiece *The
Gold Rush*, II-659

Christian Science Monitor Is Founded,
The, I-209

Civil War Rivets the Attention of the
United States, *The*, V-2657

Classic Screwball Comedy Reaches Its
Height in Popularity, The, II-951

Classic *The Wizard of Oz* Opens, The,
III-1109

Cohan's *Little Johnny Jones* Premieres,
I-108

Coppola Revives Gangster Films with
The Godfather Trilogy, V-2265

Cosby Show Makes Television History,
The, V-2532

Coward's *Design for Living* Epitomizes
the 1930's, II-936

Cranbrook Academy Begins a History of
Design Excellence, II-610

Crane Publishes *The Bridge*, II-851

Dallas Popularizes the Prime-Time Soap
Opera, V-2418

Davis' *Birth of the Cool* Recordings
Spawn 1950's Cool Jazz, III-1438

Davis' *Bitches Brew* Vitalizes Jazz-Rock
Fusion, IV-2153

Dean Becomes a Legend in *Rebel
Without a Cause*, IV-1640

Decline of the Big Three Networks
Becomes a Fall, The, V-2554

Deconstructivists Exhibit at the Museum
of Modern Art, V-2614

Denishawn School of Dance Opens in
Los Angeles, The, I-390

Design for the Real World Reorients Industrial Design, V-2208

Diary of a Country Priest Inspires Readers, *The*, II-1026

Dick Van Dyke Show Popularizes Situation Comedy, *The*, IV-1908

Dickinson's Poems Are Published in Full for the First Time, IV-1662

Disney Emerges as an Architectural Patron, V-2646

Disney Releases *Snow White and the Seven Dwarfs*, II-1053

Disney's *Fantasia* Premieres and Redefines the Boundaries of Animation, III-1195

Do the Right Thing Establishes Lee as a World-Class Director, V-2641

Dr. No Launches the Hugely Popular James Bond Series, IV-1913

Dog Soldiers Portrays Vietnam in Fiction, V-2315

Dragnet Is the First Widely Popular Police Show, III-1531

Dreiser's *Sister Carrie* Shatters Literary Taboos, I-39

Dreyfuss Designs the Bell "300" Telephone, II-1057

Dylan Performs with Electric Instruments, IV-2038

Easy Rider Captures the Spirit of 1960's Youth, IV-2158

Ellington Begins an Influential Engagement at the Cotton Club, II-739

Ellison's *Invisible Man* Is Published, III-1541

Empire State Building Opens as the World's Tallest Building, The, II-880

Esslin Publishes *The Theatre of the Absurd*, IV-1871

E.T.: The Extraterrestrial Breaks Box-Office Records, V-2491

Federal Theatre Project Promotes Live Theater, The, II-989

Female Directors Attain Prominence, V-2443

Festivals Mark a Peak in the Dance Created by Black Artists, V-2521

Fierstein's *Torch Song Trilogy* Meets with Unexpected Success, V-2502

First Academy Awards Honor Film Achievement, The, II-799

First Newport Jazz Festival Is Held, The, III-1617

First Pulitzer Prizes Are Awarded, The, I-407

First Successful Synthesizer Is Completed, The, IV-1785

Flintstones Popularizes Prime-Time Cartoons, *The*, IV-1840

Ford Defines the Western in *Stagecoach*, III-1115

Ford Foundation Begins to Fund Nonprofit Theaters, The, IV-1736

Forman Adapts *One Flew Over the Cuckoo's Nest* for Film, V-2320

Formation of the Blue Four Advances Abstract Painting, The, II-583

Forsyte Saga Is a Hit on Public Television, *The*, IV-2168

Fuller's First Industrial Geodesic Dome Is Erected, III-1579

German Artists Found the Bauhaus, I-463

Gershwin's *Porgy and Bess* Opens in New York, II-1016

Gershwin's *Rhapsody in Blue* Premieres in New York, II-598

Gone with the Wind Premieres, III-1154

Goodman Begins His *Let's Dance* Broadcasts, II-968

Gordy Founds Motown Records, IV-1790

Graham Debuts *Appalachian Spring* with Copland Score, III-1284

Grapes of Wrath Portrays Depression-Era America, *The*, III-1138

Great Books Foundation Is Established, The, III-1351

Great Gatsby Captures the Essence of the Roaring Twenties, *The*, II-626

Great Train Robbery Introduces New Editing Techniques, *The*, I-74

Grey's *Riders of the Purple Sage* Launches the Western Genre, I-304

Group Theatre Flourishes, The, II-874

Guare's *The House of Blue Leaves* Combines Comedy with Horror, V-2239

Guggenheim Museum Opens in a Building Designed by Wright, The, IV-1806

Gulag Archipelago Exposes Soviet Atrocities, *The*, V-2277

Gunsmoke Debuts, Launching a Popular Television Genre, IV-1668

Guthrie's Populist Songs Reflect the Depression-Era United States, II-810

Hallelujah Is the First Important Black Musical, II-772

Handy Ushers in the Commercial Blues Era, I-252

Hank Williams Performs on *The Grand Ole Opry*, III-1415

Hansberry's *A Raisin in the Sun* Debuts on Broadway, IV-1795

Happy Days Exemplifies Escapist Television, V-2305

Harlem Renaissance Celebrates African-American Culture, The, I-480

Harriet Monroe Founds *Poetry* Magazine, I-314

Heinlein Publishes *Stranger in a Strange Land*, IV-1883

Hemingway's *The Sun Also Rises* Speaks for the Lost Generation, II-696

Hendrix Releases *Are You Experienced?*, IV-2092

Henry James's *The Ambassadors* Is Published, I-96

Hill Street Blues Defines Hard-Reality Television, V-2470

Hollywood Enters Its Golden Age, II-822

Hollywood Studio System Is Transformed, The, III-1307

Honeymooners Enchants Audiences of All Ages, The, IV-1673

I Love Lucy Dominates Television Comedy, III-1525

I Spy Debuts to Controversy, IV-2044

Imagist Movement Shakes Up Poetry, The, I-326

Innovative Black Filmmakers Achieve Success, V-2565

Ives Completes His Fourth Symphony, I-425

Jantzen Popularizes the One-Piece Bathing Suit, I-491

Jasper Johns Paints the American Flag, III-1590

Jazz Singer Premieres in New York, The, II-734

Jeffersons Signals Success of Black Situation Comedies, The, V-2339

Jesus Christ Superstar Establishes the Rock Opera, V-2254

Joffrey Founds His Ballet Company, IV-1694

Joplin Popularizes the Ragtime Style, I-13

Joplin's *Treemonisha* Is Staged by the Houston Opera, V-2350

Karloff and Lugosi Become Kings of Horror, II-863

Kazan Brings Naturalism to the Stage and Screen, III-1164

Keaton's *The General* Is Released, II-691

Kelly Forges New Directions in Cinematic Dance, III-1432

Kubrick Becomes a Film-Industry Leader, IV-1989

Kukla, Fran, and Ollie Pioneers Children's Television Programming, III-1400

Lauren Creates the "Polo" Line, IV-2141

Laurie Anderson's *United States* Popularizes Performance Art, V-2517

Le Carré Rejects the Fantasy World of Secret Agents, IV-1934

Led Zeppelin Merges Hard Rock and Folk Music, V-2228

Leone Renovates the Western Genre, IV-1984

Lippmann Helps to Establish *The New Republic*, I-385

Little Caesar, Public Enemy, and *Scarface* Launch the Gangster-Film Genre, II-839

Live Aid Generates Millions for Famine Relief, V-2543

Loewy Pioneers American Industrial Design, II-777

Long Day's Journey into Night Revives O'Neill's Reputation, IV-1726

Lubitsch's *The Merry Widow* Opens New Vistas for Film Musicals, II-941

Luce Founds *Time* Magazine, II-577

Luce Launches *Life* Magazine, II-1031

McLuhan Probes the Impact of Mass Media on Society, IV-1973

Madonna Revolutionizes Popular Fashion, V-2449

Mahalia Jackson Begins Her Recording Career, III-1329

Mailer Publishes *The Naked and the Dead*, III-1373

Maltese Falcon Establishes a New Style for Crime Films, The, III-1223

Maltese Falcon Introduces the Hard-Boiled Detective Novel, The, II-793

Mapplethorpe's Photographs Provoke Controversy, V-2636

Marian Anderson Is Barred from Constitution Hall, III-1126

Marilyn Monroe Climbs to Stardom, III-1567

Mary Tyler Moore Show Examines Women's Roles, The, V-2218

M*A*S*H Reflects 1970's Sentiments, V-2271

"MASTER HAROLD" . . . and the boys Examines Apartheid, V-2496

Melville Is Rediscovered as a Major American Novelist, I-502

Minimalism Emphasizes Objects as Art, IV-1949

"Mr. Television," Milton Berle, Has the Top-Rated Show, III-1394

Mitchell Founds the Dance Theater of Harlem, IV-2110

Monterey Pop Festival Inaugurates the "Summer of Love" The, IV-2104

MTV Changes the Look of American Popular Culture, V-2475

National Endowment for the Arts Is Established, The, IV-2048

National Museum of Women in the Arts Opens Amid Controversy, The, V-2608

NBC and CBS Launch Commercial Television, III-1211

NBC Broadcasts the World Series, III-1362

NBC Launches American Television at the World's Fair, III-1143

New Criticism Holds Sway, The, III-1169

New Dance U.S.A. Festival Celebrates Contemporary Dance, The, V-2480

New York's Museum of Modern Art Is Founded, II-782

New York's SoHo Develops into a Center for Contemporary Art, V-2191

Nineteen Eighty-Four Portrays Totalitarianism and Mind Control, III-1421

O'Connor's *A Good Man Is Hard to Find* Is Published, IV-1645

Odets' *Awake and Sing* Becomes a Model for Protest Drama, II-1006

Oklahoma! Opens on Broadway, III-1256

Olivier's *Hamlet* Is Released to Acclaim and Controversy, III-1378

Our Town Opens on Broadway, III-1099

Parker's Playing Epitomizes Bebop, III-1318

Peggy Guggenheim's Gallery Promotes New American Art, III-1239

Peyton Place Brings Serial Drama to Nighttime Television, IV-2017

Pickford Becomes "America's Sweetheart," I-224

Pinter's *The Caretaker* Opens in London, IV-1861

Platoon Explores the Vietnam Experience, V-2576

Poitier Emerges as a Film Star in *The Blackboard Jungle*, IV-1650

Porter Creates an Integrated Score for *Kiss Me, Kate*, III-1404

Pound Wins the Bollingen Prize, III-1443

Pound's *Cantos* Is Published, I-445

Presley Becomes a Rock-and-Roll Sensation, IV-1705

Psycho Becomes Hitchcock's Most Famous Film, IV-1855

Pynchon's *Gravity's Rainbow* Is Published, V-2283

Radical Musical *Hair* Opens on Broadway, The, IV-2121

Radio Programming Dominates Home Leisure, II-828

Rap Goes Platinum with Run-D.M.C.'s *Raising Hell*, V-2582

Red Skelton Show Becomes a Landmark on Network Television, The, III-1520

Relevance Programs Change Entertainment Standards, V-2197

Riley Completes *In C*, IV-1979

Rivera's Rockefeller Center Mural Is Destroyed, II-957

Robbins' *Fancy Free* Premieres, III-1274

Rockefeller Center Is Completed, III-1149

Rodgers Cuts His First Record for RCA Victor, II-729

Rolling Stones Release *Out of Our Heads, The*, IV-2027

Roosevelt Administration Creates the WPA/FAP, The, II-995

Roots Dramatizes the African-American Experience, V-2397

Rosenberg Defines "Action Painting," III-1557

Ross Founds *The New Yorker*, II-648

Roth Publishes *Portnoy's Complaint*, IV-2163

Rowan and Martin's Laugh-In Is the Top Show on Television, IV-2115

Saarinen Designs Kennedy Airport's TWA Terminal, IV-1716

Sartre and Camus Give Dramatic Voice to Existential Philosophy, III-1174

Saturday Night Fever Epitomizes the Disco Craze, V-2386

Saturday Night Live Is First Broadcast, V-2355

Schnabel Emerges as a Celebrity Artist, V-2438

Schoenberg Develops His Twelve-Tone System, I-528

Scott's *Blade Runner* Is a Visual Masterpiece, V-2486

Sennett Defines the Slapstick Comedy Genre, I-230

Sesame Street Revolutionizes Children's Programming, V-2185

Seven of the Top Ten Television Series Are Westerns, IV-1768

Shange's *for colored girls . . .* Is a Landmark, V-2370

Shepard's *Buried Child* Promotes Off-Broadway Theater, V-2413

Sherlock Holmes Film Series Begins, The, III-1131

Show Boat Introduces American Musical Theater, II-745

Simon's *Biloxi Blues* Emphasizes Serious Themes, V-2537

Simpsons Debuts, Anchoring the Fledgling Fox Network, *The*, V-2652

Sinatra Establishes Himself as a Solo Performer, III-1250

Situation Comedies Dominate Television Programming, IV-1835

Sixteen Candles Starts a Wave of Teen Films, V-2527

60 Minutes Becomes the First Televised Newsmagazine, IV-2136

Social Philosophers Rediscover the Works of Hesse, IV-1829

Sondheim Uses Operatic Techniques in *Sweeney Todd*, V-2433

Sondheim's *Company* Is Broadway's First "Concept" Musical, V-2213

Sonny and Cher Comedy Hour Brings Glitz to Television, The, V-2244

Sound and the Fury Launches Faulkner's Career, The, II-805

Sound of Music Captivates Audiences, The, IV-2033

Sound Technology Revolutionizes the Motion-Picture Industry, II-761

Springsteen's *Born to Run* Reinvigorates Mainstream Rock, V-2325

Star Wars Trilogy Redefines Special Effects, The, V-2391

Stieglitz Organizes the Photo-Secession, I-63

Stormy Weather Offers New Film Roles to African Americans, III-1159

Streetcar Named Desire Brings Method Acting to the Screen, A, III-1487

Studio System Dominates Hollywood Filmmaking, The, II-833

Syndication Turns *Star Trek* into a Cult Classic, V-2260

Taylor Establishes His Own Dance Company, III-1602

Television Enters Its Golden Age, III-1465

Television Family Comedy Becomes Extremely Popular, III-1470

Temple Receives a Special Academy Award, II-1011

Ten Commandments Establishes Silent-Film Spectacle, The, II-567

Tharp Stages *Deuce Coupe* for the Joffrey Ballet, V-2288

Thriller Marks Michael Jackson's Musical Coming-of-Age, V-2512

Tiffany and Tiffany Studios Develop New Ideas in Design, I-34

Tonight Show Becomes an American Institution, The, III-1623

Top Hat Establishes the Astaire-Rogers Dance Team, II-984

GEOGRAPHICAL INDEX

Trudeau's *Doonesbury* Popularizes Topical Comic Strips, V-2223

U.S. Highball Premieres in New York, III-1279

USA Today Is Launched, V-2507

Van Gogh's *Irises* Sells for $53.9 Million, V-2603

Variety Shows Dominate Television Programming, III-1383

Violent Action-Adventure Television Series Flourish, V-2330

Von Sternberg Makes Dietrich a Superstar, II-845

Von Stroheim Films His Silent Masterpiece *Greed*, II-593

Vonnegut's *Cat's Cradle* Expresses 1960's Alienation, IV-1939

Wallace Founds *Reader's Digest*, II-549

Wanted: The Outlaws Revitalizes Country Music, V-2365

Warhol's *The Chelsea Girls* Becomes a Commercial Success, IV-2053

Webster's Third New International Dictionary Sparks Linguistic Controversy, IV-1898

Welles Broadcasts *The War of the Worlds*, III-1103

Welles's *Citizen Kane* Breaks with Traditional Filmmaking, III-1200

Westerns Dominate Postwar American Film, III-1313

Whitney Museum Is Inaugurated in New York, The, II-885

Wiesel's *Night* Recalls the Holocaust, IV-1700

William James's *Pragmatism* Is Published, I-171

Willson's *The Music Man* Presents Musical Americana, IV-1752

Wittgenstein Emerges as an Important Philosopher, I-518

Wiz Brings African-American Talent to Broadway, The, V-2334

Wonder Releases *Innervisions*, V-2294

Woodstock Music Festival Marks the Climax of the 1960's, The, IV-2180

Wright Founds the Taliesin Fellowship, II-902

Wright's *Native Son* Depicts Racism in America, III-1185

WSM Launches *The Grand Ole Opry*, II-675

Wynton Marsalis Revives Acoustic Jazz, V-2454

Young Readers Embrace *The Catcher in the Rye*, III-1493

WEST GERMANY

Boulez's *Le Marteau sans maître* Premieres in Baden-Baden, IV-1656

Grass Publishes *The Tin Drum*, IV-1780

Handke's *Kaspar* Dramatizes Language Theory, IV-2126

Ionesco's *Rhinoceros* Receives a Resounding Worldwide Reception, IV-1812

Nam June Paik Exhibits Video and Television as Art, IV-1955

Weiss's Absurdist Drama *Marat/Sade* Is Produced, IV-2005

WORLDWIDE

Columbus Day Debates Reflect Cultural Diversity, V-2673

Multiculturalism Dominates the Dance World, V-2559

PRINCIPAL PERSONAGES

Aalto, Aino Mario II-1067
Aalto, Alvar II-1067
Abraham, Nelson Ahlgren. See Algren, Nelson.
Achebe, Chinua IV-1763
Acuff, Roy II-675
Adamov, Arthur IV-1871
Adams, Carolyn III-1602
Adams, John V-2599
Adler, Lou IV-2104
Adler, Mortimer J. III-1351
Adler, Stella II-874, 1006
Adoian, Vosdanig. See Gorky, Arshile.
Aiello, Danny V-2641
Ailey, Alvin IV-1774; V-2521
Ain, Gregory III-1290
Akalaitis, JoAnne V-2571
Akoka, Henri III-1206
Akutagawa, Ryūnosuke III-1476
Albee, Edward IV-1903
Alda, Alan V-2271
Aldington, Richard I-326
Alekseyev, Konstantin Sergeyevich.
  See Stanislavsky, Konstantin.
Alexander, Ben III-1531
Algren, Nelson III-1449
Allegretti, Gus IV-1678
Allemann, Beda IV-2070
Allen, Fred II-828
Allen, Steve III-1623
Allen, Sture V-2668
Allen, Woody V-2381
Allison, Fran III-1400
Amis, Kingsley III-1454
Amsterdam, Morey IV-1908
Ancel, Paul. See Celan, Paul.
Andersch, Alfred III-1357
Anderson, Al V-2344
Anderson, Laurie V-2517
Anderson, Marian III-1126
Anderson, Robert III-1164
Andrews, Julie IV-2033
Antonio, Emile de IV-2053
Antonioni, Michelangelo III-1228
Antschel, Paul. See Celan, Paul.
Apollinaire, Guillaume I-337; IV-1812
Appel, Mike V-2325
Arbuckle, Roscoe "Fatty" I-230
Arden, John III-1454
Arlin, Harold W. I-469
Armstrong, Helen. See Melba, Nellie.
Armstrong, Lil II-670
Armstrong, Louis I-480; II-670
Arnaz, Desi III-1525
Arnaz y de Acha, Desiderio Alberto, III.
  See Arnaz, Desi.
Arness, James IV-1668, 1768
Arno, Peter II-648
Aron, Raymond III-1262
Aronson, Max I-74
Arp, Hans I-419
Arpino, Gerald IV-1694

Artaud, Antonin IV-1812, 2005
Ashley, Bernard III-1562
Ashley, Laura Mountney III-1562
Ashton, Sir Frederick IV-1962
Asimov, Isaac III-1094
Asner, Ed V-2218
Asplund, Erik Gunnar II-1067
Astaire, Fred II-984; III-1432
Astor, Mary III-1223
Astruc, Alexandre IV-1710
Atkins, Chet V-2365
Attenborough, Richard III-1551
Aubrey, James IV-1835
Auden, W. H. II-857; III-1514
Audry, Colette III-1449
Aulenti, Gae V-2588
Auric, Georges I-435
Aurness, James. See Arness, James.
Austerlitz, Frederick. See Astaire, Fred.
Averbakh, Leopold II-908
Aykroyd, Dan V-2355
Aylmer, Felix III-1378

Babbit, Milton IV-1785
Bach, Johann Sebastian IV-1818
Bachelet, Jean II-1073
Bacon, Lloyd II-925
Baker, George Pierce I-343
Baker, Josephine II-665
Bakst, Léon I-241, 263, 269, 332
Balaban, Barney III-1307
Balanchine, George II-974; III-1088, 1301; V-2459
Balanchivadze, Georgi Melitonovitch.
  See Balanchine, George.
Balcon, Michael II-946; III-1427
Baldwin, James IV-1929
Baldwin, John. See Jones, John Paul.
Baldwin, Stanley II-712
Balenciaga, Cristobal IV-1824
Ball, Hugo I-419
Ball, Lucille III-1525
Balla, Giacomo I-235
Balmain, Pierre III-1346
Band, the IV-2180
Banton, Travis II-845
Baraka, Amiri IV-2000; V-2370
Barber, Samuel III-1536
Barbera, Joseph IV-1840
Barca, Pedro Calderón de la III-1179
Barcelo, Randy V-2254
Bare, Bobby V-2365
Barr, Alfred H., Jr. II-782
Barrett, Aston "Family Man" V-2344
Barrett, Carlton V-2344
Barrett, Majel V-2260
Barry, John IV-1913
Barry, Philip I-343
Barrymore, Lionel III-1335
Bart, Ben IV-2059
Bartók, Béla I-102
Baryshnikov, Mikhail IV-1962; V-2288, 2459, 2559, 2663

Basehart, Richard III-1596
Baselitz, Georg V-2464
Basil, Colonel Wassili de III-1088
Bass, Saul IV-1855
Bates, Alan IV-1721, 1861
Baumgarner, James. See Garner, James.
Baxter, Warner II-925
Bazin, André IV-1710
Beach, Sylvia II-555
Beatty, Talley IV-1774; V-2521
Beaudouin, Eugène Elie II-1021
Beauvoir, Simone de III-1262, 1449
Beckett, Samuel III-1498, 1573; IV-1871, 1903
Beckmann, Max II-631
Beetson, Fred II-799
Behan, Brendan IV-1757
Behrens, Peter I-181, 219
Behrman, S. N. I-343
Bel Geddes, Barbara V-2418
Bel Geddes, Norman. See Geddes, Norman Bel.
Belar, Herbert IV-1785
Belasco, David I-224
Bell, Vanessa II-637
Belmondo, Jean-Paul IV-1845
Belushi, John V-2355
Benda, Wladyslaw Theodore I-452
Bendix, William III-1470
Benedict, Paul V-2339
Benny, Jack II-828
Benois, Alexandre I-241, 247
Ber, Israel. See Neumann, J. B.
Berg, Alban I-193, 367, 528; II-680, 1078
Berg, Helene II-1078
Bergman, Ingmar IV-1742
Bergman, Ingrid III-1245
Bergson, Henri I-161
Berkeley, Busby II-925; III-1432
Berle, Milton III-1394
Berlin, Irving II-984
Berlinger, Milton. See Berle, Milton.
Berman, Pandro S. II-984
Bernanos, Georges II-1026
Bernardini, Micheline III-1324
Bernhard, Karl I-219
Bernstein, Leonard III-1274; IV-1731
Berry, Chuck IV-1635
Bershad, Sheldon Leonard IV-2044
Besserer, Eugénie II-734
Beuys, Joseph V-2464
Biddle, George II-995
Billings, John Shaw II-1031
Bing, Rudolf III-1126
Bing, Samuel I-34
Birnbaum, Nathan. See Burns, George.
Bitzer, Billy I-402
Blackmur, R. P. III-1169
Blackwell, Chris V-2344
Blair, Eric Arthur. See Orwell, George.
Blake, Amanda IV-1668, 1768
Blakey, Art V-2454
Blamauer, Karoline. See Lenya, Lotte.
Blanton, Jimmy III-1617
Blasko, Béla. See Lugosi, Bela.
Blavatsky, Helena Petrovna I-286, 320

Bleyl, Fritz I-134
Bloch, Robert IV-1855
Blocker, Dan IV-1800
Bloomfield, Mike IV-2038
Blore, Eric II-984
Blum, René III-1088
Boccioni, Umberto I-235
Bochco, Stephen V-2470
Bogart, Humphrey III-1223, 1245
Bolger, Ray III-1109
Böll, Heinrich III-1357
Bond, Alan V-2603
Bonham, John V-2228
Bonnier, Louis II-654
Bono, Sonny V-2244
Boone, Mary V-2438
Boone, Richard IV-1768
Booth, George II-610
Borges, Jorge Luis III-1268; IV-1689
Bosley, Tom V-2305
Botterill, Joyce A. See Carne, Judy.
Boudin, Eugène II-718
Boulanger, Nadia I-508; II-561
Boulez, Pierre IV-1656
Boult, Sir Adrian I-90
Bourke-White, Margaret II-1031
Brahm, Otto I-145
Braine, John III-1454
Brand, Max. See Faust, Frederick.
Brando, Marlon III-1164, 1487; V-2265
Brannum, Hugh IV-1678
Braque, Georges I-204, 337
Brecht, Bertolt I-724; III-1410; IV-2005
Breen, Robert II-1016
Breton, André II-604, 750
Breuer, Lee V-2571
Breuer, Marcel IV-2064
Brickman, Marshall V-2381
Brill, A. A. I-19
Britten, Benjamin III-1296
Broccoli, Albert R. "Cubby" IV-1913
Brod, Max I-396
Broderick, Matthew V-2537
Bronson, Charles IV-1984
Brook, Peter IV-1888, 2005
Brooks, Cleanth III-1169
Brooks, Henry Sands I-24
Brooks, James L. V-2218, 2652
Brooks, John E. I-24
Brooks, Richard IV-1650
Broonzy, "Big Bill" I-252
Brown, James IV-2059
Brown, John Mason I-343
Brown, Trisha V-2480
Browne, Byron II-1001
Browning, Tod II-863
Brownlow, Kevin IV-642
Bruce, Edward II-995
Bruce, Nigel III-1131
Buch, Gunther IV-2126
Buchinsky, Charles. See Bronson, Charles.
Büchner, Georg II-680
Buckley, William F., Jr. IV-1683
Bukharin, Nikolai Ivanovich II-908

Bundmann, Emil Anton. *See* Mann, Anthony.
Buñuel, Luis II-750; III-1179; V-2310
Burel, Léonce-Henry II-642
Burgee, John V-2407
Burghoff, Gary V-2271
Burkan, Nathan I-379
Burliuk, David Davidovich I-320
Burliuk, Vladimir Davidovich I-320
Burnett, Charles V-2565
Burnham, James IV-1683
Burns, Allan V-2218
Burns, George II-828
Burns, Ken V-2657
Burns, Ric V-2657
Burroughs, William S. III-1460
Burton, LeVar V-2397
Busoni, Ferruccio I-166, 292; II-724; III-1629
Butler, Michael IV-2121
Butler, Nicholas Murray I-407
Butor, Michel III-1481
Buzzi, Ruth IV-2115

Cachin, Françoise V-2588
Cage, John III-1546; IV-1955, 1979, 2011
Cagney, James II-839
Cahill, Holger II-995
Calderwood, Stanford IV-2168
Campbell, John W., Jr. III-1094; IV-1883
Camus, Albert III-1174, 1573; IV-1742, 1812
Canby, Henry Seidel II-686
Candy, John V-2527
Canham, Erwin D. I-209
Cannell, Stephen Joseph V-2330
Cantor, Eddie II-828
Canudo, Ricciotto II-642
Canutt, Yakima III-1115
Capel, Arthur "Boy" I-474
Capra, Frank II-822, 833, 951; III-1335
Carl XVI Gustaf V-2423
Carne, Judy IV-2115
Carné, Marcel IV-1742
Carnegie, Dale II-1048
Carney, Art IV-1673
Carnovsky, Morris II-874
Carpentier, Alejo IV-2086
Carrà, Carlo I-235
Carroll, Madeleine II-946
Carruth, Hayden III-1443
Carsey, Marcy V-2532
Carson, Johnny III-1623
Caruso, Enrico I-69
Cary, Joyce IV-1763
Casey, Harry Wayne V-2386
Cash, Johnny V-2365
Castelli, Leo V-2191, 2438
Cather, Willa I-452
Celan, Paul IV-2070
Céline, Louis-Ferdinand II-890
Cendrars, Blaise I-435
Cervantes, Miguel de II-890
Cézanne, Paul I-204
Chabrol, Claude IV-1710, 1845
Chagall, Marc II-544
Chambers, Whittaker IV-1683

Chandler, Chas IV-2092
Chanel, Gabrielle "Coco" I-474
Chaplin, Charlie I-224, 230; II-659
Chaplin, Lita Grey II-659
Chapman, Graham IV-2174
Char, René IV-1656, 2070
Charles, Jacques II-665
Chase, Chevy V-2355
Chase, Lucia II-1036
Chashnik, Ilia I-413
Chatfield-Taylor, Hobart C. I-314
Chauchoin, Claudette Lily. *See* Colbert, Claudette.
Chekhov, Anton I-1
Cher V-2244
Chess, Leonard IV-1635
Chevalier, Maurice II-941
Childs, Lucinda V-2480
Chirac, Jacques V-2619
Chotzinoff, Samuel III-1536
Christian, Charlie III-1617
Christie, Agatha I-496; III-1551
Christo V-2548
Ciccone, Madonna Louise Veronica. *See* Madonna.
Clark, Carroll II-984
Clark, Les II-1053
Clark, Sir Kenneth III-1190
Clarke, T. E. B. III-1427
Cleese, John IV-2174
Clemenceau, Georges II-718
Clemons, Clarence V-2325
Clurman, Harold II-874
Cobbold, Baron Cameron Fromanteel IV-2131
Coburn, Alvin Langdon I-63
Cocteau, Jean I-435, 474, 513; II-561, 979
Cohan, George M. I-108
Cohen, Fritz A. II-920
Colbert, Claudette II-822, 951
Colin, Paul II-665
Collins, Tom III-1138
Columbus, Chris V-2527
Conley, William Lee. *See* Broonzy, "Big Bill."
Connery, Sean IV-1913
Connolly, Walter II-951
Connors, Chuck IV-1768
Conrad, Frank I-469
Conrad, Joseph I-51
Conrad, Joseph I-96
Cook, Barbara IV-1752
Cook, Paul V-2299, 2360
Cook, William. *See* Tudor, Antony.
Cooke, Alistair IV-2168
Coolidge, Martha V-2443
Cooney, Joan Ganz V-2185
Cooper, Paula V-2191
Copland, Aaron I-508; III-1234, 1284
Coppola, Francis Ford V-2265, 2428
Corbusier, Le II-869, 1021, 1067; III-1503, 1629; IV-1716, 1919, 2064
Corea, Chick IV-2153
Cornelius, Henry III-1427
Cornell, Julien III-1443
Cornwall, David John Moore. *See* Le Carré, John.
Correll, Charles II-755
Corso, Gregory III-1460

Cortázar, Julio IV-1689, 2086
Cosby, Bill IV-2044; V-2532
Cotes, Peter III-1551
Country Joe and the Fish IV-2180
Courrèges, André IV-1824
Cover, Franklin V-2339
Covici, Pascal III-1138
Cowan, Thomas H. I-469
Coward, Noël II-936
Cowell, Henry I-425
Craig, Samuel II-686
Crane, Hart II-851
Crawford, Cheryl II-874
Creedence Clearwater Revival IV-2180
Cret, Paul Philippe IV-1919
Crichton, Charles III-1427
Croly, Herbert I-385
Cronenweth, Jordan V-2486
Crosby, Bing II-828
Crosby, Stills, Nash, and Young IV-2180
Cullen, Countée I-480
Culp, Robert IV-2044
Cummings, E. E. III-1443
Cunningham, Merce III-1284; IV-2011
Curtis, Ken IV-1668
Curtiz, Michael III-1245
Cushing, Peter III-1378

Da Costa, Morton IV-1752
Dafora, Asalta V-2521
Dalí, Gala V-2310
Dalí, Salvador II-604, 750, 979; III-1179; V-2310
Dalio, Marcel II-1073
Daly, John V-2576
Danielovitch, Issur. See Douglas, Kirk.
Darwin, Charles I-161
Daven, André II-665
Davies, Arthur B. I-361
Davis, Chuck V-2521
Davis, Jim V-2418
Davis, Miles III-1318, 1438, 1617; IV-2153
Davis, Stuart II-1001
Day Lewis, Cecil II-857
Deacon, Richard IV-1908
Dean, Dizzy III-1362
Dean, James IV-1640
De Bosset, Vera II-561
Debrie, André II-642
Debussy, Claude I-332
De Butts, John Dulany V-2407
Dee, Ruby IV-1795
De Forest, Lee I-469
De Havilland, Olivia III-1154
De Kooning, William III-1557
Delaunay, Robert I-337
De Lavallade, Carmen IV-1774
DeMain, John V-2599
De Man, Paul IV-2075
De Mare, Rolf II-665
De Mille, Agnes II-1036; III-1234, 1256
DeMille, William C. II-799
DeMille, Cecil B. II-567, 833
Denham, Sergei III-1088
De Niro, Robert V-2265

Denoff, Sam IV-1908
Dent, Alan III-1378
Derain, André I-140, 156
Derrida, Jacques IV-2075
De Sica, Vittorio III-1228
Desnos, Robert I-513
D'Estaing, Giscard. See Giscard d'Estaing, Valéry.
Destouches, Louis-Ferdinand. See Céline, Louis-Ferdinand.
Diaghilev, Sergei I-113, 187, 241, 247, 269, 332, 373; II-561
Dick, Philip V-2486
Dickerson, Ernest V-2641
Dickinson, Emily IV-1662
Dietrich, Marlene II-845
Diller, Barry V-2652
DiMaggio, Joe III-1362, 1567
Dior, Christian III-1346
Disney, Roy III-1612
Disney, Walt II-1053; III-1195, 1368, 1612
Dix, Otto II-631; III-1083
Dixon, Thomas I-402
Doesburg, Theo van I-429, 458
Donat, Robert II-946
Donen, Stanley III-1432
Donoso, José IV-1689
Doolittle, Hilda. See H. D.
Dorsey, Thomas A. III-1329
Dorsey, Tommy III-1250
Dos Passos, John I-343
Dostoevski, Fyodor II-890
Doubleday, Frank Nelson I-39
Doubleday, Nelson II-686
Douglas, Kirk V-2320
Douglas, Michael V-2320
Douglas, Roy I-90
Doyle, Arthur Conan I-496
Dozier, Lamont IV-1790
Drapeau, Jean IV-2081
Dreiser, Theodore I-39
Drew, Jane III-1503
Dreyfuss, Doris Marks II-1057
Dreyfuss, Henry II-777, 1057
Dubček, Alexander IV-1967
Duchamp, Gaston. See Villon, Jacques.
Duchamp, Marcel I-349, 361, 513; III-1239
Duchamp-Villon, Raymond I-349
Duckworth, George II-637
Dudley, Caroline II-665
Duffy, Patrick V-2418
Dufy, Raoul I-263
Duke, Bill V-2565
Duncan, Isadora I-113, 187
Dunn, Douglas V-2480
Duras, Marguerite III-1481
Dürer, Albrecht V-2464
Durey, Louis I-435
Dushkin, Samuel II-561
Duvall, Robert V-2265
Dye, Dale A. V-2576
Dylan, Bob IV-2038, 2158
Dymling, Carl-Anders IV-1742
Dzerzhinsky, Feliks V-2277
Dzhugashvili, Joseph Vissarionovich. See Stalin, Joseph.

Eames, Charles II-610; III-1290; IV-1716
Eastwood, Clint IV-1984
Eckersley, Peter II-712
Eco, Umberto III-1268
Eddy, Mary Baker I-209
Edison, Thomas Alva I-74
Edwards, Bernard V-2386
Ehrenwiesen, Baroness Hildegard
    Rebay von. See Rebay, Hilla.
Einstein, Albert V-2375
Eisenman, Peter D. V-2614
Eisenstaedt, Alfred II-1031
Eisenstein, Sergei II-615, 701
Eisner, Michael V-2646
Ekerot, Bengt IV-1742
Eldridge, Roy III-1617
Elgar, Sir Edward I-214
Eliot, T. S. I-445; II-539, 851, 857; III-1169, 1443
Ellington, Duke I-480; II-739
Ellison, Ralph III-1541
Elwell, Herbert I-508
Engel, Erich III-1410
Enos, William Berkeley. See Berkeley, Busby.
Entenza, John III-1290
Epstein, Jean II-642
Epstein, Julius III-1245
Epstein, Philip III-1245
Erlanger, Abraham I-108
Ermolaeva, Vera I-413
Ernst, Max I-349; II-604; III-1239
Erskine, John III-1351
Erté I-263
Escher, Maurits Cornelius III-1268
Esher, Lord Oliver Sylvain Baliol IV-1924
Esquirol, Jean-Étienne-Dominique IV-1877
Esslin, Martin IV-1812, 1871
Eugene, Frank I-63
Evans, George III-1250
Evans, Mike V-2339

Fackenthal, Frank Diehl I-407
Fagan, Eleanora. See Holiday, Billie.
Fagan, Garth V-2521
Fairbanks, Douglas, Sr. I-224; II-799
Falck, August I-199
Fancher, Hampton V-2486
Farnsworth, Philo T. III-1143
Farrow, Mia IV-2017
Faulkner William II-805
Faure, Élie II-642
Faust, Frederick I-304
Fay, Frank J. I-119
Fay, William George I-119, 176
Feigen, Richard L. V-2191
Feininger, Lyonel I-463; II-583
Fellini, Federico III-1228, 1596
Ferber, Edna II-745
Ferlinghetti, Lawrence III-1460
Feuchtwanger, Walter. See Wanger, Walter.
Fierstein, Harvey V-2502
Finestra, Carmen V-2532
Fini, Leonor II-979
Fitzgerald, F. Scott II-626, 696
Fitzgerald, Robert IV-1645

Fitzgerald, Zelda II-626
Flanagan, Hallie II-989
Flatt, Lester III-1121
Flaubert, Gustave I-396
Fleming, Ian IV-1913
Fleming, Victor III-1109, 1154
Flower, Fordham IV-1888
Fokine, Michel I-113, 187, 241, 247, 269, 332; III-1088
Follett, Wilson IV-1898
Folsom, Frank III-1362
Fonda, Henry IV-1984
Fonda, Peter IV-2158
Fontanne, Lynn II-936
Fonteyn, Dame Margot IV-1962
Foote, Shelby V-2657
Force, Juliana Rieser II-885, 1001
Ford, Ford Madox I-445
Ford, Glenn IV-1650
Ford, Harrison V-2391
Ford, Henry, II III-1579
Ford, John III-1115, 1313
Foreman, Carl III-1340
Forman, Miloš IV-1967; V-2320
Foucault, Michel IV-1877
Fox, William II-761
Fraenkel, Michael II-963
Franck, Jean-Michel II-979
Franco, Francisco II-1062; V-2203
Franken, Al V-2355
Franklin, R. W. IV-1662
Frawley, William III-1525
Freed, Alan IV-1635
Freed, Arthur III-1109, 1432
Freeman, Harry Lawrence V-2350
Freeman, Morgan V-2565
Frege, Gottlob I-518
Fresnay, Pierre II-1073
Freud, Sigmund I-19, 309
Freund, Karl II-707; III-1525
Friendly, Edward IV-2115
Frost, Mark V-2470
Fry, Maxwell III-1503
Fuentes, Carlos III-1268; IV-1689, 2086
Fugard, Athol V-2496
Fuller, Anne Hewlett III-1579
Fuller, R. Buckminster III-1579; IV-2081; V-2208
Furse, Roger K. III-1378
Furth, George V-2213
Furtwängler, Wilhelm II-816

Gable, Clark II-951; III-1154
Gaines, LaDonna. See Summer, Donna.
Gaisberg, Frederick William I-69
Gance, Abel II-642
Garbo, Greta II-822
García Lorca, Federico III-1179
García Márquez, Gabriel IV-1689, 2086
Gardner, Erle Stanley I-496
Garland, Judy III-1109
Garmes, Lee II-845
Garner, James IV-1768
Garnier, Tony II-1021
Garvey, Marcus IV-2022
Gates, Curtis. See Curtis, Ken.

Gathing, Ezekial III-1465
Gaudí, Antonio I-257
Gaudier-Brzeska, Henri I-445
Gaultier, Jean-Paul V-2449
Gavin, John IV-1855
Gaye, Marvin IV-1790
Geddes, Norman Bel II-777, 1057
Geer, Will II-810
Gehry, Frank V-2614, 2646
Gelbart, Larry V-2271
Geldof, Bob V-2543
Genet, Jean IV-1871
Gershvin, Jacob. See Gershwin, George.
Gershwin, George II-598, 1016
Gershwin, Ira II-1016
Gestetner, Sigmund II-777
Getty, Estelle V-2502
Giacosa, Giuseppe I-29
Gibb, Barry V-2386
Gibb, Maurice V-2386
Gibb, Robin V-2386
Gibbs, Marla V-2339
Gibson, Henry IV-2115
Gide, André II-561, 620, 890
Gilbert, Ruth III-1394
Gillespie, John Birks "Dizzy" III-1318, 1617
Gilliam, Terry IV-2174
Gilman, Howard V-2663
Ginsberg, Allen III-1460
Gionfriddo, Al III-1362
Giroux, Robert IV-1645
Giscard d'Estaing, Valéry V-2588
Gish, Lillian I-402
Glass, Philip IV-1979; V-2375, 2571
Gleason, Jackie III-1470; IV-1673
Gleizes, Albert I-337
Glines, John V-2502
Glover, Danny V-2496
Godard, Jean-Luc IV-1710; IV-1845
Godfrey, Arthur III-1383
Goebbels, Joseph II-767; III-1083, 1217
Goemans, Camille V-2310
Goethe, Johann Wolfgang von I-396
Gogh, Vincent van V-2603
Goldberg, Whoopi V-2565
Goldenson, Leonard Harry III-1211, 1368, 1383, 1612
Golding, William III-1585
Goldmann, Max. See Reinhardt, Max.
Goldmark, Peter III-1211
Goldsmith, Harvey V-2543
Goldwyn, Samuel II-567
Golenor, Jack. See Gavin, John.
Golovin, Alexander I-269
Gonne, Maud. See MacBride, Maud Gonne.
González, José Victoriano. See Gris, Juan.
Goodman, Alice V-2599
Goodman, Benny II-930, 968
Goodyear, Conger II-782
Goossens, Eugene I-425
Gordillo, Luis V-2203
Gordimer, Nadine V-2668
Gordon, David V-2480
Gordon, General Charles George ("Chinese") I-214
Gordon, Mary III-1131

Gordon, Max II-936
Gordy, Berry, Jr. IV-1790; V-2294, 2512
Gorky, Arshile II-1001
Gorky, Maxim II-908
Gosden, Freeman Fisher II-755
Gossage, Howard Luck IV-1973
Gothardt, Matthias. See Grünewald, Matthias.
Gould, Harold V-2239
Gove, Philip B. IV-1898
Gowland, Gibson II-593
Graham, Bill V-2543
Graham, Martha I-390; III-1284
Grahn, Judy V-2370
Grant, Cary II-951
Grant, Jane II-648
Granville-Barker, Harley I-85
Grass, Günter III-1357; IV-1780
Grateful Dead, the IV-2180
Graves, Michael V-2646
Gray, Linda V-2418
Green, Paul II-874
Greenberg, Clement III-1557
Greene, Alexander Plunkett IV-1824
Greene, Lorne IV-1800
Greenstreet, Sydney III-1223
Gregory, Lady Augusta I-119, 176, 440
Gregory, Robert I-440
Grey, Zane I-304
Griffith, D. W. I-57, 224, 402
Gris, Juan I-337
Groening, Matt V-2652
Grofé, Ferde II-598
Gropius, Walter I-79, 181, 463; II-583, 1021, 1067; III-1503; IV-1919, 2064
Grossman, Arthur. See Freed, Arthur.
Grossman, Daniel Williams III-1602
Grossman, Jan IV-1967
Grosvenor, Hugh "Bend'or" I-474
Grosz, George II-631; III-1083
Grumbach, Antoine V-2646
Grünewald, Matthias II-816
Guare, John V-2239
Güell, Eusebio I-257
Guggenheim, Peggy III-1239
Guggenheim, Solomon R. IV-1806
Guilbert, Ann Morgan IV-1908
Guimarães Rosa, João IV-1689
Guinness, Alec III-1427; V-2391
Guinzburg, Harold K. II-686
Gumm, Frances. See Garland, Judy.
Gurdin, Natasha. See Wood, Natalie.
Gustafsson, Greta Louisa. See Garbo, Greta.
Guthrie, Marjorie II-810
Guthrie, Woody II-810

Hadden, Briton II-577
Hagman, Larry V-2418
Haigh, Kenneth IV-1721
Haines, Randa V-2443
Hakim, Tawfiq al- IV-1893
Hale, Georgia II-659
Haley, Alex V-2022; V-2397
Haley, Bill IV-1635
Haley, Jack III-1109

Hall, Anthony Michael V-2527
Hall, Arthur V-2521
Hall, Diane. *See* Keaton, Diane.
Hall, Peter IV-1888
Halpert, Edith II-1001
Hamer, Robert III-1427
Hamill, Mark V-2391
Hamilton, John. *See* Hayden, Sterling.
Hammerstein, Oscar, II II-745; III-1256
Hammett, Dashiell II-793; III-1223
Hammond, John II-930, 968; III-1329; V-2325
Hampshire, Susan IV-2168
Hampton, Lionel II-968
Handke, Peter IV-2126
Handy, W. C. I-252
Hanks, Nancy IV-2048
Hanna, William IV-1840
Hansberry, Lorraine IV-1795, 2000
Hansen, Emil. *See* Nolde, Emil.
Harbau, Thea von II-707
Harkness, Rebekah IV-1694
Harper, Ken V-2334
Harper, Valerie V-2218
Harris, Jed III-1099
Harris, Samuel I-108
Harrison, George IV-1944, 2098
Hartley, Vivian Mary. *See* Leigh, Vivien.
Harvey, Bernard "Touter" V-2344
Hašek, Jaroslav I-523
Hathaway, Henry III-1567
Haussmann, Jacques. *See* Houseman, John.
Havel, Václav IV-1967
Hawkins, Erick III-1284
Hawks, Howard II-839, 951; III-1313, 1567
Hawn, Goldie IV-2115
Hay, George D. II-675
Hayden, Sterling IV-1989
Haynes, Daniel L. II-772
H. D. I-326, 686
Hearst, William Randolph III-1200
Heckel, Erich I-134
Heckerling, Amy V-2443
Heckroth, Hein II-920
Heim, Jacques III-1324
Heinemann, Mitch I-491
Heinlein, Robert A. III-1094; IV-1883
Heizer, Michael IV-1949
Heller, Joseph IV-1866
Hellman, Lillian II-793
Helmond, Katherine V-2239
Helms, Jesse V-2636
Hemingway, Ernest II-626, 696
Hemsley, Sherman V-2339
Henderson, Fletcher I-480; II-670, 968
Hendrix, Jimi IV-2092, 2104, 2180
Henning, Paul IV-1835
Hennings, Emmy I-419
Henreid, Paul III-1245
Henri, Robert II-885
Hepburn, Katharine II-951
Herbert, Victor I-379
Herlie, Eileen III-1378
Herr, Michael V-2428
Herrmann, Bernard III-1200; IV-1855

Hersholt, Jean II-593
Hesse, Herman IV-1829
Hewitt, Don IV-2136
Heyward, DuBose II-1016
Hill, Bertha "Chippie" I-252
Hindemith, Paul II-724, 816
Hines, Earl II-670
Hinkle, Beatrice Moses I-309
Hitchcock, Alfred II-946; IV-1855
Hitler, Adolf III-1083, 1217
Hodges, Johnny II-739
Hoffmann, Josef I-79, 124
Holder, Geoffrey V-2334
Holiday, Billie II-930
Holladay, Wilhelmina (Billy) Cole V-2608
Holland, Brian IV-1790
Holland, Eddie IV-1790
Holst, Gustav I-90
Honegger, Arthur I-435
Hood, Raymond III-1149
Hope, Bob II-828
Hopkins, Harry L. II-995
Hopper, Dennis IV-2158
Horne, Lena III-1159
Horniman, Annie I-119
Horowitz, Jacob. *See* Harris, Jed.
Horst, Louis I-390; III-1284
Horton, Edward Everett II-941, 984
Horton, Lester IV-1774
Houseman, John II-989; III-1103, 1200
Houston, Gilbert "Cisco" II-810
Howard, Leslie III-1154
Howard, Ron V-2305
Howard, Sidney I-343
Howe, George IV-1919
Howe, Irving IV-2163
Howells, William Dean I-96
Hueffer, Ford Madox. *See* Ford, Ford Madox.
Huelsenbeck, Richard I-419
Hughes, Helena IV-1721
Hughes, Howard III-1307
Hughes, John V-2527
Hughes, Langston I-480; IV-2000
Hughes, Ted IV-1850
Hulme, Thomas Ernest I-161, 326, 445
Humphrey, Doris I-390
Hunte, Otto II-707
Hurok, Solomon I-187; III-1126
Husák, Gustáv IV-1967
Husayn, Taha V-2625
Huston, John III-1223
Hutchins, Robert Maynard III-1351
Huxley, Aldous II-896; III-1514

Idle, Eric IV-2174
Illica, Luigi I-29
Inge, William III-1164
Ionesco, Eugène III-1573; IV-1812, 1871, 1903
Isaacs, Godfrey II-712
Isherwood, Christopher II-857
Iskowitz, Edward Israel. *See* Cantor, Eddie.
Isozaki, Arata V-2646
Itten, Johannes I-463

PRINCIPAL PERSONAGES

Ivanek, Željko V-2496
Ives, Charles I-425

Jackson, Jackie V-2512
Jackson, Jermaine V-2512
Jackson, Mahalia III-1329
Jackson, Marlon V-2512
Jackson, Michael IV-1790; V-2475, 2512
Jackson, Tito V-2512
Jacob, Max I-337
Jacobs, Amos. *See* Thomas, Danny III-1470
Jagger, Mick IV-2027
James, Henry I-96; III-1250
James, William I-161, 171
Jamison, Judith IV-1774
Janco, Marcel I-419
Janowitz, Hans I-486
Jantzen, Carl I-491
Jarry, Alfred III-1410; IV-1812
Javacheff, Christo. *See* Christo.
Jawlensky, Alexey von II-583
Jeanneret, Charles-Édouard. *See* Corbusier, Le.
Jeanneret, Pierre II-869; III-1503
Jefferson, "Blind Lemon" I-252
Jefferson Airplane, the IV-2180
Jennings, Waylon V-2365
Jessel, George II-734
Joffe, Charles V-2381
Joffrey, Robert IV-1694; V-2288
Johns, Jasper, Jr. III-1590
Johnson, Arte IV-2115
Johnson, Caryn. *See* Goldberg, Whoopi.
Johnson, Colonel Herbert I-209
Johnson, Lyndon B. IV-2048
Johnson, Philip III-1590; V-2402, 2407, 2614
Johnson, Thomas Herbert IV-1662
Jolson, Al II-734
Jones, Brian IV-2027
Jones, Grace V-2386
Jones, James III-1373
Jones, John Paul V-2228
Jones, LeRoi. *See* Baraka, Amiri.
Jones, Quincy V-2512
Jones, Steve V-2299, 2360
Jones, Terry IV-2174
Jong, Bettie de III-1602
Jooss, Kurt II-920
Joplin, Janis IV-2104, 2180
Joplin, Lottie V-2350
Joplin, Scott I-13; V-2350
Jordan, Paul I-219
Joyce, James I-445; II-555, 851; III-1573
Judd, Donald IV-1949
Judkins, Steveland. *See* Wonder, Stevie.
Jung, Carl I-19, 309; IV-1829

Kafka, Franz I-396
Kahane, Jack II-963
Kahl, Milt II-1053
Kahlo, Frida II-957
Kahn, Louis I. IV-1919
Kahnweiler, Daniel-Henry I-204
Kajanus, Robert I-292
Kallman, Chester III-1514

Kalmus, Herbert III-1307
Kandinsky, Wassily I-275, 320, 463; II-544, 583, 718; III-1083
Kanoldt, Alexander II-631
Karajan, Herbert von I-292
Karloff, Boris II-863
Karsavina, Tamara I-241, 247, 269
Käsebier, Gertrude I-63
Kaufman, Denis. *See* Vertov, Dziga.
Kaufmann, Edgar, Jr. II-902
Kawabata, Yasunari IV-2147
Kaye, Nora II-1036
Kazan, Elia II-874; III-1164, 1340, 1487
Kazanjoglou, Elia. *See* Kazan, Elia.
Keaton, Buster II-691
Keaton, Diane V-2381
Keeler, Ruby II-925
Keeshan, Bob IV-1678
Kelly, Gene III-1432
Kendall, Willmoore IV-1683
Kennedy, Adrienne V-2370
Kennedy, Kathleen V-2491
Kennedy, Robert F. IV-1929
Kern, Jerome II-745
Kerouac, Jack III-1460
Kershner, Irvin V-2391
Kertész, Mihaly. *See* Curtiz, Michael.
Kesey, Ken V-2320
Khachaturian, Aram Ilich III-1388
Khamenei, Hojatoleslam Ali Hoseini V-2630
Khan, Abdullah Jaffa Anver Bey. *See* Joffrey, Robert.
Khan, Mohammad Ayub IV-1919
Khlebnikov, Velemir I-413
Khomeini, Ruhollah V-2630
Khrennikov, Tikhon III-1388
Khrushchev, Nikita S. IV-1747
Kiefer, Anselm V-2464
Kienzle, Raymond Nicholas. *See* Ray, Nicholas.
Kilburn, Patrick E. IV-1898
Kimball, Ward II-1053
King, Martin Luther, Jr. III-1329; V-2294
Kinney, Sharon III-1602
Kinski, Klaus IV-1984
Kintner, Robert E. III-1368
Kirchner, Ernst Ludwig I-134; V-2464
Kirkland, Gelsey V-2459
Kirstein, Lincoln II-974; III-1301
Kisselgoff, Anna V-2480
Klee, Paul I-463; II-583
Klimt, Gustav I-79, 124
Kliun, Ivan I-413
Knight, John S. V-2507
Knipper, Olga I-1
Koch, Howard III-1103, 1245
Kodály, Zoltán I-102
Koenig, Pierre III-1290
Konigsberg, Allen Stewart. *See* Allen, Woody.
Konitz, Lee III-1438
Kooper, Al IV-2038
Koreff, Nora. *See* Kaye, Nora.
Korzeniowski, Jósef Teodor Konrad Nałez. *See* Conrad, Joseph.
Kostrowitzky, Guillaume Albert Wladimir Alexandre Apollinaire de. *See* Apollinaire, Guillaume.

Kott, Gary V-2532
Koussevitzky, Serge I-508; II-561
Kozoll, Michael V-2470
Krampe, Hugh J. See O'Brian, Hugh.
Krauss, Werner I-486
Krishnan, Tatparanandam Ananda V-2543
Kristofferson, Kris V-2365
Krupa, Gene II-968
Krylenko, Nikolay V-2277
Kubelsky, Benjamin. See Benny, Jack.
Kubin, Alfred I-275
Kubrick, Stanley IV-1989
Kudriashev, Ivan I-413
Kuhn, Walt I-361
Kuleshov, Lev Vladimirovich II-615, 701
Kundera, Milan IV-1967
Küpper, Christian Emil Marie. See Doesburg, Theo van.
Kurosawa, Akira III-1476
Kusevitsky, Sergey. See Koussevitzky, Serge.

Lack, John V-2475
Laemmle, Carl I-224; II-833
La Farge, John I-34
Lagerfeld, Karl I-474
Lagerkvist, Pär IV-1742
Lahr, Bert III-1109
Lahrheim, Irving. See Lahr, Bert.
Laing, Hugh II-1036
Laloux, Victor V-2588
Lamb, William F. II-880
L'Amour, Louis I-304
Landau, Jon V-2325
Landon, Michael IV-1800
Lanfield, Sidney III-1131
Lang, Fritz II-707
Langdon, Harry I-230
Langhanke, Lucille Vasconcellos. See Astor, Mary.
Langlois, Henri IV-1710
LaPiere, Cherilyn. See Cher.
Lardner, Ring, Jr. III-1340
L'Arronge, Adolphe I-145
Larsen, Ray E. II-577
Larson, Eric II-1053
Lasche, Oskar I-219
Lasky, Jesse L. II-567
Laughlin, James III-1443
Lauren, Jerry IV-2141
Lauren, Ralph IV-2141
Laurents, Arthur IV-1731
Lawrence, D. H. I-502; II-896
Lawrence, Vera Brodsky V-2350
Leach, Archibald. See Grant, Cary.
Leach, Edmund IV-1995
Leadbelly II-810
Lear, Norman V-2197, 2234, 2339
LeBoulaire, Jean III-1206
Le Carré, John IV-1934
Leck, Bart van der I-429
Le Corbusier. See Corbusier, Le.
Ledbetter, Huddie. See Leadbelly.
Lee, Spike V-2565, 2641
Léger, Fernand I-337
Lehman, Ernest IV-2033
Leigh, Janet IV-1855

Leigh, Vivien III-1154, 1487
Lelong, Lucien III-1346
Lenin, Vladimir Ilich II-544, 615, 701
Lennon, John IV-1944, 2098
Leno, Jay III-1623
Lenya, Lotte II-724
Leonard, Sheldon IV-1908, 2044
Leone, Sergio IV-1984
Le Roy, Édouard I-161
Leroy, Mervyn III-1109
Leskov, Nikolai II-1042
Lesser, Gerald S. V-2185
Lestrange, Gisèle IV-2070
Lévi-Strauss, Claude IV-1995
Lewis, Cecil Day. See Day Lewis, Cecil.
Lewis, Clive Staples III-1607
Lewis, John III-1438
Lewis, Ralph I-402
Lewis, Wyndham I-445
Lindon, Jérôme III-1498
Lippmann, Walter I-385
Lispector, Clarice IV-1689
Lissitzky, El I-413
Little, Malcolm. See Malcolm X.
Littleton, Oliver. See Lord Chandos.
Littlewood, Joan IV-1757
Livingston, Neville "Bunny" V-2344
Llosa, Mario Vargas. See Vargas Llosa, Mario.
Lods, Marcel II-1021
Loewy, Raymond Fernand II-777, 1057; V-2208
Lomax, Alan II-810
Lombard, Carole II-951
Long, Walter I-402
Longwell, Daniel II-1031
Lönnrot, Elias I-292
Lorca, Federico García. See García Lorca, Federico.
Lord Chandos IV-1924
Lorre, Peter II-946; III-1223
Lowell, Amy I-326
Lowell, Robert IV-1645
Löwenstein, Laszlo. See Lorre, Peter.
Lowry, W. McNeil IV-1736
Lubitsch, Ernst II-941
Lucas, George V-2391
Luce, Clare Boothe II-1031
Luce, Henry R. II-577, 1031
Luening, Otto IV-1785
Lugosi, Bela II-863
Lumière, Auguste I-57
Lumière, Louis I-57
Lunacharsky, Anatoly I-320; II-544
Lunt, Alfred II-936
Lydon, John. See Rotten, Johnny.

McAvoy, May II-734
MacBride, Maud Gonne I-440
McCarthy, Joseph III-1164
McCartney, Paul IV-1944, 2098
McCorkindale, Douglas V-2507
McCullough, David V-2657
McDaniel, Hattie III-1154, 1159
McDaniels, Darryl V-2582
MacDermot, Galt IV-2121
Macdonald, Dwight IV-1898

PRINCIPAL PERSONAGES

MacDonald, Jeanette II-941
McDowell, Malcolm IV-1989
McIntosh, Winston Hubert. *See* Tosh, Peter.
Maciunas, George IV-1955
McKay, Claude I-480
Macke, August I-275
McKee, Elizabeth IV-1645
Mackendrick, Alexander III-1427
McKinney, Nina Mae II-772
McLaren, Malcolm V-2299, 2360
McLaughlin, John IV-2153
MacLeish, Archibald III-1443
McLuhan, Marshall IV-1973
McMahon, Ed III-1623
McMath, Virginia Katherine. *See* Rogers, Ginger.
McNair, Archie IV-1824
McNamee, Graham I-469
MacNeice, Louis II-857
McNeill, Claudia IV-1795
Macon, Uncle Dave II-675
Macpherson, Jeanie II-567
McWhinnie, Donald IV-1861
Madonna V-2449, 2475
Magnani, Anna III-1228
Magritte, René II-604
Mahfouz, Naquib V-2625
Mahler, Alma Maria I-7, 298
Mahler, Gustav I-7, 193, 298, 367
Maibaum, Richard IV-1913
Mailer, Norman III-1373
Makarova, Natalia V-2559
Malcom X IV-1929, 2022
Maleczech, Ruth V-2571
Malevich, Kazimir Severinovich I-320, 413; II-544
Malone, Dorothy IV-2017
Maloney, Dorothy. *See* Malone, Dorothy.
Mamet, David V-2413
Mandelstam, Osip IV-2070
Manguin, Henri Charles I-140
Mankiewicz, Herman J. III-1200
Mann, Anthony III-1313
Mann, Thomas I-396; II-588
Manson, Charles IV-1883
Mapplethorpe, Robert V-2636
Marc, Franz I-275, 320
Marco, Fatso III-1394
Mare, André II-654
Marinetti, Filippo Tommaso I-235
Markus, John V-2532
Marley, Bob V-2344
Marley, Rita V-2344
Marquand, Richard V-2391
Marquet, Albert I-140
Márquez, Gabriel García. *See* García Márquez, Gabriel.
Marsalis, Ellis V-2454
Marsalis, Branford V-2454
Marsalis, Wynton V-2454
Marsh, Mae I-402
Marshall, Penny V-2443
Marshall, Garry V-2305
Martin, George IV-2098
Martin, Dick IV-2115
Marx, Zeppo II-822
Marx, Harpo II-822

Marx, Groucho II-822
Marx, Chico II-822
Masina, Guilietta III-1596
Maskelyne, John Nevil I-57
Massine, Léonide III-1088
Mather, Frank Jewett, Jr. I-502
Mathers, Jerry III-1470
Mathison, Melissa V-2491
Matisse, Henri I-140, 156, 204, 320
Matlock, Glen V-2299, 2360
Mauriac, François IV-1700
Maxwell, George I-379
Mayakovsky, Vladimir II-787
Mayer, Louis B. II-799, 822, 833
Mayer, Carl I-486
Mazzatta, Rose-Marie. *See* Rose-Marie.
Mead, Syd V-2486
Meadows, Audrey IV-1673
Meara, Anne V-2239
Mekas, Jonas IV-2053
Melba, Nellie I-69
Méliès, Gaston I-57
Méliès, Georges I-57, 74
Melville, Herman I-502
Menjou, Adolphe II-1011
Menotti, Gian Carlo III-1536
Menzies, William Cameron III-1154
Meservey, Robert Preston. *See* Preston, Robert.
Messiaen, Olivier III-1206
Metalious, Grace IV-2017
Metcalf, Eleanor Melville I-502
Metzinger, Jean I-337
Meyerhold, Vsevolod I-1; II-787
Miaskovski, Nikolai III-1388
Miassin, Leonid. *See* Massine, Léonide.
Michaels, Lorne V-2355
Mielziner, Jo III-1164
Mies van der Rohe, Ludwig I-181, 463; IV-1716
Mifune, Toshiro III-1476
Miles, Vera IV-1855
Miley, James "Bubber" II-739
Milhaud, Darius I-435
Milius, John V-2428
Miller, Arthur III-1164
Miller, Court V-2502
Miller, Henry II-963
Miller, Paul V-2507
Mills, Irving II-739
Minnelli, Vincente III-1432
Minow, Newton III-1465; IV-1835
Miró, Joan II-604
Mitchell, Arthur I-161; IV-2110; V-2521
Mitchell, Margaret III-1154
Mitchell, Michael V-2543
Mitchell, Mitch IV-2092
Mitchell, Thomas III-1115
Mitterrand, François V-2619
Moe, Henry Allen III-1279
Moholy-Nagy, Làszlò I-463
Mokae, Zakes V-2496
Monash, Paul IV-2017
Mondrian, Piet I-429, 458
Monet, Claude II-718
Monroe, Bill III-1121

Monroe, Charlie III-1121
Monroe, Harriet I-314
Monroe, Marilyn III-1567
Monterey, Carlotta IV-1726
Monteux, Pierre I-373
Moog, Robert IV-1785
Moore, Charles V-2521
Moore, Henry III-1190
Moore, Mary Tyler IV-1908; V-2197, 2218
Moorman, Charlotte IV-1955
Mordkin, Mikhail I-187
More, Hermon II-1001
More, Kenneth IV-2168
Morgan, Harry III-1531
Morgan, J. P. I-24
Morgan, Terence III-1378
Moroder, Giorgio V-2386
Morricone, Ennio IV-1984
Morris, Mark V-2559, 2663
Morris, Robert IV-1949
Morris, Steveland. See Wonder, Stevie.
Morrisett, Lloyd V-2185
Morrison, Jeanette Helen. See Leigh, Janet.
Morrison, Marion Michael. See Wayne, John.
Mortenson, Norma Jean. See Monroe, Marilyn.
Mortimer, John V-2249
Morton, Ferdinand "Jelly Roll" I-13
Moser, Koloman I-79
Moss, Paula V-2370
Moulton, Charles V-2480
Muhammad, Elijah IV-1929, 2022
Mullenger, Donna Belle. See Reed, Donna.
Müller, Otto I-134
Mulligan, Gerry III-1438, 1617
Muni, Paul II-839
Münter, Gabriele I-275
Muradeli, Vano III-1388
Murdoch, Rupert V-2652, 2554
Murray, Jeanne. See Stapleton, Jean.
Musa, Salamah V-2625
Muthesius, Hermann I-181

Nagel, Conrad II-799
Naksznski, Nikolaus. See Kinski, Klaus.
Nash, Arthur J. I-34
Nasser, Gamal Abdel V-2625
Nathan, Syd IV-2059
Naumann, Friedrich I-181
Negulesco, John III-1567
Nehru, Jawaharlal III-1503
Neill, Beverly Louise. See Blake, Amanda.
Nelson, Ozzie III-1470
Nelson, Willie V-2365
Nemiroff, Robert IV-1795
Nemirovich-Danchenko, Vladimir I-1
Nervi, Pier Luigi IV-2064
Nesmith, Michael V-2475
Neuharth, Allen H. V-2507
Neuharth, Christina V-2507
Neumann, J. B. II-1001
Neutra, Richard III-1290
Newman, Rosalind V-2480
Newmarch, Rosa I-292
Niblo, Fred II-799

Nicholson, Jack IV-2158; V-2320
Nietzsche, Friedrich Wilhelm I-85; II-890; III-1573; IV-1829, 2075; V-2464
Nijinsky, Vaslav I-241, 247, 332, 373
Nimoy, Leonard V-2260
Nin, Anaïs II-963
Nobel, Alfred I-45; V-2423, 2594, 2668
Nobile, Federico. See Niblo, Fred.
Noble, Edward J. III-1211
Nochlin, Linda V-2608
Noguchi, Isamu III-1284
Nolde, Emil I-134; III-1083, 1217
Normand, Mabel I-230
Norris, Frank I-39
Novotný, Antoný IV-1967
Nureyev, Rudolf IV-1962; V-2559

O'Brian, Hugh IV-1768
O'Connor, Carroll V-2234
O'Connor, Flannery IV-1645
Odets, Clifford II-874, 1006
O'Donnell, May III-1284
O'Feeney, Sean Aloysius. See Ford, John.
O'Horgan, Tom IV-2121; V-2254
Oland, Warner II-734
Oldham, Andrew Loog IV-2027
Oliver, King II-670
Olivier, Sir Laurence III-1378; IV-1924
Olson, Harry F. IV-1785
O'Neal, Ryan IV-2017
O'Neill, Eugene I-343; IV-1726
Ong, Walter J. IV-1973
Oppenheimer, J. Robert IV-1939
Oppenheimer, Jess III-1525
Orff, Carl II-816
Orowitz, Eugene Maurice. See Landon, Michael.
Orozco, José Clemente II-957
Orr-Cahall, Christina V-2636
Orwell, George III-1421
Osborne, John III-1454; IV-1721
Österling, Anders IV-2147
Osumare, Halifu V-2370
Oud, Jacobus Johannes Pieter I-429

Paar, Jack III-1623
Pach, Walter I-361
Pacino, Al V-2265
Page, Jimmy V-2228
Paik, Nam June IV-1955
Paley, William S. III-1211, 1383
Palin, Michael IV-2174
Pan, Hermes II-984
Panagiotopolous, Hermes. See Pan, Hermes.
Papanek, Victor J. V-2208
Papirofsky, Yosl. See Papp, Joseph.
Papp, Joseph IV-1967; V-2571
Paris, Jerry IV-1908
Parker, Charles Christopher "Bird" III-1318, 1617
Parker, Colonel Tom IV-1705
Parker, Eleanor IV-2033
Parker, Fess III-1612
Partch, Harry III-1279
Pasquier, Étienne III-1206
Pasternak, Boris IV-1747

Pathé, Charles I-57
Patout, Pierre II-654
Paull, Lawrence G. V-2486
Pavlova, Anna I-187, 247
Paz, Octavio III-1268; IV-1995
Pears, Peter III-1296
Pease, Joseph Albert, Lord Gainford II-712
Peche, Dagobert I-79
Pechstein, Max I-134
Peebles, Mario Van V-2565
Peer, Ralph S. II-729
Pei, I. M. V-2619
Pei, Mario A. IV-1898
Penck, A. R. V-2464
Peoples, David V-2486
Perelman, S. J. II-648
Pérez-Minguez, Rafael V-2203
Perkins, Anthony IV-1855
Perkins, Maxwell II-696
Persky, Bill IV-1908
Peshkov, Aleksey Maksimovich. See Gorky, Maxim.
Peters, Curtis Arnoux, Jr. See Arno, Peter.
Peters, Jane Alice. See Lombard, Carole.
Peters, William Wesley II-902
Peterson, Oscar III-1617
Peymann, Klaus IV-2126
Pfitzner, Hans I-166
Phillips, John IV-2104
Phillips, Sam IV-1705
Piano, Renzo V-2402
Picabia, Francis I-349, 513
Picasso, Pablo I-156, 204, 337; II-1062; IV-1742
Pickens, Slim IV-1989
Pickford, Mary I-224
Piguet, Robert III-1346
Pinel, Philippe IV-1877
Pinter, Harold III-1454; IV-1861, 1871
Piñero, Emilio Pérez V-2310
Pirandello, Luigi I-534
Piscator, Erwin III-1410
Piston, Walter I-508
Pitoëff, Georges I-534
Pittman, Robert V-2475
Pitts, ZaSu II-593
Plant, Robert V-2228
Plath, Sylvia IV-1850
Pleasant, Richard II-1036
Pleasence, Donald IV-1861
Plumet, Charles II-654
Plummer, Christopher IV-2033
Podhoretz, Norman IV-1929, 2163
Poiret, Paul I-263
Poirier, Richard V-2283
Poitier, Sidney IV-1650, 1795
Polglase, Van Nest II-984
Pollock, Jackson III-1239, 1557
Pomare, Eleo V-2521
Pompidou, Georges V-2402
Poole, Elijah. See Muhammad, Elijah.
Popenoe, Charles B. I-469
Porter, Cole III-1404
Porter, Edwin S. I-57, 74
Porter, Eric IV-2168
Porter, Nyree Dawn IV-2168

Poulenc, Francis I-435
Pound, Ezra I-314, 326, 445; II-539, 555; III-1443
Powell, Anthony III-1509
Powell, Dick II-925
Pratella, Francesco Balilla I-235
Pratt, William Henry. See Karloff, Boris.
Predock, Antoine V-2646
Prendergast, Maurice Brazil I-361
Preobrajenska, Olga I-247
Presley, Elvis IV-1705
Preston, Robert IV-1752
Price, Lonny V-2496
Prince, Hal V-2213, 2433
Principal, Victoria V-2418
Prokofiev, Sergei II-914; III-1388
Proust, Marcel I-355
Prouvé, Jean II-1021
Puccini, Giacomo I-29
Pudovkin, Vsevolod Illarionovich II-701
Pulitzer, Joseph I-407
Puni, Ivan I-413
Puzo, Mario V-2265
Pynchon, Thomas V-2283

Quant, Mary IV-1824
Quinn, Anthony III-1596
Quintero, José IV-1726

Rabinowitz, Jerome. See Robbins, Jerome.
Radek, Karl II-914
Radice, Anne-Imelda V-2608
Radner, Gilda V-2355
Rado, James IV-2121
Ragni, Gerome IV-2121
Rainey, Ma I-252; II-572
Rains, Claude III-1245
Ralston, Vera. See Miles, Vera.
Rambert, Marie II-1036
Ramsey, Frank Plumpton I-518
Ransom, John Crowe III-1169
Rashad, Phylicia V-2532
Raskob, John Jacob II-880
Rathbone, Basil III-1131
Rathenau, Walther I-219
Rauschenberg, Robert III-1590; IV-2011
Ravel, Maurice I-90
Ray, Man I-349, 513
Ray, Nicholas IV-1640
Read, Herbert III-1190, 1239
Réard, Louis III-1324
Reasoner, Harry IV-2136
Rebay, Hilla IV-1806
Reberioux, Madeleine V-2588
Redding, Noel IV-2092
Redding, Otis IV-2104
Redl, Wolf R. IV-2126
Reed, Donna III-1335, 1470
Reich, Steve IV-1979
Reimann, Walter I-486
Reiner, Carl IV-1908
Reiner, Rob V-2234
Reinhardt, Max I-145, 534
Reith, John II-712
Reitherman, Wolfgang II-1053

Reitz, Dana V-2480
Remark, Erich Paul. *See* Remarque, Erich Maria.
Remarque, Erich Maria II-767
Remington, Frederic I-304
Renoir, Jean II-1073
Reynolds, Burt IV-1668
Reynolds, Gene V-2271
Rice, Tim V-2254
Rich, Matty V-2565
Richards, I. A. III-1169
Richards, Keith IV-2027
Richards, Lloyd IV-1795
Richardson, Tony IV-1721
Richter, Hans Werner I-7, 214; III-1357
Ricketts, Ed III-1138
Rietveld, Gerrit Thomas I-429, 458
Rifkin, Joshua V-2350
Riley, Terry IV-1979
Rilke, Rainer Maria I-281, 396
Rinehart, Mary Roberts I-496
Ringwald, Molly V-2527
Ritchie, John Simon. *See* Vicious, Sid.
Rittau, Günther II-707
Rivera, Diego II-957
Rivette, Jacques IV-1710
Robards, Jason IV-1984
Robbe-Grillet, Alain III-1481
Robbins, Jerome III-1274; IV-1731
Roberts, Pernell IV-1800
Robertson, Dale IV-1768
Robinson, Edward G. II-839
Robinson, Smokey IV-1790
Roche, Kevin IV-1716
Rockefeller, Abby Aldrich II-782
Rockefeller, John D., Jr. III-1149
Rockefeller, Nelson A. II-957; III-1149
Rodchenko, Alexander II-787
Roddenberry, Gene V-2260
Rodgers, Jimmie II-729
Rodgers, Nile V-2386
Rodgers, Richard III-1256
Roerich, Nikolay Konstantinovich I-241, 373
Roethke, Theodore IV-1850
Rogers, Ginger II-984
Rogers, Richard V-2402
Rogers, Samuel Shepard. *See* Shepard, Sam.
Rogers, Wayne V-2271
Rohmer, Eric IV-1710
Röhrig, Walter I-486
Roker, Roxie V-2339
Roller, Alfred I-7
Roosevelt, Eleanor III-1126
Roosevelt, Franklin D. II-828
Roosevelt, Theodore I-24
Rose, Fred III-1415
Rose-Marie IV-1908
Rosenberg, Alfred III-1217
Rosenberg, Harold III-1557
Rosenberg, Lev. *See* Bakst, Léon.
Rosenblum, Ralph V-2381
Rosenblum, Robert V-2608
Rosenstock, Sami. *See* Tzara, Tristan.
Ross, Diana IV-1790
Ross, Harold II-648

Ross, Marion V-2305
Rossellini, Roberto III-1228, 1596
Roth, Philip IV-2163
Rothchild, Paul IV-2038
Rotten, Johnny V-2299, 2360
Rouault, Georges I-140
Rowan, Dan IV-2115
Rubinstein, Arthur IV-1818
Ruhlmann, Jacques Émile II-654
Rulfo, Juan IV-1689
Runyon, Damon II-1011
Rushdie, Salman V-2630
Ruskin, John I-257
Russell, Bertrand I-518
Russell, John V-2608
Russolo, Luigi I-235

Saarinen, Eero II-610; IV-1716
Saarinen, Eliel II-610; IV-1716
Sachs, Paul II-782
Sackheim, Maxwell II-686
Sadat, Anwar el- V-2625
Safdie, Moshe IV-2081
St. Denis, Ruth I-390
Saito, Ryoei V-2603
Saks, Gene V-2537
Salinger, J. D. III-1493
Salmon, André I-337
Salpeter, Mechel. *See* Gordon, Max.
Saltzman, Harry IV-1913
Samish, Adrian IV-2017
Sandrich, Mark II-984
Sands, Diana IV-1795
Sanford, Isabel V-2339
Sardou, Victorien I-29
Sarnoff, David I-469; III-1143, 1149, 1211, 1362, 1383
Sarraute, Nathalie III-1481
Sarson, Christopher IV-2168
Sartre, Jean-Paul III-1174, 1262, 1449, 1573, 1812
Satie, Erik I-435
Saunders, Peter III-1551
Sauser, Frédéric. *See* Cendrars, Blaise.
Saussure, Ferdinand de IV-2075
Savoye, M. and Mme. Pierre II-869
Sayers, Dorothy L. I-496
Scalero, Rosario III-1536
Schaeffer, Pierre III-1629
Schaub, Johannes V-2548
Schenck, Joseph M. II-691
Scherman, Harry II-686
Scheyer, Emmy "Galka" II-583
Schiaparelli, Elsa II-979
Schippers, Thomas III-1536
Schlamm, William S. IV-1683
Schlatter, George IV-2115
Schlesinger, Bruno. *See* Walter, Bruno.
Schloezer, Tatiana I-286
Schmertz, Herbert IV-2168
Schmidt-Rottluff, Karl I-134
Schnabel, Julian V-2438
Schoenberg, Arnold I-166, 193, 367, 528; II-680, 816
Schoenmaekers, M. H. J. I-429
Scholz, Georg II-631
Schrimpf, Georg II-631

Schuch, Ernst von I-151
Schüfftan, Eugen II-707
Schuller, Gunther V-2350
Scott, Allan II-984
Scott, George C. IV-1989
Scott, Hazel III-1159
Scott, James I-13
Scott, Oz V-2370
Scott, Ridley V-2486
Scriabin, Aleksandr I-286
Scruggs, Earl III-1121
Seberg, Jean IV-1845
Seeger, Pete II-810
Seidelman, Susan V-2443
Seidensticker, Edward IV-2147
Self, Jim V-2480
Sellars, Peter V-2599
Sellers, Peter IV-1989
Selznick, David O. III-1154
Sennett, Mack I-230
Sert, Misia I-474
Severini, Gino I-235
Severinsen, Doc III-1623
Shabazz, Betty IV-2022
Shakespeare, William III-1404
Shange, Ntozake V-2370
Shankar, Ravi IV-2104
Shapiro, Karl III-1443
Shapiro, Mel V-2239
Shatner, William V-2260
Shaw, George Bernard I-85, 534
Shaw, Theodore. See Wilson, Teddy.
Shawn, Ted I-390
Sheldon, Edward I-343
Shepard, Sam V-2413
Sherwood, Robert E. I-343
Shire, Talia V-2265
Shook, Karel IV-2110
Shorter, Wayne IV-2153
Shostakovich, Dmitri II-787, 914, 1042; III-1388
Sibelius, Jean I-292
Sillitoe, Alan III-1454; V-2244, 2330, 2397, 2470
Silverman, Fred V-2244, 2330, 2397, 2470
Simenon, Georges I-496
Simmons, Jean III-1378
Simmons, Joseph V-2582
Simmons, Russell V-2582
Simon, Neil V-2537
Simon, Sam V-2652
Sinatra, Dolly III-1250
Sinatra, Frank III-1250
Singer, Alma V-2423
Singer, Isaac Bashevis V-2423
Singer, Israel Joshua V-2423
Singleton, John V-2565
Sinnott, Michael. See Sennett, Mack.
Siqueiros, David Alfaro II-957
Sjostrand, Osten V-2594
Skelton, Red III-1520
Skinner, Hugh. See Laing, Hugh.
Skouras, Spyros III-1307
Slater, Montagu III-1296
Sledd, James IV-1898
Sloan, John French II-885

Sly and the Family Stone IV-2180
Smalls, Charlie V-2334
Smith, Alfred Emanuel II-880
Smith, Bessie I-252; II-572, 670
Smith, David II-1001
Smith, Gladys Louise. See Pickford, Mary.
Smith, Harrison II-805
Smith, June Edith II-963
Smith, Kate II-828
Smith, Mamie II-572
Smith, Oliver III-1234, 1274
Snaith, William T. II-777
Snyder, Gary III-1460
Solovyov, Vladimir I-286
Solzhenitsyn, Aleksandr V-2277
Sondheim, Stephen IV-1731; V-2213, 2433
Soschka, Cyrill II-767
Soyinka, Wole V-2594
Spaak, Charles II-1073
Spelling, Aaron V-2330
Spencer, Herbert I-161
Spender, Stephen II-857
Spewack, Bella III-1404
Spewack, Samuel III-1404
Spielberg, Steven V-2491
Springsteen, Bruce V-2325
Stainer, Leslie. See Howard, Leslie.
Stalin, Joseph II-544, 908, 914, 1042; III-1388; V-2277
Stang, Arnold III-1394
Stanislavsky, Konstantin I-1
Stanton, Frank III-1211, 1465
Stapleton, Jean V-2234
Stark, John I-13
Starkey, Richard, Jr. See Starr, Ringo.
Starr, Ringo IV-1944, 2098
Stefano, Joseph IV-1855
Steichen, Edward I-63
Stein, Gertrude I-129; II-696
Stein, Leo I-129
Stein, Michael I-129
Stein, Sarah Samuels I-129
Steinbeck, Carol Henning III-1138
Steinbeck, John III-1138
Steiner, Rudolf I-320
Stella, Frank IV-1949
Sterling, Ford I-230
Stern, Robert A. M. V-2646
Stevens, Roger L. IV-2048
Stevenson, McLean V-2271
Stewart, Jimmy III-1335
Stieglitz, Alfred I-63; II-885, 1001
Stigwood, Robert V-2254
Stitch, George Ford. See Sterling, Ford.
Stockhausen, Karlheinz I-528
Stoclet, Adolphe I-124
Stokowski, Leopold I-425; III-1195
Stone, Milburn IV-1668
Stone, Oliver V-2576
Stone, Robert V-2315
Stone, Sid III-1394
Stonorov, Oscar IV-1919
Stoppard, Tom IV-1967
Storey, David III-1454
Strachey, James I-19

Straight, Willard I-385
Strange, Glenn IV-1668
Strasberg, Lee II-874, 1006
Strassberg, Isreal. See Strasberg, Lee.
Strauss, Baron George R. IV-2131
Strauss, Richard I-151, 193, 292
Straussler, Tomas. See Stoppard, Tom.
Stravinsky, Igor I-269, 373, 528; II-561, 816; III-1301, 1514
Streisand, Barbra V-2443
Strindberg, August I-199
Struthers, Sally V-2234
Sturgeon, Theodore III-1094
Süe, Louis II-654
Suetin, Nikolai I-413
Sullivan, Ed III-1383
Sullivan, John Florence. See Allen, Fred.
Summer, Donna V-2386
Suttner, Bertha von I-45
Swain, Mack II-659
Sweeney, James Johnson IV-1806
Swit, Loretta V-2271
Sydney, Basil III-1378
Sydow, Max von IV-1742
Synge, John Millington I-119, 176

Tafel, Edgar II-902
Tailleferre, Germaine I-435
Takei, Kei V-2480
Tanguy, Yves II-604
Tartikoff, Brandon V-2532
Tate, Allen III-1169, 1443
Tatlin, Vladimir I-413; II-544
Taubman, Alfred V-2603
Taylor, Deems III-1195
Taylor, Dwight II-984
Taylor, Paul III-1602
Teague, Walter Dorwin II-777, 1057
Tecosky, Morton. See Da Costa, Morton.
Temple, Shirley II-1011
Templeton, Fay I-108
Terkel, Studs III-1329
Thalberg, Irving G. II-833
Tharp, Twyla V-2288
Thomas, Danny III-1470
Thomas, Frank II-1053
Thomas, J. Parnell III-1340
Thompson, Uncle Jimmy II-675
Thomson, Virgil I-508
Thorburn, Richard V-2283
Thurber, James II-648
Tiffany, Charles Louis I-34
Tiffany, Louis Comfort I-34
Tillstrom, Burr III-1400
Tinker, Grant V-2218, 2470
Tiroff, Romain de. See Erté.
Tissé, Éduard II-615
Toklas, Alice B. I-129
Toland, Gregg III-1200
Tolkien, Christopher III-1607
Tolkien, John Ronald Reul III-1607
Tosh, Peter V-2344
Totheroh, Roland H. II-659
Townsend, Robert V-2565
Travanti, Daniel J. V-2470

Trevelyan, John IV-2131
Trevor, Claire III-1115
Tristano, Lennie III-1617
Trudeau, Garry V-2223
Truffaut, François IV-1710, 1845
Truitt, Anne IV-1949
Trumbo, Dalton III-1340
Trumbull, Douglas IV-1989; V-2486
Tudor, Antony II-1036
Tufts, Eleanor V-2608
Tuke, Samuel IV-1877
Turner, Ted V-2554
Tynan, Kenneth Peacock IV-1721, 1924
Tzara, Tristan I-419, 513

Ulman, Douglas. See Fairbanks, Douglas, Sr.
Ulyanov, Vladimir Ilich. See Lenin, Vladimir Ilich.
Unwin, Rayner III-1607
Updike, John IV-2163
Ure, Mary IV-1721
Ussachevsky, Vladimir IV-1785

Vadim, Roger IV-1710
Vallee, Rudy II-828
Van. See also entries under family names.
Van Doesburg, Theo. See Doesburg, Theo van.
Van Gogh, Vincent. See Gogh, Vincent van.
Van Cleef, Lee IV-1984
Van Doren, Carl I-502
Van Dyke, Dick IV-1908
Van Kuijk, Andreas Cornelius. See Parker, Colonel Tom.
Vance, Vivian III-1525
Varèse, Edgard III-1629
Vargas Llosa, Mario IV-1689, 2086
Vaughan Williams, Ralph I-90
Vaughan Williams, Ursula Wood I-90
Vauxcelles, Louis I-204
Veidt, Conrad I-486; III-1245
Velde, Henry van de I-181
Vereen, Ben V-2254, 2397
Vertov, Dziga II-701
Vicious, Sid V-2299, 2360
Vidor, King II-772
Vikár, Béla I-102
Villa-Lobos, Heiter IV-1818
Villa-Lobos, Lucilia Guimarães IV-1818
Village People, the V-2386
Villalta, Guillermo Pérez V-2203
Villon, Jacques I-349
Viollet-le-Duc, Eugène-Emmanuel I-257
Visconti, Luchino III-1228
Vlaminck, Maurice de I-140, 156
Vogt, A. E. van III-1094
Volonté, Gian Maria IV-1984
Von. See also entries under family names.
Von Sternberg, Josef II-845
Von Stroheim, Erich II-593, 1073
Vonnegut, Kurt, Jr. IV-1939
Voskresensky, Vasily. See Basil, Colonel Wassili de.

Wagner, Otto I-79
Wagner, Robin V-2254
Wagoner, Dan III-1602
Wagstaff, Sam V-2636

PRINCIPAL PERSONAGES

Wain, John III-1454
Wallace, DeWitt II-549
Wallace, Lila Bell Acheson II-549
Wallace, Mike IV-2136
Wallace, Ruby Ann. *See* Dee, Ruby.
Wallach, Eli IV-1984
Walsh, Raoul I-402
Walter, Bruno I-298
Walthall, Henry B. I-402
Walton, William III-1378
Wanger, Walter III-1115
Warburg, Edward II-974
Warburg, Fredric III-1421
Ward, Bond IV-1768
Ward, Geoffrey C. V-2657
Ward, Theodora IV-1662
Wärendorf, Fritz I-79
Warhol, Andy IV-2053
Warhola, Andrew. *See* Warhol, Andy.
Warm, Hermann I-486
Warner, Albert II-761
Warner, Harry II-734, 761
Warner, Jack L. II-734, 833
Warner, Sam II-734, 761
Washington, Denzel V-2565
Washington, Lula V-2521
Wasson, Ben II-805
Waterhouse, Keith III-1454
Watson, Forbes II-885
Watson, John B. II-896
Watts, Charlie IV-2027
Wayne, John III-1115, 1313
Weaver, Dennis IV-1668
Weaver, Harriet Shaw II-555
Weaver, Raymond M. I-502
Weaver, Sylvester "Pat" III-1465, 1623
Webb, Jack III-1531
Webber, Andrew Lloyd V-2254
Webern, Anton von I-193, 367, 528
Wedekind, Frank II-1078
Wegelius, Martin I-292
Weidman, Charles I-390
Weigel, Helene III-1410
Weill, Kurt II-724
Weininger, Otto I-518
Weisenfreund, Muni. *See* Muni, Paul.
Weiss, Peter IV-2005
Welles, Julia Elizabeth. *See* Andrews, Julie.
Welles, Orson II-989; III-1103, 1200
Wellman, William II-839
Welsh, John IV-1721
Werner, Thomas V-2532
Wertheimer, Pierre I-474
Westminster, Duke of. *See* Grosvenor, Hugh "Bend'or."
Westwood, Vivienne V-2299
Weyl, Walter I-385
Whale, James II-863
White, Clarence H. I-63
White, E. B. II-648
White, Katharine Sergeant II-648
White, Walter II-755; III-1159
Whiteman, Paul II-598
Whitfield, Norman IV-1790
Whitman, Walt I-90; II-851; III-1179

Whitney, Gertrude Vanderbilt II-885
Who, the IV-2104, 2180
Wiene, Robert I-486
Wiesel, Elie IV-1700
Wiesel, Shlomo IV-1700
Wiggins, Marianne V-2630
Wigley, Mark V-2614
Wilde, Oscar I-151
Wilder, Billy III-1567
Wilder, Thornton III-1099, 1164
Wildgruber, Ulrich IV-2126
Williams, Audrey Sheppard III-1415
Williams, Clarence II-572
Williams, Hank III-1415
Williams, Matt V-2532
Williams, Paulette. *See* Shange, Ntozake.
Williams, Talcott I-407
Williams, Tennessee III-1164, 1487
Williams, William Carlos I-445
Willis, Gordon V-2381
Willkie, Wendell III-1159
Willson, Meredith IV-1752
Wilson, Edmund II-626
Wilson, Robert M. V-2375
Wilson, Teddy II-930, 968
Wilson, Woodrow I-24
Winchell, Walter II-828
Winkler, Henry V-2305
Wise, Robert IV-2033
Wittgenstein, Ludwig I-518
Wittich, Marie I-151
Wolfe, Thomas I-343
Wolper, David V-2397
Wonder, Stevie IV-1790; V-2294
Wood, John S. III-1340
Wood, Natalie IV-1640
Wood, Robert D. V-2197, 2234
Woodruff, Robert V-2413
Woodthorpe, Peter IV-1861
Woolf, Leonard S. II-637
Woolf, Virginia II-637
Worley, Jo Anne IV-2115
Wrede, Stuart V-2614
Wright, Frank Lloyd II-902, 1067; IV-1806; V-2208
Wright, Olgivanna Lloyd II-902
Wright, Richard III-1185
Wyman, Bill IV-2027

Xenakis, Yannis III-1629

Yarborough, Barton III-1531
Yeats, William Butler I-119, 176, 309, 440, 445
Yoelson, Asa. *See* Jolson, Al.
Yorke, Francis R. S. IV-2064
Yorkin, Bud V-2197, 2234
Young, La Monte IV-1979
Young, Lester II-930; III-1617
Young, Robert III-1470
Young, Terence IV-1913

Zambona, Jutta Ilse II-767
Zanuck, Darryl F. II-1011; III-1131
Zaslavsky, David IV-1747
Zawinul, Joe IV-2153

CXLI

Zecca, Ferdinand I-57
Zehntbauer, John I-491
Zehntbauer, Roy I-491
Zehrfuss, Bernard II-1021; IV-2064
Zemlinsky, Alexander von I-193
Zhdanov, Andrei Aleksandrovich II-908, 914; III-1388

Ziegfeld, Florenz II-745
Ziegler, Adolf III-1083
Zimmerman, Robert. *See* Dylan, Bob.
Zola, Émile II-890
Zukor, Adolph I-224; II-567
Zworykin, Vladimir III-1143, 1211